D0216412

Communication Yearbook 35

Communication Yearbook 35

Edited by
Charles T. Salmon

Published Annually for the
International Communication Association

NEW YORK AND LONDON

First published 2011
by Routledge
711 Third Avenue, New York, NY 10017

Simultaneously published in the UK
by Routledge
2 Park Square, Milton Park, Abingdon, Oxon OX14 4RN

Routledge is an imprint of the Taylor & Francis Group, an informa business

ISSN: 0147-4642

ISBN 13: 978-0-415-89227-8 (hbk)
ISBN 13: 978-0-203-81417-8 (ebk)

Typeset in Times by
EvS Communication Networx, Inc.

Printed and bound in the United States of America on acid-free paper by
Sheridan Books, Inc.

Contents

The International Communication Association

The International Communication Association (ICA) was formed in 1950, bringing together academics and other professionals whose interests focus on human communication. The Association maintains an active membership of more than 4,000 individuals, of whom some two-thirds teach and conduct research in colleges, universities, and schools around the world. Other members are in government, law, medicine, and other professions. The wide professional and geographic distribution of the membership provides the basic strength of the ICA. The Association serves as a meeting ground for sharing research and useful dialogue about communication interests.

Through its divisions and interest groups, publications, annual conferences, and relations with other associations around the world, the ICA promotes the systemic study of communication theories, processes, and skills. In addition to the *Communication Yearbook*, the Association publishes the *Journal of Communication*, *Human Communication Research*, *Communication Theory*, *Journal of Computer-Mediated Communication*, *Communication, Culture & Critique*, *A Guide to Publishing in Scholarly Communication Journals*, and the *ICA Newsletter*.

For additional information about the ICA and its activities, visit online at www.icahdq.org or contact Michael L. Haley, Executive Director, International Communication Association, 1500 21st Ave. NW, Washington, DC 20036 USA; phone 202-955-1444; fax 202-955-1448; email ica@icahdq.org.

Editors of the *Communication Yearbook* series:

Volumes 1 and 2, Brent D. Ruben
Volumes 3 and 4, Dan Nimmo
Volumes 5 and 6, Michael Burgoon
Volumes 7 and 8, Robert N. Bostrom
Volumes 9 and 10, Margaret L. McLaughlin
Volumes 11, 12, 13, and 14, James A. Anderson
Volumes 15, 16, and 17, Stanley A. Deetz
Volumes 18, 19, and 20, Brant R. Burleson
Volumes 21, 22, and 23, Michael E. Roloff
Volumes 24, 25, and 26, William B. Gudykunst
Volumes 27, 28, and 29, Pamela J. Kalbfleisch
Volumes 30, 31, 32, and 33, Christina S. Beck
Volumes 34 and 35, Charles T. Salmon

Information Systems
Robert F. Potter, *Indiana University*

Instructional & Developmental Communication
Rebecca M. Chory, *West Virginia University*

Intercultural Communication
Ling Chen, *Hong Kong Baptist University*

Interpersonal Communication
Walid Afifi, *University of California, Santa Barbara*

Journalism Studies
Frank Esser, *University of Zurich*

Language & Social Interaction
Richard Buttny, *Syracuse University*

Mass Communication
David R. Ewoldsen, *Ohio State University*

Organizational Communication
Dennis Mumby, *University of North Carolina*

Philosophy of Communication
Nick Couldry, *Goldsmiths College, London University*

Political Communication
Yariv Tsfati, *University of Haifa*

Popular Communication
Paul Frosh, *Hebrew University of Jerusalem*

Public Relations
Craig Carroll, *University of North Carolina*

Visual Communication
Luc Pauwels, *University of Antwerp*

SPECIAL INTEREST GROUP CHAIRS

Children, Adolescents and the Media
J. Alison Bryant, *Smartypants.com*

Communication History
Jefferson Pooley, *Muhlenberg College*

Game Studies
John Sherry, *Michigan State University*

Gay, Lesbian, Bisexual, & Transgender Studies
Lynn Comella, *University of Nevada, Las Vegas*
Vincent Doyle, *IE University*

Intergroup Communication
Lisa Sparks, *Chapman University*

Editorial Board

Reviewers

Sandra Borden	*Western Michigan University, USA*
Judith Buddenbaum	*Colorado State University, USA*
Hazel Dicken-Garcia	*University of Minnesota, USA*
Susanna Dilliplane	*University of Pennsylvania, USA*
Matt Eastin	*University of Texas at Austin, USA*
Jeanne Flora	*New Mexico State University, USA*
Anat Gesser-Edelsburg	*University of Haifa, Israel*
Melanie Green	*University of North Carolina at Chapel Hill, USA*
Ingunn Hagen	*Norges Teknisk-Naturvitenskapelige Universitet, Norway*
Elaine Hatfield	*University of Hawaii, USA*
David Henningsen	*Northern Illinois University, USA*
Randy Hirokawa	*University of Hawaii, USA*
Michael Huspek	*California State University, San Marcos, USA*
Fern Johnson	*Clark University, USA*
Steven Karau	*Southern Illinois University, USA*
Peter Marston	*California State University, Northridge, USA*
Emanuel Schegloff	*University of California, Los Angeles, USA*
Cliff Scherer	*Cornell University, USA*
John Sherry	*Michigan State University, USA*
Paul Skalski	*Cleveland State University, USA*
Ida Stockman	*Michigan State University, USA*
Phillip J. Tichenor	*University of Minnesota, USA*
Pamela Whitten	*Michigan State University, USA*
Dmitri Williams	*University of Southern California, USA*
Kim Witte	*Michigan State University, USA*

Editor's Introduction

Charles T. Salmon

In the pages that follow, communication scholars representing multiple intellectual traditions and modes of scholarly inquiry join together to celebrate the richness and inherent eclecticism of our discipline. Reviews in this volume address enduring issues intrinsic to the human experience, such as language, love, family, and sexual behavior; they explore the implications of revolutionary communication technologies for such familiar concepts as anonymity, interactivity and aging; and they analyze paradigmatic differences in the study of topics ranging from media effects to discourse analysis. The result is reflection of an academic discipline that is vibrant, diverse, and exhibiting no signs of running short on ideas.

All of the sections of this volume offer important contributions to the study of communication processes, systems and effects, though one section in particular deserves special mention. The inspiration for Part I ("The Seeds of Mass Communication Research") occurred when University of Pennsylvania Professor Elihu Katz received an honorary degree (his fifth overall, at the time) from the University of Bucharest, and prepared some remarks for presentation at the ceremony. These remarks, which identified and traced the development of four foundational strands of mass communication scholarship, were adapted for inclusion in this volume. Kurt Lang, Gladys Engel Lang, and Gertrude Robinson agreed to share their recollections and observations about the early development of mass communication research and theory development as well. Mihai Coman, a communications scholar and administrator at the University of Bucharest who nominated Elihu Katz for the honorary degree, agreed to serve as discussant and synthesize these "mythological narrations" of the genesis of communication research. The result is a treasure trove of historical insight and commentary about our field's history and some of the pivotal figures and ideas that helped to shape and define generations of communication research.

Sir Isaac Newton once remarked that his perspicacity was due to "standing on the shoulders of giants." The same is true of all of us who study communication, in spite of revolutionary changes in technology that seemingly raze the communications landscape from one generation to the next. Inventions come and go, and yet as a community of scholars we retain a collective focus on enduring issues such as ownership, control, content, meaning, understanding, context, interaction, relationships, and effects regardless of the particular technological innovation in vogue at any moment. The resoluteness of this focus on these core constructs is a tribute to the enduring intellectual foundation underlying our discipline, and reason in and of itself for why the wisdom and insight of the pioneers of our field can never be forgotten.

Acknowledgments

My sincere gratitude and appreciation goes to a number of colleagues whose contributions, support and hard work made this volume possible. Cindy Gallois, Christina Holtz-Bacha, Nurit Guttman, and Joseph B. Walther provided outstanding support and sage counsel as associate editors. Discussants Peng Hwa Ang, Mihai Coman, Jon Nussbaum, and Ruth Wodak graciously volunteered their time to provide insightful commentary and perspective on their assigned chapters. The authors, editorial board members, and reviewers spent countless hours creating and refining the content that made this volume possible, consistently meeting deadlines in the process. Editorial assistants Robin Blom and Laleah Fernandez provided excellent and timely support for authors and editors throughout the entire review process. Finally, special thanks go to Jane Brown, Sahara Byrne, Kathleen Galvin, Jake Harwood, Caryn Medved, and Ruth Wodak for going above and beyond the call of duty with helping authors and improving manuscripts.

Part I

The Seeds of Mass Communication Research

CHAPTER CONTENTS

1 Ownership, Technology, Content, and Context in the Continuing Search for Media Effects

Elihu Katz

University of Pennsylvania

This chapter argues that the several traditions of communications research converge on the problem of explaining media efffects. The critical tradition emphasizes the role of media ownership in purveying false consciousness and reinforcing the status quo. Technological theorists are concerned with how media structure the ways in which we think and organize. Theorists of content are interested in the persuasive powers of the media, while the (neglected) tradition of contextual studies suggests that the key to effect is in the way in which the audience is "situated."

These comments were written for presentation upon receipt of an honorary degree from the University of Bucharest, May, 2010.

I thought it might be appropriate to say something about how our field has developed and changed in the 60-or-so years that I have been involved in it. To make these years more tangible, let me say that research for my Master's Thesis at Columbia University was completed in 1951 under the direction of Professor Leo Lowenthal. Lowenthal's presence in New York at that time reminds us that this was only a few years after World War II when he and other members of the famous Frankfurt School of Social Research found refuge in the United States, with the help of Professors Robert Lynd and Paul Lazarsfeld. Lazarsfeld himself had arrived in New York a decade or so earlier to establish an empirically minded center for social research—expanding on the one he had founded in Vienna. Thus, Columbia's Bureau of Applied Social Research in the 40s and 50s saw the convergence of Lazarsfeld's Viennese associates—among them Herta Herzog, Hans Zeisel, Marie Jahoda, and others; the Frankfurt group—Lowenthal, Theodor Adorno, Max Horkheimer, and others (Wheatland, 2009); and a group of young American sociologists, some of them the children of European immigrants, such as Herbert Hyman and Robert Merton. Contributions to the American War effort had enhanced the reputation of applied social science, and, as a result, a soon-to-be-famous cohort of graduate students, subsidized by the so-called G.I. Bill for veterans of the war, enrolled at Columbia (and other major American Universities) including Peter Blau, James Coleman, Joseph Klapper, Martin Lipset, and many others. Inspired, a least in part, by Lazarsfeld's Bureau, similar centers of empirical social science were established at Chicago, at Michigan, in Norway, in Israel, in Poland, and elsewhere.

Although the Bureau (originally, the Office of Radio Research) was affiliated with Columbia's longstanding Department of Sociology, and conducted social research in many institutional areas, it may be said to have been the birthplace of empirical research on mass communication. The name "communication" hardly existed at the time, and—to keep our perspective in place—radio was still the predominant medium of the day. Television did not really become widespread until the early 1950s—at the time of the Coronation of Elizabeth of England, if you can remember that far back.

To be fair, we should credit a number of European scholars with earlier work on communication and public opinion. The French social psychologist, Gabriel Tarde, is a prime example, having anticipated much of what Jürgen Habermas has taught us about the press, conversation, and opinion in the bourgeois public sphere (Clark, 1969; Habermas, 1989; Katz, 1992). Georg Simmel (Simmel & Wolff, 1950) is another theorist worth remembering. The Sociology Department at the University of Chicago inherited these European pioneers, and proceeded to consider the role of communication media in the social integration of American cities and their immigrant population (Kurtz, 1984). The Chicago group did important research on the newspaper as a socializing force (Carey, 1996) and posited other powerful effects of the media (Wirth, 1948). Columbia was different in that its major thrust was more socio-psychological and heavily methodological, contributing to the design of survey research, content analysis, focused interviews, and so on. Ironically, it can be argued that Columbia's new beginnings served to undermine—rather than expand—the more sociological thrust of the thinking that had begun in Europe and Chicago!

Lazarsfeld's own work centered on the influence of the media on individual decision-making—on how individuals make up their minds for whom to vote, what to buy, how to dress, and the like, rather than on the more structural aspects of the workings of democratic society. His studies of the process of individual decision-making in the American elections of the 1940s (Lazarsfeld, Berelson, & Gaudet, 1944) and other Bureau studies of marketing, fashions, movie-going, and the shaping of political attitudes (Katz & Lazarsfeld, 1955) were likely inspired by then-current theories of "mass society," which gave rise to the idea that the media could dictate the thinking of uprooted and atomized individuals, not well-connected with each other, and made even more vulnerable by the advent of the powerful medium of broadcasting. Empirical research, however, suggested otherwise—that selective perception and interpersonal relations still played a major part in modern society, and that networks of interpersonal influence were somehow implicated even in ostensibly individualistic processes. Lazarsfeld's serendipitous discovery of the so-called "two-step flow of communication"—whereby "opinion leaders" filter what they have gleaned from the media—pointed the way back to the kind of "deliberative democracy," on which some of the earlier theorists had dwelled, albeit with a different time perspective. The Lazarsfeld group emphasized the short run, the Europeans and the Chicago School, the long run.

But even as Lazarsfeld went his own way (and perhaps turned back again), his cohorts at Columbia, regulars and guests, were going in different directions. One group, led by Herta Herzog, began to study what was then called "uses and gratifications," a theory that expanded the focus on media effects to take account also of audience motivations for choosing certain kinds of content and coming back for more (Herzog, 1944). Based on the idea that the audience also has power—at least to be selective, but also to employ the media to satisfy various needs—this work ultimately led to what is nowadays called "reception theory," in which European scholars such as Umberto Eco, Jay Blumler, and Stuart Hall played major parts. Their emphasis, like Lazarsfeld's and Herzog's, was on the interaction of media content and audience selectivity.

At the same time, the Frankfurt group, of Max Horkheimer and Theodor Adorno (2002) and Leo Lowenthal (1961) too—still on the margins of the Bureau—set out to prove that the "culture industry"—that is, media that are remotely-controlled by hegemonic power—were inducing a false consciousness of class and identity, and an affirmation of the economic and social status quo. Their emphasis was on the ways in which control of the media constrained content, and how entertainment was infested with ideology.

Here, then, are three traditions of media research that grew up almost side by side. Looking back on the development of the field, I would add two more such traditions. One focuses on the technology of the media, a tradition made famous by Canadian scholars, especially Harold Innis and Marshall McLuhan. Innis (1950), for example, distinguished between media of space that overcome distance, and media of time that reach across generations. The other tradition—largely ignored—was called "the situation of contact" by Elliot Freidson (1953) referring to the contexts, in which audiences engage the media. Traditionally, for example, the newspaper is read alone, we go to the cinema with friends, and watch TV with family.

What is common to these traditions is the concern with effect. The Columbia groups were interested in the influence of media content on short-run change of opinions and attitudes and in the role of motivations and gratification in enlisting attention and interest, in the short run. Frankfurt School members were interested in the ways in which the management of the media produced content that maintained the class structure of society in the long run. The technological theorists were interested in how the media—whether print, or broadcasting, or cinema—affected the ways we think (i.e., not what we think, but how we think). The contextualists, likewise, were not so much interested in media content, but on the effect of the typical ways in which the different media situate us at different places and among different people.

I am proposing that these traditions tend to view media as "causes" of certain kinds of "effects." And I am further suggesting that when they refer to "media" they are thinking of different aspects of the media, and, likewise, when they think of "effects," they have different effects in mind. Thus, when the Columbia schools think media, they think Content, or more precisely, persuasion; the Frankfurt School thinks ownership and organization; the Canadian School thinks technology; and the Contextualists think situation of contact. As far as effects are concerned, the Lazarsfeldians think short-run change; the Frankfurt School think reinforcement of the status quo, or in other words, non-change; the Canadians examine the organization of perception and cognition; and the Contextualists think of place, the way screen theorists think that movie theaters are designed for daydreaming.

In other words, I am suggesting that Ownership, Technology, Content, and Context are aspects of communication media, which have been treated rather separately, as take-off points for different kinds of theorizing. Of course, all these elements are interconnected as systems, but that will become clearer as we proceed.

For the rest of this chapter, I want to illustrate the workings of these traditions. I will do by considering how each of them treated television in its heyday (and again, nowadays, on its deathbed), and how each of them is now addressing the new information technologies which have descended upon us.

Context

Let me begin with Context, because this is the least familiar of the four attributes of the media, much neglected during the era of empirical mass media research. To emphasize its importance, I will dare to say that the major "effect" of broadcasting—radio and television—was to have moved politics inside the home. Politics used to take place "outside"—in the town hall or the village square or the political club or the café, that is, in the public domain. Broadcasting invited people to return home, and to sit together as family, and thus, indirectly, to tailor content to the living-room audience. Nations were united around shared content, ordinary people felt enfranchised, but politics became less ideological and more personal, and less participatory, as a result. Gradually, of course, the family audience, and even the national audience, drew apart as television sets found their way to the bedroom, and television channels multiplied. Gerbner and Gross (1976) and Putnam (1996) blame television for damaging democracy by keeping us inside, making it impossible to listen to others who do not share our opinions, and disconnecting us from collective action.

The Internet and the cell phone have refocused attention. While there is no reason to imagine that these new media will inherit the role of the press and broadcasting as agencies of national integration, the context for consuming them is now a central concern. Contextually speaking, the most striking aspect of these new media is their ubiquity and their mobility—they destroy what Joshua Meyrowitz (1985) called "the sense of place." They have taken us outside again. Moreover, they have reawakened attention to the social networks that make up society, and through which information and influence diffuse. Will these media reawaken deliberative democracy? Will they provide us with more—or perhaps fewer—connections, and make it easier—or perhaps more difficult—to hear the other sides of an argument? How shall we interpret Pablo Boczkowski's (2010) study of online news, for example, which finds that the new locus for reading the daily news is not at home, nor on the bus, but on the computer at the workplace?

Technology

Technological theorists of the media are somewhat like Context theorists, in their essential disinterest in Content. "The medium is the message," said McLuhan (1964; Katz & Katz, 1998), meaning that the brain—or, indeed, the social organization of society—are more affected by the linear technology of print, or by the pixels of digital TV, than by the stories they tell. Although he didn't much like television either, McLuhan saw television as liberating from the regimentation of print which led us, unfeelingly, on the straight and narrow path toward a goal that our superegos had set for us. McLuhan thought of television as a medium of dispersion, one that would allow more togetherness and greater freedom. His prophecies were often ridiculed by mainstream researchers, but, nowadays, technological theories are all the rage. The very idea of "global village" is part of McLuhan's legacy, first noted in James Carey's exploration of the economic implications of the telegraph (1989) whereby stockbrokers were able to trade on the same markets, even if they were located, physically, in different parts of the world. Like Context, technology also affected content, Carey suggested, by sanitizing the news so that it could be equally acceptable to publications with competing ideological commitments.

Of course, Technologists are enthralled by the new media—by its languages, and by its mobilizing potential. If it was rare for people to step away from their television sets to join others outside in public protest or even revolution, it seems a lot easier nowadays. The long vigils in Korea—when the new media were used both to mobilize large numbers and to circulate anti-government messages—are an interesting, recent example.

Content

The mainstream focus on Content was less comprehensive than one might have expected. Much study was devoted to the effectiveness of campaigns to change opinions, attitudes and actions—and, surprisingly perhaps, these efforts proved frustrating. It is, in fact, difficult to induce change in people. As far as TV genres were concerned, the mainstream study of content focused primarily on the news, and, secondly, on series and serials, and the ways in which these types of broadcasts enlist vicarious participation. Nowadays, of course, audience participation is bursting out all over. The "Reality" genre, so called, appears to be its paradigmatic form. The relations of contestants confronting competitive tasks and inviting evaluation by everybody else appears to be—along with national "media events"—one of the last hopes of togetherness TV. By now, there is a substantial body of research on reality television.

The content of the new social media—what people say to each other about themselves—seems to have attracted little interest from Content-oriented researchers. Even the deliberations of ordinary citizens—on and off the media—have enlisted only moderate attention from mainstream research. The study of the new phenomena of citizen broadcasters and bloggers, or use of the Internet as a reference tool, seems to have been passed along to the Technologists.

Ownership

Finally, let us recall that the critical research of the Frankfurt School is also seriously interested in content even though its point of departure is Ownership and management. Modifying the Marxist idea that the economic base shapes the superstructure—whether conspiratorially or not—these theorists consider that culture is not a mere reflection but an active force, or, in other words, that content is an instrument of indoctrination. The Frankfurt scholars were outraged by the ostensible classlessness of the content of radio and film, arguing, dialectically, that the only hope for the working class was in resisting cultural embourgeoisement. The classes should be encouraged to cultivate their own cultures, they seemed to be saying! Heirs of this sort of critical thinking like Gerbner, Elisabeth Noelle-Neumann (1974) and Richard Peterson (1997)—all of whom died in recent years—tried to show how this kind of false consciousness can be manipulated, and how it may manifest itself in media content.

Lately, a new generation of critical scholars has encamped under the banner of cultural studies. They are unsure about the concentration of ownership and control—for the cultural industry of newspapers and broadcasting is floundering. They are, nevertheless, interested in power and hegemonic ideologies like neo-liberalism (Grossberg, 1995; McCarthy, 2007) but the thrust of their interest, it appears, is in the right of marginalized groups to resist mainstreaming.

Let me reiterate. I attempted to locate the origins of communication research, and to propose that media "effect" was its central concern. I selected four major traditions of research, and proposed that each concentrated on a different aspect of the media as "cause" and, correspondingly, on different definitions of "effect." I tried to illustrate these differences by reference to the ways in which each tradition approached the effects of television, in its heyday and later, and how each has begun to approach the now fashionable new media.

In retrospect, and in spite of the superficiality of these observations, I tend to think that research focused on Content is being overtaken by Technology and Context, and that long-run effects are superseding the short run. These seem worthwhile changes in emphasis, since I think that we have overemphasized the study of the persuasive effects of short-run campaigns, and neglected the long run. Indeed, it will be difficult even to sum up the long-run effects of television broadcasting for lack of longitudinal research. It looks like we are off to a better start in studying the sociology of the new media. The major heir of campaign research, I would suggest, is study of the diffusion of innovation, a tradition that is experiencing rebirth, thanks to the new accessibility of social networks (Katz, 1999).

I also think that we have neglected the institutional aspect of mass communication. True, the Frankfurt School and its heirs take ownership as a starting point, but their major thesis is that the forms of control shape content, and that content shapes attitudes and ideology. We should expect much more from institutional research. In fact, we now very little about how new genres are born, and we know only little about the management of creativity. We have done too little to consider solutions to the problem of engaging citizens in national and international issues, have done too little to consider the survival of the press, and too little to bolster the independence and the potential of public broadcasting which is under threat everywhere from commercial competitors, even while the latter are losing their grip on the entire system of broadcasting and the press.

In closing, let me say that the strength of communications research lies in its interdisciplinary ties, and that the competing tendency to throw off these ties is to be resisted. Looking around any university, one can identify colleagues in other disciplines who are practicing communications research—often without knowing it. I think it is clear from this talk that I believe it is worth forging alliances with these colleagues, for our sake and for theirs. But that's another talk, for another day.

References

Boczkowski, P. (2010). *News at work: Imitation in an age of information abundance.* Chicago: University of Chicago Press.

Carey, J. (1989). *Communication as culture: Essays on media and society.* New York: Routledge.

Carey, J. (1996). The Chicago School and mass communication research. In E. Dennis

& E. Wartella (Eds.), *American communication research: The remembered history* (pp. 21–38). Mahwah, NJ: Erlbaum.

Clark, T. (Ed.). (1969). *Gabriel Tarde on communication and social influence*. Chicago: University of Chicago Press.

Freidson, E. (1953). The relation of the social situation of contact to the media in mass communication. *Public Opinion Quarterly, 17,* 230–238.

Gerbner, G., & Gross, L. (1976). Living with television: The violence profile. *Journal of Communication, 26*, 172–199.

Grossberg, L. (1995). Cultural studies vs. political economy: Is anybody else bored with this debate? *Critical Studies in Mass Communication, 12*, 72–81.

Habermas, J. (1989). *The structural transformation of the public sphere: An inquiry into a category of bourgeois society.* Cambridge, MA: The MIT Press.

Herzog, H. (1944). What do we really know about daytime radio serials. In P. Lazarsfeld & F. Stanton (Eds.), *Radio research 1942–43* (pp. 3–33). New York: Duell, Sloan and Pearce.

Horkheimer, M., & Adorno, T. (2002). The culture industry: Enlightenment as mass deception. In G. Noerr (Ed.) & E. Jephcott (Trans.), *Dialectic of enlightenment: philosophical fragments* (pp. 94–136). Stanford, CA: Stanford University Press.

Innis, H. (1950). *Empire and communications.* Oxford, UK: Oxford University Press.

Katz, E. (1992). On parenting a paradigm: Gabriel Tarde's agenda for opinion and communication research. *International Journal of Public Opinion Research, 4*, 80–85.

Katz, E. (1999). Theorizing diffusion: Tarde and Sorokin revisited. *Annals of the American academy of political and social science, 566*, 144–155.

Katz, E., & Katz, R. (1998). McLuhan: Where did he come from, where did he disappear. *Canadian Journal of Communication, 23*, 307–319.

Katz, E., & Lazarsfeld, P. (1955). *Personal influence: The part played by people in the flow of mass communication.* Glencoe, IL: Free Press.

Kurtz, L. (1984). *Evaluating Chicago sociology: A guide to the literature, with an annotated bibliography.* Chicago: University of Chicago Press.

Lazarsfeld, P., Berelson, B., & Gaudet, H. (1944). *The people's choice: How the voter makes up his mind in presidential campaigns.* New York: Duell, Sloan and Perce.

Lowenthal, L. (1961). The triumph of mass idols. In L. Lowenthal (Ed.), *Literature, popular culture and society* (pp. 109–140). Englewood Cliffs, NJ: Prentice Hall.

McCarthy, A. (2007). Reality television: A neoliberal theater of suffering. *Social Text, 25*(4), 17–41.

McLuhan, M. (1964). *Understanding media: The extensions of man.* Toronto: McGraw-Hill.

Meyrowitz, J. (1985). *No sense of place: The impact of electronic media on social behavior.* New York: Oxford University Press.

Noelle-Neumann, E. (1974). The spiral of silence: A theory of public opinion. *Journal of Communication, 24*, 43–51.

Peterson, R. (1997). *Creating country music: Fabricating authenticity.* Chicago: University of Chicago Press.

Putnam, R. (1996). The strange disappearance of civic America. *The American Prospect, 24*, 34–48.

Simmel, G., & Wolff, K. (1950). *The sociology of Georg Simmel.* Glencoe, IL: Free Press.

Wheatland, T. (2009). *The Frankfurt School in exile*. Minneapolis: University of Minnesota Press.

Wirth, L. (1948). Consensus and mass communications. *American Sociological Review, 30*, 1–15.

CHAPTER CONTENTS

2 On the Development of Communication Theory

Some Reflections

Kurt Lang and Gladys Engel Lang

University of Washington

This chapter reflects on various efforts to theorize about mass communication processes and effects, spanning an era that ranges from early paradigms to contemporary technologies. A number of theoretical approaches are presented and assessed for their emphases, limitations, and potential for increasing understanding of fundamental human and social communications phenomena.

These reflections on the development of "communication theory" begin with a simple proposition: The media of communication penetrate all sectors of modern industrial society, their influence increasingly felt even in the developing world. They touch on just about everything—on what we know, on our thoughts, our ideas, beliefs, behavior, and social relationships. Scarcely anyone one can fully escape their ubiquitous presence. Many of these effects, subtle and indirect as they may be, become manifest only over time and regardless of whether or not people try to resist them or are even aware of them. Nor is the response to the media necessarily uniform across a society. Quite to the contrary, one of the best established findings of mass communication research is how much people differ in their selection of sources and in their interpretations of content. So pervasive is media influence that a conceptualization of it as some kind of outside intrusion, some exogenous influence on people's settled lives, would be clearly erroneous. Rather, to paraphrase Edward Sapir (1931), we should see it as an inseparable element in every social pattern and every single act of social behavior. Communication, mass or interpersonal, testifies to the existence of some kind of explicit or implicit social relationship.

In looking back on our field, we cannot help but notice how narrowly focused are some of the most cited of what passes for a theory about mass communication. How confident can we be that our present knowledge of effects, despite another half-century of mass communication research, goes much beyond the cryptic summary by Bernard Berelson in 1958 at the conference of the American Association for Public Opinion Research? Our state of knowledge, at that time, so he declared, did not amount to much, only that "some kinds of communication have some kind of effects on some kinds of people in some kinds of situations." This evaluation, based on extant research, may have been on target but only insofar as he restricted his review to the variables associated with different kinds of media effects. What he failed to acknowledge were the many leads in scholarly works on the more general influence of mass communication, not just on individuals, whose responses were easily measurable in surveys, but also on the nature of social relationships and of collective action.

The above assertion may strike some readers as both vague and grandiose. We intend in this chapter to clarify it a bit by pointing to some specific inadequacies in certain earlier formulations but also to affirm the direction to which some of them point. Even a quick look backward reveals a truly impressive list of scholars who pioneered a field that got its initial impetus from the advent of cheap print. They wrote only about the "press"; the term "mass media" was still waiting to be invented. Among the more noteworthy of those concerned over its effects were Alexis de Tocqueville and John Stuart Mill, followed decades later by Gabriel Tarde (1901) with a general treatise on how the popular press had affected the essential character of public opinion and politics and, not long thereafter, by Max Weber (1910/1924) with a proposal, presented to a meeting of the German Sociological Society, for a truly monumental collaborative study of the press in all its aspects: production, distribution, finance, content, and control. Regrettably, it never got off ground. Karl Buecher (1915), within the same decade, proved more successful in founding an Institut für Zeitungswissenschaft (Institue for Newspaper Studies) at the University of Leipzig. The field did not really take off until after the first world war with the publication of a spate of studies about the multitudinous propaganda campaigns by the major belligerents. Still influential are the two books by Walter Lippmann: *Public Opinion* (1922) and *The Phantom Public* (1925).

Those were the origins of a clearly expanding field at a time when little more than the press and posters were being let loose on the masses. Its most enthusiastic proponents during the next 20 years were American, preoccupied primarily with exploring the effectiveness of persuasive communication, an interest that reflected those of advertisers and public relations and of media moguls intent on building audiences for the ever greater flood of news and commercial entertainment pouring out from the media. Some studies were motivated by a more general concern about much feared adverse influences, especially of movies on youth, (sponsored by the Payne Foundation, e.g., Blumer 1933) and detailing the stratagems of propagandists in order to advise citizens on how to resist (e.g., Doob, 1935, and studies by the Institute of Propaganda Analysis).

On the whole, these early investigations of mass communication effects were concerned mostly with the adequacy of methods to yield useful as well as valid information. As for theory and explanations, researchers drew on other disciplines—on linguistics and semiology for theories about language, signs, and meaningful symbols; on cognitive psychology for theories about the processing of information by the human mind; and on sociology for theories about interpersonal encounters. Apart from this foraging, the theorizing about specific mass communication effects came more or less as after-thoughts but these did nevertheless raise some interesting issues. Nearly all of these, it seems to us, lend themselves to easy summary in the formulaic paradigm of Harold D. Lasswell (1946) still familiar to everyone that became a mould into which Berelson, too, had cast his somewhat unflattering evaluation of the then current knowledge of mass communication effects. The paradigm consists of four queries, with two added by us to make it all-encompassing. It reads:

Who? Says What? How? To Whom? Where? So What?

Insofar as theorems about mass communication continue to focus on one or more of these six variables, as related to differences in effect, the queries retain their relevance. They refer to the characteristics of the communicator, the content transmitted, the medium, the susceptible recipients, and the circumstances in which the content is received. Yet the paradigm, its utility for presenting and generating hypotheses notwithstanding, does not quite qualify as a comprehensive model of the full range of effects that mass communication has on modern society

Admittedly, to demand an all-embracing model of all the interrelationships may be setting our sights too high but it should not inhibit us from expressing three caveats about the paradigm. The first has to do with the variety of indicators used in the search for effects in answer to the "so what" question. Thus, researchers have measured changes in knowledge, beliefs, opinions, preferences, taste, behavior, etc. to cope with a whole variety of responses—from movement toward closer conformity with the goals of the communicator or reinforcing and confirming an already existing state. Many messages do not get through at all and some, because of misunderstandings or by arousing hostility, can actually boomerang. Analysis of these and other kinds of responses, intended or unintended, have usually been conducted without much reference to anything beyond the message, content, source, or medium.

Second, estimates of larger societal consequences have generally been based on aggregations of micro-level data about individuals and limited to the circumstances in which they occurred. Examples of these are the progressive polarization in the period preceding an election, the limited effectiveness of media information campaigns, and the increases in awareness produced by saturation coverage of certain problems.

Third, and arguably the most important of the caveats, the governing paradigm of mass communication almost invariably implies a one-way flow with the media depicted as a pipeline for high volumes of content produced by professionals to woo an audience and/or to influence their ideas or behavior. Even the addition of a second supplementary step to this flow does not amount to a fundamental reconceptualization of this essentially linear model of the media as nothing but transmitters of information and entertainment.

Our critique is not meant to dispute the value of a paradigm that has guided much highly productive research. It has certainly advanced our understanding of the various ways in which people respond to and what they do with the stream of content from the media. We claim no more but no less that the model, even with the refinement it has undergone over the years, is one dimensional, that it fails to take adequate account of the reciprocities and interactions through which the members of a society construct their images of social reality. Those images will vary according to perspectives imposed by where people live and how they earn their livelihood. Be this as it may, advances in communication technology have opened a new world to all. It has, above all, fostered a greater awareness of social relationships with others—including the many nameless ones whom they are unlikely ever to encounter or even see. That these imagined relationships are nonetheless real in their consequences has been documented and aptly conceptualized by Donald Horton and R. Richard Wohl (1956) as "para-social interaction." Consumers of popular culture respond to both fictitious characters in serials and regular performers as if they were part of an intimate circle. Public figures can enter people's lives by the same route. The most persistent intruder into the collective consciousness, no matter how vaguely perceived and devoid of distinctly personal characteristics, is the image of some kind of multitude, be it of like-minded peers, of passive bystanders, of potential adversaries, of fearsome criminals preying on the innocents, or anonymous threats from subversives or terrorists. The producers of media content respond to a similar reality constructed from their own unique professional perspective, in which the mass audiences assume a large place.

Leading "Theories"?

Two approaches to the study of media effects have enjoyed the greatest currency. The one labeled agenda-setting is focused on the role of the media as sources of information and providers of contextual elaboration for recipients; the other summons up spirals of silence, in which the media mirror—not always accurately—the opinion prevalent in the multitude. In the ongoing discourse about communication, these two, more than others, are often singled out as the significant "theories" of media effects. How well do they qualify?

To begin at the beginning, communication technology makes available ever greater amounts of information. Effects are limited less by the capacity of media to store and disseminate information than by the inability of the human mind to absorb everything the media have to offer and of the social universe to share what gets through. The idea of information overload does have a short history. Given these constraints, the mass media, like all other communication channels, function —more effectively than would ever before have been possible for so large and diverse an audience—as a focus and filter of information. Early on, world attention surveys catalogued headlines to show that a small number of events enjoyed most of the limelight. Subsequent research confirmed that media coverage and public awareness were indeed correlated as were high news consumption and being informed on politics and public affairs. While the generalization will not necessarily hold for everyone in all situations, the correlations confirm that mass communication, notwithstanding its supposedly "limited effects," does have significant influence at least on the topics and issues that people are aware of, think about, are preoccupied with, talk about, and want political leaders to solve. All this comes under the umbrella of the neologism "agenda-setting."

Well-earned credit for drawing attention to and continuing to research the agenda-setting function of the media goes to Maxwell McCombs and Donald L. Shaw (1972). Nevertheless, a brief glance backward shows theirs to have been less of a discovery than a reformulation of earlier generalizations by such sociologists as Robert K. Merton and Paul F. Lazarsfeld (1948) that mass communication defines the issues that dominate electoral campaigns. Besides, the evidence for agenda-setting effects on which McCombs and Shaw drew was really quite paltry. The effect was observed only among a small number of still undecided voters, who seemed to have been moved by the issue emphasized by the media. That was really quite paltry evidence. None of this seemed to have mattered. The new concept (new to mass communication) was enthusiastically embraced and set off a chase after agenda-setting effects everywhere on any topic of general interest or interpersonal discussion. The appeal, in our opinion, came from the boost the concept gave to those reluctant to subscribe to the then popular "minimal effects" theorem. It was as an easy way to demonstrate that mass communication did, after all, have significant influence.

The scope of the theory, for all its good, nevertheless strikes us as much narrower than implied by its name. The issues that divide a public, whether inside or outside the context of a political campaign, do not come ready-made to be seized upon by eager politicians or by a press in search of an earth-shattering exposé. Issues evolve in a discourse, not all of it visible in the media, but with input by political actors testing the waters and by advocates for particular causes and constituencies. Much of this discourse is conducted with an eye toward the media and affected by estimates of how an issue is likely to play and affect public support for one side or another. A further contribution by the media to the public discourse is for politicians to send signals to other politicians opposed to or allied with themselves. Strategies are bound to clash. With no one in complete control, the contents of an issue and even the issues themselves change prior to any final ordering of priorities. Public agenda are *built* not set, so we would argue, and to assess the role of the media in agenda building requires more than matching data from surveys with trends in content. These need to be supplemented with data on participants at every level of discourse as part of an in-depth case study with issues and controversies as the unit of analysis.

Another consideration that should enter—or does enter—our searches for mass communication effects is the recognition that individuals react to media content as social beings. The tendency is to go along, to take one's cues from one's immediate surroundings, especially when in contact with intimates, but also to take cognizance of norms sanctioned by prevailing opinion on what is right and what is wrong as well as decisions sanctioned by formal vote. Also, most people are disinclined to support that which is morally discredited and, even when disagreeing, are not anxious to be damned as apostates. Elisabeth

Noelle-Neumann (1980) imputed a similar response by people who perceive themselves out of step with an altogether nameless majority. In positing a spiral of silence, she echoed and breathed new life, albeit with new theoretical ballast, into the familiar near-obsolete band-wagon hypothesis. The case she makes for the human propensity to defer to any kind of majority is predicated on several untested assumptions. Human beings, she contends, operate with a "quasi-statistical sense" of where the majority stands. Going against that majority will elicit disapproval and sanctions. And consequently that, moved by their "fear of isolation," those who feel outnumbered are moved to conceal their true views, thereby making the majority viewpoint seem more dominant than it actually is. It follows that the "majorities" depicted in the media generate a multiplier that brings the consensus without which no society can function. As a corollary, she also contended that journalists, when they disseminate a false picture of public opinion more in line with their own point of view, exert undue influence on the direction in which public opinion develops.

Evidence to support these assumptions has been less than convincing. Unable to personally engage the mass of nameless others, people have been found more likely to perceive a "false consensus" that overstates the extent to which the views prevalent in their own circles are shared across society. Information transmitted by the media concerning polls and journalistic assessments may counter this tendency but, because of contrary estimates, probably not completely. The wide resonance the spiral of silence idea has enjoyed rests less on supporting empirical evidence than on what it suggests about the interplay between the media and recipient perceptions. Spirals of silence do occur. We ourselves, back in 1952, identified a "landslide effect" ("landslide perceptions" would have been a more fitting term) triggered by the mammoth coverage of the street crowds that greeted General Douglas MacArthur upon his return home from Japan following that hero's abrupt dismissal by President Truman. Criticism by political actors was temporarily muted and opponents of the general moved cautiously (Lang & Lang 1968/2002). On events of this kind, the spiral of silence process certainly points in the right direction. Its shortcoming as a theory lies in the off-hand manner in which Noelle-Neumann fused social control as exercised in groups of intimates and in solitary communities bound by tradition, where silence out of respect for customs and norms sanctified by age is apt to prevail, with social control in a highly differentiated mass society with by many overlapping and typically crosscutting secondary relationships. In the latter, voicing discordant opinions on a public issue is usually a strategic decision more dependent on a person's definition of the situation than a personality trait.

Direct Interactions with the Media

The way the media enter people's lives—more often as welcome guests than as intruders—affects their world as they see it. Already mentioned is the familiarity with which some audience members regard persons regularly featured on the media. This, together with the witnessing of news events that attract the attention of nearly everyone, turns them into participants, even if only vicariously and, so to speak, at a distance. Para-social relationships are nevertheless real enough for people to gossip about, to approve, morally censure, and occasionally to generate letters, usually unsolicited, to the media characters. Direct interaction, but of a different kind, also occurs whenever the press shows up. Just being present at an event that may make headlines affects the attendees' behavior. The most rudimentary and obvious of such interactions with the media is the self-conscious mien and posture that subjects adopt when having their picture taken, even if only by an amateur photographer for a family album unlikely ever to be shared beyond one's circle of family and friends.

Reactions the media elicit merely by their presence, by "being there," fall under the category of reciprocal effects. We have no idea who introduced that term but such interaction occurs whenever the media show up. The chance to be on television is enough to turn ordinary pedestrians or sightseers into performers. Ramifications go beyond mere showing off. Because of competition for media attention, those seeking publicity will schedule a press conference for maximum coverage and/or stage political rallies that, well-timed and publicized, may demonstrate and, possibly, exaggerate the public support for one's cause. The initiative may come from organizers or from the media. But regardless of the specific circumstances and regardless of who sets things up, the media become the center of convergent activity, much as a magnet would, which is to say they do more than cover activities and events. They co-determine their course. Media influence is even greater on happenings that might never have taken place had nobody turned up to report them while events jointly planned with the press usually enjoy special attention and extra publicity.

Some intriguing examples of effects traceable to recipients' interactions with the mass media are scattered throughout the literature. It was W. Phillips Davison (1956), whose case study of the blockade of West-Berlin by Soviet occupation troops, an episode of cold-war politics, alerted us to the full significance of recognition by the media. In 1948/49, while that city was under siege for nearly 10 months, residents aware of the intensive coverage of their plight in the Western press came to see themselves as the strategically positioned defenders of democracy in an escalating international conflict. The coverage greatly raised their morale and strengthened their determination to hold out despite all hardships. Media recognition can also have adverse consequences, not necessarily by portraying subjects in a bad light but because publicity is also potentially seductive. Thus, Tod Gitlin (1980), once a leading activist in the protests during the 1960s, pointed to a side effect of all the attention the leaders had courted to promote their movement's political goals. The status that recurrent media attention conferred on the small number of spokesmen became a diversion; bit by bit, the value they put on being in the limelight became a distraction.

To construe such interaction effects, even when organizers and media clearly collaborate, as falsifying the real world, is to take too narrow a view. In saying so we do not mean to ignore the many past efforts (plus others likely to come) by a politically biased media management or by some group with an axe to grind, who, with or without cooperation from authorities, may fabricate or distort information to score political points. That this occurs need not distract us from the multi-faceted interplay between the media and actors that eventuates in the construction of the social universe in which people participate even if, for the most part, only "at a distance." This holds especially for the category of media events so thoughtfully analyzed by Daniel Dayan and Elihu Katz (1992) in their studies of "contests, conquests, and coronations" organized for saturation coverage when people not actually on the scene experienced the same "sense of occasion" as the ones that were. And, once the media have left their stamp on an event, this is how it will be remembered in much the same way as any other not intrinsically significant event when hailed as a "first" enters history.

Media and Reference Groups

When people react to the media, what they are really addressing is not the equipment or the media representatives but an audience behind them that, consciously or out of sheer habit, they visualize. That unseen multitude makes up a world they have learned to imagine with help from the media. To put it another way, there are occasions on which people look at themselves from the perspective that the media have opened for them. Reporters, microphones, and cameras are mere surrogates for this abstract reference group. The reference group concept, as Tamotsu Shibutani (1955) defines it, applies to "any collectivity, real or imagined, envied or despised, whose perspective is assumed by the actor" (p. 563). Though it has an established place in social psychology, few studies of mass communication ever resort to it for explanation. Herbert Gans (1957) came close in his analysis of the different audience images in the minds of the makers of the classic movie *The African Queen* and how they shaped the final product. Closer yet to the concept is an experimental demonstration by Ithiel de Sola Pool and Irwin Shulman (1959) on the influence of "imaginary interlocutors"—whether they are supportive and friendly or critical—on the content of the stories produced by experimental subjects enrolled in a course for journalists. The experiment, to be sure, addresses only the production side as does the study by Gans. Yet people who are the subjects of media attention, insofar as they present themselves as they want to be seen, are also assuming the producer roles. The classic work of Erving Goffman (1959) on self-presentation remains highly relevant.

Anticipating and analyzing the distant and geographical mass they are targeting is part of the professional communicator's job. What about everyone else? People still encapsulated in local life are incapable of viewing themselves from a broader perspective. Discovery of this all too apparent inability of villagers in the developing world led Daniel Lerner (1957) to theorize about the conditions that extended people's capacity for "empathy." The initial impetus comes from industrialization. Accompanied by mass migration from the countryside to the city that made people geographically mobile, it also laid the technological foundation for the development of mass communication. The stage was media development. The habitual exposure through the new window on a world far beyond their immediate surroundings fostered a mental mobility that enabled people to assume a variety of other perspectives. That is the area for which reference group theory would be a good guide.

We point to a recent study of communication among scientists as a telling example of how the media serve as a stand-in for a reference group. Electronic journals, easily available to those affiliated with a particular discipline, contain information on the frequency with which articles are cited. These are taken as cues to what colleagues in their field—many of them not personally known to them—consider important work. Everyone can look to the choices of "others" and use them to guide their own reading and citation of the literature. The result, as choices converge, is to increase the number of citations from a smaller number of articles. In the emerging consensus, initially "near-random" differences in the significance of studies become magnified (Evans, 2008).

Akin concepts to reference groups are the third-party effects posited by Davison (1983), whose other work we already mentioned. They are "effects" over and above the direct impact of a communication from some source (the first person) to the recipient (the second person) and derived from estimates, accurate and often totally erroneous, about the response of *others* to some content. The estimate need not be the same as one's own response or by people like oneself. But whatever the specifics, the responses of experimental subjects to the same message are affected by information or no information at all about the responses of peers or some other category of people. There is, however, more to this idea. It drives home the inherent potential of mass communications to set off a series of interactions based on assumptions and expectations about the multitude that we have become accustomed to imagine. Subsumed under this idea are the very real concerns of policy-makers, administrators, reformers, political activists, and just ordinary citizens about the possibility of third party effects. Concerns such as these drive policy just as they drive the normal public and administrative discourse.

Institutional Adaptation: Reflections on the Advent of New Media

Of the theorists so far cited, Daniel Lerner is the only one to have explicitly addressed the vast social changes associated with the arrival of the modern media. More equal access to knowledge for ordinary people, largely rural, poor, and with limited education, would allow a more equal sharing of knowledge and pave the way for a "participant society." His theory, eloquently formulated, assumed unidirectional development.

More sweeping and at the same time more sensitive to the complexity of the interrelationship between the inherent bias of every medium and social and institutional relationships is the work of Harold A. Innis (cf. 1950), an economist, who had participated in a seminar run by Robert E. Park at the University of Chicago. The major variable for him was the "bias" of a medium dependent on whether it appealed mainly to the ear and one that appealed mainly to the eye. In line with this distinction, the natural flow of spoken words favored flexibility as against the fixed nature of written texts and iconic representations. The dichotomy seems to catch the essence of the transition from a predominantly oral culture to one increasingly visual better than the partial superseding of a predominantly literary culture by media that allow for the simultaneous transmission of both sound and sight.

Dying in 1952, Innis did not live long enough to experience the full impact of the "age of television" and of the Internet. One can only speculate about what he might have said. The one thing about which we can be sure, however, is that he was never as much a technological determinist as Marshall McLuhan, his colleague at the University of Toronto, who seized upon the many leads in Innis's ruminations, would later become. The difference between their theorizing becomes clear when one considers the political aspects of "bias" evident when the arrival or spread of a medium advances the claims of challengers against established power. Some thoughtful observations by Innis on the creation, sustenance, and impairment of certain "monopolies of knowledge" (and of culture) still apply today.

The term "monopoly" implies sole possession of something valuable. Knowledge, unlike material commodities, can be shared without diminution of the initial possessor's own stock. But there surely is value in knowing something that no one else knows, unless that knowledge is made obsolete by new intellectual and cultural products. Beyond that, claims to exclusive ownership are often contested. One only needs to call to mind the incessant disputes over copyrights, shields for journalists to protect their sources, and what documents are a president's private property.

Subject to ownership rights are, on the one side, the production and collection of knowledge (input) and, on the other, its distribution and dissemination (output), a distinction Innis tended to fudge. On the input side, the most obvious but often disputed monopoly is the personal information individuals consider their exclusive personal property to be disclosed only upon authorization by its owner. Much esoteric knowledge produced or collected by specialists is similarly privileged with access restricted to accredited insiders, to those rich enough to pay for it or with the power to force disclosure. A strong, contemporary counter trend are demands for openness in the name of the general interest. Monopolies on the output side revolve around the ownership of the channels for the distribution of content. Corporate managers of the media and, to varying degrees, the state exercise control by their selection of producers, by the kinds of content they commission, and by the sources of knowledge they cultivate.

The cultural and ideological bias that reflects the manifold ties between a media establishment and politically or economically powerful elites has a central place in the theories of such neo-Marxists as Antonio Gramsci (1975) on hegemonic influence and of the circle around Theodor Adorno (Adorno & Bernstein, 2001) on the commodification of culture by an industry that, in catering to a mass market, masks the reality behind the entertainment shows. Ownership structure and media management do, of course, matter but the bias inherent in the technology of the dominant medium matters even more. The introduction of a new medium is always an unsettling influence to which economic institutions, no less than political and cultural institutions, are forced to accommodate. Thus, musical performances without patronage by the church, state, or the wealthy become part of a business run, not necessarily for profit, but to provide musicians with a living. Radio opened new opportunities, to which musicians responded by organizing. They pressured the industry to pay royalty for every song broadcast. Meanwhile, music publishers and record production companies relied on (and sometimes bribed) disk jockeys to play and ratchet up the popularity of music they owned. These arrangements gave way once new technologies empowered purchasers to download and share their own music. Television, in its turn, led to equally significant changes in sports. With everyone able to watch, the major leagues crowded out locally based teams and, with the additional revenue from telecast games, could afford the huge salaries that attract star players. So it was that competitive athletics increasingly became professionalized.

Communication monopolies, like everything else, have a limited life span. Newspapers, once the dominant medium within their respective circulation areas, ceded some power to news services based on the telegraph and telephone. The territorial monopoly built around radio, the first genuinely national medium, caused strictly local politics to become more of a sideshow, a trend reinforced with the advent of video. In their turn, the national monopolies built around traditional broadcasting are being eroded by the increasing ease of access to and speed of electronic communication. With English emerging as the lingua franca for international trade, linguistic barriers to the world-wide dissemination of content have weakened. Anglo-American news and entertainment, according to Tunstall (1977), seemed on the way to world dominance but their formulaic content, while satisficing, could not serve all idiosyncratic needs, allowing others to fill the void. Rigidity is the Achilles heel of every monopoly. We note that two decades later Tunstall (2008) himself backtracked on his earlier claim.

Among the political institutions directly affected by the progressive intrusion of the "capitalist" media, driven as they are by their own interests, into the previously privileged presidential press conference. In the pre-television era, this had been an opportunity for a small number of elite journalists for background briefings directly from the chief executive. The nature and purpose of the interaction changed. Opening remarks by the president, usually reading from a prepared statement, would be followed by questions from reporters intent on extracting something to make headlines. Party conventions, transformed into televised spectacles, have likewise lost their nominating function. New technologies make it possible for aspirants to political office, once they find enough wealthy donors or are able to attract sufficient funds from other sources, to develop their own campaign organization and staff it with communication specialists to overwhelm voters with proprietary messages. More recently, the innovative use of the Internet by such "outsiders" as President Barack Obama once was, has led to the defeat of establishment candidates. It has even begun to undercut the dominance of such an economically dominant institution as the New York Stock Exchange. Transactions no longer require a broker's physical presence: they can be conducted via the Internet at all hours of the day and night.

The idea of some kind of balance lies at the core of James W. Carey's (1969) insightful analysis of the connection between the communication revolution and the development of a national identity in an industrial society with its complex division of labor. By providing the channel through which a diverse and geographically dispersed audience shares in the events taking place in the central institutions of their society, the national media tend to support existing authority. They exert, in this respect, a homogenizing influence but also leave some space for imaginative entrepreneurs to find or carve out some niche for themselves. Outlets specialized to accommodate the many different life styles, minority interests, professions, personal tastes, and ideologies both reflect and sustain the existing diversity within the larger cultural framework. The counter trend to the centralizing tendencies in a media-rich society is grounded not only in localism. It sustains and facilitates development of non-local networks around some commonality, deviant as it may be. As societies become more segmented horizontally, residents in the same neighborhood can participate in quite different communities of interest. New ties and identities cut across localities.

Democratic Values

Does the phenomenal increase in storage capacity coupled with the possibilities for the retrieval of archived information act as an equalizer? Or does it strengthen the hegemonic control of elites? This key question, usually sidestepped by mass communication theory, has been taken up by more radical critics of current society. It is also a question to which there is no categorical answer. Starting with the collection side, we note that the purveyors of consumer goods, of news, of reading material, of all kinds of other information and entertainment, along with public and governmental institutions, have long been probing the habits, needs, and preferences of their mass clientele. Advances in data retrieval have furthered additional monitoring, often without their knowledge and consent, of what people do as a testimonial to the sovereignty of consumers. An example of how far this has gone is a project that Yahoo, developer of a powerful search engine, is about to launch. It will be tracking common words, phrases, and topics popular with web users to guide its news staff in writing stories to appeal to readers and viewers. These same data can strengthen the hand of unscrupulous users bent on exploiting existing dispositions and prejudices in order to promote some vested interest or illegitimate cause. It goes without saying that much depends on the use made of the burgeoning archival record. The 2010 mid-term elections once again produced newspaper stories based on some "dirt" from a minor, possibly long forgotten, event from the past, but somehow dug up and planted by political operators so as to damage an opponent's reputation. Spreading irrelevant but true facts devoid of all context can be as misleading as circulating outright falsehoods.

Still, most everyone stands to gain from better access to facts and information previously unrecorded and/or impossible to locate, provided, of course, they are accurate. Putting more things into the public domain is consistent with democratic ideals; it should and could be in the public interest. Yet Tichenor, Donohue, and Olien (1970) observed that the greatest information gains were concentrated among high media users, mostly the higher income and better educated groups, inevitably creating or widening an already existing "knowledge gap" between them and the rest—at least on the issues on which the respondents were queried. Gaps between information "haves" and information "have nots" have survived into the electronic age and, in some form or other, are likely to persist even after web access has reached saturation level. Active information-seekers with a commitment or professional interest in what is communicated are bound to gain most from enlargements of the knowledge base. The current electronically enriched communication environment is simply too overwhelming. Users are at the mercy of key words and labels to guide their "self-selections." As a result, we have, instead of just one knowledge gap, an increasing number of disparities. The consequences for maintaining a consensus within a participant society are hard to anticipate.

Notwithstanding the potential for abuse, mass communication has surely opened a new window for the multitude of outsiders. No longer are they completely shut out from all the negotiations and decisions at the elite level. The shield of confidentiality seems to have been pierced. Yet most of the public remain bystanders. They do not command either the administrative tools or the expertise needed to actually implement policy. Without them, ordinary people are unable to participate actively in a government whose business is conducted at a distance and remains inaccessible. To be sure, the outcomes of elections in which ordinary citizens cast votes are legally binding and there are other means and opportunities, if they care to use them, for bringing their personal preferences to bear on government. Citizens can still send letters, telegrams, email; they can sign petitions, demonstrate, boycott, even use violence in an effort to pressure those who actually govern. The power of mass communication resides in its ability to mobilize for all kinds of causes. It is there for dissident members of the elite or outside challengers ready to avail themselves of its power to rally people. But all too seldom do the demands raised in the name of some constituency express a communal consensus, one arrived at through discussion and after the full consequences of the action have become explored. Action by citizens as members of a public that extends beyond its locality differs from participation in an assembly. It replicates the aggregate of market decisions by individuals motivated to make their concerns heard. People with like preferences, if equally motivated, constitute a powerful mass but they are oriented more to their own personal interests. They do not ordinarily sacrifice private interest to further some common good.

This market analogy is not meant to be derogatory, only to highlight that, despite the legally "binding" power of elections and plebiscites, individual voters carry no responsibility for outcomes even if the consequence run counter to what the majority intended. Theirs is not a communal decision to which everyone consents, It is a "collective" decision by a mass of individuals only vaguely aware of the longer term consequences. Hardly ever does an electoral outcome carry the clear mandate pundits read into them; to get some law passed or for a reversal of policy. All too often results force winners, in order to get anything done at all, to form coalitions and to enter into compromises that few supporters would have approved before hand. The role of the public, as Walter Lippmann (1925) noted, is a very limited one. Very few citizens have either the time or the expertise to weigh policy alternatives and to assess their consequences with the thoroughness they deserve. Political strategists know this. They coin slogans and seek endorsements for candidates just as they would in promoting a commercial product.

References

Adorno, T. W., & Bernstein, J. (Ed.). (2001). *The culture industry: Selected essays on mass culture.* London: Routledge.

Blumer, H. (1933). *Movies and conduct.* New York: MacMillan.

Buecher, K. (1915). *Unsere Sache und die Tagespresse* [Our task and the daily press]. Tübingen, Germany: J.C.B. Mohr.

Carey, J. W. (1969). The communications revolution and the professional communicator. In P. Halmos (Ed.), The sociology of mass-media communicators (pp. 23–39), *Sociological Review Monograph, 13.*

Davison, W. P. (1956). Political significance of recognition via mass media: An illustration from the Berlin blockade. *Public Opinion Quarterly, 20,* 327–333.

Davison, W. P. (1983). The third-person effect in communication. *Public Opinion Quarterly, 47,* 1–15.

Dayan, D., & Katz, E. (1992). *Media events: The live broadcasting of history.* Cambridge, MA: Harvard University Press.

Doob, L. W. (1935). *Propaganda: Its psychology and technique.* New York: H. Holt.

Evans, J. A. (2008). Electronic publication and the narrowing of science scholarship. *Science, 321,* 395–399.

Gans, H. J. (1957). The creator audience relationship in the mass media: An analysis of movie making. In B. Rosenberg & D. M. White (Eds.), *Mass culture: The popular arts in America* (pp. 315–324). Glencoe, IL: Free Press.

Gitlin, T. (1980). *The whole world is watching: Mass media in the making & unmaking of the new left.* Berkeley: University of California Press.

Goffman, E. (1959). *The presentation of self in everyday life.* Garden City, NY: Doubleday.

Gramsci, A. (1975). *History, philosophy and culture in the young Gramsci.* In P. C. U. Cavalcanti & P. Piccone (Eds.). St. Louis, MO: Telos Press.

Horton, D., & Wohl R. R. (1956). Mass communication and para-social interaction. *Psychiatry: Journal for the Study of Interpersonal Processes, 19,* 215–229.

Innis, H. A. (1950). *Empire and communications.* Oxford, UK: Clarendon Press.

Lang, K., & Lang, G. E. (2002). *Television and politics.* New Brunswick, NJ: Transaction. (Original work published 1968)

Lasswell, H. D. (1946). Introduction. In B. L. Smith, H. D. Lasswell, & R. D. Casey (Eds.), *Propaganda, communication, and public opinion: A comprehensive reference guide* (pp. 1–25). Princeton, NJ: Princeton University Press.

Lerner, D. (1957). Communication systems and social systems: A statistical exploration in history and policy. *Behavioral Science, 2*(4), 266–275.

Lippmann, W. (1922). *Public opinion.* New York: MacMillan.

Lippmann, W. (1925). *The phantom public: A sequel to public opinion.* New York: Harcourt, Brace.

McCombs, M. E., & Shaw, D. L. (1972). The agenda-setting function of mass media. *Public Opinion Quarterly, 36,* 176–187.

Merton, R. K., & Lazarsfeld, P. F. (1948). Mass communication, popular taste, and organized social action. In L. Bryson (Ed.), *Communication of ideas* (pp. 95–118). New York: Harper.

Noelle-Neumann, E. (1980). *Die Schweigespirale: Öffentliche Meinung, Unsere Soziale Haut* [The spiral of silence: Public opinion, our social skin]. München, Germany: Riper.

Pool, I. de S., & Shulman I. (1959). Newsmen's fantasies: Audience and newswriting. *Public Opinion Quarterly, 23,* 145–158.

Sapir, E. (1931). Communication. In *Encyclopedia of the social sciences* (Vol. 4, pp. 78–81). New York: MacMillan.

Shibutani, T. (1955). Reference groups as perspectives. *American Journal of Sociology, 60,* 562–569.

Tarde, G. (1901). *L'opinion et la foule* [Opinion and the crowd]. Paris: Alcan.

Tichenor, P. J., Donohue, G. A., & Olien C. N. (1970). Mass media flow and the differential growth in knowledge. *Public Opinion Quarterly, 34,*159–170.

Tunstall, J. (1977). *The media are American.* New York: Columbia University Press.

Tunstall, J. (2008). *The media were American: U.S. mass media in decline.* New York: Oxford University Press.

Weber, M. (1924). Rede auf dem Ersten Deutschen Soziologentage in Frankfurt [Address to the First Conference of German Sociology in Frankfurt]. In *Gesammelte Aufsätze Zur Soziologie und Sozialpolitik* [Collected Papers on Sociology and Social Policy] (pp. 441–459). Tübingen, Germany: J.C.B.Mohr. (Original work published 1910)

CHAPTER CONTENTS

3 Thoughts on Lazarsfeld's New York "Radio Studies" from the Perspective of 2010

Gertrude J. Robinson

McGill University

This chapter explores three topics: Lazarsfeld's departure for the United States and his attempts to re-establish his academic career; another group's (Frankfurt Institute) necessity to leave Nazi Germany and its relationships with Columbia's Bureau of Social Research; and an exploration of the unacknowledged intellectual contributions of Lazarsfeld's female staff to the theoretical development of U.S. radio and mass communication studies. Among these were Lazarsfeld's two wives: Marie Jahoda and Herta Herzog, as well as Hazel Gaudet Erskine who worked on *The Invasion of Mars* (1940) and *The People's Choice* (1944), and Marjorie Fiske, who co-authored with Merton *Mass Persuasion* (1946) and became Deputy Director of Voice of America (VOA) 1949–55.

Lazarsfeld's "Radio Studies" in New York (1933–1948)

Thomas Kuhn in his path-breaking *Structure of Scientific Revolutions* (1962) makes the important point that "doing science" is a human activity like any other, involving many groups of scholars guided by different conceptual schemes. These schemes orient not only the decision as to what constitutes "evidence" for a particular group of researchers, but also the way in which evidence is collected. Kuhn's analysis suggests that it is misleading to assume that Lazarsfeld had dropped into virgin intellectual territory when he arrived in the United States with his Rockefeller fellowship in 1933. Lazarsfeld's idea to investigate radio effects, fit in well with earlier U.S. empirical concerns of which Lazarsfeld was however unaware. Advertisers were interested in establishing national markets, while Roosevelt and Goebbels' radio successes raised questions about radio's social and political implications. Harold Lasswell's propaganda work and Cantril and Allport's *Psychology of Radio* (1935) seemed to indicate that radio had stronger political impact than print (Lerg, 1977, pp. 74–76). To relate the latent social structure became Lazarsfeld and Merton's co-operative research preoccupation throughout the 1940s and 50s, during which time Elihu Katz was a graduate student at Columbia University (Lazarsfeld, 1975). Using the Bűhler's Vienna Forschungstelle (Research Institute) idea, which supported itself through research commissions, Lazarsfeld commenced to re-establish his academic status by transferring this entrepreneurial model to New York. He accomplished the transplant in three rapid stages between 1937 and 1945, an exceptional feat for a Jewish émigré. In its first incarnation it was called the Newark Research Center, where unemployment statistics were evaluated for the National Youth Administration. This was quickly transformed into the Princeton Radio Research Project (1937–40), when Lazarsfeld became co-director of the Rockefeller sponsored program with Frank Stanton and Hadley Cantril. After the loss of its premises in Newark, and a year before Lazarsfeld and Merton were simultaneously appointed to the sociology department, the Radio Project was transferred to Columbia, where it became the Office of Radio Research (1940–44; Robinson, 1990, p. 93). As of 1941 it was co-directed by two masters, whose relationship according to Sills (1979), was intense, personal and deeply meaningful to each other (pp. 226–228). The final emergence of the Bureau of Social Research was not accomplished until 1945, when the administrative relationship to Columbia was regularized and the *Bureau* became the laboratory for the Faculty of Political Science, for which the university paid 10% of the annual operating budget (Lazarsfeld, 1969, p. 333).

Lazarsfeld and his colleague, Robert K. Merton, who had been appointed to the Columbia sociology department at the same time, immediately took to each other, though they had very different working styles. Lazarsfeld, the extrovert, preferred working with younger assistants and was able to create a sense of commitment to himself which Morrison describes as similar to the close relations he had built up with his followers in the socialist Rote Falken (Red Falcons) youth organization in Vienna (Morrison, 1978). Merton, in contrast, was a more retiring but supportive scholar, who worked closely with collaborators and research assistants, often the wives of colleagues (Sills, 1979, p. 28). Between them the masters trained a number of eminent sociologists in the media phase of the Bureau, before they developed new research interests in the 1950s, with Lazarsfeld focusing on mathematical modeling and Merton, investigating the sociology of the sciences (Barton, 1982, p. 27). Among this group of young sociologists were Edward Suchman and Thelma McCormack in the 1940s, as well as William McPhee and Elihu Katz in the 1950s. The latter rescued the Personal Influence (1955) study, after C. Wright Mills and others had failed to pull the data together (Coleman, 1980, p. 166).

In 1948 Lazarsfeld resigned the co-directorship of the Office of Radio Research to become Chairman of the Sociology Department. He was succeeded first by Kingsley Davis (1948–50) and then by Charles Glock (1951–56). Davis doubled the small budget of $90,000 of the early years and stabilized the Bureau's hand-to-mouth existence with a $500,000 grant from the Air Force to study the world's cities after WWII (Barton, 1984, pp. 1–3). This meant that between 1941 and 1945 the ad-hoc staffing of the early years had slowly become regularized. The *1939 Radio Research* volume suggests that Edward Suchman had been promoted to "manager of operations" and that Lazarsfeld was aided by two pre-doctoral fellowship holders: Alberta

Curtis and Francis Holter, who were joined by three research assistants: Marjorie Fiske, Hazel Gaudet and Jeanette Sayre who continued to work on their degrees (Lerg, 1977, p. 76). During this time Merton and his assistants developed a number of key "middle range" theories to explain social communication processes. These include the nature of influentials (cosmopolitans and locals) and their role in the diffusion of mediated messages; the characteristics of the communicator (e.g., entertainer Kate Smith's "sincerity") and its relationship to message "believability," explored by Herta Herzog; and the role of social relationships (primary groups) in these processes (Marjorie Fiske). In addition, they explored the media's social functions, pioneering such ideas as the "status conferral" function, the enforcement of social norms and the media's "narcotizing dysfunctions." Lazarsfeld, in contrast, was generally more interested in the socio-psychological dimensions of action. He and his collaborators therefore explored the effects of social categories (age, sex, education, etc.) and social networks on media use and decision-making as represented by such co-authored works as *The People's Choice* (Lazarsfeld, Berenson, & Gaudet, 1944/1969) and *Personal Influence* (Katz & Lazarsfeld, 1955). The extent to which collaborators as well as Lazarsfeld's wives contributed to the "two-step flow" theory of social communication is at present unknown. Marie Jahoda worked on the Marienthal study (1933), Herta Herzog on the *Invasion from Mars* (1940) and Patricia Kendall (with Lazarsfeld) on *Radio Listening in America: The People Look at Radio—Again* (1948), exhibiting considerable research accomplishments in their own right, which will be explored in the final section of this chapter. What emerges from this evidence suggests that Lazarsfeld was not the founder of U.S. communications studies as Berelson suggests in 1959, but rather that he developed a new social science based theory of media effects at Columbia University, where another group of European intellectuals, with different theoretical assumptions had also sought refuge from Nazism (Robinson, 1990, p. 102).

The Frankfurt Institute's Transplant to New York (1934–1949)

It is important to note that in addition to Lazarsfeld's lack of knowledge about the state of sociology in the United States, he was also unaware of the fact that another European institute had sought refuge in New York. This was the Frankfurt Institute of Social Research, founded by labor historian Karl Grünberg in 1926. The core members of this group were Max Horkheimer and Friedrich Pollock as well as Herbert Marcuse, Leo Lowenthal, Theodore Adrono, Franz Neumann, Erich Fromm, and Karl Friedrich Wittfogel. All of these scholars had been born around the turn of the century and came from assimilationist Jewish backgrounds. All of them, furthermore, revolted against the bourgeois complacency of their parents and called themselves Marxists, though most of them did not join any parties during the Weimar Republic years. The group founded the *Zeitschrift für Sozialforschung* (*Journal for Social Research*), to elaborate a Marxist cultural critique of capitalist society, which they called "critical theory." When the National Socialists took over the 1931 Reichstag, this group of Jewish intellectuals began to view themselves as internal exiles" and prepared an exit strategy to leave Germany. It included the organization of a branch research office in Geneva; the transferal of the majority of Institute funds to the Netherlands and the search for a U.S. partner. The group's emigration to New York, where Columbia offered a loose institutional affiliation, similar to that in Frankfurt, occurred on the recommendation of Julian Gumpertz, an American who was Pollock's assistant (Jay, 1987, p. 56). All except Fromm, who had been lecturing in Chicago since 1932, departed at different times as exit papers became available. Horkheimer and Marcuse left in July 1934, followed by Lowenthal in August and Pollock in September, while Wittfogel and the wives and children followed last (Jay, 1973, p. 39). As the Institute members left the old continent, they conceived of their American purpose as becoming an "island of German radical thought," which would maintain a link with the country's humanist past and be available for Germany's post-Nazi reconstruction. This was expressed in the *Zeitschrift's* German language content and Marxist theoretical preoccupation (Coser 1984).

On their arrival, the Frankfurt group's financial independence (its $300,000 endowment) allowed it to offer support to some 200 émigrés, among whom were Hans Meier, Fritz Steinberg, Gerhard Meier, and Paul Lazarsfeld. In the 10 years between 1934 and 1944, furthermore, the Institute also provided approximately $200,000 to 116 doctoral candidates and 14 post-doctoral students, who were completing their degrees at Columbia University (Jay, 1973, pp. 39, 113–115). In addition, the Institute by the 1940s made itself useful by offering both guest lectures and courses through the Extension Division of Columbia University, where August Wittfogel and Leo Lowenthal lectured on fascism and the role of culture in authoritarian regimes, two domains in which the core Institute members were well versed. At the time, Lowenthal once again assumed the managing editorship of the *Zeitschrift* which was for the first time published in English as *Studies in Philosophy and Social Science* and worked on an empirical study of workers in the Weimar Republic, directed by Fromm, to explore the failure of traditional Marxism to explain the proletariat's reluctance to fulfill its historical vanguard role. This research showed that the proletariat's revolutionary potential had to be historically contextualized and that in the United States, labor had turned into a petit-bourgeois group with massive interests in the status quo (Lowenthal, 1980, pp. 61–64). Other studies on authoritarianism undertaken contemporaneously included *Studien über Autorität und Familie* (1936) and Fromm's *Escape from Freedom* (1941), as well as Adorno, Frenkel-Brunswik, Levinson, and Stanford's *The Authoritarian Personality* (1950). All together the Frankfurt group produced a total of 16 books and 91 articles, 40% of these were studies in authority, 22% philosophical treatises and 18% studies in literature, music and art (Jay, 1973, p. 342). The Horkheimer group saw Nazism as the most extreme example of a trend towards irrational domination in Western countries and no longer considered the economic sub-structure as the source of social cohesion, but instead paid increasing attention to violence and obedience in Nazism. Moreover, Adorno introduced the concept of "culture industry" and increasingly Institute members came to feel that the culture industry enslaved people in more effective and subtle ways, than did state power (Jay, 1973, p. 216).

Midway through their exile, two massive studies financed by the Jewish Labor Committee in the 1940s restored the Institute's flagging finances and provided monetary security until its return to Germany in 1949. The first study (1943–45) involving Lowenthal, dealt with the degree of anti-Semitism in American labor. It was chaired by Adolph Held, who had contacts with the AFL and CIO and various unaffiliated unions, which facilitated the collection of data in New York, California, and Detroit, Michigan. Horkheimer remembers that the conclusions were so damaging to American labor, that the Institute was reluctant to publish them (Jay, 1973, pp. 224–225). Instead, in their *Studies in Prejudice*, Adorno and his colleagues explored the character types who would be most receptive to demagogic appeals and developed a series of anti-Semitic personality scales (Jay, 1986, pp. 94–95). Bruno Bettelheim and Morris Janowitz investigated the *Dynamics of Prejudice: A Psychological and Sociological Study of Veterans* (1950), Nathan Ackerman and Marie Jahoda focused on *Antisemitism and Emotional Disorder: A Pschoanalytic Interpretation* (1950). In the final two studies, Lowenthal and Guterman's *Prophets of Deceit* (1949) the techniques of the demagogue were analyzed, while Paul Messing's *Rehersal for Destruction* (1949) presented a straightforward historical account of anti-Semitism in Germany.

Despite their ideological differences, the Frankfurt Institute and the Bureau, had research contacts, exchanged personnel and offered each other institutional help in New York. The most important research contacts were: Theodore Adorno's "On Popular Music" (1941) and Leo Lowenthal's "The Triumph of Mass Idols" (1944), which highlight both the inability of Adorno to work with Lazarsfeld, as well as the compatibility of "critical theory," with evidential analysis. Though the "critical-administrative" debate has been well rehearsed by scholars like Hanno Hardt (1991) and David Morrison (1978), they view the historical context in which it was played out too narrowly. The missing elements are not only the deteriorating personal relationships between Lazarsfeld and Adorno, but also the Frankfurt group's disinterest in Lazarsfeld's research agendas. In the summer of 1939 the Rockefeller sponsored music project, in which Adorno had introduced the concept of a "culture industry," was cancelled. Lazarsfeld's letter to Adorno mentions his extreme disappointment with the outcome of their association, commenting in the last paragraph: "You and I agree upon the superiority of some parts of your intellectual work, but you think because you are basically right somewhere, you are right everywhere" (Jay, 1973, p. 223). In retrospect it becomes clear, that few men who knew Adorno doubted his intellectual brilliance, but fewer still, and here Horkheimer is the exception, found him an easy collaborator. In spite of the termination of the project, Adorno's "The Radio Symphony" was published in Lazarsfeld/Stanton's *Radio Research 1941* volume.

Lowenthal's "The Triumph of Mass Idols" (1944), documents the idea that the culture industry is subtly enslaving and that literature needs to be used to identify the social and cultural structures that promote such enslavement. Lazarsfeld, who knew about Lowenthal's unpublished biographical studies of Emil Ludwig and Stefan Zweig, wondered whether he could apply his insights to contemporary American literary productions. This request coincided with Lowenthal's discovery that the *Saturday Evening Post* and *Colliers,* two of the most popular American consumer magazines at the time, contained biographies. Lowenthal content analyzed all issues of the magazines between 1901 and 1940 and found that in the first 20 years of the century, the heroes of the biographies were taken from the field of production: successful merchants, professionals, inventors and entrepreneurs. The biographies thus seemed to function as politico-educational stimuli to reinforce the Horatio Alger myth of personal success. By the end of the 1930s, however, the situation had changed drastically and the so-called heroes became people from show business: movie actors, radio stars, famous impresarios, singers and sportsmen, whose sole function was to entertain the reader. This the biographies did through portraying the entertainers' consumer habits and hobbies. Lowenthal concluded that these findings were evidence that in the stage of corporate capitalism, the rise of entrepreneurship increasingly turned into pure fiction; and second; that American bourgeois society had transformed itself into a consumer society, in which people were interested only in consumption. Jay observes that the Institute's critique of mass culture and its related analysis of the American authoritarian potential had a greater impact on American intellectual life than their earlier studies, because by the 1950s, local scholars like Clement Greenberg and Dwight MacDonald, through their influential journal *Politics,* began to disseminate similar critiques to a wider public (Jay, 1973, p. 217).

The most interesting contacts between the Frankfurt and Bureau groups happened in 1944, when Pollock's office had to move to smaller quarters, because the endowment had lost half of its value as a result of bad investments. At the time Lazarsfeld proposed that the Institute be integrated into his own Bureau of Social Research, where between 1944 and 1946, C. Wright Mills was overseeing the field work and initial (unsuccessful) analysis of the Decatur data, which would ultimately become Katz and Lazarsfeld's *Personal Influence* (1955). Though the Sociology Department supported the plan, Horkheimer, who was working on the *Authorian Personality* (1950) with Adorno in California, ultimately declined the offer in 1946, citing health reasons (Jay 1973, p. 220). Yet, at about the same time, Lowenthal reported to Horkheimer that there was encouraging news from Germany to invite the Institute to return to Frankfurt to help in the post-Nazi reconstruction. Negotiations concluded in 1949, when the Frankfurt university chair was restored. On Horkheimer's return, the Institute's endowment and library went with him, although only two colleagues, Adorno and Pollock, made the return trip. The other expatriates had taken out citizenship papers and decided to remain in the United States (Jay, 1973, pp. 282–283).

The Bureau's Female Researchers: Unacknowledged Contributors

My reflections on Lazarsfeld's New York research institutes have not only mentioned connections with the Frankfurt group, but also suggested that he employed many female researchers. Though it is not yet clear exactly how many were involved in the Bureau's different incarnations, a historical re-evaluation of their role is overdue. Theoretically this means that female researchers can no longer be viewed as passive window dressing on the set, but must be acknowledged as active participants in the investigative enterprise. In the field of media and communication studies, this means focusing on how gender is implicated in and constructs a particular gender system through linguistic naming practices. Though feminist theory is by no means a unified theoretical position, there are at least two common preoccupations that distinguish it from other perspectives in the social sciences and humanities. The theory offers a systematic focus on gender as a mechanism that structures both the material and the symbolic worlds in which we live. As such, gender affects *how* we speak, *who* we speak to; as well as *how we are expected* to speak and behave. Feminist theory moreover, offers an alternative perspective on power, not in terms of a unitary "force" which some group "owns," but in terms of how gender is intertwined with a multiplicity of social relations of subordination (Robinson, 1996, 2005). Gender theory explains the silence about female contributions to Lazarsfeld's radio studies, as resulting from their lack of power in the Bureau's firmament dominated by the "double suns" of Lazarsfeld and Merton. Even though there were probably more than 20 females involved in the institution's quarter century existence, lack of space permits me to concentrate on the contributions of only four: Marie Jahoda (1907–2001) and Herta Herzog (1910–2009), Lazarsfeld's first and second wives; Hazel Gaudet (1908–1975), who co-authored *The People's Choice* (1944) and Marjorie Fiske (1914–1992), who co-authored (with Merton) *Mass Persuasion* (1946) based on the Kate Smith war bond drive and later became Leo Loewenthal's second wife. Their varied autobiographies will document the extraordinary talents and theoretical contributions that this group of four women made to the field of media and communication studies.

Marie Jahoda (1907–2001)

Marie Jahoda was born in Vienna into a middle-class Jewish family and, like many other psychologists of her time, became chair of the socialist high school student organization. There she met Paul Lazarsfeld, whom she married in 1927. In 1928, she earned her teaching diploma from the Pedagogical Academy of Vienna and in 1933 her Ph.D. in Psychology from the University of Vienna. She co-authored with Lazarsfeld and Hans Zeisel the now classical study *Die Arbeitslosen von Marienthal* (1932/English 1971), which dealt with the social impact of unemployment on the capital's small district. The researchers found that unemployment not only means financial deprivation, but also has extensive socio-psychological costs, because work in modern society provides a sense of personal worth, as well as structuring family lives and rhythms. Having divorced Lazarsfeld in 1934, after he left for the United States, she was imprisoned by the Dollfuss' Austro-fascist regime in 1937, and fled to England during WWII. After her arrival in New York in 1946, she worked as a professor of social psychology at New York University (1949–58) and as a researcher for the American Jewish Committee. For them she produced with Nathan Ackerman *Antisemitism and Emotional Disorder: A Psychoanalytic Interpretation* (1950) and also participated in Theodore Adorno's work on *The Authoritarian Personality* (1950). This led to her *Studies in the Scope and Method of the Authoritarian Personality: Continuities in Social Research* (1954) with Richard Christie. As a Professor of Social Psychology at Brunel University (1958–65) she established various Psychology degree programs, including the unique four-year practice based degree, which included three practical stints (Signorelli, 1996, p. 200).

After her return to Britain, Jahoda married the Labor politician Austen Albu (who died in 1994), whom she had first met during the war and continued work in psychology as well as future studies. The University of Sussex hired her in 1965 to found the Research Center of Human Relations and made her a consultant and Visiting Professor at the Science Policy Research Unit. In the former, she developed her theory of Ideal Mental Health, which consists of five categories: time structure, social contact, collective effort or purpose, social identity or status, and regular activity. The former interest produced *Freud and the Dilemmas of Psychology* (1977) and the latter, with co-edited with Christopher Freeman, *World Futures: The Great Debate* (1978) as well as *Technology and the Future of Europe: Competition and the Global Environment in the 1990s* with Christopher Freeman, K. Pavitt, M. Sharp, and W. Walker (1991). During her husband's long last illness, Jahoda became a founding Trustee of Bayswater Institute, when her first stroke in 1990 robbed her of most of her eyesight. Yet, she continued with her reading and research for another 11 years, dying on April 28, 2001, in Sussex.

Herta Herzog (1910–2010)

Herta Herzog was also born in Vienna in August 1910 into an assimilated Jewish family and experienced WWI as a child, remembering the family's lack of food and loss of savings. In the early 1920s, Herzog's mother contracted tuberculosis and died while her father, a graduate of law school, found work in the government. Herta attended a humanistic gymnasium, where Greek and Latin were taught and entered the University of Vienna in 1928, with the intention of studying archeology. During the first year, she attended a course by

Charlotte and Karl Bühler, who had founded the Institute of Psychology at the university in 1923. The former was known for her interest in child development and the latter had made important contributions to the psychology of thinking. The Institute of Psychology was staffed with several brilliant assistants, among them Lazarsfeld (1901–1976), a mathematician who taught statistics as applied to socio-psychology and hosted a Wednesday evening "psychological practicum" where senior students presented their work or well-known scientists such as Jean Peaget and Konrad Lorenz gave lectures. For her dissertation, Herzog decided to study the new medium of radio, with Lazarsfeld suggesting she replicate a British study, which focused on the effects of the human voice and personality of radio announcers. Herzog received her Ph.D. entitled "Die Stimme und Persönlichkeit" [The Voice and Personality] in 1933 after contracting polio, for which there was no treatment at the time. Herzog survived but was paralyzed from the waist down for six months and her right arm remained permanently lame.

After completing her Ph.D., Herzog became an Assistant Professor at the Psychological Institute of the University of Vienna, taking over Lazarsfeld's classes and students. She left the country in 1935, to move to New York and marry Lazarsfeld. There she found work as a personal assistant to Robert Lynd, who was working on his *Middletown* (1929) studies and assisted Lazarsfeld with interviews in New Jersey concerning the effects of the Depression, each of which provided her with insights into the new country, and improved her English language skills. Between 1937–1943 she obtained a research position on what would become the Columbia Bureau's radio project, which Herzog found to be infused with a pioneer-like spirit. Over 30 researchers, émigré and locals, contributed to the Bureau's first three radio publications. Based on her training with the Bűlow's, Herzog developed a new audience-centered approach to the study of mass communication, investigating the gratifications listeners derive from radio programs, using the *Invasion from Mars* (1940) broadcast and other daytime serials as her primary data (Herzog, 1940, 1941, 1943).

In 1943, the head of McCann-Erickson's research department asked Herzog to become their advertising research director in the home office, where she worked on applying three new research tools: the Lazarsfeld-Stanton program analyzer, which was later also used by the U.S. military to evaluate the "Why We Fight" film series; the "pupil dilation eye camera"; as well as figure drawing tests, which were used to determine product familiarity. In 1958, Herzog was named chairperson of Marplan, the agency's newly created research operation, and in 1959 spent a year in Germany, training and consulting clients. Between 1960 and 1970, Herzog was involved in a think-tank, Jack Tinker and Partners, working on client problems concerning management development for new market strategies. Herzog retired permanently in 1970 to spend time with her ailing second husband, Paul Messing, whom she had married in 1954. Messing was a political scientist from Rutgers University, who had written on Hitler and anti-Semitism in Germany. He died in 1979 in Europe, where Herzog remained and provided a series of lectures on U.S. television and television research at the universities of Tűbingen and later in Vienna (Signorelli, 1996).

Elisabeth Perse (1996) summarizes Herzog's research achievements by pointing out that her 60-year career encompassed three phases. In the first or Columbia Bureau phase, Herzog developed a new approach, now called "uses and gratifications," which focused on three aspects of radio listenership: its gratifications; individual responses; and audience "decoding" strategies. After she joined McCann Erickson in 1943, most of Herzog's work was client sponsored and therefore not published. She did however publish a summary of radio development and an analysis of letters to the Voice of America during the war. In her European studies of *Dallas* in the 1980s, Herzog became aware of the drawbacks of her approach, in particular the textual features she had ignored. She realized that audience decoding involves an individual negotiation with the text and that texts do not necessarily constrain a dominant reading. While in Europe, she chaired a group on motivation research for the Advertising Research Foundation and in 1986, was selected as a Hall of Fame Honoree of the Market Research Council. Herzog died in August 2010 in Tirol, Austria.

Hazel Gaudet Erskine (1908–1975)

Hazel Gaudet was a fascinating and important character, who turned survey and applied research toward politics as much as anyone associated with the Bureau in the early 1940s. Along with Herta Herzog, she was part of the Princeton Radio Project, before it became the Bureau of Social Research at Columbia. She was co-author of the first two major studies published, *The Invasion of Mars* (1940) and *The People's Choice* (1944). She administered and did some of the analysis for both field studies, and especially the latter, which produced theories like the "two-step flow" and discovered the role of "influentials" in political decision-making. Between 1939 and 1941 she published six articles on selection and enjoyment of radio programs, high school students radio preferences as well as success in job searches, before going to work with the survey researcher, Elmo Wilson, first at the Office of War Information and then at CBS. She helped with C. Wright Mills' study of labor leaders *Men of Power* (1948) and critiqued and edited his *While Collar* (1951) as a colleague and close friend.

Gaudet married Mr. Erskine and moved to Reno, Nevada, in 1947, leaving academic life and turning her public energies toward politics and liberal social causes in this conservative state. She labored diligently and selflessly to protect the gains of labor and the rights of minorities, consumers and women, as well as to defend the Bill of Rights against erosion and attack (Singer, 1975–76). One of her first causes was to win legislative support for the Aid to Dependent Children program, which was granted in 1955, while agitating to increase and transfer welfare benefits from the counties to the state. Between

1952 and 1956, moreover, she supported labor unions' attempt to repeal the "right to work" bill, which tried to prohibit unionization, to no avail. She was also involved with all major campaigns, organizing for the election of Sawyer as governor, to whom she proposed the appointment of women and minorities on state boards. In 1961 she began her 14-year editorship of *The Polls* in the *Public Opinion Quarterly,* which took on such important public issues as: race relations, religious beliefs, church observance, organized religious institutions, relations between religious groups and problems of knowledge and ignorance. Beyond that, Gaudet was involved with the furtherance of civil rights, organizing the first American Civil Liberties Union (ACLU) chapter in Reno in 1966. As secretary and board member of the northern chapter and state board for nearly nine years, she performed an important role in maintaining communications within the organization. From 1970, until illness forced her to resign in the spring of 1975, Hazel was the Nevada representative on the national ACLU Board, where she promoted prison reform and mental health (Signorelli, 1996, p. 95).

Marjorie Fiske (1914–1992)

Marjorie Fiske was born in Attleboro, Massachusetts, on June 25, 1914. She graduated from Mount Holyoke College in 1935, and received her M.A. from Columbia University in 1938. That year she published the first of her many papers, co-authoring an article with Lazarsfeld that introduced "panel studies" as a new methodology. Between 1935 and 1955, when she moved to California, she was a key figure in the newly emerging field of social psychology and became one of the key research associates at the Office of Radio Research and later the Columbia Bureau. During this time she conducted a number of radio studies, interviewed listeners, administered and wrote about the "Program Analyzer" and played a major role in conducting the Kate Smith war bond drive study, which would become *Mass Persuasion: The Social Psychology of a War Bond Drive* (1946) which she co-authored with Robert K. Merton and Alberta Curtis. It probed audience "gratifications" derived from media programming, such as a sense of participation in current events and explored people's meaning-making strategies through rhetorical analysis. In these years, Fiske learned about the value of interdisciplinary research involving psychiatrists, sociologists, psychologists and anthropologists, a type of scholarship she championed for the rest of her career. At the Bureau, Fiske also published eight articles on radio station preferences, radio advertising, consumer research, educational and psychological measurement, approaches to motion picture research and comic books. In 1949, Fiske became Deputy Director of Evaluation Staff for the State Department's International Broadcasting Service, the VOA, where she met her future husband Leo Loewenthal, who was VOA research director from 1949 to 1955. It was just before this that Katz had encountered him as a teacher and M.A. advisor at Columbia. In 1953, Fiske took a position as executive director of the Ford Foundation's national planning committee on research in television and returned to the Bureau to head their Planning Committee on Media Research (Signorelli, 1996, p. 100).

After completing his position at the VOA, Lowenthal and Fiske moved to California in 1955, where he was offered a position at Berkeley University and she taught in the departments of Sociology and the School of Librarianship at the University of California. In the latter capacity she authored a report on censorship in public and high school libraries, which was awarded the annual Library Literature Award of the American and International Library Associations. Her best-known work remains her studies of middle age and adulthood, which she began upon joining the Department of Psychiatry at the San Francisco Campus in 1958. Working with large interdisciplinary teams, she sought a method that would allow the research subjects to speak for themselves. This means that the usual psychological tests and questionnaires were supplemented with detailed, narrative interviews, often repeated with the same subject over a period of years. The method yielded unusual insights concerning how men and women cope with the normal and unexpected events of middle and late life, and what promotes and impedes mental health. Fiske summarized her findings in the book with David A. Chiriboga (1990) *Change and Continuity in Adult Life*. For her life's achievements, she won awards from the Gerontological Society of America and the American Psychological Association, and was granted an honorary doctorate by Mount Holyoke College.

The biographies of Marie Jahoda, Herta Herzog, Hazel Gaudet, and Marjorie Fiske demonstrate that the Bureau's female staff were insightful and accomplished researchers, who contributed to the practical and theoretical developments of media and communication studies in the United States for which they have not yet been credited. To be able to evaluate these contributions "in the round," gender theory suggests a number of additional questions that cannot be answered from this initial and fragmentary evidence. On the level of gender structuring the material and symbolic world in which we live, it is not yet clear *how* females were treated at the Bureau and whether Merton had a more egalitarian attitude toward his female co-authors, than Lazarsfeld. It is also not known whether female's research ideas were given the same credence as those of their male colleagues, nor whether they were paid the same salaries. All of these are important issues for future study, as is the validity of Herzog's opinion, that the Columbia Bureau's radio project was infused with a pioneer like spirit, which seems to indicate that a positive working atmosphere prevailed in which both genders felt comfortable.

References

Adorno, T. W., Frenkel-Brunswick, E., Levinson, D. J., & Sanford, R. N. (1950). *The authoritarian personality*. New York: Harper & Row.

Ackerman, N., & Jahoda, M. (1950). *Antisemitism and emotional disorder: A psychoanalytic interpretation*. New York: Harper Collins.

Barton, A. H. (1982). Paul Lazarsfeld and the invention of the University Institute for Applied Social Research. In B. Holzner & J. Nehnevsjsa (Eds.), *Organizing for social research* (pp. 17–83). Cambridge, UK: Schenckman.
Barton, J. S. (Ed.). (1984). *Guide to the Bureau of Applied Social Research.* New York: Clearwater.
Bettelheim, B., & Janwitz, M. (1950). *Dynamics of prejudice: A psychological and sociological study of veterans.* New York: Harper and Row.
Cantril, H., & Allport, G. W. (1935). *The psychology of radio.* New York: Harper & Brothers.
Cantril, H., Gaudet, H., & Herzog, H. (1940). *The invasion from Mars: A study in the psychology of panic.* Princeton, NJ: Princeton University Press.
Christie, R., & Jahoda, M. (Eds.). (1954). *Studies in the scope and method of the authoritarian personality:Continuities in social research.* Glencoe, IL: Free Press.
Coleman, J. (1980). Paul Lazarsfeld. In R. K. Merton & M. W. Riley (Eds.), *Sociological tradition from generation to generation* (pp. 1–35). Norwood, NJ: Ablex.
Coser, L. A. (1984). The Institute of Social Research and critical theory in America. In L. A. Closer (Ed.), *Refugee scholars in America: Their impact and their experiences* (pp. 90–101). New Haven, CT: Yale University Press.
Fiske, M., & Chiriboga, D. A. (1990). *Change and continuity in adult life.* San Francisco: Josey Bass.
Fromm, E. (1941). *Escape from freedom.* New York: Rinehart.
Hardt, H. (1991). The conscience of society: Leo Lowenthal. *Journal of Communication, 41,* 65–85.
Jahoda, M. (1977). *Freud and the dilemmas of psychology.* London: The Hogarth Press.
Jahoda, M., & Freeman, C. (Eds.). (1978). *World futures: The great debate.* London: Robertson.
Jahoda, M., Freeman, C., Pavitt, K., Sharp, M., & Walker, W. (Eds.). (1991). *Technology and the future of Europe: Competition and the global environment in the 1990s.* London: Pinter.
Jahoda, M., Lazarsfeld, P. F., & Zeisel, H. (1932). *Die Arbeitslosen von Marienthal* [The unemployed in Marienthal] (2nd ed.). Frankfurt, Germany: Hirzel.
Jay, M. (1973). *The dialectical imagination: A history of the Frankfurt School and the Institute of Social Research 1923–1950.* Boston: Little Brown.
Jay, M. (1986). *Permanent exiles: Essays on the intellectual migration from Germany to America.* New York: Columbia University Press.
Jay, M. (1987). *The dialectical imagination. The history of the Frankfurt School & the Institute of Social Research 1923–1950.* Berkeley: University of California Press.
Katz, E., & Lazarsfeld, P. F. (1955). *Personal influence. The part played by people in the flow of mass communication.* Glencoe IN: The Free Press.
Kuhn, T. (1962). *The structure of scientific revolutions.* Chicago: University of Chicago Press.
Lazarsfeld, P. F. (1969). An episode in the history of social research. In D. Fleming & B. Baylin (Eds.), *The intellectual migration: Europe and America, 1930–1960* (pp. 270–337). Cambridge, UK: Cambridge University Press.
Lazarsfeld, P. F. (1975). Working with Merton. In L. Coser (Ed.), *The idea of social structure: Papers in honor of Robert K. Merton* (pp. 35–66). New York: Harcourt, Brace Jovanovich.

Lazarsfeld, P. F., Berenson, B., & Gaudet, H. (1969). *The people's choice: How the voter makes up his mind in a presidential campaign.* New York: Duell, Sloane & Pearce. (Original work published 1944)

Lazarsfeld, P. F., & Kendall, P. (1948). *Radio listening in America: The people look at radio again.* New York: Prentice-Hall.

Lerg, W. (1977). Paul Felix Lazarsfeld und die Kommunikationsforschung. Ein biobibliographisches Epitaph [Communications research: A bio-bibliographic epitaph]. *Publizistik, 1,* 72–87.

Lowenthal, L. (1980). *Mitmachen wollte ich nie: Ein autobiographisches Gesprächmit helmut dubiel* [I never wanted to collaborate: Conversation with H. Dubiel]. Frankfurt, Germany: Suhrkamp.

Lowenthal, L. (1944). Biographies in popular magazines. In P. F. Lazarsfeld & F. Stanton (Eds.), *Radio research, 1942–43* (pp. 34–60). New York: Duell, Sloan & Pearce.

Merton, R. K., Fiske, M., & Curtis, A. (2004). *Mass persuasion: The social psychology of a war bond drive* (3rd ed.). New York: Howard Fertig.

Messing, P. (1949). *Rehersal for destruction.* New York: Harper & Brothers.

Morrison, D. (1978). The beginning of modern mass communication research. *European Journal of Sociology, XIX,* 347–359.

Perse, E. (1996). Herta Herzog (1910–). In N. Signorelli (Ed.), *Women in communication: A biographical sourcebook* (pp. 202–210). Westport, CT: Greenwood Press.

Robinson, G. J. (1990). Paul Felix Lazarsfeld's contributions to the development of U.S. communications studies. In W. Langenbucher (Eds.), *Paul Lazarsfeld's die wiener tradition der empirischen sozial- und kommunikationsforschung* [Paul F. Lazarsfeld: The Vienna tradition of social and communication research] (pp. 89–111) Munich, Germany: Ölschläger.

Robinson, G. J. (1996). Constructing a historiography for North American communication studies. In E. Dennis & E. Wartella (Eds.), *American Communication research—the remembered history* (pp. 157–168). Mahway, NJ: Erlbaum.

Robinson, G. J. (2005). *Gender, journalism and equity: Canadian, U.S., and European perspectives.* Cresskill NJ: Hampton Press.

Signorelli, N. (1996). *Women in communications: A biographical sourcebook.* Westport, CT: Greenwood Press.

Sills, D. (Ed.). (1979). *The international encyclopedia of the social sciences, 18* (bibliographical supplement, pp. 226–228). New York: Free Press.

Singer, E. (1975/76). In memoriam: Hazel Gaudet Erskine, 1908–1975. *Public Opinion Quarterly, 39*, 571–579.

4 *Commentary* Three Accounts of the Founding Heroes of Communication Research

Mihai Coman

University of Bucharest

The three texts in this section draw upon the process enabling the birth of a scientific paradigm and upon the turn taken by the entire field under the influence of this birth. This is why they may be seen, by analogy, as "mythical" narrations of the creation of the mass communication science. Elihu Katz outlines the beginnings as in a cosmogonic myth: the intuitions of sociologists such as Georg Simmel or Robert Park or psychologists such as Gabriel Tarde and the pioneering work of Columbia School forge the universe to which the subsequent thought schools will adhere, categorized (totemically) into four great scholarly families. I am tempted to interpret Kurt Lang's and Gladys Engel Lang's text as a Promethean myth in which the monumental paths opened by golden age thinkers (Alexis de Toqueville, Stuart Mill, Max Weber, Gabriel Tarde, Karl Buecher) are put aside by the new generation which, despite the efforts to build a complex theoretical system, provide a unidimensional model that "fails to take adequate account of the reciprocities and interactions through which the members of a society construct their images of social reality" (p. 16). Meanwhile, Gertrude Robinson proposes a heroic myth of the (forgotten) pioneers of this science—women who worked in Bureau of Social Research—and thanks to whom (i.e., thanks to their gender-determined vision) some of the hypotheses or maybe even some of the guidelines of the first media-effect theory took shape. Beyond this turn to the origins, as in a mythical construction, the three chapters intersect in many ways and probably reflect the consensus in our field reached after more than half a century of scientific research and critical reflection in mass communication science.

The first common point of view springs from the fact that each study consists of an analysis of the limitations of the school initiated by Paul Lazarsfeld. Some of these are self-imposed, resulting from the decision to view mass communication as an object of scientific study, in other words, to shift the mass media discourse from speculation to empirical investigation (and by this, despite appearances, pass to a more sophisticated view). Similar to the leap from alchemy to the empirical study of matter (chemistry), Lazarsfeld's vision lays the foundations of a science: "What emerges from this evidence suggests that Lazarsfeld was not the founder of U.S. communications studies as Berelson suggests in 1959, but rather that he developed a new social science based theory of media effects" (Robinson, p. 31, this volume). "Although the Bureau (originally, the Office of Radio Research) was affiliated with Columbia's longstanding Department of Sociology, and conducted social research in many institutional areas, it may be said to have been the birthplace of empirical research on mass communication" (Katz, p. 4, this volume). But interestingly, although he is the initiator of an approach to study the media's power of influence, which is methodologically in total opposition to that advanced by the intellectual opinion of the age (articulately expressed by the thinkers of the Frankfurt School but also put forth as common sense truth by philosophers, men and women of letters, politologists and politicians), Lazarsfeld remains the prisoner of the dominant themes; he does not question the idea of mass media power but only the way it is estimated. This automatically means taking over "The governing paradigm of mass communication almost invariably implies a one-way flow with the media depicted as a pipeline for high volumes of content produced by professionals to woo an audience and/or to influence their ideas or behavior" (Lang & Lang, p. 15, this volume).

Other limitations of the paradigm result from the evolution of science and of the perspective that we have after 70 years of research. Therefore elements standing proof of the power and consistency of the project, elements generated by its development and its institutionalization, appear today as limitations or even failures; Lazarsfeld's vision encapsulated the research only in certain thematic spheres and in certain methodological options, specific rather to positivist sociology than mass communication science. Consequently, as Lang and Lang summarize, this type of research comes up against the unlimited number of indicators it can work with, of biases generated by the direct transfer of results obtained from micro-level research to generalizations valid for the whole society and the limits of defining communication as a one-way flow of information. But as Katz shows, it inherently contains, through its efforts to overcome these limitations, the major tendencies of the current paradigms: in order to explain "media power," researchers looked into the force of technologies or into the dominating projects of the (political and economic) oligarchy or in the receiver's weaknesses and/or resistance.

Another common theme is that of the influence of marginal players on the creation of the first media effect theories. On the one hand, these are the scientific models of other disciplines whose intersection with reflections generated by the first theoretical constructs in mass communication science left a mark on their evolution—even if this intersection is perhaps related to the randomness of the books read, of academic affiliations or the socio-political context in which these scholars shaped their paradigm etc. For example, Katz highlights the importance of the technological determinism promoted by the Canadian School or of the study of the reception context launched under the name of "the situation of contact" by Elliot Freidson in the subsequent outlining of the fundamental scientific paradigms from the media effect models; Lang and Lang underline the importance of certain theories such as "para-social interaction," conceptualized by Donald Horton and R. Richard Wohl; and Robinson convincingly outlines the importance of the contribution made by some female researchers such as Maria Jahoda, Herta Herzog, Marjorie Fiske, Hazel Gaudet Erskine. On the other hand, these are unpredictable social circumstances (more exactly micro-social ones) generated by institutional affiliations: see the transformations of Newark Research Center until it became more stable and subsequently the famous Bureau of Social Research; see the importance of the association, the convergences and divergencies between researchers who worked here and who then took different paths, some of them in the line of Lazarsfeld and others new ones.

The three studies all touch on the issue of evolution ranging from the multidisciplinary to the interdisciplinary nature. I borrow this distinction from the anthropologist Marylin Strathern (2005, pp. 84–87), who stressed the difference between multidisciplinarity and interdisciplinarity. The first concept brings forward "the 'integration' of different theories or methods," whereas the second one refers to "the 'inclusion' of this or that perspective." Moreover, multidisciplinarity implies a transient ownership and has little expressive effect, while interdisciplinarity always leads to ownership and promotes a strong expressive effect. Interdisciplinarity creates a discipline or a new science that needs to define a specific field, to become legitimate through institutionalization (inclusion in the university curriculum, sections in professional associations, new specific reviews and books, recognition in encyclopedias, and so on). Interdisciplinarity claims ownership over a scientific field by using diverse strategies in order to amplify its expressive effects. And, in fact, one of the main issues of these three chapters is the process through which the Columbia School designed the identity of mass communication science—imposing a specific field and legitimizing its ownership over the filed. These three studies of the beginnings show how founding heroes shaped and directed research; they legitimate the synthesis between basic sciences (linguistics, cognitive psychology, sociology, political philosophy), establish priorities in time, and thus impose the symbolic ownership of mass communication science over the field of mediated communication.

In the beginning, the randomness of history drew close two groups of thinkers who would share only their interest for a theme with mythological echoes (if we think about the reflections of Tarde or Tchakhotine): the seemingly magic power of the mass media. Between them there was an abyss which would soon become paradigmatic:

> "What is common to these traditions is the concern with effect. The Columbia groups were interested in the influence of media content on short-run change of opinions and attitudes and in the role of motivations and gratification in enlisting attention and interest, in the short-run. Frankfurt School members were interested in the ways in which the management of

> the media produced content that maintained the class structure of society in the long run" (Katz, p. 5, this volume).

For researchers raised in the tradition of sociology and social psychology, media effects were social facts; for thinkers affiliated to the Frankfurt School, these were political phenomena; for the former the effects of the press were consequences, for the latter they were a project, even a conspiracy; the former wanted to measure and the latter were concerned with accusation and pointing fingers. The two philosophies on the mission and structure of mass communication science endure to this day and many of the incompatibilities between Continental research and the American schools of thought draw their origins from them.

The multidisciplinary *ab origo* nature of mass communication science inevitably leads to a certain cosmopolitanism. Just like in the beginning, over time research borrowed concepts and methods from various disciplines, from cybernetics to psychology, linguistics to anthropology. Most of the time media scholars adopted these other theories and research methods in a euphoric way. They did not develop any critical dialogue with other scientists or with the epistemological bibliography connected to this field. Commenting on the frenzy of adopting the ethnographic methods in media studies, Marc Hobart (2005, p. 26), for example, stresses this paradoxical situation: "Significantly, media scholars invoke anthropology at precisely the point at which its scientific approaches to society prove manifestly inadequate." This tendency of media studies to always fasten its eyes on other disciplines and borrow their tools may be due to the complexity of the multi-faceted interplay between media and society; this accounts for the subtle analysis proposed by Katz—even if in the beginning the media effects were the central concern of communication research, the amplitude of the social communication phenomenon, leading to four important research fields (Context, Technology, Content, Ownership) makes our discipline focus on everything that goes on in the other sciences. From this stems the (theoretical and methodological) eclecticism specific to many schools of media studies that are frenetically looking for new concepts in order to theorize the processes specific to media field(s).

Researchers in mass communication science unanimously recognize that there no longer is a field of social life that was not permeated by communication whether only technologically enabled or enabled by technologies and mass communication professionals. This causes on the one hand mass media study to be inevitably interdisciplinary (a convergence of some scientific tools from various disciplines) and on the other hand many mass communication manifestations to function as a *fait social total* (according to the inspired wording of Marcel Mauss, 1993). The classic study conducted by Lazarsfeld on the effects of mass media in an electoral campaign shows, among others, that for the Erie County community it was a *fait social total*; the investigation (classic nowadays) on MacArthur Day in Chicago performed by Lang and Lang half a century ago would reveal such a fait social total (see the interpretation to this end in Katz & Dayan, 2003); and the media events theory put forward by Dayan and Katz (1992) and the numerous researches inspired from it deal with situations of convergence of society subsystems in a *fait social total* (total social phenomena). What does this mean?

In the post-modern world, culture is produced, transmitted, received, and re-signified through media and within media or/and mediated culture. But media are no more only a simple channel through which cultural symbols circulate; they constitute the very system that produces culture. Media are substituting traditional forms through which culture is generated, consumed, transmitted and, through their ubiquity and power, they meld culture and mediated communication. In other words, it seems that mass media constitute a cultural system of social construction of reality, and that this construction is made with instruments to mass communication language. It follows that mass media cannot be conceived of as a go-between, mediating or covering certain cultural constructs—a situation where its role is only to remodel messages designed and made by other social instances. On the contrary, this transformation (made more visible by the rapid growth of the new technologies) imposes a perspective that places mass media at the center of the process of social construction of reality, as an institution that generates specific discourses and a specific logic. Consequently, mass communication is a *fait social total* not because it is an important social reality, rather because it is Culture itself in post-modern societies.

Were the members of the Columbia School aware of such an evolution? What consequences does it have for the scientific design of mass communication studies? All three studies underline the fact that the mass media development in that age did not allow for a globalizing vision on the role of mediated communication in society. Media only meant printed press and (terrestrial) radio stations. Moreover, the dominant model was the one resulting from the intersection between the image of a mass society made by alienated individuals and the concern (dramatically amplified by the harsh realities of Nazism, communism, and the cold war) for the mass media power in determining attitudes and behaviors. To a certain extent it was the total social fact model in its hypostasis of omnipotent social control instrument (model speculatively designed by thinkers affiliated to the Frankfurt School) that the research project promoted by Lazarsfeld distinguished itself. In their wish to measure the mass media influence, the Columbia School model rejected the macro-social perspectives by confining itself to the scientifically manageable area of the micro-social. This programmatic decision could only lead to a vision of "some" as it was put forward by Berelson (1959)—"some kinds of communication have some kind of effects on some kinds of people in some kinds of situations" (p. 543). This evolution and like a *corsi e ricorsi*, the return to more speculative perspectives (labeled today as critical) show us that a theoretical model of mass communication as *fait social total* cannot be developed unless a certain monopoly of media communication over other forms of communication is accepted (just like the gift monopolizes a certain type of exchange over other forms of exchange available in a society).

We notice how the differentiation and, eventually, the separation between the Columbia School and the Frankfurt School reveal the conceptual abyss that leaves its mark on the reflection on mass communication: accepting the idea that mass communication is a *fait social total*, is therefore culture in a society conquered by communication (Miege, 1989), orients research towards the analysis of several forms of mass communication monopoly in the field of a culture and society; the rejection of this vision orients research towards micro-social and micro-cultural phenomena in which mass communication is a variable together with other variables configurating social representations and individual behaviors. This "cold war" between minimalists and maximalists defines mass communication research to this day: "The Lazarsfeld group emphasized the short run, the Europeans and the Chicago School, the long run" (Katz, p. 5, this volume).

References

Dayan, D., & Katz, E. (1992). *Media events: The live broadcast of history.* Cambridge, MA: Harvard University Press.

Hobart, M. (2005). The profanity of the media. In E. Rothenbuhler & M. Coman (Eds.), *Media anthropology* (pp. 26–35). London: Sage.

Katz, E., & Dayan, D. (2003). The audience is a crowd, the crowd is a public: Latter day thoughts on Lang and Lang's MacArthur Day in Chicago. In E. Katz, J. Durhan Peters, T. Liebes, & A. Orloff (Eds.), *Canonic texts in media research: Are there any? Should there be? How about these?* (pp. 121–136). Cambridge, UK: Polity Press.

Mauss, M. (1993). *Eseu despre dar* [The gift: Forms and functions of the exchange in archaic societies]. Iasi, Romania: Institutul European.

Miege, B. (1989). *La société conquise par la communication – I* [The company conquered by communication, Vol. 1]. Grenoble, France: Presses Universitaires de Grenoble.

Strathern, M. (2005). Experiments in interdisciplinarity. *Social Anthropology, 13,* 75–90.

Part II

Communication and Family Contexts

CHAPTER CONTENTS

5 Work and Family in Copreneurial Family Businesses

Extending and Integrating Communication Research

Jill R. Helmle, David R. Seibold, and Tamara D. Afifi

University of California, Santa Barbara

Family businesses, especially the enterprises of married couples or *copreneurial businesses*, are a unique, but largely ignored, context in which work and family domains are intrinsically intertwined. Indeed, scholars from other disciplines who study copreneurial and family businesses have called for investigations from multiple perspectives including communication. We review the literature linking *work and family life* within the arena of *married couples'* (copreneurial) *businesses* in order to lay the foundation for a *research agenda for marital, family, and organizational communication scholars* and for researchers in *other disciplines* in which family businesses and work-life integration are central. Specifically, we examine work-family linkages of copreneurs through the frameworks of *relational dialectics, boundary, work-family border,* and *structuration* theories. We also highlight findings from marital communication research—marital schemata and equity, conflict patterns, and stress contagion effects—to guide future research. Entrepreneurial, technological, and international issues are also discussed. In so doing, we set a research agenda in the area of work-family life and copreneurial family businesses for scholars in many sub-fields in communication and other disciplines.

Introduction

In 2008, the U.S. Census Bureau conducted the American Community Survey (ACS) and found that 49.2% of American households are married-couple families. Additionally, 64.5% of parents in households with children under age 6 are in the labor force, and 72% of parents in households with children between the ages of 6 and 17 are in the labor force (U.S. Census Bureau, 2008), thus revealing the need for—and potential challenge of—integrating work and family life. The challenge of integrating our work and family lives is not a recent revelation, of course. For example, the past 60 years have brought about changes in the post-World War II notions of work and family by way of marital and gender roles. In her work on breadwinning mothers, Medved (2009) suggested that social change may occur at the intersection of individuals, families, and/or organizations that choose to enact work and family in alternative forms. In general, women are more likely than men "to reduce their work-related behavioral and psychological involvement, limit their career aspirations, and forego opportunities for career development" in favor of fulfilling their family obligations (Jennings & McDougald, 2007, p. 755; also see Rothbard, 2001; Rothbard & Edwards, 2003). Often, women do not wish to make a choice between working and taking care of their families, and some go into business themselves or with their spouse as a way to balance their work and family lives (Boden, 1999; Caputo & Dolinsky, 1998; Edley, 2001). However, and notwithstanding the empowerment they attain through proprietorships, women entrepreneurs report an increased tension between balancing their work and family lives (Gill & Ganesh, 2007). When successful, it is the benefits of autonomy, and at times flexibility, associated with owning and managing one's own business that afford entrepreneurs the opportunity to integrate their work and family lives with the hope of achieving balance (Barnett & Barnett, 1988; Jennings & McDougald, 2007).

Given the multitude of families and businesses that fall within this population so acutely affected by the interplay between the work and family domains, scholars and professionals from numerous disciplines have investigated issues linking work and family: management/business (Waters & Bardoel, 2006), sociology (Wajcman, 2008), psychology (Allen, 2001), as well as child/human development and family studies (Dilworth, 2004), women's studies (Barnett & Hyde, 2001), and social policy (Fuwa & Cohen, 2007). As is evident in the extensive writings of communication scholars (e.g., Broadfoot et al., 2008; Buzzanell & Liu, 2005; Golden, 2002; Golden, Kirby, & Jorgenson, 2006; Hoffman & Cowan, 2008; Kirby, Golden, Medved, Jorgenson, & Buzzanell, 2003; Medved, 2007, 2009; Meisenbach, 2010; Petronio, 2006), studying work and family through the lens of communication has much to add to both areas of research. It has the potential to illuminate the intrinsic role of communication in the relationships and processes of work and family. It also brings to the forefront *organizational communication* and *family communication* dynamics that have been overlooked in the absence of a thorough examination of the work and family literature. As the work and family domains are intrinsically intertwined in family businesses (Ashforth, Kreiner, & Fugate, 2000), family businesses in all forms comprise an intriguing context in which to study work-family balance from a communication perspective. In particular, studying married couples who own and operate family businesses together, hereafter termed "copreneurs" (following Barnett & Barnett, 1988), encourages communication researchers to make contributions not only to the multidisciplinary fields of work-family life and of family businesses, but also to the communication discipline in the form of integrated organizational communication, marital/family communication, and interpersonal/relational communication approaches to work-family balance and copreneurship. The dual roles of family members (e.g., supervisor/mother, subordinate/child, owner/spouse, co-worker/sibling) make inherent—and potentially problematic—the boundaries of work and family, their interconnections, and how they are managed. However, family businesses, and especially copreneurial family businesses, have been overlooked or given only cursory comment in the reviews, theoretical work, and empirical research of communication scholars in their burgeoning studies of work-family links.

Overview

We propose, first, that many advances remain to be made *independently* in the areas of work-family life scholarship and of family/copreneurial business research. The potential for these gains can be found along four paths: (a) by looking at each area separately but through the lens of the other area (i.e., alternately foregrounding one and backgrounding the other); (b) by searching for where the areas share common theoretical concerns (i.e., areas of overlap); (c) by examining each area from the standpoint of relevant communication theory broadly, and from domain-specific communication research (e.g., marital, family, organizational communication studies, among others) that heretofore have not been brought to bear on each of the two areas; (d) by exploiting the potential of research from other disciplines to illuminate dynamics ignored by communication scholars but that highlight important theoretical challenges and offer relevant theoretical solutions. We suggest, second, that the areas of copreneurs' business relationships and practices, as well how these partners manage work-family life issues in their personal relationships, interpenetrate in important theoretical and practical ways. Unraveling these connections, especially their recursivity and the mediating role of communication, can best be accomplished (e) by interrogation of relevant, powerful theories. The stakeholders for these two arguments and five approaches vary widely and, thus, the potential audiences for our work here are diverse including: (a) scholars interested in the intersection of copreneurial businesses (and family businesses more broadly) and work-family life maintenance; (b) researchers interested in only one of these two areas but who may be aided through utilizing the perspective of the other area, the perspective of allied areas in communication, and/or the perspective of relevant scholarship from other disciplines; (c) investigators from other sub-areas of communication who see either copreneurship or work-family life issues (or their interpenetration) as a fruitful new arena into which to expand their own expertise; (d) scholars in other disciplines concerned with copreneurial and family businesses and/or work-family life issues who are persuaded by the value of a communication perspective.

Toward those ends and toward these audiences, we review research suggesting links between work-family life issues and married couples' (copreneurial) businesses in order to lay the foundation for a research agenda for marital, family, and organizational communication scholars who may be interested in either arena or both. By examining the well-established area in communication of work-family issues through the lens of an area new to most communication scholars (i.e., family businesses in general and copreneurial relationships in particular), we offer a different stance on work-family life scholarship and new possibilities for work-family life scholars. We also highlight findings from marital communication research—marital schemata and equity, conflict patterns, and stress contagion effects—that can guide future research for both work-family life scholars and copreneurial business researchers. Additionally, gaps in research on copreneurship related to entrepreneurship and technology and on work-family life management are identified and reframed in communication terms in order to advance these research areas in other sub-areas of our field (especially international/global communication and new media) and in other disciplines in which family businesses have been studied. Once these foundations have been laid, we address the intersection of copreneurship and communication-related work-family linkages through prominent theoretical frameworks in communication and in other fields: relational dialectics theory, boundary theory, work-family border theory, and structuration theory. A communication research agenda concerning copreneurs' management of their businesses and their work-family life issues is proposed. We believe that this research agenda may be of interest to scholars of marital/family, organizational, international, and new media communication, as well as to researchers in other fields in which family and copreneurial businesses have been studied and to scholars in disciplines in which work-family life issues have been investigated.

Family Businesses

The criteria used to define a "family business" vary widely: percentage of ownership, voting control, power over strategic direction, involvement of multiple generations, and active management by family members (Shanker & Astrachan, 1996; Sharma, 2004). Depending upon which criteria are utilized, 90% or more of the estimated 25 million businesses in the United States are family businesses that range in size from two-person partnerships to Fortune 500 companies with total members comprising roughly 62% of the U.S. workforce (Astrachan & Shanker, 2003). A family business is defined here as a venture or enterprise where two or more members of a family are involved in daily operations and/or management and where at least one family member has a majority percentage of ownership. Just as families take various forms, family businesses vary: a married couple (with/without children), parent and child (or children), siblings, or a combination of relatives (including in-laws). Next, we discuss selected research on family businesses as a foundation for our subsequent treatment of copreneurial ventures.

In much the same way that work-family and communication scholars (Clark, 2000; Seibold, 1990) have encouraged examination of the opportunities afforded by family businesses, especially those that are at the intersection of family and organizational communication, family business researchers (Bird, Welsch, Astrachan, & Pistrui, 2002; Sharma, 2004; Stewart, 2008) have called for studies to bridge to other academic disciplines and to investigate the intersection between and among scholarly domains. Bird et al. (2002) reviewed family business literature from the previous decade and ranked topics in that arena from the most to least frequently studied: succession, distinctiveness, conflict, management/strategy, helping family businesses, macro (economics/policy), and women. Debecki, Matherne, Kellermanns, and Chrisman (2009) found the most studied topics in family business research to be strategic management (goals), strategic formulation (planning, resources, and entrepreneurship and innovation), strategic implementation (structure, systems, conflict, culture, values and change), and management (leadership and succession).

While some attention has been given to family businesses in terms of an integrated family and organizational communication research agenda (Golden et al., 2006), few empirical studies have been conducted on family businesses from a communication perspective. In an exception, Seibold (1990) reported a case study of a two-generation family business and proposed further investigation of intergroup relations among family versus non-family business members, sibling rivalry, decision-making processes, leadership, conflict negotiation, power/control dynamics, and affection versus profit bases of performance assessment, among others. There also is a gap in our knowledge of centrally important work-family balance issues in family businesses. For example, Stafford and Tews (2009) contend that although business-owning families may have more control over flexibility and the "right" to have children present, these families may have a more difficult time cognitively separating work from family life and that this disjunction invites investigation of their balance strategies.

According to Sharma (2004), most family business studies of the individual in these enterprises have examined the founders (e.g., leadership styles, influence, relationships with family or non-family members) and members of the next generation (e.g., desirable successor attributes, performance enhancing factors, and family members' decision to pursue a career in the business). Non-family employees and female family employees have received relatively little research attention, although researchers have studied succession in women-owned family businesses (Cadieux, Lorrain, & Hugron, 2002) and the challenges daughters face in family business succession (Haberman & Danes, 2007; Vera & Dean, 2005). Jimenez (2009) offers several research foci regarding the role of women in family business, all of which are salient for communication scholars: women's invisibility, emotion and leadership, succession, professional career in the family firm, and running the family firm. Research questions are raised about the relationships among gender, roles in the family, and roles in the business; assumptions made by family members with regard to gender; and how parents and families socialize their children to think about the family business as well as their future involvement with the family business.

Sharma (2004) contends that family business research conducted at the interpersonal/group level emphasizes the nature and types of contractual agreements, sources of conflict and management strategies, and intergenerational transitions. With regard to conflict, Karofsky et al. (2001) suggest that family businesses are ripe for exploring unique patterns of work-family conflict due to the high integration of the work and family domains. For example, Cole (2000) distinguished among potential role conflicts, competing systems (family and business), and dual relationships. She found that, although the blending of work and family domains worked well for most participants, all respondents mentioned that there were times when they needed separation between their work and family lives. Danes and Morgan (2004) added that conflicts that arise at work or at home are woven through both contexts given the nature of the family business.

In a study of second-generation family business member attitudes, Lee (2006) observed that family adaptability (the ability of a family system to change its power structure, roles, and rules in response to situational or developmental stress) was positively correlated with organizational commitment, job satisfaction, and life satisfaction. Shumate and Fulk (2004) propose that communication is necessary for establishing roles and maintaining boundaries among the multiple roles in family businesses. We suggest that investigation of role-related processes and interactions in the context of family businesses might include role taking, role allocation, role expectations, role performance, and gender roles. Also relevant would be studies of leadership styles in business and parenting styles at home. Furthermore, communication scholars might examine what happens to the parent-child relationship when parents and children become co-workers and/or business partners, how their communication behaviors change or adapt, and the emotion and stress involved with regard to their dual-role relationship.

Eight of 217 studies of family businesses reviewed by Sharma (2004) focused on the organizational level, and research centered on the identification and management of resources. Sharma also noted "a need to understand the mechanisms family firms use to develop, communicate, and reinforce desired vision and organizational culture over extended tenures of leaders and across generations; strategies used to maintain long-term relationships with external stakeholders and other organizations; ethical dilemmas faced and resolution strategies used" (p. 22). From a work-family life and organizational communication perspective, examining how family businesses address work-life issues compared with non-family businesses may yield insights regarding organizational values and family-friendly work cultures.

Family businesses thus offer a rich opportunity for researchers from multiple disciplines and sub-areas of communication to conduct multilevel research. The possibility of examining the intersection of work and family life is fruitful, as noted by Golden et al. (2006). However, nowhere else might this intersection be more visible than in the context of the copreneurial relationship, and in which family, psychology, business, and organizational disciplines are fully integrated. While many, perhaps most, of the research possibilities we have proposed in our discussion thus far of family businesses are germane for illuminating copreneurial businesses too, in the next section we focus on only copreneurship, and from multiple research disciplines, with the aim of highlighting potential communication research.

Copreneurial Businesses

Barnett and Barnett (1988) coined the term "copreneur" to describe a married couple working together in their entrepreneurial venture. They posit that copreneuring implies a sense of equality between the two spouses in the responsibility for their business. Fitzgerald and Muske (2002) suggest copreneurs also should be defined by their shared decision-making responsibility. Barnett and Barnett propose that the term copreneurs, coentrepreneurs, and the "new Mom and Pop" can be used interchangeably. Ponthieu and Caudill (1993) clarify that copreneurs are a subset of coentrepreneurs, any two people who are in business together. We use coentrepreneurial married couple (technically accurate) interchangeably with copreneurs (our preferred usage) and the new Mom and Pop (frequently used in popular press articles).

Copreneurs are one type of family business, but one that is clearly important to the study of work and family life because of the undeniable link between the work and family domains, especially the married couple's need to negotiate a relationship that is both personal and professional. The U.S. Census Bureau (2002) found that 11.7% of all businesses are male/female owned (versus 57.4% male owned and 28.2% female owned). It is difficult to accurately determine the prevalence of copreneurship; many couples operate as copreneurs although only one spouse may be a legal owner of the company. Thompson (1990) estimated that copreneurs accounted for 1.5 million businesses, but given the latest U.S. Census Bureau (2002) statistic listed above (11.7%) copreneurs could now account for as many as 3 million businesses.

Muske and Fitzgerald (2006) contend that copreneurs are the "perfect blend of work and family" and expect them to have stronger marriages and businesses as a result (p. 195). The researchers found that copreneurs who discontinued their business were younger, had fewer employees, more children at home, and a business manager who may have had another job. The copreneurial enterprise is usually more integrated than in the traditional family business, in which only one spouse may be involved. Copreneurship can be characterized by what Cheney, Zorn, Planalp, and Lair (2008, p. 149) highlight and Bowie (1998, p. 1083) describes as the tenets of meaningful work: "1) meaningful work involves work that individuals freely agree to do; 2) allows workers to exercise their autonomy and independence; 3) enables workers to develop their rational capacities; 4) provides a wage sufficient for physical welfare; 5) supports the moral development of employees; 6) is not paternalistic in the sense of interfering with workers' conception of how they wish to obtain happiness." Helmle (2010) reported that copreneurs described their work as allowing them a sense of freedom in using their time (even though they may not always be free); having autonomy in their work; affording them the opportunity to do the work that they enjoy and about which they are passionate; and enabling them to earn a better income than they could if they were not in business for themselves. Delving more deeply into how copreneurs portray their work has the potential to make a significant contribution to the research on the meaning of work and meaningful work. For example, copreneurs' personal identities and identification with their business are fused in ways rarely found in the organizational communication literature. Researchers might compare copreneurs' and dual-career couples' and/or academic couples' communication behaviors, work-family balance strategies, and relationship maintenance.

How copreneurs communicatively manage the integration of work and family, in addition to other communication demands in their lives, warrants particular attention from scholars since work and family are the defining axes of a copreneurial relationship. Exploring the work-family issues that copreneurs encounter adds a different yet important aspect to work-family scholarship, one that is based on the negotiation of these arenas in a context that where work and family is already incredibly intertwined. We explore several potentially fruitful areas next, including the centrality and unique features of communication in the copreneurial relationship. We then turn to three areas of marital communication research that could inform our understanding of how copreneurs balance work and family (marital schemata and equity, conflict patterns, and stress contagion effects).

Communication in the Copreneurial Relationship

Marshack (1993) notes that couple-owned businesses are "fascinating examples of the interaction and interdependence of personal relationship and business partnership, or love and work," and thus that the study of coentrepreneurial couples "provides an opportunity to observe how these couples manage the balance between the two domains of love (personal relationship) and work (business partnership)" (p. 355). Marshack also emphasizes that how couples manage both domains relies on the negotiation of multiple boundaries between them as well as how they transition, both psychologically and physically, between the domains.

There are numerous advantages and disadvantages associated with a business venture with one's spouse (Barnett & Barnett, 1988; Jennings & McDougald, 2007; Nelton, 1986). Communication-relevant advantages of becoming copreneurs include: (a) enhancing their marriages by "sharing with their spouses at home and work" and "learning how to manage conflicts and reduce tension more effectively" (Marshack, 1993, p. 363); (b) the personal satisfaction, joy, and autonomy that comes from being in control and doing the work one enjoys with a partner one loves, becoming greater than the sum of their parts (Barnett & Barnett, 1988); and (c) better understanding between spouses, and greater commitment to the business (Nelton, 1986). Additionally, as Barnett and Barnett (1988) observe, entrepreneurs who go into business by themselves or with partners other than their spouse risk having the business harm their family lives because of the long hours involved in the start-up phase and the spouse not being involved nor having an understanding of what the entrepreneur is experiencing. Nelton (1986) further notes the common factors of successful copreneurs: (a) marriage and children come first; (b) the spouses demonstrate enormous respect for each other; (c) there is a high degree of close communication; (d) the partners complement each other's talents and attitudes; (e) the partners are supportive of each other; (f) they have strong family ties; (g) they compete with the world outside, not with each other; (h) they like to laugh; and (i) they keep their egos in check.

There can be disadvantages to copreneurship too. Some stem from a breakdown in communication or negative communication behaviors between the "partners": when the problems from work carry over into the home (and vice versa); when employees are confused because copreneurs have not clearly defined who is responsible or has authority over certain aspects of the business; and when couples have not adjusted to having the business as part of their relationship (Nelton, 1986). Nelton noted several stressors that copreneurs may face, including: (a) having different management styles and work habits; (b) worry and disagreement over money; (c) not being able to separate business life from personal life; (d) spousal criticism; (e) disagreement on business decisions or goals; (f) insufficient time to be a couple or family; (g) working too hard and being tired often; (h) being together too much; (i) not listening to each other; and (j) especially for women, having two jobs—being a business partner and running the household. Cole and Johnson (2007) found that even divorced copreneurs can maintain a successful business if they compartmentalize the business from their personal life. See Table 5.1 for a summary of communication-related aspects of copreneurship.

In addition to prior research focused only on copreneurs, a broader examination of the literature on marital communication has much to offer in understanding the copreneurial relationship. While there are numerous areas within the marital research that could be examined, three in particular warrant attention: (a) marital schemata and equity, (b) conflict patterns, and (c) stress contagion effects. In the following sections, we briefly discuss how each of these areas might inform the research on copreneurs, as well as the research on balancing work and family.

Marital Schemata and Equity. To unravel these aspects of copreneurial relationships, it may be useful to examine the larger historical and cultural forces that influence people's marital and family schemata. Individuals' schemata for marriage have changed over time, largely because of the women's movement and the extraordinary increase in women's participation in the workforce (Wilcox & Nock, 2007). According to Wilcox and Nock (2007), these changes were occasioned by a gender revolution and a family revolution. The *gender revolution,* which evolved out of the rise in dual career households and support for gender equality, has resulted in marriages that are more equitable in the sense that men do more childcare and household work than

Table 5.1 Communication-Related Aspects of Copreneurship

Advantages *"When things go right"*	Greater understanding of the partner's perspective
	Opportunity for high degree of close communication
	Make marriage/family a priority
	Mutual respect and support
	Compete with outside world, not each other
	Share with partner at home and at work (the good and the bad)
	More opportunity to manage conflict effectively
	Personal satisfaction of doing the work you love with your partner
	More time together than apart
	Involvement of family in business
	Flexibility to attend to family matters as they arise
	Work-family/life balance
	100% commitment to the business by both spouses
	'Two heads are better than one' – in decision-making process
	Sense of control over work and family domains
	A routine is established and there is a clear boundary between work time and family time.
Disadvantages *"When things go wrong"*	Allowing problems to carry over into other domain
	Employee confusion due to lack of clearly defined roles
	Lack of adjustment to include business as part of relationship
	Different management styles
	Disagreement over finances, business decisions, or goals
	Difficulty separating personal from professional
	Spousal criticism
	Lack of time to be a couple/family, take vacations
	Working too hard, being tired too often
	Being together too much
	Not listening to each other
	Role conflict
	Work-family/life conflict
	Life becomes 'all about the business' and conversation becomes limited to business only.

Note. Adapted from Helmle (2010), Marshack (1993), Muske and Fitzgerald (2006), and Nelton (1986).

ever before (Wilcox & Nock, 2007). Most spouses expect, at least to some extent, that both partners will contribute to the domestic labor and emotional nurturance of the family relationships (Wilcox & Nock, 2007). The *family revolution* is evident in married partners becoming more individualistic and living in a culture that has experienced a normative decline in the notion of life-long marriage. This pattern has resulted in a greater desire for emotional investment in marriage and less stability in marriage compared to marriages of earlier generations (Wilcox & Nock, 2007). Today, women are often financially independent and marry for love and for an emotional connection, and not necessarily because their partner is a good breadwinner or a potential parent. Furthermore, Fry and Cohn (2010) reported that in a 2007 study by the Pew Research Center, 22% of husbands had wives who made more money than them (compared to 4% in 1970).

Given the rise in egalitarianism and dual career households in contemporary marriages, an important question to consider is whether women are happier in these types of marriages. On one hand, the research on equity theory has found that individuals are happiest when their relationships are perceived as equitable, or when what each person contributes to the marriage is proportional to what each person receives (Guerrero, La Valley, & Farinelli, 2008; Sprecher, 2001a, 2001b; Stafford & Canary, 2006; Walster, Traupmann, Sprecher, Utne, & Hay, 1985). People tend to feel least satisfied when they believe they are under-benefited, or when they are contributing more and receiving less from the relationship and their partner is receiving more and contributing less (Sprecher, 2001a, 2001b; Walster et al., 1985). On the other hand, research suggests that people with more traditional marriages, in which the woman does the majority of the domestic labor, childcare, and relationship maintenance and the man does the outside household chores and is the primary breadwinner, tend to have more satisfying marriages than couples with more egalitarian marriages (e.g., Wilcox & Nock, 2006). These findings regarding equity and traditional marriage may seem to be contradictory. It might appear that women in more traditional marriages would be under-benefited and feel as if their marriages are inequitable. However, equity is perception-based; many women in traditional marriages may perceive their marriage as equitable. For example, the man's role as the primary breadwinner might be such an important role in the family that it is perceived as just as important as the multiple domestic roles the woman performs.

To determine whether women with more egalitarian marriages or women with more traditional gendered marriages are happier, Wilcox and Nock (2006) assessed women's marital quality using self-report data from over 5,000 married couples in the second wave (1992–1994) of the National Survey of Families and Households (NSFH). They found that for women in more traditional marriages (where they also were stay at home parents), their husbands earned at least two-thirds of the family income. When women believed in more traditional gender norms, they were happier in their marriages than women in more egalitarian marriages in which men and women shared these responsibilities. Women who reported that the distribution of household work was equitable or fair were happier than women in less equitable marriages. Wives were happier when their husbands were emotionally invested in the marriage and spent time with them and their children. Finally, women were happiest when they envisioned marriage as life-long. Wilcox and Nock (2006) argue that women in more traditional marriages may be happier than women in more egalitarian marriages because they are less stressed and more focused on their marriages by not having to balance family and a career. However, these data from the second wave of the NSFH are nearly two decades old.

Women and men also may be happier in traditional marriages than in egalitarian marriages because the gender roles within these households are clear. Within egalitarian marriages, there is greater ambiguity regarding women and men's roles. This ambiguity can produce stress and conflict. For instance, husbands may be more likely to help their wives with domestic responsibilities in egalitarian households, but there may be increased conflict because of role ambiguity regarding who is primarily responsible for taking care of the children, making dinner, or doing specific chores. Even though women are invested in their careers more than at any time in history, there is a pressure within society and families for the woman to be primarily responsible for domestic labor and maintaining family relationships. In addition, although the women's movement emphasized equality between men and women and gave women the freedom to choose career opportunities, women today may place undue pressure on themselves as a result of the women's movement to "do it all" perfectly at work and home. This pressure can be incredibly stressful when women also feel as if they come home to a "second shift" after leaving work (Hochschild & Machung, 1989, 2001).

An important issue to consider is how the aforementioned ideas of marital schemata and marriage might inform the research on copreneurs. As co-owners of a business, husbands and wives are equally invested in the business succeeding and, by definition, may have more egalitarian marriages than traditional marriages. However, as Helmle, Seibold, and Afifi (2010) found, some copreneurs balance work and family by one of the spouses being at the forefront of the business and the other being at the forefront of the family. This may allow some couples to achieve more traditional marriages even though they both work in the same business. In addition, even if husbands and wives in copreneurial relationships spend the same amount of time and have similar leadership roles at work, the flexibility of owning one's own business may allow parents, especially women, the ability to effectively balance work and family by attending to family matters during work hours (see Ashforth et al., 2000). This might provide some women the opportunity to co-own their business with their husbands, while preserving their role as primary care-givers at home. Another possibility is that husbands and wives who start a business together are more likely to espouse egalitarian ideals in the first place and, consequently, may be less strained and conflicted if they do not fit the traditional marriage schemata. Copreneurs may be less likely to have traditional marriages because they own a business together, and thus have more egalitarian marriages and less conventional gender roles. Perhaps copreneurs are more likely than other couples to reject hegemonic gender roles in favor of post-gender marriages in which home and work life management and responsibilities are split equally (see Risman & Johnson-Sumerford, 1998), largely because of their shared business arrangement. However, even if they both own the business and believe they have a more egalitarian marriage, the husband could still be primarily responsible for managing the business and the wife could be primarily responsible for managing the family (as reported by Helmle, 2010). In general, even if spouses report egalitarian marriages, women are still responsible for managing care-giving tasks, chores, and maintenance of the family (Hochschild & Machung, 1989, 2001). Thus, it may be that even if copreneurs have more egalitarian marriages than other couple types, to be tested, women can still be at the forefront of managing the family.

An interesting avenue of research would be to compare husbands' and wives' marital schemata, perceptions of equity, and marital quality in different types of work-family relationships (e.g., comparing copreneurial relationships with dual career relationships—including those who work together—and marriage where one spouse is the primary breadwinner). Do copreneurs have more egalitarian marriages compared to other couples? Is the copreneurial relationship more equitable than other work-family marriages? Are copreneurs who have more traditional marriages happier than copreneurs in more egalitarian marriages? How important is equity in the copreneurial relationship compared with the other types? If equity is important, how do copreneurs achieve it when work and family are so intertwined, and in what ways is it a communication accomplishment? The copreneurial relationship provides an interesting context in which to study these dynamics because of the complete intertwining of work and family.

The notion of marital schemata and equity corresponds to Fitzpatrick's (e.g., 1976, 1990; Fitzpatrick & Ritchie, 1994) work on couple types. Fitzpatrick (1976) discusses three different couple types: traditionals, independents, and separates (or a combination therein, referred to as a mixed couple type). Similar to the traditional marriages described above, traditional couples follow along traditional gender roles and are extremely interdependent in that they tend to engage in almost all of their activities together (Fitzpatrick & Ritchie, 1994). They use moderate disclosure and do not have very much conflict in their marriage, but will talk about issues when they arise. They are very accommodating toward each other. Independent couple types also engage in a lot of activities together, but simultaneously want to maintain their individuality and identity apart from the marriage (Fitzpatrick, 1984, 1988). They believe in sharing and companionship, but not at the expense of autonomy. People in this marital type are extremely flexible and more androgynous (Fitzpatrick, 1988). As a result, they tend to have more egalitarian views and practices regarding childrearing, household work, and breadwinning. They are more open in their disclosures and direct in their conflict discussions. Separates tend to live separate, autonomous lives within their marital relationship. The marriage is often a matter of convenience and a part of normal life, rather than maintained due to love or closeness (Fitzpatrick, 1984, 1988). Each partner enjoys autonomy and space, and the couple engages in relatively traditional gender roles. Separates tend to be more conflict avoidant and verbal sharing is deemphasized. This couple also tends to be less affectionate than the other couples types. Finally, couples can be a mix of the different couple types. For example, a common couple type is a traditional wife and a separate husband (Fitzpatrick & Ritchie, 1994).

Given that copreneurs tend to have a unique interdependency between work and family, an interesting empirical question is what couple type is the most common among copreneurs. Are these couples more traditional or independent in nature? The very structure of spouses operating a business together suggests an independent couple type. However, it might be the case that copreneurs include a couple type that is not represented by Fitzpatrick (1977, Fitzpatrick & Ritchie, 1994). For example, the fact that both the husband and wife own a business together may make them more of an independent couple type, but they might follow more traditional gender roles at home. None of Fitzpatrick's couples types allow for the blending of the two couple types for both partners. As Deutsch (1999) notes, many couples become more egalitarian over time simply because the nature of their dual career arrangement requires it. Dual career women in her sample often demanded their husbands contribute more at home because of the equitable contributions at work. It would be interesting to see if these transformations toward independent couple types and egalitarian marriages are more likely in copreneurs than other couples due to co-owning and operating their business. Does the type of business and each spouse's role in the business make the couple more likely to assume a particular couple type. For instance, if the business is a family farm, the couple may have a more traditional couple type because rural families tend to be more traditional in nature (Pitts, Fowler, Kaplan, Nussbaum, & Becker, 2009). A person's schemata for couple types also might be passed down through generations. If the business has been inherited from previous generations of the family, for example, there may be prescribed gender roles that are socialized as well.

Conflict Patterns. When a marriage is perceived as inequitable or people feel they are under-benefited, conflict and stress result (Sprecher, 2001a, 2001b; Stafford & Canary, 2006). Partners often attempt to restore equity by noting areas in the marriage they believe are the sources of inequity. In theory, when people are over-benefited, or when they are receiving more from the marriage than they are contributing compared to their partner who is contributing more and receiving less, they should also be somewhat stressed due to guilt (Walster et al., 1985). Given this stress and guilt, people who are over-benefited also should attempt to restore equity by contributing more to the relationship (Walster et al., 1985). However, women may be more likely to feel guilty if they are over-benefited and attempt to restore equity, perhaps because they are socialized as the ones who should be responsible for maintaining family relationships. In reality, partners think that they each are contributing more than one hundred percent to the marriage (Sprecher, 2001a).

One form of conflict that tends to surface when people feel their marriages are inequitable is demand-withdraw patterns. Demand-withdraw patterns occur when one spouse nags, criticizes, or demands to talk about an issue while the other spouse avoids or withdraws from the conversation (Heavey, Layne, & Christensen, 1993). The demander views the topic as important, is emotionally invested in it, and feels passionate about addressing it immediately (Caughlin & Vangelisti, 2000). The withdrawer, on the other hand, often believes that the topic is not as important as the demander thinks it is and wants to avoid it. While this pattern of conflict behavior can promote positive relational change (see Caughlin, 2002; Golish, 2003), it typically is predictive of relational dissatisfaction (Caughlin & Huston, 2002), marital distress (Schaap, Buunk, & Kerkstra, 1988), and divorce (Gottman & Levenson, 2000).

Research consistently has found that women more often are the "demanders" in romantic relationships and men are the "withdrawers" (Christensen & Heavey, 1990). Two common explanations include the sex role socialization perspective and the structural perspective. The first suggests that women have been socialized from a young age to talk about their relationship problems, and they are more likely to talk about relationship problems with their partners when they notice them (e.g., Christensen & Heavey, 1990). The social structure perspective states that because women tend to have less power than men in marriage, they are more likely to demand changes in their relationships, while men are more likely to be satisfied with the status quo (Christensen & Heavey, 1990; Heavey et al., 1993). Therefore, when women feel as if they are being under-benefited in their relationship, they are likely to demand change to gain or restore a sense of equity. Women may be more demanding in their marriage because they tend to be under-benefited and want their husbands to contribute more to the household labor and childrearing responsibilities. Yet, Caughlin and Vangelisti (2000) argue that demand-withdraw patterns also may be due to individual differences or influences (e.g., narcissism, internal locus of control, desire for change) and relational influences (e.g., both partners' demanding and withdrawing behaviors influence each other and that partners oscillate between these behaviors). In their research, Caughlin and Vangelisti found support for both of these perspectives.

As studies have shown (Perrone & Worthington, 2001; Rogers & May, 2003), balancing two careers and a family can be stressful and conflict-inducing, often the result of feelings of inequity. When both partners have careers, equity concerns may become more salient because women's increasing contributions as breadwinners in the family place greater pressure on men to reciprocate with more responsibilities in the home. Women with careers outside the home may be particularly likely to engage in demanding behaviors in an effort to balance the work-family spheres. What role do demand-withdraw patterns play in the copreneurial relationship? Are those patterns linked to feelings of inequity? Does one spouse tend to think he/she is doing more in one or both domains and subsequently engage in demanding behavior? As research on copreneurs suggests (e.g., Nelton, 1986), co-owning a business can be stressful because the spouses are balancing both domains together every day. Given partners' mutual investment in the business and mutual reliance on each other to succeed at work and home, perhaps there is greater demanding behavior on the part of both the husband and the wife compared to other couples where this unique dynamic does not exist.

Stress Contagion Effects. Another area of marital communication research that may be relevant for communication in the copreneurial relationship includes studies of stress contagion effects. Following research on work-family balance, there is considerable research on "spillover" effects that occur when the stress from work spills over into family life and vice versa (Rogers & May, 2003). When people are unable to effectively manage their work stress, it can blend into their family life and make their partner and children stressed

(Seerey, Corrigall, & Harpel, 2008). Research has focused on service-oriented industries, particularly highly stressful ones such as police officers, firefighters, emergency room nurses, and doctors (Roberts & Levenson, 2001), because of the emotional labor involved with trying to maintain a certain public image as part of one's job (Hochschild, 1983). Persons' ability to cope effectively with their emotions and stress at home and work is predictive of personal and relational health (Grzywacz, Almeida, & McDonald, 2002).

Copreneurs may be especially prone to spillover effects because their work-family domains are intrinsically connected. Copreneurs are in a unique situation because both spouses must learn to effectively manage their work and family stress simultaneously. Working and owning a business together can be extremely fulfilling because spouses can identify and empathize with each other about their work and family life, which can result in a more cohesive and satisfying marriage (Barnett & Barnett, 1988; Nelton, 1986). Many copreneurs enjoy talking about work at home because they can support each other and it affords them the flexibility to blend the two domains successful. As such, there is variation in the degree of permeability of work-family boundaries in copreneurial relationships, with some couples perceiving work and family as highly integrated (Helmle et al., 2010). The danger is when partners talk about work too much at home and wish their boundaries between work and family were more rigid. The ability to successfully regulate work-family boundaries may be rooted in expectations for these boundaries and the extent to which they are fulfilled. It also depends upon the type of talk and the extent to which talk is stressful and interfering with other parts of their life. Some copreneurs may enjoy talking with each other about their work at home, but if most of those conversations are highly stressful, talking about work could have negative spillover effects.

One area of stress and coping that addresses potential contagion effects and that could be applied to balancing work and family is communal coping. Communal coping reflects proactive behaviors that groups of people or dyads who face similar stressors use to cope together to confront adversity (Afifi, Hutchinson, & Krouse, 2006; Lyons, Mickelson, Sullivan, & Coyne, 1998). Instead of viewing coping as a psychological and unidirectional phenomenon, communal coping entails conceptualizing coping as an interdependent process that is relational and interactive (Afifi et al., 2006; Lyons et al., 1998). From a communal coping framework, a stressor is appraised and acted upon as "our problem and our responsibility" rather than as something to be managed alone (Lyons et al., 1998). Coping is co-constructed among people who are facing similar life stressors. Communal coping can have positive and negative consequences. It typically is an effective way of coping because the collective and proactive nature of communal coping builds coping efficacy and resilience (Afifi et al., 2006; Hobfoll, Schroder, & Malek, 2002; Lyons et al., 1998). Communal coping can be harmful when stress contagion effects occur or when people talk about their stress too much (i.e., verbal rumination) to each other. As Afifi et al. (2006) point out, communal coping can be destructive if the stressor becomes misplaced or if a stressor that should have been individually owned becomes jointly owned. This can be problematic if the stressor gets displaced to someone with less power in the family or marriage, who is then afraid to communicate his/her feelings of displeasure with assuming the stressor.

Communal coping has primarily been applied to groups of people experiencing similar stressors, such as natural disasters (Kaniasty & Norris, 1993), wars (Khalaf, 2002), support groups (Brashers et al., 2000), and divorce (Afifi et al., 2006). However, it also has been applied to dyads where the stressors become jointly "owned," even if the source of the stressor resides primarily with one partner, as is usually the case with chronic illnesses (e.g., Kowal, Johnson, & Lee, 2003). Communal coping could be applied to the copreneurial relationship. Given that copreneurs co-own and co-manage a business and have a family together, they are likely to experience similar stressors. The extent to which the couple copes with their stress together could affect their personal and relational health. For example, viewing their business stressors as "our problem and our responsibility" may help copreneurs build cohesion, a stronger business and couple identity, and efficacy that they can work through life's stressors together as a unit. However, verbally ruminating about their business stressors too much could increase their stress and have detrimental effects on their health and marital/family satisfaction, and potentially their ability to function effectively as business partners.

It would be interesting to examine the physiological effects of balancing work and family, particularly in copreneurial relationships. Copreneurs may be more susceptible than other couples to stress contagion effects because of the blending of work and family spheres. The work-family stress could affect the couple physiologically if it is not managed effectively. Partners' stress and coping abilities mutually influence one another (Coyne & Smith, 1994). One person's stress can spill over to another's through verbal and nonverbal communication of the stress. Verbally ruminating about stress or "extensively discussing and revisiting problems, speculating about problems, and focusing on negative feelings" (Rose, 2002, p. 1830) has been linked to anxiety, depression, and physiological arousal (Byrd-Craven, Geary, Rose, & Ponzi, 2007; Rose, Carlson, & Waller, 2007).

However, findings indicate that the support and affection that spouses give to each other can moderate or buffer the effect of the stress on their health (see Rosal, King, Yunsheng, & Reed, 2004). Or, when spouses are affectionate and support, it lessens the negative effect of the stress on their bodies. For example, Floyd (Floyd, 2006; Floyd & Riforgiate, 2009) has shown that affection can have important physiological stress reduction effects. He has found that the more affection that people give and receive, the better their health and the less affected they are by stress-inducing laboratory tasks (Floyd, Mikkelson, Hesse, & Pauley, 2007; Floyd et al., 2009). Other research has shown that when spouses or dating partners are supportive during conflict interactions, they are better able to "down regulate" after the conflict task or experience a quicker return to baseline (Heffner Kiecolt-Glaser, Loving, Glaser, & Malarkey, 2004; Priem & Solomon, 2010). Applying this to copreneurs and to couples balancing work and family, one could argue that couples who are able to be supportive of one another during stressful times may be able to counter-act some of the ill effects of the stress. In fact, operating a family business together may provide a strong foundation of support and understanding (Barnett & Barnett, 1988), which may help shield the stress and physiological effects of the stress of balancing work and family.

Our discussion thus far references the study of the copreneurial relationship as a whole (both personal and professional), as well as how copreneurs negotiate the boundaries and borders between their work and family domains to achieve balance. Next, we offer a brief review of research on work-family integration and strategies to achieve balance, emphasizing findings that are relevant for work-balance processes in copreneurial relationships and in family businesses. Thereafter, we explicate four theoretical frameworks with the potential to illuminate these work-family and communication issues in copreneurial and family businesses.

Work-Family Integration

Given technological affordances, the ability to integrate work and family lives has never been greater (Jackson, 2005). The use of mobile phones, Internet resources, email, tele/video/web-conferencing, and personal digital assistants (PDAs) enables work from almost anywhere in the world, including home. According to the Office of Personnel Management (2004), more than 23 million U.S. workers telework on a part-time or full-time basis. Bond, Thompson, Galinsky, and Prottas (2002) reported that "18% of all wage and salaried employees use a computer at home to read and send job-related email outside of regular work hours" (p. 23), a figure that doubtlessly has increased. Brannen (2005) claimed that organizations sell flexibility to their employees by allowing them to connect their work and non-work worlds through the use of technology. Furthermore, Chesley (2005) found that persistent communications use in the family domain (i.e., cell phones and pagers), rather than computer use (email and Internet), is associated with more distress, less family satisfaction, and more negative spillover from work to family and from family to work. However, in Edley's (2001) study of employed mothers, participants reported that their cell phones empowered them to stay connected with their families when they were working and/or away on business trips. Kirby et al. (2003) suggest that the use of these mobile technologies (including laptops, cell phones, PDAs) has blurred "the temporal and spatial distinctions between domains of work and family" (p. 7), and further that this blurring of boundaries is evident in a swing during the past decade from viewing work and family in terms of the container metaphor (where the work and family domains are separated, as if in different containers) to one of work-family integration. Discussion of work-family integration no longer focuses on conflict between the two domains, but emphasizes that involvement in both domains can have benefits for the individual, family, and organization (Gareis, Barnett, Ertel, & Berkman, 2009; Van Steenbergen & Ellemers, 2009).

Family-friendly organizational policies assist employees in this balancing act, and they benefit the organization by reducing absenteeism and increasing employee productivity (Konrad & Mangel, 2000). Flexible work arrangements are one example of a family-friendly organizational policy. In 2001, 28.1% of full-time wage and salary employees had flexible schedules (U.S. Census Bureau, 2003). According to a report of the National Study of a Changing Workforce (Bond et al., 2002), employees with families report higher levels of interference between their work and family lives compared to employees in 1977. However, Bond et al. found that when supportive work-life policies and practices (i.e., flexible work arrangements) are available in organizations, employees report more positive work and life outcomes (i.e., job satisfaction, commitment to employer, retention, less interference between work and family life, less negative spillover, greater life satisfaction, and better mental health). Kirby (2006) suggests that organizations that offer employees personal services (including wellness programs, employee assistance programs, and the like) are assuming a "family-like role" by showing concern for their employees' well-being, regardless of their motives for doing so. While these services may be beneficial to employees' wellness (including balance), the offering of such services by the organization continues to blur the boundaries between work and family. In Cowan and Hoffman's (2007) study of how employees construct the work-life border, participants defined work-life balance in terms of flexibility on the part of the organization. Furthermore, Ilies, Wilson, and Wagner (2009) found that on days when employees experienced higher levels of job satisfaction, they experienced more positive affect and higher levels of marital satisfaction than on days when job satisfaction was low. These findings underscore the reciprocal influence of work and family/marital life.

Another affirmation of work-family integration is evident in Ruderman, Ohlott, Panzer, and King's (2002) findings that managerial women experienced several benefits as a result of their multiple role commitments (i.e., wife, mother, manager). The authors' results suggest that the roles women play outside of work have a positive impact on their ability and performance as a manager at work. Moreover, managerial women's multiple role commitments were positively related to life satisfaction, self-esteem, and self-acceptance. Ilies et al. (2009) reported a stronger relationship between job satisfaction and positive affect when employees were more (versus less) work-family role-integrated. These findings are consistent with the claim made by Van Steenbergen and Ellemers (2009), consistent with Marks' (1977) role expansion theory, that involvement in one role can have positive effects on the performance of other roles. This positive side of role combination has only recently been acknowledged in the literature on work and family (Wayne, Randal, & Stevens, 2006). Van Steenbergen and Ellemers define work-family facilitation as "the individual's experience that participation in one role is made easier or better by virtue of participation in another role" (p. 618; also see Van Steenbergen, Ellemers, & Mooijaart, 2007). Employees who experienced more work-family conflict were found to have greater incidences of high cholesterol and obesity (Van Steenbergen & Ellemers, 2009). Furthermore, those employees who experienced more work-family facilitation were less likely to have high cholesterol and poor physical stamina.

Wierda-Boer, Gerris, Vermulst, Malinen, and Anderson (2009) used the multiple-roles perspective to investigate work-family interference in couples from Finland, Germany, and the Netherlands. Regardless of the balance strategies the couples used (e.g., equal sharing of roles and responsibilities), what correlated with work-family interference were the hours involved on tasks. Men who were actively involved in their work domain experienced the most conflict from work to the family domain, whereas women who were actively involved in the family domain experienced the most conflict from the family to work domain. Therefore, active involvement in more than one role was only problematic when there was a higher workload (or involved a high number of hours/time spent). Among couples, the distress of one partner is an important source of the other partner's distress (Barnett, 1998), yet having the support of one's family can help reduce stress in the workplace (Adams, King, & King, 1996). These findings suggest that not only do the domains of work and family overlap, but their interconnectedness can actually have adverse effects as well as benefits for individuals with roles at home and in the workplace.

Findings from an investigation by Medved, Brogan, McClanahan, Morris, and Shepherd (2006) of how parents socialize their children to think about work and family through the messages that parents communicate to them are promising for future generations. Medved et al. (2006) note that work-family socialization is interconnected and is not contained in any one domain. Messages were coded into categories representing topics surrounding work, family, and balance. Messages related to prioritizing family over work were prevalent in all topic areas. With regard to the topic of balance, the most frequent parental messages concerned work choice and choosing a particular job or career because of the time one would be able to spend with family. There were messages about which careers to avoid because of constraints placed on family time. As future generations become socialized to prioritize family and time with family over work, organizations will need to continue to respond to the increasing work-family needs of its evolving workforce. As an extension of the research by Medved et al. on work-family messages, communication scholars may find it fruitful to explore how families talk about their family businesses, what memorable messages children retain about the family business, and how those messages impact their perceptions of work and family. It also would be theoretically important and practically useful to examine the discourse of children about their parents' or family's business, the impact on their relationship with their parents/family, and their feelings about it.

Role of Culture and Gender

Most of our discussion has focused on U.S.-based studies and cultural values. However, the importance of examining non-U.S. work and family practices cannot be overstated. Coffey, Anderson, Zhao, Liu, and Zhang (2009) studied the role of work-family balance in the lives of young Chinese professionals. They found that indeed work-family balance is an important and challenging issue for the younger generation of workers and differs from previous generations. Workers who participated in the study claimed that few organizations and managers in China acknowledge the challenges and difficulties that they experience when trying to balance their work and family lives, and often do nothing to help. Choi and Chen (2006) found that while Chinese men and women report similar work demands, Chinese women report a higher level of family demands. Coffey et al. argue that more research is concerning the changing gender roles and expectations for the younger generation of Chinese professionals.

The degree of power and collectivism within a culture also may influence work-family patterns. Mortazavi, Pedhiwala, Shafiro, and Hammer (2009) studied work-family conflict in the Ukraine, Iran, and the United States. Contrary to predictions, there were no significant differences in levels of work-family conflict among those in the Ukraine, Iran, or the United States. However, the researchers found that employed women in Iran and the United States spent more hours on family responsibilities than employed men in their country of origin, and employed men in all three countries spent more time fulfilling work demands. The authors were surprised to find that employed men reported higher family to work conflict compared to employed women. One explanation is that in Iran, a collectivistic culture, it is normative that family members are responsible to care for other family members; extended family members have the responsibility of supporting and helping working mothers achieve a sense of work-family balance. Thus, in Iran, the burden of the family does not necessarily fall solely on the mother (whether employed or not). Mortazavi et al. propose that Ukrainian women may not experience high levels of family to work conflict because of their acceptance of traditional gender roles (with family demands being their responsibility). These findings suggest that the relationship between gender and work-family conflict may vary based on cultural norms and expectations for gender roles.

Craig and Sawrikar (2009) claim that as children get older, mothers begin to commit more of their time to employment and women tend to use family-friendly benefits offered by their work organizations more often than men. Findings from their study of parents in Australia suggest that women report that they do more housework and childcare than their partner, and men consistently report that they do less than an equal share of the housework and childcare. Their findings also reveal that balancing work and family becomes easier and more gender equitable as children get older (Craig & Sawrikar, 2009, p. 705). However, the equity of gender roles arises from women changing their behavior as children age, but the behavior of men stays the same. Alternatively, Johnstone and Lee (2009) apply Hakim's (2000) lifestyle preference theory to study young Australian women's aspirations for work and family. Hakim's (2000) theory contends that women fall into three categories regarding their work-family preferences. Work-centered women are highly committed to their jobs/careers and home-centered women are focused on their family life and do not aspire to be part of the workforce. What may be most salient for work-family scholars is what Hakim describes as "adaptive women." Adaptive women want a combination of (paid) work and family, but prefer to shape their work life around their family responsibilities. They are not as committed to their jobs/careers as work-centered women and are more likely to be the secondary earners in a relationship (Hakim, 2000). Johnstone and Lee (2009) found that adaptive women's responses fell between work- and home-centered women. However, adaptive women's responses on the variables of relationships, motherhood status, and area of residence closely resembled those of home-centered women. Adaptive women were the largest group in Johnstone and Lee's (2009) study and the authors suggest that policy makers and organizations learn more about this group in order to respond to the work-family needs of the younger generation of women in the workforce. We note that the adaptive women in the Johnstone and Lee (2009) investigation are strikingly similar to the majority of women copreneurs studied by Helmle (2010), a finding that bears further study. We add that the area of how copreneurs manage work-family life issues cries out for international and comparative studies of the type just surveyed in work-family arena.

Strategies for Balance

Whether the work-family interface has positive or negative effects on the individual is associated, in part, with the strategies that individuals utilize in attempting to balance work and family. Jennings and McDougald (2007) conducted a comprehensive review of research on the work-family interface in entrepreneurial contexts. Individuals' strategies for balancing work and family include: segmentation (i.e., conscious separation between the domains); compensation (i.e., more involvement in one domain in order to compensate for unhappiness in the other domain); accommodation (i.e., "individuals limit their psychological and/or behavioral involvement in one sphere to satisfy the demands of the other"); boundary management work (i.e., "principles and practices for creating, maintaining, and crossing borders between the domains"); structural role definition (i.e., "changing the expectations of others"); personal role definition (i.e., "revising one's own expectations"); and reactive role behavior (i.e., "attempting to respond to all demands") (p. 749).

Jennings and McDougald (2007) also surveyed the work of Moen and colleagues (Becker & Moen, 1999; Moen & Yu, 2000), which identified work-family interface strategies at the couple-level. Two couple-level strategies for balancing work and family when putting one partner's career at the forefront included: the traditional strategy (one partner works and the other stays at home) and the one-job/one-career strategy (one partner "takes a less demanding job so that the other can pursue his or her career more vigorously") (Jennings & McDougald, 2007, p. 749). Other strategies identified in the literature for couples who both are highly invested in their careers include: postponing children until their careers are established (or forgoing children); hiring a domestic helper to assist with child care and housework; scaling back at work (i.e., lowering expectations for advancement, hours worked, travel, etc.); and scaling back at home (i.e., lowering expectations for housework, limiting the number of children, and/or limiting time spent on other personal pursuits) (Jennings & McDougald, 2007). However, this list of strategies is not exhaustive and the implication that segmentation is even possible is questionable due to the integrated nature of the work and family domains. Jennings and McDougald (2007) contend that women have "lower boundary separation" than men and tend to move between domains in order to fulfill their multiple role commitments (p. 753). Furthermore, a gap in the work and family literature exists in that the role of *communication* is not adequately addressed in the strategies that individuals and couples use when striving to balance their work and family lives.

We seek to fill that gap by further explicating the role of communication in the process of copreneurs' strategies for managing work-family life issues. The greatest potential contributions to the work-family and family-business areas may come where the two sub-areas of the communication discipline intersect (Golden et al., 2006). Stafford and Tews (2009) suggest that taking a systems approach to studying families and businesses from a work-family perspective may reveal whether the overlap between the two domains lends itself to better functioning in both domains. The wisdom of their advice may have a parallel in a study of 732 Spanish family businesses by Basco and Perez-Rodriguez (2009), who found that businesses that incorporated the family system into their governance had more effective management of the family business (versus businesses who did not take the family component of their venture into consideration). Next, we offer a discussion of four theoretical frameworks with the potential to illuminate these work-family management processes in copreneurs' interactions.

Theoretical Frameworks

Some work and family scholars (Clark, 2000; Desrochers, Hilton, & Larwood, 2005) contend that research in the work-family area is atheoretical or is undermined by the limitations of the theories involved. We believe communication contributions to work-family integration, especially in the context of family businesses and copreneurship, may be enhanced by boundary theory, work-family border theory, relational dialectics, and structuration theory.

Boundary Theory

Working from a symbolic-interactionist perspective, Nippert-Eng (1996) developed boundary theory as a framework for interpreting the meanings that individuals assign to home and work (also see Desrochers et al., 2005). Ashforth et al. (2000) refined boundary theory by incorporating concepts from role theory and narrowing the scope to encompass role transitions and the implications of employees' preferences for work-family integration (also see Ashforth, 2001; Desrochers et al., 2005). Focusing on "micro-role transitions," which involve frequent movement between and within the work and home domains, Ashforth et al. (2000) posit that flexibility and permeability are the two key concepts involved in micro-role transitions. Flexibility refers to the "extent to which the spatial and temporal boundaries are malleable, and can be enacted in various settings and at various times" (p. 474). Family business members make multiple micro-role transitions per day, moving between their role as an employee and as a family member. Copreneurs also make multiple micro-role transitions daily, transitioning between their role as an executive and spouse (Helmle, 2010). These transitions are enabled by permeability, the extent to which a role "allows one to be physically located in the role's domain but psychologically and/or behaviorally involved in another role" (Ashforth et al., 2000, p. 474). Copreneurs have high permeability; they may transition to their role of spouse/parent or business partner in an instant regardless of location (Helmle, 2010).

Boundary theory and spillover theory were tested in the Ilies et al. (2009) study of work-family role-integration and job/marital satisfaction. The researchers found that employees with higher work-family role-integration reported increased spillover of job satisfaction to positive affect at home. In a study of work and personal life boundary management, Bulger, Matthews, and Hoffman (2007) found that those participants who have an increased ability to flex their personal life boundary also report more work enhancement of their personal life. Boundary theory invites explanation of how communication factors into how individuals "transition" between roles, as well as the part that communication plays in how individuals establish mental boundaries between work and family. Future studies might investigate linkages between the permeability of copreneurs' work and family lives and the amount of work-family balance they experience. The relationship between the flexibility to attend to family matters in the work domain (and attend to work matters in the family domain) and the amount of copreneurs' work-family balance could be studied. Is having the flexibility to deal with work matters at home or during personal time important to *both* spouses? Exploring how copreneurs' micro-role transitions impact their work-family balance is important, especially how they are communicatively managed.

Work-Family Border Theory

According to Desrochers and Sargent (2003), the main differences between boundary theory and border theory lie in their outcomes. As they see it, boundary theory is more cognitive given its concern with "the meanings people assign to home and work and the ease and frequency of transitioning between roles" (p. 2). Border theory focuses on social/relational dynamics to explain how individuals achieve work-family balance. Examining the recursive relationship of copreneurship and work-family issues through the lens of boundary and work-family border theories offers a different, yet complementary, perspective to the communication aspects of these two approaches.

Clark (2000) developed work-family border theory in response to limitations she saw in prior theory and research in the work and family arena. She posited that balance is the "satisfaction and good functioning both at work and home with minimal role conflict" (p. 751) and can be achieved in several ways depending on the similarity of work and family domains, the strength of the boundaries between these domains, and other factors such as home and workplace cultures (Desrochers et al., 2005). Clark (2000) asserted that communication is a tool that can be used to attain better work-family balance, and the theory calls for a commitment to both roles (work and family) in order to achieve the desired balance. Family business members may exhibit high levels of commitment to their roles because of stakes that are personal (i.e., marriage, family) and professional (i.e., business is their livelihood). The theory suggests that individuals are "border-crossers who make daily transitions between these two settings (work and family domains that are seen as separate entities), often tailoring their focus, their goals, and their interpersonal style to fit the unique demands of each" (Clark, 2000, p. 751). Clark (2000) added, "while many aspects of work and home are difficult to alter, individuals can shape to some degree the nature of the work and home domains, and the borders and bridges between them, in order to create a desired balance" (p. 751). Border-keepers or domain members are those who belong to the work (e.g., one's supervisors, co-workers, and subordinates) and home/family domains (e.g., one's family members). Desrochers et al. (2005) claim that border theory addresses how these boundaries divide the times, places, and people that correspond with work and family. The goals of this perspective are to "both describe why conflict exists and provide a framework for individuals and organizations to encourage better balance between work and families" (Clark, 2000, p. 764).

This theory of work-family balance readily can be applied to copreneurs, who move in and out of the work and family domains and the borders between those domains tend to blur given that a family business is one of the most highly integrated situations involving work and family (Desrochers et al., 2005; Nippert-Eng, 1996). While Clark (2000) noted that balance may be obtained through communication, she did not explain how communication impacts the balance. Communication scholars may wish to investigate how copreneurs' communication about work in the family domain (and about family in the work domain) impacts their work-family balance. Does being able to talk about work at home or on personal time with their spouse affect copreneurs' work-family balance? Future studies might investigate the relationship between the autonomy copreneurs experience in their work and their family (and business) functioning. Do copreneurs find that their autonomy in work is positively related to their family's functioning? Exploring copreneurs' commitment to their work and family roles, and whether their idea of commitment is similar or different to that of non-copreneurs, could be studied, as well as how their commitment is related to work-family balance. How do copreneurs view their spouse's commitment to the business, and does that impact their perception of how well their business is performing? With regard to recursivity, do copreneurs' feelings of work-family balance affect their perception of their family and business functioning? We propose that organizational communication scholars could look at the notion of time (e.g., work time, family time), including the public/private time divide, in terms of work-family balance. Finally, Guest (2002) noted that the analysis of borders can help illuminate the amount of control an individual has over issues affecting balance. Family business members, especially copreneurs, have more control than the average worker over their borders, and they have more choice in how they choose to balance their work and family lives, but these dynamics warrant empirical investigation.

Relational Dialectics

Examining copreneurs' work-family balance from the premise of dialectical theory, and from the relational dialectics perspective in particular, may better illuminate the communicative processes involved in copreneurial relationships than either of the two foregoing theories (each of which has origins in disciplines other than communication). Dialectical theory views relationships as an ongoing process (Baxter, 2010). Baxter (2004, 2010; Baxter & Montgomery, 1996) argues that relationships are continually in flux as a result of a continuous struggle of contradictions or dialectical tensions that are present whenever two forces are interdependent, yet mutually oppose or negate one another. Also inherent to relational dialectics theory are the ideas of praxes and totality (Baxter, 2010). Dialectical theory posits that dialectical tensions can be negotiated through communication praxes or practices and that those communication practices are a reflection of past interactions and experiences (Baxter, 2004; Baxter & Montgomery, 1996). For instance, Hoppe-Nagao and Ting-Toomey (2002) studied the communication praxes that married couples without children use to negotiate the tensions of autonomy-connection and openness-closedness. These authors found that their strategies to negotiate the autonomy-connection tension included activities and time separation, reframing, and compromise. Strategies to manage the openness-closedness tension included topic and time alternation, withdrawal, probing, anti-social behaviors, and deception. Finally, dialectical tensions occur within the totality or complete history and context of the relationship (Baxter, 2010). To understand the dialectical tensions and their ensuing complexities, one must situate them within the larger relational and social context (Braithwaite & Baxter, 2006).

Dialectical theory can be applied to families, family businesses, or married couples with businesses. According to the theory, how the dialectical tensions in copreneurs' relationships (i.e., autonomy-connection, predictability-novelty, openness-closedness) are managed through communication will contribute to the copreneurs' relational satisfaction and how they function as a marital couple. We propose that the dialectical tension of work-family also is present in copreneurs' relationships, as work and family are two interdependent forces that mutually oppose one another, and how copreneurs manage the work-family tension communicatively also will affect their sense of work-family balance. Before pursuing this idea, a fuller treatment of the relational dialectics perspective will be useful.

In her earlier work on relational dialectics theory, Baxter identified three primary dialectical tensions that people experience in their relationships: autonomy-connection, predictability-novelty, and openness-closedness (Baxter, 1988; Baxter & Simon, 1993). While research on dialectical theory has shown that there are numerous other tensions that characterize relationships, these three tensions are probably central in copreneurs' relationships too. For instance, for relationships to thrive, individuals need to experience some form of autonomy and some form of connection with their partner (Baxter & Simon, 1993). Montgomery (1993) claims that without a form of connection between two people, relationships may cease to exist and have no real identity; however, without autonomy there is no individuality or individual identity that can be a contributing part of a relationship. This dialectical tension must be managed in order to meet the autonomy and connection needs of both partners. When both spouses work in the same job, which is exacerbated within the copreneurial relationship because both spouses also own the business together, they have difficulty struggling for autonomy because they spend most of their days together (Helmle et al., 2010). Some couples take for granted the large amount of time together and experience little tension, while other couples manage this tension through segmenting their work and family boundaries or other methods (see Helmle et al., 2010). Additionally, Baxter (1990) claims the tensions experienced by couples can vary depending on their stage of development, and the tension of autonomy-connection is at its peak during relationship maintenance phases. In the copreneurial relationship, the spouses probably experience the most difficulty with balancing autonomy-connection early in their relationship when they are trying to build and maintain their family business, which requires more time together at work.

The predictability-novelty dialectical tension refers to the need for consistency in the relationship, as well as the need for novelty (i.e., spontaneity). In copreneurial relationships, the spouse-partners need to know that the other is committed to their relationship and to the business. The copreneurs should be able to trust that the other will act and communicate in ways that reflect commitment to both facets of their dual relationship. Conversely, a sense of excitement is desired in most marriages, so a certain amount of novelty is important as well. Baxter (1990) contends that this dialectical tension is most salient for couples when the relationship is in a maintenance phase. For example, this tension may be most significant for copreneurs once their business is stabilized and/or when they have been married for awhile.

Baxter (1990) suggests that the openness-closedness dialectic is most critical during the initial phases of relationships. Perhaps this also is pertinent because partners are getting to know one another and the disclosures they make have an impact on the feeling of intimacy in the relationship (Afifi & Guerrero, 2000). Partners may wish to disclose personal information in an effort to develop a closer connection to the other, yet they may not want to disclose "too much" (or negative) information about themselves that may alienate the other (Afifi & Guerrero, 2000). The dialectical tension between openness and closedness is important for the copreneurial relationship as well, as when one spouse purposely withholds information (either personal or professional) from the other because s/he knows its impact on their spouse and how that information would affect how the other performs their role of business person or family member. Barnett and Barnett (1988) confirm that copreneurs struggle with criticism or too much openness early on in their business relationship. They also report that as these working relationships mature and businesses and roles become more stable, criticism is viewed more as a helpful tool than an impediment. Copreneurs must continually manage or negotiate the openness-closedness tension as it relates to both their work and family lives.

As Baxter's recent conceptualization of relational dialectics theory (e.g., Baxter, 2004, 2010; Baxter, Braithwaite, Golish, & Olson, 2002; Braithwaite & Baxter, 2006) suggests, relationships often experience a "web of contractions" throughout the course of their relationships. Dialectical tensions are often interconnected and affect one another through dialogue and the transactional nature of relationships. There may be one overarching dialectical tension that captures the essence of the relationship, but which is then laced with a web of intricate dialectical tensions that comprise its existence (see Baxter et al., 2002 for an example). In corpreneurs' relationships, for example, a larger work-family tension may be the dominant dialectic, but it may be fueled by other sub-tensions tensions (e.g., openness-closedness, autonomy-connection).

How copreneurs communicatively manage the work-family tension is central to their relationship as spousal co-entrepreneurs. Inherent to the copreneurial relationship, business and family life are both highly valued. Copreneurs have a large professional and personal investment in their business, and it cannot be neglected or it may fail (Helmle et al., 2010). Most copreneurs became a couple before they became business partners, so it is to their personal and professional advantage to maintain a satisfying marriage (Barnett & Barnett, 1988). Therefore, how they manage the tension between the two has implications for their sense of work-family balance, as well as the success of the business and their personal relationship. If copreneurs successfully negotiate the work-family tension so that both spouses are happy with the outcome, they also may be more likely to report higher levels of work-family balance than those copreneurs who manage the tension so that only one (or neither) spouse is satisfied with the outcome. Researchers might investigate the relationship between the negotiation of dialectical tensions in copreneurs' relationships and their work-family balance, as well as their relationship satisfaction.

Structuration Theory

Institutions are constituted in members' interactional practices. Poole, Seibold, and McPhee (1996) observe that "the key to understanding (these) practices is through analysis of the *structures* that underlie them" (p. 117). Giddens (1984) distinguishes between system and structure. *Systems* are social entities, such as family businesses, engaged in interactional practices that result in observable patterns of relationships, such as hierarchies, decision making routines, and family/non-family subgroups. *Structures* are the rules and resources that members appropriate to create and maintain the system we witness. As "recipes" for acting (Giddens, 1984), rules and resources enable and constrain members' behaviors. *Rules* are tacitly known general procedures guiding them on how to function appropriately and skillfully. *Resources* include members' capabilities to command authoritative resources (social conditions and individuals) and allocatable resources (material entities). Hoffman and Cowan (2010) identified three resources and six rules 96 employees appropriated in efforts to achieve work-life balance through requests for accommodation from their organizations. Systems have patterns, such as copreneurs' apportionment of talk time about family and work when they are at home, due to members' structuring processes surrounding rules and resources (Helmle et al., 2010).

The recursive relationship between system and structure is captured in Giddens' (1984) concept of structuration, or the process by which systems are produced and reproduced through members' use of rules and resources. Poole et al. (1996) discuss key aspects of this process:

> Not only is the system produced and reproduced through structuration, but the structures themselves are, too. Structures are dualities: they are both the medium and the outcome of action. They are the medium of action because members draw on structures to interact. They are its outcome because rules and resources exist only by virtue of being used in a practice. Whenever the structure is employed, the activity reproduces it by invoking and confirming it as a meaningful basis for action. (p. 117)

The structures that enable and constrain system behaviors are thus continually being produced and reproduced in interaction. For example, Kirby and Krone (2002) demonstrated the structuration of policy in the daily discursive practices of members of a government agency that either reinforced or undermined formal work-family policies in the organization. It is in this sense that there is a duality of structure (Giddens, 1984): system and structure enable and constrain each other in interactants' behaviors.

As patterns of interaction are repeated across time and space, institutional/social relationships are formed and reinforced as recognized features of family, copreneurial, and business life. While members are knowledgeable agents, they are also subject to situated practices which work to resist complete autonomy. Instead, individuals exercise personal agency mindful of, but not necessarily or always committed to, established rules and resources.

Finally, human social activity is recursively reflexive as individuals monitor their interactions and the consequences. Family business members and copreneurs, for example, communicate with some level of knowledgeability, presumed to be necessary for reflexivity (Giddens, 1984). Structures change as a result of intended and unintended consequences, and these patterns of consequences produce institutionalized practices (Giddens, 1984).

As individuals communicate, they produce and reproduce relationships with others. Part of developing relationships involves positioning. As Giddens (1984) observes, social interaction is built on positioning of individuals in time-space relative to others. The social interaction enabling such positioning also is the very essence of organizing that constitutes copreneurial and family businesses. In their interactions, individuals create and modify the rules, or structures, underlying their relationships.

This structuring interaction occurs through members' micro-level moves to appropriate structures, patterns of members' use of structures, and modalities of structuration (Seibold & Myers, 2005). Structuring interactions can occur in discrete as well as in conjoined moves that interactants—acting individually and in tandem with others—make to appropriate structures (Seibold & Myers, 2005). In studying parents' socializing messages to their children concerning vocations, Medved et al. (2006) identified message moves that appropriate social structure and enhance their memorability through career enjoyment, work-career choice, financial necessity, work ethic, role of education, and work or family prioritization. Second, structuring can be seen in broader patterns of interaction in social systems (Seibold & Myers, 2005). For example, Golden (2009) drew upon interview accounts to uncover a larger pattern of interactions in which a high-tech organization and its employees' families enacted each other as environments relative to work-life integration policies and practices. Third, structuring can be found in the three modalities of structuration in which structures are simultaneously manifested (Seibold & Myers, 2005). As Giddens (1984) proposes, structures can simultaneously serve as norms guiding action, as facilities enabling the exercise of power, and as interpretive schemes. Indeed, structuration theory powerfully describes social institutions at the macro-level of analysis in terms of human interaction at the micro-level of analysis. Family businesses will vary as a function of interactional practices, but similarities abound in members' appropriation of larger financial, legal, educational, market, sectoral, and cultural institutions to develop situated versions of them (Poole et al., 1996). Appropriation of structural features results in different versions of institutional features being adapted to specific contexts (e.g., Mortazavi et al. 2009).

In construing this process, Giddens (1984) underscored three modalities that connect levels of human interaction with larger institutions and social structures. Institutional features may operate as interpretive schemes in communication processes, referred to as structures of *signification*. Structures of *domination* are institutional features that facilitate power and influence, invoking the resource authorization provided by political institutions and the resource allocation afforded by economic institutions. Structures of *legitimation* invoke the sanctioning of certain behaviors afforded by legal and religious institutions, as well as by ethical standards and societal customs. The distinctions among three seemingly distinct structures are largely analytical, as the three elements intersect in practice of course (Poole et al., 1996).

In a structuration theory-based study of adults co-parenting children in stepfamilies, Schrodt, Baxter, McBride, Braithwaite, and Fine (2006) found two structures of signification with respect to the divorce decree that enabled and constrained their communication: one in which the divorce decree was framed as a legal document, and another in which interpretations of the decree guided informal interactions related to their co-parenting. The first served to structure the rights and responsibilities of parenting, particularly concerning issues of finances and child access, while the second structured co-parents' decisional processes.

Utilizing the diary interview method employed by Schrodt et al. (2006), parallel investigations of signification structures associated with institutional features of business and family systems in copreneurial relationships might illuminate heretofore ignored constraints on how copreneurs balance work and family. For example, what signification structures surrounding legal matters (co-ownership of their business, co-signed contracts, joint business accounts, fiduciary responsibilities, and the like) enable and constrain married couples' power and intimacy boundaries in their business and family systems? How are tensions managed surrounding the core features of being a copreneurial/family business: percentage of ownership, voting control, power over strategic direction, involvement of multiple generations, and degree of management by partners and family members (Shanker & Astrachan, 1996; Sharma, 2004)?

In conclusion, structuration theory illuminates how copreneurial and family communication produces and reproduces social structures appropriated as meaningful bases for action within copreneurial and family businesses. Many copreneurs succeed in negotiating work-family integration, while others cannot do so given structural and institutional constraints (excessive role demands for founders, customer focus, contracts, and so forth). These complexities are exacerbated by the presence of other members in the business and therefore the constraining effects of the institutions in which they are enmeshed. Structuration theory offers explanations of the interpenetration of such structures, including their recursivity.

Notwithstanding the benefits of structuration theory (see Kirby, Wieland, & McBride, 2006) for understanding work-family integration in copreneurial and family businesses in terms of the communication dynamics by which members enact the strategies that enable the negotiation of balance, this perspective does not accomplish all that is needed in the area. Researchers also must pursue answers to more fundamental questions. Why and how does "balance" appear to have agency as a locus of concern for copreneurs and family members? Are there means for resisting it? How can the intricacies of work, relationship/family, and business intersections be made focal, above and beyond the structural features of business policies and family practices that seem so generative of balance?

Implications

We have emphasized the research opportunities for organizational and marital/family communication scholars (and other sub-fields in the discipline) in exploring the communicative dynamics of work-family balance issues in family and especially copreneurial businesses. The integration of work and family domains by means of technology and family-friendly organizational policies has been associated with such practical benefits as increased productivity, loyalty, job retention, life satisfaction, job satisfaction, and better mental health, among others (Bond et al., 2002; Jackson, 2005; Konrad & Mangel, 2000). Given the high integration of work and family in copreneurial businesses, it may be difficult for family members to create and maintain communication boundaries and borders. For example, in work on organizational development interventions for family businesses, Poza (2008) notes that "the absence of balance or clear boundaries between family, owners, and management can lead to zero-sum dynamics or 'me-ism' in family firms" (p. 557). The communication strategies that families, and copreneurs in particular, use to attempt to balance their work and family lives is ripe for exploration. Poza claims "family business members seldom examine … their organization practices, culture, or communication processes," and processes of change management, leadership succession, strategic planning, and governance of family-business relationships could facilitate more effective communication in family firms (p. 559).

Issues surrounding managing work-family life tensions also offer scholars in several sub-areas of our discipline with opportunities to inform one another each other's research. The copreneurial relationship, in particular, provides researchers a unique context in which to build on each other's work because of the equal importance of family/relational, business, and organizational domains. For example, interpersonal, marital, and family communication scholars could contribute to the study of coperneurial relationships by introducing perspectives such as we reviewed on equity, communal coping, and demand-withdraw patterns. This work would be enhanced if integrated with knowledge of the business aspects of the copreneurial relationship (Helmle, 2010; Seibold, 1990), as well as with work by other organizational scholars on structuration and work-family accommodation (Golden, 2009; Hoffman & Cowan, 2008, 2010; Kirby & Krone, 2002). Scholars working multiple research areas also would provide a clearer and more comprehensive picture of complex copreneurial work-family dynamics.

Using theory to guide research on balancing work and family also will bridge disciplines and make their research more interpretable. Boundary theory and work-family border theory can guide researchers toward better understanding how family members and copreneurs construct the communication boundaries and borders between their work and family lives. The relational dialectics perspective has the potential to reveal the inherent struggles that copreneurs face, not only in their personal relationship as spouses but in how they manage the tensions between their personal and professional work and family lives. Given the prevalence of family and copreneurial businesses in the United States that we noted at the outset, as well as those in the international studies reviewed above, the implications of studying the communicative aspects of work-family balance, as well as other communication practices, in family and especially copreneurial businesses have the numerous theoretical and practical implications we have proposed. We believe new research in this area will considerably lengthen that list of benefits and implications.

References

Adams, G. A., King, L. A., & King, D. W. (1996). Relationships of job and family involvement, family social support, and work-family conflict with job and life satisfaction. *Journal of Applied Psychology, 81*, 411–420.

Afifi, T. D., Hutchinson, S., & Krouse, S. (2006). Toward a theoretical model of communal coping in post-divorce families and other naturally occurring groups. *Communication Theory, 16*, 378–409.

Afifi, W. A., & Guerrero, L. K. (2000). Motivations underlying topic avoidance in close relationships. In S. Petronio (Ed.), *Balancing the secrets of private disclosures* (pp. 165–179). Mahwah, NJ: Erlbaum.

Allen, T. D. (2001). Family-supportive work environments: The role of organizational perceptions. *Journal of Vocational Behavior, 58*, 414–435.

Ashforth, B. (2001). *Role transitions in organizational life: An identity-based perspective*. Mahwah, NJ: Erlbaum.

Ashforth, B., Kreiner, G., & Fugate, M. (2000). All in a day's work: Boundaries and micro role transitions. *Academy of Management Review, 25*, 472–491.

Astrachan, J., & Shanker, M. (2003). Family businesses' contribution to the US economy: A closer look. *Family Business Review, 16*, 211–219.

Barnett, F., & Barnett, S. (1988). *Working together: Entrepreneurial couples*. Berkeley, CA: Top Ten Press.

Barnett, R. C. (1998). Toward a review and reconceptualization of the work/family literature. *Genetic, Social, and General Psychology Monographs, 124,* 125–182.

Barnett, R. C., & Hyde, J. S. (2001). Women, men, work and family: An expansionist theory. *The American Psychologist, 56,* 781–796.

Basco, R., & Perez-Rodriguez, M. J. (2009). Studying the family enterprise holistically: Evidence for integrated family and business systems. *Family Business Review, 22*, 82–95.

Baxter, L. (1988). A dialectical perspective on communication strategies in relationship development. In S. Duck (Ed.), *Handbook of personal relationships* (pp. 257–273). New York: Wiley.

Baxter, L. (1990). Dialectical contradictions in relationship development. *Journal of Social and Personal Relationships, 7*, 69–88.

Baxter, L. (2004). Relationships as dialogue. *Personal Relationships, 11*, 1–22.

Baxter, L. (2010). *Voicing relationships: A dialogic perspective.* Thousand Oaks, CA: Sage.

Baxter, L., Braithwaite, D. O., Golish, T. D., & Olson, L. (2002). Contradictions of interaction for wives of elderly husbands with adult dementia. *Journal of Applied Communication Research, 30*, 1–26.

Baxter, L. A., & Montgomery, B. M. (1996). *Relating: Dialogues and dialectics.* New York: Guilford.

Baxter, L. A., & Simon, E. P. (1993). Relationship maintenance strategies and dialectical contradictions in personal relationships. *Journal of Social and Personal Relationships, 10*, 225–242.

Becker, P. E., & Moen, P. (1999). Scaling back: Dual-earner couples' work-family strategies. *Journal of Marriage and the Family, 61*, 995–1007.

Bird, B., Welsch, H., Astrachan, J., & Pistrui, D. (2002). Family business research: The evolution of an academic field. *Family Business Review, 15*, 337–350.

Boden, R. J. (1999). Flexible working hours, family responsibilities, and female self-employment: Gender differences in self-employment selection. *American Journal of Economics and Sociology, 58*, 71–93.

Bond, J. T., Thompson, C., Galinsky, E., & Prottas, D. (2002). *Highlights of the national study of the changing workforce.* New York: Families and Work Institute.

Bowie, N. E. (1998). A Kantian theory of meaningful work. *Journal of Business Ethics, 17*(9/10), 1083–1092.

Braithwaite, D. O., & Baxter, L. A. (2006). "You're my parent but you're not": Dialectical tensions in stepchildren's perceptions about communicating with the nonresidential parent. *Journal of Applied Communication Research, 34*, 30–48.

Brannen, J. (2005). Time and the negotiation of work-family boundaries: Autonomy or illusion? *Time & Society, 14*, 113–131.

Brashers, D. E., Haas, S. M., Klingle, R. S., & Neidig, J. L. (2000). Collective AIDS activism and individuals' perceived self-advocacy in physician-patient communication. *Human Communication Research, 26*, 372–402.

Byrd-Craven, J., Geary, D. C., Rose, A. J., & Ponzi, D. (2007). Co-ruminating increases stress hormone levels in women. *Hormones and Behavior, 53*, 489–492.

Broadfoot, K. J., Carlone, D., Medved, C. E., Aakhus, M., Gabor, E., & Taylor, K. (2008). Meaning/ful work and organizational communication: Questioning boundaries, positionalities, and engagements. *Management Communication Quarterly, 22*(1), 152–161.

Bulger, C. A., Matthews, R. A., & Hoffman, M. E. (2007). Work and personal life boundary management: Boundary strength, work/personal life balance, and the segmentation-integration continuum. *Journal of Occupational Health Psychology, 12*, 365–375.

Buzzanell, P. M., & Liu, M. (2005). Struggling with maternity leave policies and practices: A poststructuralist feminist analysis of gendered organizing. *Journal of Applied Communication Research, 33*, 1–25.

Cadieux, L., Lorrain, J., & Hugron, P. (2002). Succession in women-owned family businesses: A case study. *Family Business Review, 15*, 17–30.

Caputo, R. K., & Dolinsky, A. (1998). Women's choice to pursue self-employment: The role of financial and human capital of household members. *Journal of Small Business Management, 36*(3), 8–17.

Caughlin, J. P. (2002). The demand-withdraw pattern of communication as a predictor of marital satisfaction over time. *Human Communication Research, 28*, 49–86.

Caughlin, J. P., & Huston, T. L. (2002). A contextual analysis of the association between demand/withdraw and marital satisfaction. *Personal Relationships, 9*, 95–119.

Caughlin, J. P., & Vangelisti, A. (2000). An individual difference explanation of why married couples engage in the demand/withdraw pattern of conflict. *Journal of Social and Personal Relationships, 17*, 523–551.

Chesley, N. (2005). Blurring boundaries? Linking technology use, spillover, individual distress, and family satisfaction. *Journal of Marriage and Family, 67*, 1237–1248.

Cheney, G., Zorn, Jr., T. E., Planalp, S., & Lair, D. J. (2008). Meaningful work and personal/ social well-being: Organizational communication engages the meaning of work. In C. S. Beck (Ed.), *Communication yearbook 32* (pp. 137–173). Thousand Oaks, CA: Sage.

Choi, J., & Chen, C. C. (2006). Gender differences in perceived work demands, family demands, and life stress among married Chinese employees. *Management and Organization Review, 2*, 209–229.

Christensen, A., & Heavey, C. L. (1990). Gender and social structure in the demand/ withdraw pattern of marital conflict. *Journal of Personality and Social Psychology, 59*, 73–81.

Clark, S. (2000). Work/family border theory: A new theory of work/family balance. *Human Relations, 53*, 747–770.

Coffey, B. S., Anderson, S. E., Zhao, S., Liu, Y., & Zhang, J. (2009). Perspectives on work-family issues in China: The voices of young urban professionals. *Community, Work & Family, 12*, 197–212.

Cole, P. (2000). Understanding family business relationships: preserving the family in the business. *The Family Journal: Counseling and Therapy for Couples and Families, 8*, 351–359.

Cole, P., & Johnson, K. (2007). An exploration of successful copreneurial relationships postdivorce. *Family Business Review, 20*, 185–198.

Cowan, R., & Hoffman, M. (2007). The flexible organization: How contemporary employees construct the work/life border. *Qualitative Research Reports in Communication, 8*, 37–44.

Coyne, J. C., & Smith, D. A. F. (1994). Couples coping with a myocardial infarction: Contextual perspective on patient self-efficacy. *Journal of Family Psychology, 8*, 43–54.

Craig, L., & Sawrikar, P. (2009). Work and family: How does the (gender) balance change as children grow? *Gender, Work, and Organization, 16*, 684–709.

Danes, S., & Morgan, E. (2004). Family business-owning couples: An eft view into their unique conflict culture. *Contemporary Family Therapy, 26*, 241–260.

Debecki, B. J., Matherne, C. F., Kellermanns, F. W., & Chrisman, J. J. (2009). Family business research in the new millennium: An overview of the who, the where, the what, and the why. *Family Business Review, 22*, 151–166.

Desrochers, S., Hilton, J., & Larwood, L. (2005). Preliminary validation of the work-family integration-blurring scale. *Journal of Family Issues, 26*, 442–466.

Desrochers, S., & Sargent, L. (2003). *Boundary/border theory and work-family integration, A Sloan work and family encyclopedia entry.* Retrieved January 31, 2007, from http://wfnetwork.bc.edu/encyclopedia_entry.php?id=220

Deutsch, F. M. (1999). *Having it all: How equally shared parenting works.* Cambridge, MA: Harvard University Press.

Dilworth, J. L. (2004). Predictors of negative spillover from family to work. *Journal of Family Issues, 25*, 241–261.

Edley, P. (2001). Technology, working mothers, and corporate colonization of the lifeworld: A gendered paradox of work and family balance. *Women and Language, 24*, 28–35.

Fitzpatrick, M. A. (1976). *A typological examination* of *communication in enduring relationships.* Unpublished doctoral dissertation, Temple University.

Fitzpatrick, M. A. (1977). A typological approach to communication in relationships. In B. Rubin (Ed.), *Communication yearbook 1* (pp. 263–275). New Brunswick, NJ: Transaction.

Fitzpatrick, M. A. (1984). A typological approach to marital interaction: Recent theory and research. In L. Berkowitz (Ed.), *Advances in experimental social psychology 18* (pp. 1–47). Orlando, FL: Academic Press.

Fitzpatrick, M. A. (1988). *Between husbands and wives.* Newbury Park, CA: Sage.

Fitzpatrick, M. A. (1990). Models of marital interaction. In H. Giles & W. I. Robinson (Eds.), *Handbook* of *language and social psychology* (pp. 433–450). New York: Wiley.

Fitzgerald, M. A., & Muske, G. (2002). Copreneurs: An exploration and comparison to other family businesses. *Family Business Review, 15*, 1–16.

Fitzpatrick, M. A., & Ritchie, L. D. (1994). Communication schemata within the family: Multiple perspectives on family interaction. *Human Communication Research, 20*, 275–301.

Floyd, K. (2006). Human affection exchange XII. Affectionate communication is associated with diurnal variation in salivary free cortisol. *Western Journal of Communication, 70*, 47–63.

Floyd, K., Boren, J. P., Hannawa, A. F., Hesse, C., McEwan, B., & Veksler, A. E. (2009). Kissing in marital and cohabitating relationships: Effects on blood lipids, stress, and relationship satisfaction. *Western Journal of Communication, 73*, 113–133.

Floyd, K., Mikkelson, A. C., Hesse, C., & Pauley, P. M. (2007). Affectionate writing reduces total cholesterol: Two randomized, controlled studies. *Human Communication Research, 33*, 119–142.

Floyd, K., & Riforgiate, S. (2009). Affectionate communication received from spouses predicts stress hormone levels in healthy adults. *Communication Monographs, 75*, 351–368.

Fry, R., & Cohn, D. (2010). New economics of marriage: The rise of wives. Retrieved from http://pewresearch.org/pubs/1466/economics-marriage-rise-of-wives.

Fuwa, M., & Cohen, P. N. (2007). Housework and social policy. *Social Science Research, 36*, 512–530.

Gareis, K. C., Barnett, R. C., Ertel, K. A., & Berkman, L. F. (2009). Work-family enrichment and conflict: Additive effects, buffering, or balance? *Journal of Marriage & Family, 71*, 696–707.

Giddens, A. (1984). *The constitution of society: Outline of the theory of structuration.* Berkeley: University of California Press.

Gill, R., & Ganesh, S. (2007). Empowerment, constraint, and the entrepreneurial self: A study of white women entrepreneurs. *Journal of Applied Communication Research, 35*, 268–293.

Golden, A. G. (2002). Speaking of work and family: Spousal collaboration on defining role-identities and developing shared meanings. *Southern Communication Journal, 67*, 122–141.

Golden, A. G. (2009). Employee families and organizations as mutually enacted environments: A sensemaking approach to work-life interrelationships. *Management Communication Quarterly, 22*, 385–415.

Golden, A., Kirby, E., & Jorgenson, J. (2006). Work-life research from both sides now: An integrative perspective for organizational and family communication. In C. S. Beck (Ed.), *Communication yearbook 30* (pp. 142–195). Mahwah, NJ: Erlbaum.

Golish, T. D. (2003). Stepfamily communication strengths: Examining the ties that bind. *Human Communication Research, 29*, 41–80.

Gottman, J. M., & Levenson, R. W. (2000). The timing of divorce: Predicting when a couple will divorce over a 14-year period. *Journal of Marriage and the Family, 62*, 737–745.

Grzywacz, J. G., Almeida, D. M., & McDonald, D. A. (2002). Work-family spillover and daily reports of work and family stress in the adult labor force. *Family Relations, 51*, 28–36.

Guerrero, L., La Valley, A. G., & Farinelli, L. (2008). The experience and expression of anger, guilt, and sadness in marriage: An equity theory explanation. *Journal of Social and Personal Relationships, 25*, 699–724.

Guest, D. (2002). Perspectives on the study of work-life balance. *Social Science Information, 41*, 255–279.

Haberman, H., & Danes, S. M. (2007). Father-daughter and father-son family business management transfer comparison: Family FIRO model application. *Family Business Review, 20*, 163–184.

Hakim, C. (2000). *Work-lifestyle choices in the 21st century: Preference theory.* Oxford, UK: Oxford University Press.

Heavey, C. L., Layne, C., & Christensen, A. (1993). Gender and conflict structure in marital interaction: A replication and extension. *Journal of Consulting and Clinical Psychology, 61*, 16–27.

Heffner, K. L., Kiecolt-Glaser, J. K., Loving, T. J., Glaser, R., & Malarkey, W. B. (2004). Spousal support satisfaction as a modifier of physiological responses to marital conflict in younger and older couples. *Journal of Behavioral Medicine, 27*, 233–254.

Helmle, J. R. (2010). *Copreneurs and communication: Work-family balance in married couples' family businesses.* Unpublished doctoral dissertation, University of California, Santa Barbara.

Helmle, J. R., Seibold, D. R., & Afifi, T. A. (2010). *Relational dialectics and work-family balance in copreneurial businesses: A mixed methods study.* Manuscript submitted for publication.

Hobfoll, S. E., Schroder, K. E. E., & Malek, M. (2002). Communal versus individualistic construction of sense of mastery in facing life challenges. *Journal of Social and Clinical Psychology, 21*, 362–400.

Hochschild, A. (1983). *The managed heart: Commercialization of human feeling.* Berkeley: University of California Press.

Hochschild, A., & Machung, A. (1989). *Working parents and the revolution at home.* London: Piatkus.

Hochschild, A., & Machung, A. (2001). Men who share the second shift. In J. Henslin (Ed.), *Down to earth sociology: Introductory readings* (11th ed., pp. 395–409). Free Press. New York.

Hoffman, M. F., & Cowan, R. L. (2008). The meaning of work/life: A corporate ideology of work/life balance. *Communication Quarterly, 56*, 227–246.

Hoffman, M. F., & Cowan, R. L. (2010). Be careful what you ask for: Structuration theory and work/life accomodation. *Communication Studies, 61*, 205–223.

Hoppe-Nagao, A., & Ting-Toomey, S. (2002). Relational dialectics and management strategies in married couples. *Southern Communication Journal, 67*, 142–159.

Hylmö, A. (2006). Telecommuting and the contestability of choice. *Management Communication Quarterly, 19*, 541–569.

Ilies, R., Wilson, K. S., & Wagner, D. T. (2009). The spillover of daily job satisfaction onto employees' family lives: The facilitating role of work-family integration. *Academy of Management Journal, 52*, 87–102.

Jackson, M. (2005). The limits of connectivity: Technology and 21st-century life. In D. F. Halpern & S. E. Murphy (Eds.), *From work-family balance to work-family interaction: Changing the metaphor* (pp. 13–150). Mahwah, NJ: Erlbaum.

Jennings, J. E., & McDougald, M. S. (2007). Work-family interface experiences and coping strategies: Implications for entrepreneurship research and practice. *Academy of Management Review, 32*, 747–760.

Jimenez, R. M. (2009). Research on women in family firms: Current status and future directions. *Family Business Review, 22*, 53–64.

Johnstone, M., & Lee, C. (2009). Young Australian women's aspirations for work and family: Individual and sociocultural differences. *Sex Roles, 61*, 204–220.

Kaniasty, K., & Norris, F. H. (1993). A test of the social support deterioration model in the context of natural disasters. *Journal of Personality and Social Psychology, 64*, 395–408.

Karofsky, P., Millen, R., Yilmaz, M., Smyrnios, K. X., Tanewski, G. A., & Romano, C. A. (2001). Work-family conflict and emotional well-being in American family businesses. *Family Business Review, 14*, 313–324.

Khalaf, S. (2002). *Civil and uncivil violence: A history of the internationalization of communal conflict in Lebanon*. New York: Columbia University Press.

Kirby, E. (2006). "Helping you make room in your life for your needs": When organizations appropriate family roles. *Communication Monographs, 73*, 474–480.

Kirby, E., Golden, A., Medved, C., Jorgenson, J., & Buzzanell, P. M. (2003). An organizational communication challenge to the discourse of work and family research: From problematics to empowerment. In P. Kalbfleisch (Ed.), *Communication yearbook 27* (pp. 1–44). Mahwah, NJ: Erlbaum.

Kirby, E., & Krone, K. (2002). "The policy exists but you can't really use it": Communication and the structuration of work-family policies. *Journal of Applied Communication Research, 30*, 50–77.

Kirby, E. L., Wieland, S., & McBride, M. C. (2006). Work-life communication. In J. Oetzel & S. Ting-Toomey (Eds.), *Handbook of conflict communication* (pp. 327–357). Thousand Oaks, CA: Sage.

Konrad, A., & Mangel, R. (2000). The impact of work-life programs on firm productivity. *Strategic Management Journal, 21*, 1225–1237.

Kowal, J., Johnson, S. M., & Lee, A. (2003). Chronic illness in couples: A case for emotionally focused therapy. *Journal of Marital and Family Therapy, 29*, 299–319.

Lee, J. (2006). Impact of family relationships on attitudes of the second generation in family business. *Family Business Review, 19,* 175–191.

Lyons, R. F., Mickelson, K., Sullivan, J. L., & Coyne, J. C. (1998). Coping as a communal process. *Journal of Social and Personal Relationships, 15,* 579–607.

Marks, S. P. (1977). Multiple roles and role strain: Some notes on human energy, time and commitment. *American Sociological Review, 42*, 921–936.

Marshack, K. (1993). Copreneurial couples: A literature review of boundaries and transitions among copreneurs. *Family Business Review, 6*(4), 355–369.

Medved, C. E. (2007). Investigating family labor in communication studies: Threading across historical and contemporary discourses. *Journal of Family Communication, 7,* 225–243.

Medved, C. E. (2009). Constructing breadwinning-mothering identities: Moral, personal, and professional positioning. *Women's Studies Quarterly, 37,* 140–156.

Medved, C. E., Brogan, S. M., McClanahan, A. M., Morris, J. F., & Shepherd, G. J. (2006). Family and work socializing communication: Messages, gender, and ideological implications. *Journal of Family Communication, 6*, 161–180.

Meisenbach, R. J. (2010). The female breadwinner: Phenomenological experience and gendered identity in work/family spaces. *Sex Roles, 62*, 2–19.

Moen, P., & Yu, Y. (2000). Effective work/life strategies: Working couples, work conditions, gender, and life quality. *Social Problems, 47,* 291–326.

Montgomery, B. M. (1993). Relationship maintenance versus relationship change: A dialectical dilemma. *Journal of Social and Personal Relationships, 10*, 205–223.

Mortazavi, S., Pedhiwala, N., Shafiro, M., & Hammer, L. (2009). Work-family conflict related to culture and gender. *Community, Work & Family, 12*, 251–273.

Muske, G., & Fitzgerald, M. A. (2006). A panel study of copreneurs in business: Who enters, continues, and exits? *Family Business Review, 19,* 193–205.

Nelton, S. (1986). *In love and in business: How entrepreneurial couples are changing the rules of business and marriage.* New York: Wiley.

Nippert-Eng, C. (1996). *Home and work.* Chicago: University of Chicago Press.

Office of Personnel Management. (2004). *The status of telework in the federal government 2004.* Washington, DC: Author.

Perrone, K., & Worthington, E. (2001). Factors influencing ratings of marital quality by individuals within dual career marriages: A conceptual model. *Journal of Counseling Psychology, 48*, 3–9.

Petronio, S. (2006). Impact of medical mistakes: Navigating work-family boundaries for physicians and their families. *Communication Monographs, 73*, 462–467.

Pitts, M. J., Fowler, C., Kaplan, M. S., Nussbaum, J., & Becker, J. C. (2009). Dialectical tensions underpinning family farm succession planning. *Journal of Applied Communication Research, 37,* 59–79.

Ponthieu, L., & Caudill, H. (1993). Who's the boss? Responsibility and decision making in copreneurial ventures. *Family Business Review, 6*, 3–17.

Poole, M. S., Seibold, D. R., & McPhee, R. D. (1996). The structuration of group decisions. In M. S. Poole & R. Y. Hirokawa (Eds.), *Communication and group decision making* (2nd ed., pp. 114–146). Thousand Oaks, CA: Sage.

Poza, E. J. (2008). Organization development in family-owned and family-controlled companies. In T. G. Cummings (Ed.), *Handbook of organization development* (pp. 553–572). Thousand Oaks, CA: Sage.

Priem, J., & Solomon, D. H. (2010). *Relational uncertainty and physiological stress responses: Reactions to hurtful and supportive messages from a dating partner.* Manuscript submitted for publication.

Risman, B. J., & Johnson-Sumerford, D. (1998). Doing it fairly: A study of postgender marriages. *Journal of Marriage and the Family, 60*, 23–40.

Roberts, N. A., & Levenson, R. W. (2001). The remains of the workday: Impact of job stress and exhaustion on marital interaction in police couples. *Journal of Marriage and Family, 63*, 1052–1067.

Rogers, S. J., & May, D. C. (2003). Spillover between marital quality and job satisfaction: Long-term patterns and gender differences. *Journal of Marriage and Family, 65*, 482–495.

Rosal, M. C., King, J., Yunsheng, M., & Reed, G. (2004). Stress, social support, and cortisol: Inverse associations? *Behavioral Medicine, 30*, 11–21.

Rose, A. (2002). Co-rumination in the friendships of boys and girls. *Child Development, 73*, 1830–1843.

Rose, A. J., Carlson, W., & Waller, E. M. (2007). Prospective associations of co-rumination with friendship and emotional adjustment: Considering the socio-emotional trade-offs of co-rumination. *Developmental Psychology, 43*, 1019–1031.

Rothbard, N. P. (2001). Enriching or depleting? The dynamics of engagement in work and family roles. *Administrative Science Quarterly, 46*, 655–684.

Rothbard, N. P., & Edwards, J. E. (2003). Investment in work and family roles: A test of identity and utilitarian motives. *Personnel Psychology, 56*, 699–729.

Ruderman, M. N., Ohlott, P. J., Panzer, K., & King, S. N. (2002). Benefits of multiple roles for managerial women. *Academy of Management Journal, 45*, 369–386.

Schaap, C., Buunk, B., & Kerkstra, A. (1988). Marital conflict resolution. In P. Nollar & M. A. Fitzpatrick (Eds.), *Perspectives on marital interaction* (pp. 203–244). Clevedon, UK: Multilingual.

Schrodt, P., Baxter, L. A., McBride, M. C., Braithwaite, D. O., & Fine, M. (2006). The divorce decree, communication, and the structuration of co-parenting relationships in stepfamilies. *Journal of Social and Personal Relationships, 23*, 741–759.

Seerey, B. L., Corrigalli E. A., & Harpel, T. (2008). Job-related emotional labor and its relationship to work-family conflict and facilitation. *Journal of Family and Economic Issues, 29*, 461–477.

Seibold, D. (1990). Management communication issues in family businesses: The case of Oak Ridge Trucking Company. In B. Sypher (Ed.), *Case studies in organizational communication* (pp. 163–176). New York: Guilford.

Seibold, D. R., & Myers, K. K. (2005). Communication as structuring. In G. J. Shepherd, J. St. John, & T. Striphas (Eds.), *Communication as … Perspectives on theory* (pp. 143–152). Thousand Oaks, CA: Sage.

Shanker, M., & Astrachan, J. (1996). Myths and realities: Family businesses' contribution to the US economy. *Family Business Review, 9*, 107–123.

Sharma, P. (2004). An overview of the field of family business studies: Current status and directions for the future. *Family Business Review, 17*, 1–36.

Shumate, M., & Fulk, J. (2004). Boundaries and role conflict when work and family are collocated: A communication network and symbolic interaction approach. *Human Relations, 57*, 55–74.

Sprecher, S. (2001a). A comparison of emotional consequences of and changes in equity over time using global and domain-specific measures of equity. *Journal of Social and Personal Relationships*, *18*, 477–501.

Sprecher, S. (2001b). Equity and social exchange in dating couples: Associations with satisfaction, commitment, and stability. *Journal of Marriage and the Family, 63*, 599–613.

Stafford, K., & Tews, M. J. (2009). Enhancing work-family research in family businesses. *Family Business Review, 22*, 235–238.

Stafford, L., & Canary, D. (2006). Equity and interdependence as predictors of relationship maintenance strategies. *Journal of Family Communication, 6*, 227–254.

Stewart, A. (2008). Who could best complement a team of family business researchers – Scholars down the hall or in another building? *Family Business Review, 21*, 279–293

Thompson, K. D. (1990). Married … with business. *Black Enterprise, 20*(9), 46–52.

U.S. Census Bureau (2002). Survey of business owners (SBO). Retrieved March 14, 2008, from http://www.census.gov/csd/sbo/cbsummaryoffindings.htm

U.S. Census Bureau, Statistical Abstract of the United States (2003). *No. 606. Persons on flexible schedules*. Washington, DC: U.S. Census Bureau.

U.S. Census Bureau (2008). *American community survey (ACS)*. Retrieved January 12, 2009, from http://www.factfinder.census.gov

Van Steenbergen, E. F., & Ellemers, N. (2009). Is managing the work-family interface worthwhile? Benefits for employee health and performance. *Journal of Organizational Behavior, 30*, 617–642.

Van Steenbergen, E. F., Ellemers, N., & Mooijaart, A. (2007). How work and family can facilitate each other: Distinct types of work-family facilitation and outcomes for women and men. *Journal of Occupational Health Psychology, 12*, 279–300.

Vera, C., & Dean, M. (2005). An examination of the challenges daughters face in family business succession. *Family Business Review, 18*, 321–345.

Wajcman, J. (2008). Life in the fast lane? Towards a sociology of technology and time. *British Journal of Sociology, 59*, 59–77.

Walster, E., Traupmann, J., Sprecher, S., Utne, M., & Hay, J. (1985). Equity and intimate relations: Recent research. In W. Ickes (Ed.), *Compatible and incompatible relationships* (pp. 91–118). New York: Springer-Verlag.

Waters, M. A., & Bardoel, E. A. (2006). Work-family policies in the context of higher education: Useful or symbolic? *Asia Pacific Journal of Human Resources, 44*, 67–82.

Wayne, J. H., Randal, A. E., & Stevens, J. (2006). The role of identity and work-family support in work-family enrichment and its work-related consequences. *Journal of Vocational Behavior, 69*, 445–461.

Wierda-Boer, H., Gerris, J., Vermulst, A., Malinen, K., & Anderson, K. (2009). Combination strategies and work-family interference among dual-earner couples in Finland, Germany, and the Netherlands. *Community, Work & Family, 12*, 233–249.

Wilcox, W. B., & Nock, S. L. (2006). What's love got to do with it?: Equality, equity, commitment, and women's marital quality. *Social Forces, 84*, 1321–1345.

Wilcox, W. B., & Nock, S. L. (2007). 'Her' marriage after the revolutions. *Sociological Forum, 22*, 104–111.

CHAPTER CONTENTS

6 An Alternative Approach to Family Communication

Studying the Family from a Group Communication Perspective

Stephenson J. Beck, Amy N. Miller, and Whitney A. Frahm

North Dakota State University

Family communication and group communication scholars have largely worked independently of each other, despite calls for collaboration (Socha, 1999; Turner, 1970). Family communication research has generally followed the interpersonal communication tradition, with primary emphasis on dyadic relationships in the family. Up until the last decade, group communication scholars have generally focused on task-oriented, zero-history groups (Keyton, 1999). However, due to the theoretical and methodological evolution of both family and group communication research, this chapter argues that the present is an appropriate time for collaboration, and, more specifically, that three group-oriented theories (social identity theory, theory of transactive memory, faultline theory) and subsequent research on these theories would prove fruitful to family communication scholars' understanding of family interaction. Five theoretical concepts within these three theories are explored, with specific future research suggestions offered. Collaboration across artificially-created topical boundaries, such as family and group communication, enables researchers to focus on communication itself (Burleson, 1992).

Few areas of the communication discipline have been developing faster than family communication; over the past few decades, "enormous strides have been made in our understanding of how communication affects, and is affected by, family members and their relationships" (Vangelisti, 2004, p. ix). Certainly family communication is not a new area of focus. Interpersonal communication scholars and others (e.g., mass communication scholars) have studied different aspects of family member interaction for years. However, over the past two decades family communication has seen renewed emphasis as a unique subset apart from interpersonal communication. Evidence of this emphasis is demonstrated by the addition of the family communication division in the National Communication Association in 1995 (Whitchurch & Dickson, 1999), as well as handbooks and journals designed specifically for family communication research (e.g., *Handbook of Family Communication*, *Journal of Family Communication*).

Overall, the majority of family communication research has targeted different theoretical dimensions and variables (e.g., privacy management, uncertainty management, disclosure, dialectical tensions) in dyadic family relationships (e.g., husband-wife, parent-child, sibling-sibling). This research perspective is consistent with interpersonal communication assumptions, with many scholars using already existing interpersonal theories and approaches to deductively analyze a unique (i.e., family) context. However, the family is not merely a new context for interpersonal communication studies; families are unique in their own right. Extending from that premise, Whitchurch and Dickson (1999) point out that Rogers (1972) and Fitzpatrick's (1976) dissertations are considered milestones in family communication research because they are truly family-oriented, and not simply an interpersonal communication study "'translated' to the context of the marital dyad" (Whitchurch & Dickson. 1999, p. 692).

However, the focus on dyadic communication in families oversimplifies (or worse, neglects) the unique dynamic that multiple family members bring to family interaction. Although some families consist of two individuals, most families encompass more, with extended family relationships often reaching double digits. These increased family sizes, along with the different communication dynamics associated with increased group sizes, paints a potentially different picture of family communication than that offered by dyadic communication approaches and theories. Indeed, several disciplines (e.g., psychology, sociology) have pursued a more holistic approach to family research (e.g., family systems theory, Bowen, 1978; cohesion and adaptability model, Olson, Russell, & Sprenkle, 1989). Although there are several areas in the field of communication that have moved beyond dyads (e.g., family rituals, martial conflict influence on the family, social networks and dating), few have directly taken a group communication approach.

Small group scholars have argued that a dialogue between small group researchers and family scholars would be beneficial for both group and family communication research (Socha, 1999, 2009; Turner, 1970); in light of this, a panel session at the 2009 National Communication Association convention was devoted to the topic. Group experiences first occur in families (Socha, 1999), and because of this, family communication scholars have historically called for a greater emphasis on families as a system, with less focus on the individual (Benson, Berger, & Mease, 1975; Petronio & Braithwaite, 1993). Despite the recognition of group dynamics in the family context, there has been little interaction between family and small group communication researchers (Socha, 1999). There are many reasons for this disconnect; however, three important reasons include the oversimplified methodological designs used by early group scholars (e.g., zero-history groups), family communication researchers' overreliance on their interpersonal communication origins (Socha, 1999), and difficulties involved in gaining access to multiple family members.

We argue that the present is a perfect time for uniting family and group communication research. We believe this is the case for two reasons. First, with the growing importance and prominence of family communication research, it may be advantageous to investigate how non-dyadic communication perspectives, specifically group approaches, offer insight into family interaction. Families have the same characteristics that group scholars use to define groups; hence, families are groups. For example, families meet all five group characteristics set forth by Keyton (2006). Families often involve more members than dyadic communication, allowing for hidden communication (i.e., interaction that excludes certain family members) and coalition formation. Families have goals that can be both task- and relationally-oriented. Families create an evolving identity through their group interactions, and family identity is often used to differentiate between ingroups and outgroups. Family members are interdependent with one another in many ways, including emotionally, socially, fiscally, and in terms of security. In addition, both formally- (e.g., parent/child relationships, husband/wife relationship) and informally- (e.g., favored child) created family structures are simultaneously negotiated through interaction.

Importantly, since families are the first group to which most individuals are exposed, family life likely influences members' experiences in other groups. Thus, a family is more than simply another type of group. Families are a *unique* type of group, which creates a personal foundation for future social interactions and is "the most salient group context for understanding relational communication" (Gastil, 2010, p. 171).

Second, the evolution of group communication research is presently in a more suitable state to produce meaningful insights into how families interact. Early group communication research primarily dwelled on task-oriented, zero-history groups, neglecting groups with relational purposes (Keyton, 1999). Over the past two decades, Putnam and Stohl's (1990) notion of bona fide groups has encouraged group scholars to analyze groups in their natural contexts. Frey's (2003) edited volume shares many ways that group researchers have accounted for contextual influence, essential to understanding family dynamics. Although group communication researchers have struggled with a multitude of methodological concerns that emerge when studying groups (Poole, Keyton, & Frey, 1999), advances in method creation (mostly qualitative) and statistical packages have greatly improved upon the methodological attempts used to understand zero-history groups decades ago.

What we propose in the rest of this chapter are several ways that group communication theory and research can provide a unique and enhanced perspective on family interaction. Certainly this relationship can work both ways (i.e., family communication theories can also benefit group communication research); however, we take a unidirectional approach in order to take an initial step toward linking the two areas. Our purpose is to highlight several lines of group research, portray how the "group" orientation of these approaches offers something new to family communication research, and then provide a few specific avenues for future research. In doing so, we also hope to push communication scholars to talk across institutionally-created boundaries (e.g., interpersonal, organizational, political) and explore overlapping theoretical constructs that are investigated across the discipline but with differing conceptual labels.

For our purposes, we have selected five areas of group research within three theories. Several theoretical approaches could have been used (e.g., motivated information sharing, group development, functional theory of decision making); however, we believe the three theoretical approaches presented here are strong exemplars of how group research can benefit studies on family interaction. First, we will examine social identity theory, which explores identity creation and maintenance in groups. Specifically, we will highlight shared identity and deviance. Next, we will look at the theory of transactive memory, concentrating on the areas of system position and information sharing. Finally, we will explore faultline theory, specifically focusing on factors that influence faultline salience. These three theories have been used in other types of communication research, but the majority of studies have followed a group communication orientation. Additionally, there are areas within each theory that could likewise be explored other than the concepts introduced in this chapter. Our hope is not only to show how a group communication perspective can provide new paths for family communication scholars, but also how it can complement already existing lines of family communication research.

Social Identity Theory

A potentially fruitful avenue for family research is through social identity theory (Tajfel & Turner, 1979). Since the initial work of Tajfel and Turner, social identity has been expanded upon by Abrams, Hogg, and colleagues. Social identity posits that the existence of a group is contingent upon shared identity among its members (Abrams, Hogg, Hinkle, & Otten, 2005). Social identity develops when group members see themselves as a joint entity and begin referring to themselves as a collective unit (Hogg, Abrams, Otten, & Hinkle, 2004). Social identity theory examines the influence of external factors (e.g., society and culture) that cause social identity to trump personal identity (Poole, Hollingshead, McGrath, Moreland, & Rohrbaugh, 2004).

According to the social identity perspective, group identity is present when two or more members of a group have the same understanding of their collective characteristics and their separation from other outgroups (Hogg et al., 2004). When group identity is prominent for members, they try to make a distinction between their socially desirable ingroup and those belonging to the undesirable outgroup (Abrams et al., 2005).

Ingroups and outgroups are determined by *prototypes*, or “fuzzy sets of interrelated attributes that simultaneously capture similarities and structural relationships within groups and differences between groups, and prescribe group membership related behavior” (Hogg et al., 2004, p. 253). Prototypes are representations of ideal group members, and group identification is heavily tied to prototypes (Hogg et al., 2004). For example, group membership and identification is more prominent and group leadership is rated as more effective when the group leader is perceived as prototypical (Hogg et al., 2004). When members identify strongly with their ingroup, compliance with the norms of the group increases; interpersonal distinctiveness may be tolerated to an extent, but deviance from norms elicits strong reactions (Abrams et al., 2005).

Ingroup members differentiate themselves from outgroup members for a variety of reasons. Belonging to a group gives all members a sense of social identity, so members compete with and disparage outgroups to strengthen their ingroup identity (Hogg et al., 2004). Members attempt to positively separate their own group from other groups because their assessment of themselves is directly tied to the positive or negative assessment of the group (Hogg et al., 2004). Positive ingroup distinctiveness causes both the individual member and the ingroup as a whole to be filled with a sense of value (Abrams et al., 2005).

When ingroups strive to separate themselves from outgroups, a process of *social categorization* occurs. "Social categorization of other people perpetually assimilates them to the relative ingroup or outgroup prototype and thus perpetually accentuates prototypical similarities among people in the same group and prototypical differences between people from different groups" (Hogg, 2001, p. 187). When outgroup members are categorized by ingroup members, they become *depersonalized*: these outgroup members become a nameless entity and are simply known by the features of their outgroup (Hogg et al., 2004).

Although there are many avenues for analyzing family communication from a social identity perspective, we chose two specific theoretical approaches upon which to elaborate. First, we explore shared identity, using the initial endeavors of family communication scholars Jordan Soliz, Jake Harwood, and their colleagues as a foundation. Then we turn to deviance research and highlight its connection to family communication. We will provide an overview of each theoretical approach, and then explore how two specific theoretical constructs associated with each approach could enhance family communication research.

Shared Identity

Family researchers have started to connect group identity and the family through the concept of *shared family identity* (Rittenour & Soliz, 2009; Soliz, 2007; Soliz & Harwood, 2006). Shared family identity is achieved when family members perceive one another in a way that minimizes intergroup distinctions (Soliz, 2007). The relationships in families are similar to that of small groups, as families have intergroup and intragroup relationships (Soliz & Harwood, 2006). "The family is inherently a shared ingroup for all members, but family members also possess identities signifying intergroup boundaries within the family" (Soliz & Harwood, 2006, p. 88).

The social identity perspective posits that the "group is in the individual," rather than the "individual is in the group" (Abrams et al., 2005, p. 100). The perspective focuses on the realities that exist within individuals in groups (Abrams et al., 2005). This concept of individual realities corresponds to individual identities; these personal identities morph into social identities when group membership is significant for an individual (Abrams et al., 2005). The development of shared social identity leads to members' desire to differentiate their ingroup from the outgroup (Hogg et al., 2004). Ingroup/outgroup differentiation is especially important in a family setting, as shared identity can be achieved when members feel as if they are part of a collective ingroup with minimal intragroup differentiation.

The ingroup's desire to positively differentiate from the outgroup can be very powerful. As the realities and values of the ingroup become a part of members' identities, they begin to feel the emotions experienced by other members of the ingroup (Gordijn, Yzerbyt, Wigboldus, & Dumont, 2006). Members are more likely to negatively evaluate wrongdoing when they see the perpetrator as a member of the ingroup in order to maintain positive identity. Gordijn, Wigboldus, and Yzerbyt (2001) found that those observing unfair behavior of a group member became angrier when the similarities of the perpetrator to other group members were emphasized rather than the differences. Members of the ingroup are likely to negatively evaluate all behaviors displayed by members of the outgroup regardless of the context; ingroup members are held to a higher standard, and are more likely to be ostracized by other ingroup members if the positive image of the group is threatened.

Although a sense of social identity and the subsequent need to positively differentiate the ingroup from the outgroup may occur on some level for all members, the levels of identification among members may vary (Jetten, Spears, & Manstead, 1997). Those who identify highly with the group are more likely to follow group norms and strive to maintain a positive identity for the ingroup (Jetten et al., 1997). High identifiers are more likely to embrace the prototypes set forth by the ingroup than those with a lower level of identity (Gordijn et al., 2006). The group as a whole experiences a sense of shared identity among all members when the members feel connected to the emotions of other members, have a high level of identification, and follow group norms (Gordijn et al., 2001; Gordijn et al., 2006; Jetten et al., 1997). A strong sense of identity in the ingroup heightens the need to separate from any outgroups that may exist (Hogg et al., 2004).

The impact of identity and ingroup/outgroup differentiation has been studied in a variety of contexts, including health and family communication. Health communication offers a valuable context to study ingroups and outgroups; individuals afflicted by illness are forced to negotiate the change from a non-patient (ingroup) to a patient (outgroup) (Ethier & Deaux, 1994; Jackson, Tudway, Giles, & Smith, 2009). Additionally, the level of identification people have with their families can determine the responsibility they take for their health. Those with higher family identification may be more aware of their family medical history and take preventative measures (Harwood & Sparks, 2003).

Specifically, connections between cancer and identification have been studied (Harwood & Sparks, 2003). Group membership is inherently linked to cancer diagnoses; for example, certain ethnic groups are at higher risk for certain forms of cancer, and cervical cancer is a disease unique to women. Family communication may also be affected after a cancer diagnosis; the patient may feel an increased level of identification due to expressions of support from the family, or could feel like part of the outgroup because of the disease (Harwood & Sparks, 2003). Furthermore, the groups that individuals identify with in their daily lives can influence their health. Individuals who identify with others who regularly engage in high-risk behavior will find it more difficult to stop their own negative behaviors. For example, smokers who strongly identify with other smokers will struggle with quitting (Harwood & Sparks, 2003).

Researchers have begun to integrate small group and family research in terms of identity, but so far it has been limited to stepfamilies (Banker & Gaertner, 1998), grandparent-grandchild relationships (Harwood, Raman, & Hewstone, 2006; Soliz, 2007; Soliz & Harwood, 2003, 2006), and in-laws (Rittenour & Soliz, 2009). Within families, intergroup and intragroup distinctions exist (Soliz & Harwood, 2006). Intergroup and intragroup distinctions can impact shared family identity. "Perceptual intergroup differentiation is accompanied by intragroup differentiation that focuses on norms that legitimate individuals' beliefs about positive in-group distinctiveness" (Marques, Abrams, & Serodio, 2001, p. 445). For example, families strive to distinguish themselves from other family groups through their own particular norms (intergroup differentiation); within the family itself, there are certain practices and behaviors that members traditionally follow to maintain their ingroup identity (intragroup differentation).

An example of a relationship that has intergroup and intragroup attributes is a grandparent/grandchild relationship; the grandparent is part of the intergroup (family), but also has an intragroup differentiation from the grandchild because of age, which can be a significant feature that may disturb the ingroup (Soliz & Harwood, 2006). Communication between grandparents and grandchildren that emphasized age (i.e., conversations about age and personal history) was negatively associated to relational closeness (Harwood et al., 2006). Soliz and Harwood (2006) argue that grandchildren may distance themselves from grandparents to heighten intragroup differentiation in order to emphasize their youth and separation from an aging population. This finding demonstrates how family relationships can be negatively influenced by intragroup differentiation.

Future Research in Shared Family Identity

Two productive avenues to advance social identity theory in family communication are investigating different family relationships and analyzing the multiple, simultaneous perceptions family members have of their family identity. As previous research has only investigated grandparent/grandchild, mother-in-law/daughter-in-law, and stepfamily relationships, there is a need for additional exploration of how identity functions in family groups. Parent/child, sibling/sibling, and spouse/spouse relationships (as well as cohabiting couples) all are worth investigating, as they each represent unique aspects of an ingroup. Thus, a key contribution of investigating social identity in families is to gain a better understanding about what makes families unique from other group types. Whereas other groups may have long histories, no groups start earlier than families, at least in terms of children. This unique nature of identity needs to be compared to research in non-family ingroups; comparison across these types of group may provide us a better understanding of family dynamics.

In addition, family relationships that involve adopted individuals make very salient locations for identity investigations. Adopted adolescents are likely to experience adjustment difficulties and identity issues because information about their biological parents or cultural background may be unknown (Rueter, Keyes, Iacono, & McGue, 2009). Adoptive families are likely to experience identity challenges as they explore new territory with their adopted child, including parental expectations from the child and potential cultural differences (Galvin, 2003). In addition, messages from individuals outside of the adoptee's family may serve to disconfirm family identity within the family (Suter, 2008).

While shared family identity is contingent upon creating a collective family identity through fewer intragroup distinctions, shared identity within groups calls for as much positive intergroup distinctiveness as possible so the group itself is perceived as unique. Adoptive families will undoubtedly strive to integrate the adopted child within their immediate and extended family; with older children, communicative openness about the adoption process helps to build shared family identity (Jones & Hackett, 2007). However, adoptive families may also strive to make their family distinctive while integrating an adoptive child. For example, family routines and rituals play an important role in building identity (Fiese et al., 2002). A routine, such as specified bedtimes for children, or a ritual, such as inside jokes about topics particular to the family, communicates two messages that distinguish one family from another: "this is what needs to be done" (routines) and "this is who we are" (rituals) (Fiese et al., 2002, p. 382).

The prevalence of "open adoption" provides areas for future research. As many adoptions today allow the adopted child and family to have contact with the birth family, the identity negotiation for both families could be studied (Siegel, 2003). Further study of how adoptive families both minimize intergroup relations and distinguish their own group would bridge small group and family communication research.

In addition to studying the shared identity in a wider variety of family relationships, it would be beneficial to study how "subgroups" in the family work to create a larger shared identity. For example, when a couple gets married, their separate identities from their families of origin must merge to create a new *hybrid* identity. When a couple has children, this hybrid identity is passed to the child through the parents. Analyzing the manner in which this new identity is transferred to children would be beneficial not only because it moves family analysis past the dyad, but also because it problematizes the notion of identity creation and explores how "shared" identities may be perceived differently. Clearly this approach would be beneficial to other subgroups and family relationship types that involve more than two family members (e.g., parents-children, siblings-siblings, extended family-immediate family).

Of course, to pursue such a course, methodologies must be used or created that explore family identification and are not restricted to dyadic relationships. Specifically, utilizing methodologies that investigate the individual, dyad, and group-level of analysis (e.g., hierarchical linear modeling) may provide valuable insight into how families are negotiating identity. Family identification is not a static entity that is consistent across all family members; family members are consistently negotiating their own perception of family identity. Thus, methodologies that consider individual levels of analysis can consider these nuances in family identification, and treat the family as a group.

Deviance

Deviance provides a contrasting element to social identity that could provide insight into family communication. "Deviant members are people who are not very prototypical and therefore not liked (social attraction) or trusted as much as more prototypical members" (Hogg et al., 2004, p. 263). Deviant group members put the group's identity at risk and violate norms, as they do not represent the group's prototype (Hogg et al., 2004; Wellen & Neale, 2006). Deviance offers a unique danger to ingroups. Status threats can emerge externally, but "a poor performance or the negative behaviour [sic] of an ingroup member can jeopardize the ingroup reputation" (Castano, Paladino, Coull, & Yzerbyt, 2002, p. 366).

Member deviance has garnered significant attention by group scholars (Bown & Abrams, 2003; Castano et al., 2002; Marques et al., 2001; Marques, Robalo, & Rocha, 1992; Marques & Yzerbyt, 1988; Marques, Yzerbyt, & Leyens, 1988; Wellen & Neale, 2006). Specifically, the manner in which ingroup members respond to ingroup deviance has been explained by the "black sheep hypothesis" (Marques et al., 1988). According to this hypothesis, "judgments about likeable and unlikeable ingroup members should yield more extreme positive and negative evaluations than judgments about similarly unlikeable outgroup members" (Marques et al., 1988, p. 4). Ingroup members have positive feelings toward their group, and therefore expect other members to display suitable characteristics; deviance from group norms detracts from the value of the group, explaining extreme reactions to ingroup deviance (Marques et al., 2001). The level of ingroup identification also contributes to the perception of ingroup deviance, as higher levels of identification cause members to perceive deviants as less typical (Castano et al., 2002).

Ingroup deviance and the black sheep hypothesis have a profound influence on groups; specifically, deviance from group norms negatively affects perceptions of group members. Deviance of group norms has been negatively associated with likeability (Bown & Abrams, 2003; Marques et al., 2001; Wellen & Neale, 2006). Wellen and Neale (2006) found participants reading fictional workplace examples about deviant colleagues rated deviant colleagues less favorably than those participants who read about normative colleagues. Furthermore, members who displayed positive characteristics were valuable to other group members; deviance from norms reduced personal attractiveness (Bown & Abrams, 2003). In addition to negatively influencing likeability, ingroup deviance can also affect cohesiveness. Group members are likely to consider group deviants when formulating their perceptions of group cohesion, as deviant behaviors take prominence in group interactions (Wellen & Neale, 2006).

From a family perspective, research on deviance has primarily focused on the relationships that influence deviant behavior and the negative outcomes associated with deviance in adolescents (Aseltine, 1995; Freisthler, Byrnes, & Gruenewald, 2009; Higgins & Boyd, 2008; Lonardo, Giordano, Longmore, & Manning, 2009; Miller, Loeber, & Hipwell, 2009; Stormshak, Comeau, & Shepard, 2004). Adolescents' relationships with parents have an effect on adolescent deviance, as overly harsh parenting practices have been found to contribute to deviant behavior; parental deviance also plays a role in a child's deviant behavior (Lonardo, et al., 2009; Miller et al., 2009). Additionally, deviant siblings may subsequently predict deviancy in other siblings (Stormshak et al., 2004). Deviant behavior, which can be influenced by familial relationships, manifests itself in antisocial behavior, drug use, and alcohol use (Aseltine, 1995; Freisthler et al., 2009; Stormshak et al., 2004).

Future Research on Deviance in Families

Two avenues for future research in familial deviance exist in the black sheep hypothesis and in examining the benefits of family deviance. A conceptual link between identity and deviance within both small groups and the family is the black sheep hypothesis (Marques et al., 1988). The expression "s/he is the 'black sheep' of the family" is common when referencing a member who does not conform to the norms of the rest of the family. Thus, the family is an appropriate and logical context in which to study the black sheep hypothesis, a phenomenon that ironically has been studied in small groups but not in families.

Deviancy runs counter to normative views of the family. Most families strive to make themselves unique from other families through the use of rituals (Kiser, Bennett, Heston, & Paavola, 2005) and strive to maintain a positive identity for their ingroup. Yet there may be members within families that deviate from group norms (Lonardo et al., 2009). These "black sheep" are likely to experience negative evaluations from the other members of their ingroup (their family).

Since deviants threaten group norms and identity, they often cause problems and distress in families (Marques et al., 2001). Future research on deviance within the family could examine deviance as more than just "bad behavior," but a contradiction to prototypicality (Hogg et al., 2004; Wellen & Neale, 2006). Using this approach, deviant behavior is based on the norms of each family; thus, deviancy in one family would not necessarily be deviant in another. Future research would be beneficial not only to analyze how "black sheep" negotiate their identity within the family, but to also investigate attempts of deviants to find other groups with norms consistent with their "bad behavior" and with whom they wish to identity.

Although research investigating deviant behavior has tended to investigate the negative effect such behavior has on deviants and ingroups, it may be helpful to examine deviance in a positive light within families. For example, Hornsey and Imani (2004) found criticism within groups to aid group life. Discussion about group norms and the violation of those norms may lead to a better understanding of how group members perceive one another and their family. It may be helpful to examine everyday deviancy that may occur in families as a natural, constructive process that could improve family identity.

Similarly, deviancy may provide an opportunity to explicitly discuss issues that are often ignored or neglected. There are many reasons why family members engage in deviant behavior, and individual family members are likely to have a variety of perceptions about the deviancy. The member could be replicating deviance previously witnessed in a parent or sibling (Lonardo et al., 2009; Stormshak et al., 2004). The member could also be reacting to the harsh response received when a deviant act was committed, as deviant ingroup members receive severe feedback in accordance with the black sheep hypothesis (Marques et al., 1988). These explanations, usually applied to group contexts, could provide meaningful explanations for family member deviance and potential avenues for future research.

Theory of Transactive Memory

Individuals within groups communicate with each other because of relational and task goals (Bales, 1950). One specific goal that groups have is information management (Wegner, 1987). For the group to be effective, group members must find a way to store and re-access information. According to Wegner (1987), the process of memory occurs in three stages. In the encoding stage, information enters the memory. During the storage stage, the information is kept within an individual's memory, and during the retrieval stage, the information is brought to the forefront and utilized by the individual. Because individuals can choose to store items in either internal or external storage, memory can have both internal and external manifestations (Wegner, 1987). If a daughter asks her father about his wedding, the father may be able to remember portions of the answer. But if and when the father consults with his wife (external source), he is able to give an answer that is well beyond his internal store of knowledge.

According to Monge and Contractor (2003), "knowledge networks are distributed repositories of knowledge elements from a larger knowledge domain that are tied together by knowledge linkages within and between organizations" (p. 198). Transactive memory systems are a kind of knowledge network; they are sets of individual memory systems in addition to the communication that occurs between those individuals (Wegner, Giuliano, & Hertel, 1985). Thus, marriage can bring together individual memory systems to create a type of transactive memory system.

The transactive memory system begins when each member of the system becomes aware of other members' areas of expertise (Wegner, 1987). In a family, one member may remember close friends' birth dates, while another may be good at remembering where certain documents are filed. When the external storage is a transactive memory system, individuals must know who in the system possesses the information and how to ask the other individual for the information.

Previous research has shown that the extent to which people within groups know who possesses information affects both the group's communication and decision quality (Hollingshead, 1998a, 1998b). When individuals have increased levels of intimacy, there is a resulting cognitive interdependence on each other, which results in more accurate and intricate transactive memories. Therefore, it is logical to assume that there is great potential for accurate and efficient transactional memory systems within a family unit. When group members come together with their individual knowledge, integrative processes allow the group members to share existing information to create new knowledge. In return, effective exchanges of information reinforce perceptions that the transactive memory system is effective; successful transactive memory systems affirm the value of remembering as a group.

Two areas of transactive memory theory that could be helpful in family communication research are in the areas of transactive memory system positions and information sharing. Since family member positions are similar to other groups in that they are both formally (e.g., parent, child) and informally (e.g., favorite child) created, we discuss how researchers can investigate how an individual's placement within a family influences family interaction. Next, we consider several family variables that could potentially influence information exchange.

Transactive Memory System Positions

When group members make decisions about who will know what information within a group, often the default assumption is to base the decision on an individual's role or position in the group (Jackson & Klobas, 2008). Group members tend to believe that an individual's position says something about the kind of information they are likely to possess and be willing to manage. Therefore, position or status within a group may directly influence information responsibilities within the transactive memory system.

Groups need all members to participate in information sharing for transactive memory systems to work effectively. Participation in a transactive memory system requires that people share information so that it flows freely from point to point in the network (Monge & Contractor, 2003). However, this participation may not always occur. As such, individuals at certain positions within the group or organization may or may not receive all needed information.

Groups may also require certain individuals within the group to be in specific positions in order for the overall system to function. Because of the kinds of tasks different groups perform, it is important that certain individuals within the group have mastery of the transactive memory system. It is imperative that these individuals know which members of the group possess what kinds of information in order to access it quickly. When individuals in key positions within the group do not have a command of the transactive memory system, the group overall may suffer (Wegner, 1987).

However, when group members do not have a command of other group members' expertise because of hierarchy or group size, the group members may adapt differently. When a group becomes too large to maintain one transactive memory system, multiple transactive memory systems may be created (Anand, Manz, & Glick, 1998). Then, certain members of each transactive memory system will maintain some knowledge of what is contained in other transactive memory systems to keep the systems within the larger group linked.

Future Directions on Transactive Memory System Positions in Families

When group or family members engage in a transactive memory search, the position within the family group gives certain individuals an advantage, such as more accurate mental models of the transactive memory system (Brandon & Hollingshead, 2004). Individuals who communicate frequently with other family members or are considered to be a parent figure likely have a more precise knowledge of others' expertise and more access to information. Therefore, it is likely that members who are central to family systems have more influence in transactive memory systems.

Of course, the nature of this potential advantage may largely depend on the type of connections salient to the occasion. Although connections are often considered in terms of who talks to whom (communication ties), other ties, such as formal, affective, cognitive, material, and proximity (Katz, Lazer, Arrow, & Contractor, 2004) may be more salient for certain situations. For example, pooling family members' insights and information concerning the best place to eat dinner may not be as important as having a material tie to whoever is driving the car. In this situation, having a tie to a family member with a car and money trumps other potential ties. The way individuals determine which ties become salient in a certain context, especially in relation to family structure, is another fruitful avenue for future research.

As there is high potential for jealousy in sibling relationships (Parrott, 1991), disputes among family members about family positioning may emerge. A parent who asks a son for specific information about sports may draw the ire of a jealous sibling who wishes he or she was considered the repository for sports knowledge. Competition for family positioning may be a fruitful area to investigate how family structure is created. Since transactive memory systems work best with the free flow of information (Monge & Contractor, 2003), any motivation to restrict or manipulate information flow for individual gains (i.e., improved family positioning) may impede transactive memory effectiveness.

Future research should also explore how positions and roles within the family determine what information family members are expected to retain. It is possible that expectations of family members change as their roles change within the family system. As a daughter becomes a mother herself, the expectations of the areas in which she is expert may differ from when she was younger. In addition, parentified children, or children who assume adult roles when parents cannot fulfill family responsibilities, may be expected to retain information related to both parent and child roles. However, in some family systems, these expectations may not change as the individual's family role changes. Future research would benefit from examining how a position in the family correlates with expectations from family members as to the role of the individual in the transactive memory system.

Information Sharing

Transactive memory systems work because of social perceptions (Wegner, 1987). We know what we enjoy, care about, or are knowledgeable about. In the process of interacting within a group, we learn what others know about and care about. Therefore, we perceive ourselves as well as other individuals as having the capacity to retain certain pieces of information about select topics. Transactive memory systems work because each member of the group recognizes these attributes in others and in themselves, and therefore is willing to take responsibility for that information.

According to Wegner (1987), when a transactive memory system is effectively operating within a group, ownership of information is not left up to chance. Even when no one within the group has a direct responsibility for a certain kind of information (e.g., because no one is an expert in that area, because this kind of information has never entered the group before), a channel for processing that information must still exist within the group. Either implicitly or explicitly, all information that enters into the group is the responsibility of someone in the group.

However, information will not necessarily be retrieved in the same form that it was in when it was presented to the individual. First, group members may alter the information as it is being encoded (Anderson & Reider, 1979). During the course of a vacation, one family member may describe a vacation as horrible. Although the trip may not have been entirely bad in retrospect, the information is now encoded in the group's memory as a negative experience. Second, retelling of the information may alter the original information (Hayes-Roth & Thorndyke, 1979). When a family member tells the story of the vacation, he or she may get some details incorrect. This retelling may convince the individual who encoded the information that his or her memory of the event is faulty. Therefore, the false account becomes the newly-encoded true account.

Future Research on Information Sharing in Families

Transactive memory systems can exist at multiple levels within the family. Families that involve stepparents and stepchildren or multiple family groups that comprise a larger extended family must merge transactive memory systems. Healey, Hodgkinson, and Teo (2009) found that in multiteam systems effective performance was based on the development of transactive memory at two levels: intra-team and inter-team. If the team members do not create a transactive memory system (intra-team), the system cannot operate effectively. Similarly, if individual teams cannot create a transactive memory system across the teams (inter-team), the multiteam system cannot operate effectively. The storage and retrieval of information in these transactive memory systems depends on the character of the communication processes within these groups (Hollingshead, 1998b,c). Investigating how families merge transactive memory systems, as well as families that have members who are part of two different family transactive memory systems (e.g., a woman is a daughter in her family of origin, but the wife and mother of her husband and her children), would benefit both transactive memory research and family communication research.

The nature of relationships also affects how communication impacts collective recall. Hollingshead (1998c) found that the closeness of group members' relationships and the strategies of collective retrieval moderate the impact of communication on collective recall. In addition, the strategies for information retrieval are dependent on the extent to which individuals know each other (Hollingshead, 1998a, b). Since family relations are often more intimate than any other type of relationship, highly successful family transactive memory systems and outcomes would be predicted.

A good example of this finding is Wegner, Erber, and Raymond's (1991) study of real-life romantic couples compared to opposite sex strangers on memory tasks. The study showed that familiar couples tend to have higher levels of agreement on individual expertise than stranger couples (Wegner et al., 1991). In addition, familiar couples function better than stranger couples in group memory tasks. The researchers posited that familiar couples have a transactive memory system that leads them to automatically delegate knowledge responsibilities, allowing them to perform more efficiently on memory tasks.

However, there is a caveat to this finding. Even though transactive memory theory argues that face-to-face communication allows groups to ultimately know all knowledge possessed by group members, there may be reasons that such open information exchange is unlikely. Peltokorpi (2008) cites hidden profile research, arguing that group members may have reasons to keep information from the general group (see Stasser & Titus, 2003). Additionally, there may be certain types of information that may both significantly influence a family member and be difficult for that family member to share (e.g., military couples, Merolla, 2010). In light of these findings and others (e.g., Wittenbaum, Hollingshead, & Botero, 2004), Peltokorpi argues that more research must be conducted to understand exactly how face-to-face communication functions in the creation of transactive memory systems.

Although transactive memory is most often associated with transactive memory theory, transactive memory systems are frequently studied using network theory (Borgatti & Cross, 2003; Contractor, Wasserman, & Faust, 2006; Katz et al., 2004). Transactive memory systems have been defined as "cognitive networks in which people and their expertise represent network nodes, with network ties [...] presenting other's awareness of that expertise" (Peltokorpi, 2008, p. 381). The network approach to transactive memory systems may also allow for a more thorough understanding of how interactive/social information seeking processes occur (Hollingshead, 1998a). In addition, this approach may be beneficial for analyzing geographically dispersed families and how they manage information.

Faultline Theory

Faultlines divide groups into subgroups based on group members' characteristics (Roberson & Colquitt, 2005; Silberstang & Hazy, 2008). A faultline is present when two or more subgroups exist within a larger group because of shared attributes, such as demographic characteristics, common interests, or similar ideologies (Jackson & Joshi, 2010). The theoretical argument for the existence of faultlines is consistent with social identity and self-categorization theories (Tajfel & Turner, 1986) and similarity-attraction theory (Byrne, 1971). However, according to faultline theory, in order for the overall group to split into subgroups, the task or context must contain some form of faultline-relevant element that makes that difference salient.

As such, faultlines are one way to conceive of the differences that may cause intragroup distinctions discussed in social identity theory. However, rather than analyzing how prototypes lead to ingroups and outgroups, faultline research focuses on how certain characteristics become salient in a given context, leading to group division. Such divisions lead to separate subgroups; as a result, members communicate with similar members and become more selective in their communication with others.

Group faultlines "depend[s] on the compositional dynamics of the multiple demographic attributes that can potentially subdivide a group" (Lau & Murnighan, 1998, p. 325). Differences between members of a group may cause select members to distance themselves from other group members, while similarities can cause higher levels of cohesion between those members. As such, faultlines in groups can push some group members apart and yet bring others together (Silberstang & Hazy, 2008). However, faultlines may remain dormant for years or possibly never be activated. Group members may never perceive a potential faultline characteristic as pertinent, or never enter a situation or context where the characteristic becomes salient.

The faultline perspective on groups is a fairly new approach to understanding how diversity functions within groups and organizations (Jackson & Joshi, 2010). Rather than focus on the overall diversity present in groups, the faultline perspective emphasizes those differences among members that will likely elicit the formation of distinct subgroups (Lau & Murnighan, 1998). Minichilli, Corbetta, and MacMillan (2010) found that faultlines existed within family-run organizations between family member employees and non-family member employees. Minichilli et al. argued that family member employees tended to share similar group norms, rituals, educational levels, and beliefs while non-family member employees experienced exclusion from the family culture. The faultline became salient due to the family-oriented nature of the business, as family member employees maintained the business as an extension of the family culture and non-family member employees rejected this emotional attachment to the business and the rituals associated with it.

The strength of faultlines within groups can vary. Faultlines become stronger when more attributes are aligned in the same way (Lau & Murnighan, 1998). The strength of faultlines depends on the number of individual attributes apparent to members, the way an individual's attributes align with other individuals' attributes, and the number of potential subgroups (Lau & Murnighan, 1998). Thus, Lau and Murnighan warn against reducing subgroups to one, more apparent characteristic. Examining only one attribute within a group prevents insight into how multiple variables interact. Faultlines are strongest when multiple attributes are strongly aligned and relatively few subgroups have the potential to form. They are weakest when attributes are not aligned, providing the potential for multiple subgroups to form.

There are two primary types of faultlines: social category-based faultlines and information-based faultlines, each of which has different implications for groups (Bezrukova, Jehn, Zanutto, & Thatcher, 2009). Social category-based faultlines are those faultlines based on a demographic characteristic, whereas information-based faultlines concern attributes such as education or work experiences. Bezrukova et al. (2009) argue that it is the informational characteristics that tend to influence groups more because they directly relate to different tasks and decisions.

While faultlines are often categorized as problematic, information-based faultlines may also be positive, leading to better decision-making (Cramton & Hinds, 2005). Bezrukova et al. (2009) found that, while the strength of social category-faultlines negatively affected group performance, information-based faultlines were not associated with poor performance. However, the researchers offer a caveat; if there is high faultline distance in either social categorization or in information-based faultlines, there may be negative effects (e.g., power struggles, competition, difficulties in communicating).

Faultline Salience

Context plays an important role in determining what faultline characteristics become salient (Jackson & Joshi, 2010). There are a variety of potential faultline characteristics in groups, depending on the similarities and differences among group members (Lau & Murnighan, 1998). The type of group task is important in determining which characteristics become salient. If the task concerns work-family balance issues, gender subgroups may be more salient, whereas if the task concerns government issues, political subgroups may be more apparent. When all members of a group are working on a task together, the group identity and cohesion may reduce the potential for faultlines to become salient (Polzer, Crisp, Jarvenpaa, & Kim, 2006). Herein lies the value of the faultline perspective: a focus on the simultaneous evaluation and alignment of multiple diversity dimensions (Trezzini, 2008). Rather than emphasizing one area of diversity within a group, the faultline perspective argues that group members evaluate multiple facets of diversity within a group concurrently. Additionally, while the potential for multiple subgroups to form is recognized in the faultline perspective, these subgroups are not treated as automatically present.

One factor that may determine faultline salience is faultline distance (Bezrukova et al., 2009). Faultline distance refers to how different two subgroups are from one another. The age distance between a subgroup of high schoolers and a subgroup of college-age individuals would be relatively small, but the distance would be large in comparison to a subgroup of retirees. Therefore, the likelihood of the faultline between the high schoolers and the retirees becoming salient is much higher than the likelihood of the faultline between the high schoolers and the college-age individuals becoming salient.

Diversity will likely affect a group's functioning negatively when the group members are aware of the dissimilarities present within the group (van Knippenberg, De Dreu, & Homan, 2004). The diversity present within a group is most likely to cause problems in the group's performance when there are several dimensions of diversity combined to create faultlines (Thatcher, Jehn, & Zanutto, 2003). Additionally, those groups who have strong faultlines will have more intragroup conflict and less satisfaction (Bezrukova, Thatcher, & Jehn, 2007).

Beyond the problems of information coordination, salient faultlines within groups can also lead to competition for resources (Li & Hambrick, 2005). Rather than group members viewing resources as something for the group, group members may attempt to get resources only for their specific subgroup. As such, the group is not only ineffective at accomplishing tasks, it is also competing with itself, deferring progress.

Future Research on Faultline Salience in Families

There are a many ways that communication scholars can analyze faultline creation and salience in families. Children are generally raised to hold the same values, beliefs, and ideals as their parents. Parents often believe that their children will hold on to their religious, social, and political views. However, as children begin to engage in different educational and life experiences, these views may change and diverge from their parents. These differences are not readily apparent; they only become manifest through talk. When differences become manifest, the family climate may become defensive.

However, children with diverse experiences may also bring in new ideas and new ways of thinking that will benefit the family. When members of a family unit have different levels and types of education, work in different occupations, or generally take a different life path, other members of the family may be enriched by their knowledge and experiences. Future research examining how these faultlines emerge and become salient will be beneficial for communication scholars.

Faultlines influence communication patterns across networks. Perceived faultlines within groups reduce the ability of the group to coordinate information, a process which is crucial for performance and member satisfaction (Shen, Gallivan, & Tang, 2008). Even though family goals may be different (i.e., more relational, less formal) than the task groups studied in previous research, faultlines may still prove detrimental to desired outcomes. This may be especially true when trying to coordinate or share information. Thus, considering how faultlines interfere with transactive memory systems may prove fruitful to examining the ability of families to accomplish positive relational outcomes.

Previous research has shown that perceived faultlines based on social categories can be positive in some cases. As mentioned previously, stepfamily research has pointed to the difficulty of managing blended families. It may be useful to investigate how families attempt to overcome faultlines that may be manifest more easily than others. Instead of investigating how a faultline may prevent a stepfamily from uniting because it is always salient, it may be valuable to investigate how families try to prevent faultlines from emerging. Research on collusion in groups has shown that sometimes individuals collude in order to continue conflict, because the conflict is related to their identity (Zartman, 2005). Similarly, rather than problematizing the differences between family members, it could be beneficial for family communication scholars to understand when these differences benefit the family unit and bring about positive consequences.

Analyzing faultlines in blended families is a natural step for family communication scholars; there are many examples of existent research on stepfamily systems (King, 2009; Schrodt, 2003; Schrodt et al., 2007). While some families blend with relative ease, other families never truly come together as a larger family unit. Additionally, other variables relative to the family (e.g., size, family type, proximity) may influence a family's ability to keep a faultline dormant. Similar to our suggestions for information-based faultlines, future research should focus on how faultline distance in each of these social categories impacts how salient the faultline becomes or remains.

Last, there are a variety of faultlines that have yet to be examined in research. For example, genetics and the ability to transmit a disease may influence how family members see one another. In a study on the transmission of Huntington Disease, Sobel and Cowan (2003) found that genetics tests and subsequent discoveries of disease carriers had great potential to influence how family members identified with one another. "When their siblings tested positive or were already symptomatic, their bond with siblings, forged by the common threat of disease, was broken" (p. 50). Thus, any characteristic that could potentially divide families needs to be considered as a faultline.

Conclusion

In this chapter, we have elaborated upon several potential ways that group communication theories can benefit family communication scholars. Due to its interpersonal roots, family communication scholars have primarily investigated dyadic relationships in families, although recently there has been a greater frequency of studies investigating family units of more than two individuals. Clearly, interpersonal research has flourished in investigating the family; however, we believe group communication scholars have much to offer family research as well. In this chapter, we have elaborated upon two areas of social identity theory (shared identity and deviance), two areas of the theory of transactive memory (system position and information sharing), and one area in faultline theory (faultline salience) that could be fruitful frameworks for understanding interaction among family members. Certainly, these are not the only ways that group theories can benefit family communication research. Other areas studied by group scholars, such as conflict, decision making, and group development, could be equally beneficial to our understanding of family communication. We believe that the five subareas suggested in this chapter will produce strong future research lines due to their potential to produce immediate theoretical development and application.

The main premise of our argument is that analyzing the family as a whole will lead to more fruitful and holistic research findings. Often family studies do not focus on the family as a whole (Punyanunt-Carter, 2008; Wright, 2009); rather, husband-wife or father-daughter relationships are isolated. However, the idea that family relationships can be understood as a dyad is "an artificial construction of researchers" (Paley, Cox, & Kanoy, 2001, p. 264). There are several family scholars who have begun to approach families as more than dyads (e.g., Kellas & Trees, 2006; Miller-Day, 2004). Neglecting a group communication perspective when considering the family prevents a more thorough understanding of how multiple family members perceive, interpret, and negotiate meaning through family interaction. Thus, a group communication perspective surmounts the oversimplified approaches of past research, problematizing the unique dynamic that makes a family and family.

In addition to the benefits listed previously, there are several general ways that a group communication approach can prove beneficial to family communication scholars. First, many group communication research areas have been largely unstudied in families. For example, transactive memory systems have been studied in groups because they often involve decision making, which makes it a natural place to explore information management. However, family members are often associated with different types of knowledge, and provide another context which to study information management. Thus, one of the benefits of this approach is to provide new lines of research for family communication researchers.

Second, group and family communication researchers have studied similar concepts in different contexts using different labels. However, due to differing contexts and perspectives, comparison across these areas is largely absent. By comparing and contrasting findings across group and family literature, a fuller theoretical understanding of these concept areas will emerge. Additionally, it will allow scholars to talk across the artificially created semantic barriers we have in the communication discipline.

Last, investigating the family context is an appropriate way to extend group communication theory. The family is a unique type of group, differing from other groups in terms of history, identity, and culture. Hypothesizing and testing group communication theory claims in families will help us better understand if group communication theory claims are context or communication oriented. If differences are found between families and other groups, then the differences will provide researchers with a better understanding of the uniqueness of the family context. If similarities are found between families and other groups, then the similarities will speak to group communication processes than span contextual boundaries. This last point is consistent with other communication scholars who have challenged researchers to focus less on institutionally-created areas of communication (e.g., interpersonal, organizational, political) and more on what is fundamental and unique about communication itself (Burleson, 1992). Thus, opportunities for group and family communication scholars to collaborate should likewise be pursued.

References

Abrams, D., Hogg, M. A., Hinkle, S., & Otten, S. (2005). The social identity perspective on small groups. In M. S. Poole & A. B. Hollingshead (Eds.), *Theories of small groups: Interdisciplinary perspectives* (pp. 99–137). Thousand Oaks, CA: Sage.

Anand, V., Manz, C. C., & Glick, W. H. (1998). An organizational memory approach to information management. *Academy of Management Review, 23*, 796–809.

Anderson, J., & Reider, L. (1979). Elaborative processing explanation of depth of processing. In L. S. Cermak & I. M. Craik (Eds.), *Levels of processing in human memory* (pp. 385–403). Hillsdale, NJ: Erlbaum.

Aseltine, R. H. (1995). A reconsideration of parental and peer influences on adolescent deviance. *Journal of Health and Social Behavior, 36,* 103–121.

Bales, R. F. (1950). *Interaction process analysis.* Cambridge, MA: Addison Wesley.

Banker, B. S., & Gaertner, S. L. (1998). Achieving stepfamily harmony: An intergroup-relations approach. *Journal of Family Psychology, 12*, 310–325.

Benson, L., Berger, M., & Mease, W. (1975). Family communication systems. *Small Group Behavior, 6*, 91–104.

Bezrukova, K., Jehn, K. A., Zanutto, E. L., & Thatcher, S. M. B. (2009). Do workgroup faultlines help or hurt? A moderated model of faultlines, team identification, and group performance. *Organization Science, 20*, 35–50. doi: 10.1287/orsc.1080.0379

Bezrukova, K., Thatcher, S. M. B., & Jehn, K. A. (2007). Group heterogeneity and faultlines: Comparing alignment and dispersion theories of group composition. In L. Thompson & K. J. Behfar (Eds.), *Conflict in organizational groups: New directions in theory and practice* (pp. 57–92). Evanston, IL: Northwestern University Press.

Borgatti, S. P., & Cross, R. (2003). A relational view of information seeking and learning in social networks. *Management Science, 49,* 432–445. doi: 10.1287/mnsc.49.4.432.14428

Bowen, M. (1978). *Family therapy in clinical practice*. New York: Jason Aronson.

Bown, N., & Abrams, D. (2003). Despicability in the workplace: Effects of behavioral deviance and unlikeability on the evaluation of in-group and out-group members. *Journal of Applied Social Psychology, 33*, 2413–2426.

Brandon, D. P., & Hollingshead, A. B. (2004). Transactive memory systems in organizations: Matching tasks, expertise, and people. *Organization Science, 15*, 633–644. doi: 10.1287/orsc.1040.0069

Burleson, B. R. (1992). Taking communication seriously. *Communication Monographs, 59,* 79–86.

Byrne, D. (1971). *The attraction paradigm*. New York: Academic Press.

Castano, E., Paladino, M. P., Coull, A., & Yzerbyt, V. Y. (2002). Protecting the ingroup stereotype: Ingroup identification and the management of deviant group members. *British Journal of Social Psychology, 41,* 365–385.

Contractor, N. S., Wasserman, S., & Faust, K. (2006). Testing multitheoretical multilevel hypotheses about organizational networks: An analytical framework and empirical example. *Academy of Management Review, 31*, 681–703.

Cramton, C. D., & Hinds, P. J. (2005). Subgroup dynamics in internationally distributed teams: Ethnocentrism or cross-national learning? In B. Staw & R. Kramer (Eds.), *Research in organizational behavior* (Vol. 26, pp. 231–263). Oxford, UK: Elsevier Science.

Ethier, K. A., & Deaux, K. (1994). Negotiating social identity when contexts change: Maintaining identification and responding to threat. *Interpersonal Relations and Group Processes, 67,* 243–251.

Fiese, B. H., Tomcho, T. J., Douglas, M., Josephs, K., Poltrock, S., & Baker, T. (2002). A review of 50 years of research on naturally occurring family routines and rituals: Cause for celebration? *Journal of Family Psychology, 16*, 381–390.

Fitzpatrick, M. A. T. (1976). *A typological examination of communication in enduring relationships*. Unpublished doctoral dissertation, Temple University, Philadelphia, PA.

Freisthler, B., Byrnes, H. F., & Gruenewald, P. J. (2009). Alcohol outlet density, parental monitoring, and adolescent deviance: A multilevel analysis. *Children and Youth Services Review, 31,* 325–330.

Frey, L. R. (Ed.). (2003). *Group communication in context: Studies of bona fide groups* (2nd ed.). Mahwah, NJ: Erlbaum.

Galvin, K. (2003). International and transracial adoption: A communication research agenda. *Journal of Family Communication, 3*, 237–253. doi: 10.1207/S15327698jfc0304_5

Gastil, J. (2010). *The group in society.* Los Angeles: Sage.

Gordijn, E. H., Wigboldus, D., & Yzerbyt, V. (2001). Emotional consequences of categorizing victims of negative outgroup behavior as ingroup or outgroup. *Group Processes & Intergroup Relations, 4*, 317–326.

Gordijn, E. H., Yzerbyt, V. Y., Wigboldus, D., & Dumont, M. (2006). Emotional reactions to harmful intergroup behavior. *European Journal of Social Psychology, 36,* 15–30.

Harwood, J., & Sparks, L. (2003). Social identity and health: An intergroup communication approach to cancer. *Health Communication, 15,* 145–159. doi: 10.1207/S15327027HC1502_3

Harwood, J., Raman, P., & Hewstone, M. (2006). The family and communication dynamics of group salience. *Journal of Family Communication, 6*, 181–200. doi: 10.1207/s15327698jfc0603_2

Hayes-Roth, B. & Thorndyke, P. W. (1979). Integration of knowledge from text. *Journal of Verbal Learning and Verbal Behavior, 18*, 91–108.

Healey, M. P., Hodgkinson, G. P., & Teo, S. (2009, June). *Responding effectively to civil emergencies: The role of transactive memory in the performance of multiteam systems.* Paper presented at the International Conference on Naturalistic Decision Making, London.

Higgins, G. E., & Boyd, R. J. (2008). Low self-control and deviance: Examining the moderation of social support from parents. *Deviant Behavior, 29*, 388–410. doi: 10.1080/01639620701588339

Hogg, M. A. (2001). A social identity theory of leadership. *Personality and Social Psychology Review, 5*, 184–200.

Hogg, M. A., Abrams, D., Otten, S., & Hinkle, S. (2004). The social identity perspective: Intergroup relations, self-conception, and small groups. *Small Group Research, 35,* 246–276. doi: 10.1177/1046496404263424

Hollingshead, A. B. (1998a). Distributed knowledge and transactive processes in groups. In M. A. Neale, E. A. Mannix, & D. H. Gruenfeld (Eds.), *Research on managing groups and teams* (Vol. 1, pp. 105–125). Greenwich, CT: JAI Press.

Hollingshead, A. B. (1998b). Retrieval processes in transactive memory systems. *Journal of Personality and Social Psychology, 74,* 659–671.

Hollingshead, A. B. (1998c). Communication, learning, and retrieval in transactive memory systems. *Journal of Experimental Social Psychology, 34,* 423–442.

Hornsey, M., & Imani, A. (2004). Criticizing groups from the inside and the outside: An identity perspective on the intergroup sensitivity effect. *Personality and Social Psychology Bulletin, 30,* 365–383. doi: 10.1177/0146167203261295

Jackson, L., Tudway, J. A., Giles, D., & Smith, J. (2009). An exploration of the social identity of mental health inpatient users. *Journal of Psychiatric and Mental Health Nursing, 16,* 167–176. doi: 10.1111/j.1365-2850.2008.01361.x

Jackson, P., & Klobas, J. (2008). Transactive memory systems in organizations: Implications for knowledge directories. *Decision Support Systems, 44*, 409–424. doi: 10.1016/j.dss.2007.05.001

Jackson, S. E., & Joshi, A. (2010). Work team diversity. In S. Zedeck (Ed.), *APA handbook of industrial and organizational psychology: Volume II* (pp. 651–686). Washington, DC: APA.

Jetten, J., Spears, R., & Manstead, A. S. (1997). Strength of identification and intergroup differentiation: The influence of group norms. *European Journal of Social Psychology, 27*, 603–609.

Jones, C., & Hackett, S. (2007). Communicative openness within adoptive families: Adoptive parents' narrative accounts of the challenges of adoption talk and the approaches used to manage these challenges. *Adoption Quarterly, 10*, 157–178. doi: 10.1080/10926750802163238

Katz, N., Lazer, D., Arrow, H., & Contractor, N. (2004). Network theory and small groups. *Small Group Research, 35*, 307–332. doi: 10.1177/1046496404264941

Kellas, J. K., & Trees, A. R. (2006). Finding meaning in difficult family experiences: Sense-making and interaction processes during joint family storytelling. *Journal of Family Communication, 6*, 49–76. doi: 10.1207/s15327698jfc0601_4

Keyton, J. (1999). Relational communication in groups. In L. R. Frey, D. S. Gouran, & M. S. Poole (Eds.), *The handbook of group communication theory and research* (pp. 192–222). Thousand Oaks, CA: Sage.

Keyton, J. (2006). *Communicating in groups: Building relationships for group effectiveness* (3rd ed.). New York: Oxford University Press.

King, V. (2009). Stepfamily formation: Implications for adolescent ties to mothers, nonresident fathers, and stepfathers. *Journal of Marriage and Family, 71*, 954–968.

Kiser, L. J., Bennett, L., Heston, J., & Paavola, M. (2005). Family ritual and routine: Comparison of clinical and non-clinical families. *Journal of Child and Family Studies, 14*, 357–372. doi: 10.1007/s10826-005-6848-0

Lau, D. C., & Murnighan, J. K. (1998). Demographic diversity and faultlines: The compositional dynamics of organizational groups. *Academy of Management Review, 23*, 325–340.

Li, J., & Hambrick, D. C. (2005). Factional groups: A new vantage on demographic faultlines, conflict, and disintegration in work teams. *Academy of Management Journal, 48*, 794–813.

Lonardo, R. A., Giordano, P. C., Longmore, M. A., & Manning, W. D. (2009). Parents, friends, and romantic partners: Enmeshment in deviant networks and adolescent delinquency involvement. *Journal of Youth and Adolescence, 38*, 367–383. doi: 10.1007/s10964-008-9333-4

Marques, J. M., Abrams, D., & Serodio, R. G. (2001). Being better by being right: Subjective group dynamics and derogation of in-group deviants when generic norms are undermined. *Journal of Personality and Social Psychology, 81*, 436–447.

Marques, J. M., Robalo, E. M., & Rocha, S. A. (1992). Ingroup bias and the "black sheep" effect: Assessing the impact of social identification and perceived variability on group judgements [sic]. *European Journal of Social Psychology, 22*, 331–352.

Marques, J. M., & Yzerbyt, V. Y. (1988). The black sheep effect: Judgmental extremity towards ingroup members in inter- and intra-group situations. *European Journal of Social Psychology, 18*, 287–292.

Marques, J. M., Yzerbyt, V. Y., & Leyens, J. P. (1988). The "black sheep effect": Extremity of judgments towards ingroup members as a function of group identification. *European Journal of Social Psychology, 18*, 1–16.

Merolla, A. J. (2010). Relational maintenance during military deployment: Perspectives of wives of deployed US soldiers. *Journal of Applied Communication Research, 38*, 4–26. doi: 10.1080/00909880903483557

Miller, S., Loeber, R., & Hipwell, A. (2009). Peer deviance, parenting and disruptive behavior among young girls. *Journal of Abnormal Child Psychology, 37,* 139–152. doi: 10.1007/s10802-008-9265-1

Miller-Day, M. A. (2004). *Communication among grandmothers, mothers, and adult daughters: A qualitative study of maternal relationships.* Mahwah, NJ: Erlbaum.

Minichilli, A., Corbetta, G., & MacMillan, I. C. (2010). Top management teams in family-controlled companies: 'Familiness', 'faultlines', and their impact on financial performance. *Journal of Management Studies, 47,* 205–222. doi: 10.1111/j.1467-6486.2009.00888.x

Monge, P. R., & Contractor, N. S. (2003). *Theories of communication networks.* New York: Oxford University Press.

Olson, D. H., Russell, C., & Sprenkle, D. H. (Eds.). (1989). *Circumplex model: Systemic assessment and treatment of families* (3rd ed.). New York: Haworth.

Paley, B., Cox, M. J., & Kanoy, K. W. (2001). The young family coding interaction scheme. In P. K. Kerig & K. M. Lindahl (Eds.), *Family observational coding systems: Resources for systemic research* (pp. 263–278). Mahwah, NJ: Erlbaum.

Parrott, W. G. (1991). The emotional experiences of envy and jealousy. In P. Salovey (Ed.), *The psychology of jealousy and envy* (pp. 3–31). New York: Guilford Press.

Peltokorpi, V. (2008). Transactive memory systems. *Review of General Psychology, 12,* 378–394. doi: 10.1037/1089-2680.12.4.378

Petronio, S., & Braithwaite, D. O. (1993). The contributions and challenges of family communication to the field of communication. *Journal of Applied Communication Research, 21,* 103–110.

Polzer, J. T., Crisp, C. B., Jarvenpaa, S. L., & Kim, J. W. (2006). Extending the faultline model to geographically dispersed teams: How collocated subgroups can impair group functioning. *Academy of Management Journal, 49,* 679–692.

Poole, M. S., Hollingshead, A. B., McGrath, J. E., Moreland, R. L., & Rohrbaugh, J. (2004). Interdisciplinary perspectives on small groups. *Small Group Research, 35,* 3–16. doi: 10.1177/1046496403259753

Poole, M. S., Keyton, J., & Frey, L. R. (1999). Group communication methodology: Issues and considerations. In L. R. Frey, D. S. Gouran, & M. S. Poole (Eds.), *The handbook of group communication theory and research* (pp. 213–260). Thousand Oaks, CA: Sage.

Punyanunt-Carter, N. M. (2008). Father-daughter relationships: Examining family communication patterns and interpersonal communication satisfaction. *Communication Research Reports, 25,* 23–33. doi: 10.1080/08824090701831750

Putnam, L. L., & Stohl, C. (1990). Bona fide groups: A reconceptualization of groups in context. *Communication Studies, 41,* 248–265.

Rittenour, C., & Soliz, J. (2009). Communicative and relational dimensions of shared family identity and relational intentions in mother-in-law/daughter-in-law relationships: Developing a conceptual model for mother-in-law/daughter-in-law research. *Western Journal of Communication, 73,* 67–90. doi: 10.1080/10570310802636334

Roberson, Q. M., & Colquitt, J. A. (2005). Shared and configural justice: A social network model of justice in teams. *Academy of Management Review, 30,* 595–607.

Rogers, L. E. (1972). Dyadic systems and transactional communicaion in a family context (Doctoral dissertation, Michigan State University). *Dissertation Abstracts International, 33,* 11A. (University Microfilms No. 73-12, 810).

Rueter, M. A., Keyes, M. A., Iacono, W. G., & McGue, M. (2009). Family interactions in adoptive compared to nonadoptive families. *Journal of Family Psychology, 23,* 58–66.

Schrodt, P. (2003). *A typological examination of stepfamily communication schemata.* Unpublished doctoral dissertation, University of Nebraska, Lincoln.

Schrodt, P., Braithwaite, D. O., Soliz, J., Tye-Williams, S., Miller, A., Normand, E. L., & Herrigan, M. M. (2007). An examination of everyday talk in stepfamily systems. *Western Journal of Communication, 71*, 216–234. doi: 10.1080/10570310701510077

Shen, Y., Gallivan, M., & Tang, X. (2008, December). *The influence of subgroup dynamics on knowledge coordination in distributed teams: A transactive memory system and group faultline perspective.* Paper presented at the Proceedings of the International Conference on Information Systems, Paris, France.

Siegel, D. (2003). Open adoption of infants: Adoptive parents' feelings seven years later. *Social Work, 48,* 409–419.

Silberstang, J., & Hazy, J. K. (2008). Toward a micro-enactment theory of leadership and the emergence of innovation. *The Innovation Journal: The Public Sector Innovation Journal, 13,* 1–18.

Sobel, S., & Cowan, C. B. (2003). Ambiguous loss and disenfranchised grief: The impact of DNA predictive testing on the family as a system. *Family Process, 42*, 47–57.

Socha, T. J. (1999). Communication in family units: Studying the first "group." In L. Frey (Ed.), *The handbook of group communication theory and research* (pp. 475–492). Thousand Oaks, CA: Sage.

Socha, T. J. (2009, November). *Children and communication development: Missing links between family and group communication.* Paper presented at the annual meeting of the National Communication Association, Chicago, IL.

Soliz, J. (2007). Communicative predictors of a shared family identity: Comparison of grandchildren's perceptions of family-of-origin grandparents and stepgrandparents. *Journal of Family Communication, 7*, 177–194. doi: 10.1080/15267430701221636

Soliz, J., & Harwood, J. (2003). Perceptions of communication in a family relationship and the reduction of intergroup prejudice. *Journal of Applied Communication Research, 31*, 320–345. doi: 10.1080/1369681032000132582

Soliz, J., & Harwood, J. (2006). Shared family identity, age salience, and intergroup contact: Investigation of the grandparent-grandchild relationship. *Communication Monographs, 73,* 87–107. doi: 10.1080/03637750500534388

Stasser, G., & Titus, W. (2003). Hidden profiles: A brief history. *Psychological Inquiry, 14*, 304–313.

Stormshak, E. A., Comeau, C. A., & Shepard, S. A. (2004). The relative contribution of sibling deviance and peer deviance in the prediction of substance abuse across middle childhood. *Journal of Abnormal Child Psychology, 32*, 635–649.

Suter, E. A. (2008). Discursive negotiation of family identity: A study of U.S. families with adopted children from China. *Journal of Family Communication, 8*, 126–147. doi: 10.1080/15267430701857406

Tajfel, H., & Turner, J. C. (1979). An integrative theory of intergroup conflict. In W. G. Austin & S. Worchel (Eds.), *The social psychology of intergroup relations* (pp. 33–47). Monterey, CA: Brooks/Cole.

Tajfel, H., & Turner, J. C. (1986). The social identity theory of inter-group behavior. In S. Worchel & L. W. Austin (Eds.), *Psychology of intergroup relations* (pp. 2–24). Chicago: Nelson-Hall.

Thatcher, S. M. B., Jehn, K. A., & Zanutto, E. (2003). Cracks in diversity research: The effects of diversity faultlines on conflict and performance. *Group Decision and Negotation, 12*, 217–241. doi: 10.1023/A:1023325406946

Trezzini, B. (2008). Probing the group faultline concept: An evaluation of measures of patterned multi-dimensional group diversity. *Quality and Quantity, 42,* 339–368. doi: 10.1007/s11135-006-9049-z

Turner, R. H. (1970). *Family interaction.* New York: Wiley.

Van Knippenberg, D., De Dreu, C. K. W., & Homan, A. C. (2004). Work group diversity and group performance: An integrative model and research agenda. *Journal of Applied Psychology, 89*, 1008–1022.

Vangelisti, A. L. (2004). Preface. In A. L. Vangelisti (Ed.), *Handbook of family communication* (pp. ix–xii). Mahwah, NJ: Erlbaum.

Wegner, D. M. (1987). Transactive memory: A contemporary analysis of the group mind. In B. Mullen & G. R. Goethals (Eds.), *Theories of group behavior* (pp. 185–208). New York: Springer-Verlag.

Wegner, D. M., Erber, R., & Raymond, P. (1991). Transactive memory in close relationships. *Journal of Personality and Social Psychology, 61,* 923–929.

Wegner, D. M., Giuliano, T., & Hertel, P. (1985). Cognitive interdependence in close relationships. In W. J. Ickes (Ed.), *Compatible and incompatible relationships* (pp. 253–276). New York: Springer-Verlag.

Wellen, J. M., & Neale, M. (2006). Deviance, self-typicality, and group cohesion: The corrosive effects of the bad apples on the barrel. *Small Group Research, 37*, 165–186. doi: 10.1177/1046496406286420

Whitchurch, G. G., & Dickson, F. C. (1999). Family communication. In M. B. Sussman, S. K. Steinmetz, & G. W. Peterson (Eds.), *Handbook of marriage and the family* (pp. 687–704). New York: Plenum Press.

Wittenbaum, G. M., Hollingshead, A. B., & Botero, I. C. (2004). From cooperative to motivated information sharing in groups: Moving beyond the hidden profile paradigm. *Communication Monographs, 71*, 286–310. doi: 10.1080/0363452042000299894

Wright, P. J. (2009). Father-child sexual communication in the United States: A review and synthesis. *Journal of Family Communication, 9,* 233–250. doi: 10.1080/15267430903221880

Zartman, I. W. (2005). Analyzing intractability. In C. Crocker, F. Hampson, & P. Aall (Eds.), *Taming intractable conflicts* (pp. 47–64). Washington DC: United States Institute of Peace Press.

CHAPTER CONTENTS

7 Older People and New Communication Technologies

Narratives from the Literature

Margaret Richardson, Theodore E. Zorn, and C. Kay Weaver

University of Waikato

The chapter reviews the literature on older people and new communication technologies, focusing particularly on their experiences with personal computers and the Internet. The review covers the scholarly literature published primarily between 1990 and 2010. We organize the review around a series of narratives identified as prominent in the literature. Three master narratives dominate the ways in which the relationships between older people and computers have been represented: *the enabling machine and isolated elders, the potential divider and marginalized seniors, and the desirable commodity and grey consumers.*

The chapter is structured as follows: First, we introduce the narrative perspective that guides the approach to this review. We then outline each master narrative in turn, synthesize and present a critical commentary on the literature that supports that narrative. Finally, we identify gaps and limitations in the literature reviewed, and suggest an agenda for future communication research on older people and new communication technologies.

Introduction

One of the "big stories" (Phoenix & Sparkes, 2009) of our time is the domestication of personal computers and the Internet and the integration of this technology into people's daily lives. In this story, adults over 60 years of age are frequently presented as marginal and often as problematic characters because of their lack of use of the technology, but also a significant untapped market for computer hardware, software, and online products and services. In this chapter, we review and critique these and other ways in which older people and computers have been "storied" in the literature from a narrative approach. This approach identifies the key ways in which the relationships between older people and computers have been represented by researchers and how these representations reflect and reproduce culturally shared master narratives. Similar to Meyrowitz (2008), who explored how the research literature on media influence narrates human experience in particular ways, we "attempt to look beneath each research edifice to a foundational narrative" (p. 644) on which the research has been constructed. Our goal is not to demonstrate that any one of narratives is superior to the others. There is significant value and credibility in each of the narratives, but each in its own way is also limited. Through the narrative analysis, we highlight these limitations, and identify how a fuller, more complete and complex view of older people's relationships to computers may be gained. We begin by outlining the narrative perspective through which we view the literature and organize the review. Next, we indicate the method used for identifying the narratives around which the literature review coheres. This is then followed by our review of and critical commentary on the literature from within each identified narrative perspective. We close by offering suggestions for future research.

The Narrative Perspective

Whether in the form of big stories—stories of landmark events or major societal changes—or small stories—stories of mundane things in everyday occurrences (Phoenix & Sparkes, 2009)—narratives are widely understood to be a fundamental aspect of the socially constructed ordering of reality and a primary means by which humans organize and make sense of themselves and their experiences (e.g., Bruner, 1990; Fisher, 1984; MacIntyre, 1981; Richardson, 1990). In a myriad of forms, such as fairy tales, fables, and novels, and through a variety of media, including books, newspapers, movies, and research reports, stories surround and consume us. Stories also entertain and inform us and, explicitly or implicitly, guide our actions, shape our identities, and mold who we are as individuals and collectives as well as expectations about how we ought to behave individually and collectively (e.g., Bruner, 1990; Fisher, 1985; Fulford, 1999; Weick, 1995).

There are different levels of narrative storytelling that serve different interpretative needs. Lyotard (1979) introduced the idea of a master narrative—also termed "grand or meta-narrative"—which is a dominant, culturally shared story that provides a comprehensive explanation of experience and knowledge and a sense of authority to smaller stories of everyday interaction. In what follows, we identify three prominent master narratives that undergird thinking about the relationship between aging and computers. Significantly, each of these is underpinned by the common discursive construction of old age as a period of physical and mental deficit and decline (Coupland, 2003, 2004; Gullette, 1997; Westerhof & Tulle, 2007), combined with a further discursive framing of the development and widespread adoption of new technologies as making a significant contribution to social and human progress (e.g., Smith, 1994). In the next section we outline the process we used for identifying the narratives in the literature.

Scope and Process of the Review

Through our research into older people's experiences with computers (Richardson, Weaver, & Zorn, 2005; Weaver, Zorn, & Richardson, 2010; Zorn,

Richardson, Weaver, & Gilbert, 2010), we developed substantial familiarity with the scholarly literature in this area and the variety of perspectives on the relationship between older people and computers commonly adopted in research studies. For the purposes of this review, we sought to supplement and test this existing understanding with a thorough and systematic search of the literature. Consequently, we searched multiple databases for articles in the area published since 1990, a date we identified as an appropriate starting point given its common association with the widespread introduction of personal computers (Kim, 2008; Wagner, Hassanein, & Head, 2010). The following keywords were used in this search: *elderly people, older people, elderly, elders, older adults, seniors, senior citizens, ageing, aging,* and *technology, Internet, computers, communication technology, information and communication technology,* and *ICT.*

Given our interest in communication and the need to limit the scope of the review, the search was used to specifically identify literature on older people's experiences with personal computers and the Internet. That is, we excluded literature focusing on surveillance and monitoring technology in nursing homes, as well as some aspects of research into telemedicine, and older people's use of non-personal technologies such as ATMs (automatic teller machines), and a range of assistive technologies and "smart home" devices.

Consequently, in terms of its relevance to communication scholarship, this review has importance, first, because it focuses on technologies—the computer and the Internet—that are primarily used for communication and information searching (Carpenter & Buday, 2007; Fox, 2004; Venkatesh, 2008) and, second, because the narrative approach we use frames the investigation in explicitly communicative terms. In support of the first point, multiple studies have demonstrated that computers are used by older people primarily for communication via the Internet.[1] For example, research by Fox (2004), Russell, Campbell, and Hughes (2008) investigated the uses elders made of computers, and focused entirely on Internet-based communication. More specifically, Fox's (2004) survey of older Americans found that of those who used the Internet (22%), most used it almost exclusively for email and information searches. Similarly, other studies, such as Russell et al. (2008) and Hilt and Lipschultz (2004) have found that email is one of the most common and significant uses of the Internet among older people, while still others, such as McMillan, Avery, and Macias (2008) and Rideout (2005) have found that searching for health information is a popular activity. While most such studies are based in the English-speaking countries, studies in Asia have also established that elders use computers significantly for communication purposes. For example, Kanayama (2003) found that Japanese elders participated in virtual communities, and Xie (2008) found Chinese elders using voice chat rooms, instant messaging, and online forums.

Methodologically, narrative analyses of the literature, like other critical and interpretive approaches, stand in contrast to normative (Alvesson & Deetz, 2000) approaches such as meta-analyses and content analyses. As Lieblich,

Tuval-Mashiach, and Zilber (1998) argued, "Narrative research...differs significantly from its positivistic counterpart in its underlying assumptions that there is neither a single, absolute truth in human reality nor one correct reading or interpretation of a text. The narrative approach advocates pluralism, relativism, and subjectivity" (p. 2). However, as these authors also note, this does not mean "anything goes." Researchers are responsible for explaining their research procedures. Thus, the procedures we used for identifying narratives from the literature gathered during the course of our own research and the ensuing systematic data base searches involved interrogation, categorization, and creativity. In terms of interrogation, we looked at each article in turn and asked a series of questions, adapted from Östlund (2004): (a) How is the older person represented here? (b) How is computing technology represented? (c) How is the relationship between older people and computers and its consequences described? Through these questions, the articles were sorted and categorized, and then creatively labeled to capture the principal representations of relationships between older people and computers and to highlight the range and general thrust of narratives in that category. The outputs from this process are three sets of master narratives that hang together plausibly and cohesively (Riessman, 1993). We acknowledge that, as with any interpretive process, the outputs are subjective and contestable (Alvesson & Deetz, 2000) and present an obvious platform for debate about alternative possible constructions. The categorizations and critique are also intentionally provocative, since it is our goal to challenge researchers to explore new and alternative ways of investigating and narrating the relationship between older people and computers. Therefore, the final section of the chapter provides some suggestions as to the directions for future research in terms of different and/or emerging narratives deserving of further exploration.

Before exploring the three master narratives, it is important to clarify the use of some key terms. In this review, we use *stories* and *narratives* interchangeably, but make a distinction between these terms and *master narratives.* We use the term *older people* interchangeably with the terms *elders*, and *senior citizens.* We also adopt the specific term used by researchers to categorize the research participants in their particular studies. We use the term *computers* to include personal/home computers (PCs) and the access to the Internet that this technology facilitates.

Narratives from the Literature

Three master narratives dominate the ways in which computers and older people have been presented in the literature. One narrative is that of *the enabling machine and isolated elders* in which computers have been identified as a tool that can extend the capabilities and social networks of elders, once obstacles to its use have been overcome. A second narrative is that of *the potential divider and marginalized seniors.* This narrative focuses attention on computers as essential to the development of information societies and corresponding concerns, especially from governments, about how some groups, such as senior citizens, may be marginalized in such societies because of their lack of computer use and skills. Often embedded in the discourse of the digital divide, research emanating from this narrative tends to focus on the relative computer use of seniors compared to other groups and identifying the barriers that prevent older people's computer use. A third narrative is that of *the desirable commodity and grey consumers* in which computers have been identified as invested with symbolic meaning as a "must have" personal technology, and older people as a large and relatively untapped target market for computer hardware, software and online products and services. Each of these narratives is discussed below, first through a synthesis of the literature included under the umbrella of the particular narrative, and then through a critical commentary on the merits and limitations of that literature.

The Enabling Machine and Isolated Elders

Much of the empirical work conducted on older peoples' experiences with computers and the Internet falls within the *enabling machine and isolated elders* narrative. Indeed, this is the most frequently occurring of the master narratives identified in the literature and one produced through micro-level research studies of older people's interactions with computers in a social context where computer and Internet use have become commonplace. The major thrust of this body of work is a concern with identifying ways in which computing technologies can benefit individual older people and assist in their overcoming the physical, mental, and social challenges that aging brings. That is, the underlying narrative presents the computer and the Internet as a potential solution for, and to, the problem of elders who are characterized as declining in abilities and, consequently, increasingly isolated from others by being unable to fully participate in their own communities and wider society.

This is a narrative that is premised on a discourse of age as a period in which we move into deficit and decline, and the individual as inevitably a victim of this process. And yet it brings to this story a plot in which, if elders can become active agents, reconnecting with others and with society, they can stave off such deficit and decline through the deployment of technologies, and their quality of life will improve. A successful narrative resolution to the elder person's "problems" sees them living independently and remaining connected to friends, family, and the world beyond the home through the computer. Within this narrative framing, it is as if the computer offers the older person an opportunity for a Second Life.

Given the underlying narrative of the enabling machine and isolated elders, the primary focus of the studies in this cohort is identifying the transformative benefits of computer use for older people. In particular, such studies focus on how computer use can support social connectedness, autonomy, and functional independence, and thereby enhance the quality of older people's lives.

Synthesis of the Literature

Computer use has been purported to benefit older people in a variety of ways. Studies of benefits have been particularly concerned with the relationship between use of computers/Internet and quality of life enhancement. Research indicates that elders' perceptions of quality of life include being socially connected to others, including those who can provide help and social support, and being able to retain functional independence and control over one's life (Gabriel & Bowling, 2004; Wilhelmson, Andersson, Waern, & Allebeck, 2005). These two dimensions are commonly associated with older people's use of computers and the Internet and contribute to the identification of the technology as an enabling machine for elders.

Social Connectedness and Quality of Life

Social connectedness, which encompasses communicative interaction, including for social support, is one of the most significant potential quality of life benefits of computer/Internet use for elders identified in the research literature. Such connectedness—through the use of email and other forms of computer-mediated communication that bring the possibility of increased frequency of social contact—is purported to reduce the risk of loneliness and depression and enhance the quality of life among older people. Many studies have found evidence to support this claim, although that finding is by no means universal.

In support of the argument that computer use enhances the quality of life via social connection, Czaja, Guerrier, Nair, and Landauer (1993) found that the use of an electronic text messaging system enhanced social interaction and morale among women in a community in South Florida, especially those who lived alone and spent extensive amounts of time at home. In a similar vein, Cody, Dunn, Hoppin, and Wendt's (1999) study of participants in a WebTV training program found that those who remained in the 4-month course until the end experienced increased feelings of social connectedness and a greater sense of social support.

Richardson et al. (2005) also found that the benefit most frequently identified in their focus group studies of senior computer users in New Zealand was a sense of connectedness that came with increased contact with family, children and grandchildren through email. Similarly, Gatto and Tak's (2008) small (58 respondents) survey of SeniorNet members in one of the southern states of the U.S. found connectedness to be one of the most frequently mentioned benefits. Likewise Waldron, Gitelson, and Kelley's (2005) 4-year longitudinal study with residents of a planned retirement community in the U.S. Sun Belt found that email communication facilitated the maintenance of long distance relationships with family and friends, as well as their adjustment to a retirement community lifestyle. Interestingly, Thayer and Ray (2006) found that contact with family and friends actually increased as a result of Internet use.

Other research, too, has found communication via the Internet beneficial not just in terms of maintaining existing social relationships (Harwood, 2004) but also in developing new companionship and supportive relationships (Furlong, 1989; Wright, 2000). For instance, Wright (2000), studied satisfaction with both Internet and non-Internet-based relationships for social support purposes among members of the SeniorNet community in the United States. He found that those who spent more time per week communicating online were more satisfied with their Internet support networks than were those who spent less time communicating on the Internet. Wright concluded that for those who spent a great deal of time on the Internet, there was the potential for relatively strong relationships to form, even among those who only knew each other through the Internet. Kanayama's (2003) study of the online experiences of elderly Japanese in a seniors-only environment found participants comfortable using the Internet to find friends and connect socially with others. Interview participants in this study described their online exchanges as an affectionate and supportive way to share stories and listen to others.

However, other studies have raised questions about the beneficial effects of computer use on social connectedness. For instance, White et al.'s (1999) study of the effects of training and Internet use on loneliness reduction among residents in a retirement community in North Carolina identified an initial trend toward decreased loneliness after 2 weeks, but no significant findings after 5 months. A second study by White et al. (2002) with a larger group of participants (39 compared with 15) found no statistically significant effects on loneliness. Additionally, Chen and Persson's (2002) study of young and older adults, did not find a positive effect of Internet use on the psychological well-being of older adults.

Some research has attempted to go beyond simple positive or negative effects and has pointed to more complex explanations of computer use and its effects on connectedness and well-being. For instance, Sum, Mathews, Pourghasem, and Hughes' (2009) online survey of older people identified Internet use for communication with known others as having positive effects on social relationships, whereas using it to find new people and for entertainment purposes were direct predictors of *less* well-being. The complex nature of computer use effects is also reflected in Torp, Hanson, Hauge, Ulstein, and Magnusson's (2008) Norwegian study, in which informal care-givers of frail elderly people living at home were provided Internet access and training. The caregivers, who were themselves 60-plus, reported extensive use of the Internet as a result of the study, with more social contacts as well as increased support from other caregivers, all of which were particularly valued by the participants and point to beneficial outcomes of the technology's use. However, the quantitative measures employed in the study did not reveal any reduction in caregiver stress as a result of Internet use.

A challenge for research on the social benefits of computer use is parsing out the effects of the social context of computer use. For instance, Karavidas, Lim, and Katsikas (2005) examined the effects of computer use on older members of computer clubs in Florida. They found that computer use was correlated to increased self-efficacy, lower computer anxiety, and to overall life satisfaction. In addition to the use of the technology itself, the authors also pondered the implicit and subtle benefits of social networks on life satisfaction, noting that older adults who belong to computer clubs confer and teach each other computer skills and that this networking may indirectly and positively affect their life satisfaction. Tatnall and Lepa (2003) and Zorn et al. (2010) similarly found that older people's social situations and interaction networks significantly influenced their reactions to a technology. Trocchia and Janda (2000) found, for instance, that older individuals' responses to technology adoption or rejection were guided by the predominant stance of the reference group to which the individual is affiliated. Reference groups with positive attitudes towards technology, such as SeniorNet clubs in which older people teach older people how to use computers and the Internet are examples of this in that members of such organizations act as sources of information and advice, for instance, about good websites to visit, how to deal with Internet security issues, as well as being positive role models, for others (Furlong, 1989; Richardson et al., 2005).

Although the relationship between computer use and its effects is clearly a complex matter, older people themselves are represented by research as perceiving and experiencing the technology as an important enabler of social connectedness. Similarly, as we now turn to discuss, older people perceive computers as additionally beneficial in assisting the retention of an independent lifestyle and, consequently, in enhancing their quality of life.

Functional Independence and Quality of Life

The potential of computers/Internet to help older people operate independently and interact successfully both inside and outside the home has been identified as a key benefit of the technology and potential contributor to quality of life enhancement (Czaja & Lee, 2003). Functional independence can be enabled by computer use in tangible ways, such as giving older people access to information for solving problems (such as health concerns) and in more intangible ways, such as enhancing older people's sense of self-efficacy. There is evidence both for and against the claim that computer use facilitates well-being via functional independence.

Several studies have focused on the tangible ways that computers enable functional independence for older people. While acknowledging that social connection purposes were far more prevalent for elders, Carpenter and Buday (2007) found record keeping and management of finances as valued uses for some elders. Additionally, a number of studies have focused on how computing can assist in bringing senior citizens into closer proximity to a range of material they might well not otherwise access. For example, Vuori and Holmlund-Rytkönen's (2005) survey of Finnish elders found that using the Internet made life easier and more comfortable in that it brought knowledge, information, products and services within easy reach of individuals in a fast and inexpensive way. Importantly, access to such information can support lifestyle changes as Lindsay, Bellaby, Smith, and Baker (2008) found when they introduced coronary heart disease patients to a new computer, a 1-year subscription to broadband, and access to a purpose-built health portal for heart disease. In particular, and as a direct a result of exposure to the health portal, patients reported changing their diet significantly, including eating "bad foods" less often.

Regarding benefits related to self-efficacy, McConatha, McConatha, and Dermigny (1994) examined the effects of interactive computer-based education and training on the rehabilitation of long-term care residents over a six month period. They found that participants experienced increased feelings of control and an overall sense of well-being through their use of computers. Similarly, McMellon and Schiffman (2002) found that older people who became computer literate and used the Internet for activities such as emailing, information searching, and interacting with new people, institutions, and interest groups, experienced increased individual and social empowerment as a consequence of their lives feeling more enriched and their world views expanded. Shapira, Barak, and Gal (2007) found analogous beneficial results of Internet use for a group of adults with a mean age of 80 years old who were trained in computer operation. Those who used the Internet were found to be less depressed and lonely, as well as more satisfied with life, more in control and more pleased with their quality of life than members of a comparison group. Follow-up interviews found that participants felt proud of themselves for learning an innovative technology, they felt updated and "in the know," and experienced positive feelings and an elevated self-image. These perceptions highlight the potential symbolic value of computers for older people, including the ability to view themselves as active participants in the modern world (Blit-Cohen & Litwin, 2004; White & Weatherall, 2000). This is a matter we take up again in the third narrative, *the desirable commodity and grey consumers.*

However, while a number of studies have provided evidence that computer use improves overall quality of life via functional independence, other studies raise questions about this relationship. For instance, Mellor, Firth, and Moore (2008) found negative effects of computer use on self-esteem and several other measures of well-being in their small intervention study in Australia, although participants reported positive experiences in interviews. In one of the most ambitious and rigorous studies on these issues, Slegers, Van Boxtel, and Jolles (2008) adopted a randomized, controlled intervention study to examine the causal relationship between computer use, autonomy, and well-being among Dutch elders. They found that using computers and the Internet had no significant effects on everyday functioning, well-being or mood. Both Mellor et al. (2008) and Slegers et al. (2008) point to methodological issues as at least a partial explanation for the discrepant findings compared to previous studies. Both conclude that some benefits of computer use may not be easily assessed psychometrically. Slegers and colleagues go further, suggesting that previous studies that found benefits differed in important ways from their study. The earlier studies tended to use volunteer participants who may be more motivated to use the Internet; have substantial attrition rates, and thus fail to measure the effects on the participants who dropped out early; often drew participants from care facilities, who may have a different set of needs from healthy, mobile elders; and fail to account for the effects of social contact in intervention groups.

In sum, the results of empirical research are mixed in terms of the beneficial effects of computer and Internet use on older people's quality of life and well-being. It seems likely that some elders do enjoy increased social connectedness and functional independence. However, the effects do not seem to be universal.

In relation to the underpinning narrative of the *enabling machine and isolated elders*, "benefit studies" narrate the positivity of the computer-elder relationship in terms of the perceived potential benefits of computer use for communicating, building social networks, and facilitating caring and supportive relationships, as well as facilitating independent lifestyles. These perceived benefits, as well as concerns that older people have been slow to take up computing (Fox, 2004, 2006; Fox et al., 2001) and the consequent risk they face in being alienated from an increasingly computerized society, have prompted researchers to investigate barriers to elders' computer/Internet use and how they might be overcome, an issue we take up in the second narrative.

Critical Commentary

The technology-related version of the *enabling machine and isolated elders* narrative portrays computers as benign machines enabling often frail and isolated older people to live independent lifestyles and yet remain connected to the wider world. Within this narrative, old age is depicted as a problem in need and capable of being fixed or compensated for by computing. The underpinning plot line here is essentially that of the relationship between an older person-*victim* and the computer as their potential *savior.*

As Östlund (2004) points out, elders are often subjects of other people's ageist, sometimes paternalistic, sometimes patronizing, preconceptions about their needs and capabilities. Such preconceptions can include implicit and generalized assumptions that elders are a homogeneous group who, as a result of failing physical and mental health, endure limited mobility, spend most of their time at home, have few opportunities to socialize, and are in need of constant care. It is from within this framework that old age is constructed as a social problem that lends itself to technology-based solutions (Östlund, 2004). Indeed within the literature that examines the relationship between older people and computers, researchers seem enthusiastic about "the potential of technology to support and change society" (Dickinson & Gregor, 2006, p. 752). Consequently, in their zeal to improve the lives of elders, some researchers even highly romanticize the benefits of computing, portraying it as unique in its ability to bring support, companionship, and a degree of independence and autonomy to older people. The statement by Hough and Kobylanski (2009) that "Clearly, technology can assist in making the golden years truly golden" (p. 39) is a case in point.

Some research studies have indeed served to demonstrate that technology can offer many older people new opportunities for social connectedness that enhance their individual lifestyles. Furthermore, this coupling of technology and older people can constructively challenge and perhaps even help overturn stereotypically negative narratives about older people as feeble and isolated that in turn work to compound their inability to participate in and contribute to society (Cutler, 2005).

However, in portraying the computer as the older person's savior, the *enabling machine and isolated elder* narrative is in danger of presenting an overly optimistic view of computing technology's ability to solve the difficulties that some older people experience in becoming less physically able and consequentially more isolated. In this context, there is also a danger of blaming older people who do not take up the mantle of computing technologies for their own isolation and failure to participate in society when isolation and failure to participate is in part a consequence of social structures that have increasingly hidden old people away rather than facilitated their ongoing involvement and presence in society and in our communities.

To some degree, the depiction of computer as savior is not unique to older people. Rather, it reflects a generalized utopian and hyperbolic view of ICTs (Howcroft, 1999) that assumes that the use of computers by all people, including elders, is highly desirable and produces dramatically improved outcomes. As Henwood et al. argue, "Many 'information society' enthusiasts, both academics and policymakers, claim that the use of ICTs will relieve people of drudgery, improve access to information and entertainment and result in greater social justice" (2000, p. 4). However, while this view is not limited to older people, we would argue that, combined with a view of older people as increasingly feeble and isolated, it takes on added power. Especially noteworthy is how this narrative sits in stark contrast with the multiple ways in which this technology has been critically portrayed in other academic literature (see, for example, Carter & Weaver, 2003, pp. 137–161) most notably in relation to other demographic groups such as children, where the technology has often been seen as having potentially detrimental impacts on their personal safety, well-being, and innocence (e.g., Buckingham, 1997, 2002; Selwyn, 2003).

We would argue that a more moderate representation of the benefits of computer use for older people might be more realistic. Such an approach would tend to focus on identifying ways in which *some* technologies could be usefully deployed to meet *some* needs of *some* older people, as researchers (e.g., Rogers & Fisk, 2006; Fisk & Rogers, 1997) are doing. A more holistic approach would explore not only benefits, but also the risks, pitfalls, and negative consequences that elders might experience and not attribute these to the individual deficiencies of older people. Additionally, such a pragmatic approach might present a more nuanced analysis in which the presumed usefulness of the technology for this group is qualified in terms of particular uses and contexts, along with the acknowledgement that in some situations, technological solutions are unnecessary.

The narrative of *the enabling machine and isolated elders*, while commonly told, is but one story of older people's relationships with computers identified in the literature—albeit the most dominant. We now turn to another body of empirical work that contributes to the second master narrative we identified in the literature, that of *the potential divider and marginalized seniors.*

The Potential Divider and Marginalized Seniors

The second master narrative, *the potential divider and marginalized seniors*, brings together what we define as *gap* and *barrier* studies. Gap studies draw attention to the gap between the number of older people who use the Internet compared with the number of younger people, as well as the gap *within* the old age category itself, for example, between the young-old and the old-old in terms of their Internet use. Barrier studies attempt to explain this gap, particularly in terms of psychological factors, and they tend to identify ways in which such barriers might be addressed. This narrative emerges from two primary concerns: first, that non-use of a technology pervasive throughout society has the potential to marginalize those who cannot or do not use it leaving them without the resources to access information and services increasingly delivered via the Internet; and second, that old age should not be a barrier to participation in society.

This master narrative is one constructed predominantly in response to national government and international policy concerns with matters related to social inclusion. In its original manifestation this master narrative revolved round the issue of *the digital divide* and associated rhetoric which positioned those on the wrong side of the digital divide as at risk of social exclusion (e.g., Norris, 2001; Phipps, 2000). This applied to contexts of, for example, employment, use of e-government services and representation, as well as the emerging online public sphere.

The notion of the digital divide has been heavily critiqued for its simplistic technological determinism and binary absolutism (Ganesh & Barber, 2009). Yet, conceptually it has been commonly employed to categorize groups in society according to their use/non-use of computers and the Internet and, therefore, their social status (Murdock, 2002; Selwyn, 2004a). The *potential divider and marginalized seniors* master narrative is, therefore, embedded in macro social, political, and economic contexts and offers a story in which a successful narrative resolution is one in which not only the individual computer user, but society as a collective and in its many manifestations (e.g., families, employers, health providers, government, businesses, and media) benefit from everybody's participation in the world of computers and the Internet. At this point it would be negligent not to also note that all nations' levels of Internet connectivity are measured for the purposes of OECD rankings, and that such rankings impact on levels of investment that countries are able to attract (Ganesh & Zorn, in press). This is then a master narrative that at least *portrays* the national collective gains of computing/Internet use as high on the political agenda.

Synthesis of the Literature

Our review of studies in relation to this narrative is organized over two sections. We begin with reports of the existence of a grey gap between older people's and younger people's take-up and use of the Internet, followed by research that has identified differences in Internet use within the older age category itself, including between the young-old and the old-old, older men and older women, and older adults with more or less education. Next, we review studies that have identified barriers to technology take-up, particularly in terms of attitudes and the key ways these barriers might be addressed.

The Grey Gap. Research has consistently pointed to age as an important variable in determining access to and use of the Internet, with such use declining significantly in the older age groups (e.g., Fox, 2004, 2006; Fox et al., 2001; Lenhart, 2003; Lenhart, Rainie, Fox, Horrigan, & Spooner, 2000; Smith et al., 2010; Statistics New Zealand, 2004). Fox (2006), for instance, found that a significantly lower percentage of older Americans go online compared with those in the younger age groups—34% over the age of 65 compared with 89% of 18- to 28-year-olds, 86% of 29- to 40-year-olds, 78% of 41- to 50-year-olds, 72% of 51- to 59-year-olds, and 54% 60- to 69-year-olds. A survey conducted in New Zealand at a similar point in time (Statistics New Zealand, 2004) also found disproportionately lower levels of Internet use among the older age population. The New Zealand survey found that households with at least one occupant aged over 65 were the least likely to have access to the Internet (17%) compared with households in which at least one person was aged between 45–54 years (63%) who were the most likely to have access to the Internet.

Ongoing survey research, particularly in the United States, indicates that while younger people remain the dominant group on the Internet (Jones & Fox, 2009), greater numbers of older people are going online. For example, Jones and Fox (2009) point out that one of the fastest growing segments of the U.S. Internet population is 70- to 75-year-olds with 45% of this age group currently going online compared with 25% in 2005. Fox (2006), however, cautions that much of the recent growth in Internet numbers among the older age groups has come, not from older non-users suddenly going online, but from long-term users of the Internet aging and moving into this older age category. It is therefore important to recognize that while differences remain in terms of older people's and younger people's adaptation to new technologies—the so-called generational digital divide (Negroponte, 1995; Norris, 2001; Tapscott, 1998)—significant differences also exist *within* the older age category itself in terms of experiences with and uses of the Internet, a matter we turn to now.

Inside the Grey Gap. Research has identified differences in adoption of the Internet among subgroups of the older age category, particularly in terms of three socio-demographic factors: age, gender, and education. Age-related differences in Internet use have been observed, for instance, in relation to the young-old and the old-old. For instance, Rideout's (2005) telephone survey of adults over 50 years of age in the United States found that 70% of 50- to 64-year-olds had gone online at some stage to use the Internet or send emails compared with 31% of seniors over 65 years of age. He also found that individuals aged 75 years and over were much less likely to have ever gone online than were their younger age peers, aged 65–74 (18% compared to 41%). Rideout also found that seniors in the 50–64 years of age category used the Internet as a source for health-related information more than they used TV or books for this purpose, whereas those over 65 were much less inclined to consult or trust the Internet for this same purpose. Similar age-based patterns in Internet behavior were observed by Fox (2004) who found that 50- to 58-year-olds (Baby Boomers) were more like 28- to 39-year-olds (Generation X) in their use of the Internet than they were like 59- to 68-year-olds (Mature). Specifically, this research found that 75% of Generation X Internet users and 75% of Baby Boomer Internet users get news online, compared to 67% of Mature Internet users, and that 59% of Generation X Internet users and 55% of Baby Boomer Internet users conduct research online for their jobs compared to 30% of Mature Internet users.

In the studies described above, chronological age is used as a marker of difference between Internet users. However, it is important to recognize that that there is also likely to be a cohort effect due to differential experience with computers among the age groups studied. For example, Baby Boomers are more likely to have used computers at work than older cohorts. Research shows that at least some of the identified differences between age groups may be attributable to experience or familiarity with the technology (e.g., Jay & Willis, 1992; Lagana, 2008). Similarly, differential experience may result, for example, from receiving higher educational qualifications (e.g., Carpenter & Buday, 2007) and the exposure to new technologies that this education brings. This suggests that chronological age alone is insufficient to explain use or non-use of the Internet and other factors are likely to be key facilitators and impediments.

Gender is a second potentially distinguishing characteristic of older Internet users. Rideout (2005), for example, found that men were more likely to have gone online than women (38% compared with 25%). While Fox (2004) found that women were as likely as men to be *wired seniors*, that is, to have used the Internet. Karavidas et al. (2005), on the other hand, found gender differences in computer knowledge and use between older men and older women in their study of participants recruited from computer clubs in Florida. In particular, the authors identified female respondents as not enjoying the same level of comfort with computers nor the same knowledge about them as male respondents, even though both groups used computers at the same rate.

Rosenthal (2008) also found women's lack of self-confidence as a significant obstacle in their learning how to use the Internet.

It is perhaps valuable to explore such expressions of self-confidence, or its absence, in relation to socially constructed gendered expectations. This is demonstrated through Richardson et al.'s. (2005) research of older computer users in three SeniorNet clubs in New Zealand in which the authors found similarities and differences in the ways in which men and women articulated their computer-related experiences. Specifically, both older men and women expressed initial emotional discomfort in learning how to use computers. However, women were more inclined to openly express this in terms of a *fear* of the technology, while men tended to express *frustration* with the technology and a determination to master it. Arguably, such research highlights the need for more nuanced and contextualized appreciation of older Internet users than is currently provided by user surveys.

Education is a third factor identified as significant in whether or not older people use the Internet. Rideout (2005), for example, found that seniors with only, or less than, a high school education were much less likely to have ever gone online than were seniors with a college degree (18% compared with 60%). Other studies (e.g., Ahn, Beamish, & Goss, 2008; Carpenter & Buday, 2007; Karavidas et al., 2005) have also found that seniors with higher levels of education were more comfortable with and more knowledgeable about computing than those with less education.

Research that has plotted Internet usage and the characteristics of Internet users has thus identified a gap between older and younger Internet users, as well as within-group differences in age, gender, and education in adapting to new technologies like the Internet. But knowing that fewer older people than younger people use the Internet is not enough. It has also been important to understand *why* such a gap exists. In the next section we review research that has attempted to explain why older adults, for whom some would argue (e.g., Charness & Holley, 2004; Norris, 2001) the Internet seems well suited because it offers the potential to reduce social isolation, enhance functional independence, and increase quality of life (as discussed in the first narrative) are less likely than other demographic groups to avail themselves of it. For these explanations we turn to what we term "barrier studies."

Barriers to Computer Use. Barrier studies can be grouped into two broad categories: (a) those focused on attitudes, perceptions of need and usefulness, concerns about the technology's potential negative effects, and computer-related anxiety; and (b) those focused on abilities, including the effects of age-related changes in physical and mental ability on technology use.

Attitude studies include the attitude of others towards older people's use of computers. Ryan, Szecthman, and Bodkin (1992), for instance, found that the negative biases of others towards older people's engagement with computers were likely to limit elders' opportunities and inclinations to take-up such activities. In addition, studies have shown that elders' own attitudes to the technology are likely to influence their responses to it. For instance, positive attitudes towards computers have often been associated with computer use and negative attitudes with non-use, although this relationship is by no means a simple one. For instance, White and Weatherall's (2000) interview-based study with SeniorNet members in New Zealand found that participants' positive attitudes towards computers and their views on its perceived usefulness were key influences in decisions to become involved with computers. Czaja et al. (1993) also found that perceptions of usefulness were important factors in predicting computer use among their sample of older women trialing an electronic text messaging system.

On the other hand, having no interest in or need for the technology, while a common predictor of non-use (e.g., Selwyn, Gorard, Furlong, & Madden, 2003) can also be indicative of a less straight forward relationship. For instance, Millward's (2003) study with older people in the U.K. found lack of interest as a key reason for not using the Internet. But in-depth interviews with participants led Millward to conclude that showing a lack of interest in the technology was a defensive substitute for the real reason that participants did not use the Internet–that is, they did not know how to use it. This finding suggests that attitudes towards computers may be quite complex; a finding reiterated in other studies. For instance, Selwyn's (2004b) U.K.-based interview study with adults over 65 years of age found that non-users held simultaneously positive and negative views of computers and the Internet. On the one hand, they acknowledged the *miraculous* nature of the technology. On the other hand, they struggled to find a useful or pleasurable place for the computer in their lives, either as a tool or a hobby. Weaver et al.'s (2010) study with older non-users in New Zealand also found that participants recognized the potential usefulness of computers for older people, but rejected personal use of computers themselves, indicating a complex relationship between perceptions of usefulness and decisions to actually take-up and use the technology.

A second factor impacting older people's decisions to use or not use computers and the Internet is concerns about potential negative consequences of that use. Commonly identified concerns include feelings of vulnerability and insecurity in terms of exposure to viruses, worms, and junk mail, and concerns about privacy (Carpenter & Buday, 2007; Richardson et al., 2005; Vuori & Holmlund-Rytkönen, 2005). Lenhart et al. (2000) found that 54% of the surveyed sample of older people not online considered the Internet to be a dangerous thing. In addition, Rideout (2005) found that trust was an issue in relation to Internet-sourced information. He found, for example, that 46% of seniors surveyed did not trust the Internet "at all" to provide accurate information about important health issues. Vuori and Holmlund-Rytkönen's (2005) study in Finland found a fear of becoming addicted to the Internet as a concern that worked to discourage use. Meanwhile, McMellon and Schiffman's (2002) research conducted in the United States and Richardson et al.'s (2005) study conducted in New Zealand both found senior Internet users as experiencing feelings of guilt in relation to how much time they spent on the Internet to the detriment of activities and interactions with others in the offline world.

A third factor impacting older people's use of computers and the Internet is computer-related anxiety and low levels of confidence in their ability to use the technology (Marquié, Jourdan-Boddaert, & Huet, 2002). Studies of computer-related anxiety have found that older adults with higher levels of computer anxiety express less interest in the technology (Ellis & Allaire, 1999), in learning to use the technology (Temple & Gavillet, 1990), and in actually using the technology (Czaja et al., 2006). However, studies also show that anxiety levels among older learners diminish over time and their confidence with the technology and their use of it increases provided their experiences with it are positive (e.g., Cody et al., 1999; Jay & Willis, 1992; Lagana, 2008; Morris, 1994).

Research identifies that one of the major ways in which computer-related anxiety diminishes and confidence with computers increases is through training programs that attend not only to teaching computer skills and knowledge but also to supporting learners and creating relaxed learning environments. For instance, Jay and Willis's (1992) study using an experimental design found that computer comfort and efficacy increased as a result of supportive training structured to encourage success in operating the computer. Other studies conducted by Irizarry, Downing, and Elford (1997), Lagana (2008), and Temple and Gavillet (1990) have found that effective methods for teaching older adult computer learners include small classes, individualized help, slow-paced presentations and using instructors from same age cohort.

Research also points to the importance of interface design in reducing computer-related anxiety based on perceptions that the technology is too complicated to use (e.g., Charness & Holley, 2004). Carpenter and Buday's (2007) research with residents in a naturally occurring retirement community in the United States, for instance, found that one of the most common reasons participants gave for underutilization of computers is their perceived complexity. This finding suggests the need to make computers more *age-friendly* by designing the technology to place minimal demands on working memory and using navigational aids to support the user (Czaja et al., 2006). Indeed this is a focus of the specialist field of "human factors research" which is increasingly developing research-based guidelines for technology design in relation to older users (see, e.g., Fisk & Rogers, 1997; Rogers & Fisk, 2006).

In relation to the underpinning narrative of the *potential divider and marginalized seniors,* "gap and barrier" studies narrate the gap between younger and older people in terms of Internet use and the challenges of the computer-elder relationship in terms of fear and anxiety and the potential risk of social isolation.

Critical Commentary

The *potential divider and marginalized seniors* narrative, drawing on the discourse of the digital divide, portrays older people who do not have access to computers and the Internet and/or the skills to use this technology as potentially at risk in modern society. Research does indeed show age as a significant factor in predicting computer and Internet use and, because computer use across the age groups decreases with increasing age, there is a clear gap between older and younger people in terms of the technology's use. What remains far from clear, however, is the extent to which those seniors who do not use computers and the Internet are actually socially disadvantaged by this.

Indeed, researchers such as Loges and Jung (2001) and Selwyn et al. (2003), have questioned the framing of older people's non-use of computers as problematic. Loges and Jung (2001) argue that the "presumption that seniors who do not gain Internet access are [thereby] deprived of a resource for enhancing their lives" (p. 536) is inconsistent with the way many older people live their lives. In a similar vein, Selwyn et al. (2003) argued that "The government and others must accept that, in its present forms, ICT is not universally attractive to, or universally needed by, older adults … and it is folly to expect universal take-up by older adults" (p. 579). Indeed, not using computers, Selwyn and Gorard (2008) and others (e.g., Hill, Beynon-Davies, & Williams, 2008) argue, is a sensible and pragmatic decision by those for whom the technology is simply not relevant. It may even be, as Weaver et al. (2010) state, an act of empowerment, "a self-conscious and active decision not to act upon a social narrative that presents computers and computing as adding value to how their lives can be lived" (p. 713).

If, in fact, it is arguable whether the use of computers is a "crucial prerequisite to living in the Information Society" (Selwyn & Gorard, 2008, p. 27), then the universality of the *potential divider and marginalized seniors* narrative is questionable. This suggests that research is needed that explicitly focuses on whether older people who do not use computers are missing out on opportunities for social inclusion and involvement, or whether they have other avenues through which they participate in civil society and culture. Indeed, whether their non-use of computers translates *at all* into social disadvantage is an important area for future research.

The Desirable Commodity and Grey Consumers

A third master narrative of older people and computers identified from the literature is one in which older people are constructed as *grey consumers*—as members of a large and growing market segment whose discretionary income and leisure time positions them as lucrative potential targets for selling computer hardware, software and online products and services. This narrative is produced out of mostly marketing-oriented research conducted in relation to older people as consumers and technology. The studies that make up this literature are primarily concerned with identifying, differentiating, and strategizing how to encourage the market segment of older people that they should buy computer-related products, Internet connections, and/or participate in online shopping activity.

This is a master narrative that, like the two discussed above, would come to a successful conclusion with older people becoming active and confident computer users. Yet within this master narrative, it is older people's willing identification as *consumers* of computing technology and online offerings that is of prime importance to the narrative closure, and the ability to have older people think that the act of participating in the purchasing and use of technology will invigorate their self-perceptions and others' perceptions of them.

Synthesis of the Literature

Our review of studies in relation to this narrative is organized over two sections: first, we background aspects of a consumer-based society that contribute to the construction of computers as *desirable commodities,* and then outline three key ways in which they are portrayed as such in relation to older people; second, we review how the scholarly research literature has engaged with the issue of older people as a potential market for computer and associated technology and online products. We close with a critical commentary on this literature.

The phenomenon of consumer culture is about "living in a society in which the mass production, marketing and consumption of goods on a global scale are the fundamental economic imperatives of everyday life" (Hepworth 1996, p. 19). Within such a culture, consumption is not just concerned with the production, distribution, and acquisition of commodities, but is also a process in which meanings are produced and consumed, and identities expressed and displayed (Mackay, 1995) in relation to a particular system of values (Baudrillard, 2001). Consumer goods in such a system are particularly significant for what they represent, that is, for their symbolic connotations (Haddon, 2000; Mackay, 1997; Morley, 2003). Consumer items are thus containers of meaning, expressions of personal style and taste, as well as signs of affluence (Baudrillard, 2001). They can be read, according to Blaikie (1999), as positional goods, for example, as ways of defining social identity and differentiating members of one social group from another.

We would suggest that computers, in the narrative of the *desirable commodity and grey consumers*, can be read as positional goods that confer three meanings in particular on older people—that is, opportunities to demonstrate *being modern, being young,* and *being competent*. These meanings are important in that they highlight the transformative potential of computers for older people's *identities*, particularly the opportunity to avoid appearing old and declining, and to conform to a more acceptable public image: that of appearing up-to-date and "near-young" (Westerhof & Tulle, 2007).

Older people in several studies have reported that using computers and the Internet is a way to feel that they are *being modern* and participating in the modern world (Blit-Cohen & Litwin, 2004; McMellon & Schiffman, 2002; White & Weatherall, 2000), and keeping up to date and not being left behind (Richardson et al. 2005). Indeed, Richardson et al.'s (2005) New Zealand study of older computer users identifies this feeling of "keeping up" as important because it is associated with having control over and being actively involved in one's environment as well as contributing to an enhanced self-image and self-confidence through perceptions of self-relevance. Somewhat similarly, from their study of older adults who participated in a computer training course in Israel, Shapira et al. (2007) concluded that "Browsing the Internet contributed to feelings of being constantly 'in' and updated, which elevated a personal sense of belonging" (p. 482). This desire to keep up was also reflected in Blit-Cohen and Litwin's (2004) finding that older computer users tended to be future-oriented and welcoming of new challenges while their non-computer using peers tended to dwell on the past and be less willing to engage in new opportunities. Adding strength to such research findings, Rosenthal (2008) found that a large majority (81%) of a group of older women learning to use the computer cited "the desire to keep up with the rest of the world" (p. 614) as a central motivating factor.

In terms of *being young*, while technology is typically developed by younger people for the use of younger people and marketed at younger age groups (Kemper & Lacal, 2004), some older people have reported that going online has provided them a sense of a new lease on life (e.g., Richardson et al., 2005) as well as the opportunity to be seen on an equal footing with younger generations (e.g., Treguer, 2002). Participants in McMellon and Schiffman's (2002) study in the United States considered that being online kept their minds active and young, while participants in Shapira et al.'s (2007) study perceived that learning how to use the Internet, an activity associated with young people, made them feel proud of themselves, and gave them "perhaps even a glimmer of returned youth" (p. 482). Whatever the cause, there is evidence to suggest that older people who take up computing and Internet use are often enthusiastic users of the technology (Fox, 2004; OCLC Report, 2007) and, most importantly, their use of this technology often seems to make a difference in terms of their positivity about life (Chen & Persson, 2002).

In terms of *being competent*, research has found that learning to use computers can serve to demonstrate to older people themselves as well as to others that older people are still mentally capable of engaging with a new and complex innovation. Ryan and colleagues (1992), for example, found in a study conducted in Ontario, Canada, that older adults who engaged in computer activities were considered by young adults to be atypical for their age and more competent than their younger non-computer using age peers. The authors concluded that older adults could overcome general negative expectations for competence by choosing to use computers. It is worthy of note that, whereas computers in the *enabling machine and isolated elders* master narrative were identified as beneficial for individuals, including because they provided older people with enhanced functional capacity, Ryan et al.'s finding points to computers as conferring upon older people a *status* that marks them as positively different from and more competent than non-computer using same-age peers in that they demonstrate the ability to keep up with social change. The marketing research indicates that marketers are clearly aware of the symbolic status that computer use can confer on users and have investigated opportunities for promoting the technology to older consumers. Hough and Kobylanski's (2009) research conducted in the United States, for example, found that value-expressive reference group affiliation, such as using the Internet as a means of conveying a young and hip self-image, is an avenue which marketers can fruitfully exploit to promote computers/the Internet to the grey market.

Market-related research into older people and computers has focused primarily on the motivational and attitudinal characteristics of this older group and ways to market to them. A number of studies have focused on factors that would make elders more likely to engage in Internet shopping. For example, Iyer and Eastman's (2006) large survey of elders in the United States found that those who have a more positive attitude about the Internet, are confident in their ability to use the Internet, are comfortable using the Internet, and are experienced in using computers are more likely to engage in online shopping. Reisenwitz, Iyer, Kuhlmeier, and Eastman (2007) found that seniors who were more prone to nostalgia were less likely to engage in online shopping; the implications identified were that marketers needed to focus on elders' need for nostalgia in their promotion of Internet-based goods and services, such as buying vintage products and looking up past acquaintances. The same study also found that seniors who had more Internet experience were less risk averse and purchased more online, with the lesson being that getting seniors to use the Internet more will gradually reduce their risk aversion and increase online consumption. Interestingly, Eastman and Iyer's (2004) U.S. study found that more educated seniors were less willing to shop online. The authors speculated that this may be because more educated seniors were more likely to be aware of possible security and safety risks on the Internet than were less well educated users, and this awareness may have discouraged buying online.

Beyond identifying factors that might facilitate older people's online shopping, marketing research has also focused on factors that facilitate the use of computers more generally. While similar to the research differentiating users from nonusers in the *potential divider and marginalized seniors* narrative, the focus in this research is on identifying leverage points for marketers to use in selling computer products and services. For example, Trocchia and Janda's (2000) interview-based study with older computer users and nonusers attempted to identify motivational and attitudinal characteristics that differentiated the two groups and identify opportunities for marketing the Internet to seniors. They found the increased likelihood of experiencing mobility problems and the desire for enhanced social relations among some older users as characteristics that marketers could exploit. Similarly, Hough and Kobylanski (2009) applied the "four Ps" of marketing (product, price, place, and promotion) to identify the most effective marketing methods for influencing grey consumers to engage with computers. Drawing from Trocchia and Janda's (2000) findings and other recent research, they concluded that product was the most important of the four Ps; specifically, marketing designed to emphasize the computer's ease of use, and benefits for social connection were most likely to be effective. Finally, Eastman and Iyer (2004) found that having convenient training sites, past experience with the Internet, and higher income and education all make Internet use more likely. This suggests that among the more important leverage points for marketers are making Internet introduction and training convenient and inexpensive.

Critical Commentary

The literature that combines to create the *desirable commodity and grey consumers* master narrative depicts the grey market as increasingly significant to marketing and wider corporate business interests. The sale of products such as computers and Internet access to this group involves not only persuading older people of the technology's instrumental value, but even more significantly, of its symbolic value—its desirability. For example, marketing research points to the opportunity for older computer users to be socially perceived as younger than their non-computer using peers, as modern and up-to-date, and as capable and competent. Yet, very evident in how the marketing field imagines older people might be interpellated as consumers of computing hardware, software, and online products and services is the advocating of the exploitation of ageist discourses and tactics. That is, research encourages marketers to persuade older people that they can avoid being perceived as the age that they really are if only they participated in the consumption of new technologies. In these terms, old age is represented in this narrative as a spent force and not a time of life that anyone would willingly want to experience and positively identify with.

Within the *desirable commodity and grey consumers* master narrative, being near-young is a condition that can seemingly be achieved through the transformative potential of computers, which enable older people to be—and to be seen to be—keeping up with changes in the modern world. There are definite benefits in keeping up as evidenced by the enthusiasm conveyed by many computer users (e.g., Fox, 2004; OCLC Report, 2007). However, there are also downsides, in that, older people are encouraged to perceive their aging negatively and symbolic consumption as a means of "holding back the years." A more positively constructive marketing approach might be one that supports older people to regard and value themselves as autonomous individuals making independent choices about how they will age and how they will invest their time and energy, as well as their dollars.

Directions for Future Research

The studies identified above contribute to knowledge about older people's relationships with computers in important ways, particularly in terms of highlighting the benefits of computer use for members of this demographic group and the ways in which barriers to their learning and using the technology might be overcome. Limitations and gaps in this literature, however, provide significant opportunities for future research. It is to these areas we now turn using the narrative approach as a framework for the discussion.

Narrative and Sensemaking

In employing a narrative framework, we drew on a research tradition that seeks to understand how people make sense of social life. One goal of our project has been to demonstrate the utility of a narrative framework for shedding light on the assumptions and meaning-making process of researchers and others as we explore older people's uses of computers.

Relatively little attention has been paid to the sense-making processes in which older people engage in relation to new technologies, such as computers, the Internet, and other communication devices, like mobile phones. There are exceptions, but even these tend to be focused on how to exploit older people for marketing purposes (e.g., Hough & Kobylanski, 2009; Trocchia & Janda, 2000). Communication scholars, with their tradition of focusing on meaning-making, would seem to be in a particularly good position to ask questions such as: What narratives do older people draw on in making sense of computers? How do they test and negotiate the appropriateness of the selected narratives? Indeed, what narratives do they reject and why? What are the similarities and differences between different age groups, different ethnic and cultural orientations, and different genders in this sense-making process? What contributes to these differences and similarities? While some research has begun to tease out such narratives (Weaver et al., 2010), much more work remains to be done.

Alternative Stories of Aging and Technology

There are similarities and also differences in the storylines of the three master narratives that we identified in the literature. The similarities include consistent referencing of the master narrative of deficit and decline to inform the characterization of the older person, and the master narrative of the transformative potential of technology to inform the representation of the computer. The latter elevates the computer to a savior role, while the former reduces the older person to a limited and very often needy role. The differences include variation in tone from optimistic and zealous, to questioning, to potentially exploitative.

In relation to the depiction of the computer in these narratives, the studies reviewed here have tended to present the technology as pivotal in the modern world—as a "panacea for everyday problems" and a "cause of human wellbeing" (Smith, 1994, p. 23), and a source of salvation for many older people (Glanz, 1997). An underpinning story, or theory, is that of technological determinism—of technology as an undeniable and unstoppable force acting on society in predictable, inevitable ways (e.g., Bromley, 1997; Heilbroner, 1994; Henwood et al., 2000). The power of this story is such that it is not seen as a story, but as a fact, and attention is concentrated on how to help older people adapt to technology.

Technological determinism and the presumed positivity of the elder-computer relationship highlights the lack of critically oriented research on older people and computers, and the lack of attention paid to possible negative consequences of computers for older people (Kim, 2008; Weaver et al., 2010). While some researchers (e.g., Dickinson & Gregor, 2006; Loges & Jung, 2001; Östlund, 2004; Selwyn, 2004b; Selwyn et al., 2003) have critiqued the overly optimistic claims of computer benefits, the critical voice has remained relatively silent. There is a need to understand why this should be the case and whose needs are being served and/or not being served by this apparent silence. If, as Fox (2006) indicates, there is evidence to suggest that older people are relatively innocent users of the Internet and less inclined than younger people to take precautions against, for example, software fraud, then it is necessary to point out that there are potentially negative consequences of this technology for older people and they need to be aware of this and educated in how to protect themselves against such practices.

Thus, researchers should be encouraged to draw on alternative narratives in investigating the elder-computer relationship, and we would urge that both critical and creative approaches be brought to the fore.

Intersectionality and Within-Group Differences

The studies reviewed in this chapter have very frequently represented older people in essentialized, simplistic, even stereotypical ways (Hazan, 2000). For example, they are invariably and only, old. They were rarely seen in other ways, for example, as experienced, interesting, creative, resourceful, and "ageful" individuals (Andrews, 1999; Westerhof & Tulle, 2007). They were also only rarely studied in terms of within-group differences, for example, as different from each other as a result of class, culture, ethnicity, gender, circumstance, or life course experience and how these differences might intersect to produce more complex and tension-filled stories, along with a greater range of computer-related experiences and identities. Instead, in these largely unidimensional storylines, older people were presented as a broadly homogeneous group of aging bodies marked (or marred) similarly by the aging process.

Such a view is limited and partial and presents opportunities as well as challenges for future research. Specifically, it highlights the need to appreciate diversity, including in terms of the individuality and uniqueness of older adults' experiences across the life course, as well as in relation to their roles as members of ethnic and cultural communities, and the ways in which their socialization, class, education, and gender might contribute to their experiences of aging and their responses to new technologies. This suggests a need for researchers to go beyond convenience samples of elders in seniors-only computer clubs, retirement villages, and assisted-living facilities, and seek out the experiences of elders in a wider range of locations, settings, and roles, in order to learn about the influences of these situations on their experiences, perceptions, and worldviews. Our recent study of older people who were also Maori and Mormon provides an example of how research might investigate intersectionality and dimensions such as religion and ethnicity alongside age as influences on attitudes and experiences with computers (Zorn et al., 2010).

Longitudinal Studies Reflecting Individual and Societal Changes

It should not be controversial to suggest that studying the computer use and attitudes of 65-year-olds in 2011 is quite different from doing the same research 10 years earlier. There are obvious cohort differences: The 2011 group members were in their 30s when personal computers were introduced and in their 40s when the Internet first attained popular use, and thus much more likely to have worked with computers. There are also obvious differences in the cultural context; that is, there have been substantial changes in the degree to which computers and the Internet are becoming an integral part of the social fabric globally in the past 10 years (e.g., consider the accessibility of broadband and mobile Internet devices and the prominence of online banking). As these examples show, the social context of the elder-computer interaction is dynamic and evolving.

Furthermore, individuals' responses to technology change with experience. For example, Kraut and colleagues (1998) published two studies that garnered a great deal of attention, with the first showing negative effects of Internet use on social involvement and psychological well-being, and the second showing that 3 years later these negative effects had dissipated (Kraut et al., 2002). Less well known but closer to our focus is a study by Mellor et al. (2008), which found older people's responses to Internet use evolved over a 12-month period with measures of self-esteem, well-being, and social connectedness showing ups and downs over the period, and for those who remained with the project (8 out of 20 participants), self-esteem increased slightly while perceptions of social connectedness did not increase at all. Snapshot studies of older people's experiences with computers have their place, but it is critically important for researchers to go beyond these designs and make longitudinal, contextualized assessments. Of particular interest to communication scholars are how patterns of interaction evolve as technologies change and elders gain experience with those technologies.

Conclusion

In this chapter, studies of older people's relationships with computers have been reviewed over a period of two decades. The presumed beneficial effects of computers have remained constant over time. There are, however, clear limitations in this portrayal in that older people are predominantly presented as aging bodies in need of technological assistance or, alternatively, as members of a growing aging population with the presumed time and monetary resources to spend on leisure activities, such as surfing the Web. These largely optimistic accounts overlook possible negative consequences of technology use in favor of ideological positions that associate computers with positive aging outcomes, including social connectedness and functional independence. The need to problematize this one-sided, positive rendering of the elder-computer relationship is pressing, as is the need to investigate multiple possible ways in which older people, in a range of different circumstances and settings, make sense of new technologies and choose, or not, to incorporate them into their everyday lives. Social constructionist approaches, including narrative approaches such as the one we have used here, offer alternatives to instrumental perspectives and open up opportunities for conversing about a subject that has been largely closed down by voices in support of prevailing notions regarding technology and positive aging. Such approaches are likely to enrich our understanding, add more color, and greater levels of variation and complexity to the often overly simplistic storying of this relationship currently available.

Acknowledgments

The research was partially funded by the New Zealand Foundation for Research Science and Technology, contract number UOWX0306. We thank our Department of Management Communication Research Syndicate members Shiv Ganesh, Debashish Munshi, and Mary Simpson for their valuable comments on an earlier version of this chapter.

Notes

1. It is important to note that, since the 1990s, literature on computer use has consistently been conflated with Internet use. Given this trend and studies showing computers are used primarily for Internet-based communication, we often refer for simplicity's sake to *computer use* but intend that to include Internet use.

References

Ahn, M., Beamish, J. O., & Goss, R. C. (2008). Understanding older adults' attitudes and adoption of residential technologies. *Family and Consumer Sciences Research Journal, 36*(3), 243–260.

Alvesson, M., & Deetz, S. (2000). *Doing critical management research*. London: Sage.

Andrews, M. (1999). The seductiveness of agelessness. *Ageing & Society, 19*, 301–318.

Baudrillard, J. (2001). *Selected writings*. Edited and introduced by Mark Poster. Cambridge, UK: Polity Press.

Blaikie, A. (1999). *Ageing and popular culture*. Cambridge, UK: Cambridge University Press.

Blit-Cohen, E., & Litwin, H. (2004). Elder participation in cyberspace: A qualitative analysis of Israeli retirees. *Journal of Aging Studies, 18*, 385–398.

Bromley, H. (1997). The social chicken and the technological egg: Educational computing and the technology/society divide. *Educational Theory, 47*(1), 51–65.

Bruner, J. (1990). *Acts of meaning*. Cambridge, MA: Harvard University Press.

Buckingham, D. (1997). Electronic child abuse? Rethinking the media's effects on children. In M. Barker & J. Petley (Eds.), *Ill effects: The media/violence debate* (2nd ed., pp. 63–77). London: Routledge.

Buckingham, D. (2002). The electronic generation? Children and new media. In L. A. Lievrouw & S. Livingstone (Eds.), *Handbook of new media: Social shaping and consequences of ICTs* (pp. 77–89). London: Sage.

Carpenter, B. D., & Buday, S. (2007). Computer use among older adults in a naturally occurring retirement community. *Computers in Human Behavior, 23*, 3012–3024.

Carter, C., & Weaver, C. K. (2003). *Violence and the media*. Buckingham, UK: Open University Press.

Charness, N., & Holley, P. (2004). The new media and older adults: Usable and useful? *American Behavioral Scientist, 48*(4), 416–433.

Chen, Y., & Persson, A. (2002). Internet use among young and older adults: Relation to psychological well-being. *Educational Gerontology, 28*, 731–744.

Cody, M. J., Dunn, D., Hoppin, S., & Wendt, P. (1999). Silver surfers: Training and evaluating Internet use among older adult learners. *Communication Education, 48*, 269–286.

Coupland, J. (2003). Ageist ideology and discourses of control in skincare product marketing. In J. Coupland & R. Gwyn (Eds.), *Discourse, the body, and identity* (pp. 127–150). New York, NY: Palgrave MacMillan.

Coupland, N. (2004). Age in social and sociolinguistic theory. In J. F. Nussbaum & J. Coupland (Eds.), *Handbook of communication and aging research* (pp. 69–90). Mahwah, NJ: Erlbaum.

Cutler, S. J. (2005). Ageism and technology. *Generations, 29*(3), 67–72.

Czaja, S. J., Charness, N., Fisk, A. D., Hertzog, C., Nair, S. N., Rogers, W. A., & Sharit, J. (2006). Factors predicting the use of technology: Findings from the Center for Research and Education on Aging and Technology Enhancement (CREATE). *Psychology and Aging, 21*(2), 333–352.

Czaja, S. J., Guerrier, J. H., Nair, S. N., & Landauer, T. K. (1993). Computer communication as an aid to independence for older adults. *Behaviour & Information Technology, 12*(4), 197–207.

Czaja, S. J., & Lee, C. C. (2003). The impact of the internet on older adults. In N. Charness & K. W. Schaie (Eds.), *Impact of technology on successful aging* (pp. 113–133). New York: Springer.

Dickinson, A., & Gregor, P. (2006). Computer use has no demonstrated impact on the well-being of older adults. *Human-Computer Studies, 64*, 744–753.

Eastman, J. K., & Iyer, R. (2004). The elderly's uses and attitudes towards the Internet. *Journal of Marketing, 21*(3), 208–220.

Ellis, R. D., & Allaire, J. C. (1999). Modeling computer interest in older adults: The role of age, education, computer knowledge, and computer anxiety. *Human Factors, 41*(3), 345–355.

Fisher, W. R. (1984). Narration as a human communication paradigm. *Communication Monographs 51*, 1–22.

Fisher, W. R. (1985). The narrative paradigm. *Communication Monographs 52*, 347–367.

Fisk, A. D., & Rogers, W. A. (Eds.). (1997). *Handbook of human factors and the older adult*. San Diego, CA: Academic Press.

Fox, S. (2004) *Older Americans and the Internet*. [Online]. Retrieved February 12, 2006, from http://www.pewInternet.org/

Fox, S. (2006). *Data memo: Are 'wired seniors' sitting ducks*? Pew Internet & American Life Project. Retrieved March 18, 2010, from www.pewInternet.org/~/media//Files/Reports/2006/PIP_Wired_Senior_2006_Memo.pdf.pdf

Fox, S., Rainie, L., Larsen, E., Horrigan, J., Lenhart, A., Spooner, T., & Carter, C. (2001). *Wired seniors: A fervent few, inspired by family ties.* [Online]. Retrieved February 12, 2006, from http://www.pewInternet.org/pdfs/PIP_Wired_Seniors_Report.pdf

Fulford, R. (1999). *The triumph of narrative: Storytelling in the age of mass culture.* Toronto, Canada: Anansi Press.

Furlong, M. S. (1989). Crafting an electronic community: The SeniorNet story. *International Journal of Technology and Aging, 2*(3), 125–134.

Gabriel, Z., & Bowling, A. (2004). Quality of life from the perspective of older people. *Ageing & Society, 24*, 675–691.

Ganesh, S., & Barber, K. (2009). The silent community: Organizing zones in the digital divide. *Human Relations, 62*, 851–874.

Ganesh, S., & Zorn, T. E. (in press). Running the race: Competition discourse and broadband growth in Aotearoa New Zealand. *Media, Culture and Society.*

Gatto, S. L., & Tak, S. H. (2008). Computer, Internet, and email use among older adults: Benefits and barriers. *Educational Gerontology, 34*, 800–811.

Glanz, D. (1997). Seniors and cyberspace: Some critical reflections on computers and older persons. *Education and Aging, 12*, 69–81.

Gullette, M. M. (1997). *Declining to decline: Cultural combat and the politics of the midlife.* Charlottesville: University Press of Virginia.

Haddon, L. (2000). Social exclusion and information and communication technologies: Lessons from studies of single parents and the young elderly. *New Media & Society, 2*, 387–406.

Harwood, J. (2004). Relational, role, and social identity as expressed in grandparents' personal websites. *Communication Studies, 55*, 300–318.

Hazan, H. (2000). The cultural trap: The language of images. In J. F. Gubrium & J. A. Holstein (Eds.), *Aging and everyday life* (pp. 19–24). Malden, MA: Blackwell.

Heilbroner, R. (1994). Technological determinism revisited. In M. R. Smith & L. Marx (Eds.), Does technology drive history? *The dilemma of technological determinism* (pp. 67–78). Cambridge, MA: MIT Press.

Henwood, F., Wyatt, S., Miller, N., & Senker, P. (2000). Critical perspectives on technologies, in/equalities and the information society. In S. Wyatt, F. Henwood, N. Miller, & P. Senker (Eds.), *Technology and in/equality: Questioning the information society* (pp. 1–18). London: Routledge.

Hepworth, M. (1996). Consumer culture and social gerontology. *Education and Aging, 11*(1), 19–39.

Hill, R., Beynon-Davies, P., & Williams, M. D. (2008). Older people and Internet engagement: Acknowledging social moderators of Internet adoption, access and use. *Information Technology & People, 21*, 244–266.

Hilt, M. L., & Lipschultz, J. H. (2004). Elderly Americans and the Internet: Email, TV news, information and entertainment websites. *Educational Gerontology, 30*, 57–72.

Hough, M., & Kobylanski, A. (2009). Increasing elder consumer interactions with information technology. *Journal of Consumer Marketing, 26*(1), 39–48.

Howcroft, D. (1999). The hyperbolic age of information: An empirical study of internet usage. *Information, Communication & Society, 2*, 277–299.

Irizarry, C. Downing, A., & Elford, C. (1997). Seniors-on-line: Introducing older people to technology. *Australasian Physical & Engineering Sciences in Medicine, 20*(1), 39–43.

Iyer, R., & Eastman, J. K. (2006). The elderly and their attitudes toward the Internet: The impact on Internet use, purchase, and comparison shopping. *Journal of Marketing Theory and Practice*, *14*(1), 57–67.

Jay, G. M., & Willis, S. L. (1992). Influence of direct computer experience on older adults' attitudes toward computers. *Journal of Gerontology*, *47*(4), 250–257.

Jones, S., & Fox, S. (2009). *Generations online in 2009.* Pew Research Centre. [Online]. Retrieved August 13, 2010, from http://pewresearch.org/pubs/1093/generations-online

Kanayama, T. (2003). Ethnographic research on the experience of Japanese elderly people online. *New Media & Society*, *5*, 267–288.

Karavidas, M., Lim, N. K., & Katsikas, S. L. (2005). The effects of computers on older adult users. *Computers in Human Behavior, 21*, 697–711.

Kemper, S., & Lacal, J. C. (2004). Addressing the communication needs of an aging society. In R. Pew & S. Van Hemel (Eds.), *Technology for adaptive aging* (pp. 131–149). Washington, DC: National Academics Press.

Kim, Y. S. (2008). Reviewing and critiquing computer learning and usage among older adults. *Educational Gerontology*, *34*, 709–735.

Kraut, R., Kiesler, S., Boneva, B., Cummings, J., Helgeson, V., & Crawford, A. (2002). Internet paradox revisited. *Journal of Social Issues, 58*(1), 49–74.

Kraut, R., Patterson, M., Lundmark, V., Kiesler, S., Mukophadhyay, T., & Scherlis, W. (1998). Internet paradox: A social technology that reduces social involvement and psychological well-being? *American Psychologist, 53*, 1017–1031.

Lagana, L. (2008). Enhancing the attitudes and self-efficacy of older adults toward computers and the Internet: Results of a pilot study. *Educational Gerontology*, *34*, 831–843.

Lenhart, A. (2003). *The ever-shifting Internet population: A new look at Internet access and the digital divide*. [Online]. Retrieved November 16, 2004, from http://www.pewInternet.org

Lenhart, A., Rainie, L., Fox, S., Horrigan, J., & Spooner, T. (2000). *Who's not online: 57% of those without Internet access say they do not plan to log on*. [Online]. Retrieved February 12, 2006, from http://207.21.232.1103/pdfs/Pew_Those_Not_Online_Report.pdf

Lieblich, A., Tuval-Mashiach, R., & Zilber, T. (1998). *Narrative research: Reading, analysis and interpretation*. Thousand Oaks, CA: Sage.

Lindsay, S., Bellaby, P., Smith, S., & Baker, R. (2008). Enabling healthy choices: is ICT the highway to health improvement? *Sociological Abstracts, 12*, 313–331.

Loges, W. E., & Jung, J-Y. (2001). Exploring the digital divide: Internet connectedness and age. *Communication Research*, *28*, 536–562.

Lyotard, J. F. (1979). *The postmodern condition: a report on knowledge* (G. Bennington & B. Massumi, Trans.). Manchester, UK: Manchester University Press.

MacIntyre, A. (1981). *After virtue: A study in moral theory.* Notre Dame, IN: University of Notre Dame Press.

Mackay, H. (1995). Theorising the IT/society relationship. In N. Heap, R. Thomas, G. Einon, R. Mason, & H. Mackay (Eds.), *Information technology and society* (pp. 41–53). London: Sage in association with the Open University.

Mackay, H. (1997). Consuming communication technologies at home. In H. Mackay (Ed.), *Consumption and everyday life* (pp. 261–311). London: Sage.

Marquié, J. C., Jourdan-Boddaert, L., & Huet, N. (2002). Do older adults underestimate their actual computer knowledge? *Behaviour & Information Technology, 21*(4), 273–280.

McConatha, D., McConatha, J. T., & Dermigny, R. (1994). The use of interactive computer services to enhance the quality of life for long-term care residents. *The Gerontologist, 34*, 553–556.

McMellon, C. A., & Schiffman, L. G. (2002). Cybersenior empowerment: How some older individuals are taking control of their lives. *Journal of Applied Gerontology, 21*, 157–174.

McMillan, S. J., Avery, E. J., & Macias, W. (2008). From have nots to watch dogs: Understanding Internet health communication behaviors of online senior citizens. *Information, Communication & Society, 11*, 675–697.

Mellor, D., Firth, L., & Moore, K. (2008). Can the Internet improve the well-being of the elderly? *Ageing International, 32*(1), 25–42.

Meyrowitz, J. (2008). Power, pleasure, patterns: Intersecting narratives of media influence. *Journal of Communication, 58*, 641–663.

Millward, P. (2003). The 'grey digital divide': Perception, exclusion and barriers to access to the Internet for older people. *First Monday, 8*(7). Retrieved June 2003, from http://www.firstmonday7.org/issues/issue8_7/millward/index.html

Morley, D. (2003). What's 'home' got to do with it? Contradictory dynamics in the domestication of technology and the dislocation of domesticity. *European Journal of Cultural Studies, 6*, 435–458.

Morris, J. M. (1994). Computer training needs of older adults. *Educational Gerontology, 20*, 541–555.

Murdock, G. (2002). Debating the digital divides. *European Journal of Communication, 17*, 385–390.

Negroponte, N. (1995). *Being digital*. London: Hodder & Stoughton.

Norris, P. (2001). *Digital divide: Civic engagement, information poverty, and the Internet worldwide*. Cambridge, UK: University of Cambridge Press.

OCLC Report to the membership (2007). *Sharing, privacy and trust in our networked world*. [Online]. Retrieved April 28, 2009, from http://www.oclc.org/reports/sharing/deafult.htm

Östlund, B. (2004). Social science research on technology and the elderly — Does it exist? *Science Studies, 17*(2), 44–62.

Phipps, L. (2000). New communication technologies: A conduit for social inclusion. *Information, Communication & Society, 3*(1), 39–68.

Phoenix, C., & Sparkes, A. C. (2009). Being Fred: Big stories, small stories, and the accomplishment of a positive aging identity. *Qualitative Research*, *9*(2), 219–236.

Reisenwitz, T., Iyer, R., Kuhlmeier, D. B., & Eastman, J. K. (2007). The elderly's internet usage: An updated look. *Journal of Consumer Marketing*, *24*, 406–418.

Richardson, L. (1990). Narrative sociology. *Journal of Contemporary Ethnography, 19*(1), 116–135.

Richardson, M., Weaver, C. K., & Zorn, T. E. (2005). 'Getting on': Older New Zealanders' perceptions of computing. *New Media & Society*, *7*, 219–246.

Rideout, V. (2005). *E-health and the elderly: How seniors use the Internet for health information*. Kaiser Family Foundation. [Online]. Retrieved 18 June, 2010, from http://ww.kff.org/

Riessman, C. K. (1993). *Narrative analysis*. Newby Park, CA: Sage.

Rogers, W. A., & Fisk, A. D. (2006). Cognitive support for elders through technology. *Generations, 30*(2), 38–43.

Rosenthal, R. L. (2008). Older computer-literate women: Their motivations, obstacles, and paths to success. *Educational Gerontologist, 34*, 610–626.

Russell, C., Campbell, A., & Hughes, I. (2008). Aging, social capital and the Internet: Findings from an exploratory study of Australian 'silver surfers'. *Australasian Journal on Aging, 27*(2), 78–82.

Ryan, E. B., Szechtman, B., & Bodkin, J. (1992). Attitudes toward younger and older adults learning to use computers. *Journal of Gerontology: Psychological Sciences, 47*(2), 96–101.

Selwyn, N. (2003). Doing IT for the kids: Re-examining children, computers and the information society. *Media, Culture & Society, 25*, 351–378.

Selwyn, N. (2004a). Reconsidering political and popular understandings of the digital divide. *New Media & Society, 6*, 341–361.

Selwyn, N. (2004b). The information aged: A qualitative study of older adults' use of information and communications technology. *Journal of Aging Studies, 18*, 369–384.

Selwyn, N., & Gorard, S. (2008, February). What computers can't do for you. *Adults Learning*, 26–27.

Selwyn, N., Gorard, S., Furlong, J., & Madden, L. (2003). Older adults' use of information and communication technology in everyday life. *Ageing & Society, 23*, 561–582.

Shapira, N., Barak, A., & Gal, I. (2007). Promoting older adults' wellbeing through Internet training and use. *Aging & Mental Health, 11*(5), 477–484.

Slegers, K., van Boxtel, M. P. J., & Jolles, J. (2008). Effects of computer training and Internet usage on the well-being and quality of life of older adults: A randomized, controlled study. *Journal of Gerontology: Psychological Sciences, 63B*(3), 176–184.

Smith, M. R. (1994). Technological determinism in American culture. In M. R. Smith & L. Marx (Eds.), *Does technology drive history? The dilemma of technological determinism* (pp. 1–35). Cambridge, MA: MIT Press.

Smith, P., Smith. N., Sherman, K., Goodwin, I., Crothers, C., Billot, J., & Bell, A. (2010). *The Internet in New Zealand*. Auckland, New Zealand: The World Internet Project New Zealand Institute of Culture, Discourse, & Communication. [Online]. Retrieved March 26, 2010, from http://www.wipnz.aut.ac.nz

Statistics New Zealand (2004). *Report on the digital divide in New Zealand*. Retrieved from Statistics New Zealand website: http://www.stats.govt.nz/domino/external/pasfull/pasfull.nsf/7cf46ae26dcb6800cc256a

Sum, S., Mathews, R.M., Pourghasem, M., & Hughes, I. (2009). Internet use as a predictor of sense of community in older people. *Cyberpsychology & Behavior, 12*(2), 235–239.

Tapscott, D. (1998). *Growing up digital: The rise of the net generation*. New York, NY: McGraw-Hill.

Tatnall, A., & Lepa, J. (2003). The Internet, e-commerce and older people: An actor-network approach to researching reasons for adoption and use. *Logistics Information Management, 16*(1), 56–63.

Temple, L. L., & Gavillet, M. (1990). The development of computer confidence in seniors: An assessment of changes in computer anxiety and computer literacy. *Activities, Adaptation & Aging, 14*(3), 63–76.

Thayer, S. E., & Ray, S. (2006). Online communication preferences across age, gender, and duration of Internet use. *Cyberpsychology & Behaviour, 9*, 432–440.

Torp, S., Hanson, E., Hauge, S., Ulstein, I., & Magnusson, L. (2008). A pilot study of how information and communication technology may contribute to health promotion among elderly spousal carers in Norway. *Health and Social Care in the Community, 16*(1), 75–85.

Treguer, J-P. (2002). *50+ marketing: Marketing, communicating and selling to the over 50s generations.* New York, NY: Palgrave.

Trocchia, P. J., & Janda, S. (2000). A phenomenological investigation of Internet usage among older individuals. *Journal of Consumer Marketing, 17*(7), 605–616.

Venkatesh, A. (2008). Digital home technologies and transformation of households, *Information Systems Frontiers, 10*(4), 391–395.

Vuori, S., & Holmlund-Rytkönen, M. (2005). 55+ people as internet users. *Marketing Intelligence & Planning, 23*(1), 58–76.

Wagner, N., Hassanein, K., & Head, M. (2010). Computer use by older adults: A multi-disciplinary review. *Computers in Human Behavior, 26*, 870–882.

Waldron, V. R., Gitelson, R., & Kelley, D. L. (2005). Gender differences in social adaptation to a retirement community: Longitudinal changes and the role of mediated communication. *Journal of Applied Gerontology, 24*(4), 283–298.

Weaver, C. K., Zorn, T. E., & Richardson, M. (2010). Goods not wanted: Older people's narratives of computer use rejection. *Information, Communication & Society, 13*, 696–721.

Weick, K. E. (1995). *Sensemaking in organizations.* Thousand Oaks, CA: Sage.

Westerhof, G. J., & Tulle, E. (2007). Meanings of aging and old age: Discursive contexts, social attitudes, and personal identities. In J. Bond, S. Peace, F. Dittmann-Kohl, & G. J. Westerhof (Eds.), *Ageing in society: European perspectives on gerontology* (pp. 235–255). London: Sage.

White, H., McConnell, E., Clipp, E., Bynum, L., Teague, C., Navas, L., … Halbrecht, H. (1999). Surfing the net in later life: A review of the literature and pilot study of computer use and quality of life. *Journal of Applied Gerontology, 18*(3), 358–378.

White, H., McConnell, E., Clipp, E., Branch, L. G., Sloane, R., Pieper, C., & Box, T. L. (2002). A randomized controlled trial of the psychosocial impact of providing internet training and access to older adults. *Aging & Mental Health, 6*(3), 213–221.

White, J., & Weatherall, A. (2000). A grounded theory analysis of older adults and information technology. *Educational Gerontology, 26*, 371–386.

Wilhelmson, K. Andersson, C., Waern, M., & Allebeck, P. (2005). Elderly people's perspectives on quality of life. *Ageing & Society, 25*, 585–600.

Wright, K. (2000). The communication of social support within an on-line community for older adults: A qualitative analysis of the SeniorNet community. *Qualitative Research Reports in Communication, 1*(2), 33–43.

Xie, B. (2008). Multimodal computer-mediated communication and social support among older Chinese Internet users. *Journal of Computer-Mediated Communication, 13*, 728–750.

Zorn, T. E., Richardson, M., Weaver, C. K., & Gilbert, E. (2010). Technology uptake among older, Mormon Maori: Themes, tensions, and intersections. *Australian Journal of Communication, 37*(1), 1–16.

8 *Commentary* Moving Beyond Our Scholarly Comfort Zones

Jon F. Nussbaum

The Pennsylvania State University

Communication scholars, for the most part, are not known for their game changing, paradigm shifting, innovative theoretical explorations far removed from the safe comfort zones of our established theoretical ground. We tend to hold our theoretical knowledge base and methodological tool kit very close to our collective chest and rigorously question any foray into new territory. We are taught that science is a slow moving process with very few moments of significant, transformational change. I have been witness to numerous researchers "spinning" their data to somehow fit into their theory of how communication works. The scholarly innovators in our midst are few. Even suggesting a modification of the standard theory or approach can be met with generations full of skeptical insults and reviewer feedback that often crosses the line of professional decorum. With all due respect to former President Jimmy Carter, our scholarly comfort zone reinforces a theoretical and methodological malaise.

The three chapters published within Part II of this volume attempt to move communication scholarship out of our theoretical and methodological comfort zone. Each chapter provides evidence for not only an expansion of current theory and methodology, but provides for the beginning of a significant transformation toward appropriate interdisciplinary scholarship. While these three chapters will not entirely destroy our disciplinary malaise, the core of each provides the reader with numerous opportunities to move beyond the tried and true toward some rather interesting theoretical and methodological possibilities.

Helmle, Seibold, and Afifi discuss the rather puzzling fact that family businesses, especially businesses operated by married couples or copreneurial businesses, have largely been ignored by scholars across multiple disciplines who investigate work and family life. We are asked to consider the possibility of utilizing and integrating the rather extensive scholarly contributions of organizational communication and family communication to better understand the work and family dynamic of married couples who run family business. Research in the domain of family businesses from numerous disciplines along with current scholarly perspectives within organizational communication and family communication (concentrating on the marital relationship) is reviewed within the context of work and family life. Of special importance, within this general review, is a discussion of the relationship and business advantages for copreneurs, the review of marital schemata and equity literature within the communication discipline that provides an argument for a couple type not previously found within the literature, and a discussion of communal coping and the possibility of unique stressors affecting the couple not only relationally but physically as well. The chapter concludes with a proposal that communication contributions to work-family integration may be enhanced by considering the previous work of scholars writing within boundary theory, work-family border theory, relational dialectics, and structuration theory.

Beck, Miller, and Frahm argue that family communication scholars and small group communication scholars, who have traditionally not integrated their theories or methodologies, could not find a more appropriate time to collaborate and in doing so would enhance the understanding of both families and small group interaction. Three theoretical approaches associated with small group communication (social identity theory, the theory of transactive memory, and faultline theory) are summarized and offered as perspectives that family communication scholars may find valuable. Family researchers have not often investigated the entire family unit or have made decisions to limit their study of family dynamics to dyadic interaction because of the complex methodological issues that arise once one attempts to collect and analyze data from three, four, five, and larger family interactants. The underlying assumption of the chapter is that to understand how the entire family interacts, family communication scholars may find the theoretical and methodological expertise of small group researchers who have had experience investigating more than dyadic interaction quiet useful. Small group researchers have not studied, for the most part, individuals with a long interactive history or who maintain close relationships across an entire life span. Thus, the unique dynamics of the family can be a context that may enhance the theory and methodology of small group scholars as well.

Richardson, Zorn, and Weaver discuss the recent literature addressing how older adults utilize and are affected by new communication technologies. The chapter is organized around three master narratives that dominate this literature: the enabling machine and isolated elder narrative, the potential divider and marginalized senior narrative, and the desirable commodity and grey consumer narrative. The social constructivist position investigating the relationship between older adults and their use of new communication technology offers an alternative perspective with which to view both the negative and positive accounts of growing old within a society dominated by new technologies. Social gerontologists have investigated the various ways older adults are marginalized or stereotyped within our modern, technologically advanced society (Harwood, 2007). These ageist attitudes and behaviors are often associated with the construction of unnecessary barriers that limit our ability to achieve a high quality of life throughout the life span (Nussbaum, Federowicz, & Nussbaum, 2009). In addition, mass communication scholars have published an expansive literature on the use and affects of new technologies upon every aspect of human behavior. However, an active scholarly discussion of older adults and new technology is just beginning. As a matter of fact, undergraduate students within my Communication and Aging classes are often shocked that older adults would ever want to utilize new communication technologies. This perception, by a relatively small sample of young adults, is rather disparate from the scientific literature indicating that any assumption that older adults wish to avoid new technology is largely a fallacy (Rogers & Fisk, 2010). While it may be true that older adults are less likely to use technology when compared to younger adults (Czaja et al., 2006), once older adults adopt a new technology these older adults use it as frequently as younger adults (O'Brien et al., 2008).

The three chapters share several common content themes, but more importantly, serve to move communication theory and methodology toward more impactful, reality-grounded, interdisciplinary scholarship. Each set of authors attempt to move us from our theoretical and methodological comfort zones by grounding this movement in well established theory and method. The suggested moves beyond comfort do include some rather innovative and clever maneuvering.

Each chapter highlights families (directly or indirectly) and the interaction that takes place within the family as a significant context for communication scholarship. The study of family communication is relatively new not only within the formal discipline of communication but in the larger area of family studies. I have been in numerous recent faculty interactions where family scholarship has been criticized for being an atheoretical step-child of interpersonal scholarship. Prioritizing the importance of family communication as a unique scholarly enterprise is in itself a somewhat controversial statement. The three chapters individually provide an excellent rational that family businesses not only exist but are complex and exciting contexts to study communication, that family communication is much more than dyadic interaction or some combination of numerous dyads, and that new communication technologies can serve to maintain social connectiveness (family contact) for at least a segment of younger-older adults who have lost some face-to-face interactive mobility.

Each chapter reinforces the notion that group membership in an age category, a small group, or a business is much more than a linear process or an individual difference. The various theories directly referenced (dialectics, structuration, shared identity, transactive memory, and narrative and sense making) view communication as a process that both constructs and manages our interactive environment. Families, businesses and age categories are negotiated entities best understood by scholars who accept the notion that communication cannot be fully understood within our familiar static, linear perspectives. This type of innovative thinking requires innovative methodologies to capture process. Therefore, each chapter also opens a discussion for communication scholarship to become much more accepting of methodological diversity. I take this to mean that we must become much more tolerant of methods and procedures that emerge to systematically answer research questions related to development, growth, single cases, and direct observation in the context where actual families live or older adults attempt to master new technology. The loss of total control, overemphasizing internal validity, and "ideal researcher objectivity" are not always the sine-qua-non of scholarly achievement.

The most important contribution of these three chapters to our collective knowledge base beyond the specific content found within each is the emphasis on multi-theoretical and multi/interdisciplinary interphases to better understand the communication process. The three general contexts that frame these chapters (family businesses, family interaction, and older adulthood) require communication scholars to venture far beyond the journals published by our national or international associations. At times, we find it extraordinarily difficult to read and to even consider publishing outside of our own sub-disciplinary boundaries. Why would a small group of communication scholars or an organizational communication scholar read the *Journal of Family Communication*? This leap of scholarly inquiry seems near impossible. Now, to think of small group communication scholars or organizational communication scholars publishing their findings within the *Journals of Gerontology* or the *Academy of Management Journal* boggles the mind. Yet, communication scholars who are truly interested in understanding the interactive dynamics of these particular contexts are not fully informed until they do move outside of their limited reading base and begin engaging scholars investigating similar phenomena in other disciplines. As an individual who studies the communication behavior of older adults, often within the contexts of family and health care organizations, my world has always included interdisciplinary literature and various joint appointments in far reaching corners of the academy. These ventures are often not easily initiated and not initially reinforced. However, the payoff in expanded scholarly possibilities is enormous. Quite simply, we know more about the behavior of humans when we actively engage across disciplinary boundaries. These three chapters point us toward the benefits of interdisciplinary theoretical mingling.

In a rather indirect manner, the three chapters also suggest a much broader, multi-methodological approach toward answering the context based research questions that will emerge from the mingling of interdisciplinary perspectives. How do we capture the work and family dynamic of the married couple managing their own business? How do we measure three, four, five, or many more family members from different generations attempting to solve a problem that demands an unpopular decision? Finally, how do we investigate the short- and long-term affects of older adults utilizing Facebook or other social networking technology to become more engaged with society? The current, popular, most taught methodological procedures within our discipline will simply not answer the questions the authors of these chapters suggest we answer. To be a tad bold, surveys and experiments must be supplemented with trips to the "field" and long hours, months, and possibly years of focused observations. Process, change, development, and complex interactive dynamics are not easily understood or measured. Communication scholars are not often as well equipped as scholars in other disciplines to design a longitudinal investigation that captures the dynamic nature of human interaction. The three chapters within this section of *Communication Yearbook 35* set the agenda and call for theoretical and methodological action that will move us beyond our comfort zones toward a richer understanding of communication.

References

Czaja, S. J., Charness, N., Fisk, A. D., Hertzog, C., Nair, S. N., Rogers, W. A., & Sharit, J. (2006). Factors predicting the use of technology: Findings from the Center for Research and Education on Aging and Technology Enhancement (CREATE). *Psychology and Aging, 21,* 333–352.

Harwood, J. (2007). *Understanding communication and aging: Developing knowledge and awareness.* Los Angeles: Sage.

Nussbaum, J. F., Federowicz, M., & Nussbaum, P. D. (2009). *Brain health and optimal engagement in older adulthood.* Girona, Spain: Editorial Aresta.

O'Brien, M. A., Olson, K. E., Charness, N., Czaja, S. J., Fisk, A. D., Rogers, W. A., & Sharit, J. (2008, June). *Understanding technology usage in older adults.* Paper presented at the proceedings of the 6th International Conference of the International Society for Gerotechnology (ISG08) (CD-ROM Paper No. ICT-014). Pisa, Italy.

Rogers, W. A., & Fisk, A. D. (2010). Toward a psychological science of advanced technology design for older adults. *Journal of Gerontology: Psychological Sciences, 65B*(6), 645–653.

Part III

Perspectives on Communication and Language

CHAPTER CONTENTS

9 Theorizing Language Attitudes

Existing Frameworks, an Integrative Model, and New Directions[1]

Howard Giles

University of California at Santa Barbara

Mikaela L. Marlow

University of Idaho

Since the innovative work of Labov and Lambert in the 1960s, scholars have approached the study of language attitudes from a variety of perspectives. Multidisciplinary research has significantly enhanced our understanding of the cognitive and affective variables that shape language attitudes and communicative behaviors. After reviewing this empirical work, the chapter examines the major theoretical models that have emerged in this field of inquiry. A new integrative model of language attitudes is then proposed, along with suggestions for future research with respect to sense-making.

The Romanian philosopher Emil Cioran (1911–1995) once said: *We inhabit a language rather than a country.*

(Rakić, Steffens, & Mummendey, in press)

Introduction

There is a robust literature showing that speakers' voices are potent cues for listeners to socially categorize, stereotype, and form impressions of them (e.g., Ko, Judd, & Blair, 2006; Ko, Judd, & Stapel, 2009; Scherer, 1979; Zuckerman & Driver, 1989). In this vein, many of these texts make the point that Latin origins of the word *personality* referred "to sounding through." That people have, or rather are attributed as having, a so-called "accent" has been a social issue and concern in everyday parlance, popular culture, and in many professional contexts for a very long time. One of us (HG) has been the recipient of comments, some humorous and other derogatory, about his "accent" on more than a daily basis—and this for 20-plus years. A recent web-search on "reactions to people's accents," for instance, triggered well over 4 million hits. The international diversity of these websites is itself intriguing, ranging from how accents can "hold you back" and are unsuitable for classroom teaching, to those offering programs to eliminate them, to those on YouTube with video-clips of comedians taking others to task for having accents and other speech styles. Tellingly, the victim of a crime was recently reported in an American newspaper as describing her male perpetrator as "5-foot-6 to 5-foot-8, young, white and *with no accent*" (our italics; Santarelli, 2010, p. A10). In other words, how one speaks and its significant meanings, together with the reactions and decisions they garner is an incontestably significant communicative issue. In this chapter, we overview multidisciplinary research undertaken on social evaluations of languages and speech styles (an area of inquiry called "language attitudes") over more than 50 years, with a particular focus on and critique of the array of theoretical frameworks that it has attracted more recently. The ultimate aim of this is to propose an integrative heuristic model that can guide future research agendas. Before moving into the language attitudes literature, a brief history of social attitude research is provided to locate language attitudes in this more general terrain.

Research on Social and Language Attitudes

Social Attitudes

Attitudes are central to the human experience and play a pervasive role in everyday interactions (e.g., Fazio & Olson, 2003), influencing self-presentations and our interactions with others. The impressions one develops about another person's beliefs, capabilities, and social attributes are guided by many social cues, an important one of which is another's speech style. Within the last hundred years, substantial inquiry has been devoted to understanding the role of attitudes in predicting human behavior (see Maio & Haddock, 2010). The 1920s witnessed social science research that was concerned with measuring attitudes (McGuire, 1985) and Thurstone and Likert constructed the Equal Appearing Interval and Likert scales. These measurement approaches were considered substantial contributions because they demonstrated that attitudes, as unobservable subjective entities, could be measured in a quantifiable way. In 1934, La Piere (1934) found that attitudes may not necessarily predict human behavior. His work documented that although a majority of restaurant establishments in the United States reported that they would not serve a Chinese couple, when actually faced with the situation, a majority of restaurants did. This suggested that although attitudes may predict behavior under certain conditions, people may not always act in accord with them (Wicker, 1969; for a more axiomatic account of the relationship between attitudes and performances, see Kaiser, Byrka, & Hartig, 2010).

After World War II, increasing attention was devoted to the role of attitudes vis à vis broader social and political events. In this way, Lewin, Asch, Festinger, and Sherif studied attitude processes inherently connected to intergroup dynamics, such as power, conformity, and social dominance. Adorno, Frenkel-Brunswik, Levinson, and Sanford (1950) sought to understand what factors might lead people to develop anti-Semitic attitudes and authoritarianism. Around this time, attitudes began to be conceived and assessed in terms of a tripartite structure (Katz & Stotland, 1959; Rosenberg & Hovland, 1960) that featured reported thoughts, feelings, and behaviors regarding a given topic. Subsequently, the cold war and telecommunication innovations—specifically television—motivated people like Hovland, Janis, and Kelley (1953) to explore the factors that explain how and why attitudes can change over time. This research was very influential in the field of social psychology and significantly impacted the design of models of attitude change and social influence.

In 1957, Festinger introduced cognitive dissonance theory to better understand the ways in which certain incongruent beliefs and attitudes may motivate people to change them. He argued that when people hold diverging beliefs or attitudes, they experience a negative emotional state called dissonance. When people feel such cognitive disequilibrium, they may be moved to reduce this by changing one of their attitudes, which will then lead them to establish a state of consonance. This era also brought forth research concerning the reasons why people may hold certain attitudes and, according to Smith, Bruner, and White (1956) and Katz (1960), they served several functions including appraisal, value, identification, and social compliance. This work enabled practitioners the ability to develop persuasive appeals that were consistent with an individual's attitude function.

During the mid-1960s, attitudes research began to emphasize the role of social cognition, or the ways in which people make sense of messages. This approach focused attention on the introspective and reasoning processes that influence attitudes and behavior. For instance, Ajzen and Fishbein (e.g., 1980) developed the theory of reasoned action to predict behavioral dispositions based upon attitudes. This theory, and others that followed (e.g., in the health domain), sought to understand the effects that attitudes have on behavior. In the 1980s, Petty and Cacioppo (e.g., 1986) introduced the elaboration likelihood (ELM), and Chaiken (1980) proffered the heuristic-systematic (HSM), models. The former suggested that people are persuaded by either central (focused thought/evidence) or peripheral (superficial cues/less thought) routes, while HSM proposed that people engage in either systematic (careful consideration of message content) or heuristic (less careful consideration) processes while being persuaded. These dual process models have greatly enhanced knowledge about attitude change (Maio & Haddock, 2007), with the last several decades producing a plethora of studies assessing attitude strength, stability, and change (see Wilson, Lindsey, & Schooler, 2000). Strong attitudes have been shown to be persistent, resistant to change, and influence message processing and subsequent behavior (Krosnick & Petty, 1995).

Understandably, this body of literature has impacted the kinds of language attitude research and theory that will be introduced next. In it, we will encounter the tripartite structure of language attitudes and the link between them and linguistic actions, the cognitive processing and persistence of them, as well as their social functions (see Giles & Coupland, 1991a).

Language Attitudes

A number of techniques have been adopted to study language attitudes, such as the direct elicitation of them from conceptual labels of language varieties and the drawing of maps of linguistic variation and social meaning (see Preston, 1993, 1998; Ryan, Giles, & Hewstone, 1988). However, the most popular of these is the matched-guise technique (MGT) developed by Lambert, Hodgson, Gardner, and Fillenbaum (1960), and since adopted in many cultures around the globe. Its seminal impact can be gauged, in part, by the fact that Tajfel (1959) published a critique of it a year before it was actually published. The MGT, along with Labov's subjective reaction test (2006), excited a burgeoning of interest in language attitudes as witnessed in journal and convention issues devoted to the topic (e.g., Cooper, 1974, 1975; Giles & Edwards, 1983; Kristiansen, Garrett, & Coupland, 2005; Ryan, Giles, & Bradac, 1994; Shuy & Fasold, 1969). The MGT was devised to explore the ways in which a speaker's language, dialect, or accent influences trait attributions of them (Lambert et al., 1960), and work in this vein continues to this day (e.g., Cargile, Takai, & Rodriguez, 2006; Dailey, Giles, & Jansma, 2005; Garrett, Coupland, & Williams, 2003; Gluszek & Dovidio, 2010a; Rakić, Steffens, & Mummendey, in press).

MGT experiments present listeners with passages or utterances read by bilingual or bidialectal persons who can authentically adopt various guises of the targeted languages varieties; sometimes the stimulus varieties involve even code-switching or shifting between them (Garner & Rubin, 1986; Lawson & Sachdev, 2000). This procedure has the advantage of experimental control, since all extraneous variables (e.g., prosodic, paralinguistic, and emotional investment) are purportedly held constant across the guises evoked. In other words, and albeit not without criticism over the years (e.g., Grondelaers, van Hout, & Steegs, 2010), the technique assures that differences across guises are based upon the features of the language variety per se rather than the vocal differences that often exist among speakers. Listeners are then required to rate the speaker on a variety of subjective attributes found to represent the multidimensionality of raters' trait schemas (Cuddy, Fiske, & Glick, 2008; Mulac, Hanley, & Prigge, 1974; Zahn & Hopper, 1985). On occasion, more novel dependent measures are invoked, such as drawing visual images of the target speakers (e.g., Giles, Harrison, Creber, Smith, & Freeman, 1983). Thus, empirical attention has been accorded variation amongst listener-raters, such as their socio-demographics, personality differences, and social identities, but this has not yielded any really robust advances or caveats (see Cargile & Giles, 1997).

Research using the MGT (as well as other elicitation procedures) has found that *non*standard language varieties are evaluated less favorably than their standard counterparts on competence (e.g., intelligence, ambition, and confidence) as well as dynamism (e.g., lively, enthusiastic, and talkative) traits (for overviews, see Giles & Billings, 2004; Giles & Edwards, 2010; Lippi-Green,

1997). Indeed, the stronger, or broader, the perceived nonstandard accent, the more negative the social evaluations (Gluszek, Newheiser, & Dovidio, in press; Ryan, Carranza, & Moffie, 1977) that ensue, with the perceived quality of the message content and its comprehensibility being downgraded, as well (Giles, 1973; Gluszek, Newheiser, & Dovidio, in press). Examples of standard varieties would be British Received Pronunciation, Parisian French, and Castilian Spanish, whereas nonstandard speakers would be those identified from lower socioeconomic strata who spoke more regional, or nonnative (Gluszek & Dovidio, 2010b) varieties of these languages; for a discussion of standard-nonstandard distinctions, see Edwards and Jacobsen (1987), and for different standards evolving in different contexts, see Kristiansen (2001). These patterns can endure in a rather stable fashion across decades, and hence persist despite a kaleidoscope of political and socioeconomic changes (e.g., Bishop, Garrett, & Coupland, 2003; Genesee & Holobow, 1989).

Moreover, and in a very compelling way, these effects transcend mere *reported* evaluations (see below) to other more applied kinds of social decision-making that can have significant real world consequences (Kalin, 1982). Such meaningful outcomes include: a speaker's persuasiveness (Giles, Williams, Mackie, & Rosselli, 1995; Tsalikis, DeShields, & LaTour, 1991); the recall of speaker's information (Gill & Badzinski, 1992); employment suitability for high to low status jobs (e.g., Giles, Wilson, & Conway, 1981); presumed guilt in a simulated courtroom set-up (Dixon & Mahoney, 2004); teacher comprehensibility in the classroom (e.g., Gill, 1994); and evaluations of speakers' other written products (e.g., Piché, Michlin, Rubin, & Sullivan, 1977). In addition, language attitudes have also been found to be potent in more naturalistic field settings with respect to *behavioral* cooperativeness (Giles & Farrar, 1979; Kristiansen & Giles, 1992), and even locating rental facilities (Purnell, Isdardi, & Baugh, 1999). In all the above cases, speaking with a standard accent has been shown to produce favorable outcomes over the use of nonstandard varieties which themselves can represent a social hierarchy (with respect to foreign and regional accented speakers in Australia and the United States, see Ball, 1983; Mulac, 1975). Language attitudes then may profoundly influence the access and opportunities one encounters during home, educational, and professional interactions (e.g., Kalin, 1982; Matsuda, 1991).

In many cases, people who speak nonstandard varieties may consensually accept the negative status and competence evaluations assigned to them by others. Such evaluative stances may take their toll on young nonstandard speaking children. Research is beginning to emerge suggesting that people are not shy about criticizing the language varieties of others (Marlow & Giles, 2010). In fact, Trudgill (1975) found that some educators told students that their speech was "wrong … bad … careless … sloppy … slovenly … vulgar … gibberish" (p. 63; see also, Edwards & Mckinnon, 1987). Furthermore, nonstandard speakers have, in some contexts, been shown to even exaggerate the negative valence associated with nonstandard varieties accorded them by standard speakers (e.g., Lambert et al., 1960), labeled as the "minority group reaction" (see Lambert, 1967) as well as "linguistic insecurity" (Labov, 2006; Preston, 1999). Considering that language can be an integral part of an individual's social identity, the negative repercussions associated with denigrating one's speech may be particularly disturbing. As Halliday (1968) acknowledged, "a speaker who is made ashamed of his own language habits suffers a basic injury as a human being" (p. 165). It comes as no surprise then that Ryan (1979) asked the logical questions: why do low status speech varieties continue to exist? Why is it that the speakers of such languages fail to employ a variety that will grant them more status? Indeed, the modern day media ensure that all individuals are somewhat aware of and are able to access standard varieties (Edwards, 1999).

Critically, those who speak nonstandard varieties are upgraded on traits of socially attractiveness (or benevolence) and, hence, viewed as more friendly, generous, and likeable than their standard speaking counterparts (Linn & Pichè, 1982; Luhman, 1990). Interestingly too, male nonstandard speakers are upgraded over standard speakers in terms of masculinity (Giles & Marsh, 1979) and are considered more skilled at tasks requiring manual labor (e.g., Giles et al., 1992). Nonstandard speakers communicating with each other in this code can enhance feelings of ingroup solidarity as well as positively distinguish themselves from outgroup (standard) speakers who might be perceived as arrogant, pompous, and the like (Bourhis, Giles, & Tajfel, 1973). Furthermore, Giles and Edwards (2010) suggested that people who adapt their speech towards the standard variety may risk social marginalization. For instance, a Mexican American who speaks English may be called a *vendido*, a sell-out, while a French Canadian who attempts to speak English may be labeled as a *vendu*.

Nonstandard varieties can carry covert prestige (Marlow & Giles, 2008; Trudgill, 1974) and are legitimated in the community contexts in which it is the speech norm (see Giles, Katz, & Myers, 2006). In fact, Edwards (2001) suggested that linguistic necessity may motivate some people (and others on propitious occasions) to adopt the standard varieties of languages with which they do not identify with or feel comfortable speaking. For instance, Marlow and Giles (2008) demonstrated that multiethnic locals in Hawai'i adapt to Standard English during work and educational interactions out of necessity, despite the fact that they prefer to speak the local Pidgin, Hawai'i Creole English.

It is noteworthy that listener-judges are willing to assert language attitudes after quite minimal exposure to the stimulus passages to which they are required to react (Williams, 1976). Accordingly, questions were raised in the literature about the social origins of language and accent use: whether certain language varieties were upgraded because of their natural intrinsic aesthetic qualities or whether the attributions were internalized during the socialization process (Bradac & Giles, 1991); the so-called inherent value and imposed norm hypotheses, respectively. In an article entitled, "Italian is beautiful, German is ugly," Giles and Niedzielski (1998) reviewed empirical tests of these positions supporting the latter hypothesis. Indeed, very early in the lifespan, children express quite complex understandings of some of the relationships among dialect, ethnicity, foreignness, and economics (see Day, 1982; Floccia, Bulter, Girard, & Goslin, 2009; Girard, Floccia, & Goslin, 2008), schema that often persist into later life (Giles, Henwood, Coupland, Harriman, & Coupland, 1992). Additionally, it has been found that, by only 5 months old, children are already sensitive to dialectal variations (Nazzi, Jusczyk, & Johnson, 2000) and that, other speakers' accents are evaluatively more potent than their race to 5- and 6-year-olds (Kinzler, Corriveau, & Harris, in press; Kinzler, Dupoux, & Spelke, 2007; Kinzler, Shutts, DeJesus, & Spelke, 2009). Referring to their own empirical work with adults, Rakić et al. (in press) found that "it was rather irrelevant for participants what targets looked like; it mainly mattered whether they were speaking with an accent or not. In this case it was almost as if participants became blind to the visual category information in the presence of more meaningful auditory category information."

Not unrelatedly, Labov (1976) studied African American Vernacular English (AAVE) and helped scholars to recognize the general linguistic validity of all dialects. Until Labov's work, AAVE had been consistently devalued by the white middle class, and those who spoke this variety were often victims of prejudice. Labov, in critiquing prior work on methodological grounds, demonstrated AAVE was not at all a debased language variety. Furthermore, he propounded the view that the Black community is verbally rich and, similar to oral cultures globally, supports and rewards individuals who are particularly linguistically talented. Most importantly, Labov documented the rule-governed nature of AAVE. This seminal work attests to the fact that nonstandard dialects are not, despite popular assumptions to the contrary, *sub*-standard varieties, anymore than standard dialects should be considered "proper" or correct models (see Ray, 2009). Yet despite these conceptual and theoretical inroads, negative attitudes toward speakers of AAVE continue to exist (e.g., Cargile et al., 2006) and research has documented that individuals who speak this way are consistently down-graded with regards to status traits like wealth or education when compared to standard American Network English speakers (Garner & Rubin, 1986; Irwin, 1977; Johnson & Buttny, 1982; Speicher & McMahan, 1992).

Moderating these distinctive evaluations of nonstandard and standard speakers, the nature of the social and verbal contexts (e.g., topic of the stimulus passage, social status of the speaker, and the setting in which the ratings are gleaned) can influence speech evaluations (Giles & Johnson, 1986; Ryan & Carranza, 1975). Perhaps not surprisingly, people attend to factors such as a speaker's presumed motivations, attributed intentions, and avowed goals when evaluating the speech of others. Likewise, speakers may also be evaluated on a range of other speech characteristics beyond language, dialect, and accent, including powerful/less speech, pitch, pausing, lexical diversity, and self-disclosure (for a review, see Bradac, 1990). Variables such as these have been independently and simultaneously manipulated with other speaker characteristics (e.g., socio-economic status). For example in one study, the least favorable evaluations were expressed towards people of low lexical diversity, nonstandard accent, and working class background (Giles et al., 1981). It should also be noted that work on the so-called "retroactive speech halo effect" (Thakerar & Giles, 1981) has shown that having social background information on speakers influences how they are perceived to sound. In other words, not only do nonstandard language varieties suggest lowered attributed competence but knowledge of the latter can induce listeners to hear someone as more nonstandard and slower in speech rate (see also, Ball et al., 1982).

In sum, language attitudes research around the world suggests that people stereotype speakers' personal and social attributes, and develop meaningful conclusions about others, based upon their language, dialect, and accent usage (Edwards, 1999). Generally, standard language varieties grant people access to political, economic, and social forums, while nonstandard language varieties impart stigma upon speakers (Gluszek & Dovidio, 2010b). People may adopt standardized languages to access economic or social resources among other social capital and, in the second language acquisition literature, favorable attitudes towards another variety (as well as its speakers) facilitates native-like proficiency in it (e.g., Dörnyei, 2003; Gardner, in press). Nonetheless, we have seen that a considerable cache exists amongst nonstandard speakers who can reap somewhat different, but just as valuable, communicative and social rewards.

Language Attitudes Models: The Early Years

All this notwithstanding, Giles and Ryan (1982) acknowledged that "language attitudes as an area of sociolinguistic inquiry has been criticized for amassing descriptive data ad infinitum" (p. 222). These scholars in their epilogue chapter—and in their companion prologue contribution to the same volume—proposed two organizational frameworks as a modest step towards enriching this area conceptually. The first is depicted in Figure 9.1 (Ryan, Giles, & Sebastian, 1982), and while devised a couple of decades ago, the social positions of the language varieties implicated there probably have some currency to this day. The vertical dimension features how standard-nonstandard a dialect or accent is construed as being and the dynamic horizontal dimension indicates the extent to which a variety is decreasing or increasing in terms of its group vitality (see Abrams, Barker, & Giles, 2009; Bourhis & Landry, 2008). The vitality of a variety would be operationalized in terms of perceptions of its speakers' status, numbers of its users, and the institutional support it has garnered. Arguably, nonstandard varieties that are becoming increasingly vital are heard in more formal status-stressing situations as well in as solidarity-stressing situations (see Figure 9.2 for hypothetical scenarios). In this way, speakers of such accents might not suffer attributional denigrations of competence as much as those nonstandard speakers with a stable low or decreasing vitality. Speakers of standard varieties that appear to be decreasing in vitality would likely not

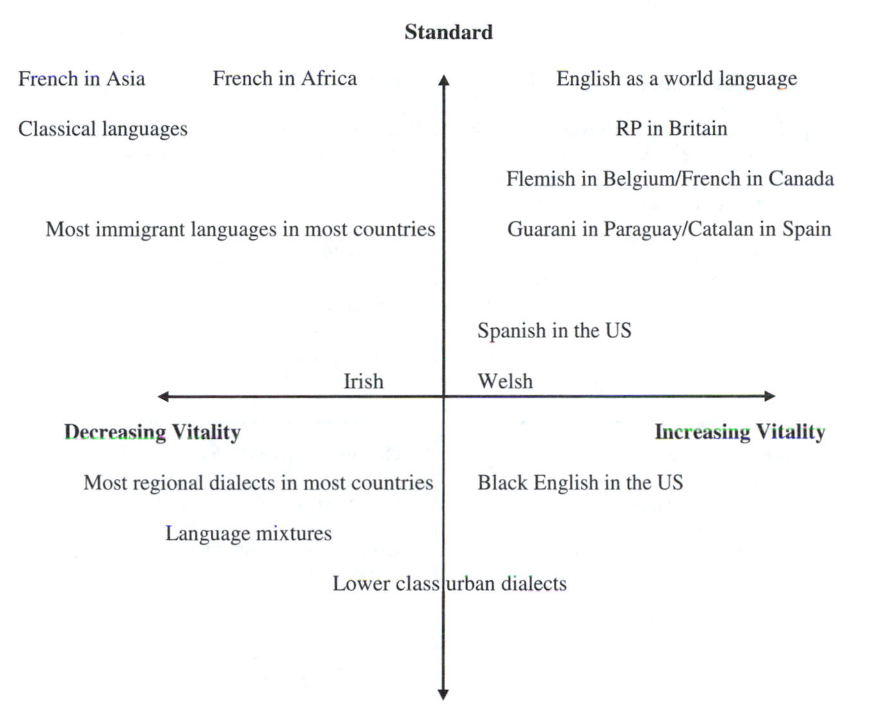

Figure 9.1 Sociostructural factors affecting language attitudes (Ryan, Giles, & Sebastian (1982, p. 6). Reproduced by permission of Hodder Education.

have as much attributed competence and status as those with a stable high or ever-increasing vitality. Potent examples here would be French and English in Quebec where the former has increased in standardization and vitality in recent times, while the momentum towards the use of English has declined (Bourhis, Montreuil, Helly, & Jantzen, 2007).

The other model (Ryan & Giles, 1982) highlighted two important dimensions of context, namely a situation's status- and solidarity-stressing features (see suggested prototypes of these in Figure 9.2) and its person and group centeredness, and the kinds of trait attributions that would be triggered by them. Person-centered conversations are likely to focus on the individuals' idiosyncratic experiences, impressions, and ideas while, in contrast, group-centered interactions might include people who belong to the same ingroup discussing how to respond to an external threat or challenge from a relevant outgroup (see Tajfel & Turner, 1986). Ryan and Giles claimed this model was useful given that most studies about language attitudes have been conducted in environments that are classified as status-stressing, such as schools. They suggested that research should be expanded to account for language attitudes and practices in other locations that would be considered more collective, including

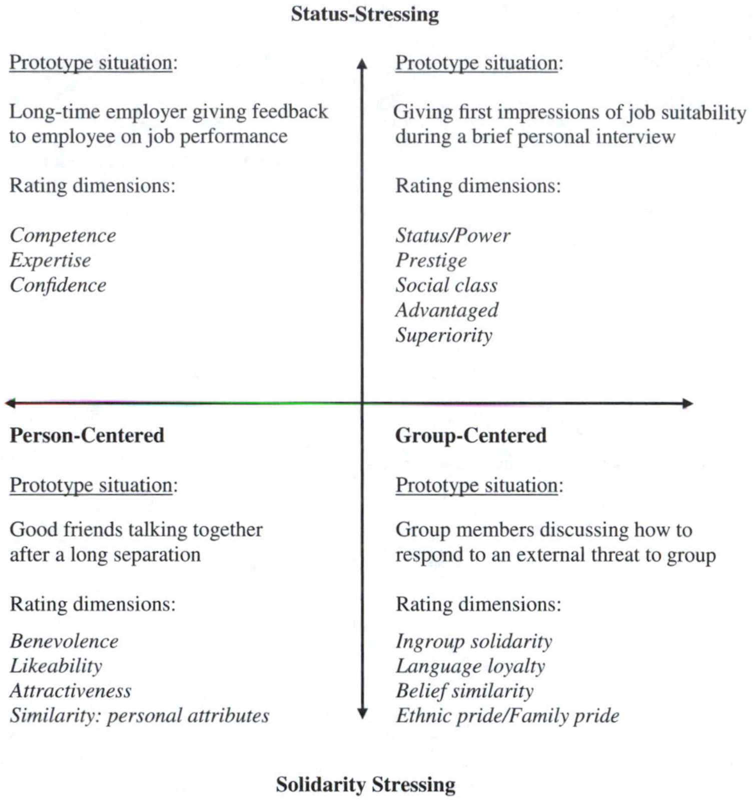

Status-Stressing

Prototype situation:	Prototype situation:
Long-time employer giving feedback to employee on job performance	Giving first impressions of job suitability during a brief personal interview
Rating dimensions:	Rating dimensions:
Competence *Expertise* *Confidence*	*Status/Power* *Prestige* *Social class* *Advantaged* *Superiority*
Person-Centered	**Group-Centered**
Prototype situation:	Prototype situation:
Good friends talking together after a long separation	Group members discussing how to respond to an external threat to group
Rating dimensions:	Rating dimensions:
Benevolence *Likeability* *Attractiveness* *Similarity: personal attributes*	*Ingroup solidarity* *Language loyalty* *Belief similarity* *Ethnic pride/Family pride*

Solidarity Stressing

Figure 9.2 Language attitude situations and evaluative ratings (Giles & Ryan, 1982, p. 220). Reproduced by permission of Hodder Education.

community centers, family discussions, and so forth (see Giles et al., 2006). Interestingly, not only have these models not been the subject of empirical scrutiny or further refinement, but the dimensions therein have not resurfaced in other scholars' subsequent models (as will be seen). Nonetheless, we contend that these dimensions warrant theoretical attention.

The need for and value of these organizational frameworks aside, Giles and Ryan (1982) were not implying that theoretical models were not already in existence, as Lambert's (e.g., 1967) initial development of the MGT was built on the following theoretical premise: language features → social categorization → trait attributions (see also, Robinson, 1972). Around the same time as the clarion call for more theoretical development, Gallois, Callan, and Johnstone (1984) speculated about *which* social categorizations would be the ones assuming salience in context. They argued that when the social distance between prevailing ethnic groups in the community was small or when listeners' ethnic affiliations were peripheral to their identities (Giles & Johnson, 1986), other speech markers than ethnolinguistic ones (e.g., gender-related cues) might assume prominence in dictating social categorizations and attending trait attributions.

For their part, Berger and Bradac (1982), invoking their own uncertainty reduction theory, proposed that there were other variables (e.g., perceived similarity) beyond mere social categorization mediating the language-attribution relationship. In particular, they focused on the ways in which listeners used language varieties as socially diagnostic cues to lend (oftentimes stereotypically) the speaker's characteristics more predictable (see also, Gudykunst & Ting-Toomey, 1990). Importantly, Berger and Bradac suggested that listeners' use of language (and other) features to reduce uncertainty about speakers allowed the former more relevant information as to how to communicate with the latter more appropriately. In this same vein, Giles and Powesland's (1975) early rendition of speech accommodation theory had acknowledged the role of language attitudes in determining speakers' communicative choices. More specifically, they argued that speakers' convergent or divergent inclinations toward or away from each other was, at least in part, predicated on prior language attitudes they had formed of their partners. Of course, the relationship between interpersonal accommodation and language attitudes is more of a symbiotic process in that being the recipient of perceived accommodative acts is part and parcel of listeners' social evaluative processes (Street & Hopper, 1982), and particularly in terms of whether such moves adhere or not to contextual norms. Bradac (1990) proposed that listeners respond positively (i.e., attributed high competence and social attractiveness) to convergence, which conforms to established norms and the converse when divergence violates them.

The strength of these early models lay in providing not only conceptual schemas in which to embed language attitudes (e.g., contextual and normative dimensions), but also began to unpack the ways in which listeners came about the language attitudes they reported. Thereafter, language attitudes began to take on a more vital role in models of interpersonal *communication* (e.g., Giles & Street, 1985) as well as miscommunication (Hewstone & Giles, 1986) more generally. All this was manifest in terms of highlighting (language attitude) schemas as being prime resources for constructing self- as well as couple-presentations in the company of others (Giles & Fitzpatrick, 1984). In tandem with these developments, more processual models of language began to emerge that took into account interactions between the nature of the message, mediating cognitions and affect, the immediate and larger-scale contexts and their histories, and wider communicative outcomes and social consequences; it is to these we move next. While being insightful, and sometimes springboarding off each other, processual frameworks seem to have highlighted different phenomena and processes and have not always, arguably, built upon each other's insights to sufficient measure. Our integrative model ultimately attempts to resolve these issues. While space precludes more details of the models to be overviewed next, their unique features are highlighted as well as the relationships between them.

Process Models of Language Attitudes

An Intergroup Perspective on Language Attitudes

One model did that did acknowledge the Ryan et al. (1982) orthogonal dimensions of the socio-structural context (standardization and group vitality), was that of Ryan, Hewstone, and Giles (1984). They were intrigued by the fact that different language attitude profiles had emerged across different intergroup contexts, and speculated about the historical relationships between dominant and subordinate groups (Language Varieties 1 and 2, respectively [LV1 & LV2]; see Figure 9.3). Following Ryan et al. (1982), at least four such patterns were identified and related to the dependent variable clusters, status and solidarity (or social attractiveness); see also, Bradac (1990).

Pattern A is where there is preference by both groups for the dominant group's speech styles and reflected in favorable status (e.g., intelligence and ambition) and solidarity (e.g., benevolence and sociability) traits. In these settings, minority language varieties maintain very low vitality and standardization and yield general feelings of ingroup denigration. Pattern B is where there

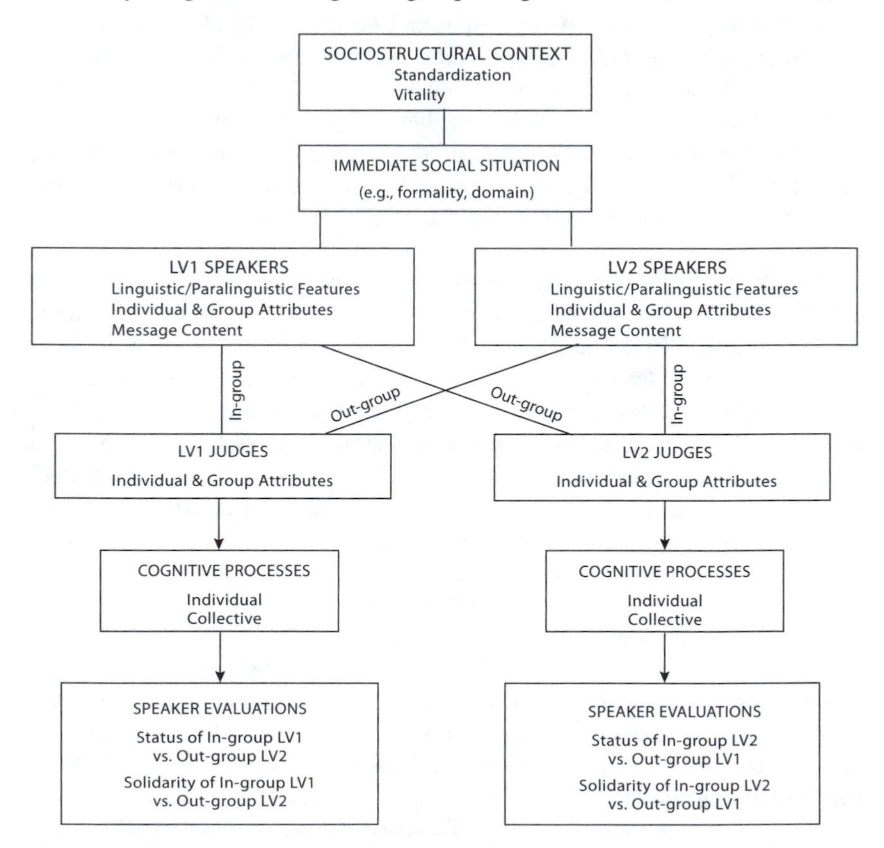

Figure 9.3 Speaker evaluations by in-group and out-group members (Ryan, Hewstone, & Giles, 1984, p. 144). Reproduced by permission of SpringerVerlag Publishers.

is a status preference for the dominant group's speech style, yet both minority and majority groups convey a solidarity preference for their own ingroup's patterns. This profile can be seen among minority language speakers when they are unable or unwilling to adapt to dominant language norms, either because they lack fluency in the outgroup code or because in-group sanctions discourage the use of the dominant language (Hogg, D'Agata, & Abrams, 1989). Pattern C is characterized by ingroup preferences for both status and solidarity traits. Ryan et al. (1982) argued that this pattern develops when the minority language group realizes that they, as individuals, are being evaluated unfavorably by other groups, based upon their collective membership; this likely occurs when the ethnolinguistic vitality of the minority group is high. Also, people who speak the dominant language variety begin to understand that they have privileges and advantages based on unfair, socially illegitimate historical circumstances. Pattern D takes place when there is a consensually-agreed upon status preference for speakers of the dominant language variety and a solidarity preference for speakers of the minority variety.

An important point emerging from this rather complex analysis was that the same profile could function socio-psychologically quite differently for the groups involved. For instance, Pattern B might be processed as a means of justifying the status quo for the majority group, but as one of social creativity for the minority group. Ryan et al. (1982) related the minority group profiles to Tajfel and Turner's (1986) identity maintenance strategies, such that profiles A, B (with D), and C represented social mobility, creativity, and competition, respectively. In this way (and see Figure 9.3), it was argued that listener raters' evaluations of an outgroup speaker *could* sometimes be mediated by processing that person as an individual but, more likely (and as initialed in Lambert's early model above), cognitively processed more collectively as a representative of the outgroup; for parallel appeals to this same distinction, but in terms of settings; see Giles and Ryan (1982) and Gudykunst and Ting-Toomey (1990).

Furthermore, Ryan et al. (1984) acknowledged that different members of the same social group could express the patterns differently given that they were construing the intergroup context in variable ways (see Giles & Johnson, 1987). They also emphasized that the public expressions of a language attitude profile by one group could spur counter-reactive measures by the other. The potency of this model is that it conceptualizes different language attitude patterns as reflections of the ongoing intergroup dynamics occurring and evolving between groups in contact.

The Staged Discursive Event Model of Language Attitudes

In a context celebrating the diverse work of Lambert, Giles, and Coupland (1991b) re-conceived of the MGT as a series of interlocking processes. This model had a number of distinctive features. These related to the production and guising of different social categories on audiotape as well as the reporting of them by raters. While not contesting their traditional authenticity (although the supposed social neutrality of the controlled textual content was), Giles and Coupland (1991b) suggested that even the readings of prose from written origins were constructed, and goal directed, so as to convey particular personas matched to the genre at hand. These so-called "discursive concerns," in turn, could be interpreted by listeners according to prevailing intergroup schemas and norms of how texts should be performed (see Giles et al., 1992). They argued that "…the more denuded a stimulus text is of contextual specificity, the more assiduous, variable, and creative will be the contextual inventiveness of listener-judges" (Giles & Coupland, 1991b, p. 32). It was also underscored that the evaluative process should be conceived as separate from the way in which the attitudes were being rarified and mindfully reported—as basic messages in a particular context.

In the integrative model that concludes this chapter, Giles and Coupland's (1991b) interlocking model is elaborated beyond the MGT paradigm and acknowledges the insights of later theoreticians about language attitudes more generally and including the models discussed below.

Social/General Process and Communication Ecology Models of Language Attitudes

The social process model by Cargile, Giles, Ryan, and Bradac (1994) afforded due attention to the communicative (as well as other behavioral) outcomes of language attitudes not evident in the prior models. This time, however, the focus was skewed more towards the interpersonal (rather than the intergroup) context of the speaker-listener connect (see Figure 9.4). In this way and appeal-

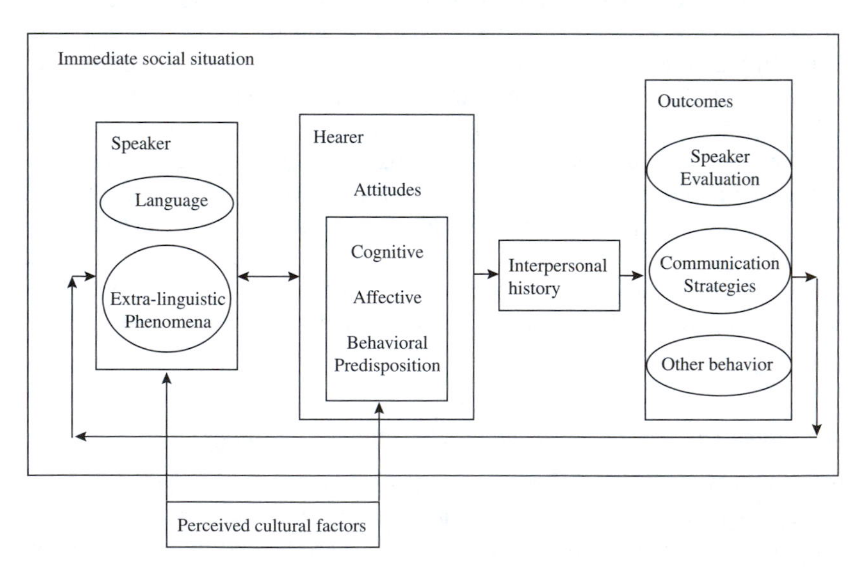

Figure 9.4 Social process model of language attitudes (Cargile, Giles, Ryan, & Bradac, 1994, p. 214). Reproduced by permission of Elsevier Publishers.

ing to more naturalistic settings beyond the task-oriented laboratory, they highlighted the role of the relational history of interactions that could have previously taken place between the speaker and listener. For instance, people who have maintained an intimate or friendly working relationship for a long period of time are more likely to be accustomed to and, thereby, overlook the accents of friends or co-workers.

Cargile et al. (1994) also acknowledged, and in many ways echoed Street and Hopper's (1982) earlier treatise, that the way in which a speaker is *perceived* to "be" and "sound," as well as the perceived cultural factors prevailing, will influence language attitudes more than the actual speech behaviors physically voiced. In addition to accent and other verbal signals, they drew attention to extra-linguistic phenomena, such non-verbal displays (e.g., gestures) that could potentially reinforce, mitigate, or interact with the language variety spoken for language attitude studies with static or dynamic visual features of the speakers available (Aboud, Clément, & Taylor, 1974; Elwell, Brown, & Rutter, 1984; Rakić et al., in press; Williams, 1976). An important aspect of their general process model, and in line with the classic social attitudes literature overviewed at the outset, was that besides cognitions and stereotypes being the focus of the language attitude process so, too, were the emotions and behavioral dispositions evoked (see Giles et al., 1995).

This model was later elaborated by Bradac, Cargile, and Hallett (2001) and Cargile and Bradac (2001). Their intent in their model refinement was to draw attention to the ways in which speakers' language varieties are selectively attended to and processed as information. Regarding the former, their model suggested that individual attitudes may motivate people to attend more to certain types of information during interactions. For instance, someone who fears or dislikes people of other racial groups may attend to the racial background of that speaker during that exchange. However, a person who enjoys foreign accents may not attend to racial background, yet may notice the type of accent one is speaking with (Rakić et al., in press). Social expectations may also guide stimuli selection (Burgoon, 1978) in that listeners will often attend to cues that align with their expectations of a particular situation. For example, participants in a new dating relationship may be unsure about the short- and long-term intentions of the other and, hence, may attend to nonverbal (and verbal) cues to gauge how the other person feels towards them.

Goals also influence what kinds of information people attend to and which information they overlook. Cargile and Bradac (2001) employed an illustrative scenario in order to demonstrate the powerful influence that goals have during impression formation:

> For example, for some parole board members the goal of imprisonment is the protection of society from criminals; for others, it is rehabilitation... One official with the protection goal may attend to a criminal's nonstandard accent and believe that he or she is a member of a particular social group stereotypically associated with the traits of cruelty and

> remorselessness. Another official with the rehabilitation goal may hear, at the same time, a criminal's slow rate of speech and redundant vocabulary, allowing attributions to be made about the criminal's impoverished educational upbringing. (p. 364)

In this situation, each official maintains a distinct goal that will influence which information they attend to, which information they overlook and, ultimately, which conclusions they form about people. Clearly, the attributions people make about the actions of others will also influence the kinds of behaviors they respond with. The consequences of situations like these may be especially dire in cases of criminal trials and/or sentencing (Frumkin, 2007).

Information processing—akin to the notion of assessing another's interpretive competence in communication accommodation theory (see Giles & Coupland, 1991a)—is one of the final stages through which listener's progress during the general process model of language evaluations. Using different nomenclature yet reminiscent of person- versus group-centered settings, inter-individual versus intergroup interactions, and individual versus collective processing referred to above, Cargile and Ryan modeled the notion that listener-raters are influenced by individuating information and stereotypes when they develop impressions of others (Brewer, 1988; Fiske & Neuberg, 1990). Individuating information relates to personal idiosyncrasies or special characteristics, while stereotypes or group-based information refers to pre-existing associations that people may have between speech (accent) or nonverbal stimuli (race) and trait attributions (e.g., education, status, and attractiveness).

In addition, this so-called general process model (see Figure 9.5) subscribes to the view that listeners may process information in automatic or controlled ways; see also, the central versus peripheral processing model of Cacioppo and Petty (1982). Automatic processing develops unintentionally, often as the result of a set of associations that are well established in a person's cognitive schema. As a result, automatic processing often occurs without much cognitive effort or elaboration. In contrast, controlled processing involves cognitive elaboration and deliberation, such as in the case when someone negatively evaluates another's accent, yet refrains from expressing criticism based upon their desire to be polite (Marlow, 2010). Finally, Cargile and Bradac (2001) articulated how functional biases could play a significant role in shaping the language attitudes of listeners. These biases could include the individual needs that a listener may have to enhance personal or social esteem and, by these means, language attitudes are not mere reactions to social stimuli but, rather, are expressed to fulfill wider personal or group needs. Relatedly, Tajfel (1981) noted that people may rely upon impressions of others to develop, preserve, or defend group-based value systems. In a similar vein, Giles and Coupland (1991a, b), calling upon the Billig's (1987) rhetorical psychological approach, argued that language attitudes may be fruitfully analyzed as one component fitting into the larger structure of listener-judges' particular *argumentative* stances on a social issue. In any case, the theoretical power of these social and process models are that

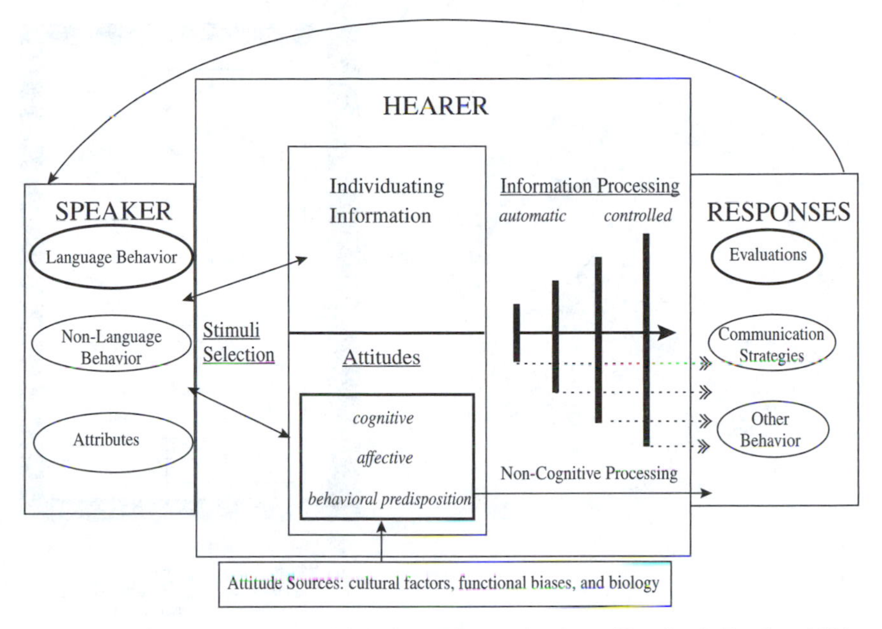

Figure 9.5 General process model of speaker evaluations (Cargile & Bradac, 2001, p. 358). Reproduced by permission of Sage Publications and The International Communication Association.

they have called attention to important relational dynamics, affective states, information processing, and communicative outcomes.

Inspired by Cargile and Bradac (2001), Giles et al.'s (2006) communication ecology model sought to develop further the social origins of language attitudes within the intricacies of people's localized social contexts. First, their model suggested that an individual maintains interpersonal networks with family, friends, and other ingroup members. Accordingly, one person does not stand alone and, instead, is embedded in meso-level interactions with their local networks that are considered to be responsible for introducing and reinforcing existing language attitudes. The communication ecology model suggests that such meso-level interactions influence how recipients evaluate a speaker's linguistic and extra-linguistic cues (e.g., accent and gestures) based on language attitudes (see Figure 9.6).

Second, the meso-macro level accounts for information gathered from neighbors and friends, local media, and community organizations. Media consumption and interpersonal interactions have been found to be responsible, at least partially, for the misperceptions individuals bring to interactions with outgroup members (Matei, Ball-Rokeach, & Qiu, 2001). Furthermore, this model identifies the importance of the communication action context which consists of local features that can enable or constrain communication between or within nodes of storytelling networks. Once again then, language attitudes should not be sterilized as mere responses to a pre-determined multidimen-

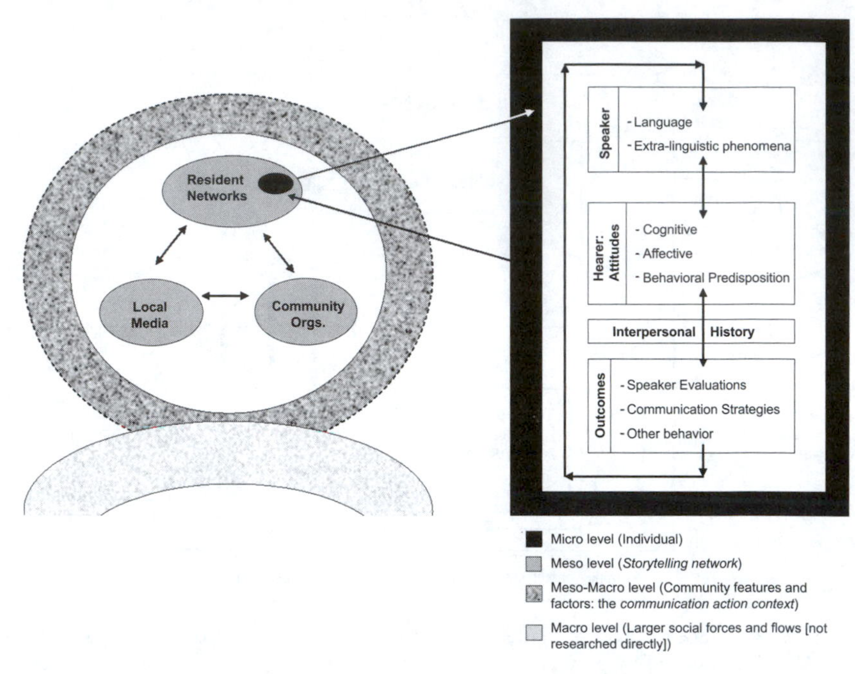

Figure 9.6 A communication ecology model of language attitudes (Giles, Katz, & Myers, 2006, p. 42). Reproduced by permission of the journal, *Moderna Språk.*

sional evaluative structure, but can be more free-flowing structures fulfilling needs within a community.

Giles et al. (1991b) articulated an array of ecological factors that are the ingredients of localized contexts and include the physical makeup of the urban grid (e.g., streets and freeways), locations that serve as gathering places for people (e.g., parks, libraries, and community centers) and may contribute to psychological comfort or fear during conversations with others. The meso-level also identifies the importance of economic features, such as the time and resources available to engage in conversation with others in the community. Technological access and knowledge, in addition to available transportation, may influence how much daily contact individuals have with other residents in their communities. The macro-level would include factors greater than those at the community level, such as the relative status afforded to certain language or ethnic groups, immigration trends, national laws and policies, in addition to enduringly-felt historical events. The value of this communication ecology model lies in its enabling a more holistic approach to understanding how each of the listed factors collectively interact to influence and socialize people's language attitudes and communication outcomes.

Model of the Stigma of Non-Native Accents

With a focus on the stigma attached to the language varieties of non-native accented speakers, Gluszek and Dovidio (2010b) highlighted several factors that may help or hinder their effective communicativeness, including accent strength, subjective comprehensibility, and objective comprehensibility. Accent strength refers to the comparative linguistic distance between two people that is causing one of them to be perceived as speaking in a "different" or marked manner (see also, Myers-Scotton, 1998). Subjective comprehensibility refers to the extent to which listener-judges perceive that they are able to understand speakers, despite their accents. Objective comprehensibility is the degree to which raters are actually able to understand the person who is considered to have an accent (see Figure 9.7).

The model suggested that listeners evaluate those who speak with a non-native accent, at least in part, based upon their perceptions of their attributed control over progress to learn the host language. In other words, people who maintain colloquially so-called "heavy accents" may be evaluated critically by native speakers who believe that they are not making the necessary effort to learn the standard language more fluently (see Simard, Taylor, & Giles, 1976). In addition, these scholars acknowledged the powerful influence of individual goals, situational variables, and socio-cultural context, and also resurrected the interpersonal focus back into the theoretical fray. Contemporaneously, the socio-cultural context included a consideration of socio-political change factors. For example, during times of international conflict and terrorist activity, Western societies can become more critical of foreigners from the Middle East and, hence, may be more likely to express negative speech evaluations and approve of others who voice similar concerns.

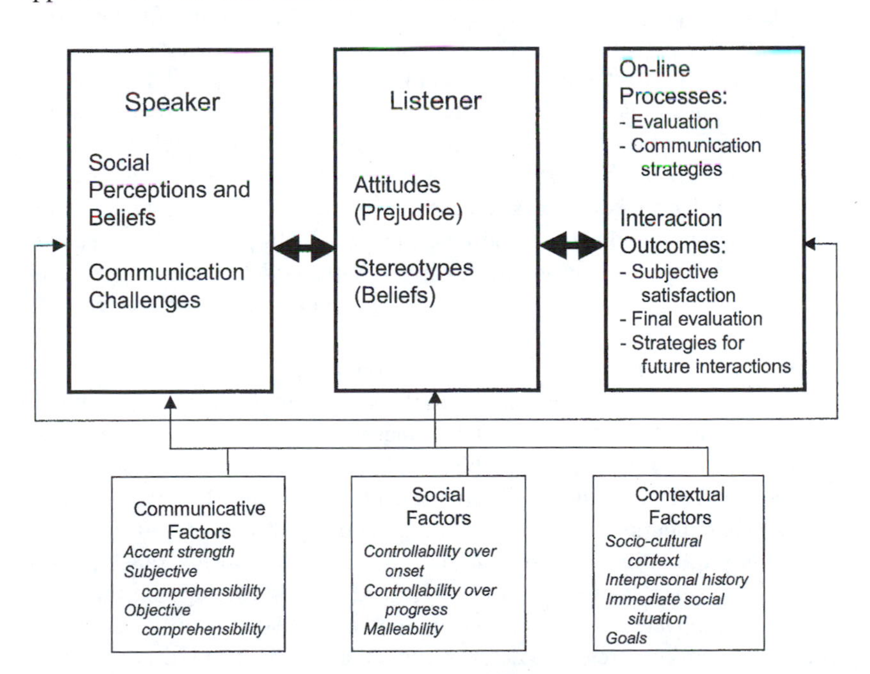

Figure 9.7 Model of the stigma of non-native accents (Gluszek & Dovidio, 2010b, p. 220). Reproduced by permission of Sage Publications.

Gluszek and Dovidio (2010b) also proposed that researchers should expand existing work on language attitudes to include interactional outcomes. They developed the term "on-line processes" to address the impressions, evaluations, and response strategies people employ during accent-based interactions. Such conversations could be evaluated based upon their outcomes and the constructs of interactional satisfaction, as well as communicative strategies for interacting in the future assumed prominence. This framework is important as it elevates additional interactional outcomes for modeling as well as highlights the importance of perceptions of speakers' comprehensibility, together with presumptions about their controllability of this. Curiously perhaps, stigma is not afforded schematic status in the model and it does not address the ways in which non-native accented individuals respond when others convey approval or criticism based upon their speech behaviors (see Meisenbach, 2010). Language praise and criticism have, thus far, been overlooked within language attitudes arena and it is to such issues that the last model reviewed addresses.

Receiver Model of Language Evaluation and Feedback

A feature of Marlow's (2010) model was that it was built on the presumption that language attitudes (e.g., stigmatic ones) do not always lie fallow in the minds of listener-judges or on the pages of questionnaire surveys - as our opening statement attested. They can also become the fodder for interpersonal "attacks" on the speaker. Poignantly for the present purposes, Kowalski (1997) suggested that people routinely encounter ostracism, embarrassment, complaining, and guilt during their interactions with others. Relatedly, Marlow and Giles (2008, 2010) showed that locals in Hawai'i were criticized by others who perceived that they were attempting to elevate their individual status by speaking Standard English, rather than Hawai'i Creole English. Marlow and Giles also found that respondents reported frequent incidents and experiences of speech criticism across professional, educational, social, and familial contexts. Drawing upon these findings, Marlow (2010) proposed the receiver model of language evaluation and feedback. This model attempts to account for factors influencing the ways in which people make sense of speech criticism (see Figure 9.8).

The first stage of the model depicts factors relating to the individual personality (e.g., self-esteem and experiential history with past criticisms) and the context in which the criticism has taken place (including power differentials). For instance, certain people may been more likely to accept criticism from their parents than from their subordinate co-workers. For Marlow (2010), the situation construct consists of the actual topic being discussed and the verbal words and phrases one uses to criticize, while non-verbal messages involve proxemic, oculesic, haptic, or paralinguistic strategies. She argued that criticism that is delivered with face-saving and supportive non-verbal cues may evoke less cognitive stress and defensiveness than outright and direct criticism that is conveyed with antagonism.

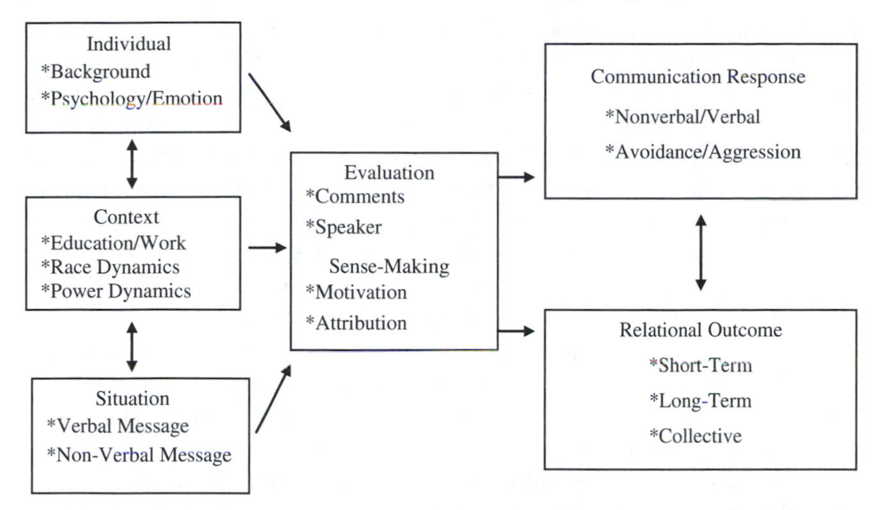

Figure 9.8 Receiver model of language evaluation and feedback (Marlow, 2010, p. 147). Reproduced by permission of VDM Verlag Dr. Müller Aktiengesellschaft & Co. KG.

Although not afforded any real discussion in the textual description of the model, the second stage of it identifies sense-making as having an important mediating role between reception of the criticism and responses to it. As such, this aspect of the model is deserving of further consideration and we delve further into this in our final integrative model below. In any case, someone who is seen to be highly critical of others will probably be less desirable as a friend or confidante, while one who is quick to praise will, other things being equal, likely be more popular in social or professional situations. In terms of attributions following speech criticism, it is likely that people who develop positive explanations for such criticism (e.g., my co-worker or boss just wants me to be successful at this organization) will respond more favorably than people who assign negative explanations (e.g., my co-worker or boss thinks that he is superior and is trying to insult me). Also, it seems important to address the ways in which internal versus external attributions may shape sense-making and subsequent reactions (Martinko, Harvey, & Douglas, 2007). For instance, someone who concludes that their co-worker or boss is criticizing their speech based upon organizational regulations for standard speech in the workplace (external attribution) may be more open to criticism and modifying their speech than someone who assumes that their co-worker or boss is attempting to elevate themselves above others because they are on a "power-trip" (internal attribution).

Following speech criticism events, and although rarely investigated in language attitude studies (see, however, Garrett et al., 2003), it is plausible that *narrative* sense-making (which now could feature as a further outcome option in Figure 9.8) may shape people's future understandings of language practices. It has been found that when people make sense of stressful experiences by constructing a written account of them, they experience a greater sense of well-being and health (e.g., Pennebaker, 1997; Sloan & Marx, 2004). More specifically, research has suggested that people who experience traumatic events may benefit, both physically and psychologically, when they develop narratives about the incident (Frattaroli, 2006). This benefit has been explained, at least in part, based upon a person's ability to release or let go of negative memories following the narrative exercise (McAdams, 1993). Narrative processes also allow people to organize and integrate an experience, in terms of the self, and may promote a more refined ability to effectively control and express themselves during stressful situations (Frattaroli, 2006), such as being the recipient of deeply-wounding speech criticisms. Indeed, we would now advocate a feedback pathway from outcomes to sense-making in Marlow's model to acknowledge the potential for re-appraisals and this is afforded conceptual status in our own model below.

The outcome stage of Marlow's model addresses communication responses and relational outcomes that may develop as a result of language criticism. Drawing from her own research that undergirded her model, Marlow (2010) found that multiethnic locals in Hawai'i responded to a hypothetical criticism vignette ranging from avoidance to aggressiveness. Avoidant individuals would look away or walk away from the critical person, while emotional and verbally aggressive responses included statements like: "You know what?! F*$% you & your 'English'. Don't be so F*$%'n stupid & arrogant! I don't criticize you so be fair to me & don't down size my language!" In the most extreme situations, informants responded to the critical person with physical threats: "Say what scrub? Don't let me catch you after work!" Qualitative reports also suggested that criticism responses may be complex and nuanced—and this was evident in situations when people predicted that their response to the criticism would be to smile and tell the critical person to "take it easy." This model is an important development for analyses of language attitudes and draws attention to how communicators manage being recipients of critical responses to their speech styles; it is, of course, somewhat constrained by its focus on one side of the interactional equation, namely the receiver.

The Integrative Model of Language Attitudes

Each of the foregoing models has highlighted valuable variables and processes, many of whose unique features appear in summary form in Table 9.1. In an attempt to assuage the proliferation of yet more models while coalescing advances in prior frameworks, we are proposing our own integrative, heuristic model that acknowledges the processes inherent in a MGT-like study as well as language attitudes in real time conversations. To accomplish this, we significantly embellish and rework the interlocking structure of Giles and Coupland's (1991b) model.

The novel essence of this more holistic approach is that it moves beyond MGT-constrained generalizations about the field that were insightful in their

Table 9.1 A Typology of Language Attitude Models

Models	*Unique Features*
Ryan et al. (1982)	Standardness-nonstandardness/ increasing-decreasing group vitality
Gudykunst & Ting-Toomey (1990)	Uncertainty reduction/perceived similarity/ interindividual-intergroup contexts
Ryan & Giles (1982)	Status-group-stressing situations
Bradac (1990)	Communication accommodation/norm adherence
Ryan et al. (1984)	Language attitude patterns/intergroup strategies, histories
Giles & Coupland (1991b)	Genres/stimulus construction/textual interpretations
Cargile et al. (1994)	Nonverbals/interpersonal history/communicative strategies
Cargile et al. (2001)	Automatic-planning processing/conversational goals/ attitude functions
Giles et al. (2006)	Community networks, organizations
Gluszek & Dovidio (2010)	Comprehensibility/relational outcomes/stigma
Marlow (2010)	Criticism/reciprocal responses

own time (see Bradac, 1990). In other words, language attitudes are much more than anonymous reports on questionnaires, produced on demand about unknown speakers in socially sterile, task-oriented settings. Rather, they can also sometimes be manifest as communicative strategies managed to react to others' voices and expressed language ideologies while, at other times, feature more creatively as cogent elements within stories told, arguments rendered, and personas performed. Furthermore and as below, we would contend that sometimes couples, peers, and others can jointly negotiate their positions about each other's speech practices and concomitant evaluations. In any case, language attitudes typically fulfill vital personal, rhetorical, and social needs whose origins are borne out of past, yet evolving, community network involvements, perceived relational trajectories, and beliefs about past intergroup histories and their on-going dynamics (see Figure 9.9).

Although the model has a transactional sequencing, we outline its elements in a linear fashion for the sake of parsimony. Figure 9.9 summarily details many of the ingredients and dimensions implicated at each stage in the structure. No claim is made as to the exhaustiveness of the components or pathways inherent in the model, and, clearly, there is room for expanding and, ultimately, fine-tuning. As found in prior models and coalesced herein, the extra-textual climates reflect a rich panoply of micro- and macro-constraints and forces (from governmental politics to the presence of significant others). Important here is the accumulated history of being the recipient of language attitudes conveyed by others as well as self-perceptions of one's own participation in targeting others in similar ways. Due attention is afforded message production dynamics

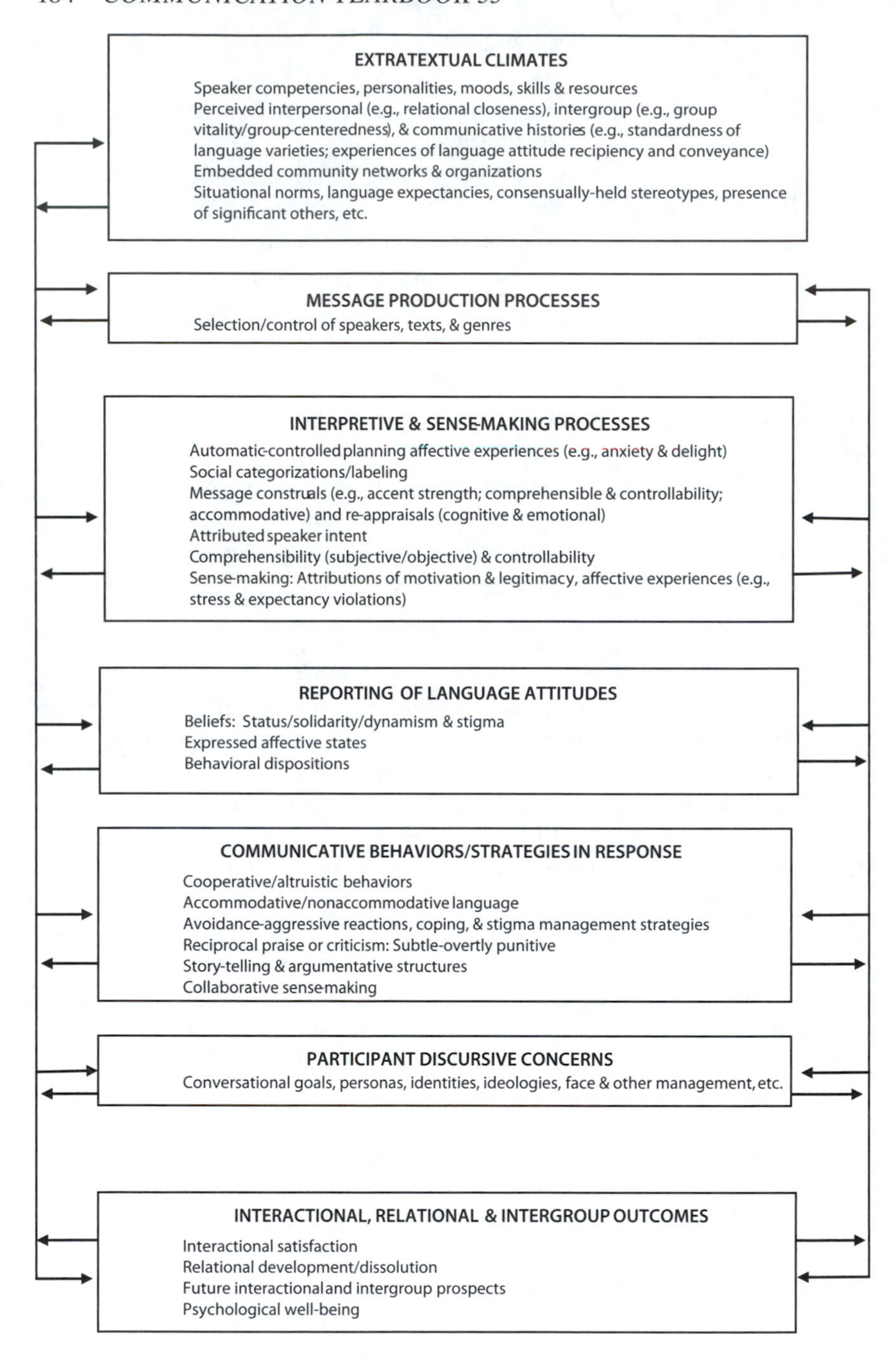

Figure 9.9 An integrative model of language attitudes

as is the role of interpretive and sense-making processes, including subjective and objective comprehensibility. Indeed, although the empirical gauntlet has still to be picked up (Giles & Coupland, 1991b), exploring how speakers and their texts are selected, and how stimulus speakers project what kinds of image are still valued pursuits to engage. The reporting of language attitudes—so endemic to MGT studies—is conceptually separated from other communicative strategies and behaviors, with participants' discursive goals influencing all other phases of the model. Last, an array of social outcomes in terms of the ongoing interaction and relationship as well as intergroup consequences are modeled, including those of relational and psychological well-being, and the re-appraisal of sense-making and its attending emotions is recognized, even as a nonconscious process (Williams, Bargh, Nocera, & Gray, 2009). Of course, such re-appraisals will likely provoke further repercussions and pathways can be re-ignited in cyclic fashion at will.

According sense-making a central phase at different stages of our model, it is important to appeal to the ample research that has explored the ways in which people do try and make sense of their interactions and relationships with others (Burgoon & Hale, 1984; Dillard, Solomon, & Palmer, 1999) and, therefore, has potential insights for future language attitudes research and theory. In fact, scholars have suggested that sense-making during intercultural communication is one of the most critical issues for future research (Oetzel & Ting-Toomey, 2006). As such, several theoretical perspectives have been developed to address this issue, including expectancy violations theory (Burgoon & Hale, 1988), discrepancy arousal theory (Cappella & Greene, 1982), relational framing theory (Dillard, Solomon, & Samp, 1996), and the functional approach to nonverbal messages (Patterson, 1983), to name a few. Each of these approaches assumes that people derive information about their relationships with others based upon their communicative interactions—and also language attitudes—and that people engage in interactions with pre-conceived expectations that influence how they perceive a given situation.

According to Planalp (1985) and Planalp and Rivers (1996), people are guided by their expectations, which will influence what information people extract from a given interaction (Dillard et al., 1996). Knowledge about a particular person, situation, or speech style will assist people in making sense of a situation and in predicting future interactions (Honeycutt, Cantrill, Kelly, & Lambkin, 1998). Such expectations have been referred to with a variety of terms, including mental models (Miller & Read, 1991), frames (Dillard et al., 1996), schemas (Planalp & Rivers, 1996), and memory structures (Honeycutt et al, 1998), yet the common assumption of each approach assumes that people process relational information based upon pre-conceived expectations for individuals and situations.

According to cognitive appraisal theory, people cope with stressful situations in diverse ways (Lazarus, 1991), especially with regards to emotional experiences (Duhachek, 2005). Cognitive, attitudinal, and behavioral issues influence the ways in which people cope, make sense of, and respond during stressful situations (Carver & Scheier, 1994; Lazarus & Folkman, 1984). Lazarus (1991) suggested that people process messages based upon primary (goal relevance, congruence, and ego involvement) and secondary appraisals (emotional response to an outcome, coping ability, and future expectations). From this perspective, people who perceive that they have sufficient coping skills and resources to deal with a situation will experience less cognitive and emotional stress than someone who does not perceive they have the ability to cope with it. Given that stigma management strategies can be variable and very stressful (see Meisenbach, 2010), coping skills, affective experiences, and expectancy violations assume conceptual status in Figure 9.9.

Epilogue

This chapter has reviewed the history and development of language attitudes research and highlighted leading models attending it, all of which have features of theoretical virtue. Consequently, an integrative model has been proposed that, at the very least, can provide a heuristic checklist for the kinds of variables and processes experimentalists as well as those more naturalistically-inclined can manipulate, control, measure, and/or observe. Obviously, given its systemic character, the model as a whole cannot be put to empirical test. That said, many of its paths are worthy of further elaboration and, by that token, a plethora of future directions can be embraced. Toward that end, we prioritize and present a manageable set of interrelated research avenues constituting a coherent programmatic agenda based on or arising from Figure 9.9.

First, our model recognizes the role of sense-making as playing important mediating roles in the immediate formulation of language attitudes, communications (positive-negative) to the speaker, and the recipient's reply to those, as well as further exchanges beyond those. Clearly, even the prototypical MGT evaluative process requires empirical scrutiny beyond the early attention afforded attributions of perceived speaker-listener similarities, and the like. Listener-judges' sense-making of the speaker's goals in the prevailing situation, attributed effort expended by the speaker appropriately in style and accommodativeness of the message content, the latter's alleged comprehensibility and its attending cognitive and affective load required for sense-making are all interlocking sequences of the interpretive work involved.

Second, research needs to be devised exploring when which types of messages are communicated about another's speech style in social networks even beyond that of the target speaker, and how recipients of these messages (e.g., presence and reactions of those present or overheard) are perceived and responded to. Relatedly, many facets of the sense-making process hitherto unexplored in this genre of work could be considered important, and one of these may be the concept of legitimacy. In this vein, Newell and Stutman (1988) suggested that perceptions of complaint legitimacy are important factors that influence how a confrontational interaction develops (and for perceived legitimacy in an intergroup context see, for example, Terry, Pelly, Lalonde, &

Smith, 2006). Not surprisingly, research has found that people are more likely to initiate complaints when the situation is one where they perceive it is their responsibility or right to do so (Newell & Stutman, 1991). Also, people who are perceived to be legitimate in these confrontations are met with more positive and cooperative responses than those who are not perceived to be legitimate and/or are a mistrusted source (Hullett & Tamborini, 2001). In sum, and while affording consideration of the emotive tone attending or evolving from these kinds of interactions, the perceived legitimacy-illegitimacy of a speaker's style of speaking and recipients' messages of praise or condemnation of it are candidates for further investigation and theorizing.

Third, the area of language attitudes has not really ever entertained the notion that language attitudes may be socially negotiated and are not always static responses elicited in a social vacuum. Of relevance here is that past research has suggested that participating in collaborative sense-making may promote one's ability to understand and cope with difficult relational interactions (Fiese & Sameroff, 1999; Holmberg, Orbuch, & Veroff, 2004; Pratt & Fiese, 2004). For instance, Kellas, Trees, Schrodt, LeClair-Underberg, and Willer (2010) found that collaborative sense-making between husbands and wives about stressful events predicted greater mental health for husbands. Konid Kellas and Trees (2005, 2006) found that collaborative sense-making is most often productive under conditions of so-called interactional sense-making. They include communication behaviors that reflect engagement (involvement of partners), turn-taking (negotiating speech and conversation), perspective-taking (confirming the other's point of view), and coherence (unified and joint telling of a story). These behaviors have been found to enhance familial adaptability, cohesion, and satisfaction (Koenig Kellas, 2005; Trees & Koenig Kellas, 2009). Given that collaborative sense-making tends to enhance health, well-being, and relational stability, it would seem important to determine when and how sense-making influences people's perceptions of criticism, why it might be successful, unsuccessful, or even counter-productive, and to document the variable ways it is communicatively managed.

In conclusion, most people today encounter and interact with others from different cultures, classes, and language groups on a regular basis. Mass media and global economies have brought us together, sometimes unwillingly, to communicate across personal, social, and public contexts. Such intensified coming-together of various language and culture groups has created new opportunities and demands for both speakers and listeners. Understanding the perceptions and attitudes that develop during intergroup speech encounters presents real opportunities for collaborative communication that is meaningful and rewarding. The research outlined above, however, has corroborated the potential for misunderstanding, language criticism, and attitudinal division during intergroup encounters. Economically and relationally, the widespread costs of such human misunderstanding and attitudinal discord are largely immeasurable and (as we noted above) can have, disturbingly affective significance at a very young age. Much of the research cited herein attempts to understand these questions and, figuratively stand in the gap, to provide ideas for future research. We acknowledge the cogent work of all authors and colleagues who have contributed to this chapter by formulating prior models, and encourage other scholars to continue inquiry into language attitudes and outcomes. Much ground has been covered, yet, there is still much to be discovered during interpersonal and intergroup interactions.

To return full circle to our opening sentiments, a recent meta-analysis of the language attitudes domain has demonstrated the overriding power of a standard accent for its speakers in terms of attributed competence (Fuentes et al., under review). Perhaps it is time to proactively utilize social networking and new communication resources to dispel and offer remedial options for what are often speech stereotypes with cumulatively disturbing repercussions, thereby alleviating some of the social harm inflicted on those enduring linguistic insecurities.

Note

1. We express our appreciation to four anonymous reviewers and the editor for their comments on earlier drafts of this manuscript and, again, to the latter for his patience.

References

Aboud, F., Clément, R., & Taylor D. M. (1974). Evaluational reactions to discrepancies between social class and language. *Sociometry, 37,* 239–250.

Abrams, J. R., Barker, V., & Giles, H. (2009). An examination of the validity of the Subjective Vitality Questionnaire. *Journal of Multilingual and Multicultural Development, 30*, 59–72.

Adorno, T. W., Frenkel-Brunswik, E., Levinson, D. J., & Sanford, R. N. (1950). *The authoritarian personality.* New York: Harper & Row.

Ajzen, I., & Fishbein, M. (1980). *Understanding attitudes and predicting social behavior.* Englewood Cliffs, NJ: Prentice Hall.

Ball, P. (1983). Stereotypes of Anglo-Saxon and non-Anglo-Saxon accents: Some exploratory Australian studies with the matched guise technique. *Language Sciences, 5,* 163–183.

Ball, P., Byrne, J. L., Giles, H., Berechree, P., Griffiths, J., McDonald, H., & McKendrick, I. (1982). The retroactive speech stereotype effect: Some Australian data and constraints. *Language and Communication, 2*, 277–284.

Berger, C. R., & Bradac, J. J. (1982). *Language and social knowledge.* London: Academic Press.

Billig, M. (1987). *Arguing and thinking: A rhetorical approach to social psychology.* Cambridge, UK: Cambridge University Press.

Bishop, H., Garrett, P, & Coupland, N. (2003). Conceptual accent evaluation: 30 years of accent prejudice in the UK. *Acta Linguistic Hefniensia, 37,* 131–154.

Bourhis, R. Y., Giles, H., & Tajfel, H. (1973). Language as a determinant of Welsh identity. *European Journal of Social Psychology, 3*, 447–460.

Bourhis, R. Y., & Landry, R. (2008). Group vitality, cultural autonomy and the wellness of language minorities. In R.Y. Bourhis (Ed.), *The vitality of the English-speaking communities of Quebec: From community decline to revival* (pp. 185–211). Montréal, Canada: CEETUM, Université de Montréal.

Bourhis, R. Y., Montreuil, A., Helly, D., & Jantzen, L. (2007). Discrimination et linguicisme au Québec: Enquête sur la diversité ethnique au Canada. *Canadian Ethnic Studies, 39*, 31–49.

Bradac, J. J. (1990). Language attitudes and impression formation. In H. Giles & W. P. Robinson (Eds.), *The handbook of language and social psychology* (pp. 387–412). Chichester, UK: Wiley.

Bradac, J. J., & Giles, H. (1991). Social and educational consequences of language attitudes. *Moderna Språk, 85*, 1–11.

Bradac, J. J., Cargile, A. C., & Hallett, J. S. (2001). Language attitudes: Retrospect, conspect, and prospect. In W. P. Robinson & H. Giles (Eds.), *The new handbook of language and social psychology* (pp. 137–155). Chichester, UK: Wiley.

Brewer, M. B. (1988). A dual process model of impression formation. In T. K. Srull & R. S. Wyer (Eds.), *Advances in social cognition* (pp. 1–36). Hillsdale, NJ: Erlbaum.

Burgoon, J. K. (1978). A communication model of personal space violations: Explication and initial test. *Human Communication Research, 4*, 129–142.

Burgoon, J. K., & Hale, J. L. (1984). The fundamental topic of relational communication. *Communication Monographs, 51*, 193–214.

Burgoon, J. K., & Hale, J. L. (1988). Nonverbal expectancy violations: Model elaboration and application to immediacy behaviors. *Communication Monographs, 55*, 58–79.

Cacioppo, J. T., & Petty, R. E. (1982). Language variables, attitudes, and persuasion. In E. B. Ryan & H. Giles (Eds.), *Attitudes toward language: Social and applied contexts* (pp. 189–207). London: Academic Press.

Cappella, J. N., & Greene, J. O. (1982). A discrepancy-arousal explanation of mutual influence in expressive behavior for adult and infant-adult interaction. *Communication Monographs, 45*, 89–114.

Cargile, A. C., & Bradac, J. J. (2001). Attitudes toward language: A review of speaker-evaluation research and a general process model. In W. B. Gudykunst (Ed.), *Communication yearbook 25* (pp. 347–382). Mahwah, NJ: Erlbaum.

Cargile, A. C., & Giles, H. (1997). Understanding language attitudes: Exploring listener affect and identity. *Language and Communication, 17*, 195–217.

Cargile, A. C., Giles, H., Ryan, E. B., & Bradac, J. J. (1994). Language attitudes as a social process: A conceptual model and new directions. *Language and Communication, 14*, 211–236.

Cargile, A. C., Takai, J., & Rodriguez, J. I. (2006). Attitudes toward African-American Vernacular English: A U.S. export to Japan? *Journal of Multilingual and Multicultural Development, 27*, 443–456.

Carver, C. S., & Scheier, M. F. (1994). Situational coping and coping dispositions in a stressful transaction. *Journal of Personality and Social Psychology, 66*, 184–195.

Chaiken, S. (1980). Heuristic versus systematic information processing and the use of source versus message cues in persuasion. *Journal of Personality and Social Psychology, 39*, 752–766.

Cooper, R. L. (Ed.). (1974). Language attitudes I [Special issue]. *International Journal of the Sociology of Language, 3*.

Cooper, R. L. (Ed.). (1975). Language attitudes II [Special issue]. *International Journal of the Sociology of Language, 6*.

Cuddy, A. J. C., Fiske, S. T., & Glick, P. (2008). Competence and warmth as universal trait dimensions of interpersonal and intergroup perceptions: The stereotype content model and the BIAS map. In M. P. Zanna (Ed.), *Advances in experimental psychology* (Vol. 40, pp. 61–149). New York: Academic Press.

Day, R. R. (1982). Children's attitudes toward language. In E. B. Ryan & H. Giles (Eds.), *Attitudes towards language variation: Social and applied contexts* (pp. 116–131). London: Edward Arnold.

Dailey, R. M., Giles, H., & Jansma, L. L. (2005). Language attitudes in an Anglo-Hispanic context: The role of the linguistic landscape. *Language and Communication, 25*, 27–38.

Dillard, J. P., Solomon, D. H., & Palmer, M. T. (1999). Structuring the concept of relational judgments. *Communication Monographs, 66*, 49–61.

Dillard, J. P., Solomon, D. H., & Samp, J. A. (1996). Framing social reality: The relevance of relational judgments. *Communication Research, 23*, 703–723.

Dixon, J. A., & Mahoney, B. (2004). The effects of accent evaluation and evidence on perceptions of a suspect's guilt and criminality. *Journal of Social Psychology, 144*, 63–74.

Dörnyei, Z. (2003). *Attitudes, orientations and motivations in language learning.* Oxford, UK: Blackwell.

Duhachek, A. (2005). Coping: A multidimensional, hierarchical framework of responses to stressful consumption episodes. *Journal of Consumer Research, 32,* 41–53.

Edwards, J. R. (1999). Refining our understanding of language attitudes. *Journal of Language and Social Psychology, 18,* 101–110.

Edwards, J. R. (2001). Languages and language learning in the face of world English. *Profession (Annual of the Modern Language Association),* 109–120.

Edwards, J. R., & Jacobsen, M. (1987). Standard and regional standard speech: Distinctions and similarities. *Language in Society, 16,* 369–380.

Edwards, J. R., & McKinnon, M. (1987). The continuing appeal of difference as deficit: A Canadian study in a rural context. *Canadian Journal of Education, 12*, 330–349.

Elwell, C. M., Brown, R. J., & Rutter, D. R. (1984). Effects of accent and visual information on impression formation. *Journal of Language and Social Psychology, 3,* 297–299.

Fazio, R. H., & Olson, M. A. (2003). Implicit measures in social cognition research: Their meaning and use. *Annual Review of Psychology, 54*, 297–327.

Festinger, L. (1957). *A theory of cognitive dissonance*. Evanston, IL: Row, Peterson.

Fiese, B. H., & Sameroff, A. J. (1999). The family narrative consortium: A multidimensional approach to narratives. *Monographs for the Society for Research in Child Development, 64,* 1–36.

Fiske, S. T., & Neuberg, S. L. (1990). A continuum of impression formation, from category-based to individuating processes: Influences of information and motivation on attention and interpretation. In M. Zanna (Ed.), *Advances in experimental social psychology 23* (pp. 1–74). San Diego, CA: Academic Press.

Floccia, C., Butler, J., Girard, F., & Goslin, J. (2009). Categorization of regional and foreign accents in 5- to 7-year-old British children. *International Journal of Behavioral Development, 33,* 336–375.

Frattaroli, J. (2006). Experimental disclosure and its moderators: A meta-analysis. *Psychological Bulletin, 132*, 823–865.

Frumkin, L. (2007). Influences of accent and ethnic background on perceptions of eyewitness testimony. *Psychology, Crime and Law, 13,* 317–331.

Fuentes, J. N., Gottdiener, W., Martin, H., Tracey C. Gilbert, T. C., & Giles, H. (under review). A meta-analysis of the effects of speakers' accents on social evaluations.

Gallois, C., Callan, V. J., & Johnstone, M. (1984). Personality judgements of Australian Aborigines and white speakers: Ethnicity, sex, and context. *Journal of Language and Social Psychology, 3,* 39–57.

Gardner, R. C. (in press). *The socio-educational model of second language acquisition.* New York: Peter Lang.

Garner, T., & Rubin, D. L. (1986). Middle class Blacks' perceptions of dialect and style shifting: The case of southern attorneys. *Journal of Language and Social Psychology, 5,* 33–48.

Garrett, P., Coupland, N., & Williams, A. (2003). *Investigating language attitudes: Social meaning of dialect, ethnicity and performance.* Cardiff: University of Wales Press.

Genesee, F., & Holobow, N. E. (1989). Change and stability in intergroup perceptions. *Journal of Language and Social Psychology, 8,* 17–38.

Giles, H. (1973). Communicative effectiveness as a function of accented speech. *Speech Monographs, 40,* 330–331.

Giles, H., & Billings, A. (2004). Language attitudes. In A. Davies & E. Elder (Eds.), *Handbook of applied linguistics* (pp. 187–209). Oxford, UK: Blackwell.

Giles, H., & Coupland, N. (1991a). *Language: Contexts and consequences.* Belmont, CA: Brooks/Cole.

Giles, H., & Coupland, N. (1991b). Language attitudes: Discursive, contextual and gerontological considerations. In A. G. Reynolds (Ed.), *Bilingualism, multiculturalism, and second language learning: The McGill Conference in honor of Wallace E. Lambert* (pp. 21–42). Hillsdale, NJ: Erlbaum.

Giles, H., & Edwards, J. R. (Eds.). (1983). Language attitudes in multicultural settings. *Journal of Multilingual and Multicultural Development, 4* (2 & 3), 81–96.

Giles, H., & Edwards, J. R. (2010). Attitudes to language: Past, present, and future. In K. Malmkjaer (Ed.), *The Routledge linguistics encyclopedia* (3rd ed., 35–40). London: Routledge.

Giles, H., & Farrar, K. (1979). Some behavioral consequences of accented speech. *British Journal of Social and Clinical Psychology, 18,* 209–210.

Giles, H., & Fitzpatrick, M. A. (1984). Personal, group, and couple identities. Towards a relational context for the study of language attitudes and linguistic forms. In D. Schiffrin (Ed.), *Meaning, form and use in context: Linguistic applications* (pp. 253–277). Washington, DC: Georgetown University Press.

Giles, H., Harrison, C., Creber, C., Smith, P. M., & Freeman, N. H. (1983). Developmental and contextual aspects of British children's language attitudes. *Language and Communication, 3,* 1–6.

Giles, H., Henwood, K., Coupland, N., Harriman, J., & Coupland, J. (1992). Language attitudes and cognitive mediation. *Human Communication Research, 18,* 500–527.

Giles, H., & Johnson, P. (1986). Perceived threat, ethnic commitment, and inter-ethnic language behavior. In Y. Kim (Ed.), *Interethnic communication: Recent research* (pp. 91–116), Newbury Park, CA, Sage.

Giles, H., & Johnson, P. (1987). Ethnolinguistic identity theory: A social psychological approach to language maintenance. *International Journal of the Sociology of Language, 63,* 69–99.

Giles, H., Katz, V., & Myers, P. (2006). Language attitudes and the role of communication infrastructure. *Moderna Språk, 100*, 38–54.

Giles, H., & Marsh, P. (1979). Perceived masculinity and accented speech. *Language Sciences, 1*, 301–315.

Giles, H., & Niedzielski, N. (1998). Italian is beautiful, German is ugly. In L. Bauer & P. Trudgill (Eds.), *Language myths* (pp. 85–93). London: Penguin.

Giles, H., & Powesland, P. F. (1975). *Speech style and social evaluation.* London: Academic Press.

Giles, H., & Ryan, E. B. (1982). Prolegomena for developing a social psychological theory of language attitudes. In E. B. Ryan & H. Giles (Eds.), *Attitudes towards language variation* (pp. 208–223). London: Edward Arnold.

Giles, H., & Street, R. L., Jr. (1985). Communicator characteristics and behavior: A review, generalizations, and model. In M. Knapp & G. R. Miller (Eds.), *The handbook of interpersonal communication* (pp. 205–262). Beverly Hills, CA: Sage.

Giles, H., Williams, A., Mackie, D. M., & Rosselli, F. (1995). Reactions to Anglo- and Hispanic-American accented speakers: Affect, identity, persuasion, and the English-only controversy. *Language and Communication, 14*, 102–123.

Giles, H., Wilson, P. J., & Conway, A. (1981). Accent and lexical diversity as determinants of impression formation and employment selection. *Language Sciences, 3*, 92–103.

Gill, M. M. (1994). Accent and stereotypes: Their effect on perceptions of teacher and lecture comprehension. *Journal of Applied Communication Research*, *22*, 348–361.

Gill, M. M., & Badzinski, D. (1992). The impact of accent and status on information perception and recall formation. *Communication Reports, 5*, 99–105.

Girard, F., Floccia, C., & Goslin, J. (2008). Perception and awareness of accents in young children. *British Journal of Developmental Psychology, 26,* 409–433.

Gluszek, A., & Dovidio, J. F. (2010a). Speaking with a nonnative accent: Perceptions of bias, communication difficulties, and belonging to the United States. *Journal of Language and Social Psychology, 29*, 224–234.

Gluszek, A., & Dovidio, J. F. (2010b). A social psychological perspective on the stigma of non-native accents in communication. *Personality and Social Psychology Review, 14,* 214–237.

Gluszek, A., Newheiser, A-K., & Dovidio, J. F. (in press). Social psychological orientations and accent strength. *Journal of Language and Social Psychology, 30.*

Grondelaers, S., van Hout, R., & Steegs, M. (2010). Evaluating regional accent variation in Standard Dutch. *Journal of Language and Social Psychology, 29*, 101–116.

Gudykunst, W. B., & Ting-Toomey, S. (1990). Ethnic identity, language and communication breakdown. In H. Giles & W. P. Robinson (Eds.), *The handbook of language and social psychology* (pp. 309–328). Chichester, UK: Wiley.

Halliday, M. (1968). The users and uses of language. In J. A. Fishman (Ed.), *Readings in the sociology of language* (pp. 160–172). The Hague: Mouton.

Hewstone, M., & Giles, H. (1986). Social groups and social stereotypes in intergroup communication: A review and model of intergroup communication breakdown. In W. B. Gudykunst (Ed.), *Intergroup communication* (pp. 10–26). London: Edward Arnold.

Hogg, M. A., D'Agata, P., & Abrams, D. (1989). Ethnolinguistic betrayal and speake evaluations across Italian Australians. *Genetic, Social, and General Psychology Monographs, 115*, 155–181.

Holmberg, D., Orbuch, T. L., & Veroff, J. (2004). *Thrice-told tales: Married couples tell their stories*. Mahwah, NJ: Erlbaum.

Honeycutt, J. M., Cantrill, J. G., Kelly, P., & Lambkin, D. (1998). How do I love thee? Let me consider my options: Cognitions, verbal strategies, and the escalation of intimacy. *Human Communication Research, 25*, 39–63.

Hovland, C. I., Janis, I. L., & Kelley, H. H. (1953). *Communication and persuasion: Psychological studies of opinion change*. New Haven, CT: Yale University Press.

Hullett, C. R., & Tamborini, R. (2001). When I'm within my rights: An expectancy-based model of actor evaluative and behavioral responses to compliance-resistance strategies. *Communication Studies, 52,* 1–16.

Irwin, R. B. (1977). Judgments of vocal quality, speech fluency, and confidence of southern black and white speakers. *Language and Speech, 20*, 261–266.

Johnson, F. L., & Buttny, R. (1982). White listeners' responses to 'sounding black' and 'sounding white': The effects of message content on judgments about language. *Communication Monographs, 49*, 33–49.

Kaiser, F. G., Byrka, K., & Hartig, T. (2010). Reviving Campbell's paradigm for attitude research. *Personality and Social Psychology Review, 14*, 351–367.

Kalin, R. (1982). The social significance of speech in medical, legal and occupational settings. In E. B. Ryan & H. Giles (Eds.), *Attitudes toward language: Social and applied contexts* (pp. 148–163). London: Academic Press.

Katz, D. (1960). The functional approach to the study of attitudes. *Public Opinion Quarterly, 24*, 163–204.

Katz, D., & Stotland, E. (1959). A preliminary statement to a theory of attitude structure and change. In S. Koch (Ed.), *Psychology: A study of science* (Vol. 3, pp. 423–475). New York: McGraw Hill.

Kellas, J. K., Trees, A. R., Schrodt, P., LeClair-Underberg, C., & Willer, E. K. (2010). Exploring links between well-being and interactional sense-making in married couples' jointly told stories of stress. *Journal of Family Communication, 10*, 174–193.

Kinzler, K. D., Corriveau, K. H., & Harris, P. L. (in press). Children's selective trust in native accent speakers. *Developmental Science.*

Kinzler, K. D., Dupoux, E., & Spelke, E. S. (2007). The native language of social cognition. *The proceedings of the National Academy of the United States of America, 104,* 12577–12580.

Kinzler, K. D., Shutts, K., DeJesus, J., & Spelke, E. S. (2009). Accent trumps race in guiding children's social preferences. *Social Cognition, 27,* 623–624.

Ko, S. J., Judd, C. M., & Blair, I. V. (2006). What the voice reveals: Within- and between-category stereotyping on the basis of voice. *Personality and Social Psychology Bulletin, 32,* 806–819.

Ko, S. J., Judd, C. M., & Stapel, D. A. (2009). Stereotyping based on voice in the presence of individuating information: Vocal femininity affects perceived competence but not warmth. *Personality and Social Psychology Bulletin, 35,* 198–211.

Koenig Kellas, J. (2005). Family ties: Communicating identity through jointly told stories. *Communication Monographs, 72*, 365–389.

Koenig Kellas, J., & Trees, A. R. (2005). Rating interactional sense-making in the process of joint storytelling. In V. Manusov (Ed.), *The sourcebook of nonverbal measures: Going beyond words* (pp. 281–294). Mahwah, NJ: Erlbaum.

Koenig Kellas, J., & Trees, A. R. (2006). Finding meaning in difficult family experiences: Sense-making and interaction processes during joint family storytelling. *Journal of Family Communication, 6*, 49–76.

Kowalski, R. M. (1997). *Aversive interpersonal behaviors.* New York: Plenum.

Kristiansen, T. (2001). Two standards: One for the media and one for the school. *Language Awareness, 10,* 9–24.

Kristiansen, T., Garrett, P., & Coupland, N. (Eds.). (2005). Subjective processes in language variation and change. *Acta Linguistic Hafniensia, 37,* 1–250.

Kristiansen, T., & Giles, H. (1992). Compliance-gaining as a function of accent: Public requests in varieties of Danish. *International Journal of Applied Linguistics, 2,* 17–35.

Krosnick, J. A., & Petty, R. E. (1995). Attitude strength: An overview. In R. E. Petty & J. A. Krosnick (Eds.), *Attitude strength: Antecedents and consequences* (pp. 1–24). Hillsdale, NJ: Erlbaum.

La Piere, R. (1934). Attitudes versus actions. *Social Forces, 13,* 230–237.

Labov, W. (1976). *Language in the inner city.* Philadelphia: University of Pennsylvania Press.

Labov, W. (2006). *The social stratification of English in New York City, 2nd ed.* New York: Cambridge University Press.

Lambert, W. E. (1967). A social psychology of bilingualism. *Journal of Social Issues, 23,* 91–109.

Lambert, W. E., Hodgson, E. R., Gardner, R. C., & Fillenbaum, S. (1960). Evaluation reactions to spoken languages. *Journal of Abnormal and Social Psychology, 60,* 44–51.

Lawson, S., & Sachdev, I. (2000). Codeswitching in Tunisia: Attitudinal and behavioral dimensions. *Journal of Pragmatics, 32,* 1343–1361.

Lazarus, R. S. (1991). *Emotion and adaptation.* New York: Oxford University Press.

Lazarus, R. S., & Folkman, S. (1984). *Stress, appraisal, and coping.* New York: Springer.

Linn, M. D., & Pichè, G. L. (1982). Black and white adolescent and preadolescent attitudes toward Black English. *Research in the Teaching of English, 16,* 53–69.

Lippi-Green, R. (1997). *English with an accent: Language, ideology, and discrimination in the United States.* New York: Routledge.

Luhman, R. (1990). Appalachian English stereotypes: Language attitudes in Kentucky. *Language in Society, 19,* 331–348.

Maio, G. R., & Haddock, G. (2007). Attitude change. In A. W. Krugkanski & E. T. Higgins (Eds.), *Social psychology: Handbook of basic principles* (2nd ed., pp. 565–586). New York: Guilford.

Maio, G. R., & Haddock, G. (2010). *The psychology of attitudes and attitude change.* London Sage.

Marlow, M. L. (2010). *Race, power, and language criticism: The case of Hawai'i.* Saarbrücken, Germany: VDM Verlag Dr. Müller Aktiengesellschaft & Co.

Marlow, M. L., & Giles, H. (2008). "Who you tink You, talkin Propah?": Pidgin demarginalized. *Journal of Multicultural Discourses, 3,* 53–68.

Marlow, M. L., & Giles, H. (2010). 'We won't get ahead speaking like that!': Expressing managing language criticism in Hawai'i. *Journal of Multilingual and Multicultural Development, 31,* 237–251.

Martinko, M. J., Harvey, P., & Douglas, S. C. (2007). The role, function and contribution of attribution theory to leadership: A review. *Leadership Quarterly, 18,* 561–585.

Matei, S., Ball-Rokeach, S., & Qiu, J. L. (2001). Fear and misperception of Los Angeles urban space: A spatial-statistical study of communication-shaped mental maps. *Communication Research, 28*, 429–463.

Matsuda, M. J. (1991). Voices of America: Accent, antidiscrimination law, and a jurisprudence for the last reconstruction. *The Yale Law Review, 100*, 1329–1467.

McAdams, D. P. (1993). *The stories we live by: Personal myths and the making of the self.* New York: William Morrow.

McGuire, W. J. (1985). Attitudes and attitude change. In G. Lindzey & E. Aronson (Eds.), *Handbook of social psychology* (3rd ed., Vol. 2, pp. 233–346). New York: Random House.

Meisenbach, R. J. (2010). Stigma management communication: A theory and agenda for applied research on how individuals manage moments of stigmatized identity. *Journal of Applied Communication Research, 38,* 268–292.

Miller, L. C., & Read, S. J. (1991). On the coherence of mental models of persons and relationships: A knowledge structure approach. In G. J. O. Fletcher & F. D. Fincham (Eds.), *Cognition in close relationships* (pp. 69–99). Hillsdale, NJ: Erlbaum.

Mulac, A. (1975). Evaluation of the speech dialect attitudinal scale. *Speech Monographs, 42*, 184–189.

Mulac, A., Hanley, T. D., & Prigge, D. Y. (1974). Effects of phonological speech foreignness upon three dimensions of attitude of selected listeners. *Quarterly Journal of Speech, 60*, 411–420.

Myers-Scotton, C. (1998). *Codes and consequences: Choosing linguistic varieties.* New York: Oxford University Press.

Nazzi, T., Jusczyk, P., & Johnson, E. (2000). Language discrimination by English-learning 5-month-olds: Effects of rhythm and familiarity. *Journal of Memory and Language, 43*, 1–19.

Newell, S. E., & Stutman, R. K. (1988). The social confrontation episode. *Communication Monographs, 55,* 266–285.

Newell, S. E., & Stutman, R. K. (1991). The episodic nature of social confrontation. In J. A. Anderson (Ed.), *Communication yearbook 14* (pp. 359–413). Thousand Oaks, CA: Sage.

Oetzel, J. G., & Ting-Toomey, S. (2006). *The Sage handbook of conflict communication: Integrating theory, research, and practice.* Thousand Oaks, CA: Sage.

Patterson, M. L. (1983). *Nonverbal behavior: A functional perspective.* New York: SpringerVerlag.

Pennebaker, J. W. (1997). *Opening up: The healing power of emotional expression.* New York: Guilford.

Petty, R. E., & Cacioppo, J. T. (1986). The elaboration likelihood model of persuasion. In L. Berkowitz (Ed.), *Advances in experimental social psychology, 19* (pp. 123–205). New York: Academic Press.

Pichè, G. L., Michlin, M., Rubin, D., & Sullivan, A. (1977). Effects of dialect-ethnicity, social class and quality of written compositions on teachers' subjective evaluations of children. *Communication Monographs, 44,* 60–72.

Planalp, S. (1985). Relational schemata: A test of alternative forms of relational knowledge as guides to communication. *Human Communication Research, 12*, 3–29.

Planalp, S., & Rivers, M. (1996). Changes in knowledge of personal relationships. In G. J. O. Fletcher & J. Fitness (Eds.), *Knowledge structures in close relationships: A social psychological approach* (pp. 299–324). Hillsdale, NJ: Erlbaum.

Pratt, M. W., & Fiese, B. H. (2004). Families, stories, and the life course: An ecological context. In M. W. Pratt & B. H. Fiese (Eds.), *Family stories and the life course: Across time and generations* (pp. 1–24). Mahwah, NJ: Erlbaum.

Preston, D. R. (1993). Folk dialectology. In D. R. Preston (Ed.), *American dialect research* (pp. 333–378). Philadelphia, PA: John Benjamins.

Preston, D. R. (1998). They speak really bad English down south and in New York City. In L. Bauer & P. Trudgill (Eds.), *Language myths* (pp. 139–149). London; Penguin.

Preston, D. R. (1999). A language attitude approach to the perception of regional variety. In D. R. Preston (Ed.), *Handbook of perceptual dialectology* (pp. 359–373). Amsterdam: Benjamins.

Purnell, T., Isdardi, W., & Baugh, J. (1999). Perceptual and phonetic experiments on American English dialect identification. *Journal of Language and Social Psychology, 18*, 10–30.

Rakić, T., Steffens, M. C., & Mummendey, A. (in press). Blinded by the accent! The minor role of looks in ethnic categorization. *Journal of Personality and Social Psychology.*

Ray, G. (2009). *Language and interracial communication in the United States: Speaking in Black and White.* New York: Peter Lang.

Robinson, W. P. (1972). *Language and social behavior.* Harmonsworth, UK: Penguin.

Rosenberg, M. J., & Hovland, C. I. (1960). Cognitive, affective, and behavioral components of attitudes. In C. I. Hovland & M. J. Rosenberg (Eds.), *Attitude organization and change: An analysis of consistency among attitude components* (pp. 1–14). New Haven, CT: Yale University Press.

Ryan, E. B. (1979). Why do low-prestige varieties persist? In H. Giles & R. N. St. Clair (Eds.), *Language and social psychology* (pp. 145–157). Oxford, UK: Blackwell.

Ryan, E. B., & Giles, H. (Eds.). (1982). *Attitudes towards language variation: Social and applied contexts.* London: Edward Arnold.

Ryan, E. B., & Carranza, M. A. (1975). Evaluative reactions of adolescents towards speakers of standard English and Mexican American accented English. *Journal of Personality and Social Psychology, 31,* 855–863.

Ryan, E. B., Carranza, M. A., & Moffie, R. W. (1977). Reactions towards varying degrees of accentedness in the speech of Spanish-English. *Language and Speech, 20*, 267–273.

Ryan, E. B., Giles, H., & Bradac, J. J. (Eds.) (1994). Recent studies in language attitudes. *Language and Communication, 14*, 211–312.

Ryan, E. B., Giles, H., & Hewstone, M. (1988). The measurement of language attitudes. In U. Ammon, N. Dittmar, & K. J. Mattheier (Eds.), *Sociolinguistics: An international handbook of the science of language* (Vol. II, pp. 1068–1081). Berlin: de Gruyter.

Ryan, E. B., Giles, H., & Sebastian, R. J. (1982). An integrative perspective for the study of attitudes toward language variation. In E. B. Ryan & H. Giles (Eds.), *Attitudes toward language variation* (pp. 1–19). London: Edward Arnold.

Ryan, E. B., Hewstone, M., & Giles, H. (1984). Language and intergroup attitudes. In J. R. Eiser (Ed.), *Attitudinal judgment* (pp. 135–160). New York: Springer.

Santarelli, C. (2010, September 15). Goleta rape claim under investigation. *Santa Barbara News-Press,* pp. A1 & A10.

Scherer, K. R. (1979). Personality markers in speech. In K. R. Scherer & H. Giles (Eds.), *Social markers in speech* (pp. 147–210). Cambridge, UK: Cambridge University Press.

Shuy, R., & Fasold, R. W. (Eds.) (1969). *Language attitudes: Current trends and prospects*. Washington DC: Center for Applied Linguistics.

Simard, L., Taylor, D. M., & Giles, H. (1976). Attribution processes and interpersonal accommodation in a bilingual setting. *Language and Speech, 19,* 374–387.

Sloan, D. M., & Marx, B. P. (2004). Taking pen to hand: Evaluating theories underlying the written disclosure paradigm. *Clinical Psychology: Science and Practice, 11,* 121–137.

Smith, M. B., Bruner, J. S., & White, R. W. (1956). *Opinions and personality*. New York: Wiley.

Speicher, B., & McMahan, S. (1992) Some African-American perspectives on Black English vernacular. *Language in Society, 21*, 383–407.

Street, R. L., Jr., & Hopper, R. (1982). A model of speech style evaluation. In E. B. Ryan & H. Giles (Eds.), *Attitudes toward language: Social and applied contexts* (pp. 175–188). London: Academic Press.

Tajfel, H. (1959). A note on Lambert's "Evaluational reactions to spoken language." *Canadian Journal of Psychology, 13,* 86–92.

Tajfel, H. (1981). Social stereotypes and social groups. In J. C. Tunrer & H. Giles (Eds.), *Intergroup behavior* (pp. 144–167). Oxford, UK: Blackwell.

Tajfel, H., & Turner, J. C. (1986). An integrative theory of intergroup conflict. In S. Worchel & W. G. Austin (Eds.), *Psychology of intergroup relations* (pp. 2–24). Chicago: Nelson-Hall.

Terry, D. J., Pelly, R. N., Lalonde, R. N., & Smith, J. R. (2006). Predictors of cultural adjustment: Intergroup status relations and boundary permeability. *Group Processes and Intergroup Relations, 9,* 249–264.

Thakerar, J. N., & Giles, H. (1981). They are — so they speak: Noncontent speech stereotypes. *Language and Communication, 1,* 251–256.

Trees, A. R., & Koenig Kellas, J. (2009). Telling tales: Enacting family relationships in joint storytelling about difficult family experiences. *Western Journal of Communication, 73,* 91–111.

Trudgill, P. (1974). *The social differentiation of English in Norwich*. Cambridge, UK: Cambridge University Press.

Trudgill, P. (1975). *Accent, dialect and the school*. London: Edward Arnold.

Tsalikis, J., DeShields, O. W., & LaTour, M. S. (1991). The role of accent on the credibility and effectiveness of the salesperson. *Journal of Personal Selling and Sales Management, 6,* 31–41.

Wicker, A. W. (1969). Attitudes versus actions: The relationship of verbal and overt behavioral responses to attitude objects. *Journal of Social Issues, 25*, 41–78.

Williams, F. (1976). *Explorations of the linguistic attitudes of teachers*. Rowley, MA: Newbury House.

Williams, L. E., Bargh, J. A., Nocera, C. C., & Gray, J. R. (2009). The unconscious regulation of emotion: Nonconscious reappraisal goals modulate emotional reactivity. *Emotion, 9,* 847–854.

Wilson, T. D., Lindsey, S., & Schooler, T. Y. (2000). A model of dual attitudes. *Psychological Review, 107,* 101–126.

Zahn, C. J., & Hopper, R. (1985). Measuring language attitudes: The speech evaluation instrument. *Journal of Language and Social Psychology*, *4*, 113–123.

Zuckerman, M., & Driver, R. E. (1989). What sounds beautiful is good: The vocal attractiveness stereotype. *Journal of Nonverbal Behavior, 13,* 67–82.

CHAPTER CONTENTS

10 Communicating Love

A Sociocultural Perspective

Elisabeth Gareis and Richard Wilkins

Baruch College/CUNY

When communicating love, what is the right thing to do or say, when, where, by whom, and to whom? This chapter focuses on how love is expressed across culture and time. Following a review of definitions of love (including the questions of prototypicality, universality, and social construction), the chapter details historical and contemporary practices, in particular communication variables (such as mode, context, and gender), cultural dimensions, and recent changes in the use of verbal love expression in a number of cultures. The chapter concludes by grounding the prevailing understandings of love within the dialectics of expression versus restraint, autonomy versus unity, and role versus personal.

In recent years, there has been a renewed interest among communication scholars in the topic of cultural communication and its influence on the expression of emotion. Dissatisfaction with the conceptualization of emotion as removed from its cultural context has sparked much of this renewed interest. Scholars have begun to speak of emotion as a kind of cultural discourse, thus placing it within a category of experience that is formed within linguistic, social, cultural, and historical orders. In other words, the psychosomatic domain of emotional experience contains states, such as anger, sadness, and love; and these emotions are expressed and interpreted in situated contexts. In this review, we will draw on studies focusing on the emotion of love and use them as an entry point into a commentary on the situated feelings of people, thus showing that social and cultural realities are reproduced and negotiated in the communication of emotions (Lutz, 1988).

Consider an episode of the American TV program *60 Minutes* that focuses on Finland (Tiffin, 1993). The lead narrator and journalist Morley Safer introduces the audience to Finns who "in their natural state," are "brooding" and "private, grimly in touch with no one but themselves, the shyest people on earth, depressed and proud of it." In one segment of the program, the locution "I love you" and its use in Finnish culture are discussed by Ms. Schultz (a female, American journalist living in Finland), Jan Knutas (a Finnish, male, literary critic), and Arja Koriseva (a celebrated, Finnish, female, tango singer):

Safer: Do people tell each other that they love each other?
Schultz: No, oh my God, no, no. Not … even lovers.
Knutas: Well, I'd say you could say it once in a lifetime.… Say, you have been married for 20 years; perhaps your spouse is on her death-bed, you could comfort her with saying "I love you,"…
Safer: (laughs)
Knutas: It's not funny.
Koriseva: It's easier to me to say, like, to my boyfriend that "I love you" [in English].… We have heard it on TV, in movies; it's easier to me to say "I love you" than "mina rakastan sinua," it doesn't [sound] very nice if I say "I love you" in Finnish.
Safer: You look slightly embarrassed when you say it in Finnish.
Koriseva: Yeah—we don't use "I love you" so much as you do. You love almost everybody (laughs). When a Finnish guy or man says "I love you," he really means it.

A source of asynchrony in the above extract is the relative degree to which Americans and Finns think that they are either emotionally expressive or emotionally restrained. When Safer asks if Finns tell each other that they love each other, Schultz's response is no, not even lovers. Compare this to ubiquitous love expression in the United States, and from the American perspective, Finns can appear cold and unfeeling. The phenomenon finds an explanation in the cultural variation within semantic networks, which implies that interactants cannot assume that a word or a sentence has the same meaning in different societies (Kagan, 2007). A growing body of communication research has also begun to explore the concept of *key words*; that is, words that say something "significant and revealing" about a culture (Wierzbicka, 1997, p. 16). One may argue that *love* is such a key word for American culture, and that the above reference to *love* in English usage evokes features of what Varenne (1977) calls the American "love story," that is, the ideas that specifically tie American society together: individualism, community, and love. In so doing, the dialogue lays out the conditions for how persons relate to one another in U.S. culture and can thus serve as a basis for evaluating Finns. For the Finn however, a lack of verbal love expression is not so much a matter of internal feelings, but a larger commentary on the moral, cultural, and political life of the community (Wilkins, 2007).

The study of love as a situated understanding of an emotion is a relatively new area of investigation. Much about the communication of love in different cultures and relationships ranging from friendship to marriage remains unknown (Gareis & Wilkins, in press; Kline, Horton, & Zhang, 2008; Seki, Matsumoto, & Imahori, 2002; Wilkins & Gareis, 2006).

As it is difficult to separate experience from expression, this chapter sets the stage with a definitional section that includes taxonomies and conceptualizations of the experience of love. While we are aware of the politically informed and critical work on the experience of love, such as that of Ahmed (2003, 2004), the major purpose, however, is not the nature of love as a phenomenon or experience, but research into the social and cultural construction of love and its communication. The core of the chapter thus focuses on love expression—its historical and contemporary practices, including the impact of culture and recent culture change.

Love is sometimes felt but not expressed; other times, love is expressed only nonverbally; and still other times, it is communicated verbally, with or without nonverbal manifestations. In the verbal realm, a healthy daily dose of verbal "I love you's," for some, communicates individuality, happiness, and community. For others, expressing love verbally too often, cheapens the deeply felt emotion and undermines its significance. There is also dispute about how much love should be revealed given the current development of a relationship, and how love can be expressed in relationships outside of romance and marriage. Just what is the right thing to do or say, when, where, by whom, and to whom?

Definition of Love

Beall and Sternberg (1995, p. 424) describe love as "a multidimensional construct that includes behavior as well as feelings and thoughts." Depending on one's academic orientation and point of view, different aspects of this construct can be highlighted. Biologists, for example, see love as a function of hormones, neurotrophins, and pheromones serving procreation and maternal attachment (Fisher, 2004), social scientists focus on social and cultural behaviors, and theologians on the divine essence of love. Illustrating this diversity, the *Merriam-Webster Online Dictionary* lists nine different definitions for the term *love* (Love, 2009), including affection, sexual embrace, and adoration for God. To arrive at a working definition for our purposes, it helps to take a closer look at various taxonomies and conceptualizations of love.

Taxonomies of Love

Serving to express anything from a preference for fast-food hamburgers to one's deepest felt affection, the word *love* is one of the most used, but—as some may argue—also most misused words, a word to which completely different meanings are allotted. Indeed taxonomies of love often feature a seemingly indefinite number of subcategories. Ancient Greek differentiation, for example, centered around *eros* (passionate, sensuous love), *agape* (selfless, unconditional love), and *philia* (love of friends, family, and community), but also included *storge* (natural affection, such as parental love), *nomos* (love of God), *xenia* (hospitality, love of strangers), and *epithymia* (libido, desire) (Lindberg, 2008; Singer, 1987). After ancient Europe's center of gravity shifted from Greece to Rome, the Latin term *caritas* (signifying love of God and love of neighbor) joined the vocabulary of love in the 4th century CE (Lindberg, 2008).

Modern taxonomies also recognize prevalent types of love. Fromm (1956) identifies five types of love: *brotherly* (i.e., love for fellow human being), *motherly, erotic, self-love,* and *love of God.* Maslow (1962) sees only two types of love, *deficit love* (dependent) and *being love* (between self-actualized individuals). Likewise, Hatfield (1988) as well as Shaver, Wu, and Schwartz (1991) differentiate between two major forms: *companionate* (or *affectional*) and *passionate* (or *romantic*) love. With a nod to the classical taxonomies, Lee (1973, 1977, 1988), in his color-of-love theory, names six love styles: eros, agape, and storge (here, in the social psychology tradition, defined as friendship love), as well as *pragma* (practical love, as in marriage for economic purposes), *mania* (manic love, marked by jealousy and doubt), and *ludus* (game-playing love with many partners, emotions not taken seriously). A number of studies explore Lee's love styles (e.g., Bailey, Hendrick, & Hendrick, 1987; Davis & Latty-Mann, 1987; Hendrick & Hendrick, 1986, 1989; Hendrick, Hendrick, & Adler, 1988; Kanemasa, Taniguchi, & Daibo, 2004; Levy & Davis, 1988; Sternberg, 1986, 1997). The resulting valuation continuum places eros on the affirmative end of the love style spectrum, followed by agape, mania, pragma, and ludus on the negative end.

Taxonomies provide a glimpse into the difficulty of conceptualizing love. When comparing love styles on opposite ends of the spectrum—such as agape, which correlates with kindness and affection, and ludus, which correlates with hostility, conflict, and lack of affection (Davis & Latty-Mann, 1987; Kanemasa et al., 2004)—the question arises whether or not some types of love are part of the same emotion or instances of two different emotions. This question becomes especially relevant when comparing love across cultures. Wierzbicka (1999a, p. 31) cautions that the categorization of emotions depends "largely on the language through the prism of which these emotions are interpreted."

Conceptualizations of Love

Components Western research on the components of love often assumes that love is a positive force and that love comprises companionate as well as passionate elements. Thus, Webster's primary (and positive) definition of love is "a strong affection for another" (Love, 2009). Rubin (1970) found that love is marked by the components of needing, caring, and trusting. In Argyle and Henderson (1985), being open, honest, caring, understanding, and trustworthy were all associated with love between friends and spouses. Similarly, Fehr (1988) lists the components of trust, caring, honesty, friendship, respect, and concern for the other's well-being.

Not all cultures, however, see love as positive. Shaver et al. (1991) conducted a study in which American, Italian, and Chinese informants grouped emotions into positive or negative categories. Predictably, the American and Italian respondents considered love positive and chose many of the same subordinate components (including affection, fondness, liking, and caring for companionate love; and passion, excitement, and longing for passionate love). The Chinese respondents—although they recognized *some* positive aspects of love—emphasized negative or sad components of love (including unrequited love, nostalgia, sorrow, and pity).

Wierzbicka (1999a), reports that in many languages, love-like emotions appear to be "linked with thoughts of 'bad things' happening to people, and so to be akin, in some ways, to 'pity,' 'compassion,' 'sadness,' and even 'anguish' rather than to 'happiness' or 'joy'" (p. 52). In addition to the Chinese focus on sad love, the Micronesian Ifaluk concept of *fago* (Lutz, 1988) and Russian *žalost* (Wierzbicka, 1999a) could be glossed as sad or sorrowful, loving compassion.

An even more pronounced counterexample to positive Western conceptualizations of love can be found among the Nyimba in Nepal (Levine, 1981). In Buddhist tradition, emotional attachments, especially sexual attachments, are considered a vice, as they are identified with the desire for material goods and thought to produce mental suffering and inevitable sorrow. The Nyimba therefore do not have a term for the sexual "love" of husbands, wives, or lovers; nor is there any positive valuation of love in general. Even the bond between parents and children—although it translates into *compassionate love* (Tib. *snying rje*)—is more likened to the Buddhist concept of disinterested concern that is prescribed towards all sentient beings than to the high-attachment parent-child relationships common in the West.

In contrast to the Nyimba rejection of sexual relations as a form of love, much of Western literature focuses on passionate love. Sternberg's (1986) triangular theory of romantic love identifies the components of passion (euphoria, sexual passion), intimacy (honesty, understanding), and commitment (devotion, sacrifices). Aron and Westbay (1996) confirm Sternberg's theory and rank the three factors according to importance: intimacy (highest), commitment (second), and passion (lowest), for both men and women. Lemieux and Hale (1999) agree that intimacy is highest for both genders, but found that passion is second for men and commitment second for women. Sternberg suggests, in his theory of love as a story, that people develop stories about what a loving relationships should be like, and seek to fulfill the stories in their lives. The triangular and love-as-story theories combine to form the duplex theory of love (Sternberg, 2006).

Various scales have also been devised to measure romantic love. Lee's (1973) love styles are the basis for Hendrick and Hendrick's (1986) well-standardized love attitude scale (LAS). The relationship rating form (RRF) by Davis (2001) uses six scales as well, but is not based on Lee's love styles. The scales cover viability (trust, acceptance, respect), intimacy (mutual confiding and understanding), care (mutual assistance, sacrifices, concern for partner's welfare), passion (fascination, exclusiveness, sexual intimacy), satisfaction (mutual enjoyment, success, positive esteem), and conflict/ambivalence. Another widely used measure, the Sternberg triangular love scale (STLS; 1997), determines which of the three components of intimacy, passion, and commitment prevails in a given relationship.

Different types of love can either be seen as quantitatively different (i.e., the same but present in different concentrations), or as qualitatively different (i.e., possessing distinct properties) (Grau, 1998).With respect to the difference between love in friendship versus love in intimate relationships, Davis and Todd (1982) come down in between, having found that friendship and love overlap in 9 out of 11 traits. Only the traits of fascination and exclusivity (which together constitute passion) were different. Davis and Todd also determined that couple relationships and best friendships (irrespective of gender) were more similar than best and second-best friendship. As to individual components, caring is the most consistently mentioned aspect of love and can thereby be regarded as a major building blocks of prototypical love.

Prototypicality and Love in Religion When assessing which type of love comes closest to an ideal in the West, romantic love has been found the happiest (Levy & Davis, 1988) but not the most prototypical. In a study by Fehr and Russell (1991), participants were asked to rate specific types of love on a scale ranging from extremely good to extremely poor example of love. Maternal love received the highest prototypicality ranking, followed by parental, friendship, sisterly, romantic, and 15 additional types of love (brotherly, familial, and sibling love; affection; committed love; love for humanity; spiritual, passionate, and platonic love; self-love; sexual love; patriotic love; love of work; puppy love; and infatuation). As Wierzbicka (1999a) states: "It seems possible that all languages have some word or words implying a desire to do good things for someone else, presumably modeled, prototypically, on the relationships between mothers and their children" (p. 53). Maternal love has not always held the top prototypicality ranking, however. While "today's North American college students regard a mother's love, not love of God, as the prototype for the concept love; medieval monks and nuns would have reversed this profile" (Kagan, 2007, p. 123).

Worldwide, love in the prototypical sense plays a central role in religion. Whether stated explicitly or implied, prototypical love in the form of compassion and selfless devotion are part of all major religions. For example, a core value of the Judeo-Christian tradition is charity, which serves "as a synonym for love, either as God's love for man or man's reciprocal love for God expressed in acts of love for fellow men" (Charity, 1987, p. 224). Critics of the notion that charity equals love point out that throughout history, the motivation for charity included not only selfless altruism, but also social obligation, righteousness, a desire for fame, inner satisfaction, and the desire to imitate divinity (Charity, 1987). Luhmann (1986) further argues that caritas (or loving God in the other person) is easy, "because it can disregard the characteristics of individuals" (p. 79).

Both Buddhism and Hinduism have the concepts of *kama* (sensuous love that tends to be selfish) and *karuna* (selfless compassion). In addition, the belief in *karma* (actions that shape past, present, and future) promotes good deeds and assistance to those in need (Charity, 1987). Buddhism also has the concept of *yuan* (fated or predestined love), which signifies that relationships have their root in countless numbers of lifetimes and are outside the control of the human mind. When individuals meet, their karmic selves meet, and it is yuan that determines who will be involved with whom (Chang & Holt, 1991).

Finally, in Islam, humans are "to serve God by means of good works, including almsgiving, … kindness, and good treatment of parents, orphans, and the elderly" (Charity, 1987, p. 224). It also deserves mention that within Islam, Sufism is known for the tenet that God is lover and beloved, and for its ecstatic poems on the joy and liberating power of love.

Recently, Pope Benedict XVI has devoted two encyclicals to love. In *Deus Caritas Est* (2005), he reconciles eros and agape, which are often defined as love that is wanting (and non-Christian) versus love that is giving (and Christian). Benedict asserts that eros and agape cannot be truly separated. Eros desires happiness, and in approaching the other, changes into the desire to care for the other, into agape. On a larger scale, Benedict evokes a connection between love and economic justice in his encyclical *Caritas in Veritate* (2009). Reminiscent of Marcuse (1955), who pitted life instinct against death instinct and proclaimed that only eros can eliminate repression (including capitalistic repression), Benedict deplores that self-love and self-interest are the governing principles of mainstream economics and calls for distributive justice and authentic love to replace current modus operandi of liberal capitalism (Nirenberg, 2009).

The life-affirming view that pure love doesn't focus on the self, but solely wants what is good (Benedict XVI, 2005) echoes through history and cultures, and is often at the core of calls for a world governed by love. The following excerpt from Martin Luther King, Jr.'s Nobel Peace Prize acceptance speech (King, 1964, para. 3) is one example for such a call:

> Sooner or later all the people of the world will have to discover a way to live together in peace, and thereby transform this pending cosmic elegy into a creative psalm of brotherhood. If this is to be achieved, man must evolve for all human conflict a method which rejects revenge, aggression, and retaliation. The foundation of such a method is love.

Universality and Social Construction Concerning the universality of love, it helps to distinguish between the experience of love, conceptualizations, and the words and expressions linked to love in a given language (Wierzbicka, 1999a). Beall and Sternberg (1995) offer the following theories: (a) love is a universal experience (all people experience love the same way) and has a universal definition (all cultures define love and different types of love the same way), (b) love is a universal experience and has a culturally determined definition, (c) love is a culturally determined experience and has a universal definition, (d) love is a culturally determined experience and has a culturally determined definition.

EXPERIENCE The jury is still out whether the phenomenon of love itself is universal. On one hand, according to the naturalist view, sexual attraction and attachment (especially maternal attachment) are based on universal physiological processes that are necessary for the survival of the species (Fisher, 2004). In support of universality Beall and Sternberg (1995) found that the experience of passionate love was not only the same across cultures, but also across gender. Likewise, Lee's (1973) love styles as well as Hendrick and Hendrick's (1986) love attitude scale (LAS) have been validated cross-culturally (Cho & Cross, 1995; Kanemasa et al., 2004; Matsui et al., 1990; Neto et al., 2000). In similar research on the relationship between passionate and companionate love styles and subjective well-being, Kim and Hatfield (2004) found no difference between U.S. and Korean participants. Domestically, Doherty, Hatfield, Thompson, and Choo (1994) determined that various U.S. ethnic groups did not differ in the intensity of love they felt. Likewise, Contreras, Hendrick, and Hendrick (1996) found only modest love attitude differences among groups of Anglo American and (bicultural as well as Hispanic-oriented) Mexican American couples. The groups did not differ in passionate, altruistic, or friendship-based love, and they were also similar in relationship satisfaction. Finally, Jankowiak and Fischer (1992) documented that romantic love exists in a broad spectrum of cultures. The study suggests that romantic love constitutes a human near-universal, although it is possibly more encountered in the industrialized West, where people have more time to cultivate subjective experiences. Romantic love may be muted by other cultural variables, but never entirely repressed.

On the social constructionist end of the spectrum, Ratner (1989), looking at emotions in general, claims that the natural character of human emotionality has been lost because human emotion experiences and expressions are uncoupled from eliciting events, and emotions are therefore controllable social construction rather than automatic response. Others (e.g., Izard & Buechler, 1980) support the notion that some emotions are universal (including surprise, anger, and fear) but don't count *love* among them.

CONCEPTUALIZATIONS. There is broad agreement that conceptualizations of love are culturally determined. Hsu (1985) and Doi (1963, 1973), for example, contend that passionate love is a Western construct, incompatible with Asian values and at least traditionally unknown in China and Japan. Likewise, Potter (1988) discusses marriage in rural China in terms of altruism, mutual aid, and good works, rather than as romantic love in the Western sense. In contrast, Schneider (1980), in his classic work on the culture of American kinship, writes about conjugal love and cognatic love as cultural units. Conjugal love is the erotic component uniting the opposites of male and female, whereas cognatic love preserves the differentiated and differentiating parents and their children and is wholly without an erotic aspect. Both types of love can be freely translated as "enduring diffuse solidarity" (Schneider, 1980, p. 50). Kinship, for the American, is not just a matter of classifying relatives, it is also a matter of how people relate to one another—with love playing a crucial role.

Many of the studies favoring a culturally determined view of love center around the topic of romantic love. Comparing Chinese, Hong Kong, and British respondents on love styles and the Chinese concept of yuan (fated and predestined love), Goodwin and Findlay (1997) found that, although Chinese and British participants agreed on several items, the Chinese were more endorsing of yuan as well as of practical and altruistic love. In the same vein, Moore (1998) explains that love in Chinese society is tempered by additional characteristics, such as the need for parental approval and the importance of appropriate behavior. In other research, Russians, Japanese, and Americans were similar in many love attitudes and experiences, but also showed cultural differences (Sprecher, Aron, Hatfield, Cortese, Potapova, & Levitskaya, 1994). The Russians were less likely to require love as a basis for marriage, the Japanese disagreed on certain romantic beliefs, and the Americans showed a greater preference for secure attachment. Studying French and U.S. American attitudes toward romantic love, Simmons, Wehner, and Kay (1989) found that the French believed more strongly in traditional romantic love, rating it a more a more ideal and desirable experience than U.S. Americans. On the other hand, Simmons, von Kolke, and Shimizu (1986) determined that U.S. and German respondents evaluated romantic love significantly more positively than the Japanese; Germans were most romantic, followed by Americans, and then Japanese.

It appears that Westerners endorse passionate love beliefs and styles more than Asians, who tend towards companionate and pragmatic beliefs about love (Kline et al., 2008). The phenomenon finds a partial explanation in the differences between individualistic and collectivistic cultural values, including the importance placed on self-fulfillment versus group harmony and the greater preference for love marriages versus arranged marriages (Levine, Sato, Hashimoto, & Verma, 1995). Bierhoff (1991) also explains, however, that in Western cultures, pragmatic love has fallen out of favor only recently, and that it still flourishes in other cultures, because it may be a necessity to choose partners on the basis of practical traits, such as economic status. Indeed, the prevalence of romantic love seems integrally tied to economic factors. In the United States in 1967, for example, 76% of women and 35% of men said they'd be willing to marry someone they didn't love (Kephart, 1967). More recently, with fewer women financially dependent on men, only 9% of women and 14% of men said that they would marry someone they did not love (Allgeier & Wiederman, 1991). Likewise, middle- and upper-class U.S. Americans tend to score higher in the belief that passionate love is necessary for marriage than lower-class informants (Sprecher & Toro-Morn, 2002).

The social constructivist approach argues that there is not one particular reality that is simultaneously experienced by all people, but that symbolic representation and social sharing differ across cultures (Beall & Sternberg, 1995). Cultures may invent specialized emotion concepts, focus heavily on some emotions, and distort or suppress others (Shaver et al., 1991). The way people perceive, select, and organize love into a concept also changes over time and varies from culture to culture and person to person (e.g., Barsalou,

1987; Bierhoff, 1991; Ochs, 1986). Landis and O'Shea (2000) add that "in even a presumably homogeneous group, there will exist consistent subgroups of subjects who will see the world in fundamentally distinct patterns from each other" (p. 769). In a study of the experience of passionate love, for example, they found that the experience differed more when rural and urban subgroups from the same culture than when rural (or urban) groups from different cultures were compared. Landis and Shea recommend that scholars should not define groups a priori but determine commonalities based on individual differences.

SEMANTICS Goddard and Wierzbicka (2007) count feel and want among 60 or so semantic primes; that is, atomic elements of language that have lexical equivalents in all languages and cannot be paraphrased in simpler terms. Although love is not a prime, Wierzbicka (1999a) believes that all languages may recognize the emotion of love. Using the culture-free natural semantic metalanguage (NSM), which consists of only primes, Goddard (2003, p. 121) creates the following molecular definition of love:

X loves person Y =
X thinks good things about Y
X wants to do good things for Y
X wants good things to happen to Y
X often thinks about Y
when X thinks about Y, X often feels something good

Goddard and Wierzbicka's work indicates that a semantic universal related to love may exist, but further research is needed on the matter.

Another method of investigating the semantics of love is to study the lexical networks surrounding the concept. Kagan (2007), for example, contends that emotions, such as fear and anger have a more extensive and richer semantic network than serene and empathic emotions. Likewise, Wierzbicka (1999a), in reference to the aborigines in Australia, suspects that tranquil emotions don't have the same degree of verbal representation as their less tranquil counterparts. Of interest also are cross-cultural overlaps in semantic and conceptual networks. Shaver et al. (1991), for instance, found that joy or bliss is connected with individual achievement in the United States, but with love in Italy.

Love Expression

While the *experience* of love has been a central topic in social psychology for some time, the study of love *expression* is in its infancy. Fiehler (1990) delineates the communication processes involved in the expression of emotion as physiological (trembling, paleness), nonvocal, nonverbal (facial expression, gestures, posture), vocal, nonverbal (sounds, laughter, sighs), paralanguage (including speed), verbal (including choice of words), and conversational (discourse type, conversation management, timing). Little is known about these processes in the expression of love. Noller (1996), for example, shows that happy couples (at least in the West) express love by verbalizing or showing love. Likewise, Chapman (1992) identifies five love languages (affirmative, encouraging messages, quality time, gifts, acts of service, and physical touch), asserting that people need to hear their preferred love language(s) to be satisfied in a relationship. Egbert and Polk (2006) suggest adding common phrases of affirmation (including the locution "I love you") to Chapman's language repertoire. The proper form, context, and frequency of such love expression, however, are historically and culturally diverse.

Historical Practices in the European-American Context

Emotion expression reflects the moral, cultural, and political life of a people and can thus yield anthropological knowledge about social structure and cultural values (Lutz, 1988). In *Love as Passion,* Luhmann (1986) explicates a system theory of love based on the notion that love is a medium of communication and that any changes in the code of love reflect changes in the social system of a time and people. Using poems and novels as sources, Luhmann analyzes the semantics of passionate love in European history, and points out pivotal time periods during which the code of love changed. Although love poetry from a variety of ancient civilizations has been preserved (including from ancient Egypt) (Walker, 2004), significant evidence of love expression as a reflection of social realities does not appear until the Middle Ages.

In Europe, the 12th century saw the rise of courtly love. Troubadours and minnesingers composed love poetry that was marked by the idealization of mostly aristocratic women and the absence of explicit sensual references. Cheyette and Chickering (2005) point out, however, that courtly love was more than a sentiment, that it had political and social meanings. The French philosopher Elisabeth Badinter (1989), for example, claims that courtly love should be seen as a love expression between warriors, not between troubadour or minnesinger and noble woman. Young knights admired the wife of their master to win his love, not hers. If love expression is related to ideas about humanity, then courtly love suggests a patriarchal system that had as its main objective the strengthening of male ties, rather than showing affection toward women.

From ancient Rome to early modernity, marriage—especially in the propertied classes—was a contract for political or economic reasons and not based on emotional love or personal affinities (Beck-Gernsheim, 1986; Beyrer, 2003; Stone, 1977). It was only during the Reformation that the idea of the "companionate" marriage as kind of spiritual friendship between respectful and affectionate partners emerged (Haslett, 2004).

The changes that made companionate marriage possible, however, did not come without drawbacks. In past times, life was defined by a multitude of traditional bonds—including family, the village community, home region, religion, class, trade, and gender (Beck-Gernsheim, 1986). Even the least person was never alone and did not have to rely on him- or herself only. The Reformation introduced individualization, which resulted in liberation from constraints on one hand, but also released humans into a deep inner isolation or what Weber (2003) calls an inner homelessness.

With the gradual dissolution of the previous bonds, the longing for a safe haven increases, and we see the rise of a person-oriented stability (Beck-Gernsheim, 1986). The people in one's immediate vicinity gain in importance for one's self-confidence and well-being. Marriage gradually becomes central to the social construction of reality as well as of one's identity; and increasingly, it is in the exchange with the spouse that we are looking for ourselves. Love and identity become interwoven. Until this process is complete, however, two centuries will pass.

In the meantime, the restructuring of intimacy brings code changes that reflect pendular swings in historical attitudes. If emotionally, historical periods oscillate between ebullient and austere, the Middle Ages (at least with respect to courtly love expression) are situated on the spirited end. The Middle Ages (generally considered to last from the 5th to the 15th century) are followed by the emotionally restrained Renaissance (14th to 17th century) and Reformation (16th century), which changed into high-energy Baroque (17th century), then to the rational Enlightenment (18th century), on to the imaginative and emotional Romanticism (early 19th century), and finally to modernity.

Following the Reformation, 17th-century Baroque saw the development of a new medium of communication for intimacy. Sexual desire enters the equation in form of puzzles, games, and hide-and-seek themes in literature, and the unattainability of worshipped women shifts to women making decisions concerning their love interests (Luhmann, 1986). According to Luhmann, the code changes from idealization to paradoxicalization. Passionate love is not selfless: The lover desires the other's desire. Foremost therefore among the paradoxes is the tension between altruistic love of the other and the self-interest of desire. Other themes cropping up in the semantics of love include love as desired imprisonment, love as sweet martyrdom, and love as madness. Reflecting the spirit of Baroque, the code is marked by an "imperative of excessiveness and the claim of totality" (Luhmann, 1986, p. 68). With the introduction of sensuality, the theme of sincere versus insincere love also appears, raising questions of how to differentiate between true and pretended love.

The 18th century brings a backlash from daring, even frivolous expressiveness to a retightening of moral controls. The code adjusts toward one of intimacy as close friendship (Luhmann, 1986). Focusing on German culture, Kagel (2007) explains that friendship was of critical importance in 18th-century culture. With traditional bonds of profession and status weakened, a new social heterogeneity evolved. Friendship—usually between members of the same sex and ultimately defined by the willingness to sacrifice one's life for the friend—gained in importance and was frequently considered superior to marriage. The 18th century is also that of the letter. Literacy rates had risen and postal delivery increased from once a week in the 17th century to two to three times a week in the 18th (Beyrer, 2003). Letter theoreticians created the ideal of the "natural" private letter based on conversational tone, and an epistolary culture developed that allowed friends to express intimate feelings, including those they would not otherwise express face to face. Writing was often the sole medium of communication between friends, and many exchanged "emotionally charged letters in language later reserved for amorous heterosexual relationships" (Kagel, 2007, p. 215). For example, in 1767, Mr. Jacobi, a professor, wrote to his friend Mr. Gleim, a poet: "O mein liebster, mein bester Freund, nie sind Sie stärker geliebt worden [oh, my dearest, my best friend, you have never been loved more strongly]" (cited in Kagel, 2007, p. 219).

Before Romanticism, romantic love was rejected by theologians and adults in general as a form of imprudent folly, even madness (Stone, 1977). Wives had to be submissive and, for example, address their spouses as "husband" rather than with "demeaning endearments as … sweetheart, love, joy, or dear" (Gouge cited in Stone, 1977, p. 139). Romantic love had thrived only in literature, beginning as a purely extra-marital emotion in troubadour literature and then propagated in romances with the spread of literacy. During Romanticism—with the French Revolution in 1789 representing the threshold event—the focus on individuality starts to diminish gender differences and leads to the complete integration of love and friendship (Badinter, 1989; Luhmann, 1986). According to Luhmann (1986), the code of love during Romanticism is self-referential: Patterns, emotions, and existences are copied. After Goethe's famous letter novel *The Sorrows of Young Werther* (1774/2001) was published, for instance, young men across Europe tried to emulate the love-sick protagonist in dress and behavior, even following him into suicide (Swales, 1987).

It took another one and half centuries, however, until women in Western countries finally received full rights (Badinter, 1989). In the 1960s, birth control is widely seen as robbing men of the last vestiges of control. Mutual trust replaces control and repression. The 1960s also see a change in childcare. Psychologists, such as Carl Rogers, suggest that simply loving children wasn't enough, that they should be loved unconditionally (Kohn, 2009). Childcare is now shared between women and men, and men show equal love for children, including complex and ambivalent reactions which previously were reserved for women (Badinter, 1989). Roles and feelings mingle, and with less differentiation between the sexes, the ego becomes the most valuable good. The orientation shifts from the other to the self, and Badinter (1989) claims that, as a result, self-sacrifice—long the sine qua non, particularly of maternal love—becomes curtailed (Badinter, 1989). Where previously motherhood was defined by devotion and sacrifices, today, maternal altruism finds limits in the ego of the mother. Even greater is the restriction when it comes to spouses. Altruism is cancelled out by the wish for equivalence; and with both women and men contributing to the income of the family, equivalence lies more than ever in proofs of love and love expression.

Giddens (1992) frames the development in the 20th century as one retreating from a focus on romantic love. While romantic love is skewed in terms of power and often marked by the domestic subjugation of women, contemporary love is confluent or pure. It presumes equality between the partners in emotional give and take and rejects the for-ever and one-and-only qualities of romantic love. In its emphasis on equality and departure from traditionally established frameworks, pure love has a longer history in homosexual than heterosexual relationships. Although Giddens does not make direct reference to love expression, he theorizes that the unpredictability of confluent love—it is expected to be dissolved when it no longer serves its purpose—often causes anxiety. One could argue that this anxiety may be a factor in Badinter's (1989) observation of the increase in proofs of love and love expression.

Mirroring the progression from role-differentiation to individualization are Maier's (1998) findings on love expression and class. In the traditional milieu (working-class, rural areas), rituals are important and gender roles are still observed. Except for the ritual declaration "I love you" in courtship and during proposal, love is measured not by verbal standards but mostly through gifts, which become a satisfactory expression of love. In the familial milieu (men higher qualified, women often housewives), love is expressed by men through helping at home, consideration, and men's conscious devotion to the family. The desire for harmony and a tension-free atmosphere function as love expression, although the cultivation of this atmosphere is often the woman's job. Finally, the individualized milieu (partners both hold careers) is dominated by a focus on communication and the authentic expression of feelings. All feelings have to be shared, even the relationship can be questioned.

Several strong cross-currents are at play. Although equality, if found to promote love and sexual satisfaction (Blumstein & Schwartz, 1983), newly individualized women have higher expectations concerning an emotionally satisfying relationship than women in traditional role-oriented relationships (Beck-Gernsheim, 1986). What was an acceptable marriage to their mothers is no longer sufficient. It has also been argued that women want emotional intimacy and stronger expressivity than men do; and if they don't get it, they may divorce (Beck-Gernsheim, 1986; Schenk & Pfrang, 1983). In the United States two thirds of divorces are initiated by women (Popenoe, 2002); other industrialized countries show similar patterns (e.g., Hettlage, 1998).

The collapse of a relationship is often attributed to rule violation, including rules concerning the expression of affection (Argyle & Henderson, 1985). Luhmann contends that we have "replaced the notion of reciprocity of perspective with the (much richer and much more demanding) concept of interpersonal interpenetration" (1986, p. 174), but also that love has become foremost the validation of self-portrayal. If this is the case, how does one express love? Is Badinter (1989) correct that love expression now often consists of nothing but banalities: If he gives her attention, she has to return the favor through an equivalent gesture? Or should we ask, with Beck-Gernsheim (1986), whether liberation *and* love are actually possible? Beck-Gernsheim suggests that children may have become the last guarantor of constancy, an anchor for people's lives, and that the bond between parents and children has started to resemble romantic love, with all its embattling and consuming ramifications.

Badinter (1989) theorizes that at the root of the tensions surrounding individualization is the longing for the selfless love of the mother. As in no time before, maternal love has become the embodiment of love. People are looking for this love in their partners, but our overreaching individualism makes sacrifice and devotion more and more difficult. More than anything, we long to be loved, but are we capable to love the other for his or her own sake? We settle for subtle compromises, but the goal always is the satisfaction of the ego. As soon as the ego is hindered or feels misunderstood or alienated, the relationship loses its right to exist.

Contemporary Practices: Culture and Its Impact on Love Expression

Although not abundant, research is beginning to shed light on contemporary practices and meanings of love expression. Most of the studies do so in form of cross-cultural comparisons, focusing on communication variables, such as mode, context, and gender differences in how love is expressed.

Communication Variables

MODE. One of the most interesting variables of love communication is the mode, or form of information. How is love expressed verbally? How is it communicated nonverbally? And which one is more common?

Verbal Love Expression. Verbal love expression includes direct verbalizations (e.g., "I love you") as well as more indirect ways to communicate love (e.g., terms of endearment and other expressions of attachment, such as "I miss you"). Arguably the most common verbalization in American English is the locution "I love you." It is used in a wide variety of contexts, ranging from marriage proposals to informal leave-taking between friends on the phone. As such, it has a significantly broader category width than many equivalent expressions in other languages. Spanish, for example, uses "ti amo" only for lovers and "te quiero" for family and friends; and in German, "ich mag dich," "ich hab' dich gern," "ich hab' dich lieb," and "ich liebe dich" [I like you, I am fond of you, I hold you dear, I love you] express gradations from everyday affection to deep love (Gareis & Wilkins, in press). Verbs such as like also exist in English, but they don't seem to be commonly used.

With "I love you" being connotatively different from the equivalents in other languages, it is difficult to translate the locution. On the general topic of translatability, Osgood, May, and Miron posit (1975) that "equivalence is a goal to be sought but never really achieved [since the] semantic spheres of translation-equivalent terms overlap to varying degrees but probably never coincide in perfection" (p. 17). Translatability is especially problematic when dealing with abstract domains, such as emotions. In fact, true "translation can only occur when points of separate speech communities' lexical maps overlap on both the dimensions of referential denotation as well as affective connotation" (Donovan & Rundle, 1997, p. 228). A particular problem in this respect is polysemy, that is, incidents when words from different languages, aside from shared meanings also have additional meanings (Goddard, 2003). The Spanish word *querer* is a case in point: it translates into *love* as well as *want*. Also an issue is mode of delivery. While oral verbalizations are du jour in some cultures, in others, the verb *to love* has such exclusivity that it is used, if at all, only in writing. An example of this issue can be found in the movie *The Last Samurai* (Herskovitz & Zwick, 2003), when the American main character speaks a line in Japanese that translates into "They want to destroy what I've come to love." The character uses the Japanese verb *aiseru* [love]. Only, "Japanese would not say *love* in this context. Maybe write it, but not say it. *Aiseru* is more natural in writing than speaking" (R. Terao, 2009, September 5, personal communication).

Non-translatability is one reason why some speakers of English as a second language report that it is easier to say the words "I love you" in English than use their native-language equivalent (Wilkins & Gareis, 2006). Although gradated verbalizations of love may exist in some languages, the variations don't necessarily apply to nonromantic settings … and in some cultures, verbal love declarations even in romantic situations seem to be so rare as to represent a void in the minds of some nonnative speakers. As a result, some welcome the opportunity to avail themselves of U.S. customs and the English locution "I love you" to express feelings that would otherwise remain unspoken. Sterk (2003, para. 1), for example, recounts:

> In my lectures for Dutch as a Foreign Language I am used to ending (and when I say ending, I mean: at the end of the year, not after every lecture) by saying: "And don't forget: I love you all." I could never say this using Dutch, because it just doesn't feel right, so I say it in English.

The use of English "I love you" by nonnative speakers finds an explanation in the linguistic process of code-switching (the shifting into another language by bilinguals and other second-language speakers) (Scotton & Ury, 1977). Certain expressions are more appropriate in one language versus the other. Through code-switching, speakers can reach into a bag of emotion terms and pick out the one that is most suitable. By doing so, they can express even topics that would be taboo in the first language (Bond & Lai, 2001; Panayiotou, 2004).

In a related trend, some languages Americanize to the extent that native-language words and phrases—although they appear the same—are re-interpreted and take on U.S. connotations. Such a semantic loan has been reported in German with respect to the verb *love*. The verb has experienced a semantic shift from formerly expressing a strong, exclusive emotion to now being used in much broader contexts than before and meaning something akin to *like* (Deutsche Sprachwelt, 2005; Zimmer, 1997). If a close relationship exists between language and the interpretation of emotions (Beall & Sternberg, 1995; Derné, 1994; Wierzbicka, 1999b), then this shift in the German language may imply a change in the social construction of emotion. In times of language and culture change, it is crucial to verify denotations and connotations carefully. Perhaps a new software, called *The Love Detector*, can be of assistance at bypassing linguistic confusion and isolating the core meaning of love (Berger, 2004). The software operates on the basis of layered voice analysis, by assessing levels of emotion and whether what is said reflects certainty, uncertainty, or outright lies. The love detector shows a flower growing petals when the speaker's emotions are strong, but no petals when affection appears inauthentic.

Nonverbal Love Expression. Nonverbal love declarations can come in form of selfless actions, physical signs of affection, the exchange of gifts, and spending time together, among others (Gareis & Wilkins, in press; Kline et al., 2008). In a study on U.S. and German love expression patterns, both Americans and Germans stated that nonverbal declarations of love are more common than verbal declarations—although the preference was more marked for German respondents (Gareis & Wilkins, in press). Reasons given for the nonverbal prevalence include shyness, familial traditions, and the notion that actions are more dependably sincere than words. Shaver et al. (1991) wonder whether there may be universal action tendencies (including proximity maintenance and speaking softly) associated with certain emotions, such as love. Luhmann (1986) evokes a philosophical dimension of the use of nonverbals over verbals when he asserts that utterances separate speakers from what they say and destroy innocence in the process.

When asked what should accompany a verbal love declaration, Americans in the study by Gareis and Wilkins (in press) stressed physical accompaniments, such as hugs and kisses; Germans focused on abstract notions, such as sincerity and loyalty. Similarly, Kline et al. (2008) found that Americans use more physical contact to communicate love in both friendship and marriage than East Asians. Likewise, Horton, Kline, and Zhang (2005), in a study comparing U.S., Chinese, Japanese, and Korean culture, found that Americans, in showing love for friends and partners, seem to prefer activities (e.g., exercise, dinner, movies/concert, shopping, drinking), whereas East Asians tend towards talk activities (e.g., dinner, drinking).

CONTEXT

Relationships. Focusing on the locution "I love you," Wilkins and Gareis (2006) conducted a study with domestic and international students from different European, Asian, and Latin American countries in the United States. While the locution is used in a wide variety of U.S. relationships, the international students—irrespective of home country—indicated that in the equivalent of "I love you" in their native languages is used mostly with romantic partners. Comparing U.S. and German patterns, Gareis and Wilkins (in press) confirmed the finding. Lovers in both cultures use the locution frequently; but in all other relationships (e.g., spouses, parents/children, siblings, friends), Germans used the locution consistently less than Americans. In fact, use of the locution in nonromantic contexts seems to feel awkward to some Germans, as the following anecdote illustrates (Sterk, 2003, para. 4):

> A German student who had lived in the United States as an au pair told me she really had to get used to always having to say (and she mentioned the pressure feeling) "I love you" or "I love you, too" to her host family, children, and the parents.

And Niesen recounts (2003, para. 1):

> "Big words" are often perceived as "insincere" over here in Germany, and saying "I love you" is mainly limited to "big moments" and not an everyday, end-of-the-telephone-conversation thing. I have definitely never ever said "I love you" to even my dearest friends or even my family. This expression still seems to be limited to partners in my context.

A contradictory result is reported by Seki et al. (2002). Investigating intimacy in Japan versus the United States, they found that the Japanese in the study value direct verbalizations (such as "I love you" or "I like you") within relationships with mother, father, and same-sex best friend more than Americans. The finding is surprising, given Japanese restraint in emotional expression, and led the authors to speculate that the relatively young age of the student respondents may have skewed the results and reflected their adherence to nonconforming youth culture. In addition, the study focused only on preferred expression mode and not on frequency. Had frequency been included, the ranking would likely have been higher for U.S. Americans. When comparing highly different cultures, such as Japan and the United States, translatability or instrument mismatches are of particular importance. Sprecher et al. (1994), for example, found Japanese to be less romantic than Americans, whereas Smith (1999) highlighted the large Japanese vocabulary for effects of romantic love in another study. The transferability of the investigated concepts may be at the root of the discrepancy.

Frequency. Wilkins and Gareis (2006) report that, in some cultures, the locution "I love you" is not only restricted to romantic contexts, but also exceedingly rare. Anecdotes along the same lines can also be found in literature and popular media. Consider, for instance, the title of the book, *I Love Yous are for White People*, on growing up Vietnamese in the United States (Su, 2009), or the statement by Finnish literary critic Jan Knutas (from the introduction of this chapter) that, in Finland, one may hear the words "I love you" only once in a lifetime—on one's death bed (Tiffin, 1993).

Culture clearly impacts what is appropriate and desirable in the expression of love (Derné, 1994; Hatfield & Rapson, 2002), but reports of conscious attempts to change the context and frequency of love expression in some cultures also speak of a desire to alter existing structures. In Japan, for example, an organization called *Japan Aisaika* [devoted husband] was formed to improve Japan's troubled approach to marriage, which is often considered more a status than a relationship. The organization recently arranged so-called *shout-outs,* during which husbands line up in public and shout the words "I love you" (some for the first time) while their wives are watching. Participants report on the effects of such shout-outs (Kambayashi, 2008, p. World 1):

> "If I say to my wife, 'I love you,' she would think I'm crazy," says Hiroto, who has been married for 20 years.... Like most of his colleagues, policymaker Motoyoshi Hashizume says he rarely expressed his love to his wife, Tomoko, in their 21 years of marriage. But since the 2006 shout-out, he continues, "I more often call her by name and appreciate what my wife has been doing."

Reflecting a similar development towards higher frequency levels, Lum (1997) reports that, in a study on immigrants to the United States, love expressions increased among immigrant couples the longer they resided in the country. While Japanese husbands and immigrants may feel that they have some catching-up to do, however, other research shows that the longer a couple is married, the less they express love to each other (Swensen, Eskey, & Kohlhepp, 1984). It's only in times of crisis (e.g., cancer diagnosis) that couples report a resurgence in love expression (Swensen & Fuller, 1992).

Setting. Apart from health crises and traditional times to declare love (such as marriage proposals and weddings), love expression appears to require no special occasion. Motives and effects range from sublime, festive, erotic, or lightly said (Barthes, 1978) to appreciative, comforting, and nostalgic (Gareis & Wilkins, in press).

Likewise, there is no limit on locales, although certain culture-specific preferences seem to exist. Thus, Gareis and Wilkins (in press) found that Americans expressed love most commonly in the home, special events, and on the phone; while Germans listed the home, transportation hubs, and a park or nature areas as the most common locales.

GENDER. The declaration "I love you" is used by both genders in romantic contexts; although males tend to initiate verbal love expression in new relationships, and females use verbal love expression more in established relationships (Owen, 1987; Ting-Toomey, 1991; Wilkins & Gareis, 2006). In non-romantic contexts, females are more likely to say "I love you" across all relationship types (Wilkins & Gareis, 2006).

The second half of the 20th century saw significant changes in male/

female relationship patterns. As women gained more independence, the men's liberation movement of the 1970s encouraged men to express their feelings more openly (Farrell, 1975; Sattel, 1976) and showed that relationships in which men have a degree of femininity are happier than those in which the men are markedly masculine (Schenk & Pfrang, 1983). Although intimacy is the strongest predictor of satisfaction for both men and women (Lemieux & Hale, 1999), men, however, are still described as having a more cognitive mode of relating to the world and more of a solo perspective, causing women to feel neglected (Clark, Kleinman, & Ellis, 1994). In an interesting study on gender stereotypes, Wilde and Diekman (2005) found that in the United States and Germany, both men and women are actually showing increasing levels of masculine personality traits (e.g., independence, competitiveness, egocentrism). The gender-role changes that started with the French Revolution seem to be still in process. It is not clear yet how they will play out and what they will ultimately mean for the experience of love and love expression.

Cultural Dimensions As research on cross-cultural communication variables shows, some patterns in the United States differ from those in a variety of other cultures. Verbal love expression seems to be more common in the United States, Americans tend towards more activities and physical contact, and the category width of the locution "I love you" is broader. Differences in cultural value orientations can explain some of the variance in the expression of love (Kimura, 1998; Sprecher & Toro-Morn, 2002).

INDIVIDUALISM VERSUS COLLECTIVISM. With the United States topping the global individualism scale (Hofstede, 2001), the individualism/collectivism dimension serves as a suitable starting point for exploration. Collectivism is marked by group harmony, mutual dependence, and restraint in the expression of opinions and emotions (Doi, 1973; Hofstede, 2001; Kimura, 1998; Lum, 1997; Mesquita, 2001; Schwartz, 1990; Ting-Toomey, 1991). With respect to love, the Japanese concept of *amae* illustrates the collectivistic value orientation. Amae—often called passive love—is defined as a need of dependency and desire to be loved (Doi, 1973, 1974, 2001; Johnson, 1993). Amae therefore suggests a focus on other-reliance that allows for what might be seen as weakness in individualistic cultures. Adorno's (1962) definition of being loved as the ability to show weakness and not provoke strength comes to mind. Lutz (1988) reports a similar concept of the Micronesian Ifaluk, for whom the focus of love is on compassion for weak, dependent people.

In addition, where individualism extols romantic love and enduring feelings for one special person (Swidler, 1997), collectivism traditionally has put more weight on pragmatic aspects of love, to the point that romantic love can even be seen as having potentially detrimental effects. In Japan, for example, romantic love has at times been considered a bad omen (Simmons et al., 1986). And Derné (1994) reports that Hindu men have been known to view romantic love as a dangerous, individualistic emotion, which has the potential to tempt people away from their obligations to the larger joint families. The Hindu men in Derné's study emphasized that they enjoy the services they get from their wives (sexual and otherwise); however, they see equality (as it occurs in love marriages) as jeopardizing social relations. In their culture, arranged marriages are still the custom, the wife moves in with the husband's family, and men tell each other to ignore their wife's complaints because expressing oneself too freely creates tension. Love then is a duty-based, role-based feeling toward many in the household, not one special person. Given the strength of interdependent relationships that exist within collectivistic structures, Potter (1988) concludes that expressions of love are considered threats to the established sociocultural order.

A different picture presents itself within the family-oriented and more expressive form of Latin collectivism. Freudenfeld (2002) compared Mexican and German relationship satisfaction and found that Mexican couples had greater relationship satisfaction than German couples. This appeared to be in part due to greater levels of attachment and stronger emotion expression in Mexico. Germans tended to be less romantic than Mexicans, scored higher on mania and ludus, and defined love often as "to be loved by the partner." Mexicans, by contrast, defined love as "to feel love for the partner," indicating less self-centeredness than the German informants.

Freudenfeld (2002) explains that, until industrialization in the 18th century, all cultures were more or less collectivistic. The importance of romantic love in Western cultures therefore seems to be at least in part a result of industrialization and development (Jankowiak & Fischer, 1992; Levine et al., 1995). Today, young men and women around the world increasingly consider love a prerequisite for courtship and marriage. Sprecher et al. (1994), for example, found that recent Japanese insistence on love in marriage partners resembles that of U.S. Americans—only the Russians in the study exhibited less resolve. In a few Eastern, collectivistic, and poorer countries, romantic love seems to remain a luxury (Levine et al., 1995)

CONTEXTUALITY. Contextuality is closely related to the individualism/collectivism dimension. Individualists tend towards low-context communication and therefore verbalize feelings more than collectivists (with the exception of Latin cultures) (Freudenfeld, 2002; Schwartz, 1990; Wilkins & Gareis, 2006). Low-context individualists also assert love commitment more overtly, high-context collectivists more discreetly and implicitly (Ting-Toomey, 1991). A Japanese anecdote illustrates the contrast (R. Terao, personal communication, September 5, 2005):

> My father's teacher told me a story of students translating "I love you" into Japanese. The first day, a student translated it as "I love you"—the teacher said "wrong." The second day, a student translated it as "I like you"—the teacher said "better." The third day, a student translated it as "The moon is beautiful tonight"—the teacher said "perfect."

Contextuality increases with strength of social ties. The low contextuality in the United States can be seen as a function of the prevalence of short-term relationships and relatively high diversity (Heylighen & Dewaele, 2002), which may have an intensifying effect on the high frequency of direct love expression in the United States.

FEMININITY VERSUS MASCULINITY. Where the individualism/collectivism dimension influences the expression of love commitment and disclosure maintenance, the masculinity/femininity dimension (Hofstede, 2001) taps gender differences in intimacy expression. Studying intimacy expression in France, Japan, and the United States, Ting-Toomey (1991) found that males and females express intimacy differently in high masculine cultures, but do not differ significantly in high feminine cultures. In the study, female respondents from Japan and the United States (both more masculine than France) scored significantly higher on some intimacy expression patterns than females from France.

Argyle and Henderson (1984) conducted research on friendship rules in four cultures (U.K., Italy, Hong Kong, and Japan) and found that women in these cultures endorsed rules on showing affection more strongly than men (they emphasized self-disclosure and emotional support). Unfortunately, the study does not differentiate between the cultures, and it is not clear whether cultural dimensions or gender differences are at the root of the females' endorsement. In general, the dearth of research on the matter makes it difficult to gauge the influence of femininity/masculinity versus gender differences on love communication.

UNCERTAINTY AVOIDANCE AND LONG-TERM ORIENTATION. Uncertainty avoidance and long-term orientation (Hofstede, 2001) are other cultural dimensions with potential effect on love. In a study on U.S. and German love expression patterns, for example, Gareis and Wilkins (in press) found that more Germans than Americans experienced tension related to the expression of love. Respondents indicated that tensions were due to personal, cultural, and gender difference or due to issues of mutuality. The relatively low tolerance for uncertainty in German culture may explain the higher occurrence of tension.

Likewise, Germans seem to place greater weight on commitment and verbal love expression as a symbol of that commitment (Gareis & Wilkins, in press)—a finding perhaps reflecting their higher long-term orientation (Hofstede, 2001). Although Germans tend to be more low-context than Americans, they don't use direct love expression as freely as Americans and with as much ease in contexts that are somewhat routine (including the end of phone conversations). The finding suggests some dimensions (e.g., uncertainty avoidance and long-term orientation) may override others (e.g., contextuality) with respect to love expression.

PRIVATE VERSUS PUBLIC REALM. Last, studies have found that U.S. culture differs from a diverse number of other cultures in higher self-disclosure

(Chen, 1995; Cunningham, 1981; Jourard, 1961; Melikian, 1962; Ting-Toomey, 1991) and lower privacy concerns (Bellman, Johnson, Kobrin, & Lohse, 2004; Maynard & Taylor, 1996). Lewin (1997) conceptualized the public and private realm as a number of concentric layers, with the threshold between public and private differing between cultures. Lewin found, for example, that whereas Americans are more likely to self-disclose even to strangers and in public contexts (i.e., their public realm is relatively large), Germans tend to have a greater sense of privacy (i.e., fewer public layers). In a similar vein, Hall and Hall (1990) describe Europeans as leaning toward deep relationships which take a long time to solidify, in contrast to Americans, who are inclined toward easy familiarity. The United States seems to be unique in its large public realm, a position which may explain the liberal use of direct love verbalizations in contexts and relationships that, in other cultures, would be considered inappropriate for love expression.

An indication that love expression is becoming even more public in the United States is the trend toward marriage proposals in front of large audiences of strangers (including marriage proposals on the megatron in sports arenas and on live television). Public proposals are also on the rise in other cultures. Reichertz (1994), for example, reports that, in the popular German TV program *Traumhochzeit* [dream wedding], real people propose on live TV and are later filmed as they get married. What, some centuries ago, used to be a private affair is now often a public event. Explanations for the interest in public proposals vary. Experts point to factors that include the rise of extravagant weddings and the desire of couples, who already live together before marriage, to mark the new stage of life in dramatic ways (Schoenberg, 2007). Reichertz argues that the cultural and ritual symbol of "I love you" followed by the question of all questions has moved from the private to the extreme public realm is to secure as many witnesses as possible and thereby enhance chances of continuity (i.e., overcome divorce odds).

Verbal Love Expression: Culture Change

CAUSES. The conception of love in a given time and culture determines which thoughts and behaviors related to love are normal and desirable (Beall & Sternberg, 1995). Significant changes in this conception occurred in the second half of the last century. The 1960s revolved around the theme of love, coining maxims such as "make love not war" and "free love;" psychologists, such as Carl Rogers (1961), espoused unconditional love in parenting; feminism promoted gender equality and female self-expression (Friedan, 1963); and the men's liberation movement of the early 1970s encouraged men to express feelings more openly (Farrell, 1975; Sattel, 1976).

Modern relationships are based on equality, mutual love and understanding, and an openness of feelings, placing an increased value on communication. Looking for the conditions that promote such change in communication behavior, Bernstein (1972) posits that socioeconomic variables are a causative first step. The economic boom of the post-WWII years may therefore be a core reason for the changes in the culture of love. Romantic love has been more prevalent in the industrialized West because people have had more time to cultivate subjective experiences and to focus on emotional aspects of marriage (Gigy & Kelly, 1992; Jankowiak & Fischer; 1992). The finding that in modern Asian countries, like Japan, young people compare with Westerners in their romantic aspirations supports the economic line of reasoning (Levine et al., 1995; Sprecher et al., 1994).

Ways of speaking constitute a manifestation of cultural rules or "cultural scripts" (Wierzbicka, 1998). Trends in verbal love expression therefore serve as a tangible measure for changes in the culture of love. Reflecting the timing of the transformations in the 20th century, direct verbalizations of love did not increase in frequency and spread until after the 1960s (Gareis & Wilkins, in press). It also appears that the sociological and cultural changes started in the United States and then spread to other cultures, with changes in love expression following suit. Thus, Japanese youth value direct verbalizations of love even within nonromantic relationships (Seki et al., 2002); Germans use the locution more frequently and in more relationships now than in the past (Gareis & Wilkins, in press); and younger Mexicans appear to say "te quiero" or even "te amo" more often than before (DeNeve, 2003).

IMPACT OF TECHNOLOGY. Although more research is needed to explore the reasons and also the extent of changes around the globe, it is likely that the development toward more verbal love expression was triggered and continues to be driven by U.S. cultural exports (including movies and TV programs) (Zimmer, 1997). Overseas viewers sometimes comment on being surprised at how often people say "I love you" in U.S.-produced films and sitcoms (e.g., Niesen, 2003).

More recently—perhaps akin to the expansion of the postal service in 18th-century Europe and the resulting explosion of love expression in letters to friends (Beyrer, 2003)—the new communication technology of the 20th and 21st century (e-mail, text and instant messages, cell phones) has caused a further rise both within and beyond the United States. Contact with friends, family, and partners via ubiquitous communication devices is easy and often concludes with expressions of love. On cell phones, the expression might be a "luv ya," frequently uttered in public (Gold, 2003); and text messages are likely to end with the abbreviation *ILY* [I love you] (ILY, 2009) or an equivalent shorthand in other languages (ONE Kommunikationsunternehmen, 2001; Roesler, 2003).

PERCEPTIONS. The proliferation of love expression elicits positive reactions in some and concerns in others. In studies that gauge attitudes (Gareis & Wilkins, in press; Seki et al., 2002; Wilkins & Gareis, 2006), many U.S. and international respondents seem to welcome the changes, citing an appreciation for today's greater emotional openness and freedom to show affection. This is especially noticeable in cultures where the development toward more liberal emotion expression does not grow organically out of traditional informality, as in the United States. In Germany, for example, the increase in love expression (as well as general playfulness and familiarity) represents a relatively drastic value change (Gareis & Wilkins, in press).

There are also some, however, who deplore the changes as inflationary and as symbols of cultural decline, citing that the locution "I love you" is used casually to satisfy the wishes of one's spouse, to cover up a mistake, or to cement brittle relationships (Gareis & Wilkins, in press; Wilkins & Gareis, 2006). Negative perceptions are especially strong when speakers of languages other than English fear that Americanization is causing their language to lose the ability to differentiate (Zimmer, 1997). When the fast-food chain McDonald's, for example, launched its *I'm loving it* campaign in Germany in 2003 and translated its slogan literally into *Ich liebe es*, a national debate ensued (Ankenbrand, 2003; Herbst, 2003). Critics complained that love is an emotion too deep to be evoked for mundane objects or businesses (Hönicke, 2003), and purists warned that the exaggerated use of superlatives would ruin the language (Deutsche Sprachwelt, 2005). The discussion continued in public forums, often spurring acerbic commentary, such as by Schafrinna (2007, Comment #22):

> … the meaningful word *Liebe* [love] is being rendered harmless, and we don't notice how it creeps in. When it is as superficial as in English, it's too late.… What, by the way, do Americans say when they want to express that they truly love someone?

Adorno theorized as early as 1969 that the erosion of interpersonal distance signified a kind of "disease of contact." From an interculturalist's perspective, Simons (2003, para. 1) speculates that the mounting need to say "I love you" is the result of "increasingly low context and hence emotional incertitude" in some cultures. "Nothing is assumed, even parental love!" Similarly, Mettler von Maibom (2003) points out that trust, although indispensable in love relations, is difficult to create and maintain in increasingly technology-dependent communication. Gold (2003) specifies that, on communication technology such as the phone, one can be more honest but also lie more easily than face to face, and that a turned off device is cause for concern about possible infidelity or betrayal of friendship.

DIALECTICS OF CHANGE. When love declarations, particularly in mediated communication, appear routine, they can trigger confusion, including insecurity about the love expressions' purpose. Schank (2007, p. ST6) illustrates the feeling with a personal account:

> My mother started saying "I love you" to me only after she and my father divorced 10 years ago, but I always have the sense that she's saying it to get an "I love you" back, rather than to inform me of her love. She ends every phone conversation with it, and at this point it feels more like a stand-in for "Goodbye" than a meaningful phrase.

Similarly, a U.S. respondent in Gareis and Wilkins (in press) ruminates that "many young people end a phone conversation by saying 'luv ya.' It's hard for the listener to discern whether it is genuine or just a cliché." Perhaps an entry in the Urban Dictionary (ILY, 2009) is most telling. The dictionary list over 100 variations on the abbreviation *ILY* [I love you], including *ILY2* [I love you, too] and *ILYMAG* [I love you millions and gazillions]. In an ultimate, disingenuous twist, one of them reads *ILYJK* [I love you, just kidding].

Applying dialectical theory (Baxter & Montgomery, 1996) to the topic of culture change with respect to love expression, a number of contradictory forces seem to be at play. On part of the speaker, there is the tension between the desire to express love on one hand, and caution on the other. Age-old doubts about mutuality are amplified by newer concerns about public rejection, gender appropriateness, and, in the case of parents, the timing of love expression. Kohn (2009), for example, asserts that some experts now advise against the unconditional love for children that was advocated in the 1960s and recommend conditional parenting instead: Parents are to show affection when children are good and withhold it when they're not.

There is also tension between sincerity and ritual. Some speakers feel pressured to use the locution "I love you" in routine contexts and awkward when they say it (e.g., at the end of a phone conversations). At the same time, some assert that they truly mean it when they declare love, even if it is habitually done (Sterk, 2003). On part of the listener, there is tension between the desire for assurance and the potential vacuousness of routine declarations. The semantic ambiguity of reduced forms (the reduced pronunciation of "luv ya" or the lacking contextual clues of *ILY* in mediated communication) makes receivers wonder whether the expression is sincerely felt or merely formulaic.

Tension also exists in intercultural contexts between tradition and accommodation, when interactants come from cultures with different category widths of love locutions. An ethnic Hungarian (Wilkins & Gareis, 2006) elaborates:

> My partner is American who feels the urge of declaring his love to me verbally and nonverbally way too often. And he is hurt by my reaction or lack of response. It took me four years, but I learned that it is important to him, so I let him say it, and I say it back, surprisingly easily.... Saying "I love you" [in English] means nothing to me. I wouldn't dare say it in Hungarian to anyone. (p. 67)

Finally, on a larger scale, there is tension between the desire to maintain one's cultural and linguistic identity and the embrace of cultural change. To use the example of Germany, the fear of linguistic loss through frivolous use of love expression is in direct opposition to a widely welcomed change toward greater informality (Gareis & Wilkins, in press).

The current dialectical tensions center around the themes of intimacy versus individualization and stability versus transience. On one hand, people hope for fusion; on the other hand, they are driven by the desire for self-actualization (Bawin-Legros, 2004). Likewise, people may desire commitment and stability, but are living in times of significant sociological change. Badinter (1986) described the change as one from the importance of selfless love to a culture of self-love. According to her, altruism has morphed into mutuality, making it more and more difficult for people to sacrifice. They want to be loved as a child, but can't love like a mother.

If dialectical tensions are indicative of major personal or cultural events (Erbert, Pérez, & Gareis, 2003), the tensions related to changes in verbal love expression may represent an attempt to maintain intimacy in the face of individualization, or to counteract the emotional incertitude caused by postmodern arbitrariness with verbalizations. Despite the increase in verbal love expression, one should keep in mind that nonverbal love expression—actions speak louder than words—still seems to be the preferred mode. Taking this preference into account, could it be that the changes in verbal love expression are mainly a function of playfulness in the face of new interactive media? Or are they the tail end of the development toward greater emotional expressiveness that started in the 1960s? Time and further research will tell.

Some General Conclusions About Communication and Love

One general thematic that can be drawn from our review of the literature is that the term love has been used by many as a point of access into a study and commentary on communicative phenomena. At the micro-level analysis of everyday talk, the term *love* is an entry point into a commentary on the historical and transformational quality of a community. At the macro level, the term *love* is an outcome of sociocultural forces. As we have argued throughout, culture and love are symbiotic; one cannot exist without the other.

While there is some agreement in the literature that a prototypical form of love exists—maternal love—and at least some universal *experience* of love is manifested in attachment and sexual attraction, there does not exist any one universal definition of love. Rather, definitions of love abound. The terms used to define love range from the classical (eros, agape, philia, storge, nomos, xenia, epithymia, and caritas) to the modern (brotherly, motherly, erotic, self-love, love of God, deficit love, being love, companionate love, passionate love, practical love, manic love, and game-playing love). It is perhaps here that a theory of love can begin. Our review is aimed at promoting an understanding of love as a feature of a larger social and cultural context where "the local symbolic currency and what it will purchase in social life must be discovered in every given case" (Stewart & Philipsen, 1984, p. 211). Much like other symbolic currencies of concern such as identity, power, and institutions that have most recently been subjected to a politically informed social constructionism (Deetze, 2010), love too, needs to be relocated into a larger body of communication practices. In order for love to be subjected to interpretive analysis, we have reconceptualized it as something that is socially constituted by those very same practices. The term *love* can be one feature of the larger symbolic currency of a community of speakers. Note here the use of the phrase *can be*; it doesn't have to be. This would suggest that the term *love* is important only if we hear sayings that state that it is important (Wierzbicka, 1997). This is perhaps where some of the intercultural asynchronies on emotion in general, and love in particular, such as in the *60 Minutes* excerpt presented in the introduction, have their origin. Interlocutors in intercultural encounters presume, erroneously so, that the experience and expression of love are the same across all communities of speakers. Alternatively, we have shown that interest should fall on the particular ways in which love is accomplished, and the particular ends love serves, and to demonstrate this through an understanding of the meaningfulness of those communication practices in which love is manifested and to do so from the vantage point of the participants who produce that communication.

While the universality of some forms of love may not be in dispute, our review shows that how persons interpret and manifest the emotional experience of love will differ from one community of speakers to another. As we have identified in this chapter, the communication of love has been influenced throughout history by social developments, zeitgeist oscillations, and tensions related to culture change. These particularized historical effects appear to inform larger dialectic patterns that help formulate the beginning of a theory of love communication. The central dialectics—those which communities of speakers seem to agonize over—is the degree persons will treat love as an object of expression or restraint, of the impulse of individuals to be free or the constraints of communal life, and of role-based communication or personalized interaction. Revealed in our literature review is the working assumption that a dialectic of love mediates a basic impulse between what Burke (1969) has called *division* and *identification*, where persons situated in the ongoing dramas of social life try to divide from and identify with one another. A dialectic is an interactive sequence in which at least two contrastive sets of communicative symbols—and their meanings—are being played with, or against each other (Baxter & Montgomery, 1996; Carbaugh, 1996). This analytical tool was developed to show how identities, relational dynamics, and rhetorical choices are crafted through contrast. As we conducted our literature review on the experience and expression of love, our task was to examine the literature for a play of symbols together, and explore the motives for selecting one set of symbols rather than the other. This process of division and identification, while universal as a form of human communication, is at the same time highly localized. We therefore suggest a theory of love as a social and cultural accomplishment that centers around three dialectics. We have named these dialectics as follows: (a) expression versus restraint, (b) autonomy versus unity, (c) role versus personal.

Expression versus Restraint

As an abstract claim, a fair amount of knowledge is required of when, to whom, and how to express love. Expression and restraint can be understood as antitheses, generating a dialectic where "the resolution of tension in decision is rhetoric" (Scott, 1993, p. 18). As an example Potter (1988) has pointed out that the West has used the capacity to express emotion as the symbolic basis for social relationships. Love becomes a part of nature—a physiological process located at the core of the nervous system giving rise to a universal emotional state. Everybody experiences the state of being *in love* with a non-familiar other at least once in a lifetime (some will say if they are lucky enough). The experience of love is often synonymous with expressed love—when people say what they feel. A source of great misunderstanding is the relative degree to which a community of speakers think that they are either verbally expressive when it comes to love or verbally restrained. Few studies then, have explored the indigenous rhetoric that grounds the choice of the expression of love over its verbal restraint. The articles that we reviewed in this chapter show how identification in a community requires both knowing how to create intelligible utterances and when, to whom, and how one can incorporate the expression of love. How persons become divided and subsequently unified over the legitimacy of the expression of love and its restraint is partly the basis upon which ethnographers can describe and interpret the symbolic currencies in communication.

Autonomy versus Unity

A second dialectic is the relative degree to which a participant's experience of love is generated by the tension between the impulse of individuals to be free and the constraints of communal life. One set of assumptions guiding this experience of love is a result of physiological or societal composition. The question, what is the basis for my emotions? is very much linked to claims of either a character trait or a social trait. Some jump intuitively to a belief that emotional states express deep things about individual character and their understandings of the world. Others see the experience of love as not just an expression of an internal feeling, but as a larger commentary on the moral, cultural, and political life of the community.

Role versus Personal

A third dialectic is the relative degree to which a participant's experience of love is generated by the tension between role-based communication versus personalized interaction. Role-based experiences of love value mindful and thoughtful understandings of the functions that love serves in relationships. For the most part, this orientation to love facilitates the suspension of an interpersonal face and best enables a dutiful expression of love. Any expression of love will be a function of treating individuals as social categories such as mother, father, husband, wife, son, daughter, and may also extend beyond the familiar roles that are found within family networks to such as love for one's leaders both past and present, for God, etc. Personalized interaction involves more spontaneous verbal interactions enabling more fluid exchanges of love among participants that are divested of their socially imposed roles. When outer behaviors, such as speech, coalesce with inner feelings, interpretations of character traits are often made based on these spoken expressions of individual feeling (Wilkins, 2007). Participants value a temporal sense of time in terms of getting feedback, receiving responses to their feelings of love, and gaining general accessibility to loved ones. Expressions of love serve to elaborate on issues of personal intent since individuals by virtue of their being a person are made up of these unique feelings, ideas, and attitudes.

Research Directions

Hymes (1964) called for "studies ethnographic in basis and communicative in scope" (p. 9). With respect to communicative behavior related to love, promising lines of inquiry include those focusing on communication processes, relationships, culture, and change.

- Research is needed on the specifics of communication processes in the expression of love, including physiological, nonverbal, vocal (sounds, laughter, sighs, etc.), paralanguage (intonation, speed, etc.), verbal, and conversational processes (discourse type, conversation management, timing). Additional linguistic evidence could include "common sayings and proverbs, frequent collocations, conversational routines and varieties of formulaic or semi-formulaic speech, discourses particles and interjections, and terms of address and reference" (Goddard & Wierzbicka, 2007, p. 110). The goal of such inquiry should be to delineate a community's speech acts, events, situations, names, and structures (Bauman & Sherzer, 1974); to uncover themes in love expression (such as never-endingness, eye language, and understanding without direct communication) (Luhmann, 1986); and to define differences concerning gender, age, and personality in view of these findings. Future research should also detail the social functions of love expression. As Kline and colleagues (2008, p. 212) posit, "particular love expressions may serve simultaneous ends; persons may feel better physically and may enact relational forms that validate the other and the other's actions."
- Studies related to love often focus on romance and marriage, and within that, mostly on heterosexual human relations (Fehr & Russell, 1991). More research is needed on love and love expression in a broader variety of relationships, including friendship, parents and their children, etc. Research should also compare same- and cross-sex friends, relationships

pertaining to different sexual orientations, and love expression in generational as well as intercultural contexts.

- Thus far, cross-cultural studies on love expression have focused on the United States, East Asia, and Germany. Not only should future studies explore more cultures, but care should be taken to differentiate within subgroups in those cultures; for example, rural versus urban practice or differences between regions in a given country (Landis & Shea, 2000). To study love communication cross-culturally, culture-sensitive instruments should be developed and cultural bias equilibrated to ensure that items have corresponding meanings (Seki et al., 2002). In addition, interdisciplinary studies suggest themselves. For example, research should be conducted on whether differences in communication and culture indicate emotional experiences unique to these cultures (Donovan & Rundle, 1997) or whether changes in love declaration over time correlate with a psychological and physiological regulation of emotions matching changed conceptions of love (Beall & Sternberg, 1995).
- With the meaning and expression of love varying historically and culturally, research should continue to investigate the parameters of change. Some of this research could focus on changes in the experience of love across cultures (including the question whether love styles involving strong personal feelings, such as eros, are largely free of cultural influences and those with lower affects, such as storge, are more prone to cultural influences and change) (Neto et al., 2000). In addition, attention should be paid to culture changes related to nonverbal and verbal love expression. In particular, the locution "I love you" as a barometer of change could be further observed and the reasons for its increased use investigated. With respect to the possible influence of U.S. culture on love expression, comparisons of love expression in literature, TV programs, and films across cultures may provide a point of departure. Additional research ideas include a comparison of cultures for insight into a potential globalization effect concerning emotion expression, and a look at love declarations in other cultures over time.
- Finally, future research should continue to build and test theory. We suggest that particularly the theme of division versus identification, and the three dialectics of expression versus restraint, autonomy versus unity, and role versus personal, lend themselves for worthwhile ethnographic inquiry.

We suggest that love expression is a worthy of ongoing research. No matter what path of inquiry is chosen, research on love communication is valuable not only due to the relative scarcity of data on the topic, but also as a tool to understand and improve intercultural communication in an increasingly globalized world.

References

Adorno, T. W. (1962). *Minima moralia: Reflexionen aus einem beschädigten Leben* [Minima moralia: Reflections on a damaged life]. Frankfurt am Main: Suhrkamp.

Ahmed, S. (2003). In the name of love. *Borderlands E-Journal, 2*(3), Retrieved from http://www.borderlands.net.au/vol2no3_2003/ahmed_love.htm

Ahmed, S. (2004). *The cultural politics of emotion.* Edinburgh: Edinburgh University Press.

Allgeier, E. R., & Wiederman, M. W. (1991). Love and mate selection in the 1990s. *Free Inquiry, 11,* 25–27.

Ankenbrand, H. (September 8, 2003). McDonald's Kampagne: Ich wiege es™ [McDonald's campaign: I am weighing it™] *Spiegel Online.* Retrieved from http://www.spiegel.de

Argyle, M., & Henderson, M. (1984). The rules of friendship. *Journal of Social and Personal Relationships, 1,* 211–237. doi: 10.1177/0265407584012005

Argyle, M., & Henderson, M. (1985). The rules of relationships. In S. Duck & D. Perlman (Eds.), *Understanding personal relationships: An interdisciplinary approach* (pp. 63–84). Newbury Park, CA: Sage.

Aron, A., & Westbay, L. (1996). Dimensions of the prototype of love. *Journal of Personality and Social Psychology, 70*, 535–551. doi: 10.1037/0022-3514.70.3.535

Badinter, E. (1989). *The unopposite sex: The end of gender battle* (B. Wright, Trans.). New York: Harper & Row. (Original work published 1986)

Bailey, W. C., Hendrick, C., & Hendrick, S. (1987). Relations of sex and gender role to love, sexual attitudes, and self-esteem. *Sex Roles, 16,* 637–648.

Barsalou, L. W. (1987). The instability of graded structure: Implications for the nature of concepts. In U. Neisser (Ed.), *Concepts and conceptual development* (pp. 101–140). Cambridge, UK: Cambridge University Press.

Barthes, R. (1978). *A lover's discourse: Fragments* (R. Howard, Trans.). New York: Hill & Wang. (Original work published 1977)

Bauman, R., & Sherzer, J. (Eds.). (1974). *Explorations in the ethnography of speaking.* London: Cambridge University Press.

Bawin-Legros, B. (2004). Intimacy and the new sentimental order. *Current Sociology, 52*, 241–250. doi: 10.1177/0011392104041810

Baxter, L. A., & Montgomery, B. M. (1996). *Relating: Dialogues and dialectics.* New York: Guilford Press.

Beall, A. E., & Sternberg, R. J. (1995). The social construction of love. *Journal of Social and Personal Relationships, 12,* 417–438. doi: 10.1177/0265407595123006

Beck-Gernsheim, E. (1986). Von der Liebe zur Beziehung? Veränderungen im Verhältnis von Mann und Frau in der individualisierten Gesellschaft [From love to relationships? Changes in the relations between men and women in the individualized society]. In J. Berger (Ed.), *Die Moderne: Kontinuitäten und Zäsuren* [Modernity: Continuities and Divides] (pp. 209–233). Göttingen, Germany: Verlag Otto Schwartz.

Bellman, S., Johnson, E. J., Kobrin, S. J., & Lohse, G. L. (2004). International differences in information privacy concerns: A global survey of consumers. *Information Society, 20,* 313–324. doi: 10.1080/01972240490507956

Benedict XVI. (2005). *Encyclical: Deus caritas est.* Rome: Libreria Editrice Vaticana.

Benedict XVI. (2009). *Encyclical: Caritas in veritate.* Rome: Libreria Editrice Vaticana.

Berger, I. (2004, February 12). He loves me not, digitally. *New York Times,* p. G6.

Bernstein, B. (1972). Social class, language and socialization. In P. P. Giglioli (Ed.), *Language and social context* (pp. 157–78). Harmondsworth, UK: Penguin.

Beyrer, K. (2003). Liebespost: Die Ordnung der Gefühle bei der Beförderung [Love mail: The organization of transmitted emotions]. In B. Burkard (Ed.), *liebe.komm: Botschaften des Herzens* [love.come: Messages from the heart] (pp. 132–151). Heidelberg, Germany: Wachter Verlag.

Bierhoff, H. W. (1991). Twenty years of research on love: Theory, results, and prospects for the future. *German Journal of Psychology, 15*(2), 95–117.

Blumstein, P., & Schwartz, P. (1983). *American couples.* New York: William Morrow.

Bond, M. H., & Lai, T. M. (2001). Embarrassment and code-switching into a second language. *Journal of Social Psychology, 126*, 179–186.

Burke, K. (1969). *A rhetoric of motives.* Berkeley: University of California Press.

Carbaugh, D. (1996). *Situating selves: The communication of social identities in American scenes.* Albany: State University of New York Press.

Chang, H. C., & Holt, G. R. (1991). The concept of yuan and Chinese interpersonal relationships. In S. Ting-Toomey & F. Korzenny (Eds.), *Cross-cultural interpersonal communicating* (pp. 28–57). Newbury Park, CA: Sage.

Chapman, G. (1992). *The five love languages: How to express heartfelt commitment to your mate.* Chicago: Northfield

Charity. (1987). In M. Eliade (Ed.), *The encyclopedia of religion* (Vol. 3, pp. 222–225). New York: Macmillan.

Chen, G. M. (1995). Differences in self-disclosure patterns among Americans versus Chinese. *Journal of Cross-Cultural Psychology, 26,* 84–91. doi: 10.1177/0022022195261006

Cheyette, F. L., & Chickering, H. (2005). Love, anger, and peace: Social practice and poetic play in the ending of Yvain. *Speculum, 80,* 75–117.

Cho, W., & Cross, S. E. (1995). Taiwanese love styles and their association with self-esteem and relationship quality. *Genetic, Social, and General Psychology Monographs, 121,* 283–309.

Clark, C., Kleinman, S., & Ellis, C. (1994). Conflicting reality readings and interactional dilemmas: Love relationships: His, hers, and theirs. In W. M. Wentworth & J. Ryan (Eds.), *Social perspectives on emotion* (Vol. 2, pp. 147–175). Greenwich, CT: JAI Press.

Contreras, R., Hendrick, S., & Hendrick, C. (1996). Perspectives on marital love and satisfaction in Mexican American and Anglo-American couples. *Journal of Counseling & Development, 74*, 408–415.

Cunningham, J. D. (1981). Self-disclosure intimacy: Sex, sex-of-target, cross-national, and generational differences. *Personality and Social Psychology Bulletin, 7,* 314–319. doi: 10.1177/014616728172021

Davis, K. E. (2001). The relationship rating form (RRF): A measure of characteristics of romantic relationships and friendships. In J. Touliatos, B. Perlmutter, & G. Holden (Eds.), *Handbook of family measurement techniques* (2nd ed., Vol. 3, pp. 195–197), Thousand Oaks, CA: Sage.

Davis, K. E., & Latty-Mann, H. (1987). Love styles and relationship quality: A contribution to validation. *Journal of Social and Personal Relationships, 4,* 409–428. doi: 10.1177/0265407587044002

Davis, K. E., & Todd, M. J. (1982). Friendship and love relationships. *Advances in Descriptive Psychology, 2,* 79–122.

Deetze, S. (2010). Politically attentive relational constructionism (PARC): Making a difference in a pluralistic, interdependent world. In D. Carbaugh & P. M. Buzzanell (Eds.), *Distinctive qualities in communication research* (pp. 32–52). New York: Routledge Taylor and Francis Group.

DeNeve, C. (2003, October 9). Love. Message posted to Interculturalinsights electronic mailing list, archived at http://finance.groups.yahoo.com/group/interculturalinsights/message/6525

Derné, S. (1994). Structural realities, persistent dilemmas, and the construction of emotional paradigms: Love in three cultures. In W. M. Wentworth & J. Ryan (Eds.), *Social perspectives on emotion* (Vol. 2, pp. 281–308). Greenwich, CT: JAI Press.

Deutsche Sprachwelt. (2005). 40 Tage quasselfrei: Verzicht auf die Fast-Food-Sprache. [40 days gibberish free: Renunciation of the fast-food language]. Retrieved from http://www.deutschesprachwelt.de

Doherty, W., Hatfield, E., Thompson, K., & Choo, P. (1994). Cultural and ethnic influences on love and attachment. *Personal Relationships, 1*, 391–398. doi: 10.1111/j.1475-6811.1994.tb00072.x

Doi, T. (1963). Amae: A Key concept for understanding Japanese personality structure. In R. J. Smith & R. K. Beardsley (Eds.), *Japanese culture: Its development and characteristics* (pp. 132–139). Chicago: Aldine.

Doi, T. (1973). *The anatomy of dependence*. Tokyo: Kodansha.

Doi, T. (1974). Amae: A key concept for understanding Japanese personality structure. In T. S. Lebra & W. P. Lebra (Eds.), *Japanese culture and behavior: Selected readings*. Honolulu: University Press of Hawaii.

Doi, T. (2001). *Tsuzuki: Amae no kouzou* [Continued: The anatomy of dependence]. Tokyo: Koubundou Press.

Donovan, J. M., & Rundle, B. A. (1997). Psychic unity constraints upon successful intercultural communication. *Language & Communication, 17*(3), 219–235.

Egbert, N., & Polk, D. (2006). Speaking the language of relational maintenance: A validity test of Chapman's (1992) five love languages. *Communication Research Reports, 23*, 19–26. doi: 10.1080/17464090500535822

Erbert, L. A., Pérez, F. G., & Gareis, E. (2003). Turning points and dialectical interpretations of immigrant experiences in the United States. *Western Journal of Communication, 67*(2), 113–137.

Farrell, W. (1975). *The liberated man*. New York: Bantam Books.

Fehr, B. (1988). Prototype analysis of the concepts of love and commitment. *Journal of Personality and Social Psychology, 55*, 557–579. doi: 10.1037/0022-3514.55.4.557

Fehr, B., & Russell, J. A. (1991). The concept of love viewed from a prototype perspective. *Journal of Personality and Social Psychology, 60*, 425–438. doi: 10.1037/0022-3514.60.3.425

Fiehler, R. (1990). *Kommunikation und Emotion: Theoretische und empirische Untersuchungen zur Rolle von Emotionen in der verbalen Interaktion* [Communication and emotion: Theoretical and empirical studies on the role of emotions in verbal interactions]. Berlin: Walter de Gruyter.

Fisher, H. (2004). *Why we love: The nature and chemistry of romantic love*. New York: Henry Holt.

Freudenfeld, E. (2002). *Liebesstile, Liebeskomponenten und Bedingungen für Glück und Trennung bei deutschen und mexikanischen Paaren: Eine kulturvergleichende Studie* [Love styles, love components, and conditions for happiness and separation in German and Mexican couples: A cultural comparison]. Unpublished doctoral dissertation, Eberhard-Karls-Universität Tübingen, Germany.

Friedan, B. (1963). *The feminine mystique*. New York: Dell.

Fromm, E. (1956). *The art of loving*. New York: Harper & Row.

Gareis, E., & Wilkins, R. (in press). Love expression in the United States and Germany. *International Journal of Intercultural Relations*.

Giddens, A. (1992). *The transformation of intimacy: Sexuality, love and eroticism in modern societies*. Stanford, CA: Stanford University Press.

Gigy, L., & Kelly, J. B. (1992). Reasons for divorce: Perspectives of divorcing men and women. *Journal of Divorce and Remarriage, 18,* 169–187. doi: 10.1300/J087v18n01

Goddard, C. (2003). Thinking across languages and cultures: Six dimensions of variation. *Cognitive Linguistics, 14*(2/3), 109–140.

Goddard, C., & Wierzbicka, A. (2007). Semantic primes and cultural scripts in language learning and intercultural communication. In G. B. Palmer & F. Sharifian (Eds.), *Applied cultural linguistics: Converging evidence in language and communication research* (Vol. 7, pp. 105–124). Amsterdam: John Benjamins.

Goethe, J. W., von (2001). *Die Leiden des jungen Werther* [The sorrows of young Werther]. Ditzingen, Germany: Reclam. (Original work published in 1774)

Gold, H. (2003). Reach out and touch someone. In B. Burkard (Ed.), *liebe.komm: Botschaften des Herzens* [love.come: Messages from the heart] (pp. 152–159). Heidelberg, Germany: Wachter Verlag.

Goodwin, R., & Findlay, C. (1997). "We were just fated together" . . . Chinese love and the concept of *yuan* in England and Hong Kong. *Personal Relationships, 4*, 85–92. doi: 10.1111/j.1475-6811.1997.tb00132.x

Grau, I. (1998). Zum Unterschied zwischen Freundschaft und Liebe [On the difference between friendship and love]. *Psychologische Beiträge, 40,* 254–270.

Hall, E. T., & Hall, M. R. (1990). *Understanding cultural differences: Germans, French, and Americans*. Yarmouth, ME: Intercultural Press.

Haslett, A. (2004, May 31). Love supreme. *The New Yorker,* 76–79.

Hatfield, E. (1988). Passionate and companionate love. In R. J. Sternberg, & M. L. Barnes (Eds.), *The psychology of love* (pp. 191–217). New Haven, CT: Yale University Press.

Hatfield, E., & Rapson, R. L. (2002). Passionate love and sexual desire: Cross-cultural and historical perspectives. In A. Vangelisti, H. T. Reis, & M. A. Fitzpatrick (Eds.). *Stability and change in relationships* (pp. 306–324). Cambridge, UK: Cambridge University Press.

Hendrick, C., & Hendrick, S. S. (1986). A theory and method of love. *Journal of Personality and Social Psychology, 50,* 392–402.

Hendrick, C., & Hendrick. S. S. (1989). Research on love: Does it measure up? *Journal of Personality and Social Psychology, 56,* 784–794.

Hendrick, S. S., Hendrick, C., & Adler, N. L. (1988). Romantic relationship: Love, satisfaction, and staying together. *Journal of Personality and Social Psychology, 54,* 980–988. doi: 10.1037/0022-3514.54.6.980

Herbst, D. (September 7, 2003). Wer liebt schon seinen Arbeitgeber? [Who actually loves their employer?] *Der Tagesspiegel*. Retrieved from http://www.tagesspiegel.de

Herskovitz, M. (Producer), & Zwick, E. (Director). (2003). *The last samurai*. USA: Warner Bros.

Hettlage, R. (1998). *Familienreport: Eine Lebensform im Umbruch* [Family report: A lifestyle in upheaval]. München: Beck.

Heylighen, F., & Dewaele, J.-M. (2002). Variation in the contextuality of language: An empirical measure. *Foundations of Science, 7,* 293–340.

Hönicke, C. (September 4, 2003). Meine Pommes und ich [My French fries and I]. *Der Tagesspiegel.* Retrieved from http://www.tagesspiegel.de

Hofstede, G. H. (2001). *Culture's consequences: Comparing values, behaviors, institutions, and organizations across nations* (2nd ed.). Thousand Oaks, CA: Sage.

Horton, B., Kline, S., & Zhang, S. (2005, May). *How we think, feel and express love: A cross-cultural comparison between American and East Asian cultures.* Paper presented at the annual conference of the International Communication Association, New York, NY.

Hsu, F. L. K. (1985). The self in cross-cultural perspective. In A. J. Marsella, G. DeVos, & F. L. K. Hsu (Eds.), *Culture and self: Asian and Western perspectives* (pp. 24–55). London: Tavistock.

Hymes, D. (1964). Introduction: Toward ethnographies of communication. In J. J. Gumperz & D. Hymes (Eds.), *The ethnography of communication. American Anthropologist, 66*(6, Pt. 2), 1–34.

ILY. (2009). *Urban dictionary.* Retrieved from http://www.urbandictionary.com

Izard, C., & Buechler, S. (1980). Aspects of consciousness and personality in terms of differential emotions theory. In R. Plutchik & H. Kellerman, (Eds.), *Emotion: Theory, research, and experience* (Vol. 1, pp. 105–187). New York: Academic Press.

Jankowiak, W. R., & Fischer, E. F. (1992). A cross-cultural perspective on romantic love. *Ethnology, 31*(2), 149–155.

Johnson, F. A. (1993). *Dependency and Japanese socialization: Psychoanalytic and anthropological investigation into amae.* New York: New York University Press.

Jourard, S. M. (1961). Self-disclosure patterns in British and American college females. *Journal of Social Psychology, 54,* 315–320.

Kagan, J. (2007). *What is emotion? History, measures, and meanings.* New Haven, CT: Yale University Press.

Kagel, M. (2007). Brothers and others: Male friendship in eighteenth-century Germany. *Colloquia Germanica: Internationale Zeitschrift für Germanistik, 40,* 213–235.

Kambayashi, T. (2008, February 13). Japanese men should the oft-unsaid: "I love you." *Christian Science Monitor,* p. World 1.

Kanemasa, Y., Taniguchi, J., & Daibo, I. (2004). Love styles and romantic love experiences in Japan. *Social Behavior and Personality, 32*(3), 265–282.

Kephart, W. M. (1967). Some correlates or romantic love. *Journal of Marriage and the Family, 29,* 470–479.

Kim, J., & Hatfield, E. (2004). Love types and subjective well-being: A cross-cultural study. *Social Behavior & Personality, 32*(2), 173–182.

Kimura, T. (1998). Cultural differences between Americans and Japanese in meanings of love (gender) (doctoral dissertation, Cornell University). *Dissertation Abstracts International, 59,* 1877.

King, M. L., Jr., (1964). *The Nobel Peace Prize 1964: Acceptance speech.* Retrieved from http://www.nobelrize.org

Kline, S. L., Horton, B., & Zhang, S. (2008). Communicating love: Comparisons between American and East Asian university students. *International Journal of Intercultural Relations, 32,* 200–214. doi: 10.1016/j.ijintrel.2008.01.006

Kohn, A. (2009, September 15). When a parent's "I love you" means "Do as I say." *New York Times,* p. 5.

Landis, D., & O'Shea, W. A. (2000). Cross-cultural aspects of passionate love: An individual differences analysis. *Journal of Cross-Cultural Psychology, 31,* 752–777.

Lee, J. A. (1973). *The colors of love: An exploration of the ways of loving.* Don Mills, Ontario: New Press.

Lee, J. A. (1977). A typology of styles of loving. *Personality and Social Psychology Bulletin, 3,* 173–182. doi: 10.1177/014616727700300204

Lee, J. A. (1988). Love styles. In R. J. Sternberg & M. L. Barnes (Eds.), *The psychology of love* (pp. 38–67). New Haven, CT: Yale University Press.

Lemieux, R., & Hale, J. L. (1999). Intimacy, passion, and commitment in young romantic relationships: Successfully measuring the triangular theory of love. *Psychological Reports, 85,* 497–503.

Levine, N. (1981). Perspectives on love: Morality and affect in Nyinba interpersonal relations. In A. Mayer (Ed.), *Culture and morality* (pp. 106–125). New York: Academic Press.

Levine, R., Sato, S., Hashimoto, R., & Verma, J. (1995). Love and marriage in eleven cultures. *Journal of Cross-Cultural Psychology, 26*, 554–571. doi: 10.1177/0022022195265007

Levy, M. B., & Davis, K. E. (1988). Lovestyles and attachment styles compared: Their relations to each other and to various relationships characteristics. *Journal of Social and Personal Relationships, 5*, 439–471. doi: 10.1177/0265407588054004

Lewin, K. (1997). Some social-psychological differences between the United States and Germany. In K. Lewin, *Resolving social conflict and field theory in social research* (pp. 15–34). Washington, DC: American Psychological Association.

Lindberg, C. (2008). *Love: A brief history through Western Christianity.* San Francisco: Wiley-Blackwell.

Love. (2009). In *Merriam-Webster online dictionary.* Retrieved from http://www.merriam-webster.com/dictionary/love

Luhmann, N. (1986). *Love as passion: The codification of intimacy* (J. Gaines & D. L. Jones, Trans.). Cambridge, MA: Harvard University Press. (Original work published 1982)

Lum, J. L. (1997). Ethnic differences in the expression of affection and other emotions (doctoral dissertation, University of California, Santa Barbara, 1997). *Dissertation Abstracts International, 58,* 1596.

Lutz, C. A. (1988). *Unnatural emotions: Everyday sentiments on a Micronesian atoll and their challenge to western theory.* Chicago: University of Chicago Press.

Maier, M. S. (1998). Ländliche Galanterie [Rural gallantry]. In K. Hahn & G. Burkart (Eds.), *Liebe am Ende des 20. Jahrhunderts* [Love at the end of the 20th century] (pp. 131–153). Opladen, Germany: Leske & Budrich.

Marcuse, H. (1955). *Eros and civilization: A philosophical inquiry into Freud.* Boston: Beacon Press.

Maslow, A. H. (1962). *Toward a psychology of being.* New York: Nostrand.

Matsui, Y., Tokusa, T., Tachizawa, H., Ohkubo, H., Ohmae, H., Okamura, M., & Yoneda, Y. (1990). Scale construction of Japanese youth's love. *The Journal of the Tachikawa College of Tokyo, 23,* 13–23.

Maynard, M. L., & Taylor, C. R. (1996). A comparative analysis of Japanese and U.S. attitudes toward direct marketing. *Journal of Direct Marketing, 10*(1), 34–44.

Melikian, L. H. (1962). Self-disclosure among university students in the Middle East. *Journal of Social Psychology, 57,* 257–263.

Mesquita, B. (2001). Emotions in collectivist and individualist contexts. *Journal of Personality and Social Psychology, 80*(1), 68–74. doi: 10.1037/0022-3514.80.1.68

Mettler von Meibom, B. (2003). Liebe ist grenzenlos [Love is without borders]. In B. Burkard (Ed.), *liebe.komm: Botschaften des Herzens* [love.come: Messages from the heart] (pp. 132–151). Heidelberg, Germany: Wachter Verlag.

Moore, R. L. (1998). Love and limerence with Chinese characteristics: Student romance in the PRC. In V. C. deMunck (Ed.), *Romantic love and sexual behavior: Perspectives from the social sciences* (pp. 251–284). Westport, CT: Praeger.

Neto, F., Mullet, E., Deschamps, J. C., Barros, J., Benvindo, R., Camino, L., Falconi, A., Kagibanga, V., & Machado, M. (2000). Cross-cultural variations in attitudes toward love. *Journal of Cross-Cultural Psychology, 31*(5), 626–635. doi: 10.1177/0022022100031005005

Niesen, A. (2003, October 6). Love. Message posted to Interculturalinsights electronic mailing list, archived at http://finance.groups.yahoo.com/group/interculturalinsights/message/6468

Nirenberg, D. (2009). Love and capitalism. *New Republic, 240*(17), 39–42.

Noller, P. (1996). What is the thing called love? Defining the love that supports marriage and family. *Personal Relationships, 3,* 97–115. doi: 10.1111/j.1475-6811.1996.tb00106.x

Ochs, E. (1986). From feelings to grammar: A Samoan case study. In B. B. Schieffelin & E. Ochs (Eds.), *Language socialization across cultures* (pp. 251–272). New York: Cambridge University Press.

ONE Kommunikationsunternehmen. (2001). *Umfrage: Das Handy als Liebesbote* [Survey: The cell phone as love messenger]. Retrieved from http://presse.one.at/medienleiste/98371858422863556.doc

Osgood, C. E., May, W. H., & Miron, M. S. (1975) *Cross-cultural universals of affective meaning.* Urbana: University of Illinois Press.

Owen, W. F. (1987). The verbal expression of love by women and men as a critical communication event in personal relationships. *Women's Studies in Communication, 10*(1), 15–24.

Panayiotou, A. (2004). Switching codes, switching code: Bilinguals' emotional responses in English and Greek. *Journal of Multilingual and Multicultural Development, 25*(2&3), 124–139. doi:10.1080/01434630408666525

Popenoe, D. (2002). *The national marriage project.* New Brunswick, NJ: Rutgers University Press.

Potter, S. (1988) The cultural construction of emotion in rural Chinese social life. *Ethos, 16*(2), 181–208.

Ratner, C. (1989). A social constructionist critique of naturalistic theories of emotion. *Journal of Mind and Behavior, 10,* 211–230.

Reichertz, J. (1994). Ich liebe, liebe, liebe dich [I love, love, love you]. *Soziale Welt, 45,* 98–119.

Rogers, C. (1961). *On becoming a person.* Boston: Houghton Mifflin.

Roesler, A. (2003). 160 Zeichen der Liebe: Zur Kommunikation eines Gefühls im SMS-Format [160 signs of love: On the communication of an emotion in the instant-message format]. In B. Burkard (Ed.), *liebe.komm: Botschaften des Herzens* [love.come: Messages from the heart] (pp. 182–189). Heidelberg, Germany: Wachter Verlag.

Rubin, Z. (1970). Measurement of romantic love. *Journal of Personality and Social Psychology, 16,* 265–273.

Sattel, J. W. (1976). The inexpressive male: Tragedy or sexual politics? *Social Problems, 23,* 467–477.

Schafrinna, A. (2007, December 11). *Alle lieben Liebe. Design Tagebuch* [Everyone loves love]. Retrieved from http://www.designtagebuch.de/alle-lieben-liebe

Schank, H. (2007, September 2). The people on the bus say "shame on you". *New York Times,* p. ST6.

Schenk, J., & Pfrang, H. (1983). Aspekte des Geschlechtsrollenbildes bei Verheirateten [Aspects of the image of gender roles in married couples]. *Psychologische Beiträge, 25,* 176–193.

Schneider, D. (1980). *American kinship: A cultural account.* Chicago: The University of Chicago Press.

Schoenberg, N. (2007, January 8). Popping the question as everybody watches. *Chicago Tribune Archives News.* Retrieved from http://archives.chicagotribune.com

Schwartz, S. (1990). Individualism-collectivism: Critique and proposed refinements. *Journal of Cross-cultural Psychology, 21,* 139–157. doi: 10.1177/0022022190212001

Scott, R. (1993). Dialectical tensions of speaking and silence. *Quarterly Journal of Speech, 79*(1), 1–18.

Scotton, C. M., & Ury, W. (1977). Bilingual strategies: The social functions of code-switching. *International Journal of the Sociology of Language, 13,* 5–20.

Seki, K., Matsumoto, D., & Imahori, T. T. (2002). The conceptualization and expression of intimacy in Japan and the United States. *Journal of Cross-Cultural Psychology, 33,* 303–319. doi: 10.1177/0022022102033003006

Shaver, P. R., Wu, S., & Schwartz, J. C. (1991). Cross-cultural similarities and differences in emotion and its representation: A prototype approach. In M. S. Clark (Ed.), *Review of Personality and Social Psychology* (Vol. 13, pp. 175–212). Newbury Park, CA: Sage.

Singer, I. (1987). *The nature of love: Plato to Luther* (2nd ed.). Chicago: University of Chicago Press.

Simmons, C. H., von Kolke, A., & Shimizu, H. (1986). Attitudes toward romantic love among American, German, Japanese students. *Journal of Social Psychology, 126,* 327–336.

Simmons, C. H., Wehner, E. A., & Kay, K. A. (1989). Differences in attitudes toward romantic love of French and American college students. *Journal of Social Psychology, 129,* 793–799.

Simons, G. (2003, October 6). Love. Message posted to Interculturalinsights electronic mailing list, archived at http://finance.groups.yahoo.com/group/interculturalinsights/message/6467

Smith, J. S. (1999). From *Hiren* to *happi-endo:* Romantic expression in the Japanese love story. In G. B. Palmer & D. J. Occhi (Eds.), *Languages of sentiment* (pp. 131–150). Philadelphia: John Benjamins.

Sprecher, S., Aron, A., Hatfield, E., Cortese, A., Potapova, E., & Levitskaya, A. (1994). Love: American style, Russian style and Japanese style. *Personal Relationships, 1,* 349–369. doi: 10.1111/j.1475-6811.1994.tb00070.x

Sprecher, S., & Toro-Morn, M. (2002). A study of men and women from different sides of earth to determine if men are from Mars and women are from Venus in their beliefs about love and romantic relationships. *Sex Roles, 46*(5/6), 131–147.

Sterk, T. (2003, October 9). Love. Message posted to Interculturalinsights electronic mailing list, archived at http://finance.groups.yahoo.com/group/interculturalinsights/message/6523

Sternberg, R. J. (1986). A triangular theory of love. *Psychological Review, 93,* 119–135. doi: 10.1037/0033-295X.93.2.119

Sternberg, R. J. (1997). Construct validation of a triangular love scale. *European Journal of Social Psychology, 27,* 313–335.

Sternberg, R. J. (2006). A duplex theory of love. In R. J. Sternberg & K. Weis (Eds.), *The new psychology of love* (pp. 184–199). New Haven, CT: Yale University Press.

Stewart, J., & Philipsen, G. (1984). Communication as situated accomplishment: The cases of hermeneutics and ethnography. In B. Dervin & M. J. Voigt (Eds.), *Progress in communication sciences* (Vol. 5, pp. 177–217). Norwood, NJ: Ablex.

Stone, L. (1977). *The family, sex and marriage in England 1500–1800.* New York: Harper & Row.

Su, L. (2009). *I love yous are for white people.* New York: HarperCollins.

Swales, M. (1987). *Goethe: The sorrows of young Werther.* New York: Cambridge University Press.

Swensen, C. H., Eskey, R. W., & Kohlhepp, K. A. (1984). Five factors in long-term marriages. *Lifestyles: Journal of Changing Patterns, 7,* 94–106.

Swensen, C. H., & Fuller, S. R. (1992). Expression of love, marriage problems, commitment, and anticipatory grief in the marriages of cancer patients. *Journal of Marriage and the Family, 54,* 191–197.

Swidler, A. (1997). *Talk of love: How Americans use their culture.* Chicago: University of Chicago Press.

Tiffin, J. (Producer). (1993, February 14). *60 minutes: Tango Finlandia* [Television broadcast]. New York: CBS.

Ting-Toomey, S. (1991). Intimacy expressions in three cultures: France, Japan, and the United States. *International Journal of Intercultural Relations, 15,* 29–46. doi: 10.1016/0147-1767(91)90072-O

Varenne, H. (1977). *Americans together: Structured diversity in a midwestern town.* New York: Teachers College Press.

Walker, C. (2004). Ancient Egyptian love poems reveal a lust for life. Retrieved from http://news.nationalgeographic.com/news/2004/04/0416_040416_pyramidsongs.html

Weber, M. (2003). The protestant ethic and the spirit of capitalism [T. Parsons, Trans.]. Mineola, NY: Dover. (Original work published 1904)

Wierzbicka, A. (1997). *Understanding cultures through their key words: English, Russian, Polish, German, and Japanese.* New York : Oxford University Press.

Wierzbicka, A. (1998). German "culture scripts": Public signs as a key to social attitudes and cultural values. *Discourse & Society, 9,* 241–282. doi: 10.1177/0957926598009002006

Wierzbicka, A. (1999a). Emotional universals. *Language Design, 2,* 23–69.

Wierzbicka, A. (1999b). *Emotions across languages and cultures: Diversity and universals.* Cambridge, UK: Cambridge University Press.

Wilde, A., & Diekman, A. B. (2005). Cross-cultural similarities and differences in dynamic stereotypes: A comparison between Germany and the United States. *Psychology of Women Quarterly, 29,* 188–196. doi: 10.1111/j.1471-6402.2005.00181.x

Wilkins, R. (2007). Cultural frames: Loci of intercultural communication asynchrony in a CBS 60 Minutes news segment. *International Journal of Intercultural Relations, 31,* 243–258. doi: 10.1016/j.ijintrel.2006.03.001

Wilkins, R., & Gareis, E. (2006). Emotion expression and the locution "I love you": A cross-cultural study. *International Journal of Intercultural Relations, 30*(1), 51–75. doi: 10.1016/j.ijintrel.2005.07.003

Zimmer, D. E. (1997). *Deutsch und anders: Die Sprache im Modernisierungsfieber* [German and others: The language in modernization fever]. Hamburg: Rowohlt Taschenbuch Verlag.

CHAPTER CONTENTS

11 Critical Discourse Analysis and (U.S.) Communication Scholarship

Recovering Old Connections, Envisioning New Ones

Karen Tracy, Susana Martínez-Guillem, Jessica S. Robles, and Kimberly E. Casteline

University of Colorado, Boulder

Critical discourse analysis (CDA) is committed to showing how talk and texts serve the interests of those with power in a society. From its initially European linguistic roots, CDA has become an influential international, interdisciplinary tradition. This chapter sketches CDA's background including its theoretical roots and key scholars. Six areas in current research are illustrated, along with a sampling of CDA work around the world. The focal criticisms that have been directed at CDA scholarship are described. In closing, we suggest CDA's potential in five areas of Communication (rhetoric, critical/cultural studies, mass communication, organizational communication, and language and social interaction) and provide an appendix of CDA vocabulary.

Introduction

What is Critical Discourse Analysis (CDA)?

1. It examines the "role of discourse in the (re)production and challenge of dominance" (van Dijk, 1993, p. 249).
2. It's about "demystifying ideologies and power through the systematic ... investigation of semiotic data (written, spoken or visual)" (Wodak & Meyer, 2009, p. 3).
3. It is a "resource for people who are struggling against domination and oppression in its linguistic forms" (Fairclough, 1995a, p.1).

CDA—or discourse analysis with a critical thrust, as we prefer to characterize the approach for reasons that will become apparent—is a well-established interdisciplinary research tradition. In just 20 years, whether one treats the appearance of Fairclough's (1989) *Language and Power* or the launching of *Discourse & Society* (D&S) in 1990 as the starting point, CDA has become enormously influential. There are journals devoted to or highly welcoming of critical discourse studies (*Critical Discourse Studies, Discourse &*

Communication, Discourse & Society, Journal of Multicultural Discourses, The Journal of Language and Politics, Visual Semiotics), as well as an increasing number of texts that offer guidance about CDA (e.g., Blommaert, 2005; Bloor & Bloor, 2007; Chouliaraki & Fairclough, 1999; Gee, 1999, 2006; van Leeuwen, 2008). At the level of individual scholars, a perusal of journals reveals that CDA is increasingly a term authors use to describe their expertise.

Our aim in this chapter is to provide a thick, textured description-critique of CDA from the point of view of Communication scholars.[1] To accomplish our goals, we weave together writings about CDA, research examples, and the results of a content analysis we carried out on the last 10 years (286 articles) of D&S,[2] the most visible CDA journal. CDA is a vast area in linguistics, as evidenced by Toolan's (2002) four-volume handbook (see van Noppen, 2004, for a review). Our review focuses on critical discourse research that is most strongly linked to the field of Communication. Thus, in addition to studies from D&S, the examples of CDA studies come from the 130 article-set we identified using "critical discourse" as a keyword or as subject term in the database *Communication and Mass Media Complete*.[3]

Our chapter unfolds in the following manner: in the first section we provide background on CDA; its birth, key commitments, and current profile, its theoretical roots, and its current relationship to the field of Communication. In the second section we review the work of three key scholars, describe CDA studies in six key topical areas, and give a sense of the reach of CDA research both topically and geographically. In the third section we explore criticisms of CDA, including explication of several lively debates in journal colloquies. Finally, we suggest why scholarship in five areas of the Communication field would be strengthened if each gave serious attention to CDA work. As CDA is steeped in linguistic concepts that will be unfamiliar to some readers, the chapter concludes with an appendix that defines the most important terms.

Background on Critical Discourse Analysis

Its Birth, Key Commitments, and Current Profile

CDA, comments Norman Fairclough (1996), "developed in a particular location within a particular political situation—out of a tendency of the political left and within the new social movements (feminism, ecology, etc.) toward cultural and ideological forms of political struggle from the 1960s onward" (p. 52). A symposium among a small group of linguists (Wodak, Fairclough, van Dijk, Kress, and van Leeuwen), occurring in 1991 in Amsterdam, is often credited as the moment CDA crystallized into an intellectual approach bigger than any particular individual (Wodak & Meyer, 2009), although critically-inflected analyses of talk and text had been around for a while. In 1979 Kress and Hodge published the first edition of *Language as Ideology* in which they called upon linguists to recognize how language is an instrument of social control. Critical linguistics, the name they gave to their approach, melded socialist political commitments with the language theory of systemic functional linguistics (Halliday, 1994).

From a Communication point of view, critical linguistics functioned to lead linguistics toward beliefs about language that have long been part of our field, such as seeing language "as an instrument of control as well as communication" (Hodge & Kress, 1993, p. 6). But what critical linguistics added to the Communication commonplace was a set of linguistic tools that enhanced noticing of interesting features of talk and text. Linguistic ideas such as modality, passive verb forms, nominalization, and intertextuality (see appendix) identified concrete language practices to examine. Additionally, critical linguistics' assumption that texts always have ideational, interpersonal, and textual functions resonated well with the Communication commonplace that all messages had both content and relational levels (Watzlawick, Beavin, & Jackson, 1967). In the second edition of *Language as Ideology,* Hodge and Kress (1993) treated CDA as a better, more interdisciplinary and inviting label for their research approach.

Critical analyses of discourse appeared in several influential books (e.g., van Dijk, 1984; Wodak, 1989) and in a variety of journals in the 1980s, but until D&S began in 1990, there was no outlet that treated CDA studies as central to its scholarly mission. D&S did, and continues to do so. The 2009 D&S mission statement says that it "studies society through discourse and discourse through an analysis of its socio-political and cultural functions and implications." The discourse that D&S refers to involves concrete manifestations of talk of all types and written or multimodal texts. The journal overview goes on to say that D&S "is a critical journal. It favours contributions that pay attention to the detailed analysis of social and political relations of power, dominance and inequality, and to the role of discourse in their legitimation and reproduction in society."[4] Although D&S favors critical discourse studies, it does not offer sharp definitional boundaries. In addition to studies that strongly and overtly position an author with the politically disenfranchised against the powerful, there are many studies in which authors adopt what we would describe as "soft critical" or a critically-inflected stance. By virtue of the social-political topic investigated, an author reveals subtle sympathies toward the less powerful, but, at the same time, his or her central claim is only slightly political.

CDA initially developed in Europe among scholars who were linguists, a fact reflected in today's scholarly progeny. Although CDA scholarship is carried out around the world and across disciplines, its center remains linguistic and European. Table 11.1 shows the disciplines and regions of authors resulting from an examination of D&S articles, 2000–2009.

CDA is often referred to as a "method," but it is better conceived as a theory/method (Chouliaraki & Fairclough, 1999), an umbrella label for a loose federation of discourse approaches that share a progressivist political commitment and some theoretical roots. In 2004, in the opening editorial of the journal *Critical Discourse Studies*, the editors argued for "studies" as a more accurate description to capture this loose federation character, rather than

Table 11.1 Disciplines and Regions of Authors for 286 D&S Articles, 2000–2009

Academic Departments	
Linguistics/Languages	39.2%
Communication/Journalism/Media Studies	11.9%
Psychology	9.8%
Sociology	7.0%
Political Science or Anthropology or Business/Marketing	6.6%
Hybrid Departments	25.5%
Region of the World	
Europe, UK	27.6%
Europe, Continental	18.5%
North America	26.2%
Asia	9.1%
Australia/New Zealand	8.4%
Central/South America	3.5%
Other Regions (e.g., Russia)	2.8%
Multiple Regions (for co-authored works)	3.8%

"analysis," which suggests CDA involves a particular method (Fairclough, Graham, Lemke, & Wodak, 2004, p. 3).

Critical discourse analysis, similar to other critical approaches in communication, has an interest in exposing how inequalities are naturalized. Van Dijk (1986) suggested that any scholarly tradition that appended "critical" to its name was committing itself to asking "further questions, such as those of responsibility, interests, and ideology. Instead of focusing on purely academic or theoretical problems, it starts from prevailing social problems, and thereby chooses the perspective of those who suffer most, and critically analyses those in power" (p. 4). This is centrally true of the diverse types of critical approaches in communication. But, in contrast to other kinds of critical studies in Communication—for example, critical race studies (Flores, 2009), critical rhetoric (McKerrow, 2009), critical ethnography (Vannini, 2009), or critical organizational communication (Ganesh, 2009)—critical discourse analysis has a relatively inductive, empirical thrust. Communication scholars who define themselves as critical, in fact, might see CDA studies as theoretically light, i.e., not sufficiently engaging with critical theory ideas before moving to analysis of texts.

What distinguishes CDA from other critical approaches is its attention to the analysis of text. CDA studies analyze the content and design of written texts or oral exchanges, drawing on language, interaction, and semiotic concepts, all the while attending to the context in which a discourse was produced. Analysis of text is the hallmark of critical discourse analysis. In our content analysis of 10 years of D&S, the vast majority (95.5%) of studies included textual excerpts and analysis/commentary.

A CDA study may analyze oral or written texts, research interviews, or multimodal texts such as web pages (see Table 11.2), but written texts such as newspapers or institutional documents are most common. This text preference is not surprising given the political, language-oriented focus of CDA: 47% of the articles in D&S analyzed written texts. Although language features are the main foci in CDA, the study of multimodal or visual texts is an important area of interest (e.g., Kress, 2006; Kress, Leite-Garcia, & van Leeuwen, 1997; Kress & van Leeuwen, 2001). Hodge and Kress (1988) labeled their approach to multimodal communication "social semiotics" to distinguish it from structural approaches that assumed signs had fixed meanings, and from other CDA approaches that were less attentive to visual aspects of texts.

CDA is relatively inductive compared to other kinds of critical approaches, but it is relatively deductive when compared to its neighboring *discourse* approaches such as conversation analysis (Drew, 2005), ethnography of communication (Philipsen & Coutu, 2005) or action-implicative discourse analysis (Tracy, 2005). CDA anchors its analyses in the ideas of critical theorists shaped by Marxism such as Althusser, Habermas and Gramsci, and a variety of social theorists including Foucault, Bourdieu, Giddens, and Bakhtin (see "Theoretical Roots" section), even though any particular study may not explicitly acknowledge these intellectual precursors. Hammersley (1997) noted that "the term 'critical' began life as a euphemism" (p. 244). Because Marxism was a taboo word, particularly in the American context, "critical" came into fashion as the preferred description for approaches growing out of Marxism.

The families of approaches that inhabit CDA quarters differ from each other in significant ways, but they also possess commonalities. CDA approaches tend to share: (a) a focus on social problems; (b) a weighing in politically on the side of the underdog or for progressive interests; (c) a close textual examination of how linguistic and semiotic practices contribute to problems; (d) an assumption that power relations are (partly) discursive, with discourse both shaping and being shaped by situations, institutions, and social structures; and (e) a belief that discourse is always doing ideological work, i.e., advancing and naturalizing the interests of dominant groups (Wodak & Fairclough, 1997).

There are scholars who analyze discourse to develop critical claims, but who do not label their work as CDA. U.S.-based anthropological linguists and sociolinguists studying law and society, such as Philips (1998), Mertz (1998, 2007), Bucholtz (2009) and Berk-Seligson (2009) would fall into this category.

Table 11.2 Kinds of Discourse Analyzed for 286 D&S Articles, 2000–2009

Discourse Type	*Percent*
Written Texts	46.9%
Oral and Naturally-Occurring (Interactive or Monologic)	30.1%
Research Interviews	9.4%
Other (Combinations, Multimodal or Visual Foci) or N/A	13.6%

In addition, numerous critically-oriented researchers have paid close attention to language and attended to how news items were structured in such a way to produce the appearance of objectivity while obscuring the subjective choices made when constructing the text. One of the earliest such scholars was French semiologist Roland Barthes (1957), followed by other semiologists (Fiske, 1988, 1996; Fiske & Hartley, 1978; Hartley, 1982, 1992, 1996), and cultural studies scholars (Hall, 1972; Hall, Critcher, Jefferson, Clarke, & Roberts, 1978). Although none of these scholars label themselves as critical discourse analysts, they all perform discourse analysis with a critical thrust.

Theoretical Roots

As noted previously, compared to other discourse analytic approaches, CDA emphasizes the importance of theoretical assumptions for building relevant analyses. Thus, rather than starting with the text as the main source of knowledge/claims, CDA scholars tend to reflect on the abstract concepts and frameworks that guide their inquiries before they turn to examining particular examples. CDA scholars see their deductive methodology as allowing them to be explicit about their own positioning while at the same time maintaining scientific rigor, something that, according to them, inductively-oriented discourse analysts fail to do. As Fairclough (2009) explains, "it is important not only to acknowledge [our perceptions on social matters] rather than affecting a spurious neutrality about social issues, but also to be open with one's readers about where one stands" (p. 4). From this perspective, "the scientific investigation of social matters is perfectly compatible with committed and 'opinionated' investigators…and being committed does not excuse [scholars] from arguing rationally or producing evidence for [their] statements" (p. 4). Beginning with theoretical background on societal processes, according to CDA scholars, also enables an analyst to build better connections between discourse's microstructures and the macrostructures of social institutions and society.

One maxim, with which all CDA scholars would agree, is that language is a social practice (Wodak & Meyer, 2001). This view can be traced back to the writings of Vygotsky (1986), Volosinov (1973), Vico (1948), and Williams (1977). Although this approach to language seems commonsensical today, it was developed to overcome the conceptualization of language as a mere reflection of an external, objective reality. For CDA scholars, language is mostly conceptualized as "practical material activity," which is both produced by and generative of reality (Williams, 1977, p. 38). Language, in other words, is both constituted and constitutive.

The endorsement of a constitutive view of language is closely tied to treating people's experiences as ideological, recognizing that discourses are produced, used, and understood for particular purposes. Ideology, as Huspek (1993) describes it, drawing particularly on Pierre Bourdieu (1984), "inscribes itself in and through discourse, taking the form of privileged words and meanings that, disguised as basic semantic constituents of a natural language, legitimize the conditions of their use, and so reproduce the relations of power that are at their basis" (p. 1).

This emphasis on the ideological bases of our experience is often explored in CDA through Gramsci's (1971) conception of hegemonic processes. Gramsci developed the concept of hegemony to account for the reality of Western Europe in the 1920s and 1930s, where, in spite of the unequal distribution of resources, the working class-led revolution predicted by orthodox Marxism had not occurred. According to Gramsci, the reasons for this were found in the ways in which modern states ruled, not through direct coercion, but by winning the proletariats' consent. This was done through a series of ideological processes which resulted in the promotion and acceptance of a set of values, a "common sense" which, although supported by most, reflected the interests of only a few. In the realm of CDA, "hegemony" and "common sense" are typically used as more general analytic terms to explain the pervasiveness of inequality by looking at how they make ideological processes more effective. As explained by Fairclough (2009), "ideology is the most effective when its workings are less visible. If one becomes aware that a particular aspect of common sense is sustaining power inequalities at one's own expense, it ceases to be common sense, and may cease to have the capacity to sustain power inequalities" (p. 71).

Another conceptual framework from which to approach power dynamics, this time without emphasizing relations of domination, is the one provided by Michel Foucault (1972), especially through his notions of discourse and orders of discourse. Discourse, according to Foucault, represents a framework to historicize powerful claims of truth of normalized knowledge: about human nature, the sense of teleological history, or the more specific domain of the various scientific disciplines. Discourses are systems of possibility that constitute subjects by setting the limits within which those subjects can both think and act (Philp, 1985). "Orders of discourse" refers to increasingly abstracted levels of discourse and social practice. The first and most concrete level is what Fairclough (1992) calls the text. Texts are the focal pieces of talk (e.g., job interviews) or written documents (letters of recommendation) that are being analyzed. Specific texts, then, are part of a larger discursive practice (e.g., professional hiring activities) that include other texts and rules of interpretation. Discursive practices, in turn, are part of even larger discourses, for instance, the discourse of capitalism in 21st-century Western societies. Gee (1999) offers a simpler version of Foucault's idea, dividing discourses into only two types. There are little-d discourses, what Fairclough called texts, and there are big-D discourses. Big-D discourses refer to sets of beliefs and societal practices that go beyond any individual text: they are the networks of beliefs that organize a domain of life such as medicine, government, law, or family.

The localized understanding of power present in hegemonic-oriented accounts contrasts with the emphasis on the diffused nature of power relations in studies influenced by the "poststructuralist turn." This theoretical issue has also been taken up by CDA scholars. As Chouliaraki and Fairclough (1999) argue,

> We agree with the post-structuralist view that all social practice is embedded in networks of power relations, and potentially subordinates the social subjects that engage in it, even those with 'internal' power. At the same time, we believe that the view of modern power as invisible, self-regulating and inevitable subjecting … needs to be complemented with a view of power as domination [that] establishes causal links between institutional social practices and the positions of subjects in the wider social field. (p. 24)

Thus, and in spite of the influences of Foucaldian notions of discourse, CDA has adamantly resisted the post-structuralist turn so enthusiastically embraced by many of the other intellectual projects influenced by critical theory. Instead, CDA scholars have, for the most part, remained faithful to a realist approach that emphasizes the interrelationship of discourse and orders of discourse with social structures and a material world. Under this view, the world and discourses are dialectically related, and "the impact of discursive practice depends upon how it interacts with the preconstituted reality" (Fairclough, 1992, p. 60). Thus, the theoretical core of CDA continues to rely on notions of material outcomes that may change the current social order in which particular groups systematically benefit from the exploitation of others.

The (U.S.) Communication Field and CDA

Until recently CDA as a clearly identified tradition has been largely invisible in U.S. departments of Communication. Reasons for this can be tied to the particular ways in which specialization areas have been defined and have evolved. Critical/cultural studies, as this expertise area tends to be labeled, is lively in both the International Communication Association (ICA) and the National Communication Association (NCA). In both critical/cultural studies and CDA, key critical theorists (e.g., Antonio Gramsci, Jurgen Habermas) and cultural studies scholars (e.g., Raymond Williams, Stuart Hall) are identified as heritage influences, but in critical/cultural studies, there is usually little attention to interaction and language when looking at texts. An exception to this generalization is the work of Michael Huspek, who has advocated for a critical ethnography of communication (Huspek, 1989/90), written about key critical theorists (e.g., Huspek, 1993, 1997), and analyzed resistance discourse in working class communities (Huspek & Kendall, 1991). Yet, if Ono's (2009) review of critical/cultural studies is treated as a barometer of recent work in the area, it is significant that discourse ideas are noticeably absent. There is not a single citation to any of the language and discourse concepts that inform CDA scholarship.

On the other side of the aisle—Communication scholars who study language, interaction and texts—there has been equally profound inattention to critical theory ideas. Language and Social Interaction (LSI) scholars, as this specialization area is called at both ICA and NCA, have largely ignored CDA.

The Handbook of Language and Social Interaction (Fitch & Sanders, 2005) has not a single chapter on CDA and barely mentions it as a discourse tradition.[5] But in the last few years there have been changes. The *Encyclopedia of Communication Theory* included a short entry on CDA (Cramer, 2009) and the Language and Social Interaction Division at ICA now explicitly lists critical discourse analysis as within the division's purview.

CDA Scholars and Topics

Critical discourse scholars adopt politically evaluative stances; they also select for study sites in which issues of injustice seem an obvious focus (Meyer, 2001). Thus, CDA researchers privilege interaction and texts in institutional sites over those in interpersonal contexts, and they give explicit attention to categories of people who are devalued by the larger society. These foci are evident in the work of the three influential CDA scholars and in the research topics that are currently lively. In our D&S analysis, 59% of studies examined one or another marginalized identity category, with race/ethnicity/nationality being the most common, and gender second (see Table 11.3). In terms of the institutional contexts that CDA scholars studied, educational and media/political contexts were the most common.

Three Influential CDA Scholars

Analysis of talk or text that shows how power is naturalized, invisibly supporting the interests of dominant groups, is one way to define CDA. But as with "conversation analysis"—which initially referred to any language-focused analysis of conversational exchanges (e.g., Craig & Tracy, 1983) but later came to be restricted to analyses informed by Emanuel Schegloff and Harvey Sacks (for overviews, see Hutchby & Wooffitt, 1998; ten Have, 1999)—CDA has

Table 11.3 Identity and Context Foci for 286 D&S Articles, 2000–2009

Type of Identity	
Race/Ethnicity/Nationality	28.7%
Gender	13.3%
Sexual Orientation	3.1%
Social Class	2.4%
Other	11.5%
No explicit identity focus	40.9%
Institutional Contexts of Discourse	
Education (K-12, Universities, Training)	46.9%
Media/political	35.7%
Corporate	9.4%
Health-Related	6.6%
Other	1.4%

also come to be strongly linked to the analytic approaches of a small set of scholars, Norman Fairclough, Teun van Dijk, and Ruth Wodak being the most prominent. In our analysis of D&S, 66% of the articles cited one or more of these three scholars. Thus, although critical and critically-inflected analyses of discourse do not necessarily cite their critical theory grandparents, they do cite CDA's immediate parents. Each of these scholars in the parental generation has crafted a relatively distinct way of doing critical discourse analysis.

Of these three leading scholars, Fairclough (1995a) has written most extensively about CDA as an enterprise, including its theoretical grounding (e.g., Fairclough, 1992) and its method, which draws heavily on Foucauldian notions of discourse and on Raymond Williams's (1977) dialectic understanding of power relations (e.g., Fairclough, 2003, 2004). He has also addressed how to integrate theory and method in order to promote social change (e.g., Fairclough, 2006). When critiques are leveled at CDA, it is Fairclough's work that is the most frequent target (e.g., O'Regan, 2006; Toolan, 1997; Widdowson, 1998).

The *discourse* part of Fairclough's CDA has been strongly influenced by systemic functional linguistics, the linguistic approach (see Eggins, 1994, for an overview) that gives particular attention to how syntactic features of language, such as nominalization, modality, and passive verb form (see the appendix for definitions) hide agency and normalize the actions of the powerful. Fairclough's work in the 1990s included research on media (e.g., Fairclough, 1995b), norms and culture (e.g., Fairclough, 1992), and marketing and institutions (e.g., Fairclough, 1993). Fairclough's particular brand of CDA emphasizes transdisciplinarity, dialectics, semiotics, and interdiscursivity. For instance, Fairclough (2002) has focused on the role of discourse in contemporary social changes, especially globalization, neo-liberalism, new capitalism, and the knowledge economy.

In contrast to Fairclough, van Dijk's (2008a, 2009) approach to CDA is strongly cognitive. Before he turned to critical discourse analysis, van Dijk published influential work with Walter Kintsch on discourse comprehension (van Dijk & Kintsch, 1983). Van Dijk's cognitive science commitments set his work apart from other CDA scholars, as well as many other discourse analysts. Van Dijk (2008a) has criticized systemic functional linguistics, Fairclough's language theory grounding, for its inadequate analysis of context and for its anti-mentalist leanings. In addition to Fairclough, discourse analysts such as Antaki (2006), Kitzinger (2006), and Maynard (2006) also regard cognition as an explanatory concept to be avoided. In contrast, van Dijk (see also Chilton, 2004, Wodak, 2006) argues that an understanding of discourse must attend to cognition: "It is through mental models of everyday discourse such as conversation, news reports, and textbook that we acquire our knowledge of the world, our socially-shared attitudes and finally our ideologies and fundamental norms or values (van Dijk, 2001, p. 114).

Van Dijk has applied his framework to the study of ethnic prejudice in everyday talk and elite discourse. His books, *Prejudice in Discourse* (1984) and *Communicating Racism* (1987), paved the way for a series of studies related to the ways in which (White) speakers reproduce racism in ordinary conversation. For example, in his discussion of stories about immigrants in the Netherlands and the United States (van Dijk, 1993), he shows how storytelling is controlled by mental categories such as the group membership of the story teller, and thus how narratives about other ethnic groups typically serve the purpose of highlighting an *Us* versus *Them* dichotomy.

Finally, Wodak has developed another approach within CDA, which she labels the "discourse-historical approach" (Reisigl & Wodak, 2001). This approach integrates "all available information on the historical background and the original sources in which discursive 'events' are embedded" by exploring how particular genres of discourse change over time (Wodak, 2002, p. 149). Similar to Fairclough, Wodak has been extensively involved in defining CDA as an approach to discourse (Wodak & Chilton, 2007; Wodak & Meyer, 2009; Weiss & Wodak, 2007). But, in addition to systemic functional linguistics, which Fairclough privileges, Wodak's critical analyses are more likely to also make use of ideas from linguistic pragmatics, argumentation theory, ethnography, rhetoric, and corpus linguistics (Baker et al., 2008; Wodak, 2007).

For instance, in her book *Disorders of Discourse* Wodak (1996) emphasized the necessity of examining text and context equally. Her studies in the 1996 collection show how discursive practices such as doctor-patient communication, school committee meetings, or watching the news are usually "disordered," in the sense that the unproblematic routine expected by the participants is often broken in different ways. These "disordered discourses" are not accidental, but they "serve certain functions of exclusion, power, justification or legitimation" (Wodak, 2002, p. 170). The main consequence of these disordered processes is that patients, parents, or less educated audiences are systematically, through specific discursive moves, left outside of the different power structures, with no possibility of intervening in them except to reinforce the unequal dynamics.

Wodak has also investigated how national identities and collective memories are discursively constructed (e.g., Wodak & Kovacs, 2004; Wodak & Richardson, 2009); the ways in which racist discourse operates in elite and everyday contexts (e.g., Reisigl & Wodak, 2001); and the dynamics of inclusion and exclusion in the discourse of immigration in Austria and in the rest of Europe (e.g., Delanty, Jones, & Wodak, 2008).

It is not simply the trajectories of these scholars that are of interest, but the directions in which others, especially in Communication, have taken their ideas. Fairclough has influenced critical organizational communication studies (Deetz, Heath & MacDonald, 2007; Mumby & Clair, 1997). Putnam and Cooren (2004), for instance, draw on Fairclough's definition of discursive events as social practice and his notion that textuality in multiple forms produces and reproduces organizational life. Van Dijk's claim that being seen as a "racist" must be accounted for in making comments potentially seeable as racist has been applied to other sorts of pejorative language, including a study of homophobic comments by teens that has been analyzed by Thurlow (2001). In his article on CDA and metaphor, Hart (2008) cites the discourse-historical perspective as an important influence on his thinking and media scholars in Communication that study immigration and race (e.g., Graham, Keenan & Dowd, 2004) also build upon Wodak's work.

As these examples show, the works of Fairclough, van Dijk, and Wodak have stimulated critical analyses of discourse. In order to provide a sense of the breadth of current CDA scholarship, we next review studies in six key areas, many influenced by these scholars.

Ethnic Prejudice

A significant number of critical approaches to discourse address questions of racism and ethnic prejudice. Following the influential work by van Dijk (1984, 1987), authors from different fields have offered insights into the structure, functions, and implicit ideologies of racist discourses and their implications for contemporary societies. Some of these analyses have focused on the communication of racism in (new) media outlets (Erjavec, 2001; Harding, 2006; Teo, 2000) whereas others concentrate on how ethnic prejudice is reproduced in political settings (Blackledge, 2006; LeCoteur, Rapley, & Augoustinos, 2001). There is also a consistent body of studies that deals with discriminatory processes in organizations (Campbell & Roberts, 2007; Tannock, 1999; Tilbury & Colic-Peisker, 2006) and more recently a great deal of attention has been addressed toward the role that schools play in the dissemination of stereotypes and ethnocentrism, for example through the content and form of textbooks (Augoustinos, Tuffin, & Every, 2005; Bonilla-Silva & Forman, 2000; Eriksson & Aronsson, 2005; Kalmus, 2003). In the realm of everyday interaction, different studies have analyzed discursive moves used to avoid potential negative judgments or the functions of disclaimers when engaging in explicitly prejudiced talk (Billig, 1985; Kleiner, 1998; Tileaga, 2005; Wetherell & Potter, 1993).

In media studies, most CDA analyses attempt to show how the representation of minorities in mediated discourse reinforces negative stereotypes and fosters inequalities among groups. Simmons and Lecoteur (2008), for example, compare the ways in which two different "riots"—one involving indigenous community members, and the other non-indigenous ones—were covered by Australian media. Their analysis concentrates on discourses around "the possibility of change" in order to show how, in the case of the indigenous riot, change was not presented as a possible outcome, whereas the reports on the non-indigenous riot did present "change" as an achievable goal.

In political communication, most efforts have been directed to looking at how the rhetoric used by institutions and its representatives may contribute to hegemonic processes in the construction of racial and ethnic categories. In relation to this, authors are increasingly focusing on the challenges that the "new racism" with its subtle but pervasive strategies, posits for the construction of an effective anti-racist discourse. Every and Augoustinos (2007) discuss the ways in which parliamentary speeches of Australian politicians who oppose allegedly racist asylum-seeking laws engage in a "socially delicate conversational act." This practice involves the careful management of the tension between avoiding direct accusations of racism while at the same time defending the interests of marginalized groups.

CDA scholars have predominantly analyzed how media talk implicitly supports racism, but there is a modest counter-voice exploring how speakers challenge racist discourse. For example, Del Teso-Craviotto (2008) explores how Argentinean immigrants to Spain participated in an Internet discussion that challenged, as well as supported, "xeno-racism," a particularly prominent form of discrimination on the rise in Europe based on wealth rather than biology or appearance.

Immigrants and Nation-Building

Another topic of interest for critically-oriented discourse scholars is immigration, a phenomenon usually seen as linked to dynamics of inclusion and exclusion. Consequently, the concepts of nation and citizenship are often discussed together with those of immigration and immigrants. For instance, Erjavec (2009) shows how discursive moves in media outlets define citizenship in ways that exclude undesirable bodies. Analyses of immigration have exposed the systematic incorporation of ethnic or cultural elements in mediated discussions of this issue (Adeyanju & Neverson, 2007); the pervasiveness of prejudice and negative stereotypes about immigrants in the media (KhosraviNik, 2009; Santa Ana, 1999); and the non-neutrality of sites, such as immigration policies (Gales, 2009; García Agustín, 2008; Schmidt, 2002) and political discourse (Charteris-Black, 2006; Lario Bastida, 2008; Mehan, 1997).

With regards to nation-building and representation, CDA scholars have concentrated on the following questions: How are national identities constructed and legitimized through discursive practices? For what purposes are particular national identities invoked? Most of these studies have explored elite sites such as political speeches (e.g., Lazar & Lazar, 2008; Ruiseco & Slunecko, 2006), parliamentary debates (Fuchsel & Martin Rojo, 2003; Kosic & Triandafyllidou, 2004), and the mass media (Higgins, 2004), although some of Wodak's work (e.g., de Cillia, Reisigl, & Wodak, 1999) explored the ways in which national identities are challenged or created in everyday interaction.

Recently, the discursive treatment of asylum seekers has been a topic of special interest. Goodman and Speer (2007), for example, explore membership categorization terms in talk about asylum seekers through an examination of media texts belonging to the public domain. In these texts, they "examine how members of the asylum debate use the term 'asylum seeker', how different categories of asylum seeker are formulated, reformulated, and used, and how members use, contrast, and combine categories to construct asylum seekers as more or less deserving of support, sympathy, or punitive measures" (p. 168).

These authors analyze newspaper articles, pamphlets, and a range of televised political shows to display how participants in the "asylum seeker debate" systematically rely on category distinctions that form the basis for their different arguments. Asylum seekers are discursively distinguished from or conflated with "refugees," "illegal immigrants," or "economic migrants" depending on the position that speakers take in the controversy. These discursive practices, they argue, concentrate society's attention on whether asylum seekers are legitimate subjects, thus diverting attention from other debates such as a discussion of how these people can receive help.

Gender

There are many analyses of discourse and gender that are critical or critically inflected. The *Handbook of Language and Gender* (Holmes & Meyerhoff, 2003), to cite just one anthology, includes chapters on identity and representations (Weatherall & Gallois, 2003), sexual assault adjudication (Ehrlich, 2003), language ideologies (Cameron, 2003), and women's self-reference (Wagner & Wodak, 2006). Gender as it plays itself out in politics, media, and marketing is important (e.g., Bergvall & Remlinger, 1996; Caldas-Coulthard & van Leeuwen, 2002; Fairhurst, 1993; Kuo, 2003; Lazar, 2000; Shaw, 2000), as is identification of the subtle ways women are treated differently than men.

Trix and Psenka (2003), in a cleverly titled article called "Exploring the Color of Glass," examined 312 recommendation letters for faculty positions in schools of medicine for male and female applicants. Combining some simple quantitative counts with analyses of different sections of the letters, the authors show that letters written for women not only are generally shorter but use gender terms more often (lady vs. man), use more linguistic tokens that raise doubt (e.g., hedges, instances of faint praise), and praise women using a large number of grindstone adjectives such as "hardworking," "conscientious," or "dependable."

One visible CDA scholar studying gender and discourse is Deborah Cameron (1998, 2006). Cameron has been an outspoken critic of Tannen's (1990) much popularized "two cultures" view of gender that treats men and women as having misunderstandings because they come from different cultures. Take a dinner table conversation where the husband says to his wife, "Is there any ketchup, Vera?" Although this utterance is stated as a question rather than an order, most observers will hear it as a directing the wife to go get the ketchup. If the same utterance had been said by a child, however, it is likely to be heard as a request for information warranting a response such as "Yes, it's on the bottom shelf of the cupboard." Men and women, Cameron (1998) argues, do not differ in their ability to speak (or interpret) directly or indirectly. Rather, they differ in their assumptions about how gender should affect interacting parties: "As long as the right contextual conditions apply, there will be no ambiguity about what the [indirect] strategy means, because participants take for granted one person's entitlement to request an item and the other's responsibility to provide it" (p. 449). In work situations, if men do not understand women giving orders indirectly—the style women are expected to exhibit more—it is because men do not believe women should be in positions superior to them.

A critically-inflected study is illustrated in Stokoe and Smithson's (2002) analysis of how gender categories enter talk. Gender, they note, may be explicitly oriented to in talk. In explicit orientations someone may self-initiate repair to find a more gender-neutral word. This occurs in cases in which the "generic female parent" is used in talk about parenting, i.e., always pairing "child" with "mother," defaulting to the "she" pronoun when talking about parenting or childcare, or even using "mother" to stand in for "parent." But at times a speaker will self-repair and add "father" or "parent." Gender may also be oriented to in subtle ways. For example, in recounting a workplace experience, a woman said, "I think the best thing is to, is to reduce the hierarchy so that your boss is not, some guy that you don't, you hate talking to, but someone you, some, just another guy who you work with" (Stokoe & Smithson, 2002, p. 232, simplified transcript). In this example, "guy" functions in a similar way to the generic male pronoun. And just as the generic "he" was once (and often still is) treated as a genderless stand-in for "he or she," "guys" is currently often taken as a gender-neutral group term that can relate to males and females.

A growing area in CDA is feminist critical discourse analysis. The latter, represented in work by Lazar (e.g., 2000, 2005), analyzes discourse as producing and perpetuating sexism and gender inequality. Lazar (2007) articulates five principles of a feminist critical discourse analysis: (a) *feminist analytical activism*—the purpose of critique is to create social transformation; (b) *gender as ideological structure*—ideologies about male-female differences structure the division of labor and simple mapping of biology and gender; (c) *complexity of gender and power relations*—interpretations of inequality are complicated and contingent, and need to be studied in subtle as well as blatant manifestations; (d) *discourse in the (de)construction of gender*—discourse and social practice reciprocally shape one another in creating and questioning gendered identities; and (e) *critical reflexivity as praxis*—being reflective about practice is necessary among institutional participants as well as feminists.

Gender studies also intersect with sexuality, and the ways in which sexuality and gender are caught up in the performance of identity. Kitzinger, for example, has explored how speakers enact themselves as heterosexuals (2005a, 2005b). Fine (2003) looked at sex education in a middle school and how the teacher moves the conversation away from talk of desire, and toward talk about disease and pregnancy prevention. Thorne and Coupland (1998) focus on how same-sex dating advertisements market sex and self-gendered identities. By analyzing the specific wording people use in commodifying their sexual selves, people creatively use the constraints of the genre to articulate idealistic identities.

News Discourse

As one of the most prominent forms of discourse in the public sphere, news journalism is a frequent object of analysis for critically-oriented discourse scholars and has been explored from several angles. In addition to the analysis of specific topics in the news such as ethnic prejudice and immigration (see sections above) scholars have studied the processes and products of news media (Bell 1991, 1997, 2003); the social effects of newspaper discourse (Locke, 2004, Matheson, 2005); as well as how the vocabulary of news reflects ruling class ideology (Chibnall, 1977; Ericson, Baranek, & Chan, 1987) such as through representations of gender (Bradby, Gabe, & Bury, 1995).

Journalistic voice has been used by many researchers to investigate news discourse (Iedema, Feez, & White, 1994; Martin & White, 2005; White, 2004, 2006). The most common news voice is the "reporter voice," which limits how explicitly authors convey their personal judgments. In essence, journalists advocate a particular value while backgrounding through a variety of discourse practices that the value is their personal stance. This process is demonstrated in a study by Caffarel and Rechniewski (2008) that compared three French news stories from *Libération*, *Le Figaro*, and *Le Monde* on the 2004 American handover of power to the interim Iraqi government. Thompson and White's (2008) *Communicating Conflict*, in which the Caffarel and Rechniewski study appears, offers cases of media coverage of politically sensitive issues around the world. By analyzing lexicogrammatical choices, evaluative positioning, ideological stances, textual organization, semantics, and journalistic voice, the media analyses show how the news texts advantage the views of those who are socially dominant. In the book *Analysing Newspapers: An Approach from Critical Discourse Analysis,* Richardson (2007) offers a useful introduction for how to begin doing such an analysis.

Attending to the visual aspects of media is equally of concern. Chouliaraki (2006) for instance, has carried out extensive work on how media visually represent war, including how visual scenes are paired with spoken narration and other language forms to frame suffering. The events of 9/11 and the subsequent "war on terror" have been one important arena for study (Chouliaraki, 2004, 2005; Hodges & Nilep, 2007), but other scenes of conflict have also garnered attention. In a recent article, Chouliaraki (2009) compares how BBC World and Arab media display the ongoing fighting in Gaza. Western suffering, she argues, is privileged over non-Western. In BBC coverage the war is displayed "through an imagery of panorama phantasmagoria and a language devoid of human agency"; … [it is] cinematic spectacle to be appreciated rather than a humanitarian catastrophe to be denounced" (p. 222). Rather than reporting "people" being killed, it is the "city" or the "compound" that suffers damage. In becoming spectacle, war becomes invisible as "a political fact that requires a response" (p. 223).

Education

In a review of CDA in education, Rogers, Malancharuvi-Berkes, Mosley, Hui, and O'Garro (2005) describe CDA's aim as being to "disrupt discourse, challenge restrictive pedagogies, challenge passive acceptance of the status quo, and reveal how texts operate in the construction of social practices" (p. 376). In our analysis of D&S, studies in education accounted for more than 45% of the context foci, with a major site for study being classrooms of all levels. Chouliaraki (1998), for instance, examined the teacher's use of modality (e.g. "think, "could," "might") in a classroom committed to a child-centered, progressive philosophy. The teacher's talk, Chouliaraki shows, worked in a subtle way to privilege ritual knowledge over substantive, ideational knowledge, thereby creating students oriented to jobs of lower status, i.e., secretarial roles, rather than those requiring creativity and autonomy.

In a study of college classrooms following the September 11 attacks, Hafen (2009) considered the complexities and implications of classroom positionings that orient to freedom, patriotism, and democracy as the uncontested status quo. She found a strong link between freedom, patriotism, and militarism in students' talk. These concepts slid into one another, as in the example, "I'm a soldier's man. I will work under the flag, fight under the flag, and I will die under the flag if necessary." Hafen explained that this jump from patriotism to nationalism and then to militarism is a "well lubricated skid" (p. 70), often exemplified in discourse about patriotism. At the same time, challenges to the dominant meaning of patriotism occurred when students used terms such as "blind," "uncritical," or "belligerent patriotism."

Educational discourse outside of classrooms has also been a focus of attention. Pitt (2002) examined how programs of family literacy preparing women to mother taught them to unquestioningly accept the role of learner and define self as always ready to drop other activities to assist their child's cognitive development. This training discourse, Pitt shows, reveals contradictions in the vision of motherhood, all the while supporting the society's capitalist ideology. Another example outside the classroom is Mehan's (2001) study of a school's educational team meeting in which a child is transformed from "normal" to "learning disabled" by virtue of the institutional weight given to the psychologist's voice over that of the teacher and parents. Other studies show how textbooks maintain dominant ideologies (Prins & Toso, 2008).

Healthcare Exchanges

CDA studies in health contexts run the gamut of methodological approaches from the most discourse-focused to those that look broadly at societal discourses (Agar, 1985). The situations analyzed also differ—from doctor-patient interviews (e.g., Binbin, 1999; Menz & Al-Roubaie, 2008), to drug testing meetings (e.g., Jenkings & Barber, 2006), to therapy sessions (see Bartesaghi,

2009 below) to considering how "medical discourse" is ideologically disseminated in texts (MacDonald, 2002).

We have made a distinction between *critical* discourse studies and *critically-inflected* discourse studies. To give that distinction greater clarity, we look at two studies analyzing healthcare exchanges that also illustrate a way to draw on conversation analytic transcription practices in the service of showing how institutional exchanges construct what is true from rhetoric "developing rituals which both create and legitimate the practices of the profession and the institution" (Sarangi & Roberts, 1999, p. 16) The two studies differ in how explicitly they represent the actions of the institution and its agents as problematic.

The explicitly critical study by Bartesaghi (2009) analyzes on-site therapy sessions in a family clinic in conjunction with the clinic's manual instructing therapists how to proceed, and the Beck Depression Inventory, a measurement tool used regularly in the clinic. Therapy, Bartesaghi argues, draws on everyday conversational practices to pursue institutional aims in less than transparent ways that delegitimize family members' framings of their experiences. Consider one exchange between a therapist and a mother about her adolescent son, the identified patient (Bartesaghi, 2009, p. 164).

T: Hmm. How do you know that there's something going on with him? How can you tell?
M: I just think there's something going on, he's acting different.
T: What do you mean, <u>different</u>?
M: <u>Withdrawn</u> from things.
T: Has he always been withdrawn from things?
M: No.
T: It seems like a couple of years ago when you first came here in '93 he was sort of sad and withdrawn. ((shows manila folder)) Here's his record.

Bartesaghi offers a line-by-line explication of the discursive features to show how the therapist's questioning constructs the mother as a poor institutional interviewee and incompetent. Her study concludes: "Psychotherapy's questioning practices exemplify asymmetric and forceful use of the resources of the question-answer pair … [T]hese resources are embedded in a covert logic of institutional authority that presupposes that clients are mysterious and unreliable" (p. 167).

Whereas Bartesaghi is straightforwardly critical of how the institutionally powerful enacted their definition of the situation, its clients, and their problems, Schubert, Hanson, Dyer, and Rapley's (2009) analysis of interviews with men who were receiving treatment at a detox center is implicitly challenging, a study we treat as *critically-inflected*. In this Australian detox center, all of the interviewed patients had received psychiatric diagnoses of ADHD (attention-deficit/hyperactivity disorder) after entering treatment for amphetamine dependence. The diagnosis and treatment of ADHD is a contested issue within the medical community, with the most common treatment being the use of dexamphetamine, what could be labeled as a "therapeutic" kind of amphetamine. In beginning their article, the authors provide background and diagnosis frequency, noting how Australia, which prescribes the drug four times more than other countries internationally, is second only to the United States, which prescribes the drug seven times more than the international average.

The focus of Schubert and colleagues' (2009) study is on the membership-term strategies the four patients use to steer away from the morally problematic identity of being an "illicit drug user" and toward the more reasonable identity of "ADHD patient." Their study's main purpose is to make visible how, in a situation where another meaning is pressing at the door, patients work to frame their actions in a positive light. At the same time, albeit implicitly, their analysis makes available a critique of the larger therapeutic-medical discourse that normalizes drug-taking and, hence, pharmaceutical companies' selling of drugs as the preferred answer to life's troubles.

Other Directions

This review and illustration of critical and critically-inflected discourse analyses in six areas by no means exhausts the topics, nor identifies the majority of studies within each area. As we noted, CDA as a research arena is attentive to social problems. As new problems arise or take their place on the world stage, CDA scholars begin to give them attention. Scollon (2005), for instance, developed a new type of CDA, what he called "nexus analysis," to examine an interconnected set of food issues in the world from consumption practices, to industrialized production systems, to global climate change and public health.

In the last five years, studies of environmental discourses have also grown (Alexander, 2009). Vannini and McCright (2007) have analyzed how reporting on the weather channel supports a dominant discourse of leisure, consumption, and capital accumulation; Carvalho (2005) has explored how climate change has been represented in prominent British newspapers; and Stamou and Paraskevopoulos (2008) have critiqued how ecotourism guidebooks conceal a consumerist essence within a superficial green wrapping.

Jan Blommaert (2005), scholar of African linguistics and popular culture, points out that most CDA research analyze data originating in present day European contexts, a fact that was corroborated in our D&S content analysis which showed that non-Western contexts comprised only 15% of the sample. But while this is true, social and political events in different countries often become the focus of a CDA study. To give examples, CDA studies in non-Western contexts have included: (a) an analysis of fifth-grade literacy discussions to show teachers' inattention to gay-lesbian themes in Brazil (Moita-Lopes, 2006); (b) an evaluation of the ideology of teachers' talk in Hong Kong English language classes (He, 2006); (c) an across-time analysis of New Year's day editorials in the Chinese *The People's Daily* (Huang & Chen, 2009); (d) an analysis of quotation patterns in ideologically opposing newspapers in Taiwan

(Kuo, 2007); (e) showing how national identity is constructed in the presidential speech of Alvaro Uribe Velez in Colombia in 2002 (Ruiseco & Slunecko, 2006); (f) looking at uses of invective in speeches of leading political party leaders in Ghana (Agyekum, 2004); (g) an evaluation of four major Japanese newspapers editorials following the September 11, 2001, attacks on the United States (Saft & Ohara, 2006); (h) showing how in Korea the United States is constructed as common cultural enemy in the controversy about the movie, *007 Die Another Day* (Lee, 2007); (i) researching power issues in the fragmented Arabic-English speech used by wealthier classes with their domestic servants in Lebanon (Haraty, Oueini, & Bahous, 2007); (j) an examination of discussions on an Al Jazeera religious talk show in Qatar about the *hijab* (head covering worn by Muslim women; Dabbous-Sensenig, 2006); (k) a study probing how the mass media propagate neoliberal policies in post-apartheid South Africa (Kariithi & Kareithi, 2007); (l) an examination in Venezuela of the issue management strategies of a corporation in the Las Cristinas mine (Brooks & Waymer, 2009); and (m) an analysis of the ideological positioning in columns from the journalist, Tafataona Mahoso in Zimbabwe (Maidza, 2008).

Criticisms of CDA

Over the more than 20 years that CDA has existed as a visible method, theory, and approach, it has not only amassed a broad array of practitioners, but has also generated a goodly number of critics. The interdisciplinary nature of CDA leaves it vulnerable to critiques from researchers who make use of the method/theory in disparate ways, as well as from scholars who critique CDA through the lens of the discipline or subdiscipline from which they come, including the different approaches within CDA. Critics of CDA (and more often than not, of Norman Fairclough's particular approach) have advanced five main claims.

It Pays Insufficient Attention to Particulars of Talk

A first issue for which CDA has been criticized, originating primarily with conversation analytic scholars, is that CDA studies pay insufficient attention to the particulars of talk. This criticism, as well as counters to it, has been played out in several journal debates. A key focus of the debates has concerned the extent to which CDA claims are adequately grounded in details of talk. Conversation analysis (CA) is strongly associated with Sacks, Schegloff, and Jefferson (see Schegloff, 2007). Core assumptions associated with conversation analysis include: (a) claims must be made on the basis of what matters to and is oriented to participants; (b) claims must be grounded in empirical data and proven through rigorous analysis on a case-by-case basis; (c) context must be relevantly oriented to based on adjacent utterances; and (d) interaction is orderly and serves to accomplish and promote conversational aims developed through talking.

The transcripts that are the starting point for analysis in CA are detailed, capturing not only *what* people say, but also *how* people say things, including vocal stress, pauses, overlapping talk, repair, intonation, and rate of speech, all of which are represented with particular symbols and notations (see Atkinson & Heritage, 1999). CA's use of detailed transcripts flows from its commitment to minimize the role of a priori theory in interpretation. Because one never knows in advance what features of talk could be attended to by participants, it is important to capture as many specifics as possible. CA and other discourse analysts have criticized CDA analyses which they claim make inferential leaps to inequality and marginalization without grounding them sufficiently in the analysis of talk. This criticism has been the source of heated debates between Schegloff (1997, 1998, 1999a, 1999b) and critical discursive psychologists (Billig, 1999a; Wetherell, 1998), and has engendered further commentary (Mey, 2001).

In the debate, Schegloff (1997) criticized CDA for not attending to the particulars of the talk, which he argued needed to be understood in their own right before connecting them with political claims. "In the apparent multiplicity, and continuing multiplication of perspectives," Schegloff comments, "truth seems to disappear in a hall of mirrors" (p. 166). In her rejoinder, Wetherell (1998) accepts some of Schegloff's criticisms—recognizing that critical discourse studies sometimes do not engage adequately with the exigencies of talk. However, she counters, the problem with conversation analysts is that "they rarely raise their eyes from the next turn in the conversation, and further, this is not an entire conversation or sizeable slice of social life but usually a tiny fragment" (p. 402).

In the next round of the debate, Billig (1999a,b) weighed in to accuse conversation analysis of possessing a contestable view of the world that assumed cooperation and harmony and to oppose Schegloff's claim that CDA sees ideology where it is a minor or nonexistent force. CA's view, argues Billig, is not neutral, as CA frames itself, but is but one view, and a contestable one at that.

An opening remark in Schegloff's initial essay provides a nuanced sense of CA's central criticism of CDA:

> I understand that critical discourse analysts have a different project, and are addressed to different issues, and not to the local co-constructions of interaction. If, however, they mean the issues of power, domination, and the like to connect up with discursive materials, it should be a serious rendering of the material. And for conversation, and talk-in-interaction more generally, that means it should at least be compatible with what was demonstrably relevant to the parties—not necessarily their sequentially directed preoccupations, but, whatever it was, demonstrably relevant to them as embodied in their conduct. Otherwise the critical analysis will not "bind" to the data and risks ending up merely ideological. (Schegloff, 1997, p. 183)

It's Not Attentive to the (Correct) Linguistic Principles

A second kind of criticism, originating with linguists, is that CDA is inattentive to one or another important linguistic principle or theory, although which linguistic principle is forwarded varies widely. Among linguists, Widdowson (1995, 1998) is one of CDA's most outspoken critics. He argues that CDA is not rigorous or sufficiently scientific. He describes CDA methods and procedures of analysis as being akin to ideological literary criticism or literary hermeneutics, and is particularly critical of how scholars apply systemic functional linguistics in CDA. According to Widdowson, the grammar is applied piecemeal in order to forward a particular reading of the text, and he accuses CDA of not providing adequate proof for the ideological effects that are claimed.

Coming from an opposite stance is O'Regan (2006), a CDA scholar himself, who criticizes (Fairclough's version of) CDA as being inappropriately reliant on systemic functional linguistics. In essence, there is a dispute within CDA as to how ethnographic its discourse analyses should be. For O'Regan, systemic functional linguistics is an overly structural approach to language study, one that is inattentive to context in its analytic apparatus. If one wants to take the critical grounding of CDA seriously O'Regan argues, then CDA needs systematic ways to analyze context as well as texts' grammatical features. Likewise, Wodak's (1996) discourse-historical approach is an implicit criticism that Fairclough's approach is over-reliant on systemic functional linguistics and inattentive to contextual specifics. What CDA needs, argues Sarangi and Roberts (1999), is "a 'thick description' [that] reaches down to the level of fine-grained linguistic analysis and up and out to broader ethnographic descriptions and wider political and ideological accounts" (p. 1).

Besides CDA being seen as either too reliant or not reliant enough on systemic functional linguistics, it has been criticized for inadequately attending to other linguistic traditions including text linguistics (Toolan, 1997), cognitive linguistics (Chilton, 2005), and corpus linguistics (Stubbs, 1996). In our analysis of D&S, 22.1% of studies combined quantitative indices with discursive explication. So, although CDA studies might benefit from using corpus analyses more often, as Jäger (2001) argues should happen, CDA already uses quantitative methods more than most other discourse approaches do.

Its Academic Discourse is at Odds with What It Espouses

As an academic enterprise, CDA could be described as turning language back on itself to examine the practices of the ruling elites. One unexamined elite, Bar-Lev (2007) notes, is the community of academic researchers doing CDA. Employing a CDA-type analysis of two journal articles, one critiquing a speech of then-president Bush and the other analyzing Bush's response to the September 11, 2001 attacks, Bar-Lev shows that the authors engage in the same linguistic practices they accuse Bush of using. As he comments, "Where it is at least possible to argue that demonization and self-righteousness are legitimate as rhetorical tools for leaders, surely they do not belong in academic research?" (p. 183).

Billig (2003) has been an outspoken critic from within the field and has asked whether labeling critical work with acronyms like CDA might exclude outsiders and undermine the intentions of the research. He also examines ways that critical discourse is written and concludes that the use of nominalization and passivization are inappropriate by virtue of the fact that they instantiate the linguistic processes of ideology they intend to expose (Billig, 2008a). "All discourse analysts," notes Billig, "face a paradoxical situation: We investigate language, yet at the same time we use language in order to make our investigations" (p. 783).

The issue of CDA's use of nominalization became the focus of a colloquy between Billig and other CDA scholars. Billig is distorting the treatment of nominalizations, argued Martin (2008); knowledge, which means discipline-specific terms, is dependent on nominalizations, but those kinds of nominalization are different from using them to convey evaluation, which is a goal in political discourse. Fairclough (2008) and van Dijk (2008b) likewise defended CDA's use of nominalization in its own discourse. Nominalizations, they both argued, are necessary in some contexts and problematic in others. But, countered Billig (2008b), as an academic area criticizing language use in the world, CDA has a particular responsibility to be self-reflective and careful in its own language practices.

It Does Not Deliver on Its Commitments to Materiality and Agency

"Checklists of linguistic features are not…going to provide us with a reliable method of doing political analysis of texts" (Jones, 2007, p. 362); the conditions under which people are not free cannot "be elucidated by purely linguistic or discourse-analytical means" (Chilton, 2004, p. 45): so argue two scholars committed to critical analyses of discourse who feel that CDA (and especially Fairclough) have given inadequate attention to how the material world shapes and constrains discourse meanings. CDA does acknowledge the role of the material world, but for some critics the acknowledgment is not much more than lip service. The fact that social movement scholars have made no use of CDA, for instance, points to a noticeable absence of attention to CDA in a tradition where we might expect to see it.[6] Collins and Jones (2006) state the concern this way:

> The whole CDA enterprise remains problematic. It claims that communication practices play a crucial role in processes of social and political context, yet, at the same time, it eschews the kind of engagement with "history and context" which might allow that claim to be demonstrated. (p. 52)

We would note that while Collins and Jones' (2006) criticism seems reasonable if Fairclough's work is its focus, it seems less applicable if Wodak's work is the target. This underscores one issue in just about all criticisms of CDA: because CDA is such a vast and diffuse enterprise, there are few things that are categorically true of all threads of its work.

If there is a single leaning that is applicable to most threads of CDA, it would seem to be that CDA privileges structural forces over agency. How to understand the relationship between social structure and individual agency is a truly thorny issue, and it is not our intention to enter this debate very far. Suffice it to say that theorists (and academic fields) tend to privilege the intentions/agency of actors OR the constraining forces of social structures, even if they explicitly recognize that both are at work. Critical discourse analyses, as our review has illustrated, typically foreground the constraining power of social structures. CDA sees people as caught in a web of conventions that bind them, including linguistic and social-structural ones.

CDA's focus on global and macro-structures can strip people of their ability to act while distorting how meaning-making works. Cobb (1994) notes that "Intentions are central to our understanding of the relation between power and discourse, not because intentions reveal (or mask) person's moves to dominate, but because intentions construct legitimacy or delegitimacy and all their corollary consequences" (p. 133). Thus, in seeking to show how inequality is naturalized and how discourse is doing ideological work, CDA scholars, critics contend, too rigidly fix the social world and inadequately recognize the ways people maneuver, playing little-d and Big-D discourses against each other to (sometimes) change oppressive conditions.

It Assumes a Western World View in Its Analyses

In the *Journal of Multicultural Discourses,* Shi-xu (2009), the first Chinese scholar to edit an international journal in the social sciences,[7] describes the state of scholarship in "language, discourse, and communication" in this way:

> Trends of research topics and questions are not culturally independent, or intellectually neutral, but reflect particular cultural, social, professional conditions, needs, and interests.... Objects of research often come from Anglo-American or some European cultures and realities, or, otherwise, the types of research question and so principles of research interest usually emanate from the Western Cosmopolitan institutions. (p. 239)

Blommaert (2005, see also Blommaert & Bulcaen, 2000), who identifies with the central commitments of CDA, amplifies this criticism further. CDA, he argues, while giving lip service to cultural differences, treats the institutions and societies it criticizes as if the first world's way of organizing applied to all countries. This is not the case, he notes, as the majority of the world lives more like villagers in Tanzania than like inhabitants in Manchester, England, Fairclough and Wodak's current home.

What those in the Western (or global North) often fail to recognize is that contexts come in different sizes. In addition to the local (country-specific context) there is also a translocal context. Societies around the world have different statuses, power, and amounts of prestige in the international arena. An upshot of this is that the same language or interaction feature, depending on the context of the speaker, may inscribe powerlessness or cue prestige. Thus, the speaking of English by an African in Africa will be a marker of prestige whereas the same speech will be stigmatized in London and heard as a nonstandard dialect. If voice is "the capacity to accomplish desired *functions* though language" (Blommaert, 2005, p. 68), then a particularly important part of the ability is the potential for a speaker's style to be semiotically mobile, where such capacity for such mobility is "very often associated with the most prestigious linguistic resources 'world languages' such as English, literacy, and more recently multimodal internet communication" (p. 69).

We agree with Blommaert and Shi-xu's criticism that CDA scholarship assumes a Western society orientation, taking cosmopolitan institutions as its benchmark. We saw evidence of this orientation as we performed our content analysis. Most scholars using data from Western locations assume a neutral (unnamed) orientation whereas non-Western data are identified as such. At the same time, we see it as important to note that CDA scholarship is more concerned about, and doing a better job at, remedying its first world tilt than most other discourse or communication traditions.

Summary

CDA includes many different threads. At its broadest we would define it as scholarship that grounds itself in ideas from critical and social theory in order to investigate contextually-grounded questions about the harmful exercise of power and domination. CDA combines a progressivist political commitment with analysis of talk, written documents, or multimodal texts, and it uses a variety of concepts from language, discourse, conversation, interaction, semiotics, and rhetoric to make visible how the analyzed texts sustain (and occasionally overturn) problematic, unequal relationships.

Taken as a whole, we view the criticisms of CDA as signs that critical discourse analysis is alive and vibrant. Whatever its short-fallings, the fact that scholars both inside and outside of CDA feel compelled to critique it, rather than ignore it, is a clear sign of its importance and relevance within the academy. Critical discourse analysis recognizes its responsibility to be self reflective, thereby positioning itself as a tradition that can grow and continue to benefit from critique. As two of its key scholars comment, CDA

> needs to be reflexive and self-critical about its own institutional position and all that goes with it: how it conducts research, how it envisages the

> objectives and outcome of research, what relationships researchers have to the people whose social lives they are analyzing, even what sort of language books and papers are written in. (Chouliaraki & Fairclough, 1999, p. 9)

In the final section we turn our attention to the Communication field as it is structured in the United States, considering what CDA can offer to each of five main areas of research.

CDA's Potential in Five Areas of Communication Scholarship

Critical discourse analysis has much to offer Communication scholars. In this section we suggest what it can offer to five areas that are usually demarcated from each other in U.S. Communication departments: (a) rhetoric, (b) critical/cultural studies, (c) mass communication, (d) organizational communication, and (e) language and social interaction.

Rhetoric

Of all the areas of Communication, CDA would seem to link most straightforwardly to rhetorical studies. Both are centrally interested in political/mediated events, both do close textual analyses, and both eschew neutrality as a desirable stance for authors. However, the two traditions have had little to do with each other. In a recent study seeking to bridge the two, Kaufer and Hariman (2008) commented: "The traditions of European critical discourse analysis (CDA) and American rhetorical criticism grew up independently, and judging from the paucity of cross-citation practices, have remained non-interactive" (pp. 475–476). This mutual inattention is particularly striking because both rhetoricians—especially those that adhere to a "critical rhetoric" project—and critical discourse analysts draw on similar social and critical theorists.

We see the cause of this inattention as related to the larger intellectual categories to which each tradition orients. CDA sees itself as a social science; rhetoric regards itself as a humanistic enterprise. To be sure, CDA scholarship has expanded beyond linguistics, but CDA research is anchored in a *social science* notion of scholarship, and a sharply drawn one at that. For this reason, it is possible to criticize CDA scholars by describing their work as just like "literary analysis" (Widdowson, 1995). Rhetoricians, in contrast, comfortably accept that they are critics and that their unique sensibilities will shape what they notice and argue. From a rhetorical vantage point, CDA's attention to its "rigorousness" seems a strange preoccupation.

In terms of developing rhetorical ideas that resonate with discourse-interested, social science communities and with rhetorical humanistic studies, no person has been more influential than social psychologist Michael Billig. Billig (1987; Billig et al., 1988) has developed a rhetorical approach to thinking and arguing that he has used as the cornerstone for exploring critical discourse issues such as banal nationalism (Billig, 1995) or racist jokes of the Ku Klux

Klan (Billig, 2001). A recent volume (Johnstone & Eisenhart, 2008) by 12 U.S. rhetoricians suggests that this type of bridge-crossing is becoming more frequent. The authors in Johnstone and Eisenhart's volume show how their rhetorical analyses can be made more persuasive when they draw on linguistic features to back up their claims, and many rhetorical scholars develop the kinds of insights about power and discourse that are consistent with CDA's political views.

If one defines rhetoric as a set of ideas rather than as an academic community, CDA and rhetoric have been linked since CDA came into existence. In many non-U.S. departments, rhetoric and argumentation are specialty areas within linguistics, and as the appendix of discourse terms shows, CDA scholars regularly use rhetorical tropes such as metaphor, personification, and synecdoche in analyzing texts. Other contributions CDA can make to rhetorical studies is to help it develop a more international, less U.S.-centric stance, and furnish it with language-interaction concepts that can enhance analyses. Rhetoric, in turn, might show CDA how to inhabit its critical-political stance-taking role in a more comfortable manner.

Critical/Cultural Studies

Even though critical/cultural communication scholarship is best described as both an interdisciplinary and a transdisciplinary project (Ono, 2009), one could argue that both the questions asked by critical/cultural scholars and the ways of addressing them are very much linked to a rhetorical approach to Communication. This translates into a primary concern for examining public discourses in terms of the ways in which they relate to different audiences. To this, critical/cultural studies have added an emphasis on how the status quo is reproduced and/or resisted in the different realms of the public sphere, although still the specifics of exactly how linguistic devices can be related to reifying processes are not a priority in the different analyses.

Critical/cultural approaches have produced valuable insights about the necessity to incorporate all kinds of cultural practices into communicatively oriented analyses. Yet this work is too often accompanied by an assumption of the primary role of discourses in constructing reality—and the people in it—at the expense of the material world with which these discourses interact. For this reason, attending to the epistemological orientation and methodological tools that CDA offers could be fruitful at two levels: first, CDA would help to create space for a type of critical/cultural scholarship that not only engages in a critique of the social order, but which grounds this critique in systematic, close textual analysis. Second, because CDA gives attention to the tightly connected relationship between discourse and material conditions—although as noted, not all critics see it as sufficient—it could assist critical/cultural studies in bridging the gap between political/economic and cultural analyses, a project that has been identified as crucial for the next generation of critical/cultural communication scholarship (see Ono, 2009).

Mass Communication

Scholars of mass communication have a plethora of choices for approaching their objects of study and CDA offers one highly salient option in and of itself or in conjunction with other approaches. Although some media scholars might frame CDA as attending to linguistic minutiae, the kind of careful and detailed analysis that CDA promotes would be useful for mass communication scholars being able to form a deeper understanding of how mediated communication functions. Concepts like conversationalization, marketization, nominalization, and synthetic personalization, among others (see appendix), can shed light on the micro-level practices enacted by media producers to craft their messages.

Second, CDA's critical approach to mass communication can be an effective tool for highlighting the ideological construction of power relations, representations, and social identities. Ideological processes are always complex, often nuanced, and sometimes even contradictory, as media audience reception studies have shown. However, those complexities do not negate the necessity of critical analysis. Media, everyone agrees, do affect society. As media discourses continue to saturate everyday life in late-modern society, it is more important than ever to examine the ideological meanings of the texts that surround us. In essence, CDA brings to the study of mass communication a method for understanding the connection between *how* media communicate on the micro-level and *what* media communicate on the macro-level, an important connection to which more media scholars should attend.

Organizational Communication

Within organizational communication, the North American name for an organizational studies specialization (Bargiela-Chiappini, 2008), critical approaches are a well-established tradition (e.g., Deetz, 1982; Mumby & Stohl, 1991). By and large, however, scholars in this tradition have not been interested in close analysis of talk or texts. Outside the United States, analyses of text and talk have been a research focus for some time among organizational scholars who are linguists (e.g., Bargiela-Chiappini & Harris, 1997; Firth, 1994); until recently, though, there have been few critical analyses of talk or text. This division of emphasis has begun to change.

Critical organizational communication scholars have begun to argue for the importance of discourse—meaning both talk/text and larger belief systems, such as "globalization" (Fairhurst & Putnam, 2004; Putnam & Fairhurst, 2001)—and organizational scholars around the world are arguing for the value of critical analyses in organizational studies (Ainsworth & Hardy, 2004, McKenna, 2004). In a 25-year, 112-article analysis focused on the term "organizational discourse" across multiple organizational studies journals, Jian,

Schmisseur, and Fairhurst (2008) found both meanings of discourse to be alive and well. In a response to the analysis, however, Taylor (2008) counter-argued that the majority of studies were focusing on Big-D discourse. Most of the organizational studies, Taylor claimed, were exploring discourses in society, but they were not attending to the particulars of language and social interaction.

Organizational communication has a rich critical tradition and it knows how to study Big-D discourse. It could, however, do a better job building connections to discourse particulars and interactional processes. CDA offers a way for critical organizational communication scholars to deepen their understanding of how the macro-discourses of inequality that pervade organizational life are reflected in and accomplished through concrete conversations and texts.

Language and Social Interaction

Language and social interaction (LSI) is an area of Communication in which scholars interested in discourse (language, text, talk, interaction) explore issues in a diversity of communication contexts. LSI is steeped in a variety of language-related traditions, including conversation analysis, sociolinguistics, linguistic pragmatics, philosophy of language, and ethnography of speaking, although, interestingly, not systemic functional linguistics. While LSI is the name for a distinctively Communication specialization, of all areas, LSI is the most similar to the European linguistics communities from which most CDA scholars come and to whom they target their arguments. Outside the United States, in fact, most LSI communication scholars have been trained in departments of linguistics or language studies rather than in Communication.

In LSI, critical discourse analysis is a recognized approach to the study of language and social life (Tracy, 2008). At the same time, it is an approach that is on the margins of the area. We mentioned that one criticism of CDA is that it does not pay sufficient attention to the details of talk. This criticism could be turned on its head and directed back at much LSI work. LSI work, which has been especially influenced by conversation analysis, could be accused of giving too much attention to details of talk, and doing so at the expense of speaking to larger issues, including normative issues of how persons ought to act or how institutions ought to be structured. Critical discourse studies offer LSI researchers exemplars of how to give serious attention to language and interaction *and* institutionalized issues of conflict, justice, democracy, or decision making. Linking interactional moments to social issues and problems is a key part of the CDA project. CDA can help LSI bring its discursive commitments into serious conversation with social critics.

Appendix 11. A Critical Discourse Vocabulary

The CDA lexis consists of elements that draw on its critical theory/social theory roots (e.g., hegemony, orders of discourse) and from its language and discourse traditions, including corpus linguistics, sociolinguistics, systemic functional linguistics, discourse analysis, rhetoric, conversation analysis, discursive psychology, and social semiotics. Below is an alphabetical list of the more commonly used language-discourse terms in CDA research.

Term	*Definition and Illustration*	*Recent Applicaton*
Collocation	The existence of a sequence of words that co-occur more often than would be expected by chance, e.g., disease terms (plague, epidemic, disease) that occur near the word "immigrant."	Orpin (2005) uses collocation to analyze words semantically related to corruption and discovers significant ideological differences in the use of words referring to activities within Britain versus those outside of Britain.
Conversation-alization	The use of informal speech patterns—back and forth turns—in a genre normally characterized by formal speech patterns and practices.	Patrona (2006) investigates conversationalization on Greek television discussion programs and finds that presenters do not sustain neutral stances.
Dialogism	The theory that texts (and utterances) can only be understood as a part of a greater whole, that none derive meaning unitarily (Bakhtin, 1981).	Pietikäinen and Dufva (2006) use dialogism to examine the construction of ethnic identity through the interplay of individual and social discourses.
Genre	A classificatory device used to designate conventionalized characteristics. The use of language associated with a particular social activity (Swales, 1990), e.g., meeting minutes, citizen speeches at school board meetings, and college lectures.	Thurlow and Aiello (2007) analyze airline tailfin designs as a visual genre and find that they service national identity concerns while also appealing to the international market.
Interdiscursivity	The presence of diverse discourses or genres within a text (Fairclough, 1995a).	Using 60 adversarial political interviews broadcast in the United Kingdom, Hyatt (2005) shows how interdiscursivity is central to the construction of political discourse. One of his examples is the combining of education and economics discourses in a speech by Tony Blair.

Term	*Definition and Illustration*	*Recent Applicaton*
Interruption	When one speaker intrudes into another's understood talk turn, most often, but not necessarily, through overlap.	Menz and Al-Roubaie (2008) perform quantitative analysis of doctor-patient interruptions and found differences based on gender and status.
Intertextuality	The presence of elements of other texts within a text either directly (such as reported speech) or indirectly (such as irony).	Li (2009) shows how newspapers in the United States and China draw on intertextual resources to construct national identities in their reporting on U.S.-China relations.
Membership Categorization Terms	Terms for referring to persons that categorize them, and in so doing convey evaluation (Schegloff, 2007) e.g., calling an 18-year-old who is stealing "a boy" or "a man," a "shoplifter," or a "thief."	Mallinson and Brewster (2009) investigate restaurant server categorizations of patrons and the resulting production of "racetalk" and "regiontalk" in server discourse.
Metadiscourse	Discourse about discourse (Craig, 2008). The collection of textual features that organize a writer's or speaker's stance towards the content and the addressee.	Martínez-Guillem (2009) analyzes how speakers in the European Parliament engaging in argumentative communication invoke knowledge about ongoing interactions and past and future communicative events using meta-discourse.
Metaphor	A figure of speech in which one entity is represented as being another; Pervasive in language, thought, and action (Lakoff & Johnson, 2003), e.g., argument is war or time is money.	Ferrari (2007) presents a metaphor-based analysis of the persuasion strategies used by George W. Bush in post-9/11 speeches.
Metonymy	A figure of speech in which an attribute is used to refer to the whole, e.g., using the word "Washington" to refer to the U.S. government or "the crown" in reference to royalty.	Meadows (2005) analyzes metonymical references to conceptualizations of us/them in Bush administration statements about the Iraq conflict.
Mitigation Markers	Words and phrases to soften requests and orders or make assertions less direct, e.g., "if it's not too much trouble" can serve as a mitigation marker in front of "could you wash the dishes."	Kendall (2004) examines mitigation practices at a radio network and shows how they function to create gendered identities.

(*continued*)

Appendix 11. A Continued

Term	*Definition and Illustration*	*Recent Applicaton*
Modality	The degree of surety about an event, action, or situation (Palmer, 2001). The phrases "it might be a dog," "it must be a dog," and "it is a dog" represent varying degrees of modality.	Lillian (2008) investigates types of modality used in two conservative non-fiction texts by Canadian authors and finds that one constitutes persuasion and the other constitutes manipulation.
Nominalization	The use of an adjective, adverb, or verb as the head of a noun phrase or the process of producing a noun from another part of speech. For example, the verb evaluate can be used in the phrase "we will evaluate the data" or nominalized in the phrase "an evaluation will occur."	Bonnin (2009) analyzes the meanings, uses, and effects of the nominalized entity "reconciliation" in the context of religion and politics in Argentina.
Passivization	The process of transforming the subject of a sentence from an active agent to an object. For example, the sentence, "John moved the table" is constructed such that John is the subject and performer of the actions whereas the sentence, "The table was moved by John" is constructed such that John is an object.	Oteíza and Pinto (2008) show how passivization and other techniques are used to highlight some actors and processes while silencing others in Chilean and Spanish history textbook discussions of dictatorships and subsequent transitions to democracy.
Personification	The process of attributing human qualities to non-living entities, e.g., "the state is proud of her heroes."	Rojo (1995) analyzes the personification of the first Gulf War conflict in terms of good and evil.
Recontextual-ization	The process of transferring an element of a text—e.g., an argument, a quote—to a new context in order to give it new meaning. For example, using Hamlet's "To Be or Not To Be" speech within the context of a debate about the existence of Israel.	Hodges (2008) examines George W. Bush administration officials' and White House journalists' recontextualization of words spoken by General Peter Pace in order to contest each others' claims to the truth in regards to Iranian involvement in Iraq.
Reported Speech	One person's words as quoted or paraphrased by another person, e.g., "I was talking to Jim and he went, 'I won't do it.'"	Stokoe and Edwards (2007) examine the formulation of talk about ethnicity and race through reported speech in U.K. neighborhood disputes.

Term	*Definition and Illustration*	*Recent Applicaton*
Speech Act	The social function performed by an utterance. A question could be a compliment, a reprimand, a request for information.	Jiang (2006) analyzes the types of speech acts enacted during press conferences on the North Korea nuclear crisis and found that the frequency and distribution of requests and refusals occurred in conjunction with ideological and cultural indicators.
Synecdoche	A figure of speech in which a part refers to the whole (e.g., workmen as "hired hands").	Adams, Towns, and Gavey (1995) analyze synecdoche and other devices in male discourses about violence towards women that allow them to justify positions of dominance.
Synthetic Personalization	The process of treating mass or impersonal audiences as individuals (Fairclough, 1995a), e.g., fast food restaurants wishing customers to "have a nice day."	Grabowski (2007) identifies how financial institutions create relationships with readers, viewers, and the environment through synthetic personalization.

Notes

1. When we are referring to the field of Communication, we capitalize the "C" and leave unsaid the modifier, "U.S." In the United States, Communication as a field is sharply distinguished from linguistics, business, psychology, etc. Our comments need to be read as focused on the United States.
2. We coded 60 articles of the 286 articles to check reliability. Disagreements were resolved through discussion. In some cases the source of the disagreement raised an interesting interpretation issue. Department affiliation was coded only for the first author and reliability was 85%. Disagreements revolved around whether a department should be classified as communication or a hybrid program. Many non-U.S. program names included communication as part of a larger department name. In resolving disagreements we included these programs in the communication field category. There was 92% agreement for discourse kind, and context was 77%. Coding reliability for identity was 80%, and disagreements related to two issues of conceptual interest. The United States and the U.K. tended to not mark their nationality in keywords but other countries did. Much of the research in non-U.S. and non-U.K. countries was no more identity-focused than that in the U.S. or U.K. The other area of disagreement concerned the "other" versus "non-identity" categories; we coded studies that labeled categories—refugees, alcoholics, politicians—as other.
3. We searched *Communication and Mass Media Complete* for the same 10-year period that we did for *Discourse & Society. Discourse & Society* is one of the journals included in the database so there was overlap, although it was modest. *Communication and Mass Media Complete* includes full coverage of 380

journals and selected coverage of 200 others. Of note, very few of the communication journals sponsored by the International Communication Association, the National Communication Association, or regional U.S. communication journals had critical discourse articles. Most of the articles appeared in multidisciplinary journals with links to language study, linguistics, or culture.

4. Quoted from the back jacket of D&S of the May, 2009, Volume 20.
5. Although the handbook does not foreground CDA, its key authors are cited.
6. Our thanks to an anonymous reviewer for this observation.
7. See http://www.h-net.org/announce/show.cgi?ID=145338.

References

Adams, P., Towns, A., & Gavey, N. (1995). Dominance and entitlement: The rhetoric men use to discuss their violence towards women. *Discourse & Society, 6*, 387–406.

Adeyanju, C. T., & Neverson, N. (2007). "There will be a next time": Media discourse about an "apocalyptic" vision of immigration, racial diversity, and health risks. *Canadian Ethnic Studies, 39*, 79–105.

Agar, M. (1985). Institutional discourse. *Interdisciplinary Journal for the Study of Discourse, 5*, 147–168.

Agyekum, K. (2004). Invective language in contemporary Ghanaian politics. *Journal of Language & Politics, 3*, 345–375.

Ainsworth, S., & Hardy, C. (2004). Critical discourse analysis and identity: Why bother? *Critical Discourse Studies, 1*, 225–259.

Alexander, R. J. (2009). *Framing discourse on the environment: A critical discourse approach*. New York: Routledge.

Antaki, C. (2006). Producing a "cognition." *Discourse Studies, 8*, 9–15.

Atkinson, J. M., & Heritage, J. (1999). Jefferson's transcript notation. In A. Jaworski & N. Coupland (Eds.), *The discourse reader* (pp. 158–166). London: Routledge.

Augoustinos, M., Tuffin, K., & Every, D. (2005). New racism, meritocracy and individualism: Constraining affirmative action in education. *Discourse & Society, 16*, 315–340.

Baker, P., Gabrielatos, C., Khosravinik, M., Krzyzanowski, M., McEnery, A. M., & Wodak, R. (2008). A useful methodological synergy? Combining critical discourse analysis and corpus linguistics to examine discourses of refugees and asylum seekers in the UK press. *Discourse & Society, 19*, 273–306.

Bakhtin, M. (1981). *The dialogic imagination*. Austin: University of Texas Press.

Bargiela-Chiappini, F. (2008). Discourse and/or communication: Living with ambiguity. *Discourse and Communication, 2*, 327–332.

Bargiela-Chiappini, F., & Harris, S. J. (1997). *Managing language: The discourse of corporate meetings*. Amsterdam: John Benjamins.

Bar-Lev, Z. (2007). Mrs. Goldberg's rebuttal of Butt et al. *Discourse & Society, 18*, 183–196.

Bartesaghi, M. (2009). Conversation and psychotherapy: How questioning reveals institutional answers. *Discourse & Society, 11*, 153–177.

Barthes, R. (1957). *Mythologies*. Paris: Éditions du Seuil.

Bell, A. (1991). *The language of news media*. Oxford, UK: Blackwell.

Bell, A. (1997). The discourse structure of news stories. In A. Bell & P. Garrett (Eds.), *Approaches to media discourse* (pp. 64–104). Oxford, UK: Blackwell,

Bell, A. (2003). Poles apart: Globalisation and the development of news discourse in the twentieth century. In J. Aitchison, & D. Lewis (Eds.), *New media language* (pp. 7–17). London: Routledge.

Berk-Seligson, S. (2009). *Coerced confessions: The discourse of bilingual police interrogations*. Berlin: Mouton de Gruyter.

Bergvall, V., & Remlinger, K. (1996). Reproduction, resistance, and gender in educational discourse: The role of critical discourse analysis. *Discourse & Society, 7*, 453–579.

Billig, M. (1985). Prejudice, categorization and particularisation. *European Journal of Social Psychology, 15*, 79–103.

Billig, M. (1987). *Arguing and thinking: A rhetorical approach to social psychology* (1st ed.). Cambridge, UK: Cambridge University Press.

Billig, M. (1995). *Banal nationalism*. London: Sage.

Billig, M. (1999a). Whose terms? Whose ordinariness? Rhetoric and ideology in conversation analysis. *Discourse & Society, 10*, 543–557.

Billig, M. (1999b). Conversation analysis and the claims of naivety. *Discourse & Society, 10*, 572–576.

Billig, M. (2001). Humour and hatred: The racist jokes of the Ku Klux Klan. *Discourse & Society, 12*, 267–289.

Billig, M. (2003). Critical discourse analysis and the rhetoric of critique. In G. Weiss & R. Wodak (Eds.), *Critical discourse analysis: Theory and interdisciplinarity* (pp. 35–46). London: Palgrave Macmillan.

Billig, M. (2008a). The language of critical discourse analysis: The case of nominalization. *Discourse & Society, 19*, 783–800.

Billig, M. (2008b). Nominalizing and denominalizing: A reply. *Discourse & Society, 19*, 829–841.

Billig, M., Condor, S., Edwards, D., Gane, M., Middleton, D., & Radley, A. (1988). *Ideological dilemmas*. London: Sage.

Binbin, Z. (1999). Asymmetry and mitigation in Chinese medical interviews. *Health Communication, 11*, 209–215.

Blackledge, A. (2006). The racialization of language in British political discourse. *Critical Discourse Studies, 3*, 61–79.

Blommaert, J. (2005). *Discourse: A critical introduction*. Cambridge, UK: Cambridge University Press.

Blommaert, J., & Bulcaen, C. (2000). Critical discourse analysis. *Annual Review of Anthropology, 29*, 447–466.

Bloor, M., & Bloor, T. (2007). *The practice of critical discourse analysis: An introduction*. London: Arnold.

Bonilla-Silva, E., & Forman, T. A. (2000). "I am not a racist but…": Mapping white college students' racial ideology in the USA. *Discourse & Society, 11*, 50–85.

Bonnin, J. E. (2009). Religious and political discourse in Argentina: The case of reconciliation. *Discourse & Society, 20*, 327–343.

Bourdieu, P. (1984). *Outline of a theory of practice* (R. Nice, Trans.). Cambridge, UK: Cambridge University Press.

Bradby, H., Gabe, J., & Bury, M. (1995). 'Sexy docs' and 'busty blondes': Press coverage of professional misconduct cases brought before the General Medical Council. *Sociology of Health and Illness, 17*, 458–476.

Brooks, K. P. de., & Waymer, D. (2009). Public relations and strategic issues management challenges in Venezuela: A discourse analysis of Crystallex International Corporation in Las Cristinas. *Public Relations Review, 35*, 31–39.

Bucholtz, M. (2009). Captured on tape: Professional hearing and competing entextualizations in the criminal justice system. *Text & Talk, 29*, 503–523.

Caffarel, A., & Rechniewski, E. (2008). When is a handover not a handover? A case study of ideological opposed news stories. In E. Thomson & P. White (Eds.), *Communicating conflict: Multilingual case studies of the news media* (pp. 25–50). London: Continuum.

Caldas-Coulthard, C. R., & Van Leeuwen, T. J. (2002). Stunning, shimmering, iridescent: Toys as the representation of gendered social actors. In L. Litosseliti & J. Sunderland (Eds.), *Gender identity and discourse analysis* (pp. 91–108). Amsterdam: John Benjamins.

Cameron, D. (1998). "Is there any ketchup, Vera?": Gender, power and pragmatics. *Discourse & Society, 9*, 437–455.

Cameron, D. (2003). Gender and language ideology. In J. Holmes & M. Meyerhoff (Eds.), *The handbook of language and gender* (pp. 447–467). Malden, MA: Blackwell

Cameron, D. (2006). Performing gender identity: Young men's talk and the construction of heterosexual masculinity. In A. Jaworski & N. Coupland (Eds.), *The discourse reader* (2nd ed., pp. 419–432). London: Routledge.

Campbell, S., & Roberts, C. (2007). Migration, ethnicity and competing discourses in the job interview: Synthesizing the institutional and personal. *Discourse & Society, 13*, 243–271.

Carvalho, A. (2005). Representing the politics of the greenhouse effect. *Critical Discourse Studies, 2*, 1–29.

Charteris-Black, J. (2006). Britain as a container: Immigration metaphors in the 2005 election campaign. *Discourse & Society, 17*, 563–581.

Chibnall, S. (1977). *Law-and-order news: An analysis of crime reporting in the British press*. London: Tavistock.

Chilton, P. (2004). *Analyzing political discourse: Theory and practice*. London: Routledge.

Chilton, P. (2005). Missing links in mainstream CDA: Modules, blends and the critical Instinct. In R. Wodak (Ed.), *New agenda in (critical) discourse analysis: Theory, methodology and interdisciplinarity* (pp. 19–51). Philadelphia: John Benjamins.

Chilton, P. (2007). Missing links in mainstream CDA: Modules, blends and the critical instinct. In R. Wodak & P. Chilton (Eds.), *A new research agenda in (critical) discourse analysis: Theory and interdisciplinarity* (2nd ed., pp. 19–52). Amsterdam: John Benjamins.

Chouliaraki, L. (1998). Regulation in 'progressivist' pedagogic discourse: Individualized teacher-pupil talk. *Discourse & Society, 9*, 5–32.

Chouliaraki, L. (2004). Watching September 11th: The politics of pity. *Discourse and Society, 15*, 185–198.

Chouliaraki, L. (2005). The soft power of war: Political and media discourses on the Iraq war. *Journal of Language and Politics, 3*, 1–10.

Chouliaraki, L. (2006). *Spectatorship of suffering*. London: Sage.

Chouliaraki, L (2008). Symbolic power of transnational media: managing the visibility of suffering. *Global Media and Communication, 4*, 329–351.

Chouliaraki, L (2009). Witnessing war: Economies of regulation in reporting war and conflict. *The Communication Review, 12*, 215–226.

Chouliaraki, L., & Fairclough, N. (1999). *Discourse in late modernity: Rethinking critical discourse analysis*. Edinburgh: Edinburgh University Press.

Cobb, S. (1994). A critique of critical discourse analysis: Deconstructing and reconstructing the role of intention. *Communication Theory, 4*, 132–152.

Collins, C., & Jones, P. E. (2006). Analysis of discourse as "a form of history writing": A critique of critical discourse analysis and an illustration of a cultural-historical alternative. *Atlantic Journal of Communication, 14*, (1/2), 51–69.

Craig, R. T. (2008). Meta-discourse. In W. Donsbach (Ed.), *International encyclopedia of communication* (Vol. VII, pp. 3107–3109). Oxford, UK: Wiley-Blackwell.

Craig, R. T., & Tracy, K. (Eds.). (1983). *Conversational coherence: Form, structure, and strategy*. Beverly Hills, CA: Sage.

Cramer, J. M. (2009). Critical discourse analysis. In S. L. Littlejohn & K. A. Foss (Eds.), *Encyclopedia of communication theory* (pp. 220–223). Los Angeles: Sage.

Dabbous-Sensenig, D. (2006). To veil or not to veil: Gender and religion on Al-Jazeera's Islamic law and life. *Westminster Papers in Communication & Culture, 3*(2), 60–85.

De Cillia, R., Reisigl, M., & Wodak, R. (1999). The discursive construction of national identities. *Discourse & Society, 10*, 149–173.

Deetz, S. A. (1982). Critical interpretive research in organizational communication. *The Western Journal of Speech Communication, 46*, 131–149.

Deetz, S., Heath, R., & MacDonald, J. (2007). On talking to not make decisions: A critical analysis of organizational talk. In F. Cooren (Ed.), *Interacting and organizing: Analyses of a management meeting* (pp. 225–244). Mahwah, NJ: Erlbaum.

Del Teso-Craviotto, M. (2008). Gender and sexual identity authentication in language use: The case of chat rooms. *Discourse Studies, 10*, 251–270.

Delanty, G., Jones, P., & Wodak, R. (2008). *Migration, identity, and belonging*. Liverpool, UK: University of Liverpool Press.

Drew, P. (2005). Conversation analysis. In K. Fitch & R. Sanders (Eds.), *Handbook of language and social interaction* (pp. 71–102). Mahwah, NJ: Erlbaum.

Eggins, S. (1994). *An introduction to systemic functional linguistics*. London: Pinter.

Ehrlich, S. (2003). Coercing gender: Language in sexual assault adjudication processes. In J. Holmes & M. Meyerhoff (Eds.), *Handbook of language and gender* (pp. 645–671). Oxford, UK: Blackwell.

Ericson, R. V., Baranek, P. M., & Chan, J. B. L. (1987). *Visualizing deviance: A study of news organizations*. Milton Keynes, UK: Open University Press.

Eriksson, K., & Aronsson, K. (2005). "We're really lucky": Co-creating "us" and the "other" in school booktalk. *Discourse & Society, 16*, 719–738.

Erjavec, K. (2009). The "Bosnian war on terrorism." *Journal of Language & Politics, 8*, 5–27.

Every, D., & Agoustinos, M. (2007). Constructions of racism in the Australian parliamentary debates on asylum seekers. *Discourse & Society, 18*, 411–436.

Every, D., & Agoustinos, M. (2008). Constructions of Australia in pro- and anti-asylum seeker political discourse. *Nations & Nationalism, 14*, 562–580.

Fairclough, N. (1988). Discourse representation in media discourse. *Sociolinguistics, 17*, 125–139.

Fairclough, N. (1989). *Language and power*. Essex, UK: Longman.

Fairclough, N. (1992). *Discourse and social change*. Cambridge, UK: Polity Press.

Fairclough, N. (1993). Critical discourse analysis and the marketization of public discourse: The universities. *Discourse & Society, 4*, 133–168.

Fairclough, N. (1995a). *Critical discourse analysis: The critical study of language*. Harlow, UK: Pearson Education.

Fairclough, N. (1995b). *Media discourse*. London: Edward Arnold.

Fairclough, N. (1996). A reply to Henry Widdowson's "Discourse analysis: A critical view." *Language & Literature, 5*, 49–56.

Fairclough, N. (2002). Language in new capitalism. *Discourse & Society, 13*, 163–166.

Fairclough, N. (2003). *Analysing discourse: Textual analysis for social research*. London: Routledge.

Fairclough, N. (2004). Critical discourse analysis in researching language in the new capitalism: Overdetermination, transdisciplinarity and textual analysis. In L. Y. C. Harrison (Ed.), *Systemic functional linguistics and critical discourse analysis* (pp. 103–122). New York: Continuum.

Fairclough, N. (2006). *Language and globalization*. London: Routledge.

Fairclough, N. (2008). The language of critical discourse analysis: Reply to Michael Billig. *Discourse & Society, 19*, 811–819.

Fairclough, N. (2009). *Language and power*. London: Longman.

Fairclough, N., & Wodak, R. (1997). Critical discourse analysis. In T. A. van Dijk (Ed.), *Discourse as social interaction* (pp. 258–284). London: Sage.

Fairclough, N., Graham, P., Lemke, J., & Wodak, R. (2004). Introduction. *Critical Discourse Studies, 1*, 1–7.

Fairhurst, G. T. (1993). The leader-member exchange patterns of women leaders in industry: A discourse analysis. *Communication Monographs, 60,* 321–351.

Fairhurst, G. T., & Putnam, L. (2004). Organizations as discursive constructions. *Communication Theory, 14*, 5–26.

Ferrari, F. (2007). Metaphor at work in the analysis of political discourse: Investigating a 'preventative war' persuasion strategy. *Discourse & Society, 18*, 603–625.

Fine, M. (2003). Sexuality, school, and adolescent females: The missing discourse of desire. In A. Darder, B. Marta, & D. T. Rodolfo (Eds.), *The critical pedagogy reader* (pp. 296–321). New York: Routledge.

Firth, A. (Ed.). (1994). *The discourse of negotiation: Studies of language in the workplace*. London: Pergamon/Elsevier Science.

Fiske, J. (1988). Critical response: Meaningful moments. *Critical Studies in Mass Communication, 5,* 246–251.

Fiske, J. (1996). *Media matters: Race and gender in US politics*. Minneapolis: University of Minnesota Press.

Fiske, J., & Hartley, J. (1978). *Reading television*. London: Methuen.

Fitch, K., & Sanders, R. (2005). *Handbook of language and social interaction*. Mahwah, NJ: Erlbaum.

Flores, L. (2009). Critical race theory. In S. L. Littlejohn & K. A. Foss (Eds.), *Encyclopedia of communication theory* (Vol. 1, pp. 231–234). Los Angeles: Sage.

Foucault, M. ([1969]1972). *The archaeology of knowledge*. London: Routledge.

Fuchsel, H. G., & Martín Rojo, L. (2003). Civic and ethnic nationalistic discourses in Spanish parliamentary debates. *Journal of Language & Politics, 2*, 31–70.

Gales, T. (2009). 'Diversity' as enacted in us immigration politics and law: A corpus-based approach. *Discourse & Society, 20*, 223–240.

Ganesh, S. (2009). Critical organizational communication. In S. L. Littlejohn & K. A. Foss (Eds.), *Encyclopedia of communication theory* (pp. 226–230). Los Angeles: Sage.

García Agustín, O. (2008). Fronteras discursivas: Las políticas migratorias de inclusión y exclusión en la Unión Europea [Discursive borders: migration policies of inclusion and exclusion in the European Union]. *Discurso y Sociedad, 2,* 742–768.

Gee, J. P. (1999). *An introduction to discourse analysis: Theory and method.* London: Routledge.

Gee, J. P. (2006). *An introduction to discourse analysis: Theory and method.* (2nd ed.). London: Routledge.

Goodman, S., & Speer, S. A. (2007). Category use in the construction of asylum seekers. *Critical Discourse Studies, 4*, 165–185

Grabowski, I. (2007). Consumed by consumerism: The pervasive discourse of financial institutions. *Language and Ecology, 2*, 1–15.

Graham, P., Keenan, T., & Dowd, A. M. (2004). A call to arms at the end of history: A discourse–historical analysis of George W. Bush's declaration of war on terror. *Discourse & Society, 15*, 199–221.

Gramsci, A. (1971). *Selections from the prison notebooks.* London: Lawrence and Wishart.

Hafen, S. (2009). Patriots in the classroom: Performing positionalities post 9/11. *Communication and Critical/Cultural Studies, 6*, 61–83.

Hall, S. (1972). The determination of news photographs. *Working Papers in Cultural Studies, 3*, 53–89.

Hall, S., Critcher, C., Jefferson, T., Clarke, J., & Roberts, B. (1978). *Policing the crisis: Mugging, the state, and law and order.* London: Macmillan.

Halliday, M. A. K. (1994). *Introduction to functional grammar* (2nd ed.). London: Edward Arnold.

Hammersley, M. (1997). On the foundation of critical discourse analysis. *Language & Communication, 17*, 237–248.

Haraty, N., Oueini, A., & Bahous, R. (2007). Speaking to domestics in Lebanon: Power issues or misguided communication. *Journal of Intercultural Communication, 14.* Retrieved from http://www.immi.se/intercultural

Harding, R. (2006). Historical representations of aboriginal people in the Canadian news media *Discourse & Society, 17*, 205–235.

Hart, C. (2008). Critical discourse analysis and metaphor: Toward a theoretical framework. *Critical Discourse Studies, 5*, 91–106.

Hartley, J. (1982). *Understanding news.* London: Methuen.

Hartley, J. (1992). *The politics of pictures: The creation of the public in the age of popular media.* London: Routledge.

Hartley, J. (1996). *Popular reality: Journalism, modernity, popular culture.* London: Arnold.

He, A. (2006). Subject matter in Hong Kong primary English classrooms: A critical analysis of teacher talk. *Critical Inquiry in Language Studies, 3,* 169–188.

Higgins, M. (2004). The articulation of nation and politics in the Scottish press. *Journal of Language & Politics, 3,* 463–483.

Hodge, R., & Kress, G. (1988). *Social semiotics* (2nd ed.). Ithaca, NY: Cornell University Press.

Hodge, R., & Kress, G. (1993). *Language as ideology* (2nd ed.). London: Routledge.

Hodges, A. (2008). The politics of recontextualization: Discursive competition over claims of Iranian involvement in Iraq. *Discourse & Society, 19,* 483–505.

Hodges, A., & Nilep, C. (2007). *Discourse, war and terrorism.* Amsterdam: John Benjamins.

Holmes, J., & Meyerhoff, M. (2003). Different voices, different views: An introduction to current research in language and gender. In J. H. M. Meyerhoff (Ed.), *Handbook on language and gender* (pp. 1–17). Oxford, UK: Basil Blackwell.

Huang, Y., & Chen, J.-p. (2009). Discursive democratization in Mainland China: A diachronic study of the New Year's editorials in the People's Daily. *Journal of Asian Pacific Communication, 19*, 199–217.

Huspek, M. (1989/90). The idea of ethnography and cultural critique. *Research on Language and Social Interaction, 23*, 293–302.

Huspek, M. (1993). Dueling structures: The theory of resistance in discourse. *Communication Theory, 3*, 1–25.

Huspek, M. (1997). Toward normative theories of communication with reference to the Frankfurt school: An introduction. *Communication Theory, 7*, 265–276.

Huspek, M., & Kendall, K. (1991). On withholding analysis of the political vocabulary of a 'non-political' speech community. *Quarterly Journal of Speech, 77*, 1–19.

Hutchby, I., & Wooffitt, R. (1998). *Conversation analysis: Principles, practices, and applications*. Malden, MA: Polity Press.

Hyatt, D. (2005). Time for a change: A critical discoursal analysis of synchronic context with diachronic relevance. *Discourse & Society, 16*, 515–534.

Iedema, R., Feez, S., & White, P. R. (1994). *Media literacy (write it right literacy in industry research project — stage 2*. Sydney, Australia: Metropolitan East Disadvantaged School Program.

Jäger, S. (2001). Discourse and knowledge: Theoretical and methodological aspects of a critical discourse and dispositive analysis. In R. Wodak & M. Meyer (Eds.), *Methods of critical discourse analysis* (pp. 32–62). Thousand Oaks, CA: Sage.

Jenkings, N. K., & Barber, N. (2006). Same evidence, different meanings: Transformation of textual evidence in hospital new drugs committees. *Text and Talk, 26*, 169–189.

Jian, G., Schmisseur, A. M., & Fairhurst, G. (2008). Organizational discourse and communication: The progeny of Proteus. *Discourse & Communication, 2*, 299–355.

Jiang, X. (2006). Cross-cultural pragmatic differences in the US and Chinese press conferences: The case of the North Korea nuclear crisis. *Discourse & Society, 17*, 237–257.

Johnstone, B., & Eisenhart, C. (Eds.). (2008). *Rhetoric in detail*. Amsterdam: John Benjamins.

Jones, P. E. (2007). Why there is no such thing as "critical discourse analysis." *Language & Communication, 27*, 337–368.

Kalmus, V. (2003). 'Is interethnic integration possible in Estonia?': Ethno-political discourse of two ethnic groups *Discourse & Society, 14*, 667–697.

Kariithi, N., & Kareithi, P. (2007). It's off to work you go! *Journalism Studies, 8*, 465–480.

Kaufer, D., & Hariman, R. (2008). Discriminating political styles as genres: A corpus study exploring Hariman's theory of political style. *Text & Talk, 28*, 475–500.

Kendall, S. (2004). Framing authority: Gender, face, and mitigation at a radio network. *Discourse & Society, 15*, 55–79.

KhosraviNik, M. (2009). The representation of refugees, asylum seekers and immigrants in British newspapers during the Balkan conflict (1999) and the British general election (2005). *Discourse & Society, 20*, 477–498.

Kitzinger, C. (2005a). "Speaking as a heterosexual": (How) does sexuality matter for talk-in-interaction? *Research on Language and Social Interaction, 38*, 221–265.

Kitzinger, C. (2005b). Heteronormativity in action: Reproducing the heterosexual nuclear family in after-hour medical calls. *Social Problems, 52*, 477–498.

Kitzinger, C. (2006). After post-cognitivism. *Discourse Studies, 8*, 67–83.

Kleiner, B. (1998). The modern racist ideology and its reproduction in "pseudo-argument" *Discourse & Society, 9*, 187–215.

Kosic, A., & Triandafyllidou, A. (2004). Representations of the European Union and the nation(-state) in Italian party discourse. *Journal of Language and Politics, 3*, 53–80.

Kress, G. (2006). *Reading images: The grammar of visual design*. London: Routledge.

Kress, G., & Hodge, R. (1979). *Language as ideology*. London: Routledge and Kegan Paul.

Kress, G., & van Leeuwen, T. (2001). *Multimodal discourse*. Oxford, UK: Hodder Arnold.

Kress, G., Leite-García, R., & van Leeuwen, T. (1997). Discourse semiotics. In T. A. van. Dijk (Ed.), *Discourse as structure and process* (pp. 257–291). London: Sage.

Kuo, S. H. (2003). Involvement vs detachment: Gender differences in the use of personal pronouns in televised sports in Taiwan. *Discourse Studies 5*, 479–494.

Kuo, S. (2007). Language as ideology: Analyzing quotations in Taiwanese news discourse. *Journal of Asian Pacific Communication, 17*, 281–301.

Lakoff, G., & Johnson, M. (2003). *Metaphors we live by* (rev. ed.). Chicago: University of Chicago Press.

Lario Bastida, M. (2008). Crónica crítica del debate político sobre migraciones en España [Critical account of the political debate on migration in Spain]. *Discurso y Sociedad, 2*, 769–798.

Lazar, A., & Lazar, M. M. (2008). Discourse of global governance: American hegemony in the post-cold war era. *Journal of Language & Politics, 7*, 228–246.

Lazar, M. M. (2000). Gender discourse and semiotics: The politics of parenthood representations. *Discourse & Society, 11*, 373–400.

Lazar, M. M. (2007). Feminist critical discourse analysis: Articulating a feminist discourse praxis. *Critical Discourse Studies, 4,* 141–164.

Lazar, M. M. (Ed.). (2005). *Feminist critical discourse analysis: Gender, power and ideology in discourse*. London: Palgrave.

LeCouteur, A., Rapley, M., & Augoustinos, M. (2001). "This very difficult debate about WIK": Stake, voice and the management of category memberships in race politics. *British Journal of Social Psychology, 40*, 35–57.

Lee, J. S. (2007). North Korea, South Korea, and *007 Die Another day. Critical Discourse Studies, 4*, 207–235.

Li, J. (2009). Intertextuality and national identity: Discourse of national conflicts in daily newspapers in the United States and China. *Discourse & Society, 20*, 85–121.

Lillian, D. L. (2008). Modality, persuasion and manipulation in Canadian conservative discourse. *Critical Approaches to Discourse Analysis across Disciplines, 20*, 1–16.

Locke, T. (2004). *Critical discourse analysis*. New York: Continuum.

MacDonald, M. N. (2002). Pedagogy, pathology and ideology: The production, transmission and reproduction of medical discourse. *Discourse & Society, 13*, 447–468.

Maidza, N. (2008). Many faces of regime change politics: A critical analysis of a delection of Mahoso's African focus articles. *Nawa: Journal of Language & Communication, 2*, 89–104.

Mallinson, C., & Brewster, Z. W. (2009). "Blacks and bubbas": Stereotypes, ideology, and categorization processes in restaurant servers' discourse. *Discourse & Society, 16*, 787–807.

Martin, J. R. (2008). Incongruent and proud: De-vilifying 'nominalization'. *Discourse & Society, 19*, 801–810.

Martin, J. R., & Rose, D. (2003). *Working with discourse: Meaning beyond the clause*. London: Continuum.

Martin, J. R., & White, P. R. (2005). *The language of evaluation: Appraisal in English*. London: Palgrave.

Martínez-Guillem, S. (2009). Argumentation, metadiscourse and social cognition: Organizing knowledge in political communication. *Discourse & Society, 20*, 727–746.

Matheson, D. (2005). *Media discourses: Analysing media texts*. New York: Open University Press.

Maynard, D. W. (2006). Cognition on the ground. *Discourse Studies 8*, 105–115.

McKenna, B. (2004). Critical discourse studies: Where to from here? *Critical Discourse Studies, 1*, 9–39.

McKerrow, R. (2009). Critical rhetoric. In S. L. Littlejohn & K. A. Foss (Eds.), *Encyclopedia of communication theory* (Vol. 1, pp. 234–237). Los Angeles: Sage.

Meadows, B. (2005). Distancing and showing solidarity via metaphor and metonymy in political discourse: A critical study of American statements on Iraq during the years 2004–2005. *Critical Approaches to Discourse Analysis across Disciplines, 1*, 1–17.

Mehan, H. (1997). The discourse of the illegal immigration debate. *Discourse & Society, 8*, 249–270.

Mehan, H. (2001). The construction of an LD student: A case study in the politics of representation. In M. Wetherell, S. Taylor, & S. J. Yates (Eds.), *Discourse theory and practice* (pp. 345–363). London: Sage.

Menz, F., & Al-Roubaie, A. (2008). Interruptions, status and gender in medical interviews: The harder you brake, the longer it takes. *Discourse & Society, 19*, 645–666.

Mertz, E. (1998). Linguistic ideology and praxis in US law school classrooms In B. Schieffelin, K. A. Woolard, & P. V. Kroskrity (Eds.), *Language ideologies: Practice and theory* (pp. 149–162). New York: Oxford University Press.

Mertz, E. (2007). *The language of law school: Learning to "think like a lawyer."* New York: Oxford University Press.

Mey, I. (2001). The CA/CDA controversy. *Journal of Pragmatics, 33*, 609–615.

Meyer, M. (2001). Between theory, method and politics: Positioning of the approaches to CDA. In M. Meyer & R. Wodak (Eds.), *Methods of critical discourse analysis* (pp. 14–31). London: Sage.

Moita-Lopes, L. P. (2006). Queering literacy teaching: Analyzing gay-themed discourses in a fifth-grade class in Brazil. *Journal of Language, Identity & Education, 5*, 31–50.

Mumby, D. K., & Clair, R. P. (1997). Organizational discourse. In T. van Dijk (Ed.), *Discourse studies. Volume 2. Discourse as social interaction* (pp. 181–205). London: Sage.

Mumby, D. K., & Stohl, C. (1991). Power and discourse in organization. *Discourse & Society, 2*, 313–332.

Ono, K. A. (2009). Critical/cultural approaches to communication. In W. F. Eadie (Ed.), *21st century communication: A reference handbook* (Vol. 1, pp. 74–81). Los Angeles: Sage.

O'Regan, J. P. (2006). The text as a critical object: On theorizing exegetic procedures in classroom-based critical discourse analysis. *Critical Discourse Studies, 3*, 179–209.

Orpin, D. (2005). Corpus linguistics and critical discourse analysis: Examining the ideology of sleaze. *International Journal of Corpus Linguistics, 10*, 37–61.

Oteíza, T., & Pinto, D. (2008). Agency, responsibility and silence in the construction of contemporary history in Chile and Spain. *Discourse & Society, 19*, 33–358.

Palmer, F. R. (2001). *Mood and modality.* Cambridge, UK: Cambridge University Press.

Patrona, M. (2006). Conversationalization and media empowerment in Greek television discussion programs. *Discourse & Society, 17*, 5–27.

Philips, S. U. (1998). *Ideology in the language of judges: How judges practice law, politics, and courtroom control.* New York: Oxford University Press.

Philipsen, G., & Coutu, L. M. (2005). The ethnography of speaking. In K. Fitch & R. Sanders (Eds.), *Handbook of language and social interaction* (pp. 355–380). Mahwah, NJ: Erlbaum.

Philp, M. (1985). Michel Foucault. In Q. Skinner (Ed.), *The return of grand theory in the human sciences* (pp. 65–81). Cambridge, UK: Cambridge University Press.

Pitt, K. (2002). Being a new capitalist mother. *Discourse & Society, 13*, 251–267.

Prins, E., & Toso, B. W. (2008). Defining and measuring parenting for educational success: A critical discourse analysis of the parent education profile. *American Educational Research Journal, 45*, 555–596.

Putnam, L. L., & Cooren, F. (2004). Alternative perspectives on the role of text and agency in constituting organizations. *Organization, 11*, 323–333.

Putnam, L. L., & Fairhurst, G. T. (2001). Discourse analysis in organizations: Issues and concerns. In F. M. Jablin & L. L. Putnam (Eds.), *The new handbook of organizational communication* (pp. 78–136). Thousand Oaks, CA: Sage.

Reisigl, M., & Wodak, R. (2001). *Discourse and discrimination.* London: Routledge.

Richardson, J. E. (2007). *Analysing newspapers: An approach from critical discourse analysis.* Houndmills, UK: Palgrave Macmillan.

Rogers, R., Malancharuvi-Berkes, E., Mosley, M., Hui, D., & O'Garro, G. (2005). Critical discourse analysis in education: A review of the literature. *Review of Educational Research, 75*, 365–416.

Rojo, L. M. (1995). Division and rejection: From the personification of the gulf conflict to the demonization of Saddam Hussein. *Discourse & Society, 6*, 49–80.

Ruiseco, G., & Slunecko, T. (2006). The role of mythical European heritage in the construction of Colombian national identity. *Journal of Language & Politics, 5*, 359–384.

Saft, S., & Ohara, Y. (2006). The media and the pursuit of militarism in Japan: Newspaper editorials in the aftermath of 9/11. *Critical Discourse Studies, 3*, 81–101.

Santa Ana, O. (1999). "Like an animal I was treated": Anti-immigrant metaphor in US public discourse. *Discourse & Society, 10*, 191–224.

Sarangi, C., & Roberts, C. (Eds.). (1999). *Talk, work and institutional order: Discourse in medical, mediation and management settings.* Berlin: Mouton de Gruyter.

Schegloff, E. A. (1997). Whose text? Whose context? *Discourse & Society, 8*, 165–187.

Schegloff, E. A. (1998). Positioning and interpretative repertoires: Conversation analysis and post-structuralism in dialogue - reply to Wetherell. *Discourse & Society, 9*, 413–416.

Schegloff, E. A. (1999a). "Schegloff's texts" as "Billig's data": A critical reply. *Discourse & Society, 10*, 558–572.

Schegloff, E. A. (1999b). Naiveté vs. sophistication or discipline vs. self-indulgence: A rejoinder to Billig. *Discourse & Society, 10*, 577–582.

Schegloff, E. A. (2007). *Sequence organization in interaction: A primer in conversation analysis*. Cambridge, UK: Cambridge University Press.

Schmidt, R. (2002). Racialization and language policy: The case of the USA. *Multilingua, 21*, 141–161.

Schubert, S. J., Hanson, S., Dyer, K. R., & Rapley, M. (2009). "ADHD patient" or "illicit drug user"? Managing medico-moral membership categories in drug dependencies services. *Discourse & Society, 20*, 499–516.

Scollon, R. (2005). The discourses of food in the world system: Toward a nexus analysis of a world problem. *Journal of Language & Politics, 4*, 465–488.

Shaw, S. (2000). Language, gender and floor apportionment in political debates. *Discourse & Society, 11*, 401–418.

Shi-xu. (2009). Editorial. *Journal of Multicultural Discourses, 4*, 239–241.

Simmons, K., & Lecoteur, A. (2008). Modern racism in the media: Constructions of 'the possibility of change' in accounts of two Australian 'riots.' *Discourse & Society, 19*, 667–687.

Stamou, A. G., & Paraskevopoulos, S. (2008). Representing protection action in an ecotourism setting: A critical discourse analysis of visitors' books at a Greek reserve. *Critical Discourse Studies, 5*, 35–54.

Stokoe, E., & Edwards, D. (2007). 'Black this, black that': Racial insults and reported speech in neighbour complaints and police interrogations. *Discourse & Society, 18*, 337–372.

Stokoe, E., & Smithson, J. (2002). Gender and sexuality in talk-in-interaction: Considering conversation analytic perspectives. In P. McIlvenny (Ed.), *Talking gender and sexuality: Conversation, performativity and discourse in interaction* (pp. 79–110). Amsterdam: John Benjamins.

Stubbs, M. (1996). *Text and corpus analysis*. Oxford, UK: Blackwell.

Swales, J. M. (1990). *Genre analysis: English in academic and research settings*. Cambridge, UK: Cambridge University Press.

Tannen, D. (1990). *You just don't understand: Women and men in conversation*. New York: Ballantine.

Tannock, S. (1999). Working with insults: Discourse and difference in an inner-city youth organization. *Discourse & Society, 10*, 317–350.

Taylor, J. R. (2008). Communication and discourse: Is the bridge language? Response to Jian et al. *Discourse & Communication*, *2*, 347–352.

ten Have, P. (1999). *Doing conversation analysis*. London: Sage.

Teo, P. (2000). Racism in the news: A critical discourse analysis of news reporting in two Australian newspapers. *Discourse & Society, 11*, 7–49.

Thompson, E. A., & White, P. R. R. (Eds.). (2008). *Communicating conflict: Multilingual case studies of the news media*. London: Continuum.

Thorne, A., & Coupland, J. (1998). Articulations of same-sex desire: Lesbian and gay male dating advertisements. *Journal of Sociolinguistics*, *2*, 233–257.

Thurlow, C. (2001). Naming the "outsider within": Homophobic pejoratives and the verbal abuse of lesbian, gay and bisexual high-school pupils. *Journal of Adolescence, 24*, 25–38.

Thurlow, C., & Aiello, G. (2007). National pride, global capital: A social semiotic analysis of transnational visual branding in the airline industry. *Visual Communication, 6*, 305–344.

Tilbury, F., & Colic-Peisker, V. (2006). Deflecting responsibility in employer talk about race discrimination. *Discourse & Society, 17*, 651–676.

Tileaga, C. (2005). Accounting for extreme prejudice and legitimating blame in talk about the Romanies. *Discourse & Society, 16*, 603–624.

Toolan, M. (1997). What is critical discourse analysis and why are people saying such terrible things about it? *Language and Literature, 6*, 83–103.

Toolan, M. (2002). *Critical discourse analysis: Critical concepts in linguistics*. London: Routledge.

Tracy, K. (2005). Reconstructing communicative practices: Action-implicative discourse analysis. In K. Fitch & R. Sanders (Eds.), *Handbook of language and social interaction* (pp. 301–319). Mahwah, NJ: Erlbaum.

Tracy, K. (2008). Language and social interaction. In W. Donsbach (Ed.), *International encyclopedia of communication* (pp. 2645–2655). Oxford, UK: Wiley-Blackwell.

Trix, F., & Psenka, C. (2003). Exploring the color of glass: Letters of recommendation for female and male medical faculty. *Discourse & Society, 14*, 191–220.

van Dijk, T. A. (1984). *Prejudice in discourse*. Amsterdam: John Benjamins.

van Dijk, T. A. (1986). *Racism in the press*. London: Edward Arnold.

van Dijk, T. A. (1987). *Communicating racism. Ethnic prejudice in thought and talk*. Newbury Park, CA: Sage.

van Dijk, T. A. (1993). *Elite discourse and racism*. Newbury Park, CA: Sage.

van Dijk, T. A. (2001). Multidisciplinary CDA, a plea for diversity. In R. Wodak & M. Meyer (Eds.), *Methods of critical discourse analysis* (pp. 95–120). London: Sage.

van Dijk, T. A. (2008a). *Discourse and context: A sociocognitive approach*. Cambridge, UK: Cambridge University Press.

van Dijk, T. A. (2008b). Critical discourse analysis and nominalization: Problem or pseudo-problem? *Discourse & Society, 19*, 821–828.

van Dijk, T. A. (2009). *Society and discourse*. Cambridge, UK: Cambridge University Press.

van Dijk, T. A., & Kintsch, W. (1983). *Strategies of discourse comprehension*. New York: Academic Press.

van Leeuwen, T. (2008). *Discourse and practice: New tools for critical discourse analysis*. Oxford, UK: Oxford University Press.

van Noppen, J.-P. (2004). CDA: A discipline come of age? *Journal of Sociolinguistics, 8*, 107–126.

Vannini, A. (2009). Critical ethnography. In S. L. Littlejohn & K. A. Foss (Eds.), *Encyclopedia of communication theory* (Vol. 1, pp. 223–226). Los Angeles: Sage.

Vannini, P., & McCright, A. M. (2007). Technologies of the sky: A socio-semiotic and critical analysis of televised weather discourse. *Critical Discourse Studies, 4*, 49–74.

Vico, G. (1948). *The new science*. New York: Ithaca.

Volosinov, V. N. (1973). *Marxism and the philosophy of language*. New York: Seminar press.

Vygotsky, L. S. (1986). *Thought and language*. Cambridge, MA: The MIT Press.

Wagner, I., & Wodak, R. (2006). Performing success: Identifying strategies of self-presentation in women's biographical narratives. *Discourse & Society, 17*, 385–411.

Watzlawick, P., Beavin, J. H., & Jackson, D. D. (1967). *Pragmatics of human communication*. New York: Norton.

Weatherall, A., & Gallois, C. (2003). Gendered identity: Complexities/intersections. In J. Holmes & M. Meyerhoff (Eds.), *Handbook of language and gender* (pp. 487–508). Oxford, UK: Basil Blackwell.

Weiss, G., & Wodak, R. (Eds.). (2007). *Critical discourse analysis: Theory and interdisciplinarity in critical discourse analysis.* London: Palgrave.

Wetherell, M. (1998). Positioning and interpretative repertoires: Conversation analysis and post-structuralism in dialogue. *Discourse & Society, 9*, 387–412.

Wetherell, M., & Potter, J. (1993). *Mapping the language of racism: Discourse and the legitimation of exploitation.* New York: Columbia University Press.

White, P. R. (2004). Subjectivity, evaluation and point of view in media discourse. In C. Coffin, A. Hewings, & K. O'Halloran (Eds.), *Applying English grammar: Functional and corpus approaches* (pp. 229–246). London: Arnold.

White, P. R. (2006). Evaluative semantics and ideological positioning in journalistic discourse. In I. Lassen, J. Strunck & T. Vestergaard (Eds.), *Mediating ideology in text and image: Ten critical studies* (pp. 37–67). Amsterdam: John Benjamins.

Widdowson, H. G. (1995). Discourse analysis: A critical view. *Language & Literature, 4*, 157–172.

Widdowson, H. G. (1998). The theory and practice of critical discourse analysis. *Applied Linguistics, 19*, 136–151.

Williams, R. (1977). *Marxism and literature.* Oxford, UK: Oxford University Press.

Wodak, R. (1989). *Language, power, and ideology: Studies in political discourse.* Amsterdam: John Benjamins.

Wodak, R. (1996). *Disorders of discourse.* London: Longman.

Wodak, R. (2002). Fragmented Identities: Redefining and recontextualizing national identity. In P. Chilton & S. Christina (Eds.), *Politics as text and talk: Analytic approaches to political discourse.* Amsterdam: John Benjamins.

Wodak, R. (2006). Mediation between discourse and society: Assessing cognitive approaches in CDA. *Discourse Studies, 8*, 179–190.

Wodak, R. (2007). Discourses in European Union organizations: Aspects of access, participation, and exclusion. *Text & Talk, 27*, 655–680.

Wodak, R., & Chilton, P. (2007). *A new agenda in critical discourse analysis, 2nd ed.* Amsterdam: John Benjamins.

Wodak, R., & Fairclough, N. (1997). Critical discourse analysis. In T. A. van Dijk (Ed.), *Discourse as social interaction* (pp. 258–284). London: Sage.

Wodak, R., & Kovacs, A. (2004). National identities in times of supra-national challenges: The debates on NATO and neutrality in Austria and Hungary *Journal of Language & Politics, 3*, 209–246.

Wodak, R., & Meyer, M. (Eds.). (2001). *Methods of critical discourse analysis.* London: Sage.

Wodak, R., & Meyer, M. (Eds.). (2009). *Methods of critical discourse analysis* (2nd ed.). London: Sage.

Wodak, R., & Richardson, J. E. (2009). On the politics of remembering (or not). *Critical Discourse Studies, 6*, 231–235.

12 *Commentary* Discourse, Context, and Interdisciplinarity

Ruth Wodak

University of Lancaster

1. Dimensions of Comparison

The three contributions I was asked to discuss cover relevant social phenomena from very different perspectives: on the one hand, language attitudes consciously and subconsciously co-determine our perceptions of others in all possible contexts; on the other, the expression of emotions, such as love, governs in manifold ways our interpersonal relationships, our behaviors, and our activities. And third, critical problem-oriented qualitative research, as illustrated by many approaches in Critical Discourse Analysis (CDA), offers an entry point to investigate salient factors co-determining our daily lives. Thus, the three chapters in this section differ significantly in that one chapter reviews research on a specific phenomenon (love), the second chapter reviews research on an important factor which accompanies all communication (language attitudes), whereas the third contribution discusses a particular school in the domain of Discourse Studies (Critical Discourse Analysis), which could be employed and applied to study both love or attitudes towards language use. Hence, the three chapters have to be regarded as belonging to different dimensions of scholarly work: oriented towards specific social phenomena (as objects of investigation) in contrast to theoretical and methodological approaches which could be used to study such phenomena.

In all three chapters, however, it becomes obvious, that—although the theoretical and methodological approaches differ significantly (see below)—the context of an utterance (such as social, cultural, historical, genre-specific, language-specific, peer-group specific, organizational, gender-specific, class-specific, and so forth) has a major impact on both decisions on how to study a phenomenon as well as on the enactment and realisation of attitudes, discourses, and emotions. It is thus not surprising that the chapters all foreground contextual factors and attempt to integrate them into existing (or new) research models.

In my necessarily brief considerations, I will thus focus on the salience of theorizing and operationalizing context in communication studies. Such a focus entails, I claim, both interdisciplinary research and the study of authentic, natural occurring communication, be it written, oral, or visual. Studying semiosis (or meaning-making in context) further implies integrating qualitative and quantitative methodologies and methods, and various modes of data sampling and collection (Titscher, Wodak, Meyer, & Vetter, 2000; Wodak & Krzyżanowski, 2008). Most importantly, I would like to point to the communication model which underlies context-dependent approaches: it is important to transcend simple sender-receiver models and to account for the complexity of language games (i.e., texts in context) (Wittgenstein 1967; Wodak 2008, 2009; Reisigl & Wodak 2009) in research on communication.

2. The Salience of Context

The concept of context has accompanied text linguistics, linguistic pragmatics, sociolinguistics, discourse studies, and CDA for many years (e.g., Beaugrande & Dressler 1981; Cicourel 1992; Wodak 1996, 2000; Wodak et al., 1990). Even the anthropologist Bronislaw Malinowski (1923, p. 206) emphasized that utterances can only be understood if their context is taken into consideration:

> [the utterance itself] becomes only intelligible when it is placed within its context of situation … which indicates on the one hand that the concept of context has to be broadened and on the other that the situation in which words are uttered can never be passed over as irrelevant to the linguistic expression….

At the same time, the Russian philosopher and linguist V. N. Volosinov (1973, p. 95) stated that

> Verbal communication can never be understood and explained outside of … connection with a concrete situation.… Language acquires life and historically evolves … in concrete verbal communication, and not in abstract linguistic system of language forms, nor in the individual psyche of speakers.

In spite of such theoretically relevant insights in the 1920s and 1930s, it took some time until modern mainstream linguistics actually took the detailed analysis of 'context' seriously. For example, Noam Chomsky restricted his theory of transformational grammar to context-isolated sentences; context was thus viewed as positioned outside of systematic research, part of performance and unpredictable in its impact on language behavior (Chomsky, 1965). At the outset of sociolinguistics in the 1970s, context was first operationalized only via static variables such as age, sex, social class, and so forth; linguistic units were then correlated statistically with these variables to illustrate the interdependence of language use and context, thus not accounting for the processual dynamics of all verbal and non-verbal interaction (Labov, 1972; Bernstein, 1987).

Apart from Ludwig Wittgenstein's Philosophical Investigations (1967) and the work by John Austin and John Searle who launched speech act theory and claimed that concepts only gained meaning in context, sociologists such as Aaron Cicourel (1992, p. 309) influenced the development of context-oriented research in (socio)linguistics and pragmatics:

> Observers or analysts, like participants of speech events, must continually face practical circumstances that are an integral part of all research or everyday living. As researchers, we obviously privilege some aspects of a context while minimizing or ignoring other conditions. The observer is obligated to justify what has been included and what has been excluded according to stated theoretical goals, methodological strategies employed, and the consistency and convincingness of an argument or analysis…

Thus, scholars of linguistic pragmatics started studying communicative actions. However, even in such micro-linguistic research the wider situational contexts as well as the co-text of utterances were usually neglected although important theoretical notions such as presupposition or implicature necessarily imply context-oriented in-depth analysis (Chilton, 2004; Johnstone, 2007; Schiffrin, 1994; Wodak, 2007). Another important and influential approach to context, Conversational Analysis, which has its roots in ethnomethodology, only integrates aspects of context into the analysis which are explicitly indexed by the speakers in a conversation (see Schegloff 1987; chapter 11, this volume). All other dimensions of context are viewed as speculative and thus not included into the analysis.

Some recent theoretical approaches in CDA such as by van Dijk (2001, 2008; see below) propose a socio-cognitive approach to the analysis of context. Context is linked to presupposed knowledge as well as to belief systems and presuppositions of the participants of a conversation. In this vein, van Dijk (2001, p. 11) emphasized that

> People not only form mental models of the events they talk about, but also of the events they participate in, including the communicative event of which their ongoing discourse is an inherent part….These subjective, mental representations of the communicative event and the current social situation as it constrains current discourse, will be called context models, or simply "contexts."

I claim, while drawing on the necessarily very briefly summarized research on context above, that the analysis of both love and language attitudes as realized in text and talk would be substantiated by drawing on systematic approaches to context which would also link to theories of neighboring disciplines, in the sense of an integrative interdisciplinarity (Wodak & Weiss, 2004). I will come back to this claim below when presenting approaches to context in CDA in more detail, such as the four-level model of context in the discourse-historical approach (DHA) in CDA (Richardson & Wodak, 2009a, b; Wodak, 2001, 2009).[1]

2.1 Context and Critical Discourse Analysis

All forms of Critical Discourse Analysis have roots in a synthesis of influences including: Rhetoric, Text linguistics, Anthropology, Philosophy, Socio-Psychology, Cognitive Science, Literary Studies and Sociolinguistics, as well as Applied Linguistics and Pragmatics (Wodak & Meyer, 2009). They have at least seven dimensions in common (van Dijk, 2008): an interest in naturally occurring language; a focus on larger units of analysis other than words and sentences (e.g., texts, discourses, conversations, and speech acts); an extension of linguistics beyond sentence grammar to encompass action and interaction; extension to non-verbal interactions; a focus on the dynamics of interaction over time; an interest in the role of context on language use; and analysis of language use via tools of text grammar (e.g., topics, turn-taking, argumentation, rhetoric, pragmatics). In order to address complex social problems, all forms of CDA are also inherently problem-oriented and interdisciplinary.

Van Dijk (2008) has put forward a radically new theory of discursive context as a construct that exists within the heads of participants. This critical, socio-cognitive theory of 'context models' has three principal components. First, they are based on experience and hierarchically structured, effectively acting as a heuristic guide for the individual to make sense of a communicative situation. They are therefore implicit and presupposed, influencing talk and text in indirect ways. Second, they are shared by individuals within groups, thus allowing for the fast mutual interpretation of relevant aspects of unique events and the production and comprehension of discourse. Third, the genre of the communicative situation is frequently known in advance, allowing participants to make presuppositions and thus engage in the purposeful production of appropriate texts and talk.

Van Dijk's novel conceptualization of discourse context is helpful to Social Science (Communication) researchers because it fundamentally challenges the narrow focus of many studies on the immediate, isolated text. It also overcomes the simplistic and flawed assumption that separates out the factors that might influence discourse at the micro- and the macro-level. However as van Dijk points out, because this context model is sociocognitive, it, obviously, cannot be directly observed. Hence, he proposes three methods to uncover the effects of this unobservable context model across different communicative situations: (a) the systematic comparison of cases; (b) controlled experiments; and (c) the observation of everyday situations. The problem therefore is not so much theoretical as methodological.

These suggested possibilities take us back to the three chapters under discussion. When studying language attitudes, most research has to date focused on experiments which allow for a controlled standardization of informants' responses (see chapter 9, this volume). However, as the authors rightly argue, existing models have not been able to account for many relevant factors which might influence language attitudes and do not allow the integration of the informants' sense making of specific contexts. Thus, it seems that controlled experiments have clear limitations if one would like to understand and explain language attitudes, their functions and impact, in concrete everyday and organizational contexts. To achieve such explanatory power, van Dijk's third proposal would need to be considered, namely the observation of everyday situations.

Such a study would, however, transcend the frequently used experimental setting and lead to more qualitatively oriented research which would have to include detailed and in-depth discourse analysis of very specific contexts and texts. The model proposed by Giles and Marlow (chapter 9, this volume) illustrates — heuristically, as all such necessarily abstract diagrams—dimensions, processes, and factors which might be relevant. The plethora of factors of different kinds (psychological, ideological, cultural, sociopsychological, and so forth) points to the necessity of an interdisciplinary study which would integrate ethnography, participant observation, tape-recording (or video-taping) of specific discursive events, interviews with the participants, etc.; i.e., triangulation of methods and methodologies, and a range of theoretically and epistemologically very different approaches. In any case, a systematic way of examining the manifold influences of contextual constraints on manifestations of language attitudes seems necessary for relevant research on language attitudes. Studying the expression of emotions also implies, as Gareis and Wilkins (chapter 10, this volume) suggest taking into account a range of cultural, gender-specific, class-specific, group-specific, and historical factors, apart from genre-inherent characteristics (i.e., love is expressed and performed in significantly different ways, in popular culture TV soaps or films or in everyday concrete situations, in fiction or reality, in hetero- or homosexual relationships, and in different cultures across the globe). Literary scholars, psychologists, psychoanalysts, historians, sociologists, media scholars, cultural studies and communication scholars all have developed different approaches to, and concepts of, emotions and of their display, performance, and enactment. Emotions can be explicitly expressed or latently inferred, they can be verbalized or depend on gaze or gestures, and so forth. The cultural traditions and politeness conventions governing the expression of emotions in public or private have to be investigated in detail. Indeed, similar expressions might indicate different emotions in different cultural and situational contexts; they are clearly context-dependent in their meaning and illocutionary effect. Thus, any in-depth study which would attend to all the factors mentioned in the chapter by Gareis and Wilkins would need to integrate a systematic contextual analysis apart from some standardized categorization via a range of clearly defined variables through experiments, surveys or questionnaires. As emotions can be and frequently are expressed latently, indirectly, or nonverbally, any quantitative content-analysis or corpus-linguistic analysis would certainly not suffice.

2.2 *A Multi-Level Model of Context*

Although Tracy, Martínez-Guillem, Robles, and Casteline rightly mention important challenges to CDA approaches and some important limitations of CDA research to date (chapter 11, this volume), the context of utterances has always been investigated in related studies, albeit in different ways (see summary of van Dijk's conceptualization above). In this chapter, I would like to focus briefly on DHA, which has made the systematic analysis of context and its dialectical relationships to meaning-making to one of its priorities.

The DHA enables analysis of the historical (i.e., intertextual) dimension of discursive practices by exploring the ways in which particular genres of discourse are subject to change through time, and also by integrating social theories to explain context. Following Foucault (1972), historical context can also mean the history and subsystem of meetings and narratives in an organization or any other institutional or every day event; intertextuality can, for example, also encompass the media reporting about specific events over time which are all interrelated in complex way through the recontextualization of quotes, arguments, or specific stances and positions (Triandafyllidou, Wodak, & Krzyżanowski, 2009). Consequently, history can involve studying how language use changes over shorter timescales, for example, during one meeting (over a certain amount of time) or over several meetings, as part of latent and manifest rules and norms that serve to rationalize, explain, and make sense of organizational events (e.g., Lalouschek, Menz, & Wodak, 1990; Mumby & Clair, 1997; Wodak, 1996). Or history can indicate how perceptions of specific events have changed over time due to conflicting narratives and accounts of a specific experience—a phenomenon which can be frequently observed in the discursive construction of national or transnational identities (Heer, Manoschek, Pollak, & Wodak, 2008; Wodak, De Cillia, Reisigl, & Liebhart, 2009).

The DHA has already been used in various organizational contexts (e.g., courtroom interactions, crisis intervention centers, hospitals, political (transnational) organizations, media studies, bureaucracies, and schools (Muntigl, Weiss, & Wodak, 2000; Krzyżanowski & Oberhuber, 2007 Wodak, 1996, 2009;) and in the analysis of identity politics in different regional and national contexts (Unger, 2010). Given that it is ideal for looking at the way in which actors deploy discursive knowledge, mobilize representations, and get their views accepted in a "muscular" way in the process of organizational communication, for example, this approach has great potential to contribute to communication discourse research. For instance, Kwon, Clarke, and Wodak (2009) have recently shown that DHA can be used to shed new light on how meaning and action in organizations is shaped discursively through power, hegemony, and ideology, by giving researchers the methodological and theoretical traction they need to examine how personal social power develops through naturally occurring talk in strategic discussion. This ability to link critical theory with rigorous empirical investigation is a crucial feature of DHA.

Conceptually, the empirical event under investigation such as love or language attitudes in a very specific setting could be viewed as a phenomenon that has discursive manifestations across four heuristic levels of context (Wodak, 2009):

1. the immediate, text of the communicative event in question (e.g., the conversation between friends or a negotiation between managers, thus a particular detailed transcript of talk);
2. the intertextual and interdiscursive relationship between utterances, texts, genres and discourses (e.g., transcripts of individual interviews with the respective participants involved in the conversation or negotiation, other conversations with the same participants in different settings, reports about the on-going negotiations in minutes or emails, and so forth);
3. the extralinguistic social (e.g., physical gestures, facial expressions, postures, etc.) and environmental (e.g., room size and layout) variables and institutional frames (e.g., latent or formal hierarchical structure, informal power relations in a friendship, cultural constraints and conventions, etc.) of a specific context of situation (derived, for example, from observer notes and reflections on direct observations of the communicative event); and
4. the broader sociopolitical and historical context which discursive practices are embedded in and related to (e.g., knowledge derived from ethnography study of the relationships, aspects of the broader social and cultural macro-environment that influence the talk and conversations).

Understanding the empirical phenomenon as being embedded in hierarchical levels of context then allows researchers to unpack the relationship between the motivations (e.g., underlying agendas, ingrained attitudes and practices) of the respective actors and their actions (i.e., what they say and do). Thus, the analysts would be able to make sense of the process of meaning construction and also understand and explain the effects of emotions or of language attitudes. In this way, the DHA with its multilevel concept of context could have significant potential for providing new insights into particular social phenomena under context-sensitive conditions (Clarke, Kwon, & Wodak, in press).

3. Perspectives

The linguistic and discursive turns in communication studies are certainly very timely and welcome. Taking these turns seriously, however, implies integrating approaches from Discourse Studies, CDA, pragmatics, and sociolinguistics which have all developed into multidisciplinary or interdisciplinary fields. Moreover, it is obvious that we need to conceptualize communication in all its forms as multi-determined, situated, fluid and dynamic, and dependent of many different, historical, social, socio-psychological, ideological, collective and individual factors. As social phenomena are complex, multiple theoretical and methodological approaches are necessary for adequate research. To be able to understand and explain such complexity, new theories and methodologies and their innovative integration are called for which transcend the traditional (frequently Euro-centric or Anglo-centric) disciplinary boundaries.

Notes

1. Recently, DHA in CDA has been successfully combined with *Begriffsgeschichte* (or conceptual history) as developed by Reinhart Koselleck (1989; see Stråth & Wodak, 2009). *Begriffsgeschichte* traces the change of meanings of individual concepts across historical periods while focussing on historical sources of all kinds and deconstructing *semantic fields* in which the respective concepts are embedded. Such an analysis could, of course, prove most fruitful in the analysis of concepts such as love over time in different cultures and languages.

References

Bernstein, B. (1987). Social class, codes and communication. In U. Ammon, N. Dittmar, & K. J. Mattheier (Eds.), *Sociolinguistics: An international handbook of the science of society* (Vol. 1, pp. 563–579). Berlin: de Gruyter.

Chilton, P. (2004). *Analysing political discourse. Theory and practice.* London: Routledge.

Chomsky, N. (1965). *Aspects of a theory of syntax.* Boston: MIT Press.

Cicourel, A. (1992). The interpretation of communicative contexts: Examples from medical encounters. In A. Duranti & C. Goodwin (Eds.), *Rethinking context: Language as an interactive phenomenon* (pp. 291–310). Cambridge, UK: Cambridge University Press.

Clarke, I., Kwon, W., & Wodak, R. (in press). A contextensitive approach to analysing talk in meetings *British Journal of Management.*

de Beaugrande, R., & Dressler, U. W. (1981). *Introduction to text linguistics.* New York: Longman.

Foucault, M. (1972). *The archeology of knowledge.* London: Routledge.

Heer, H., Manoschek, W., Pollak, A., & Wodak, R. (Eds.). (2008). *The construction of history. Remembering the war of annilihation.* Basingstoke, UK: Palgrave.

Johnstone, B. (2007). *Discourse analysis* (2nd ed.). Oxford, UK: Blackwell.

Koselleck, R. (1989) *Vergangene Zukunft. Zur Semantik geschichtlicher Zeiten* [Past future. On the semantics of historical time]. Frankfurt, Germany: Suhrkamp.

Krzyżanowski, M., & Oberhuber, F. (2007). *(Un)Doing Europe: Discourses and practices of negotiating the EU constitution* (Vol. 35). Bern, Switzerland: Peter Lang.

Kwon, W., Clarke, I., & Wodak, R. (2009). Organizational decision-making, discourse, and power: Integrating across contexts and scales. *Discourse & Communication, 3,* 273–302.

Labov, W. (1972). *Language in the inner city.* Philadelphia: University of Pennsylvania Press.

Lalouschek, J., Menz, F., & Wodak, R. (1990). *Alltag in der Ambulanz* [Daily routine in an outpatients' ward]. Tübingen, Germany: Niemeyer.

Malinowski, B. (1923). The problem of meaning in primitive languages. In C. K. Ogden & I. A. Richards (Eds.), *The meaning of meaning* (pp. 146–152). New York: Harcourt.

Mumby, D. K., & Clair, R. P. (1997) Organizational discourse. In T. A. Van Dijk. (Ed.), *Discourse as social interaction* (Vol. 2, pp. 181–205). London: Sage.

Muntigl, P., Weiss, G., & Wodak, R. (2000). *European Union discourses on un/employment. An interdisciplinary approach to employment policy-making and organisational change.* Amsterdam: John Benjamins.

Reisigl, M., & Wodak, R. (2009). The discourse-historical approach. In R. Wodak & M. Meyer (Eds.), *Methods of critical discourse analysis* (2nd rev. ed., pp. 87–121). London: Sage.

Richardson, J. E., & Wodak, R. (2009a). The impact of visual racism: Visual arguments in political leaflets of Austrian and British far-right parties. *Controversies, 2,* 45–77.

Richardson, J. E., & Wodak, R. (2009b). Recontextualising fascist ideologies of the past: Rightwing discourses on employment and nativism in Austria and the United Kingdom. *Critical Discourse Studies, 4,* 251–267.

Schegloff, E. (1987). Between micro and macro: Contexts and other connections. In J. Alexander, B. Giesen, R. Munch, & N. Smelser (Eds.), *The micro-macro link* (pp. 207–236). Berkeley: University of California Press.

Schiffrin, D. (1994). *Approaches to discourse.* Cambridge, UK: Blackwell.

Stråth, B., & Wodak, R. (2009). Europe-discourse-politics-media-history: Constructing crises. In A. Triandafillydou, R. Wodak, & M. Krzyzanowski (Eds.), *Europe in crisis: The European public sphere and national media in the post-war period* (pp. 15–33). Basingstoke, UK: Palgrave.

Titscher, S., Wodak, R., Meyer, M., & Vetter, E. (2000). *Methods of text and discourse analysis.* London: Sage.

Triandafyllidou, A., Wodak, R., & Krzyżanowski, M. (2009). (Eds.). *Europe in crisis: The European public sphere and national media in the post-war period.* Basingstoke, UK: Palgrave.

Unger, J. (2010) Legitimating inaction: Differing identity constructions of the Scots language. *European Journal of Cultural Studies, 13*(1), 99–118.

van Dijk, T. A. (2001). Discourse, ideology and context. *Folia Linguistica,* XXX/1-2, 11–40.

van Dijk, T. A. (2008). *Discourse and context: A sociocognitive approach.* Cambridge, UK: Cambridge University Press.

Volosinov, V. I. (1973). *Marxism and the philosophy of language.* London: Seminar Press. (Original work published 1928)

Wittgenstein, L. (1967). *Philosophische Untersuchungen* [Philosophical investigations]. Oxford, UK: Blackwell.

Wodak, R. (1996). *Disorders of discourse.* London: Longman.

Wodak, R. (2000). From conflict to consensus? The co-construction of a policy paper. In P. Muntigl, G. Weiss, & R. Wodak (Eds.), *European Union discourses on unemployment. An Interdisciplinary approach to employment policy-making and organisational change* (pp. 73–114). Amsterdam: John Benjamins.

Wodak, R. (2001). The discourse-historical approach. In R. Wodak & M. Meyer (Eds.), *Methods of critical discourse analysis* (pp. 63–95). London: Sage.

Wodak, R. (2007). Pragmatics and critical discourse analysis. *Pragmatics and Cognition, 15*(1), 203–225.

Wodak, R. (2008). Introduction: Discourse studies — important concepts and terms.

In R. Wodak & M. Krzyżanowski (Eds.), *Qualitative discourse analysis for the social sciences* (pp. 1–29). Basingstoke, UK: Palgrave.

Wodak, R. (2009). *The discourse of politics in action: Politics as usual.* Basingstoke, UK: Palgrave.

Wodak, R., Pelikan, J., Nowak, P., Gruber, H., De Cillia, R., & Mitten, R. (1990). *"Wir sind alle unschuldige Täter!" Diskurshistorische Studien zum Nachkriegsantisemitismus* ["We all are innocent perpetrators!" Discourse historical studies on post-war anti-Semitism]. Frankfurt, Germany: Suhrkamp.

Wodak, R., & Weiss, G. (2004). Möglichkeiten und Grenzen der Diskursanalyse: Konstruktion europäischer Identitäten [Possibilities and limitations of discourse analysis: Construction of European Identities]. In O. Panagl & R. Wodak (Eds.), *Text und Kontext: Theoriemodelle und methodische Verfahren im transdisziplinären Vergleich* [Text and context: Theoretical models and methodologies in the interdisciplinary comparison] (pp. 67–86). Würzburg, Germany: Königshausen & Neumann.

Wodak, R., & Krzyzanowski, M. (Eds.). (2008). *Qualitative discourse analysis for the social sciences.* Basingstoke, UK: Palgrave.

Wodak, R., & Meyer, M. (2009). Critical discourse analysis: history, agenda, theory and methodology. In R. Wodak & M. Meyer (Eds.), *Methods of critical discourse analysis* (2nd ed., pp. 1–33). London: Sage.

Wodak, R., De Cillia, R., Reisigl, M., & Liebhart, K. (2009). *The discursive construction of national identity* (2nd rev. ed.). Edinburgh: Edinburgh University Press.

Part IV

Emerging Perspectives on Issues of Enduring Importance

CHAPTER CONTENTS

13 Anonymous Communication

Unmasking Findings Across Fields

Craig R. Scott

Rutgers University

Stephen A. Rains

University of Arizona

Muge Haseki

Rutgers University

Research examining anonymous communication has a rich history spanning several academic fields and numerous decades. Despite this broad and longstanding interest, few attempts have been made to summarize the body of scholarship on anonymous communication. This chapter reviews research on anonyms communication from journalism, organization studies, economics, information systems, psychology, social psychology, computer-mediated communication, and education—tracing the findings related to three process (i.e., participation, influence, and feedback) and outcome (i.e., trust, performance, and identification) variables. The findings reflect the diversity of ways in which anonymity is conceptualized and operationalized across fields. Although the results related to several of the variables are mixed, there is sufficient evidence to suggest that anonymity facilitates participation and undermines trust.

From anonymous Puritan attacks against the Anglican Church in the 1500s to a wide range of unsigned paintings and writings through much of recorded history, and from the pseudonymously published Federalist Papers over two centuries ago to the millions of unidentified online messages today, anonymous communication has occurred, and its merits debated, in numerous countries at numerous times. Despite this history, and a general view that anonymity is a basic right of free speech in most democracies (Bronco, 2004), Crews (2007) suggests the "long tradition of anonymous communications faces an image problem in today's age of spam, computer viruses, spyware, denial-of-service attacks on websites, and identity theft" (p. 97). Indeed, one of the key reasons anonymous communication is especially relevant today is due to the rise of new information and communication technologies (ICTs)—especially the Internet—which is distinctive in part because of the anonymity it affords many of its users (Bargh & McKenna, 2004; Turkle, 1995). As Bronco (2004) notes, communication technology makes anonymity more possible on one level, while simultaneously making communication more identifiable through logs, profiles, and other identifying information.

Other forces have led to a renewed sense of interest in anonymous communication. Ongoing debates about anonymous news sources and unidentified leaks have grown with the proliferation of alternative media and a more competitive push toward breaking news quickly. Corporate scandals (e.g., Enron) have led to passage of the Sarbanes-Oxley Act in the United States, which requires provision of anonymous means (e.g., anonymous telephone tiplines) for organizational members to report wrongdoing (Walker, 2004). Another major force stems from heightened concerns about security and calls for accountability following the events of September 11, 2001. Although several scholars have noted that identification technologies have greatly expanded in recent years (cf. Marx, 2001), Bronco (2004) underscores this point, explaining that "judicial and organizational officials are increasingly likely to take actions limiting one's privacy and to provide identifying information in the name of national security—all of which erodes anonymity" (p. 127). This in turn has led to resistance in the form of new types of technologies designed to protect anonymity (Saco, 2002).

Considered together, these influences make anonymous communication an important topic for scholars across a number of fields. Though the concept is generally understood, it is somewhat complex and often confused with related constructs such as privacy.[1] Anonymous (1998) suggests the following definition for anonymity relevant to communication research: "the degree to which a communicator perceives the message source is unknown and unspecified" (p. 387). Source knowledge refers to issues of familiarity and knowing one by name and/or sight. Specification refers to the range of possible communicators (e.g., member of some small club, anyone online). Anonymous also claims anonymity is usefully considered as both technical and perceptual, and that it is more continuous than absolute. Indeed, confidentiality (when some know one's identity, but agree not to share with others) and pseudonymity (where one uses a persistent alternate identity that does not necessarily correspond to one's legal identity) both represent partial anonymity. Marx (1999, 2004) also offers useful sociological work on types of identity knowledge, which speaks directly to what makes individuals more or less anonymous when communicating. In addition to one's name, these include demographics, location information, networks/relationships, objects owned, what one does, what one believes/feels, photos/images, and other trace information. Even with its obvious relevance to the discipline of communication, anonymity is a cross-disciplinary topic studied in several different fields, including psychology, economics, journalism and education. Anonymity is examined using a variety of methods and range of assumptions. Yet, relatively few works have attempted to theorize or summarize research in this area. One notable exception is a series of articles emerging from a 1997 conference and published in a special issue of *The Information Society* (Froomkin, 1999; Kling, Lee, Teich, & Frankel, 1999; Marx, 1999; Nissenbaum, 1999; Teich, Frankel, Kling, & Lee, 1999; Wayner, 1999). At about the same time, a theoretical model of anonymous communication was published in the communication literature (Anonymous, 1998). Several years later, Rains and Scott (2007) published a model of receiver responses to anonymous communication and Christopherson (2007) offered a literature review of anonymity in Internet social interactions. Finally, Morio and Buchholz (2009) proposed a hierarchical structure of anonymity conditions specific to online interaction. Despite the value of all this scholarship, none is comprehensive in its efforts to describe, review, and/or theorize anonymous communication.

Our goal is to review major strands of research about anonymous communication in a single chapter, and analyze/synthesize findings across fields and research traditions to offer suggestions for moving forward on this important contemporary topic. Such an effort will ideally reveal a clearer, research-based picture of the processes and outcomes linked to anonymous communication—as well as identify key gaps in our knowledge and potential points of integration. We begin with our literature review in each of eight major disciplinary and interdisciplinary research areas. We conclude by identifying and discussing several areas of overlap in our findings and then suggesting directions for future research. Figure 13.1 illustrates the specific topics and fields examined in this chapter.

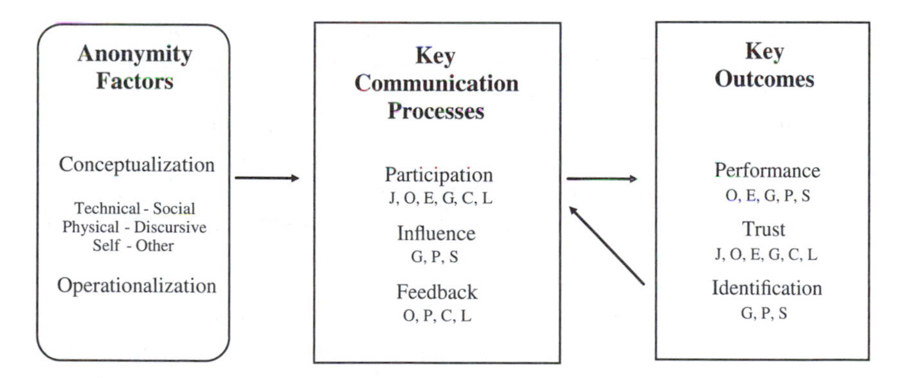

Figure 13.1 Descriptive model of anonymous communication research.
Note. Letter codes for each process and outcome refer to the research traditions containing relevant findings: J = Journalism, O = Organization/Management Studies, E = Economics, G = Group Support Systems from Information Systems, P = Psychology, S = SIDE in Social Psychology, C = Computer-Mediated Communication, and L = Education (Learning).

Anonymous Communication

In order to assess the scope of peer-reviewed research examining anonymous communication, a broad search of EBSCO databases was first conducted.[2] The results of that effort led us to concentrate on original research in eight substantial areas within and across several research traditions: journalism, organization/management studies, economics, information systems (specifically group support systems, or GSSs), psychology, social psychology (especially social identity and deindividuation [SIDE] studies), interdisciplinary work on computer-mediated communication, and education. We have excluded research on technical protocols for designing anonymous computer systems as well as any research about the role of anonymity in the research process itself. We have also excluded research about anonymity from legal and literary studies, which is typically not original social scientific research comparable to that reported here. In an attempt to make sense of a sizable body of research that spans multiple different research traditions across several decades, we organize the review around three topics for each area of literature. These topics emerge primarily from the findings that cut across these areas. However, they are also consistent with other theoretical work, meta-analyses, and overviews of anonymity more generally (e.g., Anonymous, 1998; Bronco, 2004; Marx, 1999, 2004; Pinsonneault & Heppel, 1997; Postmes & Lea, 2000; Rains & Scott, 2007). Figure 13.1 provides a graphic representation of the research examined here and the research traditions relevant to each topic.

First, we begin by looking at the conceptual and operational definitions of anonymity. These include distinctions between key types of anonymity studied in the various fields: technical and social anonymity; physical and discursive anonymity; and self and other anonymity. *Technical anonymity* refers to anonymity (ostensibly) conferred by a feature of a technology, and *social anonymity* is the degree of anonymity that individuals perceive the technology actually offers. *Physical anonymity* occurs when one cannot see or is otherwise unaware that others are physically present, and *discursive anonymity* involves not being able to identify the name of a particular source or attribute a message to a particular source. *Self anonymity* is a sender's perception that he or she is anonymous to others, and *other anonymity* refers to a receiver's perception of a sender's anonymity. Central to these distinctions is the notion that anonymity is sometimes considered to be a discrete construct (i.e., individuals are either fully identified or completely anonymous) and other times considered to be continuous (i.e., individual may be relatively more or less identified). Additionally, this includes an analysis of the various ways in which anonymity is measured, manipulated, and otherwise assessed in this research.

Second, we examine three communication processes that seem relevant to much of this literature. Specifically, we examine three variables—each of which underscores a tension in the literature on anonymous communication; i.e., arguments exist suggesting that anonymity facilitates and or undermines the processes discussed here. *Participation* involves the level of contribution one perceives can be made as well as the actual quantity of messages communicated. Here we examine the ways in which anonymity supports and/or undermines an environment or situation that fosters individual involvement and contribution Research on *influence* focuses on factors involving the persuasion of others; thus, we broadly construe it to include research ranging from leaders who shape others' views to processes of choice shift as various group dynamics alter individual decisions. The research reported here involves the ways that anonymity facilitates and/or mitigates ability to impact the perceptions, attitudes, or behaviors of others. Finally, *feedback* processes concern efforts to evaluate another's performance or otherwise communicate information about one's own performance. The research here focuses more specifically on those instances where anonymity encourages and/or diminishes the exchange of evaluative information.

Third, we examine three key outcomes related to anonymity and anonymous communication. Although research points to several consequences linked to anonymity, we concentrate on a smaller set linked to traditional outcome measures and those more regularly tied to anonymity. *Performance* represents a traditional research outcome assessing quantity or quality of various forms of output. Here we examined the positive and negative implications of anonymity for this key measure of task accomplishment. *Trust* assessments are more specific to anonymous communicators and/or their messages, and pertain to issues of believability, credibility, and/or legitimacy. The research reported here analyzes how anonymity enhances and/or diminishes perceptions of communicators and their messages. Similarly, issues of *identification* as it pertains to a sense of connection and identity are also examined here—even though it is usefully viewed as both an outcome of anonymous interaction and as more of a process factor (see Scott, Corman, & Cheney, 1998).

Before we begin our review, two clarifications are needed. First, the research traditions we review do not necessarily cover all six processes and outcomes examined; however, as Figure 13.1 helps illustrate, each of these literatures addresses at least two key areas. Second, we seek to include both sender- and receiver-focused perspectives on anonymous communication when reviewing this research because that best reflects the variation in this literature as it addresses these key processes and outcomes.

Journalism

Anonymity has received a considerable amount of attention in journalism research. Source anonymity has been argued to be "an interesting dilemma for journalists … many look upon the practice as, at best, a 'necessary evil'" (Wulfemeyer, 1985, p. 81). Much of the research on anonymity in journalism involves conducting content analyses to determine the use and prevalence of anonymous sources in news reporting. A few studies cited below manipulate anonymity as an independent variable to evaluate how news stories that include an anonymous source are perceived by readers. Throughout this work, anonymity is typically studied in regard to a particular news source cited within a news story. Though anonymity is not frequently defined, it is conceptualized in journalism research as a continuous construct referring to sources who are unnamed or have their identity "veiled" (Culbertson, 1976). Anonymity is operationalized through the use of pseudonyms, non-specific attributions (e.g., "senior officials"), and/or citing a source without including the name of a specific person. In this section, we review literature focusing on the implications of anonymity in journalism for participation and trust.

Participation. An avenue to explore the implications of anonymity for participation in the context of journalism is to consider how and when anonymous sources are used in news reporting. Several content analyses have been conducted to address this issue, focusing mostly on the use of anonymous sources in newspapers. In general, the findings from research conducted during the past 35 years suggest that anonymity is a staple of news reporting. Anonymous sources have been used in 54% of analyzed stories from the *New York Times* and the *Washington Post* (Culbertson, 1975) and between 70% and 81% of analyzed stories in *Newsweek* and *Time* (Culbertson, 1976; Wulfemeyer, 1985). Wulfemeyer (1985) analyzed one randomly selected issue per month of *Time* and *Newsweek* during 1982 and reported a mean of approximately 4 anonymous attributions per story. In a more recent study, Martin-Kratzer and Thorson (2007) conducted an analysis of 16 newspapers and 7 television news programs sampled during 2003 and 2004. Forty-one percent of the television network news stories analyzed and 21% of newspaper stories analyzed included at least one anonymous.

Several studies have examined the use of anonymous sources in addressing a general news topic or particular news event. Uses of anonymous sources in stories about international news and war, in particular, have been considered. Blankenburg (1992) examined stories published in the *New York Times,* the *Washington Post,* and the *Los Angeles Times*, reporting that 23%–30% of national and international news stories printed in the main news section included an anonymous source in February, 1990, and 26%–35% did so in February, 1991. Sheehy (2008) found that 70% of all stories about foreign news published on page one of the the *Washington Post* during even-numbered years from 1970 to 2000 included an anonymous source. Moreover, there is some evidence that anonymous sources are more likely to be used in stories about war than in non-war stories (Blankenburg, 1992; Martin-Kratzer & Thorson, 2007).

Research also has examined the use of anonymity in reporting about specific events. Anonymity has been examined in news coverage following the September 11 (Reynolds & Barnett, 2003) and anthrax (Swain, 2007) attacks, celebrity trials (Carpenter, Lacy, & Fico, 2006), the 2004 Democratic primary (Zeldes, Fico, & Lacy, 2008), U.S.-China relations (Chang, 1989), and international incidents (Algraawi & Culbertson, 1987). These studies found greater uses of anonymous sources in sports-section stories about crime and vice or salaries (Blankenburg, 1992), stories about high-profile crimes (Carpenter et al., 2006), stories with speculation and conflicting reports (Swain, 2007), and depending on the specific news organization reporting (Reynolds & Barnett, 2003) or the nationality and type of sources included in the story (Algraawi & Culbertson, 1987).

In addition to the general use of anonymous sources in news reporting, researchers have examined the various labels applied to anonymous sources and to whom these labels are applied. Culbertson's (1975) analysis of the *New York Times* and the *Washington Post* showed that the most common labels used to describe anonymous sources were: "officials," "spokesman," and "sources." Of note, the word "anonymous" was the least frequently used label. "Official" and "aide" were the most common labels found in two studies of *Time* and *Newsweek* (Culbertson, 1976; Wulfemeyer, 1985). Research has also examined the entities that may serve as anonymous sources. In two studies, Culbertson (1975, 1976) found that persons were the most common anonymous sources followed by organizations, media institutions, and nations. In Chang's (1989) study of front-page articles in the *New York Times* and the *Washington Post* from 1950 to 1984 about U.S. policy regarding China, the most commonly cited sources were from the Executive Branch followed by unnamed sources, China, and Congress. Finally, a few studies have been conducted considering the utility and implications of anonymity for allowing sources and reporters to share confidential or private information. Gassaway (1988) conducted interviews with 15 individuals who had served as a confidential news source. Most of the respondents indicated that one motivation for serving as an anonymous source was to make information available to the public. The respondents also indicated being selective about the specific reporters with whom they shared information. An outcome of such selectivity is that 11 of the 15 respondents had their confidentiality maintained by the reporter.

St. Dizier (1985) surveyed two different groups of newspaper reporters during 1974 and 1984. All of the journalists reported using anonymous sources in 1974 and 97% did so in 1984. However, reporters felt significantly less hampered by not using anonymous sources and were significantly more likely to consult with their editor prior to using an anonymous source in 1984 than in 1974.

Trust. Beyond assessing the frequency with which anonymous sources are used in news reporting, several studies have examined the impact of source anonymity on perceptions of the general quality of news stories and sources. One issue of interest in this research has been perceptions of different labels used to refer to an anonymous source (Adams, 1962, 1964; Riffe, 1979). Adams (1962) reported some variation in the acceptability of source labels, with "the U.S. Government" and "the government" as the two most acceptable sources, and "indications," "trustworthy indications," and "political leaders" as the three least acceptable. Riffe (1979) attempted to replicate and extend

Adams' (1962) work. His findings suggest the possibility that perceptions of some anonymous source labels may have changed over time; 7 of the 18 labels originally used by Adams (1962) were perceived to be significantly less acceptable in 1979 than in 1960. Of those seven sources, three referred explicitly to government: "the U.S. government," "the government," and "a high government official." "Indications" was the only label rated significantly more acceptable in 1979.

Story attribution has also been experimentally manipulated and tested in several studies (Adams, 1964; Culbertson & Somerick, 1976; Fedler & Counts, 1981; Hale, 1984; Smith, 2007; Sternadori & Thorson, 2009). Participants read a story in which source attribution is manipulated and then register their perceptions of the story and or source. The results of this research generally suggest that stories with anonymous sources may be perceived no differently than stories with identified sources (Adams, 1964; Culbertson & Somerick, 1976; Hale, 1984; Smith, 2007). Stories with anonymous sources were rarely rated more (Fedler & Counts, 1981) or less (Sternadori & Thorson, 2009) positively than stories with identified sources or no sources at all.

In contrast to the experimental studies examining the influence of source anonymity, the results of Culbertson and Somerick's (1976) cross-sectional survey suggests that perceptions of anonymous sources in news may be more varied. When asked about anonymous news sources in general, more than two-thirds of participants reported them to be less believable than identified sources—though 14% said that they were *more* believable. Further, respondents were presented with a list of pro and con arguments and asked to rate, overall, whether anonymous news sources are good and bad. Almost two-thirds of participants reported that anonymous sources are good.

Organization/Management Studies

Research addressing anonymity in an organizational context tends to center on two topics primarily: whistleblowing (and other reports of wrongdoing) or various assessment/feedback programs. A smaller set of studies examines ethics or anonymity more generally. This research—which employs survey questionnaires, interviews, field experiments, and other methods—occurs in several developed countries and is most commonly published in business/management journals.

Anonymity in this research tradition is both a predictor and outcome variable as well as a theme emerging in more qualitative studies. Thus, anonymity (and some identified comparison group) is operationalized in a variety of ways: use of real names with details or an assumed name without details (Park, Blenkinsopp, Oktem, & Omurgonulsen, 2008), name or not (Bamberger, Erev, Kimmel, & Oref-Chen, 2005; Roch & McNall, 2007), individualized reports vs. group summaries (Antonioni, 1994), perceived confidence in ability to preserve one's anonymity (Miceli, Roach, & Near, 1988), in-person vs. telephone channels (Ayers & Kaplan, 2005; Kaplan, Pany, Samuels, & Zhang, 2009), through scenarios where others are described as unidentified or identified (Bloom & Hautaluoma, 2001), etc. The only research to define anonymity, for readers or study participants, uses a more general definition not unique to this research tradition: "Anonymous communication occurs when the identity of the sender of a message is not known or specified for the receiver of that message. It is based on people's perceptions" (Scott & Rains, 2005, p. 167). In this section we review the role of anonymity in organizations as it pertains to participation, feedback, performance and trust.

Participation. Some of the strongest evidence that anonymity facilitates participation comes from the research on whistleblowing and reporting of wrongdoing. In a large study of federal agency employees, Miceli et al. (1988) found that respondents who are more aware of complaint channels and more confident identity would not be revealed were more likely to blow the whistle. This was especially true for anonymous whistleblowing via internal channels, and somewhat less so for confidence in identity not being revealed when whistleblowing anonymously via external channels. Kaplan et al.'s (2009) experiment with MBA students reporting fraud found that participants were more likely to report wrongdoing to an anonymous telephone hotline than to a nonanonymous internal audit department—and reporting intentions to the hotline grew stronger as personal costs of anonymous reporting declined. Shawver and Clements (2008), in a study of accounting professionals, reported, "if guaranteed their anonymity, accounting professionals are more likely to blow the whistle internally for being asked to approve the performance report with the highest dollar value," which led them to conclude "employees may not be comfortable disclosing their identities when reporting unethical actions of higher dollar amounts" (p. 35). In a similar study with graduate business professionals, Ayers and Kaplan (2005) found no difference in intentions to use a nonanonymous or anonymous reporting channel; however, the study did find that anonymous reporting intentions are primarily based on cost-benefit analysis (and such costs are lower with anonymous reporting mechanisms).

Anonymity may promote participation beyond whistleblowing also. Schwartz's (2004) interview study of employees, managers, and ethics officers at several large Canadian organizations suggested that having an anonymous phone line serves a purpose, especially when one is uncomfortable talking to his/her manager. Scott and Rains (2005) reported two studies that explore anonymous organizational communication more broadly and more directly. Their research documented at least some use of a wide range of anonymous forms ranging from suggestion boxes, anonymous calls, and anonymous feedback to unsigned messages, anonymous computer-mediated communication (CMC), and whistleblowing.

There is some evidence in the organization/management literature that anonymity may be particularly valuable for encouraging participation among certain marginalized groups. Kaplan et al.'s (2009) finding that participants were more likely to report wrongdoing to an anonymous telephone hotline than to a nonanonymous internal audit department was stronger for women than men. Although there were some gender differences (e.g., males were more likely than females to use remailers) and variations in organizational type (e.g., public sector employees more likely than others to be regular users of various forms of anonymous organizational communication) in Scott and Rains's (2005) study, the quality of one's relationships with others was most consistently linked to use of anonymity in the workplace. Scott and Rains reported that quality of relations with one's supervisor were lower for users than nonusers of four anonymous forms: whistleblowing, electronic group meeting systems, unidentified comments in suggestion boxes, and anonymous emails/remailers.

Feedback. Several studies have examined the tension between anonymity and accountability during upward appraisals (e.g., conducting a performance review of one's supervisor). Antonioni's (1994) experimental field study of 38 managers and 183 subordinates in an insurance company examined anonymous feedback (included summary reports with no individual information) and what he called accountable feedback (provided the individually completed assessments to the managers). As predicted, managers in the accountability condition evaluated the feedback process more favorably than did managers in the anonymity group; conversely (but as predicted), subordinates in the anonymity condition rated the feedback process more favorably than did their counterparts in the accountability group. Post-study debriefing comments suggested that fear of reprisal was the primary reason subordinates preferred anonymous feedback. Although the study had no independent measure of accuracy, subordinates in the accountability group rated their managers' leadership more positively than did subordinates using anonymous appraisal. Roch and McNall (2007) also examined this issue, but with 315 industrial and organizational psychology students evaluating their professor—and with rather different results. Although half the students wrote their names on evaluations and half did not, a perceptual measure of how anonymous students felt was used in the analysis (as expected, students in a no name condition felt more anonymous than did those in a named condition). Contrary to predictions, perceptions of anonymity were (a) uncorrelated with feelings of accountability and (b) linked to slightly higher performance ratings.

Other research has examined peer feedback and assessment, with somewhat mixed findings. Arnold, Shue, Kritt, Ginsburg, and Stern (2005) conducted focus groups with medical school students about peer assessment, and anonymity emerged as a key theme strongly linked to willingness to participate in peer assessment. On the positive side, students believed anonymity protects the student evaluator and the peer being evaluated, minimizes discomfort of facing one's peer directly, reduces accusations of tattling, and may reduce disruptions to relationships as well as encourage more candid and honest appraisal. However, anonymous assessment also created concerns about disclosing identity, retaliation, verification of information, accountability and responsibility, allowing venting and vendettas, not taking evaluations seriously, and not forcing people to confront others. Focus group participants suggested a confidential system may be a reasonable compromise that "offers the prospect of verification and thus accountability but retains the anonymity of the student evaluator" (p. 822). In a different study, Bloom and Hautaluoma's (2001) experiment with college students reacting to workplace scenarios failed to find any interaction between anonymity and feedback valence in terms of influence on either affective reactions or intentions to improve. Garbett, Hardy, Manley, Titchen, and McCormack's (2007) qualitative case study of a clinical nursing term refining a 360-degree feedback process suggested that anonymity is not essential to providing supportive and critical feedback (though candor and detailed feedback may take additional time to develop without it); overall, both anonymous and more identified forms of feedback were found to be useful.

One of the more interesting examinations of anonymity and peer assessment comes from workers employed in a kibbutz-owned manufacturing firm in Israel (Bamberger et al., 2005). The study examined anonymous (no name) and nonanonymous (confidential, but included name of evaluator) assessment of others over time and related those to supervisory ratings. Bamberger et al. found "following the implementation of peer assessment, the mean composite peer ratings received by those assigned to the nonanonymous condition were significantly higher than those assigned to the anonymous condition in both Time 2 and Time 3" (p. 363); furthermore, this effect of anonymity on peer assessments increased over time. More interesting, and consistent with their prediction, "supervisory assessments of those employed in departments in which peer assessment was conducted on a nonanonymous basis were significantly higher ($p < .05$) than those employed in departments in which the assessment was conducted anonymously" (p. 365). This was true for three of four group process criteria at T2 (initiative, motivation, teamwork) and all four at T3 (including mentoring). Similarly, supervisory-rated productivity behaviors increased in both the anonymous and nonanonymous conditions from T2 to T3, but were significantly stronger in the nonanonymous condition at both times. These findings led the authors to conclude that "our results suggest that whereas anonymous peer appraisal procedures may be well institutionalized in organizations and in fact preferred by raters, their utility should not be taken as a given" (p. 372). Consequently they call for the "the elimination of rater anonymity" as a way to improve peer assessment (p. 373).

Scott and Rains (2005) coded open-ended questionnaire responses from organizational members related to when use of anonymity was seen as appropriate, and clearly several of these link to assessment/feedback: complaints/suggestions about organization/management, complaints/criticisms about coworkers, organizational surveys, performance feedback (for peers or supervisors), and general suggestions. The second study Scott and Rains (2005) report focused on appropriateness issues surfacing in the first study. Based on 98 working adult respondents to an online questionnaire, six appropriateness situations emerged (from most to least appropriate): organizational assessment, formal evaluations, technology use, informal evaluations, general use, and firing. Older respondents viewed anonymity for formal and informal evaluations as less appropriate, and quality of relations with coworkers was negatively correlated with appropriateness of anonymous informal evaluations.

Performance. The organization/management research related to anonymous communication also has implications for performance outcomes. There is some evidence that whistleblowing and fraud reporting are less effective when done anonymously. Price's (1998) research about anonymous and pseudonymous reports of scientific wrongdoing suggested that the portion of anonymous complaints is small (8%)—perhaps because few of these are judged as adequately substantiated. In this research, only 1 of 13 anonymously reported cases with substantive concerns actually resulted in a finding of scientific misconduct. Related to this, Miceli et al. (1988) found that seriousness of wrongdoing was somewhat more linked to identified whistleblowing (though overall, seriousness is more tied to use of external channels than identification/anonymity choices). Additionally, they found no support for their prediction that anonymous whistleblowers expect greater responsiveness to their complaints.

Trust. Finally, two studies have considered the relationship between anonymity and trust in management/organizational research. Callison (2001) noted that anonymous generic sources were actually rated as more trustworthy than a source identified as a public relations spokesperson. Additionally, trust in others not to reveal identity and organizational climate were both factors influencing decisions to anonymously blow the whistle in a survey of federal agency employees (Miceli et al., 1988).

Economics

Anonymity has also been of interest in the economics literature as a factor influencing group coordination, bargaining/negotiation, and/or collaboration. It is often studied in the context of group games, including auctions, prisoner's dilemma, dictator games, power-to-take games, the Groves' mechanism, one-shot trust games, and coin toss games. Almost all of these studies consist of experiments. In some cases, an anonymous treatment is compared with identification and no-identification at all. In some cases, though, treatment is one-way identification where only one participant can identify the other, or with two-way identification where both participants visually identify one another. We review research examining anonymous communication in economics, focusing particularly on the implications of anonymity for participation, performance, and trust.

Participation. Research related to anonymity and participation suggests that the implications of anonymous communication are linked to specific features of the experimental games used in economics studies. In auctions, for example, anonymous bidding might encourage bidders to participate by making collusion more difficult. Bajari and Yeo (2009) examined the relationship between anonymous bidding and the frequency of anti-competitive bidding strategies in the Federal Communication Commission (FCC) spectrum auctions. During anonymous bidding the identity of the bidder, the bid amounts other than the standing high bid, the initial level, and changes of each bidder's eligibility, were not revealed until the auction ended. Their findings suggest that anonymous bidding makes collusion considerably more difficult because it disguises bidder identity—limiting enforcement of collusive agreements by cartels. In dictator games, there is evidence that information about the identity of the recipient can increase donations (Bohnet & Frey, 1999; Eckel & Grossman, 1996). Bohnet and Frey (1999) compared an anonymous treatment, a one-way identifiability treatment in which dictators could identify their respective recipients, and a two-way identifiability treatment where both dictators and recipients could visually identify each other. Dictators retained more of the money when there was total or partial anonymity than the two-way identifiability condition. The authors concluded that one-way identifiability "transforms anonymous, faceless entities into visible, specified human beings, i.e., identifiable victims" (p. 339). Along these lines, Eckel and Grossman (1996) reported similar findings. Dictators offered more money to an established charity than an anonymous student.

Anonymity has also been shown to influence participation in intergroup competitions. In these types of games, the benefits associated with winning the competition are often shared jointly by the members—regardless of the level of their contribution to the group's success. Bornstein and Rapoport (1988) tested the effects of group discussion prior to playing the game on contribution towards the provision public goods during the game. They found evidence that, when the decision is anonymous, discussion prior to the game enhanced contributions made during the game.

Performance. Anonymous preplay communication moderated the coordination and collusion strategies in budgeting mechanisms. Arnold, Ponick, and Schenk-Mathes (2008) explored the effects of anonymous communication on the Groves mechanism and a profit sharing scheme in a corporate budgeting context. Under the Groves mechanism, a manager's compensation is determined by "his own division's actual profit as well as by the expected profits that all other divisions report to headquarters *ex ante*" (p. 38), whereas under a profit sharing scheme it is determined by overall firm profit. Within this framework, the role of anonymous communication in overcoming coordination failures and improving resource allocation was tested experimentally. Under the profit sharing scheme, anonymous preplay communication improved coordination and reduced inefficient resource allocation. Under the Groves mechanism, however, anonymous preplay communication led to stable collusion strategies of the participants.

Trust. Economics literature suggests that anonymous group games can make trustworthiness difficult among group members. Some studies focused on the role of institutions in anonymous games, examining how institutions can induce a reporter to tell the truth, and thus, affect his/her trustworthiness in anonymous group games. Bohnet and Baytelman (2007) suggested that when institutions make betrayal more costly, trustors' beliefs about trustees' trustworthiness increase. That is, trustors are willing to send more and trustees to return more in conditions other than an anonymous one-shot environment. Similarly, Boudreau, McCubbins, and Coulson (2009) studied choices made by individuals after receiving information from an anonymous individual in the coin toss game. The results of this study showed that participants tend to trust an anonymous reporter who shares common interests or who was made trustworthy by an institution, but not anonymous sources that have conflicting interests.

Information Systems: GSSs

Anonymous communication has received a fair amount of attention in the Information Systems literature and, in particular, scholarship focusing on group support systems (GSSs). GSSs are technologies that facilitate group work (for a review, see Scott, 1999). Anonymity is a key feature of many GSSs. Anonymity is conceptualized and operationalized in different ways throughout GSS research. The most common way of conceptualizing anonymity is in the form of technical anonymity provided by a GSS; technical anonymity is operationalized by removing group members' names from their contributions (i.e., discursive anonymity) and/or physically separating group members from one another (i.e., physical anonymity). Social anonymity is relatively infrequently studied in GSS research. In the following sections, the role of anonymity in GSS research is considered focusing on the implications of anonymity for participation, influence, performance, trust, and identification.

Participation. There is evidence to suggest that anonymity has both positive and negative consequences for participation in GSS groups. Several studies have reported findings consistent with the claim that anonymity facilitates participation in GSS groups relative to GSS groups without anonymity or groups meeting face-to-face. In terms of gross or overall discussion participation, Postmes and Lea (2000) reported in their meta-analysis that anonymous GSS groups generated a greater total number of statements than identified GSS groups. Additionally, Scott (1999) reported participants in a discursive anonymity condition made more contributions than discursively identified members. There is also some evidence of differences in regard to specific forms of participation. Anonymous groups have been found to ask a greater number of solution-related questions (Jessup, Connolly, & Galegher, 1990; Jessup & Tansik, 1991), make a greater number of solution clarifications (Jessup et al., 1990; Jessup & Tansik, 1991), generate a greater number of controversial ideas (Cooper, Gallupe, Pollard, & Cadsby, 1998), and, among minority opinion members, discuss greater amounts of previously unshared information (McLeod, Baron, Marti, & Yoon, 1997) than identified GSS groups or groups meeting face-to-face (FtF).

Two specific forms of participation have received a fair amount of attention in prior research. First, anonymity has been argued to facilitate idea generation through removing group members' fear of evaluation and encouraging participation (Connolly, Jessup, & Valacich, 1990; Cooper et al., 1998). Although a few experimental studies have found evidence that anonymous groups generate a greater number of unique (i.e., non-redundant) ideas or solutions in brainstorming tasks than identified groups (Connolly et al., 1990; Cooper et al., 1998), others have reported no differences between anonymous and identified groups (Jessup et al., 1990; Jessup & Tansik, 1991; Pissarra & Jesuno, 2005; Sosik, 1997; Valacich, Dennis, & Nunamaker, 1992). Evidence from case studies is no more consistent. Anonymity has been reported to be effective (de Vreede & Mgaya, 2006; Trauth & Jessup, 2000) and ineffective (Trauth & Jessup, 2000) in facilitating idea generation. Perhaps the most consistent findings regarding the impact of anonymity on idea generation comes from meta-analytic studies. Postmes and Lea (2000) found no difference between identified and GSS groups in regard to the number of original solutions generated. Moreover, anonymity did not significantly moderate the relationship between idea generation and GSS use in two other meta-analyses (Lim, Yang, & Zhong, 2007; Rains, 2005).

Second, an ostensibly more consistent finding regarding participation in GSS research is that anonymous group members are more inclined to share critical comments than identified members. In their meta-analysis, Postmes and Lea (2000) found that anonymous groups generated a greater number of critical comments than identified groups. This finding, however, requires a qualification. That is, critical comments are assumed to be both destructive and constructive in the body of GSS research. In a few studies (e.g., Connolly et al., 1990), both of these perspectives are combined into a category representing "expression[s] of opposition to a proposal with, or without, evidence or arguments (e.g., 'That's a terrible idea' or 'That will never work because…')" (Valacich et al., 1992, p. 59). The key difference between the two types of criticisms is that one is unsubstantiated and might be considered a personal attack, whereas the other offers supporting evidence and, thus, has the potential to advance the group's discussion. There is some evidence that, in comparison with identified groups, anonymous groups make more negative and destructive critical comments (Jessup et al., 1990; Sosik, 1997), more constructive critical comments (Reinig & Mejias, 2004), and an amalgamation of both (Connolly et al., 1990; Valacich et al., 1992). Other studies have found no differences between anonymous and identified groups in constructive (Jessup et al., 1990; Jessup & Tansik, 1991) or destructive (Reinig & Mejias, 2004) critical comments.

Influence. Several studies have been conducted examining influence behaviors and processes in GSS groups. Although Rains's (2005) meta-analysis showed that anonymity did not moderate the relationship between GSS use and influence equality, normative influence, nor decision shifts, other research suggests that anonymity might be important for decision shifts, individuals holding minority opinions, and leadership. In regard to decision shifts, at least two studies have reported differences between anonymous GSS groups and identified GSS groups or groups meeting FtF. The anonymous GSS group made more conservative decisions in Hiltz, Turoff, and Johnson's (1989) study, whereas Karan, Kerr, Murphy, and Vinze (1996) found evidence of a "cautious shift" (p. 189) only in groups meeting FtF. A more recent study conducted by Sia, Tan, and Wei (2002, study 2) suggests that the type of anonymity offered by a GSS is important to consider. They reported significant interaction effects for discursive and physical anonymity on choice shift and preference change (both of which assess decision shifts). Greater choice and preference shift occurred in the conditions with discursive but without physical anonymity and with physical but without discursive anonymity than in the condition without physical or discursive anonymity (i.e., the FtF/identified GSS condition).

Anonymity has also been examined as a factor that might impact the expression and influence of minority opinions. There is some evidence that anonymity facilitates (Lim & Guo, 2008; McLeod et al., 1997) and mitigates (Kahai, 2009) the expression of members holding a minority opinion. Compared to minority opinion holders in identified GSS groups or groups meeting FtF, those using an anonymous GSS have been found to present more unshared information and repeat unshared information more frequently (McLeod et al., 1997) and report lower uncertainty, greater satisfaction, higher decision quality, and conform less (Lim & Guo, 2008). Yet, there is also evidence that anonymity may have limitations for members holding minority opinions. McLeod et al. (1997) reported that perceptions of unshared information were most negative in the anonymity condition. Moreover, Kahai (2009) found that, when initial opinions differed in a group, participants who were introduced prior to the study and had discursive anonymity during the decision-making task generated significantly fewer counter-normative arguments and greater agreement than in identified GSS groups and GSS groups where members had discursive anonymity but were not introduced prior to the study.

A final dimension of influence that has been examined in research on anonymity and GSSs is group leadership. In studies testing interactions between assigned leadership (George, Easton, Nunamaker, & Northcraft, 1990) or transformational leadership (Sosik, 1997; Sosik, Kahai, & Avolio, 1998) and anonymity on group processes and outcomes, there are relatively few significant findings. George et al. (1990) found that groups were more satisfied when both anonymity and designated leadership were either present or absent than when anonymity was present but a designated leader was absent or when anonymity was absent but a designated leader was present. Sosik et al. (1998) found that, in the low transformational leadership condition, members of the anonymous groups demonstrated more flexibility than participants in identified groups. Flexibility was defined in their study as the number of different approaches used to generate the group's solution. Sosik (1997) reported no significant interactions between transformational leadership and anonymity for any of the outcome variables he tested. Related to group influence, Rains (2007) conducted an experiment examining perceptions of the credibility and influence of anonymous group members. He reported that, controlling for social (i.e., perceived) anonymity, participants viewed a technically anonymous confederate to be significantly less persuasive than an identified confederate.

Performance. Although group performance is frequently measured in GSS research, the effects related to anonymity are unclear. The findings from three meta-analyses underscore the inconsistent findings in research examining the impact of anonymity. Postmes and Lea (2000) reported no differences between anonymous and identified GSS groups in regard to decision quality or perceived effectiveness. Additionally, Lim et al. (2007) reported that anonymity was not a significant moderator of decision quality or time to reach decisions. In contrast, Baltes, Dickson, Sherman, Bauer, and LaGanke (2002) found that anonymity moderated the relationship between GSS use and group effectiveness, and between GSS use and time to reach a decision. Anonymous groups were less ineffective and took longer to reach a decision than identified groups.

Trust. GSS research related to trust takes a message-receiver perspective and examines perceptions of anonymous group members. Evidence from quantitative (Hayne, Pollard, & Rice, 2003; Hayne & Rice, 1997) and qualitative (Dennis, 1994; Scott, Quinn, Timmerman, & Garrett, 1998) studies suggests that, despite the discursive anonymity provided by GSS technologies, members make attributions about the identity of others in their group. Hayne and Rice (1997) found that, although attributions about a comment author's identity were made frequently, the accuracy of such attributions was low. Attribution accuracy ranged from 39%–83% among the anonymous groups in Hayne et al.'s (2003) study, and total prior communication with one's group was positively associated with attribution accuracy. Beyond making inaccurate attributions, Scott et al. (1998) reported that members of the groups they analyzed actively tried to circumvent the technical anonymity provided by the GSS. Participants identified themselves by signing their comments, including specific or unique information that would help others identify them, and asking for responses from specific members of the group. Finally, Rains (2007) found, controlling for social (i.e., perceived) anonymity, participants viewed a technically anonymous confederate to be significantly less trustworthy and to have less goodwill toward the group than an identified confederate.

Identification. The impact of anonymity on group member identification has been investigated in a few studies. Bhappu, Griffith, and Northcraft (1997) examined identification with one's ingroup and outgroup, but found no differences between the FtF, anonymous GSS, or identified GSS conditions. Scott (1999) tested the influence of physical and discursive anonymity on perceptions and expressions of identification. There was a significant interaction for the two types of anonymity on perceptions of group identification. Participants reported the greatest identification in the groups that were physically hidden but were discursively identified and the least identification when groups were physically hidden and had discursive anonymity. There were three differences in expressions of identification. Participants in physically visible groups made more expressions of group identification than in groups with hidden participants. Discursively anonymous members made more expression of disidentification or no identification and fewer statements of multiple identifications than participants in groups whose names were used.

Psychology

Anonymous communication research in psychological literature focuses on issues such as anti-social behavior, social identity, attributions, choice shift, and commitments. Most of the studies consist of experiments. Anonymity was tested in a variety of ways; however, many of the studies operationalized anonymity by not allowing participants to see one another's behavior. Although there are a number of studies spanning decades examining anonymity and various behaviors (e.g., shocking/punishing others, altruism/helping), we focus on research examining more communicative behaviors and processes. Specifically, we examine how anonymity relates to influence, feedback, performance and identification.

Influence. One body of psychology research examined choice shift in anonymous and nonanonymous conditions. Bell and Jamieson (1970) found a choice shift in a public discussion condition, but no shift occurred in an anonymous condition. In this study, anonymity is manipulated by the social comparison information—either subjects did not sign their names to forms or they didn't know each others' pretest scores and no one endorsed a specific preference during discussion. Cotton and Baron (1980) reported mixed findings when they manipulated anonymity while holding social comparison information constant. That is, sometimes there was no statistical difference between anonymous and public conditions on risky shift, but in one study the anonymous ballot condition suggested the largest risky shift.

Feedback. Research suggested that anonymity affects the extent the subjects are critical with their feedback. Lindskold and Finch (1982) examined to what extent participants complied with a demand to critically evaluate group members when there is a counterpressure from the group and they are anonymous or identified The results showed that, with high group counterpressure and without the protection of anonymity, subjects who were demanded to critically evaluate group members were no more critical than the subjects in the low demand condition. Also, the results suggested that, in the low demand condition, anonymous subjects were less critical than identified participants.

Performance. Some research has examined the role of anonymity in predicted and actual task performance. Pezzo, Pezzo, and Stone (2006) explored the impact of making predictions either orally to a familiar experimenter or anonymously (nothing was said and the decision was written down) and how that might relate to the planning fallacy (where people expect to finish a task more quickly than they actually do). The discrepancy between the predicted and actual completion of a take-home portion of the task was significantly smaller in the anonymous condition. Predicted and actual completion times for participants making anonymous predictions were significantly correlated, but these variables were not correlated for those in the identified condition.

Identification. A few studies have examined anonymity using social identity theory and/or self-categorization theory. This work is related to research on the SIDE model, but does not involve CMC. Barreto, Spears, Ellemers, and Shahinper (2003) conducted an experiment with Portuguese immigrants living in the Netherlands examining identification with native and host countries as a function of audience (native or host) and anonymity (respondents provided name and address to be identifiable or provided no personal information to be anonymous). As predicted, the Portuguese respondents reported stronger identification with their native national group when anonymous to that audience than when identifiable to it. Similarly, identification with the host Dutch national group was stronger when participants' responses were anonymous to that audience than when identifiable to it. Smith, Terry, and Hogg (2007) report two studies examining group identification and norms under conditions of anonymity and identifiability. In the first, they found that, "High identifiers reported stronger intentions to engage in attitude-consistent behavior in anonymous response conditions … than in [identified] response conditions… This pattern was reversed for the low identifiers…" (p. 245). In the second study, identity salience was added to the experiment. The results show that, for low-salience participants, the effects of norms were greater when participants were identified; however, for high-salience participants, the effects of norms were greater for anonymous participants.

Social Psychology: SIDE Studies

An important extension of the work done in psychology can be found in the mostly social psychological research related to the SIDE model. Anonymity is important because it provides one of the key ways to create deindividuation—a condition in which individuals are not viewed or recognized as individuals. In examining the role of identity salience as it interacts with anonymity, the SIDE model has produced counter-intuitive, yet compelling, explanations for the effects of anonymity. In short, when a social identity is salient, anonymity can actually enhance that identity (because individuating features are obscured), which leads to behavior in line with group norms (rather than antinormative, uninhibited behavior; Postmes, Spears, Sakhel, & de Groot, 2001). Because anonymity can be created via CMC, work using the SIDE model has regularly mixed anonymity and CMC.

These studies differ from others reviewed in this chapter in at least three key ways. First, these studies are non-U.S. focused (with multiple studies from Netherlands, Australia, Great Britain, and Germany) and conducted by a smaller set of influential scholars. More specifically, this area is heavily influenced by the work of Douglas and McGarty (2001, 2002), who published two sets of studies with language abstraction as the outcome variable, and research more relevant to our review here by Postmes, Spears, and Lea (2002; Spears, Lea, Corneliussen, Postmes, & Haar, 2002). Second, the work in this area is overwhelmingly experimental in nature and predominantly uses undergraduate subjects. Consequently, anonymity in these studies is almost always a manipulated independent variable. Third, even though anonymity itself is not explicitly defined as a variable or construct in these studies, it is operationalized in ways that place primary emphasis on physical (i.e., *visual*) communication. Indeed, the use of simple pictures or not is the most common way of creating anonymous and identified conditions; however, studies have also used two-way synchronous video vs. CMC text only (Lea, Spears, & de Groot, 2001) and even manipulated anonymity with photos taken from videotapes of students (see Walther, Slovacek, & Tidwell, 2001; yet this is not framed as a SIDE study, per se). Although a number of studies use SIDE, the research relevant here has implications for influence, performance, and identification.

Influence. Sassenberg and Postmes (2002) explored differences between anonymity of a group (showing or not showing pictures of group) and anonymity of the self (showing or not showing picture of self to others) in online discussions. Neither anonymity type influenced choice shift or agreement independently; however, there were interaction effects. When the self was anonymous, social influence was stronger in anonymous group conditions than identified ones; this pattern was reversed when the self was identifiable to others in the group.

A follow-up study with actual group communication among students again suggested interaction effects: when the self was anonymous, group anonymity led to greater choice shift in the direction of the group norm compared with identifiable groups; conversely, when the self was identifiable, the choice shift was greater when the group was identifiable than when it was anonymous. As predicted, more violations of local coherence occurred in the identifiable self condition than in the anonymous self condition.

Postmes et al. (2001) tested the SIDE model and concluded that anonymity obscures individual inputs, thus enhancing the salience of group norms. Again manipulating anonymity by presenting pictures of group members or withholding them, anonymous groups favored prosocial solutions when they were primed prosocially and favored efficiency-oriented solutions when primed accordingly; however, this was not true for the identified groups. Their second study measured group norms and atmosphere directly and focused on an efficiency vs. neutral prime for these norms. As expected, anonymous groups perceived a more efficiency oriented group norm than did identifiable groups; similarly, anonymous groups had more efficiency-oriented solutions and used more efficiency-oriented words than did identifiable groups. As the authors conclude, "visually anonymous groups appear to be more conducive to social influence in line with a primed group norm than identifiable groups... Results show that the effect of visual anonymity on normative behavior is mediated by identification with the group" (p. 1252).

Sassenberg and Boos (2003) examined groups communicating FtF (visually identified) and through CMC (visually anonymous) to test the basic predictions of SIDE in interacting groups. Counter to their prediction, when social identity was salient FtF groups showed greater attitude change than did the more anonymous CMC groups. In a second study, all groups interacted via CMC but some could see one another (nonanonymous) and some could not (anonymous). When participants received a reference norm for their larger category, nonanonymous groups showed greater attitude change away from the group norm than did those in the anonymous condition; findings were reversed for those who did not receive a reference norm for their larger superordinate category.

Performance. The third study reported by Douglas and McGarty (2002) asked participants to respond (identified or anonymous) to a message from someone at the university about student attitudes toward work/leisure. Identified respondents reported they were better able to show opposition to university staff views than were anonymous respondents. Tanis and Postmes (2007) looked at cues to identity (through presence or absence of portrait pictures and a name) as students interacted in simulated dyads online. They found, in a study using actual group interaction via online chat and assessed performance, that those in the cues condition were less satisfied with their performance than those in the no-cues situation. The authors explain "it is not so much the identifiability of the other that produced these effects found, but the identifiability to the other" (p. 966). Tanis and Postmes (2008) continued this work using the same cues manipulation and online dyadic chat from their previous work. Results suggested participants with cues were less satisfied with performance as compared to those interacting without cues.

Identification. In SIDE research identification is sometimes an outcome factor. For example, Sassenberg and Postmes's (2002) exploration of differences between anonymity of a group (showing or not showing pictures) and anonymity of the self (showing or not showing picture of self to others) in online discussions revealed respondents reported greater group unity when the group was anonymous than when group members were identifiable; however, anonymity of the self did not influence this measure. Also, group identification was stronger in the anonymous groups in a study by Postmes et al. (2001). Tanis and Postmes (2008) found that in the condition with cues participants perceived less shared identity compared to conditions lacking cues.

However, SIDE research more commonly treats identification as more of a mediating or moderating variable or as part of what is manipulated in the efforts to make social identities more salient. As Postmes et al. (2001) conclude, "Results show that the effect of visual anonymity on normative behavior is mediated by identification with the group" (p. 1252). Tanis and Postmes (2008) report a second study where they sought to further examine conditions where the inability to form personalized impressions were beneficial. Using a manipulation designed to heighten identification with one's university, Tanis and Postmes found that presence of cues was linked to less ambiguous impressions and somewhat more positive impressions of the other. More interesting is the finding that when no cues were present, social identification with the larger university group was strongly associated with the emergence of a dyadic shared identity (yet this does not happen in the condition with cues present). Their summary explanation helps capture a key contribution of SIDE research as it relates to anonymity:

> Study 2 confirmed our prediction that the effects of cues to personal identity depend on identification with the overarching group. When cues to personal identity are absent, identification with the superordinate group positively affects feelings of shared identity and performance. When cues to personal identity are present, identification has no effect. (p. 106)

Computer-Mediated Communication

Beyond the GSS studies from the Information Systems tradition and the SIDE studies from Social Psychology, there is a more diffuse body of interdisciplinary research examining anonymity in various forms of computer-mediated communication (CMC). Even after excluding numerous studies that hold anonymity constant and/or treat anonymity as a defining feature of CMC without ever measuring or examining anonymity itself (see, for example, a series of related studies by Lee, 2004, 2005, 2006, 2007a, 2007b, 2007c), this remains a sizable and diverse literature. These general CMC studies were published in a range of journals, used several different methods, and were conducted in several different countries even though the majority were still U.S.-based (which is potentially of concern given findings that U.S. users indicate a greater preference for identifiability in online posts than is found in some other cultures; see Morio & Buchholz, 2009). The nature of this research was diverse in two other important ways. First, it covered a sizable array of communication technologies (including email, online discussion forums, online ads and dating sites, games, chat, instant messaging, phone services, blogs, texts, and social network sites) that do not all share the same underlying characteristics (e.g., synchronicity, interactivity, capacity; see Lievrouw & Finn, 1996).

Second, anonymity was not explicitly defined as a construct in this research. However, it was operationalized in markedly different ways across this research—revealing multiple forms of anonymity and raising concerns about comparisons across those different studies. For example, these operationalizations included real name CMC vs. anonymous CMC (Adrianson, 2001; Westerman, 2008); no information vs. real name and additional information (Qian & Scott, 2007); no photo vs. revealing actual photo (Qian & Scott, 2007); anonymous CMC technologies vs. identifiable CMC technologies; pseudonym vs. real name (Jaffe, Lee, Huang, & Oshagan, 1999); anonymous vs. nickname (Morio & Buchholz, 2009); anonymous chat vs. identified instant messaging (Kang & Yang, 2006); visible vs. invisible (Joinson, 2001); online vs. public (Coffey & Woolworth, 2004); and even large city anonymous vs. small-town identifiable (Gudelunas, 2005). CMC research is considered focusing on the implications of anonymity for participation, feedback, and trust.

Participation. Several CMC studies examine some form of participation. For example, Qian and Scott (2007) surveyed bloggers about their use of both visual and discursive anonymity as they related to self-disclosure. Bloggers posted under all six different discursive anonymity options (ranging from no identifying information to using a real name plus other identifying information) and all but one of the six visually anonymous options (ranging from no photo to revealing actual photos). Visual anonymity was not statistically linked to amount of self-disclosure, but discursive anonymity was. With the exception of the one extreme group that revealed even more than their real name, the authors report "generally the more identification information given on one's blog, the less self-disclosive people seem to be" (p. 1436). Joinson (2001) reported a pair of relevant studies experimentally manipulating visual anonymity where it did influence self-disclosure. In the study comparing FtF interactants with visually isolated CMC users, CMC dyads engaged in significantly more self-disclosure than participants in the FtF condition. In a second study manipulating visual anonymity entirely within CMC interaction, the presence of a picture of one's interaction partner led to significantly less self-disclosure than in the condition where visual anonymity was maintained—a finding they link to heightened private self-awareness in that condition. Waskul and Douglass (1997) used content analysis, surveys, interviews and participant observation to analyze a large commercial online chat service—with several themes in the research pointing to potentially greater participation: freedom to be oneself; openly expressing oneself; identity experimentation and construction of multiple selves; and no barriers to communication because people are not blinded by age, sex, nationality, or race.

Other studies suggest greater participation is linked to anonymous CMC, for at least certain types of users. Colvin, Chenoweth, Bold, and Harding's (2004) survey of adult caregivers and online social support pointed to two relevant findings: easier to relate to anonymous others online, and ability to express oneself in a nonjudgmental atmosphere. An analysis of email messages from young people with learning disabilities revealed these individuals "were more comfortable talking about their disabilities anonymously than they were in real-life situations" (Raskind, Margalit, & Higgins, cited in Samuels, 2007, p. 12). Morahan-Martin and Schumacher (2003), in a survey of undergraduates in courses requiring Internet use, found that lonely users found online anonymity to be liberating. Other studies of both children and adults have noted that shier individuals value online anonymity (Livingstone & Helsper, 2007; Scharlott & Christ, 1995); indeed, Scharlott and Christ's online survey of users on the marriage market intermediary Matchmaker concluded "the ability to communicate with others without revealing details about oneself enables the shier user to interact without fear of rejection;" this tool thus allows "users to communicate in ways that in other contexts they might feel too socially inhibited to do" (p. 199). Peter and Valkenburg (2007) used a survey of adults in the Netherlands to confirm that individuals with high dating anxiety and low physical self-esteem value the anonymity of online communication more than do individuals low in dating anxiety and high in physical self-esteem. In addition to the previous studies, several others examined gender differences related to anonymity in CMC. Kang and Yang (2006) compared instant messaging (IM) avatars (where users go by real name typically) and Internet Relay Chat (IRC) avatars (where users are generally anonymous) through user surveys. They found that females express imaginary identity on anonymous IRC avatars more than do males (but gender does not affect realism of identity of more identified IM avatars). Thus, anonymity enhances participation generally—especially for certain (sometimes marginalized) groups.

In some instances, the type of participation facilitated by anonymity may be seen as less socially desirable. Livingstone and Helsper (2007), in a nationwide survey and interviews with children and youth in the U.K., found that valuing anonymity online was positively correlated with sensation-seeking, lower life satisfaction, more frequent Internet communication, and risky behaviors such as meeting online friends offline. In their study of cyberbullying (Mishna, Saini, & Solomon, 2009), middle school (grades 5–8) students participated in focus groups and claimed anonymity facilitated bullying and allowed the aggressor to hide behind the keyboard. The students suggested "anonymity lets individuals behave in ways they might not otherwise and that would not otherwise be tolerated" (p. 1224). However, we note that much of the cyberbullying that actually occurred involved others the student could identify. As Mishna et al. note, "the cyber bullying often occurred in the context of their social groups and relationships, for example boyfriend/ girlfriend, 'best' friend, and other friends and classmates. Analysis of the participants' comments revealed that the students often discover the identity of the individual who bullies them online…" (p. 1226).

Feedback. Feedback has been much less examined in this research. However, Adrianson's (2001) experimental study with student groups using email found FtF communication included more feedback than in an anonymous CMC condition (but not greater than the CMC with real names condition).

Trust. The only outcome among those we examined that is regularly considered here are issues related to trust. In Henderson and Gilding's (2004) interviews with chatroom users about online friendships, respondents pointed to limited cues producing lack of accountability, widespread deceit and betrayal, and inability to establish reputation (but note that pseudonyms could allow for that). A minority of respondents (5%) reported drawbacks to anonymity in a survey study of Internet-based social support for adult caregivers that centered on questions of sincerity, truthfulness and ability to verify one's claims (Colvin et al., 2004). Waskul and Douglass (1997) used content analysis, surveys, interviews and participant observation to analyze a large commercial online chat service—concluding that anonymity was an important element in this online tool. However, frustration and concern also emerged about those very benefits, especially when they resulted in misrepresentation, deceit, game playing, etc. We see each of these findings as suggesting anonymity reduced trust online.

Education

Anonymous communication has been studied in the education literature, with much of this work focusing on the implications of anonymity for computer-mediated collaboration and learning. Education studies involving anonymity use a wide range of research methods, including: content analysis, survey questionnaires, interviews, focus groups, participant observation, and experiments. Anonymity is most often operationalized as a technical feature of communication technologies such as synchronous chat systems, email, and electronic bulletin boards. In most of the cases, anonymity is conceptualized as a continuous construct and manipulated with the use of no-identity (anonymous) or a created-identity (nickname). We review research examining anonymous communication in education in the following paragraphs, focusing particularly on the implications of anonymity for participation, feedback, and trust.

Participation. Several scholars have found evidence that anonymity makes individuals more comfortable and, thus, may facilitate participation in computer-mediated learning environments (Ahern & Durrington, 1995; Gallagher-Lepak, Reilly, & Killion, 2009; Roselli & Brophy, 2006; Yu, 2009; Yu & Liu, 2009). Yu and Liu (2009), for example, they had participants use their real name, be anonymous (no name), or use a created identity (nickname) during an online question construction and peer assessment task. Most students preferred either being anonymous or using a pseudonym in completing the task. A preference for or comfort with anonymity in the context of participation was also reported in studies of nursing students (Gallagher-Lepak et al., 2009), English as a second-language (ESL) writing classes (DiGiovanni & Nagaswami, 2001; Sullivan & Pratt, 1996), and among undergraduate engineering students (Roselli & Brophy, 2006).

Feedback. In addition to allowing individuals to feel more comfortable participating, there is some evidence that anonymity may be particularly important for sharing and receiving feedback. Tuzi (2004) reported that students made more macro level revisions following anonymous feedback adding new information and revising structures at clause, sentence, and paragraph levels. Similarly, Guardado and Shi (2007) examined students' experiences of online peer feedback in an ESL class. The essays were posted with the authors' names, but the feedback was anonymous (no name). The findings suggest that sharing feedback anonymously online allowed students to write more constructive responses. The outcomes of anonymity associated with feedback are not all positive. Guardado and Shi also found that some students perceived the anonymous online feedback to be confusing and suspected they had misunderstood the comments.

Trust. Research addressing the implications of anonymous communication for various outcomes related to trust is mixed. One of the studies showed that feedback from students and faculty promoted trust, confidence, and learning (Galagher-Lepak et al., 2009). Rovai (2002) argued that candor comes with trust as anonymous participants feel safe and subsequently expose gaps in their learning. However, other research showed that some anonymous interactions were superficial and excessive, and that the practice of over-posting in anonymous discussions is not always a means of connection but for reassurance or to gain approval (Beuchot & Bullen, 2005).

Conclusions and Future Directions

Even with our focus on research topics where there was at least some overlap in what was being examined, these eight research traditions often approach the study of anonymous communication with unique assumptions, methods, and goals. In many cases, this has resulted in findings that are difficult to compare across area. In other cases, this produces mixed or inconclusive findings.

Despite these challenges, our review does allow us to draw several conclusions about anonymous communication across these areas. We utilize Figure 13.1 to again organize these observations.

Anonymity Factors

One of the more consistent findings is that anonymity or anonymous communication is almost never conceptually defined in any of this research literature. It is treated as though familiar enough not to need defining. However, the different types of anonymity and the various operationalizations would suggest this is a problematic assumption.

There are several types and forms of anonymity found across this literature. Several research traditions focus on physical forms of anonymity (e.g., social psychology work on SIDE, psychology) while others emphasize discursive forms (e.g., GSS studies, organization/ management studies). Yet, both types are often referenced simply as anonymity. Similar differences exist for those studies that look at technical anonymity provided by a communication channel relative to more social/perceived forms of anonymity. Self and other anonymity also emerge across these areas. Additionally, we have research about confidentiality and pseudonymity, lumping it all under the heading of anonymity. In some instances, focusing on more precise forms can help reconcile seemingly inconsistent findings and clearly identify trends in the research. In the SIDE research, for example, it appears that visual anonymity[3] makes it more likely group members will follow salient group norms; however, discursive anonymity has more mixed and indirect results. For other types of anonymity and in different contexts, few comparisons have been made. It is rare, for instance, to see findings comparing technical anonymity (provided by the technology as a feature or characteristic that often treats anonymity as "on" or "off") with perceptual forms (which is more likely to represent a subjective assessment of the degree of anonymity), though manipulation checks in experimental studies would generally suggest substantial overlap with the two. Scholars conducting research in these various domains would be well served to evaluate the specific form of anonymity they are studying in the broader context of the various types of anonymity available. The typology of anonymity forms discussed in this chapter might be useful starting point for such an endeavor.

Even more important are the various operationalizations of anonymity. Beyond the fact that anonymity may emerge as a theme or finding in qualitative research, the manipulations and treatment of anonymity in experimental and certain other forms of research highlight the multi-faceted nature of this construct. Technical anonymity is quite common in the general CMC, GSS, SIDE, and education areas where technology is used to create anonymity; yet, a vast range of technologies are used to provide that anonymity (and they do not all provide the same level of protection). More interesting are the operationalizations of physical and discursive anonymity. Across these areas, pseudonyms or nicknames emerge most frequently as a way to achieve anonymity (though a few studies actually use this as a "named" online condition that is then compared to more anonymous conditions that include no name). It is worth remembering that pseudonyms provide only partial anonymity—and yet our conclusions about anonymity are based heavily on studies providing only some anonymity. Other studies across areas operationalized anonymity as a condition in which one has no name at all—but then compare that to named strangers who may be functionally anonymous to most others. In short, these various operationalizations are likely not equivalent, which may help account for some of the mixed findings across the areas examined here.

Despite the various forms and operationalizations of anonymity, a final noteworthy issue that appears to transcend scholarship on anonymous communication is the relatively limited ways in which anonymity is studied. Marx (1999, 2004) convincingly argues that anonymity should be thought of as a continuum ranging from completely anonymous to fully identified. Moreover, he identifies various types of identity information that may make one more or less anonymous. Much of the research we review focused one or two distinct types of identity information—one's name and or physical appearance. Other, more nuanced, types of identity information such as information about networks and relationships or information about beliefs and attitudes are worth considering. Examining other types of identity information that might make one more or less anonymous is critical to advance research and theorizing regarding anonymous communication.

Communication Processes

Participation. In general, the literature would suggest that anonymity facilitates participation. It encourages sources to reveal news information, it provides a form of voice for organizational members, online it may facilitate more contributions generally, and discursive anonymity may allow for more self-disclosure in CMC. Some of the strongest evidence that anonymity facilitates participation comes from the education literature; here, anonymity creates a more equitable and safe environments to present one's opinions, which allows individuals to feel less inhibited and more comfortable sharing ideas. This participation is limited in some key ways, however. Anonymity encourages participation more for controversial or major issues (e.g., whistleblowing); that participation may only occur if communicators are reasonably confident their identity will be protected, and the participation that results from anonymity may not always be socially valued (especially in CMC).

What also seems clear across this literature is that anonymity fosters participation by more marginalized groups. The general CMC literature suggests that online anonymity enables greater involvement for groups such as the learning disabled, shier/lonely users, and high anxiety individuals. At work, members who do not have strong relations with others in their organization also tend to use and value anonymity more. The journalism findings suggest that anonymous sources are more common in stories that are critical in nature—which may also link to this finding. Furthermore, some studies show that anonymity in GSSs may facilitate arguments from members holding a minority opinion (though other research suggests that anonymity makes group norms salient and mitigates minority opinions). Although relatively few studies have been conducted, there is some evidence in the GSS, general CMC, and organization/management literature that anonymity may be particularly valuable to women—who may also be marginalized in some online and workplace settings. Thus, anonymity enhances participation generally—and especially for marginalized groups.

Influence. The anonymity-related research on influence examining decision shifts, risky shifts, and attitude change can also only be described as mixed across these different bodies of research. In the psychology literature, studies have reported no statistical difference between anonymous and public conditions on risky shift; however, at least one study has reported that the largest risky shift occurred in the anonymity condition. Research examining the effects of anonymity on decision shifts in GSS groups is even more decidedly mixed: some studies show anonymity may facilitate decision shifts, other research suggests anonymity makes group norms salient and mitigates decision shifts. In the SIDE research examining this dynamic, the findings depend largely on the anonymity of those involved. In general, when the self was anonymous, group anonymity led to greater choice shift in the direction of the group norm compared with identifiable groups; when the self was identifiable, the choice shift was greater when the group was identifiable than when anonymous. Distinguishing between self and group anonymity, which was not found in the research in other areas, suggests one explanatory factor amid otherwise inconclusive findings. SIDE research also illustrates that the influence of anonymity depends on what identity may be salient for group members; thus, mixed findings may be better accounted for through efforts to understand identity salience in among anonymous interactants.

Feedback. Again, across several different literatures that examine feedback, the findings are somewhat mixed. In organization/management studies, the effects of anonymity on performance ratings are unclear. A couple of studies suggest that anonymous assessments result in lower ratings—which are not received well by those being evaluated and may ultimately be linked to lower evaluations of anonymous raters by their supervisors. Anonymity is clearly used in formal and informal feedback and seen as appropriate, but clearly with some consequences. In the education research, anonymity allows group members to share less positive, unpleasant, and/or more open feedback with each other. At least one study suggested that even though most students liked the direct and honest comments from anonymous reviewers, some found online feedback confusing and unclear. In the journalism research, stories containing an anonymous source were much more likely to include criticism than stories that did not contain an anonymous source. Conversely, at least one experimental study with student groups using email found FtF communication included more feedback than in an anonymous CMC condition (but not greater than the CMC with real names condition). Some evidence from psychology also suggests that the nonanonymous condition may produce greater punishments in evaluations of others' ideas relative to anonymous conditions. Thus, it is difficult to conclude anything definitive across these studies.

However, the feedback literature does raise a related issue cutting across this research. Consideration of to whom one is anonymous is an important, but still understudied, research area in anonymous communication. Perceptions about and use of anonymity may vary depending on whether one is the initiator or recipient of such messages—and even vary based on the type of feedback recipient (e.g., teacher vs. managers/supervisor). All this is consistent with our prior calls to more closely consider the receiver in anonymous research (see Rains & Scott, 2007). We see some of these issues illustrated in this literature when those evaluating and those being evaluated express different views of anonymity, or when peers favor anonymous peer assessment but supervisors end up rating subordinates providing anonymous peer feedback less favorably. Related to this, several different areas we reviewed have examined audience at least implicitly—and in several cases the audience has an important influence on anonymous communication or other variables. In SIDE research and some psychology research, for example, one of the key considerations examined in several studies is the different groups to whom one's identifiability or anonymity matters—especially related to one's in-group or out-group. Other literature has pointed to third parties, which could serve as an intermediary audience; for example, in situations involving confidentiality one's identity may not be known to most, but would be known to some. Each of these findings points to a similar conclusion: greater attention to the relevant audience(s) matters and may account for some of the mixed findings related to feedback (and other topics).

Outcomes of Anonymous Communication

Performance. The findings regarding the relationship between anonymity and performance are mixed (e.g., anonymous GSS groups are both more and less effective), but several pieces of evidence suggests anonymity may enhance certain measures of performance (with less evidence suggesting it diminishes performance). Findings from economics suggest improved coordination, reduced collusion and increased giving in non-strategic situations. Psychology findings point to a better match between predicated and actual performance when anonymous. The SIDE research does generally find that anonymity is linked to greater satisfaction with performance. Part of the concern here is the sizable number of ways in which a task outcome such as performance is assessed. However, it may be harder to be effective when anonymous. At least one SIDE study suggests anonymity might be less effective for showing opposition. The organization/management research also finds that whistleblowing and fraud reporting are less effective when done anonymously. Overall, there are relatively few findings that even examine this traditional outcome—and even fewer conclusive findings when they do.

Trust assessments. Based on findings across several literatures, we suggest that anonymity generally leads sources to be perceived as less credible. Economics findings suggest anonymity can make trust more difficult. The GSS research points to anonymous confederates and other anonymous online users as being less trustworthy. Even the efforts to identify anonymous individuals in that work suggests people do not trust others who are anonymous. However, it is worth noting that several journalism studies found no differences in ratings of news stories with anonymous and identified sources—and in certain specific situations anonymous sources may be more trusted than they would be in general. Similarly the economics research would suggest that third party institutions or other ways of showing common interests can enhance the trust of anonymous others.

As a related finding, we note there is some evidence to suggest that credibility perceptions of specific labels used to denote an anonymous source (e.g., "official" vs. "analyst") in journalism may vary. In related organizational work, Callison (2001) noted that anonymous generic sources were actually rated as more trustworthy than a source identified as a public relations spokesperson. This links back to issues of how anonymity is operationalized and the heavy use of pseudonyms across much of the research reviewed here.

Identification. This construct has been examined across these literatures as both an outcome of anonymous interaction and as more of a moderating factor. In the SIDE research and related psychology research, one of the more consistent findings is that identification with one's overarching group, and sometimes with one's more local group, matters substantially when cues to personal identity are not present. Thus, the influence of anonymity may depend heavily on existing identifications and salient identities for group members (and anonymity could have almost opposite influences depending on whether a more personal or social identity is salient). As an outcome variable, there are some consistent findings tied to identification, especially as related to visual anonymity. Psychology research found that participants reported stronger identification with their native nationality group when anonymous to that audience than when identifiable to them. Similarly, identification with the host nation was also stronger when responses were anonymous than when identifiable. In the GSS literature, one of the only studies to examine this found that participants reported the greatest group identification when members were physically hidden but were discursively identified. In general, physical anonymity is the type most linked to greater identification with one's group.

Summary and Future Directions

Overall, the findings paint a picture of anonymity as a construct that is both poorly defined and thus operationalized in numerous different ways. Its utility is that it fosters participation—and this is especially true for more marginalized groups who might feel too threatened or uncomfortable interacting without anonymity. But, the relationship to various influence and feedback processes is unclear, the effect on performance is at best mixed (with some evidence suggesting less effectiveness), and trust is generally diminished when communicating anonymously. Yet, identification can result from anonymity and even shape how anonymity influences other constructs. This creates in some ways a concerning contradiction in that a key way of enhancing participation (in the media, in the workplace, in the economic system, online, in groups, etc.) may not produce intended results and even contribute to diminished trust among communicators. Addressing this sort of contradiction and understanding how people manage these situations is vital for moving research forward.

Figure 13.1 not only provides one potentially useful way to organize the relevant findings across these literatures, but it also suggests several directions for future research. The heuristic value of the model helps focus attention on questions about anonymous communication *to whom, by what means,* and *through what processes.* Gaps in the current research also suggest the need to consider questions about *from whom* and *for what purpose.*

Anonymity factors include those that assess types of anonymity such as physical vs. discursive anonymity (and the many potential ways to achieve that anonymity), technical vs. social anonymity (and the recognition that anonymity is often a matter of degree rather than an absolute), and even the communication technology used (some of which afford much greater opportunity for anonymity than others). These factors also consider conceptual and operational definitions for anonymity. Together, these factors address important questions about anonymity *by what means.* Greater attention to these variables as they influence anonymity processes and ultimately outcomes is needed—but has yet to receive much attention across these research areas. Operationalizations of any online tool as anonymous would seem to overlook sizable variations between tools in norms for use and technological affordances (some tools are much more anonymous than others). Conversely, assumptions that any FtF setting or use of names makes one identified may need to be challenged—especially when zero-history strangers are interacting. Beyond the channels that provide some degree of technical anonymity, perceptual views of anonymity should continue to be examined. Anonymous's (1998) model of anonymous communication provides several useful ideas for a more social view of anonymity.

A related concern less obvious from the model addresses questions about anonymity *to whom.* Several findings suggested audience/receiver considerations guide communication efforts. Relevant issues here include whether we are anonymous to all or only some; use of confidentiality and intermediaries; and considerations about the receiver's acceptance of, expectations for, and/or reaction to (e.g., desire to identify) anonymity (see Rains & Scott, 2007). We suspect this is important at several levels. In some cases, certain institutions may know our identity, but keep it confidential so that we are effectively anonymous to others. This is comparable to the role that Internet Service Providers may play in some instances. For some, that level of partial anonymity is acceptable because it provides a user anonymity for the audience where it is most needed. In a similar vein, we want anonymity from coworkers or teachers or others to save face, but we may care less if technical experts (e.g., IT personnel) could identify us. In other cases, audience anonymity matters because we wish to be anonymous to one group but potentially identifiable to another. The work on ingroups/outgroups and internal/external others provides a useful reminder that we are not simply anonymous or not (but must consider to whom we are or wish to be anonymous). Consideration of audience and receiver preferences is vital for future research as well.

The middle part of the model focuses on communication processes that appear especially relevant to anonymous communication. We already have evidence that anonymity seems to often enhance participation—but for which audiences and under what types of anonymity? One of the clearer findings across these research areas is that more marginalized groups have the most to benefit from anonymous participation—which not only speaks to the interaction process, but anonymous sources. The findings are much more mixed about processes related to influence such as decision making and attitude change, as well as feedback. More specific consideration of anonymity types and audiences may help sort out when anonymous communication leads to certain types of decision shifts or facilitates more/less feedback. Variables such as participation, influence, and feedback help address questions about anonymous communication *through what processes* and to a lesser extent *from whom* (though past research has not heavily examined source issues, future research should do more to describe and profile communicators who choose anonymity). In addition, future research may benefit from exploring other processes closely linked to anonymous forms of interaction (e.g., uncertainty reduction efforts, attributions).

Finally, the model notes a focus on outcomes. The findings related to standard outcomes such as performance are mixed. Trust and credibility are often diminished in anonymous exchanges. However, greater connection of these outcomes to specific communication processes as well as anonymity factors (e.g., type of anonymity) may help address these concerns. The findings for identification are more consistent, but need to be examined with a wider range of relevant targets and anonymity types. Outcomes questions should help us answer questions about *for what purpose*. Answering such a question, though, should go beyond efforts to be effective or create identification and must lead anonymity scholars to begin more widely addressing other related issues such as situational appropriateness, topic suitability, and practical applications.

In conclusion, we see anonymous communication as a topic of growing importance in the world and one that continues to receive attention from somewhat scattered fields of study. As legal examinations grow, as the Internet matures, and as public opinion about accountability shifts, this topic will likely become even more important and more examined in these various fields. However, the lack of prior efforts to look across these areas leaves us with an inadequate picture of the current state-of-the-art in this area and without direction for future research on the topic. It is our hope this chapter provides both a useful summary of the existing literature on this topic and some sensemaking that inspires the next generation of scholars to build on prior efforts.

Notes

1. However, anonymity is distinct from privacy. Anonymous communication may be public or private, and it is only the identity of one or more communicators that is kept hidden.
2. An initial search of EBSCO databases using the search term "anonymity" produced well over 20,000 results—but many were an artifact of using anonymity as part of the data-collection procedure for a study (e.g., anonymous survey responses). Accordingly, we took several steps to focus the search process. We limited our searches to article abstracts, added the tem "communicat*" to all queries, and searched for variations of the words "anonymity," "pseudonym," and "unidentified." The search for "anonym*," "unident*," and "pseudonym*" each with "communicat*" produced exactly 1,600 records, which were then reviewed by one of the chapter authors to identify original research studies, eliminate nonpublished work, and begin classifying research by disciplinary areas and interdisciplinary topics. In a few instances, the articles we retrieved cited additional studies relevant to anonymous communication; we attempted to retrieve the additional studies to ensure reasonable comprehensiveness.
3. As Walther (2010) notes, studies manipulating visual anonymity may provide even more anonymity through impersonal experiences, abstract identifiers, and relatively limited interaction periods. Thus, even with relatively consistent findings, it is not always possible to know exactly how much of that is due to the visual anonymity.

References

Adams, J. B. (1962). The relative credibility of 20 unnamed sources. *Journalism Quarterly, 39,* 79–82.

Adams, J. B. (1964). Unnamed sources and the news: A follow-up study. *Journalism Quarterly, 41,* 262–264.

Adrianson, L. (2001). Gender and computer-mediated communication: Group processes in problem solving. *Computers in Human Behavior, 17,* 71–94.

Ahern, T. C., & Durrington, V. (1995). Effects of anonymity and group saliency on participation and interaction in a computer-mediated small-group discussion. *Journal of Research on Computing in Education, 28,* 133–148.

Algraawi, M. A., & Culbertson, H. M. (1987). Relation between attribution specificity and accessibility to news sources. *Journalism Quarterly, 64,* 799–804.

Anonymous. (1998). To reveal or not to reveal: A theoretical model of anonymous communication. *Communication Theory, 8*, 381–407.

Antonioni, D. (1994). The effects of feedback accountability on upward appraisal ratings. *Personnel Psychology, 47*, 349–356.

Arnold, L., Shue, C. K., Kritt, B., Ginsburg, S., & Stern, D. T. (2005). Medical students' views on peer assessment of professionalism. *Journal of General Internal Medicine, 20*, 819–824.

Arnold, M. C., Ponick, E., & Schenk-Mathes, H. Y. (2008). Groves mechanism vs. profit sharing for corporate budgeting—An experimental analysis with preplay communication. *European Accounting Review, 17*, 37–63.

Ayers, S., & Kaplan, S. E. (2005). Wrongdoing by consultants: An examination of employees' reporting intentions. *Journal of Business Ethics, 57*, 121–137.

Bajari, P., & Yeo, J. (2009). Auction design and tacit collusion in FCC spectrum auctions. *Information Economics and Policy, 21*, 90–100.

Baltes, B. B., Dickson, M. W., Sherman, M. P., Bauer, C. C., & LaGanke, J. S. (2002). Computer-mediated communication and group decision making: A meta-analysis. *Organizational Behavior and Human Decision Processes, 87*, 156–179.

Bamberger, P. A., Erev, I., Kimmel, M., & Oref-Chen, T. (2005). Peer assessment, individual performance, and contribution to group processes: The impact of rater anonymity. *Group & Organization Management, 30*, 344–377.

Bargh, J. A., & McKenna, K. Y. A. (2004). The internet and social life. *Annual Review of Psychology, 55*, 573–590.

Barreto, M., Spears, R., Ellemers, N., & Shahinper, K. (2003). Who wants to know? The effect of audience on identity expression among minority group members. *British Journal of Social Psychology, 42*, 299–318.

Bell, P. R., & Jamieson, B. D. (1970). Publicity of initial decisions and the risky shift phenomenon. *Journal of Experimental Social Psychology, 6*, 329–345.

Beuchot, A., & Bullen, M. (2005). Interaction and interpersonality in online discussion forums. *Distance Education, 26*, 67–87.

Bhappu, A., D., Griffith, T. L., & Northcraft, G. B. (1997). Media effects and communication bias in diverse groups. *Organizational Behavior and Human Decision Processes, 70,* 199–205.

Blankenburg, W. (1992). The utility of anonymous attribution. *Newspaper Research Journal, 13*(1/3), 10–23.

Bloom, A. J., & Hautaluoma, J. E. (2001). Effects of message valence, communicator credibility, and source anonymity on reactions to peer feedback. *The Journal of Social Psychology, 127*, 329–338.

Bohnet, I., & Baytelman, Y. (2007). Institutions and trust: Implications for preferences, beliefs, and behavior. *Rationality and Society, 19*, 99–135.

Bohnet, I., & Frey, B. S. (1999). Social distance and other-regarding behavior in dictator games: Comment. *The American Economic Review, 89*, 335–339.

Bornstein, G., & Rapoport, A. (1988). Intergroup competition for the provision of step-level public goods: Effects of preplay communication. *European Journal of Social Psychology, 18*, 125–142.

Boudreau, C., McCubbins, M. D., & Coulson, S. (2009). Knowing when to trust others: An ERP study of decision making after receiving information from unknown people. *SCAN, 4*, 23–34.

"Bronco" a.k.a. Scott, C. R. (2004). Benefits and drawbacks of anonymous online communication: Legal challenges and communicative recommendations. In S. Drucker (Ed.), *Free speech yearbook* (Vol. 41, pp. 127–141). Washington, DC: National Communication Association.

Callison, C. (2001). Do PR practitioners have a PR problem?: The effect of associating a source with public relations and client-negative news on audience perception of credibility. *Journal of Public Relations Research, 13*, 219–234.

Carpenter, S., Lacy, S., & Fico, F. (2006). Network news coverage of high-profile crimes during 2004: A study of source use and reported context. *Journalism & Mass Communication Quarterly, 83,* 901–916.

Chang, T-K. (1989). Access to the news and U.S. foreign policy: The case of China, 1950–1984. *Newspaper Research Journal, 10*(4), 33–44.

Christopherson, K. M. (2007). The positive and negative implications of anonymity in Internet social interactions: "On the Internet, nobody knows you're a dog." *Computers in Human Behavior, 23*, 3038–3056.

Coffey, B., & Woolworth, S. (2004). "Destroy the scum, and then neuter their families:" The web forum as a vehicle for community discourse? *The Social Science Journal, 41*, 1–14.

Colvin, J., Chenoweth, L., Bold, M., & Harding, C. (2004). Caregivers of older adults: Advantages and disadvantages of internet-based social support. *Family Relations, 53*, 49–57.

Connolly, T., Jessup, L. M., & Valacich, J. S. (1990). Effects of anonymity and evaluative tone on idea generation in computer-mediated groups. *Management Science, 36*, 689–703.

Cooper, W. H., Gallupe, B. R., Pollard, S., & Cadsby, J. (1998). Some liberating effects of anonymous electronic brainstorming. *Small Group Research, 29*, 147–178.

Cotton, J. L., & Baron, R. S. (1980). Anonymity, persuasive arguments, and choice shifts. *Social Psychology Quarterly, 43*, 391–404.

Crews, C. W. (2007). Cybersecurity and authentication: The marketplace role in rethinking anonymity—before regulators intervene. *Knowledge Technology Policy, 20*, 97–105.

Culbertson, H. M. (1975). Veiled news sources—who and what are they? *News Research Bulletin, 3,* 3–22.

Culbertson, H. M. (1976). Veiled attribution—an element of style? *Journalism Quarterly, 53,* 456–465.

Culbertson, H. M., & Somerick, N. (1976). Cloaked attribution—what does it mean to news readers? *Newspaper Research Bulletin, 1,* 3–21.

Dennis, A. R. (1994). Electronic support for large groups. *Journal of Organizational Computing, 4*, 177–197.

de Vreede, G., & Mgaya, R. J. S. (2006). Technology supported collaborative learning for higher education: Comparative case studies in Tanzania. *Information Technology for Development, 12,* 113–130.

DiGiovanni, E., & Nagaswami, G. (2001). Online peer review: An alternative to face-to-face? *ELT Journal, 53*, 263–272.

Douglas, K. M., & McGarty, C. (2001). Identifiability and self-presentation: Computer-mediated communication and intergroup interaction. *British Journal of Social Psychology, 40*, 399–416.

Douglas, K. M., & McGarty, C. (2002). Internet identifiability and beyond: A model of the effects of identifiability on communicative behavior. *Group Dynamics: Theory, Research, and Practice, 6*, 17–26.

Eckel, C. C., & Grossman, P. J. (1996). Altruism in anonymous dictator games. *Games and Economic Behavior, 16*, 181–191.

Fedler, F., & Counts, T. (1981). Variations in attribution affect readers' evaluations of stories. *Newspaper Research Journal, 2*(3), 25–34.

Froomkin, A. M. (1999). Legal issues in anonymity and pseudonymity. *The Information Society, 15*, 113–127.

Gallagher-Lepak, S., Reilly, J., & Killion, C. M. (2009). Nursing student perceptions of community in online learning. *Contemporary Nurse, 32*, 133–146.

Garbett, R., Hardy, S., Manley, K., Titchen, A., & McCormack, B. (2007). Developing a qualitative approach to 360-degree feedback to aid understanding and development of clinical expertise. *Journal of Nursing Management, 15*, 342–347.

Gassaway, B. (1988). Are secret sources in the news media really necessary? *Newspaper Research Journal, 9*(3), 69–77.

George, J. F., Easton, G. K., Nunamaker, J. F., & Northcraft, G. B. (1990). A study of collaborative group work with and without computer-based support. *Information Systems Research, 1*, 394–415.

Guardado, M., & Shi, L. (2007). ESL students' experiences of online peer feedback. *Computers and Composition, 24*, 443–461.

Gudelunas, D. (2005). Talking taboo: Newspaper advice columns and sexual discourse. *Sexuality & Culture, 9*, 62–87.

Hale, D. (1984). Unnamed news sources: Their impact on the perceptions of stories. *Newspaper Research Journal, 5*(2), 49-56.

Hayne, S. C., Pollard, C. E., & Rice, R. E. (2003). Identification of comment authorship in anonymous group support systems. *Journal of Management Information Systems, 20*, 301–329.

Hayne, S. C., & Rice, R. E. (1997). Attribution accuracy when using anonymity in group support systems. *International Journal of Human Computer Studies, 47*, 429–452.

Henderson, S., & Gilding, M. (2004). 'I've never clicked this much with anyone in my life': Trust and hyperpersonal communication in online friendships. *New Media & Society, 6*, 487–506.

Hiltz, S. R., Turoff, M., & Johnson, K. (1989). Experiments in group decision making 3: Disinhibition, deindividuation, and group process in pen name and real name computer conferences. *Decision Support Systems, 5*, 217–232.

Jaffe, J. M., Lee, Y., Huang, L., & Oshagan, H. (1999). Gender identification, interdependence, and pseudonyms in CMC: Language patterns in an electronic conference. *The Information Society, 15*, 221–234.

Jessup, L. M., Connolly, T., & Galegher, J. (1990). The effects of anonymity on GDSS group process with an idea-generating task. *MIS Quarterly, 14*, 313–321.

Jessup, L. M., & Tansik, D. A. (1991). Decision making in an automated environment: The effects of anonymity and proximity with a group decision support system. *Decision Sciences, 22*, 266–279.

Joinson, A. N. (2001). Self-disclosure in computer-mediated communication: The role of self awareness and visual anonymity. *European Journal of Social Psychology, 31*, 177–192.

Kahai, S. S. (2009). Anonymity and counter-normative arguments in computer-mediated discussions. *Group Organization Management, 34*, 449–478.

Kang, H., & Yang, H. (2006). The visual characteristics of avatars in computer-mediated communication: Comparison of Internet Relay Chat and Instant Messenger as of 2003. *International Journal of Human Human-Computer Studies, 64*, 1173–1183.

Kaplan, S., Pany, K., Samuels, J., & Zhang, J. (2009). An examination of the association between gender and reporting intentions for fraudulent financial reporting. *Journal of Business Ethics, 87*, 15–30.

Karan, V., Kerr, D. S., Murphy, U. S., & Vinze, A. S. (1996). Information technology support for collaborative decision making in auditing: An experimental investigation. *Decision Support Systems, 16,* 181–194.

Kling, R., Lee, Y., Teich, A., & Frankel, M. S. (1999). Assessing anonymous communication on the Internet: Policy deliberations. *The Information Society, 15*, 79–90.

Lea, M., Spears, R., & de Groot, D. (2001). Knowing me, knowing you: Anonymity effects on social identity processes within groups. *Personality and Social Psychology Bulletin, 27*, 526–537.

Lee, E. (2004). Effects of gendered character representation on person perception and informational social influence in computer-mediated communication. *Computers in Human Behavior, 20*, 779–799.

Lee, E. (2005). Effects of the influence agent's sex and self-confidence o informational social influence in computer-mediated communication. *Communication Research, 32*, 29–58.

Lee, E. (2006). When and how does depersonalization increase conformity to group norms in computer-mediated communication? *Communication Research, 33*, 423–447.

Lee, E. (2007a). Character-based team identification and referent informational influence in computer-mediated communication. *Media Psychology, 9*, 135–155.

Lee, E. (2007b). Effects of gendered language on gender stereotyping in computer-mediated communication: The moderating role of depersonalization and gender-role orientation. *Human Communication Research, 33*, 515–535.

Lee, E. (2007c). Wired for gender: Experientiality and gender-stereotyping in computer-mediated communication. *Media Psychology, 10*, 182–210.

Lievrouw, L. A., & Finn, A. T. (1996). New information technologies and informality: Comparing organizational information flows using the CSM. *International Journal of Technology Management, 11*, 28–42.

Lim, J., & Guo, X. (2008). A study of group support systems and the intergroup setting. *Decision Support Systems, 45*, 452–460.

Lim, J., Yang, Y. P., & Zhong, Y. (2007). Computer-supported collaborative work and learning: A meta-analytic examination of key moderators in experimental GSS research. *International Journal of Web-Based Learning and Teaching Technologies, 2,* 40–70.

Lindskold, S., & Finch, M. L. (1982). Anonymity and the resolution of conflicting pressures from the experimenter and from peers. *The Journal of Psychology, 112*, 79–86.

Livingstone, S., & Helsper, E. J. (2007). Taking risks when communicating on the internet: The role of offline social-psychological factors in young people's vulnerability to online risks. *Information, Communication & Society, 10*, 619–644.

Martin-Kratzer, R., & Thorson, E. (2007). Use of anonymous sources declines in U.S. newspapers. *Newspaper Research Journal, 28*(2), 56–70.

Marx, G. T. (1999). What's in a name? Some reflections on the sociology of anonymity. *The Information Society, 15*, 99–112.

Marx, G. T. (2001). Murky conceptual waters: The public and the private. *Ethics and Information Technology, 3*, 157–169.

Marx, G. T. (2004). Internet anonymity as reflection of broader issues involving technology and society. *Asia-Pacific Review, 11*, 142–166.

McLeod, P. L., Baron, R. S., Marti, M. W., & Yoon, K. (1997). The eyes have it: Minority influence in face-to-face and computer-mediated group discussion. *Journal of Applied Psychology, 82,* 706–718.

Miceli, M. P., Roach, B. L., & Near, J. (1988). The motivations of anonymous whistle-blowers: The case of federal employees. *Public Personnel Management, 17*, 281–296.

Mishna, F., Saini, M., & Solomon, S. (2009). Ongoing and online: Children and youth's perceptions of cyber bullying. *Children and Youth Services Review, 31*, 1222–1228.

Morahan-Martin, J., & Schumacher, P. (2003). Loneliness and social uses of the Internet. *Computers in Human Behavior, 19*, 659–671.

Morio, H., & Buchholz, C. (2009). How anonymous are you online? Examining online social behaviors from a cross-cultural perspective. *AI & Society, 23*, 297–307.

Nissenbaum, H. (1999). The meaning of anonymity in an Information Age. *The Information Society, 15*, 141–144.

Park, H., Blenkinsopp, J., Oktem, M. K., & Omurgonulsen, U. (2008). Cultural orientation and attitudes toward different forms of whistleblowing: A comparison of South Korea, Turkey, and the U.K. *Journal of Business Ethics, 82*, 929–939.

Peter, J., & Valkenburg, P. M. (2007). Who looks for casual dates on the Internet? A test of the compensation and the recreation hypotheses. *New Media & Society, 9*, 455–474.

Pezzo, S. P., Pezzo, M. V., & Stone, E. R. (2006). The social implications of planning: How public predictions bias future plans. *Journal of Experimental Social Psychology, 42*, 221–227.

Pinsonneault, A., & Heppel, N. (1997). Anonymity in group support systems research: A new conceptualization, measure, and contingency framework. *Journal of Management Information Systems, 14,* 89–108.

Pissarra, J., & Jesuino, J. C. (2005). Idea generation through computer-mediated communication: The effects of anonymity. *Journal of Managerial Psychology, 20*, 275–291.

Postmes, T., & Lea, M. (2000). Social processes and group decision making: Anonymity in group decision support systems. *Ergonomics, 43,* 1252–1274.

Postmes, T., Spears, R., & Lea, M. (2002). Intergroup differentiation in computer-mediated communication: Effects of depersonalization. *Group Dynamics: Theory, Research, and Practice, 6*, 3–16.

Postmes, T., Spears, R., Sakhel, K., & de Groot, D. (2001). Social influence in computer mediated communication: The effects of anonymity on group behavior. *Society for Personality and Social Psychology, 27*, 1243–1254.

Price, A. R. (1998). Anonymity and pseudonymity in whistleblowing to the U.S. Office of Research Integrity. *Academic Medicine, 73*, 467–472.

Qian, H., & Scott, C. R. (2007). Anonymity and self-disclosure on weblogs. *Journal of Computer-Mediated Communication, 12*, 1428–1451.

Rains, S. A. (2005). Leveling the organizational playing field—virtually: A meta-analysis of experimental research assessing the impact of group support system use on member influence behaviors. *Communication Research, 32,* 193–234.

Rains, S. A. (2007). The impact of anonymity on perceptions of source credibility and influence in computer-mediated group communication: A test of two competing hypotheses. *Communication Research, 34*, 100–125.

Rains, S. A., & Scott, C. R. (2007). To identify or not to identify: A theoretical model of receiver responses to anonymous communication. *Communication Theory, 17,* 61–91.

Reinig, B. A., & Mejias, R. J. (2004). The effects of national culture and anonymity on flaming and criticalness in GSS-supported discussion. *Small Group Research, 35*, 698–723.

Reynolds, A., & Barnett, B. (2003). This just in ... how national TV news handled the breaking "live" coverage of September 11. *Journalism & Mass Communication Quarterly, 80,* 689–703.

Riffe, D. (1979). Relative credibility revisited: How 18 unnamed sources are rated. *Journalism Quarterly, 56,* 618–623.

Roch, S. G., & McNall, L. A. (2007). An investigation of factors influencing accountability and performance ratings. *The Journal of Psychology, 141*, 499–523.

Roselli, R. J., & Brophy, S. P. (2006). Experiences with formative assessment in engineering classrooms. *Journal of Engineering Education*, *95*, 311–324.

Rovai, A. (2002). Building a sense of community at a distance. *International Review of Research in Open and Distance Learning, 3*(1), 1–16.

Saco, D. (2002). *Cybering democracy: Public space and the Internet.* Minneapolis: University of Minnesota.

Samuels, C. A. (2007). Online support seen for youths with learning disabilities. *Education Week, 26*, 12.

Sassenberg, K., & Boos, M. (2003). Attitude change in computer-mediated communication: Effects of anonymity and category norms. *Group Processes & Intergroup Relations, 6*, 405–422.

Sassenberg, K., & Postmes, T. (2002). Cognitive and strategic processes in small groups: Effects of anonymity of the self and anonymity of the group on social influence. *British Journal of Social Psychology, 41*, 463–480.

Scharlott, B. W., & Christ, W. G. (1995). Overcoming relationships-initiation barriers: The impact of a computer-dating system on sex role, shyness, and appearance inhibitions. *Computers in Human Behavior, 11*, 191–204.

Schwartz, M. S. (2004). Effective corporate codes of ethics: Perceptions of code users. *Journal of Business Ethics, 55*, 323–343.

Scott, C. R. (1999). Communication technology and group communication. In L. R. Frey, D. Gouran, & M. S. Poole (Eds.), *The handbook of group communication theory and research* (pp. 432–472). Thousand Oaks, CA: Sage.

Scott, C. R., Corman, S. R., & Cheney, G. (1998). Development of a structural model of identification in the organization. *Communication Theory, 8*, 298–336.

Scott, C. R., Quinn, L., Timmerman, C. E., & Garrett, D. (1998). Ironic uses of group communication technology: Evidence from meeting transcripts and interviews with group decision support system users. *Communication Quarterly, 46,* 353–374.

Scott, C. R., & Rains, S. A. (2005). Anonymous communication in organizations: Assessing use and appropriateness. *Management Communication Quarterly, 19,* 157–197.

Shawver, T., & Clements, L. H. (2008). Whistleblowing: Factors that contribute to management accountants reporting questionable dilemmas. *Management Accounting Quarterly, 9*, 26–38.

Sheehy, M. (2008). Foreign news stories more likely to include unnamed sources. *Newspaper Research Journal, 29*(3), 24–37.

Sia, C., Tan, B., & Wei, K. (2002). Group polarization and computer-mediated communication: Effects of communication cues, social presence, and anonymity. *Information Systems Research, 13,* 70–90.

Smith, J. R., Terry, D. J., & Hogg, M. A. (2007). Social identity and the attitude-behavior relationship: Effects of anonymity and accountability. *European Journal of Social Psychology, 37*, 239–257.

Smith, R. (2007). Impact of unnamed sources on credibility not certain. *Newspaper Research Journal, 28*(3), 8–19.

Sosik, J. J. (1997). Effects of transformational leadership and anonymity on idea generation in computer-mediated groups. *Group & Organization Management, 22*, 460–487.

Sosik, J. J., Kahai, S. S., & Avolio, B. J. (1998). Transformational leadership and dimensions of creativity: Motivating idea generation in computer-mediated groups. *Creativity Research Journal, 11*, 111–121.

Spears, R., Lea, M., Corneliussen, R. A., Postmes, T., & Haar, W. T. (2002). Computer-mediated communication as a channel for social resistance: The strategic side of SIDE. *Small Group Research, 33*, 555–574.

St. Dizier, B. (1985). Reporters' use of confidential sources, 1974 and 1984: A comparative study. *Newspaper Research Journal, 6*(4), 44–50.

Sternadori, M. M., & Thorson, E. (2009). Anonymous sources harm credibility of all stories. *Newspaper Research Journal, 30*(4), 54–66.

Sullivan, N., & Pratt, E. (1996). A comparative study of two ESL writing environments: A computer assisted classroom and a traditional oral classroom. *System, 24*, 491–501.

Swain, K. A. (2007). Outrage factors and explanation in news coverage of the anthrax letters. *Journalism & Mass Communication Quarterly, 84,* 335–352.

Tanis, M., & Postmes, T. (2007). Two faces of anonymity: Paradoxical effects of cues to identity in CMC. *Computers in Human Behavior, 23*, 955–970.

Tanis, M., & Postmes, T. (2008). Cues to identity in online dyads: Effects of interpersonal versus intragroup perceptions on performance. *Group Dynamics: Theory, Research, and Practice, 12*, 96–111.

Teich, A., Frankel, M. S., Kling, R., & Lee, Y. C. (1999). Anonymous communication policies for the Internet: Results and recommendations of the AAAS Conference. *The Information Society 15*, 71–77.

Trauth, E. M., & Jessup, L. M. (2000). Understanding computer-mediated discussions: Positivist and interpretive analyses of group support system use. *MIS Quarterly, 24*, 43–79.

Turkle, S. (1995). *Life on the screen: Identity in the age of the Internet.* New York: Simon & Schuster.

Tuzi, F. (2004). The impact of e-feedback on the revisions of L2 writers in an academic writing course. *Computers and Composition, 21*, 217–235.

Valacich, J. S., Dennis, A. R., & Nunamaker, J. F. (1992). Group size and anonymity effects on computer-mediated idea generation. *Small Group Research, 23*, 49–73.

Walker, R. S. (2004). The effect of recent US legislation and rule making on corporate compliance and ethics programmes. *International Journal of Disclosure and Governance, 1*, 138–145.

Walther, J. B. (2010). Computer-mediated communication. In C. R. Berger, M. E. Roloff, & D. R. Roskos-Ewoldsen (Eds.), *Handbook of communication science* (2nd ed., pp. 489–505). Los Angeles: Sage.

Walther, J. B., Slovacek, C., & Tidwell, L. C. (2001). Is a picture worth a thousand words? Photographic images in long term and short term virtual teams. *Communication Research, 28*, 105–134.

Waskul, D., & Douglass, M. (1997). Cyberself: The emergence of self in on-line chat. *The Information Society, 13*, 375–397.

Wayner, P. (1999). Technology for anonymity: Names by other nyms. *The Information Society 15*, 91–97.

Westerman, D. (2008). How do people really seek information about others?: Information seeking across Internet and traditional communication channels. *Journal of Computer-Mediated Communication, 13*, 751–767.

Wulfemeyer, K. (1985). How and why anonymous attribution is used by Time and Newsweek. *Journalism Quarterly, 62*, 81–126.

Yu, F. (2009). Scaffolding student-generated questions: Design and development of a customizable online learning system. *Computers in Human Behavior, 25*, 1129–1138.

Yu, F., & Liu, Y. (2009). Creating a psychologically safe online space for a student-generated questions learning activity via different identity revelation modes. *British Journal of Educational Technology, 40*, 1109–1123.

Zeldes, G., Fico, F., & Lacy, S. (2008). Context and sources in broadcast television coverage of the 2004 Democratic primary. *Mass Communication & Society, 11*, 340–356.

CHAPTER CONTENTS

14 Mass Media Effects on Youth Sexual Behavior

Assessing the Claim for Causality

Paul J. Wright

University of Arizona

Studies of the impact of the mainstream mass media on young people's sexual behavior have been slow to accumulate despite longstanding evidence of substantial sexual content in the mass media. The sexual media effects landscape has changed substantially in recent years, however, as researchers from numerous disciplines have answered the call to address this important area of sexual socialization scholarship. The purpose of this chapter is to review the subset of accumulated studies on sexual behavior effects to determine whether this body of work justifies a causal conclusion. The standards for causal inference articulated by Cook and Campbell (1979) are employed to accomplish this objective. It is concluded that the research to date passes the threshold of substantiation for each criterion and that the mass media almost certainly exert a causal influence on United States' youth sexual behavior.

In any formula for pop entertainment, the two most time-tested ingredients are sex and violence. Of course, purveyors must be careful. Too much of one or the other can attract unwanted attention and public outcries for restraint.

(O'Conner, 1990)

Entertainment mass media offerings in the United States are replete with portrayals of recreational, consequence-free sex and glorified violence (e.g., Gunasekera, Chapman, & Campbell, 2005; Kunkel et al., 2007; Sargent et al., 2002; Smith et al., 1998; Ward, 1995). While potentially fallacious (Bushman & Bonacci, 2002), the rationale driving sexual and violent productions is captured in the often stated clichés: "sex sells" and "violence sells." Although they may fill the coffers of media companies, few content patterns have drawn the ire of child advocates, moral authorities, and overseers of the public's health to the extent of media sex and violence. For instance, The Parents' Television Council was founded with the express purpose of preventing children from being "constantly assaulted" by sex and violence in the mass media (Arnston, 2005, p. 1C). Likewise, the National Council of Churches has warned that media sex and violence lead to untoward behavior among youth and "seriously threaten the quality of American life" (Associated Press, 1985, p. 3A). Similarly, members of the American Academy of Pediatrics have repeatedly advised the public about the dangers to children that accrue from exposure to media violence and sex (Guernsey, 2008; United Press International, 1986).

National surveys indicate that parents and other adults are also quite concerned about the adverse effects of media sex and violence on young people. A *Los Angeles Times* poll conducted in 1989 found that nearly two-thirds of adults believed that violence and sex in the media were "corrupting the nation" (Kaye, 1989, p. D8). A study of parents carried out by the Kaiser Family Foundation almost 20 years later generated parallel sentiment about the negative effects of media violence and sex on youth and also revealed that the majority of parents would favor stricter federal oversight of sex and violence in the media (Allday, 2007, p. A1). Corroborating these findings, data from the Pew Research Center indicate that approximately 60% of adults are "very concerned" about the effects of media sex and violence on young people (Lester, 2005). Like the lay public, academics interested in the antisocial effects of media on youth also tend to talk about media sex and media violence in the same breath (Brown & Cantor, 2000; Brown & Steele, 1995; Donnerstein & Smith, 2001; Malamuth & Impett, 2001; Ward, 2003). In sum, statements of trepidation about media sex invariably include statements of trepidation about media violence and vice versa, and sex and violence appear to be the content patterns of most concern when it comes to the role of the mass media in the behavior of youth in the United States.

Despite the prevalence of both sex and violence in mainstream mass media fare and longstanding worry about both sexual and violent depictions on youth behavior, however, only the study of media violence and aggression has a long research history. Studies of mass media violence began more than 75 years ago (Sparks & Sparks, 2002), have been conducted by some of the most distinguished social psychologists of our time (e.g., Bandura, 1965; Donnerstein & Berkowitz, 1981), and have drawn the attention of policy makers at the highest levels of the federal government (Kunkel, 2003; Wright, 2009a). More than 1,000 studies of media violence were conducted by the end of the 20th century (Strasburger & Donnerstein, 1999), and more studies of the effects of media violence continue to be published each year. Social scientists, medical doctors, and public health scholars who have reviewed the mass media violence research nearly all agree that a causal link between mass media violence and aggression has been established (Kunkel, 2003; Wright, 2009a). For instance, in a *Psychological Science in the Public Interest* article on the role of media violence in youth aggression, a team of eminent psychologists and communication researchers concluded that there is "unequivocal evidence that exposure to media violence increases the likelihood of aggressive and violent behavior in both immediate and long-term contexts" (Anderson et al., 2003, p. 81).

One would be hard pressed to find a similar statement regarding the effects of the mass media on youth sexual behavior. An official declaration about the role of mass media violence in youth aggression was made in a 1972 Surgeon General's report (Surgeon General, 1972). Conversely, a volume released in

1982 by the National Institute of Mental Health reported that "no study" had yet assessed the effect of television on youth sexual behavior (Roberts, 1982, p. 209). Instead of coming to conclusions about behavioral effects, the paucity of studies available in the past forced reviewers to conjecture about the mass media's "great potential for playing an important role in the sexual socialization of our youth" (Brown, Walsh-Childers, & Waszak, 1990, p. 68), to speculate that "studies of the impact of the media on sexual behavior very likely will find patterns of effects similar to those established for violent content" (Brown & Steele, 1995, p. 24), and to theorize why it is "likely" that the mass media "affect a child's sexual socialization" (Roberts, 1982, p. 209).

In December of 1997, the Kaiser Family Foundation brought together an esteemed group of scholars to look into possible reasons for the scarcity of studies on the effects of sexual mass media on adolescents and to make suggestions for researchers interested in the role of the mass media in sexual socialization.[1] The report that resulted from this symposium (Huston, Wartella, & Donnerstein, 1998) and the Surgeon General's call to action to promote sexual health and responsible behavior (Office of the Surgeon General, 2001) has led to an increase in empirical data regarding the effects of sexual mass media content on adolescents (Kunkel, Eyal, Finnerty, Biely, & Donnerstein, 2005). Many of these studies have been well-funded, longitudinal efforts carried out by interdisciplinary research teams comprised of established scholars such as Jane Brown (communication), the late Martin Fishbein (psychology), and Ralph DiClemente (public health).

For the first time, evidence-based statements about the impact of the mass media on youth sexual behavior are being made by social scientists. Collins et al. (2004) conclude that the magnitude of the effect of sexual television is so strong that even "a moderate shift in the average sexual content of adolescent TV viewing could have substantial effects on sexual behavior at the population level" (p. 287). Chandra et al. (2008) argue that if only "a fraction" of the association between sexual television viewing and pregnancy involvement in their prospective study is causal, "reducing the exposure of US teens to sexual content might substantially reduce teen pregnancy rates" (p. 1052). Referencing their overtime findings and the longitudinal findings of Collins et al. (2004), Ashby, Arcari, and Edmonson (2006) conclude that "television watching increases the risk of sexual initiation by adolescents" (p. 379). Bleakley, Hennessy, Fishbein, and Jordan (2008) similarly remark that their prospective findings "are consistent with others in the literature that demonstrate a causal effect of sexual content exposure on sexual behavior" (p. 458). Finally, commenting on the implications of their finding that a "media diet" high in sexual content hastens coital initiation and increases noncoital behavior, Brown et al. (2006) admonish the academic community and policymakers "not to wait decades" to conclude that the mass media are an important factor in youth sexual behavior (p. 1026).

In the introduction to the most recent synthesis of the literature on the content of sexual messages in entertainment mass media, Wright (2009b) mentioned the progression of the sexual mass media effects literature but did not review these advances in any detail. The purpose of this chapter is to address this deficiency. Specifically, this chapter assesses findings from quantitative studies that have investigated the effects of the mainstream mass media on the sexual behavior of adolescents and emerging adults in the United States. This review is limited to mainstream (i.e., non-pornographic) media studies because the effects of the mainstream mass media have been the focus of recent sexual socialization research efforts, are the primary source of current causal claims, and the near exclusive focus of longitudinal behavioral effects studies of youth in the United States (see Brown & L'Engle, 2009, for an exception).

A report of this nature is overdue. More than a decade has passed since the Kaiser conference and the Surgeon General's 2001 report. First, an overview of United States youths' sexual behavior and its consequences is provided to demonstrate the importance of research into the determinants of youth sexual behavior. Second, a multi-component perspective on mass media behavioral effects is outlined to explore how mass media influences on youth sexual behavior may occur. Third, mass media studies that have measured sexual behavior outcomes are presented. Finally, the evidence reviewed is evaluated to determine whether a causal conclusion about the effects of mass media on youth sexual behavior is warranted.

U.S. Youths' Sexual Behavior and Sex in the Mass Media

The American Academy of Pediatrics (2001) has identified precocious and unprotected youth sexual activity as a "major public health problem" (p. 191). This section presents information on the prevalence and consequences of United States youths' sexual behavior and discusses the potential role of the mass media on youth sexual decision making as suggested by content studies.

In 2007, 48% of high school students reported that they had already had sexual intercourse (Centers for Disease Control, 2008a); by the age of 19, 70% of adolescents have had sexual intercourse (Abma, Martinez, Mosher, & Dawson, 2004). Early intercourse onset has been associated with a number of negative health outcomes (American Academy of Pediatrics, 2001) but approximately 13% of females and 15% of males engage in coitus before they are 15 years old (Abma et al., 2004). Fifteen percent of high school students report having had intercourse with four or more different partners (Centers for Disease Control, 2008a). Data gathered by the Kaiser Family Foundation indicates that 36% of teens aged 15–17 have had oral sex and 66% of young adults aged 18–24 have had oral sex (Toff, Greene, & Davis, 2003).

In 2007, 39% of sexually active high school students did not use a condom during their last intercourse (Centers for Disease Control, 2008a) and previous research has found that even adolescents who do use condoms do so inconsistently (Abma et al., 2004). Only 18% of sexually active high school students report that either they or their partner used birth control pills before their last intercourse (Centers for Disease Control, 2006).

Given these figures, it is not surprising that pregnancy and STIs often go hand in hand with youth sexual activity. Eighty-two percent of teen pregnancies are unplanned and account for about 20% of the unintended pregnancies in the United States annually (Finer & Henshaw, 2006). Thirty-one percent of the adolescent female population becomes pregnant at least once before the age of 20 and about 80% of these pregnancies occur out of wedlock (Guttmacher Institute, 2006). Although the teen birth rate had been declining since 1991, recent Centers for Disease Control (CDC) data show that teen birth rates increased 3% from 2005 to 2006 (SIECUS, 2007). Although 15- to 24-year-olds comprise about 25% of the sexually experienced population, they account for nearly 50% of all new STIs each year (Weinstock, Berman, & Cates, 2004). In 2006, 14% of the people diagnosed with HIV/AIDS in states reporting to the CDC were between the ages of 13 and 24 (Centers for Disease Control, 2008b).

These data indicate that a sizable portion of United States youth are sexually active, have sex with multiple partners, engage in unsafe sex practices, and experience detrimental outcomes as a result of their sexual behavior. Why do some young people abstain from sex or engage in responsible sexual activity while other adolescents engage in indiscriminate and unsafe sex? Do the mass media highlight sexual risks and promote sexual responsibility, or do they largely ignore sexual responsibility and downplay sexual risks? Although there is variability by genre (Wright, 2009b), the answer is that by and large the mass media portray sex as a recreational, risk-free activity.

According to an American Academy of Pediatrics' report on sexuality, contraception, and the media (2001), "the average American adolescent will view nearly 14,000 sexual references per year, yet only 165 of these references deal with birth control, self-control, abstinence, or the risk of pregnancy or STDs" (p. 191). A review of sex on television by Brown et al. (1990) concluded that "contraceptives are almost never referred to or used, but women seldom get pregnant [and] men and women rarely contract sexually transmitted diseases" (p. 64). A more recent review of sex on television (Kunkel et al., 2007) reports that messages about sexual risk are still "quite limited" (p. 611) and indicates that even when sexual risk or sexual responsibility messages are present they "rarely receive primary emphasis within a program" (p. 616). Wright's (2009b) review of content studies found that "popular films contain frequent references to and depictions of sexual activity but feature very few messages about the risks and consequences associated with being sexually active" (p. 190). Wright (2009b) also reports that lifestyle magazines for teen girls (e.g., *Seventeen, YM, 'Teen*) send mixed messages about sexual responsibility and that lifestyle magazines for teen boys (e.g., *Maxim, FHM*) may be totally devoid of risk and responsibility messages. Finally, in her review and synthesis essay, Ward (2003) also concluded that the mass media give "minimal attention" to the potential negative consequences associated with sexual activity (p. 359). To conclude, content studies provide reason to believe that exposure to sexual mass media may have a disinhibiting effect on young people and do little to prompt safe sex behavior.[2]

Acquisition, Activation, Application: A Multi-Component Perspective on Mass Media Sexual Behavior Effects

No theory has been designed with the specific purpose of predicting how and when sexual media content affects young people's sexual behavior and the complete development of such a theory is beyond the scope of this review. For heuristic and descriptive purposes, however, this section presents a multi-component perspective on mass media behavioral effects to explore how mass media influences on youth sexual behavior may occur (see Figure 14.1). Results from mass media sexual socialization studies are incorporated whenever possible to link theoretical statements to actual findings. It is assumed that youth have access to the mass media and opportunities to be sexual.

The perspective draws most heavily on the theorizing of Huesmann (1986, 1988, 1998). According to Huesmann (1986), the mass media affect behavior by providing cognitive scripts which suggest what events should and should not be happening, how people should behave in response to what is or is not happening, and what the outcomes of particular courses of action should be. A scripts perspective on sexual behavior has been recommended by numerous sex researchers (Gagnon & Simon, 1973; Laws & Schwartz, 1977) and may be particularly relevant to young people's sexual decision making (Reed & Weinberg, 1984). Beyond the extension of the scripts concept to media effects

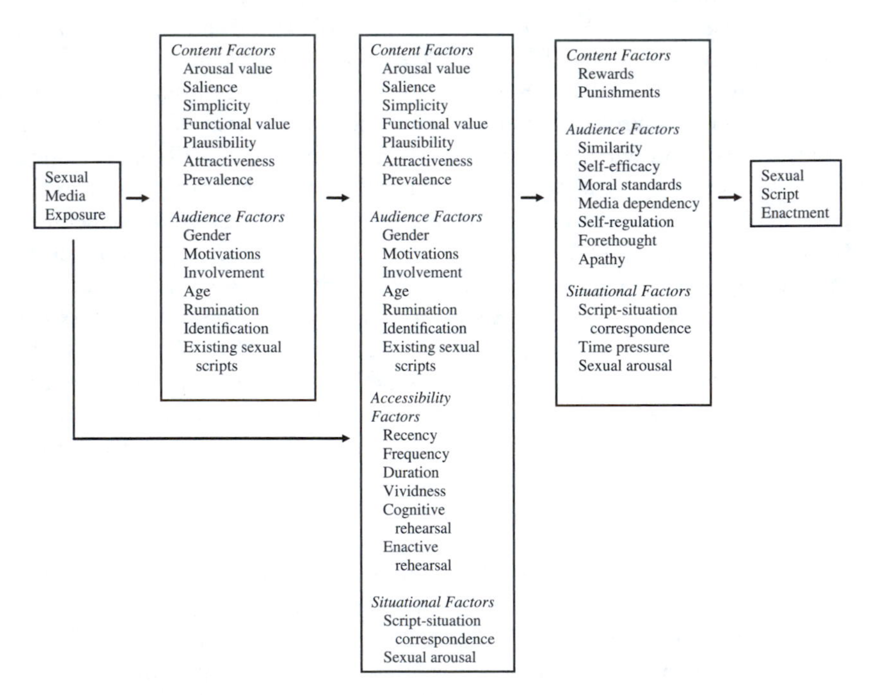

Figure 14.1 An acquisition, activation, application perspective on mass media sexual behavior effects.

theorizing, another contribution made by Huesmann is his assertion that there are really three components to the media effects on behavior process: the acquisition of behavioral scripts, the activation of behavioral scripts, and the application of behavioral scripts (Bandura, 2001, for example, focuses on acquisition and application, but not on activation).

An acquisition effect occurs when an observer learns a new behavioral script that he or she was not aware of. Adolescents can learn specific scripts from the mass media (e.g., that sex on prom night is common and a special experience) or "higher order scripts" (Huesmann, 1986, p. 131) by abstracting the general rule or philosophy guiding media models' behavior (e.g., "if sex on prom is acceptable, adolescent sex in general is acceptable"). An activation effect occurs when media exposure cues "the retrieval of already-learned … scripts" (Huesmann, 1986, p. 132). Media content may activate sexual scripts that were acquired from the mass media or from other sources. Stimuli other than the mass media may cue sexual scripts (e.g., sexual arousal, being alone with a partner), but all acquired scripts must be activated in some way in order to guide behavior (Huesmann, 1998). Activation and application are not synonymous, however. Huesmann's information processing model of observational learning (1988, 1998) allows for the possibility that activated scripts will be deemed inappropriate and discarded.

Several other conceptualizations have been suggested as relevant to sexual mass media effects. Brown and Steele (1995) have suggested that cultivation (Gerbner, Gross, Morgan, & Signorielli, 1994; Shrum, 2009) and social-cognitive theory (Bandura, 2001) can explain mass media sexual socialization. Ward (2003) has suggested the utility of "priming" concepts (p. 361) and has also employed uses and gratifications (Rubin, 2002) variables in her work. Hetsroni (2008) explores the utility of media dependency models. Tenets from all of these approaches are utilized in the present discussion. In sum, the following perspective is more integrative than novel. It is presented to explore whether a synthesis of existing theories supports the contention of mass media effects on youth sexual behavior and to provide insight into factors that may increase or decrease the likelihood of such effects.

Acquisition

A number of content and audience variables are theorized to influence the acquisition of behavioral scripts from the mass media. The primary importance of content variables on script acquisition has to do with the ability of various portrayals to catch and maintain the attention of receivers. A fundamental position of both Bandura (2001) and Huesmann (1986) is that attention is a prerequisite for learning from the mass media. Behaviors that do not attract at least a modest level of attention cannot be encoded.

To start, behaviors with arousal value, that are salient to receivers, and relatively simple may be more likely to draw the attention of and be encoded by audiences than behaviors that are not arousing, do not stand out, or are complicated to understand and follow. Studies employing physiological measures of sexual arousal such as penile tumescence (Schaefer & Colgan, 1977) and blood volume levels in vaginal blood vessels (Sintchak & Geer, 1975) have found that both males and females can be aroused by sexual media content. Studies of the impact of media sex on sexual arousal have generally used sexually explicit media as stimuli. But sexual explicitness may not linearly relate to sexual arousal for all persons (Gunter, 2002), so the types of sexually suggestive but not explicit portrayals of sexual activity that young people encounter when they attend to mainstream media may still have arousal value (Malamuth & Impett, 2001). Most sexual behaviors (e.g., kissing, petting, intercourse) that are talked about, suggested, shown (at least indirectly), and described in mass media fare are not particularly complicated to understand. Nor are scripts for who to have sex with (e.g., anybody one is highly attracted to—Ward, 1995), what to wear to be sexually attractive (e.g., next to nothing if you are a female who wants to attract a male—Seidman, 1992), or when to have sex (e.g., better to wait until at least the second date—Heintz-Knowles, 1996). Finally, sexual behavior is highly salient to adolescents (Diamond & Savin-Williams, 2009).

Second, behaviors with functional value that are portrayed in realistic ways by attractive models may be more likely to be attended to and encoded by audiences than behaviors that have little functional value, are not realistic, and are performed by nondescript individuals. The functional value of a behavior lies in its ability to create rewards or punishments for the enactor. It is more important to pay attention to behaviors that result in pronounced rewards or punishments than behaviors that result in subtle consequences or no perceptible consequences. Because the rewards (e.g., orgasm, bonding, romantic love) and punishments (e.g., HIV, physical violence, rejection) associated with sexual behavior can be quite dramatic (Bleske & Shackelford, 2001; Rotherum-Borus, O'Keefe, Kracker, & Foo, 2000; Small & Kerns, 1993; Sprecher & Regan, 1998; Stephan & Bachman, 1999; Young, Denny, Young, & Luquis, 2000), portrayals of sexual behavior likely have functional value in the eyes of youthful observers.

An important moderator of perceived sexual script functionality may be gender. Males may pay special attention to short-term sexual scripts because short-term mating strategies have been adaptive for male primates historically, females may pay special attention to long-term sexual scripts because long-term mating strategies have been adaptive for female primates historically (Malamuth, 1996). Evolved sexual predilections are not completely deterministic, however. According to Bandura (2001), "human nature is a vast potentiality that can be fashioned by direct and observational experience into a variety of forms within biological limits" (p. 266). If Bandura's (2001) model of triadic reciprocal causation is accurate, males should be able to "unlearn" evolved short-term mating preferences and females should be able to "unlearn" evolved long-term mating preferences, at least to some extent (see also MacDonald, 2008).

Evidence for the latter pattern can be found in several studies. Strouse, Buerkel-Rothfuss, and Long (1995) found a positive association between high school girls' permissive premarital sex attitudes and music video exposure. Ward and Rivadeneyra (1999) found a positive association between television viewing and female undergraduates' recreational attitudes towards sex. Female undergraduates, in an experiment carried out by Ward (2002), were more apt to look at dating as a "game" and to see women as "sex objects" after they had seen sexual prime-time dramas and sitcoms. Similarly, females who watched more sexual television expected sex to occur earlier in relationships than females who watched less television in a survey study of undergraduates' sexual expectations (Aubrey, Harrison, Kramer, & Yellin, 2003). In sum, males and females probably have evolved divergent sexual strategies that tend to direct their attention to different sexual models. Behavioral inclinations are malleable, however, and studies of mass media sexual socialization suggest that there are youthful females who pay attention to and are influenced by media portrayals that tout recreational, short-term sex. Whether males are interested in and influenced by portrayals of intimate, long-term sexual relationships in the mass media remains to be seen.

Sexual behaviors engaged in by media models may have functional value in the mediated world, but may not be encoded by receivers for purposes of behavioral enactment unless they are perceived as realistic. Several studies suggest that heightened perceptions of mass media sexual realism among young people increase the likelihood of sexual socialization effects (Baran, 1976a, b; Olson, 1994; Taylor, 2005; Ward, Merriwether, & Caruthers, 2006). Heightened realism perceptions have not always been associated with predicted sexual outcomes in mass media studies, however (Aubrey et al., 2003; Davis & Mares, 1998). From an information processing perspective, this may be because people often process media messages at low levels of criticality and do not label media portrayals as "false" at the time of encoding (Wyer & Radvansky, 1999). From an evolutionary perspective, inconsistent perceived reality findings may be due to the fact that distinguishing "fantastic" from "real" modeling events was unimportant in the environment of evolutionary adaptedness (Malamuth & Impett, 2001). As far as the attractiveness of media models is concerned, young people acknowledge that models in their preferred vehicles are typically highly attractive (Milkie, 1999).

A final content attribute that almost certainly facilitates attention and encoding is prevalence. Behavioral prevalence may increase the likelihood of encoding for several reasons. First, the more prevalent a particular behavior is the less likely it is to go unnoticed. Adolescents may vary in their desire to consume sexual media (Steele, 1999), but the prevalence of sexual portrayals across genres (Wright, 2009b) and the tremendous amounts of time adolescents spend attending to mass media content (e.g., United States youth aged 8–18 spend more than 7½ hour a day attending to entertainment media, and almost 11 hours if one considers media multitasking—Rideout, Foehr, & Roberts, 2010) make it unlikely that adolescents can avoid exposure to sexual portrayals with much success. Second, the idea of prevalence in the social learning arena may be likened to the concept of message repetition in persuasion. Message repetition is thought to facilitate attention through increased comprehension (McGuire, 1969). While the essence of most sexual scripts is straightforward, nuanced script components may require repeated exposures to be fully understood. Third, repeated exposure to a pattern of sexual portrays may facilitate encoding by eventually increasing liking for the behaviors portrayed (Zajonc, 1968). In sum, behavioral prevalence may facilitate the acquisition of behavioral scripts due to an increased ability and desire to encode modeled behaviors.

Scholars from the uses and gratifications tradition have argued for some time that the motivations for media consumption brought to the table by audience members impact what they learn from the mass media (Rubin, 2002). For instance, audiences may be motivated by escape or diversion desires (i.e., ritualized use) or may attend to media content for information acquisition (i.e., instrumental use). The latter motivation is expected to enhance effects, a supposition supported by several studies (Aubrey et al., 2003; Kim & Ward, 2004; Ward, 2002; Ward et al., 2006). To illustrate, Kim and Ward (2004) found that female undergraduates who read contemporary women's magazines to learn about sex held more stereotypical views about male sexuality (e.g., that males are sex driven and afraid of commitment) than their peers who had other reading motives. Aubrey et al. (2003) report that male undergraduates who watch sexual television for instrumental purposes have higher expectations for sexual variety in romantic relationships.

Another important uses and gratifications variable is audience involvement, or the degree to which audiences actively interpret, assess, and think about what they see, read, or hear in the mass media. Shrum (2009) has recently suggested that higher levels of involvement equate to stronger media effects for attitudinal variables. Thirty years ago Blumler (1979) argued the opposite position. Rubin (2002) adopts a more nuanced stance: audience involvement can enhance effects or reduce them, depending on the nature of the involvement. Preliminary mass media sexual socialization results support Rubin's (2002) assertion. Ward (2002) reports that male and female undergraduates who are selective, involved television viewers who speak with others about the shows they watch are more likely to hold sexually objectified beliefs about women. This finding supports the argument that "a more selective, attentive and involved state of media use … may actually be a catalyst to message effects" (Rubin, 2002, p. 535). On the other hand, Bryant and Rockwell (1994) found that 13- and 14-year-old youth who viewed television with a critical eye were not desensitized to the sexual improprieties they were shown in a longitudinal experiment. The results of this study support the position that being "skeptical" may "inhibit … outcomes" (Rubin, 2002, p. 535).

Four other audience variables should be mentioned. First, younger adolescents may not encode scripts suggested by subtle sexual messages and innuendos simply because they cannot understand them (Silverman-Watkins & Sprafkin, 1983). At the same time, sexual scripts that can be understood may hold special relevance to young audiences due to a primacy effect (Huesmann, 1986). Second, the propensity to ruminate and fantasize about sexual media content may increase the likelihood of script encoding due to increased comprehension and increased opportunity for abstract modeling (Bandura, 2001; Huesmann, 1986). Third, youth who identify with media models may be more likely to attend to and retain the sexual scripts they have observed than youth who do not identify with media models. Support for this social learning mainstay was demonstrated in an experiment by Ward, Hansbrough, and Walker (2005), who found that identification with music video persona enhanced the effect of sexist music videos on Black adolescents' sexual stereotypes. Other studies by Ward and her associates also point to the importance of identification for sexual script acquisition (Ward, 2002; Ward & Friedman, 2006; Ward et al., 2006).

Finally, sexual mass media scripts should be more readily encoded when they are at least somewhat compatible with existing sexual scripts. To illustrate, the sexual values espoused by mass media models often contradict those espoused by families (Zillmann, 1994). If content-value incongruity hinders script acquisition, it would be expected that living in a family with an open communication style and clearly defined values would buffer youth from the sexual scripts available for adoption in the mass media. Evidence in support of the mitigating effects of family values has been found by Bryant and Rockwell (1994). Because most religions emphasize relational and procreational sexual values, high levels of religiosity may also discourage the internalization of sexual scripts provided by the mass media (Strouse & Buerkel-Rothfuss, 1987).

Activation

Scripts must be active in memory in order to have an effect on behavior. An activation effect occurs when exposure to media messages cues the retrieval of an already acquired schema. Schemas "refer to any macro knowledge structure encoded in memory that represents substantial knowledge about a concept, its attributes, and its relation to other concepts" (Huesmann, 1998, p. 80). Schemas may contain beliefs, attitudes, and behavioral scripts (Fiske & Linville, 1980; Huesmann, 1998). The process of media induced schema activation is generally referred to as "priming" (Huesmann, 1998, p. 81).

During the time primed schema are activated, they may color perceptions and alter behavior. For instance, McKenzie-Mohr and Zanna (1990) found that men who already held sexually stereotyped views of women behaved more sexually than non sex-typed men towards a female confederate after being primed by sexually explicit films. Sexually explicit media may also prime male expectations of female physical attractiveness (Weaver, Masland, & Zillmann, 1984), sexual interest, and sexual permissiveness (Jansma, Linz, Mulac, & Imrich, 1997). Mainstream mass media sex studies suggest similar effects. For instance, exposure to music videos may prime positive attitudes towards premarital sex (Greeson & Williams, 1986) and more acceptance of aggressive romantic strategies (Johnson, Adams, Ashburn, & Reed, 1995) among middle and high school students, and heightened sexual attributions of others

(Hansen & Krygowski, 1994) and adversarial sexual beliefs (i.e., the belief that male/female sexual relationships are adversarial and exploitive) (Kalof, 1999) among college students.

There are three types of moderating variables in the priming process: (a) variables that increase the likelihood that particular media portrayals will generate the force required to activate scripts, (b) variables that increase the accessibility of scripts in memory, and (c) variables that increase the likelihood that particular scripts will be activated in a given situation. Examples of each class of variable are mentioned briefly to close this section.

A "first law" of media priming may be stated as follows: schema at rest will stay at rest unless sufficiently acted upon by a media message. In other words, media messages can only act as primes if audiences attend to them. Consequently, many of the content factors that were mentioned in the acquisition delineation apply here. Depictions with attractive models, that have arousal and functional value, are salient, simple, realistic, and prevalent, should be more likely to activate sexual scripts than depictions with nondescript models, that have little arousal and functional value, are not salient, are convoluted, unrealistic, and infrequent. Several of the audience variables also apply. Male and female adolescents may attend to different sexual portrayals. Audiences with instrumental motives may be more susceptible to media primes than audiences with escape or diversion motives. A certain level of decoding ability, rumination, cognitive involvement, and character identification may be required for media primes to have an activation effect. Additionally, sexual content that is highly incompatible with existing sexual schemas may be ignored.

Several variables are thought to increase the accessibility of scripts in memory. Foremost among these are recency of exposure and frequency of exposure (Roskos-Ewoldsen, Roskos-Ewoldsen, & Dillman Carpentier, 2009; Shrum, 2009). Recent exposure increases the accessibility of scripts in short-term memory. Frequent exposure may lead to long-term memory activation and scripts in long-term memory are typically highly or "chronically" accessible (Huesmann, 1998; Roskos-Ewoldsen et al., 2009). An additional factor is prime duration (Roskos-Ewoldsen et al., 2009). The longer people are exposed to a particular set of related messages, the more likely the messages are to increase the accessibility of related scripts in memory. Because sexual messages make up a significant portion of the mass media landscape and the only activity adolescents engage in more than media consumption is sleeping (Rideout et al., 2010), it seems reasonable to assume that the average adolescent has recently and frequently been exposed to sexual mass media for considerable periods of time.

A content factor that may increase the accessibility of sexual scripts primed by the mass media is vividness. Vivid content is content that is "emotionally interesting, concrete and imagery provoking, and proximate in a sensory, temporal, or spatial way" (Nisbett & Ross, 1980, p. 45). A number of authors have commented on the ever increasing vividness of sexual portrayals in the mass media (Brown & Steele, 1995; Huston et al., 1998; Malamuth & Impett,

2001; Wingood et al., 2003). Shrum (2009) has suggested that vivid portrayals increase the accessibility of related constructs in memory.

Two audience behaviors that should increase the accessibility of sexual mass media scripts are cognitive and enactive rehearsal (Bandura, 2001; Huesmann, 1986). First, cognitive behaviors such as reflection and fantasy increase the accessibility of scripts by strengthening connections between nodes and by creating new node links (Pfau, Ivanov, & Houston, 2005; Pfau, Roskos-Ewoldsen, & Wood, 2003). Second, sexual media consumption and fantasizing may be accompanied by masturbation, a form of enactive rehearsal that should increase the accessibility of rehearsed scripts to an even greater degree (Lyons, Anderson, & Larson, 1994; Malamuth & Impett, 2001). Since "the masturbating man" is the "target" of much sexual media (Strager, 2003, p. 51), accessibility effects due to solo-sex activity may be most likely to accrue for males.

Last, Huesmann (1988, 1998) identifies two situational cues that can impact the activation of sexual scripts acquired from the mass media: script-situation correspondence and arousal. All other factors being equal (e.g., accessibility), the script activated in a given situation will be the one that has the most overlap with current environmental factors. Consider the example of an adolescent heterosexual couple who has not yet engaged in coitus. He has acquired a coital script from "lad" magazines such as *Maxim* (Taylor, 2006) that emphasizes the thrill of sex in public places. She has acquired a coital script from magazines such as *Seventeen* (Carpenter, 1998) that stress that one's "first time" should take place somewhere special, such as a nice hotel. Sitting in a parked car alone will be much more likely to activate thoughts of coitus in his mind than in hers. A variable closely related to script-situation correspondence that affects script activation is script diversity, or the number of different scripts a person has witnessed and encoded (Huesmann, 1986).

The impact of script diversity on script activation is straightforward. The more varieties of mass media scripts a person has encoded the more relevant any one script will be in a particular situation and the more likely it is that a script acquired from the mass media will be activated. Though some are presented much more often than others, the variety of sexual scenarios presented in the mass media is impressive (e.g., extra-relationship sex, sadomasochistic sex, threesome sex, one-night stands, anal sex, group sex, tit-for-tat sex, coercive sex, teenage stripping, exhibitionism—Greenberg & Hofschire, 2000; Wright, 2009b). Consequently, an adolescent who attends to a variety of mass media may possess a sexual script for almost every sexual situation.

Arousal plays a role in script activation in two different ways. First, arousal shrinks the capacity of working memory and restricts memory searching which increases the likelihood that the most accessible script will be the one activated in a given situation (Huesmann, 1998). The most accessible sexual scripts for adolescents who consume large amounts of mass media should be those provided by the mass media. The accessibility of these scripts should be even more pronounced when adolescents are sexually aroused. An adolescent who is both sexually aroused and a heavy media consumer should find it difficult to access sexual scripts other than those provided by the mass media. The second way arousal may play a part in script activation is through "encoding specificity." Encoding specificity refers to the fact that cues and emotions present when information is first encoded become "associated with the encoded information and can trigger its activation in memory" (Huesmann, 1998, p. 83). If adolescents are sexually aroused when they encode mass media sexual scripts, arousal and the encoded scripts become associated. Then, when an adolescent is aroused in a sexual situation, his or her arousal will increase the accessibility of the sexual script he or she learned from the mass media.

Application

The activation of a script increases the probability it will be employed but does not guarantee it. Bandura (2001) "distinguishes between acquisition and performance because people do not perform everything they learn" (p. 274). This article distinguishes between activation and performance because activation is the liaison between script acquisition and script enactment. Huesmann's (1988, 1988) information processing model of observational learning allows for the possibility that activated scripts will be deemed inappropriate and discarded. Huesmann (1998) calls this script evaluation process "filtering." Anderson (1997) calls it a "secondary appraisal." Whatever the descriptor, the script evaluation process ultimately involves an "effortful, controlled appraisal of the situation," a "thoughtful consideration of various behavioral alternatives to the situation," and a decision that can "correct or override the primary appraisal" (Roskos-Ewoldsen et al., 2009, p. 82).

A number of factors determine whether an activated script is applied. Chief among these are the consequences a person believes will result from carrying out the script. Since most scripts are learned vicariously (Bandura, 2001), the consequences that accompany models' behavior should weigh heavily in the decision making process. Rewards should prompt behavioral matching, punishments should inhibit matching behaviors. The relationship between consequences to media models and receivers' behavioral intentions is complicated by the media schemas audiences' possess (Nabi & Clark, 2008). Nevertheless, there is evidence that different consequences lead to different effects. Collins et al. (2004) found that Black youth who viewed more television content portraying the risks associated with sex were less likely to have engaged in coitus a year later. Martino, Collins, Kanouse, Elliot, and Berry (2005) found that a prospective association between sexual television viewing and adolescents' precocious sexual behavior was mediated by adolescents' sexual outcome expectations (since media models experience positive consequences, viewers develop positive outcome expectations). Eyal and Kunkel (2008) experimentally tested the effects of different intercourse portrayals and also found that outcomes varied depending on whether characters were rewarded or punished for their behavior.

Perceptions of similarity to media models should moderate the impact of portrayed rewards and punishments. For example, a model may be punished but an observer may believe that she would be able to enact the script to better success due to skills and abilities she possess that the model does not. On the other hand, a model may be rewarded but because of perceived dissimilarities an observer may not believe he would experience the same positive outcomes. Behavioral matching is most likely when observers see themselves as similar to models and when models experiences positive consequences for their actions. Similarity leads to heightened self-efficacy, rewards lead to behavioral motivation. Exposure to sexual mass media content does lead to sexual efficacy among youth, which is in turn predictive of intercourse initiation (Martino et al., 2005). Even if observers perceive similarity between themselves and models and models experiences positive consequences for their behavior, however, observers may still decide to suppress the script in question if their internal moral standards proscribe against it. The moral and religious symbolism so often attached to sexual behavior may inhibit the enactment of the myriad casual sexual scripts in the mass media among some youth. That being said, exposure to sexual media predicts premarital sexual behavior even after the effects of variables such as religiosity and parental disapproval of unmarried sex are considered (Brown et al., 2006; Collins et al., 2004). Finally, script-situation correspondence should also figure into the filtering equation. Script contemplators should place more emphasis on the consequences that a model experienced when their situation corresponds closely with the model's situation.

Whether or not the filtering process results in the selection of a script learned from a source other than the mass media depends on whether the filterer has another script she can select. According to Rubin, dependence on the mass media for behavioral guidance "results from an environment that restricts the availability of functional alternatives" (p. 536). Parents (Wright, 2009c), educators (Brown, Steele, & Walsh-Childers, 2002), and medical professionals (Schuster, Bell, Peterson, & Kanouse, 1996) are typically reluctant sexual communicators. In the absence of alternative scripts provided by adult mentors, youth faced with sexual situations have to either use a script obtained from the mass media or a script obtained from a peer or a sibling. But in the absence of adult sexual socialization, peers and siblings are most likely imparting a script they learned from the mass media. In sum, the role of the mass media in adolescent sexual decision making may represent a classic media dependency situation (Rubin & Windahl, 1986).

Recall that the script evaluation process was purported to involve an "effortful, controlled appraisal of the situation" and a "thoughtful consideration of various behavioral alternatives to the situation" (Roskos-Ewoldsen et al., 2009, p. 82). When such systematic processing takes place, secondary appraisals may indeed be dependent on the factors just outlined. But systematic processing in social situations occurs infrequently (Bargh & Chartrand, 1999). Processing in many situations is "automatic." Automatic processing "occurs very rapidly, without using many cognitive resources and without any conscious executive decisions made about the process" (Huesmann, 1998, pp. 80, 81). Shrum (2007) concludes that "close scrutiny of all or even most of the relevant information available to a person in the course of decision making may be the exception rather than the rule" (p. 115).

Systematic processing is inhibited when people lack the ability or motivation to engage in systematic behavioral analysis (Shrum, 2009). Some individuals' capacity for systematic processing may always be limited due to an inherent lack of self-regulation and forethought capacity (Bandura, 2001). Other individuals possess these capacities but are indifferent to the negative outcomes an inappropriate script will generate for themselves and others (Huesmann, 1988).

Time pressure (Shrum, 2007) and sexual arousal (Huessmann, 1998) are situation-specific factors that should decrease the likelihood of systematic processing. Time pressure decreases the ability to process systematically, sexual arousal should decrease both the motivation and the ability to process systematically. Since spontaneity and sexual arousal are part and parcel to sexual passion and intrigue, it seems likely that a good deal of sexual script processing is automatic, irrespective of innate individual differences in forethought and self-regulation capacity. While not developed to explain script analysis, Shrum's (2009) heuristic processing model points to some possibilities for how sexual decisions are made under automatic processing conditions.

Two social cognition principles (accessibility and sufficiency) and one cognitive heuristic (availability) are key to Shrum's (2009) model. The accessibility principle states that under automatic processing conditions social decisions are made using the most accessible information in memory. The sufficiency principle states that under automatic processing conditions social decisions are made using the minimum amount of information necessary. The role of mass media exposure in script accessibility was established in some detail in the "activation" section and the ability of the mass media to provide the basic sexual script necessities has also been outlined. In sum, automatic processing should make the application of media acquired sexual scripts likely for heavy media consumers because of their accessibility in memory and their ability to guide a complete sequence of sexual behavior (i.e., what should be done, with whom, and under what circumstances).

When linked with the finding that descriptive norms influence young people's behavior (Rimal & Real, 2005), the availability heuristic provides additional insight into how exposure to sexual media may facilitate the application of media acquired sexual scripts. The availability heuristic refers to the now well demonstrated fact that under automatic processing conditions people make prevalence estimates of phenomena based on how easily they can recall a specific example from memory. High levels of exposure to youth-targeted media should make it easy to recall examples of teen sex which should lead to larger estimates of sexual behavior among young people. Perceived descriptive norms can then be used to make a quick assessment of an activated sexual script (e.g., that one should accept or initiate a sexual advance or forgo using a condom). Although she did not test the specific proposition just described, Chia (2006a, b) has provided evidence in support of the general notion that exposure to sexual media, perceived peer norms, and permissive sexual attitudes and intentions among young people are indeed intertwined.

Summary

This portion of the chapter provided a multi-component perspective on mass media behavioral effects to explore how mass media influences on youth sexual behavior may occur. It was presented to investigate whether a synthesis of existing theories support the contention of mass media effects on youth sexual behavior and to provide insight into factors that may increase or decrease the likelihood of such effects. Following Huesmann (1988, 1998), the effects process was broken down into three components: the role of the mass media in sexual script acquisition, the role of the mass media in sexual script activation, and factors that determine whether scripts acquired or primed by the mass media are actually applied in sexual situations. At each step in the process variables were described that could reduce the impact of the mass media on young people's sexual behavior.[4] By and large, however, the convergence of existing theory supports the hypothesis that exposure to sexual mass media should generally have a facilitating effect on sexual behavior. The next section of the chapter details findings of studies that have looked for empirical evidence of the impact of the mainstream mass media on U.S. youths' sexual behavior.

Effects on Sexual Behavior

Several steps were taken to obtain a comprehensive list of studies for review. First, the PsycINFO, PsycARTICLES, Communication & Mass Media Complete, MEDLINE, Web of Science, and Academic Search Complete databases were searched using combinations of the following key words and their variants: mass media, media, television, movies, magazines, music videos, sex, and sexuality. Second, relevant studies derived from the electronic search were read and cross-referenced to locate reports that had not been generated by the database search. Twenty-one studies were located that included samples of U.S. youth and measured some association between mainstream mass media consumption and sexual behavior (see Table 14.1). Nine studies were longitudinal, 16 studies were comprised of youth 18 or younger or in grade 12 or below. Studies were inspected to see the kinds of outcome variables they addressed. Five outcome themes emerged upon review: coital status, sexual experience including but not limited to coital behavior, noncoital behavior, number of sexual partners, and contraception use/STIs/pregnancy. The subsequent discussion reflects this thematic breakdown.

Table 14.1 Studies Assessing Young People's Exposure to the Mass Media and Sexual Behavior by Method, Year, Sample, and Outcome

Method	*Year and Author*	*Sample*	*Outcome*
Longitudinal survey	1991, Peterson et al.	Addolescents	Coital status
Longitudinal survey	1991, Brown & Newcomer.	Addolescents	Coital status
Longitudinal survey	2003, Wingood et al.	Addolescents	Sexually transmitted infection, Number of sexual partners
Longitudinal survey	2004, Collins et al.	Addolescents	Coital status, Noncoital behavior
Longitudinal survey	2006, Ashby et al.	Addolescents	Coital status
Longitudinal survey	2006, Brown et al.	Addolescents	Coital status, Noncoital behavior
Longitudinal survey	2008, Bleakley et al.	Addolescents	Overall sexual experience
Longitudinal survey	2008, Chandra et al.	Addolescents	Pregnancy
Longitudinal survey	2009, Hennessy et al.	Addolescents	Overall sexual experience
Cross-sectional survey	1987, Fabes & Strouse	Young adults	Number of sexual partners, Contraception use
Cross-sectional survey	1987, Strouse & Buerkel-Rothfuss	Young adults	Number of sexual partners
Cross-sectional survey	1988, Solderman et al.	Adolescents	Pregnancy
Cross-sectional survey	1995, Peterson & Kahn	Adolescents	Overall sexual experience
Cross-sectional survey	1995, Strouse et al.	Adolescents	Coital status
Cross-sectional survey	1999, Ward & Rivadeneyra	Young adults	Overall sexual experience
Cross-sectional survey	2005, Pardum et al	Adolescents	Overall sexual experience, Non-coital behavior
Cross-sectional survey	2006, Taylor	Young adults	Number of sexual partners
Cross-sectional survey	2006, Ward & Friedman	Adolescents	Overall sexual experience
Cross-sectional survey	2006, Zurbriggen & Morgans	Young adults	Coital status, Contraception use
Corss-sectional survey	2008, DuRant et al.	Adolescents	Contraception use
Cross-sectional survey	2009, Fisher et al.	Adolescents	Coital status, Noncoital behavior

Note: For sample: Adolescents = youth 18 or younger or in grade 12 or below. Young adults = college students.

Coital Status

Eight studies examined associations between mass media consumption and coital status (i.e., whether or not participants had ever engaged in sexual intercourse) (Ashby et al., 2006; Brown et al., 2006; Brown & Newcomer, 1991; Collins et al., 2004; Fisher et al., 2009; Peterson, Moore, & Furstenberg, 1991; Strouse et al., 1995; Zurbriggen & Morgan, 2006). Five of these studies were longitudinal (Ashby et al., 2006; Brown et al., 2006; Brown & Newcomer, 1991; Collins et al., 2004; Peterson et al., 1991) and three of the five longitudinal studies featured national samples (Ashby et al., 2006; Collins et al., 2004; Peterson et al., 1991). On the whole these studies provide convincing evidence that mass media consumption is related to intercourse initiation.

First, all five longitudinal studies and all three national studies found a main or moderated effect. Collins et al. (2004) surveyed a national sample of teenagers aged 12–17 in 2001 and again in 2002. Sexual media exposure was measured at T1 by assessing how frequently participants viewed 23 popular prime-time programs coded for sexual content by coders employed in Kunkel et al.'s (2003) *Sex on TV 3* study. Participants (1,292) were virgins at T1. Sexual media exposure strongly predicted intercourse initiation at T2, even after controlling for confounding variables such as age, having mostly older friends, household structure, parental education, parental monitoring, academic achievement, religiosity, mental health, sensation seeking tendencies, and engaging in deviant behavior. Probability analyses showed that "watching the highest levels of sexual content effectively doubled the next-year likelihood of initiating intercourse" (Collins et al., 2004, p. 287).

Brown et al. (2006) gathered two-wave data from 1,107 North Carolinian teenagers who were aged between 12 and 14 at T1 and 14 and 16 at T2. Sexual media exposure was assessed at T1 by examining each participant's "sexual media diet," a composite measure which gauges the sexual content of each popular television show, music album, movie, and magazine used frequently by the participant, as well as the frequency of exposure to each medium. Higher sexual media exposure scores were positively related to intercourse initiation at T2 for both Black and White participants, even after controlling for gender, socioeconomic status, parental education, and pubertal status. The effect remained for White participants after the following additional covariates were added to the model: valence of relationship with mother, parenting styles, parents' disapproval of sex, religiosity, religious attendance, school connectedness, academic achievement, and permissive peer sexual norms. Probability analyses based on the final model for Whites revealed that "white adolescents who were in the top exposure quintile to sexual content in the media were at 120% greater risk, or 2.2 times as likely, to have initiated sexual intercourse than white adolescents who were in the lowest exposure quintile" (Brown et al., 2006, p. 1025). The authors point out that the effect size for the association between sexual media exposure and intercourse initiation for Whites ($r = .30$) parallels the association between televised violence exposure and aggression (as calculated in Bushman & Anderson's, 2001, meta-analysis of the effects of television violence).

Ashby et al. (2006) utilized data from 4,808 high school students who participated in the National Longitudinal Study of Adolescent Health (Add Health). The Add Health sampling strategy ensured a nationally representative sample of seventh- through twelfth-grade students. T1 data used for this study were gathered in 1995; T2 data were gathered approximately a year later. Ashby et al. (2006) analysis included participants who were younger than 16 years old at T1 and who had never engaged in coitus. Even though a crude measure of media exposure was employed (number of hours of television viewed per day at T1), results indicated that participants who watched more than 2 hours of television per day were 1.35 times more likely to have experienced intercourse by T2 than participants who watched less than 2 hours a day.

Peterson et al. (1991) also used national data from middle and high school students and a simple measure of time spent watching television. Their analyses were based on two waves of data (T1 = 1976–77; T2 = 1981) from the National Survey of Children. Participants were aged 10–11 at T1 and were assumed to be virgins. The final T2 sample consisted of 461 respondents aged 15–16, 125 of whom reported that they had engaged in coitus. No effect of T1 television viewing on T2 intercourse status emerged for females. However, a "strong positive association" (Peterson et al., 1991, p. 111) between television viewing and intercourse status was observed for males who watched television apart from their parents. The lack of an association between television viewing and females' coital status may have been due to social desirability influences, as the authors indicate that the extent of female coitus self-reported in this data set was suspiciously low in comparison to the findings of other large scale studies.

Brown and Newcomer (1991) used the last two waves of data gathered over the course of several years (1978, 1979, 1981) from southeastern adolescents aged 13–18. Media use data were only available at T3. A proportional measure of sexual media exposure was created at T3 by dividing the amount of sexual television programming participants were exposed to by the total amount of television programming to which they were exposed. This proportional exposure measure predicted coital status at T3, even after controlling for ethnicity, gender, mother's education, puberty status, prior sexual behavior, and perceptions of pressure from friends to have sex. On the other hand, coital status and non-coital sexual behavior at T2 were unrelated to the measure of proportional sexual television viewing at T3. The authors interpret these findings to mean that "the causal direction flows from a high proportion of sexy television viewing to sexual activity rather than vice versa" but caution that the lack of a T2 sexual media exposure → T3 coital status test renders this "a tentative conclusion" (p. 87).

In addition to the evidence provided by the national and longitudinal studies, it is also instructive that five of the six studies that measured sexual media exposure found an effect (Brown et al., 2006; Brown & Newcomer, 1991; Collins et al., 2004; Fisher et al., 2009; Strouse et al., 1995). Fisher et al. (2009) sampled 1,012 Californian adolescents between 13 and 18 years of age from 10 northern and southern counties and administered computer-mediated home interviews. After controlling for age, gender, and ethnicity, a sexual cable television exposure measure that included assessments of music video, HBO, Showtime, R rated movie and Cinemax consumption positively predicted coital status. Strouse et al. (1995) found that adolescents from an unsatisfactory family environment who were heavy music video consumers were 3.7 times more likely to have had coitus than adolescents from an unsatisfactory family environment who did not watch many music videos. Zurbriggen and Morgan (2006), on the other hand, did not find an association between reality dating program viewing and coital status in their sample of college undergraduates. They attribute this null finding to the "recency of this genre of television" coupled with the fact that they assessed "the sexual past rather than the sexual present" (Zurbriggen & Morgan, 2006, p. 14). It should be noted, though, that this study did find a positive association between overall television viewing and female participants' coital status.

Sexual Experience Including but not Limited to Coital Behavior. Seven studies examined associations between mass media consumption and sexual experience including but not limited to coital behavior (Bleakley et al., 2008; Hennessy, Bleakley, Fishbein, & Jordan, 2009; Pardun, L'Engle, & Brown, 2005; Peterson & Kahn, 1995; Ward & Friedman, 2006; Ward & Rivadeneyra, 1999; Zurbriggen & Morgan, 2006). Six of these studies found a main or moderated effect. Zurbriggen and Morgan (2006)—the limitations of which were just discussed—was the lone exception. As was the case for reports of mass media consumption and coital status, these studies afford potent support for the supposition that mass media consumption is related to a range of sexual behaviors.

Bleakley et al. (2008) and Hennessy et al. (2009) were the only longitudinal studies to assess overall sexual experience. These studies represent two of the key reports to date from the Annenberg Sex and Media Study (ASAMS), a three-wave survey of youth from the greater Philadelphia area carried out by researchers at the University of Pennsylvania Annenberg School for Communication and Public Policy Center. All participants were between 14 and 16 years old at T1. Data were collected in 2005, 2006, and 2007. Sexual experience data were collected at all three waves using a lifetime sexual experience Guttman type scale with behaviors such as deep kissing and petting on the low end, and behaviors such as oral and vaginal sex on the high end. Sexual media exposure at T1 and T2 was calculated through a composite measure of exposure to a variety of popular media (e.g., highly rated television shows, magazines) and sexual content analyses of selected titles representative of each genre. Self-reports from participants were used to assess sexual content at T3, but these sexual content assessments were highly correlated with corresponding sexual content assessments from T1 ($r = .75$) and T2 ($r = .77$).

Bleakley et al. (2008) report findings from T1 and T2. Controlling for a host of variables related to teen sexual behavior (e.g., parental monitoring and supervision, unsupervised time at home, parents and peers' approval of sex, physical development, age, and relationship status), a positive association between T1 sexual media exposure and T2 sexual experience was found. Unlike Brown and Newcomer's (1991) results, however, T1 sexual experience was positively related to T2 sexual media exposure, suggesting a nonrecursive relationship (although the authors note that the T1 sexual media exposure → T2 sexual experience effect was stronger than the T1 sexual experience → T2 sexual media exposure effect, p. 457).

Data from T3 were available for Hennessy et al. (2009) analysis, allowing them to utilize individual growth modeling techniques (Singer & Willett, 2003). Age, rather than wave, was employed as the time variable because participants were different ages at each wave. This adjustment created five waves of data, as participants ranged in age from 14 to 18 across the three waves of data collection. Results from this expanded analysis yielded differential findings based on ethnicity in line with the trends uncovered by Brown et al. (2006). Specifically, while both Whites and Blacks' sexual media exposure and sexual experience intercepts positively covaried, only Whites' sexual media exposure and sexual experience scores positively covaried over time. Given the high levels of both sexual experience and sexual media exposure for Blacks at age 14 (both significantly higher than for Whites), it is possible that sexual media exposure has already exerted its influence on Black youth by the time they are 14 and that other factors (e.g., peer influence, socioeconomic circumstances) carry more predictive weight as Blacks age.

Pardun et al. (2005) surveyed 1,074 seventh and eighth graders from three southeastern public school districts. Sexual media exposure scores were derived by assessing exposure to an assortment of media that were subsequently content analyzed for sexual messages. Several sexual behavior indices were tested in this study, but a cumulative measure of "heavy sexual activity" is of interest here (Pardun et al., 2005, p. 84). This indicator of sexual experience was a summative measure of participants' lifetime encounters with heavy petting, oral sex, and coitus. Pardun et al. (2005) tested their hypotheses by pitting each genre against the others. Two-step regression analysis (age, ethnicity, gender, and socioeconomic status were entered in the first step as controls) revealed that exposure to sexual movies and magazines explained independent variance in sexual experience.

Ward and her colleagues have conducted two studies with outcome measures that assess a range of sexual behaviors. Ward and Rivadeneyra (1999) found that female college students who viewed more network comedies, dramas, and soap operas scored higher on a sexual experience scale that asked participants to describe their "current level of experience with dating and sexual relationships" (selection options ranged from "just starting out" and "some dating" to "have had several sexual relationships"; Ward & Rivadeneyra, 1999, p. 241). This association held after controlling for age, socioeconomic status, and ethnicity. Similarly, Ward and Friedman (2006) took into account several demographic controls and viewing motives and still found that music video and talk show (but not prime-time television) exposure explained unique variance in high school students' sexual experience levels (selection options ranged from no sexual experience on the low end to oral sex experience and coital experience on the high end).

Finally, Peterson and Kahn (1995) surveyed a random sample of 326 youth ranging in age from 11 to 18 from a county in Cleveland, Ohio. Their dependent variable was a Guttman scale that ranged from kissing to coitus. Their media exposure variables were a curious potpourri, ranging from exposure to music television to Harrison Ford's *Raiders of the Lost Ark*. The most intuitive measures—music television exposure and an "antisocial" media consumption scale based on exposure to deviant television programs, movies, and musical artists (antisocial judgments were made by a youth panel)—were positively related to sexual experience, even after controlling for age, gender, race, family income, educational goals, family rules, and religiosity.

Noncoital Sexual Behavior

Predictors of noncoital sexual behavior are important to study for at least three reasons. First, behaviors such as kissing, petting, and oral sex may increase the likelihood of coitus. Second, oral sex is a behavior that poses STI transmission risk. Third, more teens engage in oral sex than coitus (Abma et al., 2004). Four studies measured associations between sexual media exposure and noncoital behavior (Brown et al., 2006; Collins et al., 2004; Fisher et al., 2009; Pardun et al., 2005). Results for noncoital behavior assessments are also quite consistent with the hypothesis that mass media exposure catalyzes youth sexual behavior.

Collins et al. (2004) assessed noncoital behavior on a 1 to 5 scale (1 = kissing; 5 = oral sex). After accounting for a host of confounding variables as well as T1 noncoital behavior, sexual television exposure at T1 predicted unique variance in T2 noncoital behavior. The size of this effect rivaled the size of the intercourse initiation effect for this sample described earlier. It is important to stress that the inclusion of T1 noncoital behavior in the model creates a situation where "relationships between viewing sexual content and advancing sexual behavior (are) not attributable to the effects of developing sexual behavior on selective viewing of sexual content" (Collins et al., 2004, p. 287).

Brown et al. (2006) measured noncoital behavior in virtually the same manner as Collins et al. (2004). Brown et al. (2006) results for noncoital behavior paralleled their results for coital status. After the effect of T1 sexual behavior was accounted for, sexual media exposure at T1 predicted T2 noncoital behavior for Blacks after age, gender, socioeconomic status, parental education, and pubertal status were controlled for and for Whites after controlling for all possible covariates. The effect size for sexual media exposure on Whites' noncoital behavior (r = .38) was slightly larger than the effect size for coital initiation (r = .30). As in Collins et al. (2004), controlling for T1 sexual behavior addresses the issue of T1 sexual behavior causing both T1 sexual media exposure and T2 sexual behavior.

Fisher et al. (2009) measured whether participants in their cross-sectional study had ever engaged in oral sex. Sexual cable television exposure was positively related to oral sex status after accounting for age, gender, and ethnicity. Last, Pardun et al. (2005) included the most conservative measure of noncoital behavior. Their measure of "light sexual activity" was a summative measure of participants' lifetime encounters with behaviors such as dating, light kissing, and "French" kissing. Two-step regression analysis (age, ethnicity, gender, and socioeconomic status were entered in the first step as controls) indicated that exposure to sexual movies explained unique variance in "light" noncoital experience.

Number of Sexual Partners

Having sex with multiple partners may increase the risk of STI infection (Wagstaff et al., 1995) so assessing predictors of multiple sexual couplings is of considerable importance. Four studies were located that measured this outcome variable (Fabes & Strouse, 1987; Strouse & Buerkel-Rothfuss, 1987; Taylor, 2006; Wingood et al., 2003).

The most noteworthy study was conducted by Wingood et al. (2003). The sample for this two-wave study (one year between waves) consisted of 480 Black females aged 14 to 18 who were recruited from health classes and medical clinics. Sexual media exposure was assessed by measuring the number of rap videos participants estimated they saw in an average day, multiplied by the number of days in the week rap videos were viewed. Sexual media exposure at T1 predicted multiple sexual couplings at T2, after controlling for age, employment status, involvement in extracurricular activities, religious involvement, family structure, family's receipt of public assistance, and parental monitoring. Compared with participants with lower levels of rap video exposure, participants with high levels of exposure were twice as likely to have had multiple sexual partners by T2.

All three other studies were cross-sectional. Fabes and Strouse (1987) found that college students who rated media characters as exemplars of sexual responsibility had more sexual partners than students who rated parents and educators as their top models of sexual responsibility, although this difference did not reach conventional levels of statistical significance. Strouse and Buerkel-Rothfuss (1987) found that music television exposure and soap opera viewing positively predicted both female and male college students' sexual couplings. Taylor (2006) found that exposure to "lad" magazines (e.g., *Maxim*, *Stuff*) was positively although not significantly related to the number of sexual couplings reported by male undergraduates.

In sum, only one study that assessed number of sexual partners was prospective and only two of the four studies found a significant effect. Taken together, then, these studies provide suggestive evidence but are not as compelling as a group as the sets of studies reviewed in earlier sections.

Pregnancy/Contraception Use/STIs

It is the way sex is portrayed in the mass media—not the portrayal of sex itself—that concerns public health and developmental scholars interested in the well-being of young people. In fact, before Collins and her colleagues published their 2004 study documenting the powerful longitudinal association between exposure to television sex and adolescent sexual behavior, they published an article highlighting the possibility of television serving as a "healthy sex educator" (Collins, Elliott, Berry, Kanouse, & Hunter, 2003). As stated at the conclusion of the section on adolescent sexual behavior and health risk, though, this possibility has yet to be realized (see Wright, 2009b, however, for a discussion of how certain genres are more likely to convey risk and responsibility messages than others and Singhal, Cody, Rogers, & Sabido, 2004, for discussions of the possible power of entertainment-education in the health domain). Consequently, several authors have hypothesized positive associations between mass media consumption and outcome variables such as pregnancy, contraception use, and STIs (Chandra et al., 2008; DuRant, Neiberg, Champion, Rhodes, & Wolfson, 2008; Fabes & Strouse, 1987; Solderman, Greenberg, & Linsangan, 1988; Wingood et al., 2003; Zurbriggen & Morgan, 2006).

Chandra et al. (2008) employed the same sample as Collins et al. (2004), but had access to a third wave of data (T1 = 2001, T2 = 2002, T3 = 2004). Their outcome variable was pregnancy status, operationalized as whether or not a male in the sample had impregnated a female or a female in the sample had been impregnated a month or more after the initial data collection. Male impregnators or females who had become pregnant received the same score. Sexual media exposure was a strong predictor of pregnancy involvement, even after controlling for age, lower grades, parent education, educational goals, ethnicity, gender, household structure, deviant behavior, and intentions to have a child before the age of 22. Probability analyses showed that being in the 90th sexual media exposure percentile doubled the likelihood of pregnancy involvement (in comparison to the 10th sexual media exposure percentile). The results of this study buttress the cross-sectional findings of Solderman et al. (1988) from two decades before. These authors conducted sexual content analyses of soaps, primetime television programs, and R-rated movies popular with a sample of pregnant and non-pregnant teen girls and found that pregnant teens had more exposure to these media than their non-pregnant peers.

DuRant et al. (2008) report results from a random sample of 2,307 youth aged 16 to 20. Data were gathered via telephone interviews. Youth from 138 communities in 17 states took part in the study. The media variable of interest was exposure to professional wrestling, an extremely popular genre with highly sexualized portrayals (DuRant et al., 2008, p. 130). The outcome variable of interest was whether or not participants had ever had sexual intercourse without using birth control. Controlling for a number of confounding factors such as ethnicity, gender, family income, region of the country, fighting behaviors, and family composition, the authors found that "with each one unit increase in the number of times watched wrestling in the past two weeks, youth were 13% more likely to have had sex without birth control" (DuRant et al., 2008, p. 134).

Two other studies addressed contraceptive use. Fabes and Strouse (1987) found that college students who rated media characters as exemplars of sexual responsibility had lower rates of contraceptive use than students who rated parents and educators as their top models of sexual responsibility, although this difference did not reach conventional levels of statistical significance. Zurbriggen and Morgan (2006), on the other hand, found no association between their measures of media exposure and contraceptive use.

Only one study was located that measured an association between mass media consumption and STI status, but the results of this study are notable because the dependent variable consisted of an actual (rather than a self-report) measure of chlamydia, trichomoniasis, and gonorrhea status. Wingood et al. (2003) found that Black teen girls who watched higher levels of rap music videos at T1 were 1.5 times as likely than their more infrequently exposed counterparts to have acquired one of the STIs just listed by T2. This association was found after controlling for a host confounding variables.

In sum, associations between pregnancy status, STI contraction, lack of contraceptive use and mass media exposure have been found prospectively or nationally. On the other hand, the results of small scale cross sectional studies have not yielded significant results. Given that time is often a requirement for both sexual script acquisition and sexual script application and that national samples are the most reliable, it is concluded that the studies reviewed in this section provide moderate to strong support for the idea that mass media consumption is related to sexual behaviors and outcomes that place youth at health or developmental risk.

Assessing the Claim for Causality

Conclusions about cause depend not only on the evidence accumulated regarding a particular causal question but also on the standards used to assess causality. This chapter adopts the conditions espoused by Cook and Campbell (1979). Drawing from John Stuart Mill, Cook and Campbell (1979) invoke the familiar covariation, nonspuriousness, and temporal-sequencing criteria, but also make several additional declarations within the context of these broad standards that are especially relevant to social scientific determinations of causality. Specifically, their treatise on causation speaks to the following micro-level issues that arise when an assessment of causality is undertaken within the scope of Mill's macro-level canons: conditional effects, mediated effects, strength of association, third-variable control, the importance of theory, reverse causation, and reciprocal causation. Questions regarding conditional effects, mediated effects, and strength of association are contemplated in the discussion of the covariation criterion. Third-variable control and the importance of theory are considered in the section on nonspuriousness. Reverse and reciprocal causation are addressed in the evaluation of the temporal-sequencing requirement.

Covariation

Variables must covary in order to infer causation. In the present case, this means that studies should find that higher levels of mass media consumption are associated with higher levels of content congruent sexual behavior. Given that the mass media generally portray sex as enjoyable, exciting, and risk-free, youth who attend more frequently to the mass media should be more likely to engage in behaviors such as coitus and oral sex and should be more likely to experience the consequences that arise from unsafe sex such as pregnancy and STI contraction. Extant studies have measured these and other similar outcomes. Given that 19 out of the 21 studies reviewed found one or more positive associations between media use and content congruent sexual behavior, it appears that the covariation criterion has been met.

Conditional Effects. While many studies found main effects of media exposure on sexual behavior, several studies found only conditional effects or main effects and conditional effects. For instance, Peterson et al. (1991) found an effect conditional upon gender, Brown et al. (2006) and Hennessy et al. (2009) found that the strength of certain effects varied by ethnicity, and Fisher et al. (2009) found several effects conditional upon parental mediation. These findings suggest that mass media exposure and sexual behavior outcomes covary under certain conditions only. Does the conditional nature of the mass media exposure → sexual behavior association call into question causal assertions about this relationship? Not according to Cook and Campbell (1979). In fact, they encourage moderation exploration, arguing that "social scientists can better approximate inevitable causal connections by studying the contingency conditions that codetermine when a particular putative cause affects an outcome" (p. 15).

The issue of moderation brings up a related concern: What if media exposure is a sufficient but not necessary cause of youth sexual behavior? In other words, does the causal factor in question need to be the sole cause of the outcome of interest? Cook and Campbell (1979) address this issue with their third proposition: "The effects in molar causal laws[3] can be the result of multiple causes" (p. 33). They offer a light switch analogy to illustrate their point, as the reality that there are a number of ways to activate a light does not nullify the fact that flipping a light switch is one of these methods of activation. In relation to the present causal question, this assertion means that the possibility of factors other than the mass media uniquely impacting youth sexual decision making (e.g., Miller, Benson, & Galbraith, 2001; Wright, 2009c) does not eliminate the mass media as a legitimate causal factor.

Mediated Effects. Closely related to the issue of moderation is the issue of mediation. Can it be said that the mass media are a cause of youth sexual behavior if exposure to the mass media is only a distal cause that sets into motion ultimate, proximal causes? Cook and Campbell (1979) speak to this issue with their fifth proposition: "Dependable intermediate meditational units are involved in most strong molar laws" (p. 35). Consequently, that the mass media may exert their influence on youth through mediating variables such as sexual self-efficacy, sexual outcome expectations (Martino et al., 2005), and beliefs about peers' sexual permissiveness (Chia, 2006a,b) does not affect the mass media's status as a causal factor in youth sexual behavior.

Strength of Association. Some philosophers have argued that causation can only be inferred when there is perfect covariation between the presumed cause and effect variables. Even though the most sophisticated studies have found impressive effects sizes for the media exposure → sexual behavior relationship (e.g., Brown et al., 2006; Collins et al., 2004), none of the studies reviewed found a perfect correlation between media exposure and youths' sexual behavior. Cook and Campbell (1979) concentrate on the issue of perfect covariation in their second proposition: "Molar causal laws, because they are contingent on many other conditions and causal laws, are fallible and hence probabilistic" (p. 33). They suggest that social scientists either abandon the notion of cause in the social world or accept that the causal relationships they uncover will always be somewhat "contingent" and "probabilistic."

Nonspuriousness

The nonspuriousness criterion is met when alternative explanations for a causal association are systematically tested and dismissed. Two design considerations dramatically improve a social scientist's odds of ruling out alternative explanations: conducting studies in an environment where known confounding variables are completely under her control and randomly assigning participants to treatment conditions. In other words, the best way to address the issue of spuriousness is to conduct controlled, laboratory experiments. For ethical reasons, experimental mass media sex effects studies with teenagers and young adults that measure sexual behavior outcomes have not been conducted. In the absence of experimental opportunities, "the researcher has to explicate the specific threats to valid causal inference that random assignment [and laboratory control] rules out and then in some way deal with these threats" (Cook & Campbell, 1979, p. 9).

Third-Variable Control. Nonexperimental researchers "explicate the specific threats to valid causal inference" by including confounding third-variables in their study, and "deal with these threats" through statistical control. For example, low levels of parental monitoring might explain both high levels of sexual behavior and high levels of sexual media exposure. However, if sexual behavior and sexual media exposure are still correlated after the effects of parental monitoring are accounted for, parental monitoring has been ruled out as a confounding third-variable (Howell, 2002).

The variety of confounding variables included in studies of mass media and youth sexual behavior to date is impressive. Most of these variables have already been listed, but given the importance of eliminating third-variable explanations, the control variables included across the (arguably) most important longitudinal studies reviewed (Brown et al., 2006; Bleakley et al., 2008; Collins et al., 2004) are worth repeating: baseline sexual behavior, age, having mostly older friends, household structure, parental education, parental monitoring, academic achievement, mental health, sensation seeking tendencies, engaging in deviant behavior, gender, socioeconomic status, pubertal status, valence of relationship with mother, parenting styles, parents' disapproval of sex, religiosity, religious attendance, school connectedness, permissive peer sexual norms, unsupervised time at home, peers' approval of sex, physical development, and relationship status. That these (and other) studies found associations between mass media exposure and sexual behavior after controlling for these (and other) third-variables gives significant credence to the media exposure youth sexual behavior hypothesis.

Importance of Theory. Nonexperimental studies can never completely rule out every possible third-variable, of course. In reference to their pregnancy findings, Chandra et al. (2008) levy a purely empirical argument against the invocation of the third-variable critique: "The magnitude of the observed association is so great … that if even 20% of the prospective association that remained after controlling for covariates was causal, then sex exposure in the media would be a policy and public health arm of tremendous leverage" (p. 1052). Cook and Campbell (1979) make the case that it should require both "alternative theory *and* discordant facts" (p. 23) to depose of causal hypotheses with substantial theoretical and empirical support. In other words, third-variable critiques should be supported by established theory and empirical findings. Little, Card, Preacher, and McConnell (2009) argue that the burden of disproof should be especially heavy for causal critics who dispute the findings of well-designed longitudinal studies. In light of the shortage of alternative theory and the consistency of the findings in the studies reviewed, it is concluded that the burden of disproof regarding the question of confounding third-variables has now been shifted to the shoulders of causal critics.

Temporal-Sequencing

Mill's final criterion for causal inference is that the cause must temporally precede the effect. Seven longitudinal studies were located that found positive associations between T1 mass media exposure and T2 sexual outcomes such as intercourse initiation, sexual experience including but not limited to coitus, noncoital experience, having multiple sexual partners, and pregnancy and STI status. Most importantly, several of these studies controlled for baseline levels of the sexual outcome of interest (e.g., Brown et al., 2006; Chandra et al., 2008; Collins et al., 2004), demonstrating the role of mass media exposure in sexual behavior or outcome change over time. Because methodologists assert that longitudinal panel studies successfully address the issue of temporal-sequencing (Segrin, in press), it is concluded that this final criterion has also been met.

Reverse Causation. Can exposure to media sex be said to cause sexual behavior if engaging in sexual behavior causes youths to be interested in media sex (Bleakley et al., 2008)? To put it another way, what are the implications for a particular causal hypothesis if the cause can also be the effect and the effect can also be the cause? Cook and Campbell (1979) address this issue with their seventh proposition: "Some causal laws can be reversed, with the cause and effect interchangeable" (p. 36). To support this position they use the simple example that increases in pressure can cause increases in temperature and increases in temperature can also cause increases in pressure.

Reciprocal Causation. Similar to the issue of reverse causation is the issue of reciprocal causation:

> Moreover, some reversible relationships are what we shall call mutually reciprocating within limits, as would be the case if an increase in temperature caused an increase in pressure which, without further external stimulation, caused an increase in temperature. (Cook & Campbell, 1979, p. 17)

A reciprocal relationship between exposure to media sex and sexual behavior would be evident if exposure caused behavior which then caused exposure and if behavior caused exposure which in turn caused behavior. The results of Bleakley et al. (2008) provide suggestive evidence of a reciprocal relationship between mass media consumption and sexual behavior. As this was a two-wave panel study and three waves of panel data are required to truly assess reciprocal causation (Slater, 2007), additional research is needed to formally test this hypothesis. The primary implication of this discussion for the present study, though, is that evidence of such a causal dynamic would not have any effect on causal media exposure → sexual behavior conclusions drawn from extant two-wave studies.

Conclusion

Depictions of risk and responsibility free sex and justified, sanitized, glorified violence abound in United States mass media. Child advocates, public health officials, moral leaders, parents, and other concerned adults have for decades attributed the precocious sexual and aggressive behavior of many young Americans to exposure to sexual and violent mass media content.

Social scientists have also commented on the probable impact of sexual and violent mass media on young people's behavior. The nature of this commentary has taken different forms depending on the content pattern in question, however. Statements about the effects of mass media violence on aggressive behavior have often been definitive and confident, bolstered by scores upon scores of studies documenting associations between exposure to violence in various vehicles and elevated aggressive behavior. Statements about the effects of mass media sex on youth sexual behavior, on the other hand, have been speculative and provisional, tempered by an extremely meager base of empirical studies from which to draw conclusions. For many years, the best those called upon to comment on the effects of mass media sex could do was point to content analyses documenting the prevalence of sexual portrayals in the mass media, reference the handful of extant behavioral studies, and call for additional research. The sexual mass media effects landscape has changed substantially in recent years, however, as researchers from numerous disciplines have answered the call to address this important area of sexual socialization scholarship. For the first time, evidence-based statements about the causal effect of the mass media on youth sexual behavior have been made by social scientists. The chief purpose of this chapter was to review the subset of accumulated studies on sexual behavior effects to determine whether this body of work justified a causal conclusion. Twenty-one studies were reviewed that measured U.S. youths' mass media consumption and sexual behavior. The standards for causal inference articulated by Cook and Campbell (1979) were employed to accomplish this objective. The research to date clearly met the covariation and temporal-sequencing criteria and passed the threshold of substantiation for the nonspuriousness requirement. Consequently, this chapter concludes that the mass media almost certainly exert a causal influence on youths' sexual behavior.

Science is epistemologically alluring to so many because its focus on observable phenomena, and standardized methods of analysis promise that different scientists will come to the same conclusions when assessing a particular body of evidence. This promise can only be kept, however, when both completely unambiguous and agreed upon evaluative criteria are developed. In the case of causal assessments, the three primary criteria articulated by Cook and Campbell are well accepted. Determining the point at which a body of studies definitively "proves" each criterion has been fulfilled, on the other hand, is quite ambiguous. There is no $p < .05$, $\alpha > .70$, or power > .80 rule of thumb for scholars who tackle a causal assessment. The best they can do is provide a rationale for their conclusions on each causal criterion specified and attempt to anticipate the protestations of skeptical peers. The former chore was undertaken in the previous section, the latter chore is undertaken to close the chapter.

There are two primary threats to the position adopted by the present inquiry. The first threat has to do with third-variable control. This issue was addressed previously but is important enough that it deserves revisiting. This analysis agrees with the methodological assertion that a well-conducted laboratory experiment is the only approach that can completely eliminate third-variable confounds. It is important, therefore, to acknowledge again the third-variable problem posed by the lack of experimental studies in the present review.

However, the possibility of a yet unmeasured variable that completely explains the media sex → sexual behavior association uncovered in the studies reviewed is seen as improbable for the following reasons.

First, as outlined, the variety of potentially confounding variables accounted for in the literature to date is notable. Second, the confounds included were based on one of the larger developmental literatures: the environmental and biological predictors of youth sexual behavior (Kirby, LePore, & Ryan, 2005). Third, existing theory and associated research provide strong conceptual support for the role of the mass media in sexual script acquisition, activation, and application. Furthermore, the synthesis of existing theory undertaken in this review pointed to several factors (e.g., dependence on the media for sexual scripts, the extreme salience sex has for adolescents, sexual arousal at the time of script evaluation) that may make the role of the mass media in youth sexual behavior even more potent than in other areas of behavioral influence. Fourth, there is strong evidence that mass media exposure is related to young people's sexual beliefs and attitudes (Ward, 2003), and virtually all theories of behavior identify beliefs and attitudes as potential precursors of behavior. Moreover, unlike in the area of sexual behavior, experimental research assessing cognitive and attitudinal variables is more ethically defensible and thus more prevalent (e.g., Bryant & Rockwell, 1994; Calfin, Carroll, & Shmidt, 1993; Emmers-Sommer, Pauley, Hanzal, & Triplett, 2006; Gan, Zillmann, & Mitrook, 1997; Greeson & Williams, 1986; Hansen & Hansen, 1988; Hansen & Krygowski, 1994; Kalof, 1999; Johnson et al., 1995; Taylor, 2005; Ward, 2002; Ward et al., 2005; Ward & Friedman, 2006; Weisz, & Earls, 1995). Fifth, intentions are the most proximal determinant of behavior (Hale, Householder, & Greene, 2002) and experimental evidence indicates that exposure to sexual mass media enhance young people's intentions to engage in risky sexual behavior (Nabi & Clark, 2008). Sixth, the strength of the effects uncovered by the most sophisticated studies was potent enough that it is unlikely that any overlooked third-variable could totally eliminate these associations. Seventh, experimental designs assessing the effects of sexual media on non-sexual behaviors (e.g., aggression) have shown that sexual media can directly affect behavior (Allen, D'Alessio, & Brezgel, 1995; Lyons et al., 1994).

The second threat to the position adopted by this chapter has to do with the number of studies required to make a causal claim. Again, no definitive specifications exist for the number of total studies or the number of total participants required before one can conclude, for example, that the covariation criterion has been met once and for all. Of course, as the number of studies with similar findings expands, the chance that the body of findings can be explained by sampling error decreases and calculations can be made to assess the number of non-significant findings required to nullify an average significant effect (Orwin, 1983). But the impossibility of chance findings can never be demonstrated indisputably. More is better, but when is more enough? Cook and Campbell (1979) seem to caution against using quantity as a vital criterion when they speak of the "self-conscious concern about the limitations to causal inference that one sees when social scientists discuss individual studies" (p. 11). Speaking for communication scholars, Sparks (2006) writes that "researchers are reluctant to declare that they know anything about media effects until they have results from more than *one or two* (italics added) studies" (p. 40). The selection of "one or two" as the quantity comparison point suggests a modest quantity threshold for making an effects inference. Although only opinions, statements such as these seem to minimize the necessity of having scores of studies before coming to a causal conclusion.

It is acknowledged, then, that few studies have been conducted on mass media sex and youth sexual behavior, at least when compared to longstanding areas of media effects research such as aggression, agenda-setting, or political behavior. That comparatively fewer studies have been carried out is not considered a fatal problem, however, for the following reasons. First, the samples of many studies were sizable (e.g., seven studies had samples of more than 1,000; 12 had samples of more than 500). Second, the samples employed were diverse regionally (e.g., national studies, studies from the Northeast, Southeast, Midwest, and West), chronologically (e.g., data gathered in the 1980s, 1990s, and 2000s), ethnically (e.g., samples with Whites, Blacks, and Latinos), and developmentally (e.g., samples of pre-teens, teens, and emerging adults). Third, the longitudinal studies were wide in sampling scope, employed state of the art statistics and methods, and were conducted by teams that included some of the most qualified communication scientists and psychologists in the field. While future prospective studies could certainly parallel the sophistication of the longitudinal studies conducted to date, it seems unlikely that they could surpass it. Finally, because mass media scholars have "established strong empirical support" (Slater, 2007, p. 281) for media effects on an array cognitive, attitudinal, and behavioral outcome variables (Bryant & Oliver, 2008; Preiss, Gayle, Burrell, Allen, & Bryant, 2007), it seems less important to have legions of studies that champion a particular effects hypothesis now than when the field of media effects was developing.

The causal conclusion adopted by this analysis has different implications for different parties. For policy makers, parents, public health practitioners, educators, and others charged with the well-being of young people, the implication is clear. Exposure to sexual mass media should be considered a health threat to young people and interventions aimed at increasing parental monitoring of children's sexual mass media exposure and towards reducing the degree to which youth identify with and perceive the sexual exploits of mass media persona as realistic and acceptable should be developed and implemented (Anderson et al., 2003; see Pinkleton, Weintraub-Austin, Cohen, Chen, & Fitzgerald, 2008, for an intervention example). For social scientists, the implication of this review is that the mass media sexual effects literature has reached the point the mass media violence effects literature reached in 1982, when the National Institute of Mental Health concluded: "The research question has moved from asking whether or not there is an effect to seeking explanations for the effect" (p. 6).

Notes

1. The term "sexual socialization" refers to the full range of symbolic processes by which youth acquire sexual beliefs, attitudes and behaviors. By "full range of symbolic processes," it is meant that sexual socialization can occur through direct messages about sex (i.e., verbal statements) as well as through indirect messages about sex inferred from the behavior of others (i.e., behavioral modeling). Both forms of sexual socialization take place in the mass media and are equally predictive of adolescent sexual behavior (Collins et al., 2004).
2. There are ethnic differences in youth sexual behavior and sexual media consumption. Compared to White and Latino youth, Black youth are more likely to have intercourse before the age of 13, more likely to have multiple sexual partners, more likely to be sexually active, and less likely to get tested for HIV (Centers for Disease Control, 2008a). Black youth are also more prone to STI contraction (Centers for Disease Control, 2008c) and pregnancy (Ventura, Abma, Mosher, & Henshaw, 2004). Asian youth are the least sexually at-risk ethnic group (Grunbaum, Lowy, Kann, & Pateman, 2000). Less is known about ethnic differences in sexual mass media consumption, but Collins et al. (2004), Brown et al. (2006), and Hennessy et al. (2009) all report that Black youth consume more sexual mass media than White youth.
3. Cook and Campbell (1979) distinguish between macro (i.e., molar) and micro causal laws. "The term molar refers to causal laws stated in terms of large and often complex objects" (Cook & Campbell, 1979, p. 32). On the other hand, "micromediation refers to the specification of causal connections at a level of smaller particles than make up the molar objects" (p. 32). The statement that exposure to mass media sex is a causal factor in youth sexual behavior is a molar proposition; the various cognitive and physiological linkages between these variables identified in the acquisition, activation, application perspective on sexual mass media effects exemplify micromediational propositions.
4. Ethnicity and pubertal development—known moderators of many sexual outcomes among youth—were not specifically mentioned in the model because they are hypothesized to operate through more proximal variables that were identified (e.g., perceptions of salience, functional value, similarity, moral standards).

References

Abma, J. C., Martinez, G. M., Mosher, W. D., & Dawson, B. S. (2004). Teenagers in the United States: Sexual activity, contraceptive use, and childbearing, 2002. National Center for Health Statistics. *Vital Health Statistics 23*(24). Retrieved from http://www.cdc.gov/nchs/data/series/sr_23/sr23_024.pdf

Allday, E. (2007, June 20). Parents limiting media offerings of sex and violence. *San Francisco Chronicle,* p. A1.

Allen, M., D'Alessio, D., & Brezgel, K. (1995). A meta-analysis summarizing the effects of pornography II: Aggression after exposure. *Human Communication Research, 22,* 258–283.

American Academy of Pediatrics. (2001). Sexuality, contraception, and the media. *Pediatrics, 107,* 191–194.

Anderson, C. A. (1997). Effects of violent movies and trait hostility on hostile feelings and aggressive thoughts. *Aggressive Behavior, 23,* 161–178.

Anderson, C. A., Berkowitz, L., Donnerstein, E., Huesmann, L. R., Johnson, J. D., Linz, D., … Wartella, E. (2003). The influence of media violence on youth. *Psychological Science in the Public Interest, 4*(3), 81–106.

Ashby, S. L., Arcari, C. M., & Edmonson, M. B. (2006). Television viewing and risk of sexual initiation by young adolescents. *Archives of Pediatrics & Adolescent Medicine, 160,* 375–380.

Associated Press. (1985, September 20). Church study assails TV sex, violence. *Miami News,* p. 3A.

Arnston, J. (2005, June 23). Parents vs. TV. *Huntsville Times*, p. 1C.

Aubrey, J. S., Harrison, K., Kramer, L., & Yellin, J. (2003). Variety versus timing. Gender differences in college students' expectations as predicted by exposure to sexually oriented television. *Communication Research*, *30*, 432–460.

Bandura, A. (1965). Influence of models' reinforcement contingencies on the acquisition of imitative responses. *Journal of Personality and Social Psychology, 1,* 589–595.

Bandura, A. (2001). Social-cognitive theory of mass communication. *Media Psychology, 3,* 265–299.

Baran, S. J. (1976a). How TV and film portrayals affect sexual satisfaction in college students. *Journalism Quarterly, 53*, 468–473.

Baran, S. J. (1976b). Sex on TV and adolescent self-image. *Journal of Broadcasting, 20*, 61–68.

Bargh, J. A., & Chartrand, T. L. (1999). The unbearable automaticity of being. *American Psychologist, 54,* 462–479.

Bleakley, A., Hennessy, M., Fishbein, M., & Jordan, A. (2008). It works both ways: The relationship between exposure to sexual content in the media and adolescent sexual behavior. *Media Psychology, 11,* 443–461.

Bleske, A. L., & Shackelford, T. D. (2001). Poaching, promiscuity, and deceit: Combating mating rivalry in same-sex friendships. *Personal Relationships, 8,* 407–424.

Blumler, J. G. (1979). The role of theory in uses and gratifications studies. *Communication Research, 6,* 9–36.

Brown, J. D., & Cantor, J. (2000). An agenda for research on youth and the media. *Journal of Adolescent Health, 27,* 2–7.

Brown, J. D., & L'Engle, K. L. (2009). X-rated: Sexual attitudes and behaviors associated with U.S. early adolescents' exposure to sexually explicit media. *Communication Research, 36,* 129–151.

Brown, J. D., L'Engle, K. L., Pardun, C. J., Guo, G., Kenneavy, K., & Jackson, C. (2006). Sexy media matter: Exposure to sexual content in music, movies, television, and magazines predicts black and white adolescents' sexual behavior. *Pediatrics, 117,* 1018–1027.

Brown, J. D., & Newcomer, S. F. (1991). Television viewing and adolescents' sexual behavior. *Journal of Homosexuality, 21*, 77–91.

Brown, J. D., & Steele, J. R. (1995). *Sex and the mass media*. Menlo Park, CA: Kaiser Family Foundation.

Brown, J. D., Steele, J. R., & Walsh-Childers, K. (2002). *Preface*. In J. Brown, J. R. Steele, & K. Walsh-Childers (Eds.), *Sexual teens, sexual media* (pp. xi–xiv). Mahwah, NJ: Erlbaum.

Brown, J. D., Walsh-Childers, K., & Waszak, C. S. (1990). Television and adolescent sexuality. *Journal of Adolescent Health Care, 11,* 62–70.

Bryant, J., & Oliver, M. B. (2008). *Media effects: Advances in theory and research.* New York: Routledge.

Bryant, J., & Rockwell, S. C. (1994). Effects of massive exposure to sexually oriented prime-time television programming on adolescents' moral judgment. In D. Zillman, J. Bryant, & A. C. Huston (Eds.), *Media, children, and the family: Social scientific, psychodynamic, and clinical perspectives* (pp. 183–195). Hillsdale, NJ: Erlbaum.

Bushman, B. J., & Anderson, C. A. (2001). Media violence and the American public: Scientific facts versus media misinformation. *American Psychologist, 56,* 477–489.

Bushman, B. J., & Bonacci, A. M. (2002). Violence and sex impair memory for television ads. *Journal of Applied Psychology, 87,* 557–564.

Calfin, M. S., Carroll, J. L., & Shmidt, J. (1993). Viewing music-videotapes before taking a test of premarital sexual attitudes. *Psychological Reports, 72*, 475–481.

Carpenter, L. M. (1998). From girls into women: Scripts for sexuality and romance in Seventeen magazine, 1974–1994. *Journal of Sex Research, 35*, 158–168.

Centers for Disease Control. (2006). Youth risk behavior surveillance — United States, 2006. *Morbidity and Mortality Weekly Report, 53*(SS-5), 1–108.

Centers for Disease Control. (2008a). Youth risk behavior surveillance — United States, 2007. *Morbidity & Mortality Weekly Report, 57*(SS-4), 1–131.

Centers for Disease Control. (2008b). *HIV/AIDS surveillance report, 2006.* Atlanta, GA: U.S. Department of Health and Human Services, Centers for Disease Control and Prevention.

Centers for Disease Control. (2008c). *Sexually transmitted disease surveillance.* Atlanta, GA: U.S. Department of Health and Human Services, Centers for Disease Control and Prevention.

Chandra, A., Martino, S. C., Collins, R. L., Elliott, M. N., Berry, S. H., Kanouse, D. E., Miu, A. (2008). Does watching sex on television predict teen pregnancy? Findings from a national longitudinal survey of youth. *Pediatrics, 122*, 1047–1054.

Chia, S. C. (2006a). How peers mediate media influence on adolescents' sexual attitudes and sexual behavior. *Journal of Communication, 56,* 585–606.

Chia, S. C. (2006b). How media contribute to misperceptions of social norms about sex. *Mass Communication & Society, 9,* 301–320.

Collins, R. L., Elliott, M. N., Berry, S. H., Kanouse, D. E., & Hunter, S. B. (2003). Entertainment television as a healthy sex educator: The impact of condom-efficacy information in an episode of Friends. *Pediatrics, 112*, 1115–1121.

Collins, R. L., Elliott, M. N., Berry, S. H., Kanouse, D. E., Kunkel, D., Hunter, S. B., & Miu, A. (2004). Watching sex on television predicts adolescent initiation of sexual behavior. *Pediatrics, 114*, 280–289.

Cook, T. D., & Campbell, D. T. (1979). *Quasi-experimentation: Design & analysis issues for field settings*. Chicago: Rand McNally.

Davis, S., & Mares, M. L. (1998). Effects of talk show viewing on adolescents. *Journal of Communication, 48,* 69–86.

Diamond, L. M., & Savin-Williams, R. C. (2009). Adolescent sexuality. In R. M. Lerner & L. Steinberg (Eds.), *Handbook of adolescent psychology* (pp. 479–523). New York: Wiley.

Donnerstein, E., & Berkowitz, L. (1981). Victim reactions in aggressive erotic films as a factor in violence against women. *Journal of Personality and Social Psychology, 41*, 710–724.

Donnerstein, E., & Smith, S. (2001). Sex in the media: Theory, influences, and solutions. In D. G. Singer, & J. L. Singer (Eds.), *Handbook of children and the media* (pp. 289–307). Thousand Oaks, CA: Sage.

DuRant, R. H., Neiberg, R., Champion, H., Rhodes, S., & Wolfson, M. (2008). Viewing professional wrestling on television and engaging in violent and other health risk behaviors by a national sample of adolescents. *Southern Medical Journal, 101,* 129–137.

Emmers-Sommer, T. M., Pauley, P., Hanzal, A., & Triplett, L. (2006). Love, suspense, sex, and violence: Men's and women's film predilections, exposure to sexually violent media, and their relationship to rape myth acceptance. *Sex Roles, 55,* 311–320.

Eyal, K., & Kunkel, D. (2008). The effects of sex in television drama shows on emerging adults' sexual attitudes and moral judgments. *Journal of Broadcasting & Electronic Media, 52,* 161–181.

Fabes, R. A., & Strouse, J. (1987). Perceptions of responsible and irresponsible models of sexuality: A correlational study. *Journal of Sex Research, 23*, 70–84.

Finer, L. B., & Henshaw, S. K. (2006). Disparities in rates of unintended pregnancy in the United States, 1994–2001. *Perspectives on Sexual and Reproductive Health, 38*(2), 90–96.

Fisher, D. A., Hill, D. L., Grube, J. W., Bersamin, M. M., Walker, S., & Gruber, E. L. (2009). Televised sexual content and parental mediation: Influences on adolescent sexuality. *Media Psychology, 12,* 121–147.

Fiske, S. T., & Linville, P. W. (1980). What does the schema concept buy us? *Personality and Social Psychology Bulletin, 6,* 543–557.

Gagnon, J. H., & Simon, W. (1973). *Sexual conduct: The social sources of human sexuality.* Chicago: Aldine.

Gan, S. L., Zillmann, D., & Mitrook, M. (1997). Stereotyping effect of Black women's sexual rap on White audiences. *Basic and Applied Social Psychology, 19*, 381–399.

Gerbner, G., Gross, L., Morgan, M., & Signorielli, N. (1994). Growing up with television: The cultivation perspective. In J. Bryant & D. Zillmann (Eds.), *Media effects: Advances in theory and research* (pp. 17–41). Hillsdale, NJ: Erlbaum.

Greenberg, B. S., & Hofschire, L. (2000). Sex on entertainment television. In D. Zillmann & P. Vorderer (Eds.), *Media entertainment* (pp. 93–111). Hillsdale, NJ: Erlbaum.

Greeson, L. E., & Williams, R. A. (1986). Social implications of music videos for youth: An analysis of the content and effects of MTV. *Youth and Society, 18*, 177–189.

Grunbaum, J. A., Lowy, R., Kann, L., & Pateman, B. (2000). Prevalence of health risk behaviors among Asian American/Pacific Islander high school students. *Journal of Adolescent Health, 27*, 322–330.

Guernsey, L. (2008, September 15). Limiting, and watching, what children watch. *New York Times,* p. H4.

Gunasekera, H., Chapman, S., & Campbell, S. (2005). Sex and drugs in popular movies: An analysis of the top 200 films. *Journal of the Royal Society of Medicine, 9,* 464–470.

Gunter, B. (2002). *Media sex.* Mahwah, NJ: Erlbaum.

Guttmacher Institute. (2006). *U.S. teenage pregnancy statistics: National and state trends by race and ethnicity.* New York: Author.

Hale, J. L., Householder, B. J., & Greene, K. L. (2002). The theory of reasoned action.

In J. P. Dillard & M. Pfau (Eds.), *The handbook of persuasion* (pp. 259–286). Thousand Oaks, CA: Sage.

Hansen, C. H., & Hansen, R. (1988). How rock music videos can change what is seen when boy meets girl: Priming stereotypic appraisal of social interactions. *Sex Roles, 5*, 287–316.

Hansen, C. H., & Krygowski, W. (1994). Arousal-augmented priming effects: Rock music videos and sex object schemas. *Communication Research, 21*, 24–47.

Heintz-Knowles, K. E. (1996). *Sexual activity on daytime soap operas: A content analysis of five weeks of television programming.* Menlo Park, CA: Kaiser Family Foundation.

Hennessy, M., Bleakley, A., Fishbein, M., & Jordan, A. (2009). Estimating the longitudinal association between adolescent sexual behavior and exposure to sexual media content. *Journal of Sex Research, 46,* 1–11.

Hetsroni, A. (2008). Dependency and adolescents' perceived usefulness of information on sexuality: A cross-cultural comparison of interpersonal sources, professional sources and the mass media. *Communication Reports, 21,* 14–32.

Howell, D. C. (2002). *Statistical methods for psychology.* Pacific Grove, CA: Wadsworth.

Huesmann, L. R. (1986). Psychological processes promoting the relation between exposure to media violence and aggressive behavior by the viewer. *Journal of Social Issues, 42,* 125–139.

Huesmann, L. R. (1988). An information processing model for the development of aggression. *Aggressive Behavior, 14*, 13–24.

Huesmann, L. R. (1998). The role of social information processing and cognitive schema in the acquisition and maintenance of habitual aggressive behavior. In R. G. Geen & E. Donnerstein (Eds.), *Human aggression: Theories, research, and implications for policy* (pp. 73–109). New York: Academic Press.

Huston, A. C., Wartella, E., & Donnerstein, E. (1998). *Measuring the effects of sexual content in the media*. Menlo Park, CA: Kaiser Family Foundation.

Jansma, L. L., Linz, D. G., Mulac, A., & Imrich, D. J. (1997). Men's interactions with women after viewing sexually explicit films: Does degradation make a difference? *Communication Monographs*, *64,* 1–24.

Johnson, J., Adams, M. S., Ashburn, L., & Reed, W. (1995). Differential gender effects of exposure to rap music on African American adolescents' acceptance of teen dating violence. *Sex Roles, 33*, 597–605.

Kalof, L. (1999). The effects of gender and music video imagery on sexual attitudes. *The Journal of Social Psychology, 139*, 378–385.

Kaye, J. (1989, September 26). Most Americans slam TV sex, violence, but oppose censorship. *The Modesto Bee,* p. D8.

Kim, J. L., & Ward, L. M. (2004). Pleasure reading: Associations between young women's sexual attitudes and their reading of contemporary women's magazines. *Psychology of Women Quarterly, 28,* 48–58.

Kirby, D., Lepore, G., & Ryan, J. (2005). Sexual and risk protective factors: Factors affecting teen sexual behavior, pregnancy, childbearing and sexually transmitted disease: Which are important? Which can you change? National Campaign to Prevent Teen Pregnancy. Washington, DC: ETR Associates.

Kunkel, D. (2003). The road to the V-Chip: Television violence and public policy. In D. Gentile (Ed.), *Media violence and children* (pp. 227–245). Westport, CT: Praeger.

Kunkel, D., Biely, E., Eyal, K., Cope-Farrar, K., Donnerstein, E., & Fandrich, R. (2003). *Sex on TV 3: A biennial report to the Kaiser Family Foundation*. Menlo Park, CA: Kaiser Family Foundation.

Kunkel, D., Eyal., K., Finnerty., K., Biely, E., & Donnerstein, D. (2005). *Sex on TV 4: A biennial report to the Kaiser Family Foundation*. Menlo Park, CA: Kaiser Family Foundation.

Kunkel, D., Farrar, K. M., Eyal, K., Biely, E., Donnerstein, E., & Rideout, V. (2007). Sexual socialization messages on entertainment television. Comparing content trends 1997–2002. *Media Psychology, 9,* 595–622.

Laws, J. L., & Schwartz, P. (1977). *Sexual scripts: The social construction of female sexuality*. Hinsdale, IL: Dryden.

Lester, W. (2005, April 19). Public unhappy about on-air sex and violence. *The Associated Press*. Retrieved on March 15, 2010, from LexisNexis database.

Little, T. D., Card, N. A., Preacher, K. J., & McConnell, E. (2009). Modeling longitudinal data from research on adolescence. In R. M. Lerner & L. Steinberg (Eds.), *Handbook of adolescent psychology* (pp. 15–24). New York: Wiley.

Lyons, J. S., Anderson, R. L., & Larson, D. B. (1994). A systematic review of the effects of aggressive and nonaggressive pornography. In D. Zillman, J. Bryant, & A. C. Huston (Eds.), *Media, children, and the family: Social scientific, psychodynamic, and clinical perspectives* (pp. 271–310). Hillsdale, NJ: Erlbaum.

MacDonald, K. B. (2008). Effortful control, explicit processing, and the regulation of human evolved predispositions. *Psychological Review, 115*, 1012–1031.

Malamuth, N. M. (1996). Sexually explicit media, gender differences, and evolutionary theory. *Journal of Communication, 46,* 8–31.

Malamuth, N. M., & Impett, E. A. (2001). Research on sex in the media. What do we know about effects on children and adolescents? In D. G. Singer & J. L. Singer (Eds.), *Handbook of children and the media* (pp. 269–287). Thousand Oaks, CA: Sage.

Martino, S. C., Collins, R. L., Kanouse, D. E., Elliot, M., & Berry, S. H. (2005). Social cognitive processes mediating the relationship between exposure to television's sexual content and adolescents' sexual behavior. *Journal of Personality and Social Psychology, 89,* 914–924.

McGuire, W. J. (1969). The nature of attitudes and attitude change. In G. Lindzey & E. Aronson (Eds.), *The handbook of social psychology* (2nd ed., pp. 136–31). Reading, MA: Addison-Wesley.

McKenzie-Mohr, D., & Zanna, M. P. (1990). Treating women as sexual objects: Look to the (gender schematic) male who has viewed pornography. *Personality and Social Psychology Bulletin, 16,* 296–308.

Milkie, M. A. (1999). Social comparisons, reflected appraisals and mass media: The impact of pervasive beauty on black and white girls' self-concepts. *Social Psychology Quarterly, 62,* 190–210.

Miller, B. C., Benson, B., & Galbraith, K. A. (2001). Family relationships and adolescent pregnancy risk: A research synthesis. *Developmental Review, 21,* 1–38.

Nabi, R. L., & Clark, S. (2008). Exploring the limit of social cognitive theory: Why negatively reinforced behaviors on TV may be modeled anyway. *Journal of Communication, 58,* 407–427.

National Institute of Mental Health. (1982). Ten years of scientific progress: An overview. In D. Pearl, L. Bouthilet, & J. Lazar (Eds.), *Television and Behavior: Ten years of scientific progress and implications for the eighties* (pp. 1–8). Washington, DC: Author.

Nisbett, R., & Ross, L. (1980). *Human inferences: Strategies and shortcomings of human judgment*. Englewood Cliffs, NJ: Prentice-Hall.

O'Conner, J. (1990, June 12). Sex, violence and a leavening grace. *New York Times*. Retrieved on March 15, 2010, from http://www.nytimes.com/1990/06/12/arts/review-television-sex-violence and-a-leavening-grace.html?pagewanted=1

Olson, B. (1994). Soaps, sex, and cultivation. *Mass Communication Review, 21*, 106–113.

Office of the Surgeon General. (2001). *The Surgeon General's call to action to promote sexual health and responsible sexual behavior.* Rockville, MD: U.S. Public Health Service.

Orwin, R. G. (1983). A fail-safe N for effect size in meta-analysis. *Journal of Educational and Behavioral Statistics, 8*,157–159.

Pardun, C. J., L'Engle, K. L., & Brown, J. D. (2005). Linking exposure to outcomes: Early adolescents' consumption of sexual content in six media. *Mass Communication & Society, 8*, 75–91.

Peterson, R. A., & Kahn, J. (1995). Media preferences of sexually active and inactive youth. *Sociological Imagination, 32*, 29–43.

Peterson, J. L., Moore, K. A., & Furstenberg, F. F., Jr. (1991). Television viewing and early initiation of sexual intercourse: Is there a link? *Journal of Homosexuality, 21*, 93–118.

Pfau, M., Ivanov, B., & Houston, B. (2005). Inoculation and mental processing: The instrumental role of associative networks in the process of resistance to counterattitudinal influence. *Communication Monographs, 72*, 414–441.

Pfau, M., Roskos-Ewoldsen, D., & Wood, M. (2003). Attitude accessibility as an alternative explanation for how inoculation confers resistance. *Communication Monographs, 70*, 39–51.

Pinkleton, B. E., Weintraub-Austin, E., Cohen, M., Chen, Y., & Fitzgerald, E. (2008). Effects of a peer-led media literacy curriculum on adolescents' knowledge and attitudes towards sexual behavior and media portrayals of sex. *Health Communication, 23*, 462–472.

Preiss, R. W., Gayle, B. M., Burrell, N., Allen, M., & Bryant, J. (2007). *Mass media effects research: Advances through meta-analysis*. New York: Erlbaum.

Reed, D., & Weinberg, M. S. (1984). Premarital coitus: Developing and established sexual scripts. *Social Psychology Quarterly, 47*, 129–138.

Rideout, V. J., Foehr, U. G., & Roberts, D. F. (2010). *Generation M^2: Media in the lives of 8-to-18 year olds*. Menlo Park, CA: Kaiser Family Foundation.

Rimal, R. N., & Real, K. (2005). How behaviors are influenced by perceived norms, a test of theory of normative social behavior. *Communication Research, 32*, 389–414.

Roberts, E. J. (1982). Television and sexual learning in childhood. In D. Pearl, L. Bouthilet, & J. Lazar (Eds.), *Television and behavior: Ten years of scientific progress and implications for the eighties* (pp. 209–223). Washington, DC: National Institute of Mental Health.

Roskos-Ewoldsen, D. R., Roskos-Ewoldsen, B., & Dillman Carpentier, F. R. (2009). Media priming. An updated synthesis. In J. Bryant & M. B. Oliver (Eds.), *Media effects: Advances in theory and research* (pp. 74–93). New York: Psychology Press.

Rotherum-Borus, M. J., O'Keefe, Z., Kracker, R., & Foo, H. (2000). Prevention of HIV among adolescents. *Prevention Science, 1,* 15–30.

Rubin, A .M. (2002). The uses-and-gratifications perspective on media effects. In J. Bryant & D. Zillmann (Eds.), *Media effects: Advances in theory and research* (pp. 525–548). Mahwah, NJ: Erlbaum.

Rubin, A. M., & Windahl, S. (1986). The uses and dependency model of mass communication. *Critical Studies in Mass Communication, 3,* 184–189.

Sargent, J. D., Heatherton, T. F., Ahrens, M. B., Dalton, M. A., Tickle, J. J., & Beach, M. L. (2002). Adolescent exposure to extremely violent movies. *Journal of Adolescent Health, 31,* 449–454.

Schaefer, H. H., & Colgan, A. H. (1977). The effect of pornography on penile tumescence as a function of reinforcement and novelty. *Behavior Therapy, 8,* 938–946.

Schuster, M. A., Bell, R. M., Peterson, L. P., & Kanouse, D. E. (1996). Communication between adolescents and physicians about sexual behavior and risk prevention. *Archives of Pediatrics and Adolescent Medicine, 150,* 906–913.

Segrin, C. (in press). Panel designs. In N. J. Salkind, D. M. Dougherty, & B. Frey (Eds.), *Encyclopedia of research design.* Thousand Oaks, CA: Sage.

Seidman, S. A. (1992). An investigation of sex-role stereotyping in music videos. *Journal of Broadcasting and Electronic Media, 36*, 209–216.

Shrum, L. J. (2007). The implications of survey methods for measuring cultivation effects. *Human Communication Research, 33,* 64–80.

Shrum, L. J. (2009). Media consumption and perceptions of social reality: Effects and underlying processes. In J. Bryant & M. B. Oliver (Eds.), *Media effects: Advances in theory and research* (pp. 50–73). New York: Psychology Press.

SIECUS. (2007, December 6). *Data show teen birthrate on the rise.* Retrieved February 10, 2008, from http://www.siecus.org/media/press/press0159.html

Silverman-Watkins, L. T., & Sprafkin, J. N. (1983). Adolescents' comprehension of televised sexual innuendos. *Journal of Applied Developmental Psychology, 4,* 359–369.

Singer, J. D., & Willett, J. B. (2003). *Applied longitudinal data analysis.* New York: Oxford.

Singhal, A., Cody, M. J., Rogers, E. M., & Sabido, M. (2004). *Entertainment-education and social change: History, research, practice.* Mahwah, NJ: Erlbaum.

Sintchak, G., & Geer, J. (1975). A vaginal plethysymograph system. *Psychophysiology, 12,* 113–115.

Slater, M. D. (2007). Reinforcing spirals. The mutual influence of media selectivity and media effects and their impact on individual behavior and social identity. *Communication Theory, 17,* 281–303.

Small, S. A., & Kerns, D. (1993). Unwanted sexual activity among peers during early and middle adolescence: Incidence and risk factors. *Journal of Marriage and the Family, 55,* 941–952.

Smith, S., Wilson, B., Kunkel, D., Linz, D., Potter, W. J., Colvin, C., & Donnerstein, E. (1998). Violence in television programming overall. *National Television Violence Study, Volume 3.* Thousand Oaks, CA: Sage.

Solderman, A. K., Greenberg, B. S., & Linsangan, R. (1988). Television and movie behaviors of pregnant and non-pregnant adolescents. *Journal of Adolescent Research, 3*, 153–170.

Sparks, G. G. (2006). *Media effects research.* Belmont, CA: Thomson Wadsworth.

Sparks, G. G., & Sparks, C. W. (2002). Effects of media violence. In J. Bryant & D. Zillmann (Eds.), *Media effects: Advances in theory and research* (pp. 489–506). Mahwah, NJ: Erlbaum.

Sprecher, S., & Regan, P. C. (1998). Passionate and companionate love in courting and young married couples. *Sociological Inquiry, 68,* 163–185.

Steele, J. (1999). Teenage sexuality and media practice: Factoring in the influences of family, friends and school. *Journal of Sex Research, 36,* 331–341.

Stephan, C. W., & Bachman, G. F. (1999). What's sex got to do with it? Attachment, love schemas, and sexuality. *Personal Relationships, 6,* 111–123.

Strager, S. (2003). What men watch when they watch pornography. *Sexuality & Culture, 7,* 50–61.

Strasburger, V. C., & Donnerstein, E. (1999). Children, adolescents, and the media: Issues and solutions. *Pediatrics, 103,* 129–139.

Strouse, J. S., & Buerkel-Rothfuss, N. L. (1987). Media exposure and the sexual attitudes and behaviors of college students. *Journal of Sex Education and Therapy, 13,* 43–51.

Strouse, J. S., Buerkel-Rothfuss, N. L., & Long, E. C. (1995). Gender and family as moderators of the relationship between music video exposure and adolescent sexual permissiveness. *Adolescence, 30*, 505–521.

Surgeon General's Scientific Advisory Committee on Television and Social Behavior. (1972). Summary of findings and conclusions. In *Television and growing up: The impact of televised violence* (pp. 1–11). Washington, DC: U.S. Government Printing Office.

Taylor, L. D. (2005). Effects of visual and verbal sexual television content and perceived realism on attitudes and beliefs. *Journal of Sex Research, 42,* 130–137.

Taylor, L. D. (2006). College men, their magazines, and sex. *Sex Roles, 55,* 693–702.

Toff, H., Greene, L., & Davis, J. (2003). *National survey of adolescents and young adults: Sexual health knowledge, attitudes, and experiences.* Menlo Park, CA: Kaiser Family Foundation.

United Press International. (1986, November 5). Parents urged to censor TV sex, violence. *Pittsburgh Press,* p. A10.

Ventura, S. J., Abma, J. C., Mosher, W. D., & Henshaw, S. (2004). Estimated pregnancy rates for the United States, 1990–2000: An update. *National Vital Statistics Reports, 52,* 1–9.

Wagstaff, D. A., Kelly, J. A., Perry, M. J., Sikkema, K. J., Solomon, L. J., Heckman, T. G., & Anderson, E. S. (1995). Multiple partners, risky partners, and HIV risk among low-income urban women. *Family Planning Perspectives, 27,* 241–245.

Ward, L. M. (1995). Talking about sex: Common themes about sexuality in the prime-time television programs children and adolescents view most. *Journal of Youth & Adolescence, 24*, 595–615.

Ward, L. M. (2002). Does television exposure affect emerging adults' attitudes and assumptions about sexual relationships? Correlational and experimental confirmation. *Journal of Youth and Adolescence, 31*, 1–15.

Ward, L. M. (2003). Understanding the role of entertainment media in the sexual socialization of American youth: A review of empirical research. *Developmental Review, 23,* 347–388.

Ward, L. M., & Friedman, K. (2006). Using TV as a guide: Associations between television viewing and adolescents' sexual attitudes and behavior. *Journal of Research on Adolescence, 16,* 133–156.

Ward, L. M., Hansbrough, E., & Walker, E. (2005). Contributions of music video exposure to black adolescents' gender and sexual schemas. *Journal of Adolescent Research, 20*, 143–166.

Ward, L. M., Merriwether, A., & Caruthers, A. (2006). Breasts are for men: Media, masculinity ideologies, and men's beliefs about women's bodies. *Sex Roles, 55*, 703–714.

Ward, L. M., & Rivadeneyra, R. (1999). Contributions of entertainment television to adolescents' sexual attitudes and expectations: The role of viewing amount versus viewer involvement. *Journal of Sex Research, 36*, 237–249.

Weaver, J. B., Masland, J. L., & Zillmann, D. (1984). Effects of erotica on young men's aesthetic perception of their female sexual partners. *Perceptual and Motor Skills, 58*, 929–930.

Weinstock, H., Berman, S., & Cates, W. (2004). Sexually transmitted diseases among American youth: Incidence and prevalence estimates, 2000. *Perspectives on Sexual and Reproductive Health, 36*, 6–10.

Weisz, M. G., & Earls, C. M. (1995). The effects of exposure to filmed sexual violence on attitudes towards rape. *Journal of Interpersonal Violence, 10*, 71–84.

Wingood, G. M., DiClemente, R. J., Bernhardt, J. M., Harrington, K., Davies, S. L., Robillard, A., & Hook, E. W. (2003). A prospective study of exposure to rap music videos and African American female adolescents' health. *American Journal of Public Health, 93*, 437–439.

Wright, P. J. (2009a). An evaluation of the Federal Communications Commission's 2007 report on TV violence. *The Communication Review, 12*, 174–186.

Wright, P. J. (2009b). Sexual socialization messages in mainstream entertainment mass media: A review and synthesis. *Sexuality & Culture, 4*, 181–200.

Wright, P. J. (2009c). Father-child sexual communication in the United States: A review and synthesis. *Journal of Family Communication, 4*, 1–18.

Wyer, R. S., & Radvansky, G. A. (1999). The comprehension and validation of social information. *Psychological Review, 106*, 89–119.

Young, M., Denny, G., Young, T., & Luquis, R. (2000). Sexual satisfaction among married women. *American Journal of Health Studies, 16*, 73–84.

Zajonc, R. B. (1968). Attitudinal effects of mere exposure. *Journal of Personality and Social Psychology Monographs, 9*, 1–27.

Zillmann, D. (1994). Erotica and family values. In D. Zillman, J. Bryant, & A. C. Huston (Eds.), *Media, children, and the family: Social scientific, psychodynamic, and clinical perspectives* (pp. 183–195). Hillsdale, NJ: Erlbaum.

Zurbriggen, E. L., & Morgan, E. M. (2006). Who wants to marry a millionaire? Reality dating television programs, attitudes towards sex, and sexual behaviors. *Sex Roles, 54*, 1–17.

CHAPTER CONTENTS

15 The Business Value of Interactivity

Managing Customers in the Electronic Marketplace

Paul C. Murschetz

Cologne Business School and University of New York Tirana

By offering interactive e-commerce applications and services, and thereby actively engaging consumers in the communication process, businesses increasingly are emphasizing solid and sustainable relationships that may help them achieve competitive advantages in the electronic marketplace (Porter, 2001). As a result, one might expect a rich literature and ample empirical insights into the important issue of interactivity management in the e-commerce domain. However, my own review of this literature concludes that a clear picture of the relationship between interactivity and its impact on the business value of an organization has not emerged from previous studies. Although creating business value from interacting with customers in the electronic marketplace is far from being a new academic proposition (Amit & Zott, 2001; Armstrong & Hagel, 1996; Zeithaml, 1988), the concept warrants closer study from the perspective of e-commerce management (Jiang, Chan, & Tan, 2010; Yadav & Varadarajan, 2005a,b) in an attempt to reconcile limited and contradictory findings resulting from a variety of deficiencies. These include: inconsistent conceptual definitions of interactivity, different units and levels of analysis (i.e., the question of identifying a locus of interactivity; does it reside in the infrastructure, distribution and/or end-user technology, the communication structures and processes, and/or in the perceived consumer control over the media and communication process?), and a largely incoherent base of theory for examining relations and interdependencies between the abovementioned factors.

The primary purpose of this work is to undertake a comprehensive and necessarily interdisciplinary literature review on the concept of interactivity. I intend to broaden existing knowledge of interactivity by drawing from disparate academic fields such as media and communication theory, computer-mediated communication (CMC), marketing, advertising, and e-commerce, and thereby systematize, link, and extend familiar definitions, characteristics, types, and dimensions of interactivity from extant literature in these fields. By delineating the central properties of interactivity, I will attempt to make important strides towards the construction of an analytical bridge between interactivity and its potential for creating business value for organizations in an e-commerce context. By reviewing the scholarly debate on interactivity, I also offer ideas for future research on managerial implications of interactivity and the business value that may result from interactions between the main participants in the electronic marketplace: the business firm and the customer. Essentially, I will develop propositions as first principles of a (still to be built) conceptual model analyzing the efficacy of interactive e-commerce applications and services with regard to the business value of customer integration in the electronic marketplace. It is this nexus of considerations that motivates this work. I will view interactivity not as an objective, external property of technology with deterministic impact on adoption, usage, and performance within business firms, but as both a system- and human-related artifact of CMC interaction (Mackenzie & Wajcman, 1985; Thomas, 1992; Williams & Edge, 1996).

I first provide a literature review on interactivity. This review will proceed along the three dominant research traditions focusing on the interactivity phenomenon: technology, communication process, and user perception. This will include reviewing literature streams in the domains of media and communication studies and e-commerce. The review then focuses on discussions about impacts of interactivity on business value potential. By reviewing the e-commerce literature on this relationship, I highlight gaps in the debate on interactivity in the electronic marketplace and present some caveats as to the general validity of the concept discussed among scholars from various other backgrounds. Again, the purpose of this exercise is not only to organize ideas and material in a logical and meaningful way but also to formulate an analytical bridge from interactivity to the creation of business value in e-commerce. This conceptual model eventually will serve to develop a guiding framework for successful interactivity management. In fact, this framework will help integrating the concept of interactivity into existing frameworks of e-commerce management of customer integration in electronic commerce environments (McKay & Marshall, 2004; Turban, King, Lee, Warkentin, & Chung, 2002; Vulkan, 2003).

What is Interactivity? A Review of the Literature

Delineating the concept of interactivity is the Archimedean point from which I will begin this research itinerary. Interactivity was coined as *the* buzzword during the late 1980s and early 1990s when the multimedia euphoria fascinated politicians, economists, and researchers alike. Over the past 20 years, however, there has been little agreement among researchers on how interactivity should be conceptualized (Bucy, 2004a; Heeter, 2000; Neumann, 2008). Therefore, it is difficult to develop concrete knowledge regarding its constituent factors and consequences for computer-mediated communication (CMC) in the electronic marketplace. This makes the prospect of synthesizing and integrating the literature on the business value of interactivity rather elusive.

As has been pointed out in meta-analyses of the interactivity literature (Bruner, & Kumar, 2006; Bucy, 2004a; Rafaeli & Ariel, 2007), some of the confusion about this construct comes from lack of agreement as to its nature, role, and effects. As the doyen of interactivity research, Rafaeli (1988), put it: "Interactivity is a widely used term with an intuitive appeal, but it is an underdefined concept. As a way of thinking about communication, it has high face validity, but only narrowly based explication, little consensus on meaning, and only recently emerging empirical verification and actual role" (p. 110). Similarly, reflecting upon how interactivity is used within the context of new media, Heeter (2000, p. 2) pointed out that interactivity is an "overused, underdefined concept." Heeter referred to it as basically everything a human does.

As it stands, the academic debate about interactivity is confronted with three main difficulties. First, interactivity is a multi-discursive concept; significantly different meanings and connotations can be found according to their use within different disciplinary discourses, including sociology, media and communication studies, CMC, and computer science. Consequently, however, differences in how interactivity is observed, defined, and interpreted are significant. In fact, the academic debate about interactivity is characterized by some degree of conceptual confusion. Scholarly dispute on concept relevance and validity has never receded. Communication theory, for example, derives *interactivity* from *social interaction* in sociology and social psychology (Argyle, 1969; Blumer, 1969; Goffman, 1967). There, *interaction* is defined as mutually interdependent social action between individuals who exchange symbols and meanings in the communication process which itself is supposed to be sequential, that is actions of one person result in reactions of another person (Jaeckel, 1995). Jaeckel, who studied the origins of the term, explained that the term *interactivity* extends from *interaction* which generally means *exchange* and *mutual influence*. In general, an explanation of interactivity or interaction refers—perhaps not surprisingly—back to *action*, and in the social sciences action is presupposed to depend on an active human subject intentionally acting upon an object or another subject. However, fundamentally, this type of non-computer-based mutual or reciprocal interaction between humans has been adopting significantly contradictory meanings within competing scientific discourses. While most scholars in communication science derive the concept of interactivity from sociology and social psychology, scholars in informatics introduce interactivity by referring to software which accepts and responds to inputs from humans in an interactive human-computer dialogue (Baecker, 1980). On the other hand, the consensus among most HCI researchers is to understand interactivity as interaction between people, the computer and the human-technology interface (Hall, 1999; Helander, Landauer, & Prabhu, 1997; Lowe & Myers, 1998; Svanæs, 2000). There, interactivity is explained as a relationship between the human operator and technology. Being a multi-paradigmatic discipline, HCI's view of the concept of interactivity is vast. At the heart of technological aspects of HCI towards interactivity lie issues of interface hardware and software architecture, computer graphics, dialogue architecture, and design (Hewett et al., 1992). Seen this way, the human-computer interaction model is based on four main components: human, computer, task environment, and machine environment.

Second, interactivity is considered a multi-dimensional and multi-attribute concept, which owes to its hybrid intellectual architecture. Interactivity is defined by an array of objective, technological properties such as media and transmission technology, interactive features, and interface design. However, other dimensions of interactivity are content quality and breadth, the nature of HCI, human behavior and perceptions as well as situational and contextual aspects (e.g., task demands, organizational arrangements).

A third central caveat in discussing interactivity lies in the fact that little effort has been directed at theorizing on the effects of interactivity (Bucy, 2004a; Gleason & Lane, 2009; Sundar, 2004). Scholars in interactive advertising effectiveness research, for example, found interactivity to have a positive impact on user attitudes (Cho & Leckenby, 1999). Others argued, by contrast, that interactivity may even be detrimental to advertising effectiveness (Bezjian-Avery, Calder, & Iacobucci, 1998; Liu & Shrum, 2002). Further, the multi-dimensionality of the concept infers that research needs to be conducted to understand the effects of varying levels of interactivity of a message vehicle (e.g., a website) on an individual's capacity for effective information processing and decision-making (Bezjian-Avery et al., 1998; Cho & Leckenby, 1999; Coyle & Thorson, 2001). Moreover, research in personality differences and social and psychological factors would lead to a rich space of further possible research topics (Jee & Lee, 2002; Lin, 2003; Sohn & Lee, 2005).

Three Traditions of Interactivity

Notwithstanding these difficulties in conceptualizing interactivity, scholars developed three dominant concept traditions alongside the dominant characteristics of the phenomenon (Heeter, 2000; Jensen, 1998; Kiousis, 2002; McMillan, 2002, 2006; Quiring & Schweiger, 2008): *technology, communication process, and user perception.* Each of these characteristics locates the reference point of interactivity differently according to the nature of the participants (i.e., active or passive), the level of user or receiver control (i.e., high or low), and the center of control (i.e., human or computer) (McMillan, 2006).[1]

First, the interactivity-as-technology tradition sees interaction between humans and the computer itself (or other types of new media systems) as central to new media. Rooted in HCI research (Baecker, 1980; Baecker & Buxton, 1987; Guedj, tenHagen, Hopgood, Tucker, & Duce, 1980; Hartson, 1998; Nielsen, 2000), this tradition defines the interaction between a single human and a single computer as the most elementary form of interactivity (Shaw,

Aranson, & Belardo, 1993). As indicated above, key underlying constructs of this view of interactivity are: *bi-directionality* (McMillan, 2000; Nickerson, 1977; Noll, 2003), *bandwidth* (indicating the speed at which data are transferred using a particular network medium; Burke & Chidambaram, 1999), and *speed of response* (as explained by the *timeliness* construct described further below; Hanssen, Jankowski, & Etienne, 1996). In addition, *symmetry,* which refers here to (a) a technology characteristic where speed or data quantity transferred is the same in both directions; measured by down *and* upstream channel or bandwidth capacity by transmit time per mega bytes, and (b) a communication characteristic where the sender and receiver roles becoming virtually indistinguishable in environments such as chat rooms, bulletin boards, etc., as described in Grunig and Grunig's (1989) model of two-way symmetric communication), and *synchronicity* (similar to *speed of response* this construct refers to the extent to which a message exchange occurs in real time or is delayed; Burgoon et al., 2000; Dennis, Fuller, & Valacich, 2008; Dennis & Valacich, 1999) come to explain interactivity-as-technology. Essentially, no computer-mediated interactivity would occur without the provision of a physical return-path and adequate communication technology architecture.

The second school of thought identifies interactivity as communication process at the heart of which lies computer-mediated interaction between humans. Rooted within CMC theory, this view refers to themes of interpersonal interaction, symbolic interaction, and social interaction (Goffman, 1967; McMillan, 2006). Underlying constructs on this dimension are: *reciprocality of participants* (also discussed as *reciprocity*, *participation*, *mutual action*, *action-reaction*, and *two-way communication*; Ha & James, 1998; Gouldner, 1960; Johnson, Bruner, & Kumar, 2006), *exchange of (symbolic) messages* (whereby networked interactivity in computer-mediated communication settings goes beyond natural interactivity in that "later messages in any sequence take into account not just messages that preceded them, but also the manner in which previous messages were reactive. In this manner interactivity forms a social reality"; Rafaeli & Sudweeks, 1997, para. 8), *active user control* (Rice & Williams, 1984), *immediacy of feedback* (tools such as e-mail links that allow the receiver to concurrently communicate with the sender; Dennis & Kinney, 1998), and *participation* (defined by Laurel, 1991, p. 21, as "how immersed you are in the experience). CMC theory, in particular, stresses the way by which the communicators process social identity and relational cues (i.e., the capability to convey meanings through cues like body language, voice, tones, that is basically social information) using different media (Fulk, Schmitz, & Steinfield, 1990; Walther, 1992).

And third, interactivity is viewed to have anthropomorphic properties (Quiring, 2009). Here, interactivity refers back to action and, in the social sciences, whereby action is presupposed to depend on an active human subject intentionally acting upon an object or another subject. Interaction with objects and the creators of these objects modify their actions and reactions due to the actions by their interaction partner(s) (Jaeckel, 1995). Seen this way, interactivity is understood as a subjective mode of perception and cognition and, as interpreted from a communication theory perspective, focuses on how a receiver actively interprets and uses mass and new media messages. In the CMC literature, two key themes have emerged under this rubric: individual experiential processes of interactivity (Downes & McMillan, 2000; McMillan, 2000; McMillan & Hwang, 2002), and perceptions of individual control over both presentation and content (Bezjian-Avery et al., 1998; Hanssen et al., 1996). *Self-awareness* (i.e., the psychological factor that impacts on social interaction as mediated by CMC; Matheson & Zanna, 1998), *responsiveness* (the degree to which a user perceives a system as reacting quickly and iteratively to user input; Rafaeli, 1988), a *sense of presence* (discoursed as virtual experience made by humans when they interact with media and simulation technologies; Lee, 2004; Lombard & Ditton, 1997; Short, 1974; Short, Williams, & Christie, 1976; Steuer, 1992), *involvement* (defined as perceived sensory and cognitive affiliation with product and content; Fortin & Dholakia, 2005; Franz & Robey, 1986; McMillan, 2000; McMillan, Jang-Sun, & Guiohk, 2003; Zaichkowsky, 1986), and *perceived user control* are further constituent psychological activities on this level of discussion (Robey, 1979).

McMillan (2002, 2005; McMillan, Jang-Sun, & Guiohk, 2003), whose conceptual typology will be used more explicitly below, identified three types of interactivity in the literature. First, human-to-computer interactivity, also known as medium or man-machine interactivity, focuses on the techno-structural properties of human-computer interaction. It looks at interactivity as a machine attribute and at interaction as the process that takes place when a human user operates a machine (Jensen, 1998). HCI research addresses this type of interactivity and deals with issues of design, evaluation and implementation of interactive computing, telecommunication, and media systems for human use (Kirsh, 1997; Sears & Jacko, 2009; Sundar, Xu, & Bellur, 2010). Typical examples of features that drive HCI are search function/engine, choice of language, choice of browser support, retrieval of audio files, retrieval of moving images, adaptive interactivity in start area (personalization tools), reference to other areas of the same site, and hyperlinks to other websites (see Table 15.1). Heeter (1989) conceived of this type of interactivity as complexity of choice available and defined it as "the extent to which users are provided with a choice of available information" (Heeter, 1989, p. 222), such that when users are forced to make more choices, they are engaging in a behavior that may be described as being more interactive. Similarly, Heeter's dimension monitoring of information use which considers the potential of a system to track users' usage patterns and locates individual user profiles also falls under this category.

Stimulated by Heeter's (1989) construct of *facilitation of interpersonal communication*, *human-to-human interactivity* (also known as user-to-user interactivity), the second main *type* of interactivity, sees interactivity as mode of social interaction between participants and as natural to a communication process between and among humans (Blattberg & Deighton 1991; Goertz,

1995; Milheim, 1996). There, exchange of meaning between interaction partners takes place (Haeckel, 1998; Rafaeli, 1988; Rafaeli & Sudweeks, 1997; Williams, Rice, & Rogers, 1988). Typical examples for human-to-human interactivity in computer-mediated settings are scheduled chat sessions, newsgroup forums, subscriber blogs, reader polls on current topics, and hypertextual cross-reference to editorial content related to the current topic under surveillance.

Finally, *human-to-content interactivity* refers to the concept of interactivity as mode of the individual receiver's perception and cognition. Potential drivers among this type of interactivity are the direction of communication, the time flexibility, the sense of place, the level of control, the perceived system responsiveness, and the perceived purpose of communication (Downes & McMillan, 2000; Kiousis, 2002; McMillan, 2006). Here, typical examples are websites which allow users to add web pages, hobby or special interest pages, announcements of births, marriages, death, and reviews of games, movies, and other entertainment events. Heeter (1989) referred to this type of interactivity as *ease of adding information*. The easier it is to add information to a website, the more interactive it is supposed to be. Other facets that constitute perceived interactivity on this level are: *reciprocity*, *responsiveness*, and *speed of response* (Alba et al., 1997; Bezjian-Avery et al., 1998; Heeter, 1989).

Interactivity in Traditional and New Media

Historically, the term *interactivity* has been attributed largely to personal, face-to-face communication (Bretz & Schmidbauer, 1983; Duncan, 1989; Durlak, 1987; McMillan, 2006). Face-to-face communication between people typically is interactive, so are telephone conversations (Carey, 1989). Durlak (1987) even claimed that interpersonal communication and especially face-to-face communication is the ideal type of interactive communication: "Face-to-face communication is held up as the model because the sender and receiver use all their senses, the reply is immediate, the communication is generally closed circuit, and the content is primarily informal or 'ad lib'" (p. 744). The importance of interactivity as *distinctive* variable of mediated communication has grown with the emergence of the World Wide Web (Bucher, 2002, 2004; Huhtamo, 1998; Jensen, 1998; Manovich, 2001; Morris & Ogan, 1996) and other digital media such as interactive digital television (Jensen, 2005) and mobile media (Gao, Rau, & Salvendy, 2009; Lee, 2005).

In this chapter, I will review interactivity from a communication theory perceptive. According to Steuer (1992), traditional media refer to interactivity as "the degree to which users of a medium can influence the form or content of the mediated environment in real time" (p. 83). Steuer focused on the relationship between an individual who is both a sender and a receiver, and on the mediated environment with which he or she interacts in face-to-interface communication. Steuer suggested an alternative view of mediated communication, and draws attention to a fundamental difference with conventional media. "Traditionally, the process of communication is described in terms of the transmission of information, as a process linking sender and receiver. Media are therefore important only as a conduit, as a means of connecting sender and receiver, and are only interesting to the extent that they contribute to or otherwise interfere with transmission of the message from sender to receiver" (p. 80). In addition, Steuer claimed that "information is not transmitted from sender to receiver; rather, mediated environments are created and then experienced" (p. 80).

Jensen (1998) employed the model of information traffic patterns of Bordewijk and Van Kaam (1986) to examine *scientific images* of interactivity. Their classification system begins with what they call *allocution*, a traditional communications flow to distribute information from a centre simultaneously to many peripheral receivers. Allocution is typically one-way communication with little or no feedback or control by the recipient (e.g., public speaking, TV broadcasting). Second, *conversation* takes place when individuals interact directly with each other without intermediary, choosing partner, time, topic (e.g., talk, e-mail, telephone). The parties are equal in exchange. Further, *consultation* occurs when an individual looks for information at a central store of information (e.g., library, database, archive). Here, the receiver determines time, place, and topic. The decision is peripheral. Finally, *registration* is a process whereby a centre requests and receives information from a participant at the periphery (e.g., recording systems). Jensen (1998) adopted these patterns of information traffic to assess whether particular media are interactive or not. To achieve this, Jensen proposed to apply these information patterns to the concept of interactivity. For this, they needed to be broken down into the following four dimensions: (a) *transmissional interactivity*—a measure of media's potential ability to let the user choose from a continuous stream of information in a one-way media system without a return channel and therefore without a possibility for making requests (e.g., teletext, near-video-on-demand, be-your-own-editor, multi-channel systems, datacasting, multicasting; (b) *consultational interactivity*—a measure of media's potential ability to let the user choose, by request, from an existing selection of preproduced information in a two-way media system with a return channel (e.g., video-on-demand, online information services, CD-ROM encyclopaedias, FTP, WWW, Gopher); (c) *conversational interactivity*—a measure of a media's potential ability to let the user produce and input his/her own information in a two-way media system, be it stored or in real-time (e.g., video conferencing systems, newsgroups, e-mail, mailing lists); and (d) *registrational interactivity* if information is produced by the information consumer, but processed and controlled by the information providing centre. Jensen's taxonomy thus delivered a complex typology of the concept of 'interactivity' to reveal some central inherent properties: interactivity is functional, processual, auctorial, and situational.

Looking at interactivity from the perspective of communication studies, Hanssen et al. (1996) pioneered a slightly different approach in stating that interactivity is a multi-dimensional construct and allows for the overlapping of three dimensions that are central to interactivity. "Aspects of interactivity were clustered around three terms: (1) *equality* (containing aspects such as participants, mutual activity, role exchange, control); (2) *responsiveness* (e.g., mutual discourse, nature of feedback, response time); and (3) *functional communicative environment* (e.g., bandwidth, transparency, social presence, artificial intelligence)" (p. 71).

Heeter (2000) observed seven central aspects about interactivity when tracing developments from traditional to new media systems: "(1) information is always sought or selected not merely sent; (2) media systems require different levels of user activity (i.e., users are always active to some extent); (3) activity is a user trait as well as a medium trait. Some media are more interactive than others; some receivers are more active than others; (4) person-machine interactions are a special form of communication; (5) continuous feedback is a special form of feedback in which behavior of all users is measured on an ongoing basis by a source (e.g., videotext system) or gatekeeper (e.g., cable operator); and (6) the distinction between source and receiver is not present in all media systems; and (7) media systems may facilitate mass communication, interpersonal communication, or both." Heeter suggested domains for *designed experiences* in TV versus computer contexts such as screen resolution, input devices, viewing distance, user posture, room, number of users, and user engagement. Against this backdrop, Heeter developed a list of requirements for new and improved interactive interfaces, referring to the notions of *time*, *space*, *participation*, and *user affordances*. The idea of affordances plays an important role in the study of human-computer interaction. For Norman (1988), who adopted the term to HCI, affordances are action possibilities that are readily perceivable by an actor.

Similarly, Steuer (1992) came to define interactivity as "the degree to which users of a medium can influence the form or content of the mediated environment" (p. 80). Steuer considered interactivity (and *vividness*) as an experiential antecedent to *tele-presence*. Tele-presence, on its part, is defined as a sense of presence in a mediated environment, wherein the user experiences the computer-mediated environment as less mediated than it actually is (Steuer, 1992; Klein, 2003). Consequently, Steuer offered three dimensions of interactivity: *speed*, *range*, and *mapping*, which are all technological elements. "Speed refers to the rate at which input can be assimilated into the mediated environment; range, which refers to the number of possibilities for action at any given time; and mapping, which refers to the ability of the system to map its controls to changes in the mediated environment in a natural and predictable manner" (p. 15). A review of the literature led Fortin (1997, as cited in Dholakia, Zhao, Dholakia, & Fortin, 2000) to define interactivity as "the degree to which a communication system can allow one or more end users to communicate alternatively as senders or receivers with one or many other users or communication devices, either in real time (as in video teleconferencing) or on a store-and-forward basis (as with electronic mail), or to seek and gain access to information on an on-demand basis where the content, timing and sequence of the communication is under control of the end user, as opposed to a broadcast basis" (p. 4).

Apart from more theoretical backup, studies in web design have tried to empirically verify the effects of interactivity on media offers. Dholakia et al. (2000), for example, focused on interactivity as it affects revisits to websites. Following an extensive literature review in CMC research on interactivity, they identified six key dimensions of the interactivity construct: *user control*, *responsiveness*, *real-time interactions*, *connectedness*, *personalization/customization*, and *playfulness*. Focusing on revisits, they proposed a framework that traces the effect of interactivity dimensions through intermediate stages of perceived interactivity, social presence, empowerment, and satisfaction. A closer look at the relationship between interactivity dimensions and revisits takes into consideration four types of websites—shopping, entertainment, information, and communication.

However, it took until the advent of new information and communication technologies (ICTs) for the concept of interactivity to be developed more conceptually. In this regard, Rafaeli (1988), an often-cited expert on interpersonal and group computer-mediated communication, focused on the concept of *responsiveness* as interactive exchange and argued that interactivity is "an expression of the extent that, in a given series of communication changes, any third (or later) transmission (or message) is related to the degree to which previous exchanges referred to event earlier transmissions" (p. 111). On Rafaeli's (1988) reading, interactivity is defined as a property of the communication process itself rather than a medium, although the medium "may set upper bounds, remove barriers, or provide necessary conditions for interactivity levels" (pp. 119–120). This model uses three progressive levels in its continuum: (a) two-way communication takes place when messages are delivered both ways; (b) reactive communication also requires that a later message reacts to a previous message; (c) full interactivity requires that a later message responds to a sequence of previous messages. In this conceptual construction, *responsiveness* plays a central role. Responsiveness obviously requires that the media registers and stores information about a given user's input and actions and can then adjust to the user's wishes and distinctive characteristics. This concept of interactivity refers therefore (contrary to Rogers) primarily to the registration communication pattern. This aspect can be stated such that a media—in one sense or another—*understands* the user, and in this way approaches themes related to *smart technologies*, *artificial intelligence,* etc. Once again, interpersonal communication functions as an ideal to be measured with characteristics similar to the sociological concept of interaction, and its requirement of reciprocity.

Stressing the notion of interactivity as technology feature, Kiousis (2002) suggested that "interactivity is an attribute of the channel through which the dynamic interdependence between senders and receivers in communication becomes possible" (p. 359). In his concept explication concerning interactivity, Kiousis (2002) formulated a definition which assigns three central dimensions to interactivity: (a) the information technological structure of the medium; (b) the context of communication settings; and (c) the perception of users.

Kiousis (2002) offered the following conceptual and operational definitions of interactivity: "To restate, interactivity can be defined as the degree to which a communication technology can create a mediated environment in which participants can communicate (one-to-one, one-to-many, and many-to-many) both synchronously and asynchronously and participate in reciprocal message exchanges (third-order dependency)" (p. 379). With regard to human users, interactivity additionally refers to the ability of users to perceive the experience to be a simulation of interpersonal communication and increase their awareness of tele-presence. Operationally, interactivity is then established by three factors: technological structure of the media used (e.g., speed, range, timing flexibility, and sensory complexity), characteristics of communication settings (e.g., third-order dependency, i.e., A's response to B depends on B's prior response to A's initial communication acts, and social presence), and individual user's perceptions (e.g., proximity, perceived speed, sensory activation, and tele-presence). *Perception* is a popular category among many scholars who seek to identify the inner workings of the concept of interactivity (Lee, Barua, & Whinston, 2000; McMillan, 2000; Morrison, 1998; Sohn & Lee, 2005). Burgoon et al. (2000), for example, suggested that one way to conceptualize interactivity is that it is based on the qualitative experiences that users equate with interactivity. Morrison (1998) noted that it is important to understand how individuals perceive interactivity in order to grasp the influence of newer media technologies in their lives. McMillan and Hwang (2002) found that online users' attitudes toward websites is positively related to their perceived interactivity of the site. Lee et al. (2000) suggested that the most important thing to be examined in measuring the level of interactivity is not counting more provisions of technological features, but rather investigating how users perceive and/or experience those features. Seen from a slightly different view, Williams et al. (1988) defined interactivity as "the degree to which participants in a communication process have control over, and can exchange roles in, their mutual discourse." By mutual discourse, Williams et al. meant "the degree to which a given communication act is based on a prior series of communication acts" (pp. 10–11). By exchange of role, Williams et al. defined "the ability of individual A to take the position of individual B and thus to perform B's communication acts." Control is defined as "the extent to which an individual can choose the timing, content, and sequence of a communication act, search out alternative choices, enter content into a storage for other users, and perhaps create new system capabilities" (pp. 10–11).

User control has been conceptualized as one key component of interactivity by a number of researchers. Studying the importance of presence and active personal experience as success variable for interactive digital media, Lombard and Snyder-Duch (2001) defined "interactivity as a characteristic of a medium in which the user can influence the form and/or content of the mediated presentation or experience. It is not dichotomous (a medium is not just interactive or not), but can vary in degree (from not interactive to highly interactive) as well as type (different aspects of the form and/or content that can be influenced by the user)" (p. 2). For them, "central to the idea of interactivity is the concept of control, either of elements of the physical world or of information." They proposed that interactivity has five critical components: number of inputs acceptable; number and type of characteristics that are modifiable, range of response possible, speed of response, degree of correspondence between input and response. Drawing from studies in CMC research and communication theory, Rafaeli (1988) recounted further key elements of interactivity: bi-directionality, quick response, bandwidth, user control, amount of user interactivity, ratio of user to medium interactivity, feedback, transparency, social presence, and artificial intelligence (p. 115). However, all these dimensions fall short of explaining the intuitive appeal of interactivity that captures the ultimate essence of interactivity: user and content-oriented qualities that go beyond mere user responsiveness and reaction (p. 110). As Rafaeli and Sudweeks (1997) put it: "We note that communication is mostly about and for the purpose of interaction. Interactivity places shared interpretive contexts in the primary role. Interactivity describes and prescribes the manner in which conversational interaction as an iterative process leads to jointly produced meaning. Interactivity merges speaking with listening. And it is a general enough concept to encompass both intimate, person-to-person, face-to-face communication and other forums and forms" (para. 7).

Interactivity and e-Commerce

Adoption of the concept of interactivity within the research domain of electronic commerce can be found in studies investigating business-to-customer relationships in e-commerce research traditions (Essler & Whitaker, 2001; Kuk & Yeung, 2002; Romano & Fjermestad, 2003; Sukpanich & Chen, 2000; Yadav & Varadarajan, 2005a) and the marketing and advertising activities of firms (Blattberg & Deighton, 1991; Coviello, Milley, & Marcolin., 2001; Day, 1998; Ha & James, 1998; Iacobucci, 1998; Novak, Hoffman, & Yung, 2000; Ko, Cho, & Ro, 2005; Liu & Shrum, 2002; Webster, 1996, 1998). Naturally, the possible thematic scope of interactivity within an electronic commerce context is broad and rather scattered, discussing structural, processual, and experiential dimensions across various issues. To start with, Choi, Stahl, and Winston (1997) saw interactivity as a defining criterion for digital products: "Products that are downloaded at once or in a piecemeal fashion, such as through daily updates, can be called delivered products. Interactive products, on the other hand, are products or services, such as remote-diagnosis, interactive games, and tele-education" (p. 76). Bezjian-Avery et al. (1998) defined interactivity as part of "the immediately iterative process by which customer needs and desires are uncovered, met, modified, and satisfied by the providing firm" (p. 23). Interactivity can push users to actively engage in the communication process and thus build sustainable relationships between consumer and advertiser/message provider. Romano and Fjermestad (2003) identified a number of current and emergent technologies for internet-based electronic customer relationship management (e-CRM). They developed an e-CRM IT classification scheme from the consumer's perspective based on how consumers communicate to develop and maintain relationships via three specific levels of participation along a continuum ranging from passive to interactive. For them, interactive emergent technologies such as e-mail, forums, online focus groups, interactive interviews, survey panels, auctions, trade shows, and shopping agents are participatory. Essler and Whitaker (2001) pointed to the need of rethinking e-commerce business models impacted by interactivity in the era of cyberspace. They argued that, in the future, interactivity would drive changes from enterprise infrastructure to the so-called *interactional agitecture* described as a process of reciprocal interactivity and influence between firm and customer. Alba et al. (1997) conceptualized interactivity from an e-commerce point of view as "a continuous construct capturing the quality of two-way communication between two parties [...]. In the case of interactive home shopping (IHS), the parties are the buyer and seller. The two dimensions of interactivity are response time and response contingency. Because IHS involves electronic communication, the response can be immediate – similar to response time in face-to-face communications. Response contingency is the degree to which the response by one party is a function of the response made by the other party" (p. 38). The concept of interactivity has received considerable attention within the e-tailing domain in recent years, especially with the help of consumer behavior concepts and tools (Ballantine, 2005; Szymanski & Hise, 2000; Yoo, Lee, & Park, 2010). Within these studies, interactivity takes on manifold meanings, either as "physical interactivity between store and customer" (Merrilees & Miller, 2001), as "image interactivity (that) allows the customer to create and manipulate visual images of a product on a Web site" (Fiore & Jin, 2003), or as "interactive service quality" between the service provider's and the service receiver's expectations and perceptions (Svensson, 2003). While images on a website may enhance responses towards an online retail store (Fiore & Jin, 2003), the success of interactive features offered may depend on the consumer's level of satisfaction with the interface provided. This view was supported by Schumann who claimed: "Ultimately it is the consumer's choice to interact, thus interactivity is a characteristic of the consumer, and not a characteristic of the medium. The medium simply serves to facilitate the interaction" (Schumann, Artis, & Rivera, 2001, para. 11).

The Business Value of Interactivity

Now that I have reviewed various notions and models of interactivity, I will turn my attention to two key questions: What types and dimensions of computer-mediated interactivity create business value for both organization and consumer in the electronic marketplace? And how does interactivity, if at all, advance theoretical insights into economic analyses of interactions between buyers and sellers in the electronic marketplace?

Table 15.1 Typology of Types and Ddimension of Interactivity and Definitions of Interactivity in e-Commerce—Synoptic Overview

Types	*Dimensions of Interactivity*			*Definitions of Interactivity in e-Commerce*
	Technology	*Communication Process*	*User Perception*	
Human-to-Computer	• Navigational tools • Site search tools • Choice of language • XML-based web browsers • Links to other site content • Hyperlinks to external content	• Navigating a website • Using a search engine • Browsing a product catalogue • Choosing preferred language • Choosing preferred browser • Retrieving different types of (on-site or hyperlinked) website content	• Finding a website easy to control and engaging • Based on experience with the technology and involvement with issue	• "Products that are downloaded … can be called delivered products. Interactive products, on the other hand, are products or services, such as remote-diagnosis, interactive games, and tele-education" • Ha & James (1998) studied business websites to identify five characteristics of interactivity: *playfulness*, *choice*, *connectedness*, *information collection*, and *reciprocal communication* • "Interactive speed is a construct that contributes to flow and is based on measures such as waiting time, loading time, and degree to which interacting with the Web is 'slow and tedious'"
Human-to-Human	• Instant messaging (IM) • Email • Live or scheduled chat • Newsgroup forums • Subscriber blogs • Reader polls • Hyper-textual cross-reference to related editorial content	• Communicating with website editors and other consumers • Communicating to web editors and/or peers • Facilitating and enforcing interpersonal computer-mediated communications between and among participants	• Believing that interactive feature facilitates communication • May be based on personal interest or involvement with communication participants	• "In interactive systems, a customer controls the content of the interaction requesting or giving information.… The hallmark of these new media is their interactivity – the consumer and the manufacturer enter into dialogue in a way not previously possible" • Interactivity defined as "facility for persons and organizations to communicate directly with one another regardless of distance or time"

		• Facilitating transaction between participants		• Defined interactivity as “the degree to which two or more communication parties can act on each other, on the communication medium, and on the messages and the degree to which such influences are synchronized” • Physical interactivity, image interactivity, interactive service quality • “Ultimately it is the consumer’s choice to interact, thus interactivity is characteristic of the consumer, and not a characteristic of the medium. The medium simply serves to facilitate the interaction” • Interactivity as *interactional agitecture* described as a process of reciprocal interactivity and influence between firm and customer
Human-to-Content	• Tools that facilitate personalized content and delivery formats • Tools that allow adding web pages • Etc.	• Retaining and relinquishing control of content • Influencing the communication direction	• Believing that customized and personalized content format is interactive • User perception of positive manipulation of communication • User perception of control over content	• Image interactivity (that) allows the customer to create and manipulate visual images of a product on a website

Note: Definitions of Human-to-Computer interactivity are taken from Choi (1997), Ha & James (1998), and Novak et al. (2000). Definitions of Human-to-Human interactivity stem from Bezjian-Avery et al. (1997), Blattberg & Deighton (1991), Liu & Shrum (2002), Merrilees & Miller (2001), Fiore & Jin (2003), Svensson (2003), Schumann et al. (2001), and Essler & Whitaker (2001). The definition of Human-to-Content interactivity is credited to Fiore & Jin (2003).

Source: The author (based on McMillan, 2002, 2005, 2006)

The following key arguments have repeatedly been voiced as major drivers for change in the governance of electronic commerce relations, be it sharing business information, maintaining relationships, conducting actual business transactions and generating value streams by means of telecommunication and computer networks (Amit & Zott, 2001; Wigand, 1997).

First, the idea that business value is co-created and enhanced through the producers' interaction with their customers may be traced back to F. W. Taylor, who developed the concept of scientific management in 1911. Taylor's concept of analyzing the improved efficiency in mass production contains aspects that are relevant to the theory and practice of mass customization in the electronic marketplace. Mass customization, which is defined as "producing goods and services to meet individual customer's needs with near mass production efficiency" (Tseng & Jiao, 2001, p. 685), integrates the customers deeply into a firm's system of value creation. As a result, customer integration systems aim at combining the low unit costs of classical Taylorist mass production processes with the flexibility of individual customization (Piller, Moeslein, & Stotko, 2004).

Second, modern organization theory based on the work of Barnard (1948), the author of pioneering work in management theory and organizational sociology, has originated the idea of *relationship marketing* whereby customers are not external actors in the business communication process but an integral part of an organization's plan for survival through effectiveness and efficiency (Barnard, 1948). Third, in 1993, Normann and Ramirez published their seminal work on how new ICTs and changing consumer lifestyles transform the notion of business value from Porter's (1985) traditional model of the sequential value chain into their new model of *value constellation*. There, consumers and other partners, suppliers, etc., actively co-produce relationships along with the enterprise. In their model, the business model is meant to be actively co-created between the various actors involved. To support this, interactive network technologies would potentially open organizations towards customers' involvement for value generation. Prahalad and Ramaswamy (2000, 2002, 2003, 2004), another two comprehensive business thinkers, have further elaborated on changes in the traditional logic of governance in electronic commerce as analytically depicted by the concept of the *linear* and *horizontal value chain*. Briefly, they claim the need for producers to establish interaction platforms for *co-creating unique value with customers* (Prahalad & Ramaswamy, 2004). Only this would achieve sustainable competitive advantage for the business firm. Likewise, German and Scandinavian researchers in business and management have focused on *customer integration* (Kleinaltenkamp, Fließ, & Jacob, 1996; Lampel & Mintzberg, 1995; Wikstroem, 1996a, b), *value webs* (Reichwald, Seifert, & Walcher, 2004), and *interactive value* (Reichwald & Piller, 2009), a general research perspective on which this present study is conceptually and analytically.

The Concept of Customer Integration

The concept of *customer integration* dates back to the mid-1990s, when several researchers in management theory began to work on the belief that new technologies, increased competition, and more assertive customers are leading firms towards customization of their products and services. By integrating customers into design, research and product development, manufacturing, assembling, or sales activities, companies, it is believed, will get efficient support to improve products for more customer satisfaction, and identify and unlock new sources of revenue (Kleinaltenkamp et al., 1996). Customer integration can be defined as a value creation process where "consumers take part in activities and processes which used to be seen as the domain of the companies" (Wikstroem, 1996a, p. 360). *Value webs* enable both customers and suppliers to be co-operatively active in team-based product and process innovation activities, as well as in product design, re-design, development, and, finally, electronically mediated transactions between organizations and customers (Chesbrough, Vanhaverbeke, & West, 2006; von Hippel, 2005). Social network effects and transaction cost efficiencies resulting from these value webs are said to emerge if customers are actively involved in and integrated into the respective e-business processes (Economides, 1996; Klemperer, 2008; Yadav & Varadarajan, 2005a). In addition, the role of the customer is changing from a pure consumer of products or services to that of equal partner in a process of adding value: consumers are becoming co-producers and co-designers (Berger, Moeslein, Piller, & Reichwald, 2005; Picot, Reichwald, & Wigand, 1998; Reichwald et al., 2004; Tseng & Piller, 2003). Both e-business partners are thus tied together in these value webs. Finally and essentially, the firm's relationship with the customer, thus the business value of any customer integration, is crucially dependent on interaction with him or her.

Here, interactivity as an essential building block for enhancing an electronic commerce relationship with the customer steps in. More strongly, interactivity may even be considered as the engine of this the new fabric of interaction with the customer. Theoretically, customer integration is the ultimate form of this kind of customer orientation. Its goal is to provide customized products or services that exactly meet the desires and wishes of each individual customer (Milgrom & Roberts, 1990). Among other issues, the economic view of customer integration identifies interactive value creation as an emergent paradigm at the interface of research into strategic management, innovation management, and marketing management (Kotha, 1995; Reichwald & Piller, 2009). Hence, customer integration may become a strategic necessity of business companies as electronic transactions may impact the characteristics of these markets in ways that overall efficiency gains (e.g., lower information search costs for consumers) and/or improvements in effectiveness (e.g., greater ability of consumers to purchase products better suited to their specific needs) may result from transactions in electronic marketplaces in various industries (Bakos, 1991;

Lampel & Mintzberg, 1996; Yadav & Varadarajan, 2005b; Zeithaml, 1988). As for customer integration, companies may benefit from so-called *economies of integration* (Noori, 1990; Piller et al., 2004; Vandermerve, 2000; Wind & Rangaswamy, 2001). These are defined as "cost savings potentials as a result from the direct interaction between each customer and the firm" (Piller & Moeslein, 2002, p. 6).

Potential Impacts of Interactivity on Business Value: Some Key Propositions

Reviewing the extant literature on interactivity and business value has illustrated the complexity of studying the relationships between these two concepts. The following sample propositions offer a suggested research direction in analyzing potential impacts of interactivity on business value.

Proposition 1 [P1]: *Interactivity enhances consumer choice and thus perceived consumer value. This has a positive impact on business value.*

Reviewing the interactivity concept has shown that it potentially offers greater product choices for consumers by offering a wider range of options for consumption to customers.

Proposition 1 is supported by the following arguments as drawn from a review of the literature: First, that interactivity enhances consumer choice is plausible if one considers the importance of the technology dimension of interactivity when predicting a positive impact relationship between interactivity and consumer value. Following the interactivity as technology school of thought, which focuses on functions of features, interactivity is based on how many and what types of features are available for online users to fulfill interactive communication [see Proposition 1.1 in Table 15.2] (Steuer, 1992; Sundar, 2004). A range of theories from neighboring disciplines such as marketing science, journalism, and advertising support this proposition (Deuze, 2003; Ghose & Dou, 1998; Liu, 2003; Woodruff, 1997; Wu, 2006). There, greater choice would improve the general attractiveness of a website by improving the consumer's choice of options and active control over the type of product sought after and selected [Proposition 1.2]. On closer inspection, however, interactivity sub-dimensions may each impact differently on consumer value. *Bi-directionality*, *bandwidth*, and *synchronicity* may serve as necessary *but not sufficient* conditions for interactivity [Proposition 1.3]. As exemplified by Song and Bucy (2008), "it might be possible that one perceives communication through asynchronous e-mail as more interactive than synchronous communication through Instant Messenger (IM) even though objectively (technologically) the opposite appears true" (p. 7). Further, *timeliness* as interaction speed is perceived as a positive predictor of interactivity-induced business value [Proposition 1.4]. However, when defined as communication speed, the construct becomes particularly valuable for the consumer (Kiousis, 2002). In fact, consumers may wish to determine their own message timing and thus increase their control over technology and communication process [Proposition 1.5]

(Downes & McMillan, 2000; Kiousis, 2002). Consumer value may thus eventually depend on the perceptual aspects of interactivity that may mediate the effects of technology on certain outcomes (Bucy & Tao, 2007).

Past research has also indicated that greater *complexity of choice available* may have an effect on consumer choice difficulty and choice overload [Proposition 1.6] (Ariely, 1998, 2000; Heeter, 1989; Kim & LaRose, 2004). Interactivity thus also implies that consumers may have to afford higher amounts of effort to seek, self-select, process, use, and respond to information (Heeter, 1989; Stewart & Pavlou, 2002). In this case, consumers may have to undertake (significant) cognitive activities when trying to satisfy some need or goal (e.g., navigating the website and pulling information from it) (Heeter, 1989; McMillan & Hwang, 2002; Zaichkowsky, 1985). This may act as a further impediment on consumer value effectiveness [Proposition 1.7].

Proposition 2 [P2]: *Interactivity enhances perceived product and service quality and thus consumer satisfaction and perceived communication quality and satisfaction. This has a positive impact on business value.*

Interactivity enhances perceived product & service quality (Chen & Yen, 2004; Hsiu-Fe, 2007; Svensson, 2003; Yoo et al., 2010), and perceived communication quality and process satisfaction (Lowry, Romano Jr., Jenkins, & Guthrie, 2009).

Proposition 2 is justified by the following arguments: First, product and service quality improvements are viewed to be triggered by various forms and levels of interactivity that allow consumers using an online shopping environment to access higher product quality, gain greater control of their shopping experience, and experiences higher levels of satisfaction through more convenient shopping environments (Ariely, 2000; Chen & Dubinsky, 2002; Chen & Yen, 2004).

When linked with the interactivity concept, this proposition is mainly supported by the CMC dimension of interactivity [Proposition 2.1]. Seen this way, message-based approaches define interactivity of a particular communication message as directly responsive to, or contingent on, a previous message received (Rafaeli, 1988). As aptly exemplified by Sundar (2007), "(…) in a chat room if both people post messages without acknowledging each other's messages, then it is non-interactive. If one interactant posts a message that is a direct response to another's postings, then it is considered to be reactive. If the latter interactant then responds to this posting in a manner that takes into account not only the latest posting but also those before them, then it is considered to be responsive. For a message exchange to be fully interactive the messages should have a flow or coherence, i.e., they can be threaded together in sequence" (p. 95) [Proposition 2.2]. When consumer experience features of interactivity which provide for bi-directional and multidirectional communication, they may feel a sense of increased control not only over the communication process, but also over timing and choice of subject (Bordewijk & van Kaam, 1986) [Proposition 2.3]. As reviewed, Jensen's conversational interactivity underpins this rationale (Jensen, 1998).

Proposition 3 [P3]: *Interactivity enables participation and interpersonal communication. This has a positive impact on business value.*

Interactivity builds, facilitates, and enforces interpersonal computer-mediated communication between and among participants thereby activating and engaging them. This includes all forms of CMC processes "by which people create, exchange, and perceive information using networked telecommunication systems and facilitate encoding, transmitting, and decoding messages" (December, 1996; as cited in Romiszowski & Mason, 2004, p. 398; Soukup, 2000).

Proposition 3 builds on the following arguments: If websites make it easy for users to add information, then they empower users by making it easier for them to add information [Proposition 3.1]. Further, the degree to which interactive media systems facilitate interpersonal communication between specific customers is said to be correlated with interactivity. E-mail addresses can make communication easy between participants in the electronic marketplace [Proposition 3.2]. Discussion forums and live chat areas attract and keep consumers at a site. In addition, an interactive site may offer "synchronous communication with data transfers occurring at fractions of a second" (Kenney, Gorelik, & Mwangi, 2000, para. 17). Further, interactivity encourages the publishing of end-user's own contributions and commenting on other people's, thus increasing both the site's content and the rate of end-user engagement on various levels [Proposition 3.3]. Encouraging participation may, however, solely reside in the mind of the consumer interacting with technology. Laurel (1991), for example, made participation an experience of *feeling* mediated by a computer interface: "You either feel yourself to be participating in the ongoing action of the representation or you don't" (pp. 20–21) [Proposition 3.4].

Proposition 4 [P4]: *Interactivity customizes products, services, and exchange processes between business firm and consumer. This has a positive impact on business value.*

Customization on a website may lead to a more interactive experience for the consumer (McMillan et al., 2003). Once consumers have disclosed relevant information, an interactive site may use the collected information and then tailor it to the consumer's preferences.

Proposition 4 is justified on the following grounds: By defining *involvement* as a hybrid facet of technological and perceptual interactivity, consumers may feel higher perceived sensory, cognitive, and affective affiliation with product and site content [Proposition 4.1]. This potentially improves their perceived value of the site (Kalyanaraman & Sundar, 2006), and thus generally improves the site's stickiness, i.e., the site's ability to retain online customers and prolong the duration of each stay.

On the sell-side, interactivity is said to constitute new generation web-based interactions which, in turn, may drive new interactive Web 2.0 business models (Tredinnick, 2006; Wirtz, Schilke, & Ullrich, 2010). By developing an ongoing learning relationship with customers, businesses can tailor their product and service portfolio not only to the actual customer needs, wants, and preferences, but also according to their contribution to the firm's economic success (Melville, Kraemer, & Gurbaxani, 2004; Rangaswamy & Pal, 2003; Tseng & Piller, 2003). Interactivity may thus influence the strategic decisions of companies in producing, delivering, and exchanging products in accordance with the dynamic preferences of their consumers [Proposition 4.2]. Taking this argument further, businesses may achieve cost efficiencies when they intensify orientation towards customers by integrating them into various value creation processes (Lampel & Mintzberg, 1996; von Hippel, 2002). The customer benefits from integration when his/her social valuation of the product exceeds the price actually paid [Proposition 4.3].

Proposition 5 [P5]: *Interactivity lowers transaction costs. This has a positive impact on business value.*

Past research has shown that interactivity impacts on transaction processes and outcomes as it may reduce the transaction costs between and among the market participants (Bakos, 1991; Benjamin & Wigand, 1995; Brynolffson & Smith, 2000; Cordella & Simon, 1997). Conceptually introduced in Coase's 1937/1979 paper *The Nature of the Firm,* which analysed why firms exist, what determines the number of firms, and what firms do, and later attributed to the work of Williamson (1975, 1985), transaction costs are generally defined as costs incurred when using the market mechanism in buying or selling a good or service. Williamson based transaction cost theory on two assumptions of human behavior (*bounded rationality* and *opportunism*, i.e., results from human limits to cognitive abilities and imperfect information) and three key dimensions of transactions (*asset specificity*, *uncertainty*, and *frequency;* Williamson, 1975). *Asset specificity* terms the significance of certain assets that support a specific transaction (i.e., Williamson mentioned four types of asset specificity: *site*, *physical asset*, *human asset*, and *dedicated asset specificity*). *Uncertainty* is embodied in any kind of future action and *frequency* describes how often a specific transaction takes place. The magnitude of these five parameters determines the scale of transaction costs occurring. Typically, the *frequency* of a transaction lowers transaction costs due to economies of scale, while all other four parameters have an increasing effect whereby asset specificity carries most influence (Williamson, 1981).

Proposition 5 is supported by the following arguments: Reviewing the extant literature on interactivity alludes to the possibility that interactivity drives up the frequency of interaction and thus transactions (because of open standards, anyone can interact with anyone else), reduces transaction uncertainty (by providing a wealth of transaction-specific information), and a leads to reduction in asset specificity (e.g., through lower site specificity—the next site is only one click away) (Amit & Zott, 2001) [Proposition 5.1]. Surprisingly, however, interactivity-induced e-commerce transactions may lead to counterintuitive effects on transaction costs involved. Offering interactivity-driven B2C e-commerce goods and services may involve transaction costs that exceed efficiency thresholds on both sides of the transaction (Williamson, 1975, 1996). This "interactivity paradox" would negatively affect the welfare of both business firm and consumer (Bucy, 2004b) [Proposition 5.2]. The business may thus wish to ensure that the consumer's additional costs are kept as small as possible, while the benefits experienced through interactivity have to be clearly perceptible (Piller, 2002).

Proposition 6 [P6]: *Interactivity widens the range of strategic e-commerce management options for competitive positional advantages of business firms. This has a positive impact on business value.*

Proposition 6 relies on the following arguments: Interactivity widens a business firm's strategic options because it may help achieving product and distribution channel differentiation thereby reducing the pressure of competition from identical products or close substitutes (Bakos, 1991, 1997) [Proposition 6.1]. For customer integration to be successful, hybrid product differentiation and cost reduction strategies are necessary so as to reconcile the cost advantages of standardized production with the disadvantages of customization (Reichwald & Piller, 2000). Interactivity management may thus imply that business firms find e-business strategies that integrate market opportunities, sufficient resources to implement these strategies, and e-tailing objectives that fit their plans (Varadarajan & Yadav, 2002) [Proposition 6.2].

Table 15.2 offers an integrative view on dimensions of interactivity and their relations to potential business value impacts. Propositions to explain these relations are indexed accordingly.

Conclusion and Managerial Implications

The present reconstruction of the concept of interactivity has identified a variety of themes from various scholarly perspectives. Although there are disciplinary differences in observing, defining, and interpreting interactivity, which obviously makes comparisons of different studies difficult, interactivity must be analyzed from these multiple sources in order to soundly bridge the concept of interactivity with the concept of business value in electronic commerce research. The literature on electronic commerce has yet to treat the concept more systematically. The problems are manifold but the most pressing seems to be the nature of the concept of interactivity itself, which remains multi-faceted and difficult to operationalize.

This chapter has adopted the dominant three-dimensional view of interactivity, conceptualizing it as an intrinsic attribute of the communication technology or format, as a constituent part of a social interaction and communication process between users or between users and technology interfaces and designs, and as a process of subjective user perception (McMillan, 2002, 2005, 2006; Quiring & Schweiger, 2008). This three-dimensional approach has become the canonical standard in researching the phenomenon of interactivity (Bucy & Tao, 2007; McMillan, 2005; Gleason, 2008). I conclude from the review of current literature that interactivity must be considered as being heterogeneous in nature, covering a broad area of tools, processes, and perceptual practices in online communication.

Table 15.2 Dimension of Interactivity and Business Value Impacts including Contingencies

Interactivity Dimensions	*Business Value Impact*	*Contingencies*
Technology structure	• Interactivity enhances consumer choice and thus perceived consumer value [P1] • Greater choice leads to higher website attractiveness improving consumer choice options and active control [P1.2] • *Bi-directionality*, *bandwidth*, and *synchronicity* are necessary but not sufficient conditions for interactivity [P1.3] • *Timeliness* as positive predictor of perceived consumer value [P1.5]	• Consumer value contingent upon adequate transmission technology infrastructure and interactive features offered by a website [P1.1] • *Timeliness* as positive predictor of business value [P1.4] • Greater choice as negative predictor when consumers face choice overload [P1.6] • Greater choice as negative predictor when consumers face considerable cognitive costs [P1.7]
Communication process	• Interactivity enhances perceived quality and consumer satisfaction [P2] • Message-centric interactivity is fully effective if communication flow is achieved [P2.2] • Interactivity enables participation and interpersonal communication [P3] • Consumers feel empowerment when being able to add information [P3.1] • Interactivity facilitates interpersonal communication [P3.2] • Interactivity encourages consumer co-operation [P3.3] • Interactivity customizes products, services, and exchange processes between business firm and consumer [P4] • Interactivity drives strategic decisions of business firms in tailoring their offers toward dynamic consumer preferences [P4.2] • Interactivity enables customer integration [P4.3]	• Consumer value contingent upon CMC dimension [P1.2] • Consumer value contingent upon increased control over communication process, timing and choice of subject [P2.3] • Participation is a mere perceptual category [P3.4] • Optimal transaction cost efficiency level contingent upon both producer and consumer [P5.2] • Interactive e-business strategies contingent upon integration of market opportunities, sufficient resources to implement these strategies, and e-tailing objectives that fit business plans [P6.2]

(*continued*)

Table 15.2 Continued

Interactivity Dimensions	*Business Value Impact*	*Contingencies*
Communication process	• Interactivity lowers transaction costs [P5] • Interactivity drives up frequency of interaction, reduces transaction uncertainty, and leads to reduction in asset specificity [P5.1] • Interactivity widens the range of strategic e-commerce management options for competitive advantage [P6] • Interactivity helps achieving differentiation [P6.1]	
Consumer perception	Involvement enhances sensory, cognitive, and affective affiliation with product and website content [P4.1]	

Triangulation from multiple sources has evidenced that interactivity can have significant business value on various levels of interactivity because, essentially, companies that support interactivity can dynamically adapt to customer preferences and buying behavior. By reducing transaction costs in interactive media settings, business firms may gain competitive advantage, widen their product range through adding more interactive features, offer richer and new content channels to customers, or integrate once passive consumers into the production processes of their ventures in various ways. This, in turn, may leverage consumer trust and loyalty in the online brand of the producer's offering (Gefen, 2000; McWilliam, 2000). Online retailers may incorporate features to take advantage of the Internet's two-way communication abilities such as customer service, e-mail inquiries to sales representatives, discussion forums for customers, and voice and video applications. And customers are set to experience higher degrees of (cognitive and affective) involvement with the products and services portfolio offered (Franz & Robey, 1986; Hartwick & Barki, 1994; McMillan, 2002; Tseng & Piller, 2003). Content quality, control, convenience, and costs may well be the determinants for an effective integration. These determinants are driven by further constituents of a successful relationship: the object of integration, the communicative relationship between the business firm and the customer, the depth and familiarity of this relationship, the customer's goal and motivation to interact, and the governance of this exchange (Song & Zinkhan, 2008). But while Internet-enabled business exchange is said to lead to transaction costs efficiencies (Bakos, 1991; Benjamin & Wigand, 1995; Brynolffson & Smith, 2000; Cordella & Simon, 1997; Piller et al., 2004; Reichwald & Piller, 2009), I argue that although interactivity may potentially reduce these transaction costs, this would remain contingent upon different forms and practicalities of interactivity.

On the consumer side, the effectiveness of these forms and practicalities of interactivity will depend on perceived consumer values that are themselves driven by a bundle of antecedent forces. It seems obvious that the mere availability of interactive features and technologies do neither inherently constitute interactivity by nature nor deliver customer surplus per se. It is thus claimed that interactive features may be present on a website but "without necessarily eliciting the *perception* of interactivity. Rather, its features and interactive functionality hold the *potential* to yield the perception of interactivity for individual users under certain circumstances" (Gleason, 2008, p. 14).

To deliver real business value, interactive e-commerce managers may need to set up the following agenda according to type and dimension of interactivity offered.

Human-to-Computer interactivity management would:

- provide a site design to accommodate different browsers and settings particularly required for high-bandwidth formats to offer users innovative product promotions such as full motion video and webTV formats;
- provide consumers with tools to move between different information with the site;
- provide consumers with tools for asking questions;
- facilitate site visits for consumers whose first language is not English; and
- manage accessibility of high-bandwidth formats to provide users with innovations such as full motion video and webTV.

Human-to-Human interactivity management would imply:

- the need to communicate with customers by means of contextual marketing or sense and respond marketing, where every customer interaction or response to a communication is followed up with a series of relevant communications delivered by the right combinations of channel (web, email, phone, direct mail) to elicit a response or further dialogue (Chaffey, 2010);
- an orientation towards customers by integrating them into various value creation processes; and
- the encouragement of interaction and creation of user-generated content (Wirtz et al., 2010).

Human-to-Content interactivity management would mean to:

- create compelling and persuasive experiences to engage consumers through relevant messages and content, encouraging them to stay on the site and return;

- deliver an online presence developed to support branding and customer service quality objectives;
- provide tailored products to meet particular customer needs to make customer's comparative shopping difficult and would shift the customer's focus away from price to quality and other intrinsic values;
- personalize and customize products and services to differentiate against others (Rangaswamy & Pal, 2003);
- forge a close relationship with customers and therefore encourage them to return time and time again for additional (i.e., establish better utilization of the company's customer base); and
- let consumers self-configure their products to allow access to "sticky local information," which is aimed at the user who does not reveal a price preference (von Hippel, 1998).

Finally, more research is needed that improves the validity of analysis by generating better testable propositions (i.e., hypotheses). This would imply the establishment of a conceptual model which postulates effects between the technological, communicative, and perceptual determinants of interactivity alongside the three different types of interactivity and the perceived impacts on value on both sides of the equation, i.e., the consumer as well as the business.

Essentially, a more nuanced investigation needs to be made into the transaction cost effectiveness of interactive media and communication technologies in e-commerce settings as these costs can become critical for the overall success of the business.

Notes

1. Alternatively, academia has systematized the concept alongside actual (i.e., objectively assessed) versus perceived interactivity (Williams et al., 1988; Wu, 2005), human-to-human and human-to-media interaction (Stromer-Galley, 2004), feature-based versus perception-based interactivity (McMillan, 2002), or structural versus experiential interactivity (Liu & Shrum, 2002). Other scholars have defined interactivity as prototype (e.g., conversational media whose communication form is essentially two-way), criterion (i.e., as a certain trait or feature that must be fulfilled), and continuum (i.e., from declarative one-way to reactive two-way communication (Goertz, 1995; Jensen, 1998; Rafaeli, 1988; Rogers, 1986). Deuze (2003) translated interactivity dimensions of news websites into navigational interactivity, adaptive interactivity, and functional interactivity.

References

Alba, J. W., Lynch, J., Weitz, B., Janiszewski, C., Lutz, R., & Sawyer, A. (1997). Interactive home shopping: Consumer, retailer, and manufacturer incentives to participate in electronic marketplaces. *Journal of Marketing*, *61*, 48–53.

Amit, R., & Zott, C. (2001). Value creation in e-business. *Strategic Management Journal*, *22*(6–7), 493–520.

Argyle, M. (1969). *Social interaction*. New York: Atherton Press.

Ariely. D. (1998). Combining experiences over time: The effects of duration, intensity changes, and on-line measurements on retrospective pain evaluations. *Journal of Behavioral Decision Making, 11*, 19–45.

Ariely, D. (2000). Controlling the information flow: Effects on consumers' decision making and preferences. *Journal of Consumer Research, 27*, 233–248.

Armstrong, A., & Hagel, J. III (1996). The real value of online communities. *Harvard Business Review, 74*, 1345–1441.

Baecker, R. M. (1980). Towards an effective characterization of geographical interaction. In R. A. Guedj, P. W. T. ten Hagen, F. R. Hopgood, H. Tucker, & D. A. Duce (Eds.), *Methodology of interaction* (pp. 127–147). Amsterdam, The Netherlands: North-Holland.

Baecker, R. M., & Buxton, W. A. S. (1987) *Readings in human-computer interaction: a multidisciplinary approach*. San Mateo, CA: Kaufmann.

Bakos, J. Y. (1991). A strategic analysis of electronic marketplaces. *MIS Quarterly, 15*, 295–310.

Bakos, J. Y. (1997). Reducing buyer search costs: Implications for electronic marketplaces. *Management Science, 43*, 1676–1692.

Ballantine, P. W. (2005). Effects of interactivity and product information on consumer satisfaction in an online retail setting. *International Journal of Retail & Distribution Management, 33*, 461–471.

Barnard, C. (1948). *Organization and management*. Cambridge, MA: Harvard University Press.

Benjamin, R., & Wigand, R. (1995). Electronic markets and virtual value chains on the information highway. *Sloan Management Review*, 62–72.

Berger, C., Moeslein, K., Piller, F. T., & Reichwald, R. (2005). Co-designing modes of cooperation at the customer interface: learning from exploratory research. *European Management Review, 2*, 70–87.

Bezjian-Avery, A., Calder, B., & Iacobucci, D. (1998). New media interactive advertising vs. traditional advertising. *Journal of Advertising Research, 38*(4), 23–32.

Blattberg, R. C., & Deighton, J. (1991). Interactive marketing: Exploiting the age of addressability. *Sloan Management Review, 32*(1), 5–14.

Blumer, H. (1969). *Symbolic interactionism: Perspective and method*. Englewood Cliffs, NJ: Prentice-Hall.

Bordewijk, J. L., & van Kaam, B. (1986). Towards a new classification of teleInformation Services. *Inter Media, 14*(1), 16–21.

Bretz, R., & Schmidbauer, M. (1983). *Media for interactive communication*. Beverly Hills, CA: Sage.

Brynjolffson, E., & Smith, M. D. (2000). Frictionless commerce?, A comparison of Internet and conventional retailers. *Management Science*, *46*, 563–585.

Bucher, H.-J. (2002). The power of the audience: Interculturality, interactitvity and trust in internet communication. In F. Sudweeks & C. Ess (Eds.), *Cultural attitudes towards computer and communication* (pp. 3–14). Perth, Western Australia: Murdoch.

Bucher, H.-J. (2004). Online-Interaktivität — Ein hybrider Begriff für eine hybride Kommunikationsform [Online interactivity — a hybrid term for a hybrid form of communication]. In K. Bieber & C. Leggewie (Eds.), *Interaktivität. Ein transdisciplinärer Schlüsselbegriff* [Interactivity. A transdisciplinary key term] (pp. 132–168). Frankfurt, Germany: Campus Verlag.

Bucy, E. P. (2004a). Interactivity in society: Locating an elusive concept. *Information Society*, *20*, 375–387.

Bucy, E. P. (2004b). The interactivity paradox: Closer to the news but confused. In Bucy, E. P., & Newhagen, J. E. (Eds.), *Media access: Social and psychological dimensions of new technology use*. (pp. 47–72). Mahwah, NJ: Erlbaum.

Bucy, E. P., & Tao, C. C. (2007). The mediated moderation model of interactivity. *Media Psychology*, *9*, 647–672.

Burgoon, J. K., Bonito, J. A., Bengtsson, B., Cederberg, C., Lundeberg, M., & Allspach, L. (2000). Interactivity in human-computer interaction: A study of credibility, understanding, and influence. *Computers in Human Behaviour*, *16*, 553–574.

Burke, K., & Chidambaram, L. (1999). How much bandwidth is enough? A longitudinal examination of media characteristics and group outcomes. *MIS Quarterly*, *23*, 557–580.

Carey, J. (1989). Interactive media. In E. Barnouw (Ed.), *International encyclopaedia of communications* (pp. 328–330). New York: Oxford University Press.

Chaffey, D. (2010). *Right touching — Using contextual marketing to deliver relevant messages online*. Retrieved March 1, 2010, from http://www.davechaffey.com/Internet-Marketing/C6-Customer-Relationship-Management/right-touching-using-contextual-marketing

Chen, K., & Yen, D. C. (2004). Improving the quality of online presence through interactivity. *Information & Management*, *42*(1), 217–226.

Chen, Z., & Dubinsky, A. J. (2002). A conceptual model of perceived customer value in e-commerce: A preliminary investigation. *Psychology and Marketing*, *20*, 323–347.

Chesbrough, H., Vanhaverbeke, W., & West, J. (2006). *Open innovation: Researching a new paradigm*. Oxford, UK: Oxford University Press.

Cho, C., & Leckenby, J. D. (1999). Interactivity as a measure of advertising effectiveness: Antecedents and consequences of interactivity in web advertising. In *Proceedings of the 1999 Conference of the American Academy of Advertising* (pp. 162–179). Pullman, WA: American Academy of Advertising.

Choi, S.-Y., Stahl, D. O., & Winston, A. B. (1997). *The economics of electronic commerce*. London: Macmillan Technical Publishing.

Coase, R. H. (1979). The nature of the firm. *Economica*, *4*, 386–405. Reprinted in Kronman, A. T., & Posner, R. A. (Eds.), *The economics of contract law* (pp. 31–32). Boston: Little Brown. (Original work publishd 1937)

Cordella, A., & Simon, K. A. (1997, August). *The impact of information technology on transaction and coordination cost*. Paper presented at the Conference on Information Systems Research in Scandinavia (IRIS 20), Oslo, Norway.

Coviello, N., Milley, R., & Marcolin, B. (2001). Understanding IT-enabled interactivity in contemporary marketing. *Journal of Interactive Marketing*, *15*(4), 18–33.

Coyle, J. R., & Thorson, E. (2001). The effects of progressive levels of interactivity and vividness in web marketing sites. *Journal of Advertising*, *30*, 65–77.

Day, G. (1998).Organizing for interactivity. *Journal of Interactive Marketing*, *12*(1), 47–53.

December, J. (1996). What is computer-mediated communication? Retrieved March 25, 2005, from http://www.december.com/john/study/cmc/what.html

Dennis, A. R., Fuller, R. M., & Valacich, J. S. (2008). Media, tasks, and communication processes: A theory of media synchronicity. *MIS Quarterly*, *32*, 575–600.

Dennis, A. R., & Valacich, J. S. (1999). Rethinking media richness: Towards a theory of media synchronicity. *Proceedings of the Thirty-Second Annual Hawaii International Conference on System Science* (pp. 34–40). Washington, DC: IEEE.

Deuze, M. (2003). The web and its journalisms: Considering the consequences of different types of newsmedia online. *New Media Society, 5*, 203–230.

Dholakia, R. R., Zhao, M., Dholakia, N., & Fortin, D. R. (2000). Interactivity and revisits to web sites: A theoretical framework. RITIM working paper. Retrieved February 12, 2004, from http://ritim.cba.uri.edu/wp2001/wpdone3/wpdone3.htm

Downes, E. J., & McMillan, S. J. (2000). Defining interactivity: A qualitative identification of key dimension. *New Media & Society, 2,* 157–179.

Duncan, S. (1989). Interaction, face to face. In E. Barnouw (Ed.), *International encyclopedia of communications* (pp. 325–330). New York: Oxford University Press.

Durlak, J. T. (1987). A typology for interactive media. In M. L. McLaughlin (Ed.), *Communication yearbook 10* (pp. 743–757). Mahwah, NJ: Erlbaum.

Economides, N. (1996). The economics of networks. *International Journal of Industrial Organization, 14*, 673–699.

Essler, U., & Whitaker, R. (2001). Re-thinking e-commerce business modelling in terms of interactivity. *Electronic Markets, 11*(1), 10–16.

Fiore, A. M., & Jin, H.-J. (2003). Influence of image interactivity on approach responses towards an online retailer. *Internet Research, 13*(1), 38–48. Retrieved from http://www.emeraldinsight.com/journals.htm?articleid=863764&show=abstract

Fortin, D. R., & Dholakia, R. R. (2005). Interactivity and vividness effects on social presence and involvement with a web-based advertisement. *Journal of Business Research, 58*, 387–396.

Franz, C. R., & Robey, D. (1986). Organizational context, user involvement, and the usefulness of information systems. *Decision Sciences, 17*, 329–356.

Fulk, J., Schmitz, J., & Steinfield, C. W. (1990). A social influence model of technology use. In J. Fulk & C. Steinfield (Eds.), *Organizations and communication technology* (pp. 117–140). Newbury Park, CA: Sage.

Gao, Q., Rau, P.-L. P., & Salvendy, G. (2009). Perception of interactivity: Affects of four key variables in mobile advertising. *International Journal of Human Computer Interaction, 25*, 479–505.

Gefen, D. (2000). E-commerce: The role of familiarity and trust. *Omega: The International Journal of Management Science, 28*, 725–737.

Ghose, S., & Dou, W. (1998). Interactive functions and their impacts on the appeal of internet presence sites. *Journal of Advertising Research, 38*(2), 29–43.

Gleason, J. P. (2008, March). The responsive multi-dimensional model of interactivity. *Proceedings of the 2008 University of Kentucky GSA Symposium*. Retrieved March 30, 2008, from http://people.eku.edu/gleasonj/2008%20GSA%20paper%20_RMD%20model_.pdf

Gleason, J. P., & Lane, D. (2009, November). *Interactivity redefined: A first look at outcome interactivity theory.* Paper presented at the annual meeting of the NCA 95th Annual Convention, Chicago, IL. Retrieved February 24, 2010, from http://people.eku.edu/gleasonj/Outcome_Interactivity_Theory.pdf

Goertz, L. (1995). Wie interaktiv sind Medien? Auf dem Weg zu einer Definition von Interaktivität [How are interactive media? Towards a definition of interactivity]. *Rundfunk und Fernsehen, 43*, 477–493.

Goffman, E. (1967). *Interaction ritual*. Chicago: Aldine.

Gouldner, A. W. (1960). The norm of reciprocity: A preliminary statement. *American Sociological Review, 25*, 161–178.

Grunig, J. E., & Grunig, L. A. (1989). Toward a theory of public relations behavior of organizations: Review of a program of research. In J. E. Grunig & L. A. Grunig (Eds.), *Public relations research annual* (pp. 27–63). Hillsdale, NJ: Erlbaum.

Guedj, R. A., tenHagen, P. J. W., Hopgood, F. R., Tucker, H. A., & Duce, D. A. (1980). *Methodology of interaction*. Amsterdam, The Netherlands: North Holland.

Ha, L., & James, E. L. (1998). Interactivity reexamined: A baseline analysis of early business web sites. *Journal of Broadcasting & Electronic Media*, *42*, 457–474.

Haeckel, S. H. (1998). About the nature and future of interactive marketing. *Journal of Interactive Marketing*, *12*, 63–71.

Hanssen, L., Jankowski, N. W., & Etienne, R. (1996). Interactivity from the Perspective of Communication Studies. In N. W. Jankowski & L. Hanssen (Eds.), *Contours of multimedia: Recent technological, theoretical, and empirical developments* (pp. 61–73). London: University of Luton Press.

Hartson, H. R. (1998). Human-computer interaction: Interdisciplinary roots and trends. *Journal of Systems and Software*, *43*(2), 103–118.

Hartwick, J., & Barki, H. (1994). Explaining the role of user participation in information system use. *Management Science*, *40*(4), 440–465.

Heeter, C. (1989). Implications of interactivity for communication research. In J. L. Salvaggio & B. Jennings (Eds.), *Media use in the information age: Emerging patterns of adoption and consumer use* (pp. 53–75). Mahwah, NJ: Erlbaum.

Heeter, C. (2000). Interactivity in the context of designed experiences. *Journal of Interactive Advertising*, *1*, 4–15.

Helander, M. G., Landauer, T. K., & Prabhu, P. (Eds.). (1997). *Handbook of human-computer interaction* (2nd ed.). Amsterdam, The Netherlands: North Holland.

Hewett, T., Baecker, R., Card, S., Carey, T., Gasen, J., Mantei, M., Perlman, G., Strong G., & Verplank, W. (1992). *ACM SIGCHI curricula for human-computer interaction*. Report of the ACM SIGCHI Curriculum Development Group. New York: ACM.

Hsiu-Fe, L. (2007). The impact of website quality dimensions on customer satisfaction in the B2C e-commerce context. *Total Quality Management & Business Excellence, 18*, 363–378.

Huhtamo, E. (1998). From cybernation to interaction: a contribution to an archaeology of interactivity. In P. Lunenfeld (Ed.), *The digital dialectic: New essays on new media* (pp. 96–110). Cambridge, MA: MIT Press.

Iacobucci, D. (1998). Interactive marketing and the meganet: Networks of networks. *Journal of Interactive Marketing*, *12*(1), 5–16.

Jaeckel, M. (1995). Interaktion. Soziologische Anmerkungen zu einem Begriff [Interaction. Sociological comments on a concept]. *Rundfunk und Fernsehen*, *43*(4), 463–476.

Jee, J., & Lee, W.-N. (2002). Antecedents and consequences of perceived interactivity: An exploratory study. *Journal of Interactive Advertising*, *3*, 1–18.

Jensen, J. F. (1998). Interactivity — tracking a new concept in media and communication studies. *Nordicom Review*, *19*(1), 185–204.

Jensen, J. F. (2005). Interactive television: New genres, new format, new content. In *Proceedings of the Second Australasian Conference on Interactive Entertainment, ACM international conference proceeding series* (Vol. 123, 89–96). Sydney, Australia: Creativity & Cognition Studios Press.

Jiang, Z., Chan, J., & Tan, B. (2010). Effects of interactivity on website involvement and purchase intention. *Journal of the Association of Information Systems, 11*(1). Retrieved January 10, 2010, from http://aisel.aisnet.org/jais/vol11/iss1/1

Johnson, G. J., Bruner, G. C. II, & Kumar, A. (2006). Interactivity and its facets revisited: Theory and empirical test. *Journal of Advertising, 35*(4), 35–52.

Kalyanaraman, S., & Sundar, S. S. (2006). The psychological appeal of personalized content in web portals: Does customization affect attitudes and behavior? *Journal of Communication, 56*, 110–122.

Kenney, K., Gorelik, A., & Mwangi, S. (2000, January). Interactive features of newspapers. *First Monday, 5*(1), 3. Retrieved October 3, 2006, from http://www.firstmonday.org/issues/issue5_1/kenney/index.html

Kim, J., & LaRose, R. (2004). Interactive e-commerce: Promoting consumer efficiency or impulsivity? *Journal of Computer-Mediated Communication, 10*(1). Retrieved July 9, 2006, from http://jcmc.indiana.edu/vol10/issue1/kim_larose.html

Kiousis, S. (2002). Interactivity: A concept explication. *New Media & Society, 4*, 355–383.

Kirsh, D. (1997). Interactivity and multimedia interfaces. *Instructional Science, 25*, 79–96.

Klein, L. R. (2003). Creating virtual product experiences: The role of telepresence. *Journal of Interactive Marketing, 17*(1), 41–55.

Kleinaltenkamp, M., Fließ, S., & Jacob, F. (1996). *Customer Integration — Von der Kundenorientierung zur Kundenintegration* [Customer integration — from customer orientation to customer integration]. Wiesbaden, Germany: Gabler.

Klemperer, P. D. (2008). Network effects. In S. N. Durlauf & L. E. Blume (Eds.), *The new Palgrave: A dictionary of economics* (pp. 915–917). Basingstoke, UK: Palgrave-Macmillan.

Ko, H., Cho, C.-H., & Roberts, M. S. (2005). Internet uses and gratifications: A structural equation model of interactive advertising. *Journal of Advertising, 34*(2), 57–70.

Kotha, S. (1995). Mass customization: Implementing the emerging paradigm for competitive advantage. *Strategic Management Journal, 16*, 21–42.

Kuk, G., & Yeung, F. T. (2002). Interactivity in e-commerce. *Quarterly Journal of Electronic Commerce, 3*(3), 223–235.

Lampel, J., & Mintzberg, H. (1996). Customizing customization. *Sloan Management Review, 38*(1), 21–30.

Laurel, B. (1991). *Computers as theatre*. Reading, MA: Addison-Wesley.

Lee, C.-H., Barua, A., & Whinston, A. B. (2000). The complementarity of mass customization and electronic commerce. *Economics of Innovation and New Technology*, *9*(2), 81–110.

Lee, K. M. (2004). Presence, explicated. *Communication Theory, 14*, 27–50.

Lee, T. (2005). The impact of perceptions of interactivity on customer trust and transaction intentions in mobile commerce. *Journal of Electronic Commerce Research, 6*(3), 165–180.

Lin, C. A. (2003). An interactive communication technology adoption model. *Communication Theory, 13*, 345–365.

Liu, Y. (2003). Generating value through online interaction. Individual and situational differences. Competitive Paper Submitted to the 2003 AMS Annual Conference. Retrieved July 9, 2006, from http://jcmc.indiana.edu/ vol3/issue2/ lombard.html

Liu, Y., & Shrum, L. J. (2002). What is interactivity and is it always such a good thing? Implications of definition, person, and situation for the influence of interactivity on advertising effectiveness. *Journal of Advertising*, *31*(4), 53–64.

Lombard, M., & Ditton, T. (1997). At the heart of it all: The concept of presence. *Journal of Computer-Mediated Communication, 3*(2). Retrieved July 9, 2006, from http://jcmc.indiana.edu/ vol3/issue2/ lombard.html

Lombard, M., & Snyder-Duch, J. (2001). Interactive advertising and presence: A framework. *Journal of Interactive Advertising, 1*(2), Retrieved July 1, 2009, from http://www.jiad.org/vol1/no2/lombard/index.html

Lowe, D., & Hall, W. (1999). *Hypermedia and the web. An engineering approach.* Chichester, UK: Wiley.

Lowry, P. B., Romano Jr., N. C., Jenkins, J. L., & Guthrie, R. W. (2009). The CMC interactivity model: How interactivity enhances communication quality and process satisfaction in lean-media groups. *Journal of Management Information Systems, 26*(1), 155–195.

Mackenzie, D., & Wajcman, J. (1985). *The social shaping of technology: How the refrigerator got its hum.* Milton Keynes, UK: Open University Press.

Manovich, L. (2001). *The language of new media.* Cambridge, MA: MIT Press.

Matheson, K., & Zanna, M. P. (1998). The impact of computer-mediated communication on self-awareness, *Computers in Human Behavior, 4*(3), 221–233.

McKay, J., & Marshall, P. (2004). *Strategic management of e-business.* Brisbane, Australia: Wiley.

McMillan, S. J. (1998). Who pays for content? Funding in interactive media. *Journal of Computer Mediated Communication, 4*(1). Retrieved July 24, 2009, from http://www.ascusc.org/jcmc/vol4/issue1/mcmillan.html

McMillan, S. J. (2000). Interactivity is in the eye of the beholder: Function, perception, involvement, and attitude toward the website. In M. A. Shaver (Ed.), *Proceedings of the 2000 Conference of the American Academy of Advertising* (pp. 71–78). East Lansing: Michigan State University Press. Retrieved July 21, 2004, from http://web.utk.edu/~sjmcmill/Research/mcmillsj.doc

McMillan, S. J. (2002). A four-part model of cyber-interactivity: Some cyber-spaces are more interactive than others. *New Media and Society, 4*, 271–291.

McMillan, S. J. (2005). The researchers and the concept: Moving beyond a blind examination of interactivity. *Journal of Interactive Advertising, 5*(2), 1–4.

McMillan, S. J. (2006). Exploring models of interactivity from multiple research traditions: Users, documents, and systems. In L. L. Lievrouw & S. Livingstone (Eds.), *Handbook of new media* (pp. 205–230). London: Sage.

McMillan, S. J., & Hwang, J.-S. (2002). Measures of perceived interactivity: An exploration of the role of direction of communication, user control, and time in shaping perceptions of interactivity. *Journal of Advertising, 31*(3), 41–54.

McMillan, S. J., Jang-Sun, H., & Guiohk, L. (2003). Effects of structural and perceptual factors on attitudes toward the website. *Journal of Advertising Research, 43*, 400–409.

McWilliam, G. (2000). Building stronger brands through online communities. *Sloan Management Review, 41*(3), 43–54.

Melville, N., Kraemer, K. L., & Gurbaxani, V. (2004). Information technology and organizational performance: An integrative model of IT business value. *MIS Quarterly, 28*, 283–322.

Merrilees, B., & Miller, D. (2001) Superstore interactivity: A new self-service paradigm of retail service? *International Journal of Retail & Distribution Management, 29*, 379–389.

Milgrom, P., & Roberts, J. (1990). The economics of modern manufacturing: Technology, strategy and organization. *American Economic Review, 80*, 511–528.

Milheim, W. D. (1996). Interactivity and computer-based Instruction. *Journal of Educational Technology Systems*, *24*, 225–233.

Morris, M., & Ogan, C. (1996). The Internet as mass medium. *Journal of Communication*, *46*, 39–50.

Morrison, M. (1998). A look at interactivity from a customer perspective. In J. B. Ford & E. J. D. Honeycutt (Eds.), *Developments in marketing science 21* (pp. 149–154). Norfolk, VA: Academy of Marketing Science.

Myers, B. A. (1998). A brief history of human computer interaction technology. *ACM interactions*, *5*(2), 44–54.

Neumann, W. R. (2008). Interactivity, concept of. In W. Donsbach (Ed.), *The international encyclopedia of communication*. Retrieved October 10, 2010, from http://www.blackwellreference.com/public/tocnode?id=g9781405131995_yr2010_chunk_g978140513199514_ss44-1

Nickerson, R. S. (1977). On conversational interaction with computers. In *User-oriented design of interactive graphic systems* (pp. 101–113). New York: ACM.

Noll, A. M. (2003). Television over the Internet: Technological challenges. In E. Noam (Ed.), *Internet television* (pp. 19–30). Mahwah, NJ: Erlbaum.

Norman, D. (1988). *The psychology of everyday things*. New York: Basic Books.

Noori, H. (1990). Economies of integration: A new manufacturing focus. *International Journal of Technology Management*, *5*, 577–587.

Normann, R., & Ramirez, R. (1993). From value chain to value constellation: Designing interactive strategy. *Harvard Business Review*, *71*, 65–77.

Novak, T. P., & Hoffman, D. L. (1997). New metrics for new media: Toward the development of web measurement standards. *World Wide Web Journal*, *2*(1), 213–246.

Novak, T. P., Hoffman, D. L., & Yung, Y.-F. (2000). Measuring the customer experience in online environments: A structural modeling approach. *Marketing* Science, *19*(1), 22–42.

Nielsen, J. (2000). *Designing web usability: The practice of simplicity*. Indianapolis, IN: New Riders Publishing.

Picot, A., Reichwald, R., & Wigand, R. (1998). *Information, organization, and management: expanding markets and corporate boundaries*. New York: Wiley.

Piller, F. T. (2002). Customer interaction and digitizability — a structural approach. In C. Rautenstrauch, R. Seelmann-Eggebert, & K. Turowski (Eds.), *Moving towards mass customization: Information systems and management principles* (pp. 119–138). Berlin: Springer.

Piller, F., & Möslein, K. (2002, August). *From economies of scale towards economies of customer integration. Value creation in mass customization based electronic commerce*. Unpublished working reports of the Chair of Industrial and Business Economics at the Technical University of Munich.

Piller, F. T., Moeslein, K., & Stotko, C. (2004). Does mass customization pay? An economic approach to evaluate customer integration. *Production Planning & Control, 15*, 435–444.

Porter, M. E. (1985). *Competitive advantage: Creating and sustaining superior performance*. New York: The Free Press.

Porter, M. E. (2001). Strategy and the Iinternet. *Harvard Business Review, 79*(3), 62–78.

Prahalad, C. K., & Ramaswamy, V. (2000). Co-opting customer competence. *Harvard Business Review, 79*(1), 79–87.

Prahalad, C. K., & Ramaswamy, V. (2002). The co-creation connection. *Strategy and Business, 27,* 50–61.

Prahalad, C. K., & Ramaswamy, V. (2003). The new frontier of experience innovation. MIT *Sloan Management Review, 44*(4), 12–18.

Prahalad, C. K., & Ramaswamy, V. (2004). *The future of competition: Cocreating unique value with customers.* Boston: Harvard Business School Press.

Quiring, O. (2009). What do users associate with 'interactivity'? A qualitative study on user schemata. *New Media & Society, 11,* 899–920.

Quiring, O., & Schweiger, W. (2008). Interactivity: A review of the concept and a framework for analysis. *Communications, 33*(2), 147–167.

Rafaeli, S. (1988). Interactivity: From media to communication. In R. P. Hawkins, J. M. Wieman, & S. Pingree (Eds.), *Advancing communication science: Merging mass and interpersonal communication* (pp. 110–134). Newbury Park, CA: Sage.

Rafaeli, S., & Sudweeks, F. (1997). Networked interactivity. *Journal of Computer-Mediated Communication, 2*(4). Retrieved March 3, 2007, from http://jcmc.huji.ac.il/vol2/issue4/rafaeli.sudweeks.html

Rafaeli, S., & Ariel, Y. (2007). Assessing interactivity in computer-mediated research. In A. N. Joinson, K. Y. A. McKenna, T. Postmes, & U-D Reips (Eds.), *The Oxford handbook of internet psychology* (pp. 71–88). Oxford, UK: Oxford University Press.

Rangaswamy, A., & Pal, N. (2003). Gaining business value from personalization technologies. In N. Pal & A. Rangaswamy (Eds.), *The power of one: Gaining business value from personalization technologies* (pp. 1–9). Victoria, Australia: Trafford.

Reichwald, R., & Piller, F. T. (2000). Mass customization-Konzepte im electronic business [Mass customization concepts in electronic business]. In R. Weiber (Ed.), *Handbuch electronic business. Informationstechnologien — electronic commerce — Geschäftsprozesse* [Handbook Electronic Business. Information technologies — electronic commerce — business processes] (pp. 359–383). Wiesbaden, Germany: Gabler.

Reichwald, R., & Piller, F. T. (2009). *Interaktive Wertschoepfung: Open Innovation, Individualisierung und neue Formen der Arbeitsteilung* (Vol. 2) [Interactive value creation: Open innovation, individualization and new forms of division of labor]. Auflage. Wiesbaden, Germany: Gabler.

Reichwald, R., Seifert, S., & Walcher, D. (2004, January). *Customers as part of value webs. Towards a framework for webbed customer innovation tools* Paper presented at the Hawaii International Conference on Computer Sciences (HICSS), Maui.

Rice, R. E., & Williams, F. (1984). Theories old and new: The study of new media. In R. E. Rice (Ed.), *The new media* (pp. 55–80). Beverly Hills, CA: Sage.

Robey, D. (1979). User attitudes and management information system use. *Academy of Management Journal, 22,* 527–538.

Rogers, E. M. (1986). *Communication technology. The new media in society.* New York: Free Press.

Romano, N. C., & Fjermestad, J. (2003). Electronic commerce customer relationship management: A research agenda. *Information Technology and Management, 4,* 233–258.

Romiszowski, A., & Mason, R. (2004). Computer-mediated communication. In D. H.

Jonassen (Ed.), *Handbook of research on educational communications and technology* (pp. 397–431). Mahwah, NJ: Erlbaum.

Schumann, D. W., Artis, A., & Rivera, R. (2001). The future of ineractive advertising viewed through an IMC lens. *Journal of Interactive Advertising, 1*(2), Retrieved March 3, 2007, from http://jiad.org/article12

Sears, A., & Jacko, J. A. (2009). *Human-computer interaction fundamentals.* New York: CRC Press.

Shaw, T., Aranson, K., & Belardo, S. (1993). The effects of computer mediated interactivity on idea generation: An experimental investigation. *IEEE Transactions on Systems, Man & Cybernetics, 23*, 737–745.

Short, J. A. (1974). Effect of medium of communication on experimental negotiation. *Human Relations, 27*, 225–234.

Short, J., Williams, E., & Christie, B. (1976). *The social psychology of telecommunications.* New York: Wiley.

Sohn, D., & Lee, B. (2005). Dimensions of interactivity: Differential effects of social and psychological factors. *Journal of Computer-Mediated Communication, 10*(3). Retrieved November 10, 2005, from http://jcmc.indiana.edu/vol10/issue3/sohn.html

Song, I., & Bucy, E. P. (2008). Interactivity and Political Attitude Formation. A Mediation Model of Online Information Processing. *Journal of Information Technology & Politics, 4*(2), 29–61.

Song, J. H., & Zinkhan, G. M. (2008). Determinants of perceived web site interactivity. *Journal of Marketing, 72*, 99–113.

Soukup, C. (2000). Building a theory of multi-media CMC. *New Media & Society, 2*, 407–425.

Steuer, J. (1992). Defining virtual reality: Dimensions determining telepresence. *Journal of Communication, 42*(4), 73–93.

Stewart, D. W., & Pavlou, P. A. (2002). From consumer response to active consumer: Measuring the effectiveness of interactive media. *Academy of Marketing Science, 30*, 376–396.

Stromer-Galley, J. (2004). Interactivity-as-product and interactivity-as-process. *The Information* Society, *20*, 391–394.

Sukpanich, N., & Chen, L.-D. (2000). Interactivity as the driving force behind e-commerce. *AMCIS 2000 Proceedings* (Paper 163). Retrieved June 11, 2007, from http://ais.bepress.com/amcis2000/163

Sundar, S. S. (2004). Theorizing interactivity's effects. *The Information Society, 20*, 355–383.

Sundar, S. S. (2007). Social psychology of interactivity in human-website interaction. In A. N. Joinson, K. McKenna, & T. Postmes. (Eds.), *The Oxford handbook of internet psychology* (pp. 89–102). Oxford, UK: Oxford University Press.

Sundar, S. S., Xu, Q., & Bellur, S. (2010). Designing interactivity in media interfaces: a communications perspective. *Proceedings of ACM CHI 2010 Conference on Human Factors in Computing Systems, 1*, 2247–2256.

Svanæs, D. (2000). *Understanding interactivity: Steps to a phenomenology of human-computer interaction.* Trondheim: Norwegian University of Science and Technology (NTNU). Retrieved June 25, 2008, from http://dag.idi.ntnu.no/interactivity.pdf

Svensson, G. (2003). A generic conceptual framework of interactive service quality. *Managing Service Quality, 13*(4), 267–275.

Szymanski, D. M., & Hise, R. T. (2000). E-satisfaction: An initial examination. *Journal of Retailing, 76*, 309–322.

Taylor, F. W. (1911). *The principles of scientific management.* New York: Harper & Row.

Thomas, P. J. (1992). Introduction: The social and interactional dimensions of human-computer interfaces. In P. J. Thomas (Ed.), *The social and interactional dimensions of human-computer interfaces* (pp. 1–10). Cambridge, UK: Cambridge University Press.

Tredinnick, L. (2006). Web 2.0 and business. *Business Information Review, 23*(4), 228–234.

Tseng, M., & Jiao, J. (2001). Mass customisation. In G. Salvendy (Ed.), *Handbook of industrial engineering* (pp. 684–709). New York: Wiley.

Tseng, M. M., & Piller, F. T. (2003). *The customer centric enterprise. Advances in mass customization and personalisation*. Berlin: Springer.

Turban, E., King, D., Lee, J., Warkentin, M., & Chung, H. M. (2002). *Electronic commerce: A managerial perspective.* Upper Saddle River, NJ: Pearson Education.

Varadarajan, P. R., & Yadav, M. S. (2002). Marketing strategy and the internet: An organizing framework. *Journal of Academy of Marketing Science, 30*(4), 296–313.

von Hippel, E. (1994). Sticky information and the locus of problem solving. *Management Science, 40*, 429–439.

von Hippel, E. (1998). Economics of product development by users. *Management Science, 44*, 629–644.

von Hippel, E. (2002). Open source projects as horizontal innovation networks — by and for users. *MIT Sloan Working Paper No.* 4366-02. Retrieved March 30, 2006, from http://web.mit.edu/evhippel/www/papers/UserInnovNetworksMgtSci.pdf

von Hippel, E. (2005). *Democratizing innovation*. Cambridge, MA: MIT Press.

Vandermerve, S. (2000). How increasing value to customers improves business results. *Sloan Management Review, 42*, 27–37.

Vulkan, N. (2003). *The economics of e*-commerce. Princeton, NJ: Princeton University Press.

Walther, J. B. (1992). Interpersonal effects in computer-mediated interaction: A relational perspective. *Communication Research, 19*, 52–89.

Webster, F. E., Jr. (1996). Perspectives — the future of interactive marketing. *Harvard Business Review* (November-December), 156–157.

Webster, F. E., Jr. (1998). Commentary: Interactivity and marketing paradigm shifts. *Journal of Interactive Marketing, 12*(1), 54–55.

Wigand, R. T. (1997). Electronic commerce: Definition, theory, and context. *The Information Society, 13*, 1–16.

Wikstroem, S. (1996a). Value creation by company-consumer interaction. *Journal of Marketing Management, 12*, 359–374.

Wikstroem, S. (1996b). The customer as co-producer. *European Journal of Marketing, 30*(4), 6–19.

Williams, R., & Edge, D. (1996). The social shaping of technology. *Research Policy, 25*, 856–899.

Williams, F., Rice, R. E., & Rogers, E. M. (1988). *Research methods and the new media*. New York: Free Press.

Williamson, O. E. (1975). *Markets and hierarchies, analysis and antitrust implications*. New York: The Free Press.

Williamson, O. E. (1981). The economics of organisation: The transaction cost approach. *American Journal of Sociology, 87*, 548–577.

Williamson, O. E. (1985). *The economic institutions of capitalism: Firms, markets, relational contracting*. New York: The Free Press.

Williamson, O. E. (1996). *The mechanism of governance*. New York: Oxford University Press.

Wind, J., & Rangaswamy, A. (2001). Customerization: The next revolution in mass customization. *Journal of Interactive Marketing, 15*(1), 13–32.

Wirtz, B. W., Schilke, O., & Ullrich, S. (2010). Strategic development of business models: Implications of the web 2.0 for creating value on the internet. *Long Range Planning, 43*(2/3), 272–290.

Woodruff, R. B. (1997). Customer value: The next source for competitive advantage. *Journal of the Academy of Marketing Science, 25*(2), 139–153.

Wu, G. (2005). The mediating role of perceived interactivity in the effect of actual interactivity on attitude towards the website. *Journal of Interactive Advertising, 5*(2). Retrieved September 17, 2005, from http://www.jiad.org/ vol5/no2/wu/

Wu, G. (2006). Conceptualizing and measuring the perceived interactivity of websites. *Journal of Current Issues and Research in Advertising, 28*(1), 87–104.

Yadav, M. S., & Varadarajan, P. R. (2005a). Interactivity in the electronic marketplace: An exposition of the concept and implications for research. *Journal of the Academy of Marketing Science, 33*, 585–603.

Yadav, M. S., & Varadarajan, P. R. (2005b). Understanding product migration to the electronic marketplace: A conceptual framework. *Journal of Retailing, 81*(2), 125–140.

Yoo, W. S., Lee, Y., & Park, J. (2010). The role of interactivity in e-tailing: Creating value and increasing satisfaction. *Journal of Retailing and Consumer Services, 17*(2), 89–96.

Zaichkowsky, J. L. (1985). Measuring the involvement construct. *Journal of Consumer Research, 12*, 341–352.

Zaichkowsky, J. L. (1986). Conceptualizing involvement. *Journal of* Advertising, *15*(2), 4–34.

Zeithaml, V. A. (1988). Consumer perceptions of price, quality, and value: A means-end model and synthesis of evidence. *Journal of Marketing, 52*(3), 2–22.

16 *Commentary* From Definition to Policy Making

A Review of Sexual Behavior, Anonymity, and Interactivity

Peng Hwa Ang

Nanyang Technological University

The three chapters that comprise this section all merit a thoughtful response, from policy makers in two instances and from the academy in the third. They also offer some contrasting answers to enduring meta-quesitons in research: what purpose does the research serve and how should one get there?

All three chapters are well researched and must have consumed many hours of assistants' help in order to achieve the level of documentation they have. They illustrate well the great difficulty that social sciences such as communication have in answering seemingly simple questions regarding key concepts in the field. And if one has to prove causality, something that the natural sciences more easily take for granted, then it may be easier to move a mountain. More on that later.

Anonymous Communication

The chapter begins promisingly by observing that anonymity is part of the basic right of free speech in most democracies. Its value has been proven in journalism and in whistle-blowing circumstances. It is also useful in certain situations such as auctions and tenders, when knowing the parties involved in the bids might lead to collusion.

And right away, one sees the difficulty in researching the subject. It lies in the very definition of "anonymity." The authors, while acknowledging at various points that the term is poorly defined by researchers, adopt the definition by (I kid not) Anonymous (1998) that anonymity is "the degree to which a communicator perceives the message source is unknown and unspecified" (p. 387) and that it is both technical and perceptual, and that it is more continuous than absolute.

In essence, anonymity is a matter of degree on a scale from fully known to fully unknown. This is a contestable definition as the chapter itself suggests that there are several forms, as opposed to degrees, of anonymity. There is the anonymity where the identity of the content-producer is unknown to everyone.

This is the instance where the basic right of free speech would be applicable. In more concrete terms, it would be a Deep Throat-type news source or Pfc Bradley Manning of Wikileaks notoriety (Bumiller, 2010).

Then there is the situation where the content producer is anonymous to each other but known to the recipient of the content. Auctions would fall into this category; anonymity is intended to avoid collusion and thereby achieve a larger overall economic benefit. Whistle blowing may fall into this situation, too. After all, anonymity is intended precisely to protect the whistle blower from the person or entity complained about. Without a more precise definition, it would be impossible to proceed very far.

So what should a more robust definition of anonymity include? Two tentative suggestions emerge from the chapter: the purpose of anonymity and (for want of a better term) "the circle of anonymity"—who knows or does not know the anonymous person, or, in the summary, "anonymity to whom." They help predict some of the outcomes of using anonymity and on that basis present themselves as important. An illustration may be useful.

In the section on journalism, an anonymous source is contrasted with the public relations officer (PRO): who would one trust?—the anonymous source or the PRO? Those interviewed had apparently said they trusted the anonymous source more than the PRO, hence the utility of anonymity. But take a closer-to-real-life Wikileak of classified U.S. military information concerning Afghanistan: should one trust the anonymous source who provided the information, or the military PRO who comments on the information? Yes, the PRO has an undoubtedly biased point of view. On the other hand, the anonymous source could have been someone from the Taliban. A rational answer is to go back to the source—which is why Wikileaks put the documents online. It enables readers to verify the original documents (and also puts pressure on the news editors in case they should have any ideas of censorship (Rosen, 2010). This would seem, at least to this reviewer, a more rational outcome than preferring the anonymous source over a public relations spokesperson simply because the source is anonymous, as would seem to be indicated by Callison (2001). The strongest explanation for the phenomenon observed by Callison may be the contrast: between an anonymous source who apparently has no agenda as opposed to a PRO. In which case, why the source stays anonymous (purpose) and anonymous from whom (circle) are possibly important explanatory factors.

In short, a more precise and robust definition may be a direction for future research. Both these possible factors are in the summary section of the chapter. On the one hand, the authors' candidness about the lack of direction for future research is to be appreciated: "However, the lack of prior efforts to look across these areas leaves us with an inadequate picture of the current state-of-the-art in this area and without direction for future research on the topic" (p. 333).

There are additional areas worth investigating as well. For example, trust is a variable significant in both the statistical and social senses. While the authors conclude that anonymity undermines trust, one cannot help wonder if the argument is tautological—it is because there is a lack of trust that anonymity is deployed. The anonymity of whistle-blowers is necessary because those whistled at cannot be trusted not to act against whistle-blowers.

Trust is significant as a variable to investigate because it has been shown to be a stronger predictor of Internet penetration than income (Huang, Keser, Leland, & Shachat, 2003). If that is the case, and if anonymity does indeed undermine that same trust, then anonymity could undermine Internet penetration, with the attendant consequences of digital divide, etc.

Anonymity, however, has been demonstrated by the authors to have significant values in certain settings. Perhaps the major direction for research also is to consider the situations where anonymity has a positive contribution in economic, political and social capital terms.

Sex

In stark contrast to the research on anonymity, there is plenty of prior research on the effects of exposure to sex in media. But how does one know if there is a causal relationship? It appears to face the same difficulty as an investigation into the causal relationship between media consumption and violence. And here is where the author steps in.

Wright's chapter is a masterful demonstration of an academic study in the best sense of the word. First, he attempts to pose the relevant questions on the subject. It is a study of the United States, but how representative are the studies of the United States? Answer: The various datasets came from all regions.

Second, he asks questions that communication scholars (and perhaps only communication scholars) would ask. What are the conditional effects? What are the mediated effects? How strong are these effects? And then he closes off other possible variables, something he calls the "third variable" by ensuring there is non-spuriousness.

Finally, he draws up a template from Cook and Campbell (1979) to answer the question: what must one prove in order to prove causality? Then, he rigorously applies the template to 21 studies in the United States he has assembled.

His conclusion? "Exposure to sexual mass media should be considered a health threat to young people" (p. 375).

If the warning sounds stark, it is mitigated by the fact that policy-makers have always assumed the conclusion to be the case. Media regulators the world over regulate sexual media content as a matter of course. From a policy perspective, the interesting question, though, is whether the study can be extrapolated internationally. If so, different cultural attitudes, particularly in Europe, may warrant stricter regulation on such content targeted towards the young.

In Denmark, the reviewer was stunned to see a television channel used for cartoons for much of the day and then for soft-porn from about 8 p.m. In Germany, advertisements may feature bare-breasted women. Perhaps the different socialization towards such content may mean a different definition of what is sexual. (This is reminiscent of a class on violence in the media by the reviewer. Students from China were unanimous that kung-fu movies were not violent because it was impossible to kill another human being using the moves the actors used.)

Given the thoroughness of the chapter, are there possible loopholes or gaps?

The research methods deployed in the studies cited look robust. So that leaves data and possible bias. On the data front, the question would be the reliability of the statements by the subjects, who were often students. Could this be a case of "pluralistic ignorance" (Chia & Lee, 2008), meaning that everyone ignorantly assumes everyone else is having sexual relations and being in a setting where it is "cool" to have such relations based on perceptions from media consumption, have led to a tendency towards overstatement of having had coitus? This is pure speculation from the reviewer based on one work and so it should be taken with a bag, rather than a mere grain, of salt.

That leaves possible bias. Do these two paragraphs contain evidence of bias?

1. The lack of an association between television viewing and females' coital status may have been due to social desirability influences, as the authors indicate that the extent of female coitus self-reported in this data set was suspiciously low in comparison to the findings of other large-scale studies.
2. Fabes and Strouse (1987) found that college students who rated media characters as exemplars of sexual responsibility had more sexual partners than students who rated parents and educators as their top models of sexual responsibility, although this difference did not reach conventional levels of statistical significance.

In the first paragraph, data that disagreed with the findings is labelled "suspicious." In the second, a finding that was not statistically significant was highlighted.

This reviewer thinks not. The author has very carefully argued his case and while the term "bias" does not appear in the chapter, he seems to be fully cognisant of the issue. Unlike many articles that attempt to downplay weaknesses in their study, this points out possible flaws such as: "Non-experimental studies can never completely rule out every possible third-variable, of course" (p. 370).

Overall then, this chapter is a masterful model for other studies attempting to show causality among phenomena in communication research.

Interactivity

Unlike the study on sexual content in the media, the chapter on interactivity faces a mountain of obstacles to get started. The author begins by pointing out three problems in grappling with interactivity:

- inconsistent conceptual definitions,
- different units and levels of analysis, and
- a largely incoherent base of theory.

So, the author should be commended for even attempting what is evidently not at all a promising first step on the journey to developing a theory. In the end, more than a quarter of the chapter is devoted to discussing six major propositions and a small entourage of accompanying sub-propositions regarding interactivity and how the concept would add value to business.

It is a wholesome idea, interactivity. Modern technologies are more interactive than technologies of yore. Television today is more interactive than before because of the remote control device. A website that has more interactive features, particularly if it is on an e-commerce site, will likely be more useful than a similar site with more limited interactivity. Therefore, if one can identify the settings in which interactivity would be a welcome addition, one would be adding value to the business.

All the propositions suggest that having greater interactivity is better. There will be greater consumer choice, greater participation, lower costs, etc. Just from everyday experience, one realizes that more interactivity is better but too much to the point of complexity is not good (Schwartz, 2004). The relationship between interactivity and value suggests itself as an inverted U-shape curve where the value of interactivity rises up to an inflexion point, after which its value falls. Such a U-shape curve, were it to materialize, would help managers in deciding the degree of interactivity in their devices.

In reality, as one might suspect, things are more complex. In some settings, limited interactivity would be preferred. Take e-commerce. Every shopper would like the ability to maximize choice. Here, greater interactivity is needed for greater choice. But once the choices are made, then it is time to pay. But here, limited interactivity is desired. A one-click system to payment would be preferred. Too much interactivity at this stage, in fact, could subtract value from the business.

Further, because of conceptual confusion and the absence of a firm definition, the propositions regarding interactivity in some areas are in conflict, or at least need refining. For example, in Proposition 5, the author suggests that interactivity lowers transaction costs. But in the conclusion section, the author makes the case that "although interactivity may potentially reduce these transaction costs, these would remain contingent upon different forms and practicalities of interactivity" (p. 411). Intuitively, this is a more appealing argument from a practical, user point of view. But from an academic perspective, contingency theories have more limited utility and cry out for a meta-theory. Without even an explanatory model, it means that every change in a variable would require research to investigate the impact of that variable on the business.

The difficulties, even among the propositions for further research, raises the question: is interactivity a dead-end idea? The author's characterization and paraphrasing of one definition of interactivity as "basically everything a human being does" by Heeter (2000), who was among the very first to research the construct of "interactivity," suggests such a sweeping definition as to be impossible to operationalize.

Conclusion

Review pieces are reminders that good research is very hard to do, and they underscore the importance of having strong shoulders on which to stand when breaking new theoretical ground. The three chapters in this section advance thinking in their respective areas, in spite of the fact that each area is characterized by vastly different degrees of prior scientific conceptualization and consensus. Using an aviation analogy, one chapter is attempting a launch (through efforts to bring definitional clarity to the concept of interactivity); a second chapter is attempting to chart a course (for an emerging sub-area of scholarship on anonymity); and a third chapter is nearing a specific destination (by attempting to bring closure to an enduring and clearly defined scientific debate). Though very different types of scholarly work, all are essential components of the scholarly enterprise, and indispensible foundations on which future generations of scholars can stand and build programs of research.

References

Anonymous. (1998). To reveal or not to reveal: A theoretical model of anonymous communication. *Communication Theory, 8,* 381–407.

Bumiller, E. (2010, July 30). Army broadens inquiry into WikiLeaks disclosure. *New York Times.* Retrieved from http://www.nytimes.com/2010/07/31/world/31wiki.html?_r=1&ref=bradley_e_manning

Callison, C. (2001). Do PR practitioners have a PR problem? *Journal of Public Relations Research,13*(3), 219–234.

Chia, S., & Lee, W. (2008). Pluralistic ignorance about sex: The direct and the indirect effects of media consumption on college students' misperception of sex-related peer norms. *International Journal of Public Opinion Research, 20*(1): 52–73. doi: 10.1093/ijpor/edn005.

Cook, T. D., & Campbell, D. T. (1979). *Quasi-experimentation: Design & analysis issues for field settings.* Chicago: Rand McNally.

Fabes, R. A., & Strouse, J. (1987). Models of responsible and irresponsible sexuality: A correlational study. *Journal of Sex Research, 23,* 70–84.

Heeter, C. (2000). Interactivity in the context of designed experiences. *Journal of Interactive Advertising, 1*(1). Retrieved from http://jiad.org/vol1/no1/heeter/

Huang, H., Keser, C., Leland, J., & Shachat, J. (2003, July). Trust, the Internet, and the digital divide. *IBM Systems Journal, 4*(3), 507–518. doi:10.1147/sj.423.0507

Rosen, J. (2010). The Afghanistan war logs released by Wikileaks, the world's first stateless news organization. PressThink blog. Retrieved October 26, 2010, from http://archive.pressthink.org/2010/07/26/wikileaks_afghan.html

Schwartz, B. (2004). *The paradox of choice.* HarperCollins: New York.

About the Editor

Charles T. Salmon earned his Ph.D. in Mass Communication from the University of Minnesota in 1985, and nine years later became the first recipient of a named professorship in the College of Communication Arts and Sciences at Michigan State University. Today, he holds the Ellis N. Brandt Chair and is Past Dean of the College.

Salmon has been a Rockefeller Scholar in Residence at Villa Serbelloni, Lake Como, Italy, a Fulbright Scholar at Tel Aviv University, a Visiting Professor at the Norwegian School of Management, a UNICEF HIV/AIDS advisor in Kazakhstan, and a Visiting Scientist at the U.S. Centers for Disease Control and Prevention.

His research focuses on the intersection of public communication, public opinion, and public health, and has appeared in such journals as: *Archives of Internal Medicine, American Behavioral Scientist, Bioethics, Health Education and Behavior, International Journal of Public Opinion Research, Journal of Acquired Immune Deficiency Syndromes, Journal of Communication, Journal of Health Communication, Public Health Reports*, and *Public Opinion Quarterly*.

His books include *Information Campaigns: Balancing Social Values and Social Change*, and *Public Opinion and the Communication of Consent* (with Theodore Glasser).

About the Associate Editors

Cindy Gallois is Professor in the Faculty of Social and Behavioural Sciences at the University of Queensland. Her research centers on intergroup communication in health, organizational, and cross-cultural contexts. She has published about 150 articles, chapters, and books, and has supervised 34 successful PhD students. Her research has been continuously supported since 1987 by the Australian Research Council and National Health and Medical Research Council. She is a Fellow of the Academy of the Social Sciences in Australia and the International Communication Association, a former President of ICA and the International Association of Language and Social Psychology, a former editor of *Human Communication Research*, and current Associate Editor of the *Journal of Cross-Cultural Psychology.*

Nurit Guttman (Ph.D., Rutgers University) is Chair of the Department of Communication and Head of the Herzog Institute of Media, Politics and Society at Tel Aviv University. Her research focuses on participatory approaches to social marketing, dissemination of rights information, citizen involvement in policy issues, and entertainment television for social change. Her areas of emphasis are health, road safety and the environment. She is a former recipient of the Distinguished Researcher Award from Tel Aviv University, and a current member of Israel's National Council of Health Promotion She is the author of *Public Health Communication Interventions: Values and Ethical Dilemmas.*

Christina Holtz-Bacha is Professor of Communication at the University of Erlangen-Nürnberg, Germany. Prior to her current position she taught at universities in Mainz, Bochum, and Munich. She was a Visiting Scholar at the University of Minnesota, and a Research Fellow at the Joan Shorenstein Center on the Press, Politics and Public Policy at the John F. Kennedy School of Government, Harvard University. She is Co-Editor of the German journal *Publizistik* and has served as Chair of the Political Communication Division of ICA. She has published widely in the area of political communication and media policy. Among her most recent publications is the two-volume *Encyclopedia of Political Communication*, co-edited with Lynda L. Kaid.

Joseph B. Walther is Professor of Communication and of Telecommunication, Information Studies & Media at Michigan State University. His research focuses on computer-mediated communication in personal relationships, groups, organizational, and educational settings, in which he has published several original theories and empirical studies. He has held appointments in Psychology, Information Science, and Education in the U.S. and England. He has been an officer in the Academy of Management and the International Communication Association. He has been recognized twice with the National Communication Association's Woolbert Research Award for articles that offered new conceptualizations of communication phenomena that have influenced thinking in the discipline for more than ten years. He is an associate editor of *Human Communication Research* and the *Journal of Media Psychology.*

About the Contributors

Tamara D. Afifi (Ph.D., University of Nebraska-Lincoln) is Associate Professor in the Department of Communication at the University of California, Santa Barbara. She is an interpersonal and family communication scholar, with specific interests in (a) information regulation (secrets, avoidance, disclosure, privacy) and (b) communication patterns (e.g., stress, coping, conflict, uncertainty) in challenging life circumstances, particularly within divorced families. She is a recipient of the Young Scholars Award, from the International Communication Association, and the Distinguished Article and Knower Article Awards, from the National Communication Association, and serves as Associate Editor for the *Journal of Social and Personal Relationships*.

Peng Hwa Ang (Ph.D., Michigan State University; LL.B., National University of Singapore) is Professor and former Dean of the Wee Kim Wee School of Communication and Information at Nanyang Technological University, Singapore. In 2004, he was appointed by the U.N. Secretary General to the Working Group on Internet Governance. He later co-founded the Global Internet Governance Academic Network, for which he served as inaugural Chair. He currently serves as Chair of the non-profit organization, Asian Media Information and Communication Centre. He is the author of *Ordering Chaos: Regulating the Internet*.

Stephenson J. Beck (Ph.D., University of Kansas) is Assistant Professor of communication at North Dakota State University. His research interests deal with conflict and decision making in group communication. Specifically, he is interested in how individuals strategically adapt their messages to accomplish goals in group situations.

Kimberly E. Casteline (B.A., New York University) is a doctoral candidate in the School of Journalism and Mass Communication and a field research staff member at the Center for Media, Religion, and Culture at the University of Colorado. Her research focuses on how members of religious communities construct their media identities. For her dissertation, she is studying media engagement practices of Christian Ghanaians in several US communities as well in their native land.

Mihai Coman (Ph.D., University of Bucharest) is the inaugural Dean of the School of Journalism and Mass Communication Studies at the University of Bucharest, and considered the founder of journalism and communication education in Romania. In 2009 he was granted the Order of Cultural Merit, Romania's highest civilian award, for his contribution to the development of journalism and communication education in Romania. His books include *Pour une anthropologie des media*, *Media Anthropology* (with Eric Rothenbuhler), *Mass Media and Journalism in Romania* (with Peter Gross), and seven volumes of mythology studies.

Whitney A. Frahm (M.A., North Dakota State University) is a grant writer with Fox Consulting in Minneapolis, MN. Her research interests include interpersonal, group and health communication.

Elisabeth Gareis (Ed.D., University of Georgia) is Associate Professor of Communication Studies at Baruch College/CUNY. Her research focuses on intercultural friendship and cross-cultural comparisons of communication behaviors in close relationships. Additional interests include the scholarship of teaching and learning, second language acquisition, and the use of English as a world language. She is author of *Intercultural Friendship: A Qualitative Study*, the textbook series, *A Novel Approach* (on the use of literature and film in the language education), and numerous journal articles in the areas of intercultural communication, communication education, and second language acquisition.

Howard Giles (Ph.D., University of Bristol) is Professor of Communication at the University of California, Santa Barbara, and previously Professor of Social Psychology and Head of Psychology at the University of Bristol, England. He is current and Founding Editor and Co-Editor of the *Journal of Language & Social Psychology* and the *Journal of Asian Pacific Communication* as well as past President of the International Communication Association and the International Association of Language and Social Psychology. His research explores very different areas of applied intergroup communication research and theory, with a focus on intergenerational communication and aging across cultures and, more recently, police-civilian relations.

Muge Haseki (M.A., University of Wisconsin-Milwaukee) is a doctoral student in the School of Communication & Information at Rutgers University. Her research interests are mediated communication, social networks, and social media.

Jill R. Helmle (Ph.D., University of California, Santa Barbara) is a postdoctoral researcher at the University of California, Santa Barbara. Her research interests include work and family issues, family businesses, and marital and parent-child relationships.

Elihu Katz (Ph.D., Columbia) is Distinguished Trustee Professor of Communication in the University of Pennsylvania Annenberg School for Communication. He is a member of the American Academy of Arts and Sciences, Emeritus Professor of Sociology and Communication at Hebrew University, a Fellow of the International Communication Association, and a recipient of honorary degrees from universities in five countries. His many books include *Personal Influence* (with Paul F. Lazarsfeld), *The Uses of Mass Communication* (with Jay G. Blumler), *The Export of Meaning* (with Tamar Liebes), *Media Events* (with Daniel Dayan), and *Canonic Texts in Media Research* (with J. D. Peters, T. Liebes, & A. Orloff).

Gladys Engel Lang (Ph.D., University of Chicago) is currently Professor Emerita in communication, political science, and sociology at University of Washington, Seattle. She conducted her first communication research with the Office of War Information in Washington, D.C. in 1943, then spent some years with the Office of Strategic Services as a research analyst in England, Italy, and, after the war, in China before resuming her studies. She is author of *Etched in Memory: the Building and Survival of Artistic Reputation*, a study of visual communicators and their entry into collective memory, and co-author of three books with Kurt Lang.

Kurt Lang (Ph.D., University of Chicago) is Professor Emeritus in sociology and communications at the University of Washington, Seattle. With Gladys Engel Lang he is co-recipient of the distinguished career award of the American Association for Public Opinion Research and the Political Communication section of the American Political Science Association. He is the author of *Military Institutions and the Sociology of War*, which arose from his research for the U.S. government following World War II. With Gladys Engel Lang, he has co-authored *Politics and Television*, *Voting and Nonvoting*, and *The Battle for Public Opinion: the President, the Press, and the Polls During Watergate.*

Mikaela L. Marlow (Ph.D., University of California, Santa Barbara) is an Assistant Professor of Communication at the University of Idaho. Her work explores indigenous language survival and the ways in which intergroup differences influence language evaluations and feedback. She has published in *Journal of Multilingual and Multicultural Development* and *Journal of Multicultural Discourses*, and recently completed her first book *Race, Power, and Language Criticism: The Case of Hawai'i.*

Susana Martínez-Guillem (M.A., University of Iowa) is currently working on her Ph.D. in Communication at the University of Colorado at Boulder. Her research combines critical approaches within discourse analysis and cultural studies. Her current project examines the discursive and material aspects of European identity formation, drawing, among others, on Critical Race Theory and Whiteness studies. She is the author of "Argumentation, Metadiscourse, and Social Cognition: Organizing Knowledge in Political Communication," published in *Discourse & Society*.

Amy N. Miller (B.A. Jamestown College) is a direct-to-doctoral candidate and teaching assistant at North Dakota State University. Her research interests include family communication and workplace friendships.

Paul C. Murschetz is Professor of Media Management at Cologne Business School and Adjunct Associate Professor of Business Administration at University of New York, Tirana. He earned his Ph.D. from the Vienna School of Economics and Business Administration. He also holds a master's degree in media and communication (London School of Economics and Political Science). His current research work focuses on issues of strategic e-commerce management, media interactivity, WebTV, and effects of public financial subsidies on media firms. Research results have appeared in journals such as *The International Journal on Media Management*, the *European Journal of Communication*, and in conference proceedings of the German association of communication (DGPuK), and its expert group on media economics. Paul is founding member of the European Media Management Association (EMMA).

Jon F. Nussbaum (Ph.D., Purdue University) is Professor of Communication Arts & Sciences and Human Development & Family Studies at Penn State University. He is the Past President of the International Communication Association, former editor of the *Journal of Communication*, a Fulbright Research Fellow in the UK, Fellow of the International Communication Association and Fellow within the Adult Development and Aging Division of the American Psychological Association. Nussbaum has published 13 books and over 80 journal articles and book chapters on communication behaviors and patterns across the life span including research on family, friendship and professional relationships with well and frail older adults.

Stephen A. Rains (Ph.D., University of Texas at Austin) is Assistant Professor in the Department of Communication at the University of Arizona. His research examines new communication technologies, social influence, and health communication. His work related to anonymous communication, investigates perceptions of and responses to anonymous sources and their messages, and is published in *Communication Research, Communication Theory, Journal of Applied Communication Research*, and *Management Communication Quarterly*.

Margaret Richardson (Ph.D., University of Waikato) is a Research Fellow in the Department of Management Communication at the University of Waikato. In this capacity she has worked on a number of research projects, including researching older people's use of information and communication technologies, the uptake of broadband in rural communities, and the adoption and utilization of computers in not-for-profit organizations. Her current work focuses on the organizational communication structures and processes that impact older people's capacity to participate in and with organizations. Her work has been published in *New Media & Society* and *Information Communication & Society.*

Gertrude J. Robinson (Ph.D., Illinois) is Professor Emerita in Communications at McGill University. Robinson has published 11 books and more than 50 articles in major journals. She served as president of the Canadian Communication Association and Vice President & Treasurer of the International Association for Media and Communication Research. Robinson was Editor of the *Canadian Journal of Communication*, Senior Fellow at the Gannett Center at Columbia University and Senior Scholar at the Centre for Research on Women at the University of British Columbia. She received Phi Beta Kappa, Kappa Tau Alpha, and Dodi Robb awards for her scholarship on women.

Jessica S. Robles (M.A., University of Essex) is a doctoral student in Communication at the University of Colorado at Boulder. Her research includes interpersonal and institutional conflict, how people talk about conflict, and how moral issues are addressed in communication. She has done work on discursive strategies such as reported speech, emotion, facework, positioning, identity-work, questioning, intersubjectivity practices and argument in contexts related to healthcare, local governance, political bodies, and friendship and family talk. She is currently completing her doctoral dissertation on morality and conflict in interpersonal relationships.

Craig R. Scott (Ph.D., Arizona State University) is Associate Professor of Communication in the School of Communication & Information at Rutgers University. His research examines communication technology use, identification, and anonymous communication in the workplace. His other work related to anonymous communication specifically has been published in *Communication Theory, Management Communication Quarterly, Journal of Computer-Mediated Communication, Journal of Applied Communication Research, Western Journal of Communication, Communication Quarterly,* and the *Free Speech Yearbook.*

David R. Seibold (Ph.D., Michigan State University) is Professor of Communication in the Division of Social Sciences and co-director of the Graduate Program in Management Practice in the Technology Management Program (College of Engineering) at the University of California, Santa Barbara. His research interests include group communication and interpersonal influence, organizational innovation and change, workplace temporality, management communication, communication and family businesses, and theory-practice issues. He has been elected a Distinguished Scholar in the National Communication Association and a Fellow of the International Communication Association.

Karen Tracy (Ph.D., University of Wisconsin) is Professor of Communication at the University of Colorado at Boulder. Her research investigates the problems, discourse strategies, and situated ideals of institutional interaction of different kinds. She has studied emergency calls to the police, academic colloquia, education governance meetings, and, most recently, oral argument in appellate courts. Her work has appeared in a variety of communication and discourse journals and she is past editor of the journal, *Research on Language and Social Interaction*. She is the author of *Challenges of Ordinary Democracy: A Case Study in Deliberation and Dissent*; *Colloquium: Dilemmas of Academic Discourse*; and *Everyday Talk*.

C. Kay Weaver (Ph.D., University of Stirling) is a Professor in the Department of Management Communication at the University of Waikato, Hamilton, New Zealand. Her teaching and research interests include media and communication audiences and users, new technologies, gender and communication, and critical cultural analysis of public relations. She is co-author of *Cameras in the Commons, Women Viewing Violence, and Violence and the Media*, co-editor of *Critical Readings: Violence and the Media* and *Public Relations in Global Contexts*, and has published in journals such as *New Media & Society, Media, Culture & Society, Public Relations Review, Journal of Public Relations Research*, and *Feminist Media Studies*.

Richard Wilkins (Ph.D., University of Massachusetts, Amherst) is Associate Professor of Communication at the Weissman School of Arts and Sciences, Baruch College, CUNY. His research utilizes practices of communication as points of access into study and commentary on cultural phenomena. Using qualitative methodology in general and ethnography in particular, his work has examined cultural discourses found in symbolic forms, terms for talk, the regulation of talk, relational dialectics, face-work, strategic communication, and argumentation.

Ruth Wodak (Ph.D., University of Vienna) is Distinguished Professor of Discourse Studies at Lancaster University and the current President of the Societas Linguistica Europea. She is a recipient of the Wittgenstein Prize for Elite Researchers, the Kerstin Hellelgren Chair of the Swedish Parliament, and an honorary doctorate from Orebro University, Sweden. Her research interests focus on discourse studies; gender studies; language and/in politics; prejudice and discrimination; and on ethnographic methods of linguistic fieldwork.

Recent books include *Discourse of Politics in Action: 'Politics as Usual'* (2009); *The Politics of Exclusion* (with M. Krzyżanowski, 2009); and *Gedenken im Gedankenjahr* (with R. de Cillia, 2009).

Paul J. Wright (M.A., California State University, Fullerton) is a doctoral student in the Department of Communication at the University of Arizona (minor Family Studies and Human Development). His work on sexual socialization and sexual health has been accepted at *Communication Quarterly*, *Journal of Health Communication, Journal of Family Communication*, *Sexuality & Culture*, *Psychological Reports*, and *Sexual Addiction & Compulsivity*. He is the inaugural College of Social and Behavioral Sciences Edward I. Donnerstein Graduate Fellow.

Theodore E. Zorn (Ph.D., University of Kentucky) is Professor of Management Communication at the University of Waikato, Hamilton, New Zealand. His teaching and research interests are organizational change processes, such as IT implementation, change-related communication, and enhancing workplace well-being. Ted is currently Vice Chair of the Organizational Communication Division of the International Communication Association, past editor of *Management Communication Quarterly*, and the 2006 recipient of the International Communication Association's Frederic Jablin Award for Outstanding Member of ICA's Organizational Communication Division. He is co-author of the textbook *Organizational Communication in an Age of Globalization*, now in its second edition.

Author Index

C

I

J

K

X

Y

Subject Index

Page numbers in italic refer to figures or tables

D

Also Available from Routledge

The Handbook of Communication Ethics

Edited by George Cheney, Steve May, and Debashish Munshi

A Volume in the ICA Handbook Series

The Handbook of Communication Ethics serves as a comprehensive guide to the study of communication and ethics. It brings together analyses and applications based on recognized ethical theories as well as those outside the traditional domain of ethics but which engage important questions of power, equality, and justice. The work herein encourages readers to make important connections between matters of social justice and ethical theory. This volume makes an unparalleled contribution to the literature of communication studies, through consolidating knowledge about the multiple relationships between communication and ethics; by systematically treating areas of application; and by introducing explicit and implicit examinations of communication ethics to one another.

The *Handbook* takes an international approach, analyzing diverse cultural contexts and comparative assessments. The chapters in this volume cover a wide range of theoretical perspectives on communication and ethics, including feminist, postmodern and postcolonial; engage with communication contexts such as interpersonal and small group communication, journalism, new media, visual communication, public relations, and marketing; and explore contemporary issues such as democracy, religion, secularism, the environment, trade, law, and economics. The chapters also consider the dialectical tensions between theory and practice; academic and popular discourses; universalism and particularism; the global and the local; and rationality and emotion.

An invaluable resource for scholars in communication and related disciplines, the *Handbook* also serves as a main point of reference in graduate and upper-division undergraduate courses in communication and ethics. It stands as an exceptionally comprehensive resource for the study of communication and ethics.

HB ISBN: 978-0-415-99464-4
PB ISBN: 978-0-415-99465-1
EB ISBN: 978-0-203-89040-0